Contemporary European Politics

Revised throughout, the second edition of this comprehensive and highly respected textbook continues to provide a thorough introduction to European and European Union politics.

Pairing a genuinely comparative approach with in-depth analysis of the national, supranational, local and regional political systems of large and small countries across Europe, including Central and Eastern Europe and the Balkans, this accessible book covers history, theory, institutions, parties and party systems, and interest groups, among others.

Key topics and features of this book:

- Examines the European Union multilevel governance system and uses a regional cluster approach to highlight differences across Europe.
- Contextualises European politics in a theoretical framework explaining the major political, social and economic transformations taking place in the information age.
- A new chapter on the comparative political systems and cultures of wider Europe, particularly Russia, Ukraine, Moldova, Georgia, Belarus and Turkey.
- Engages with the latest challenges and crises facing Europe, including new streamlined chapters on parties, elections, politics and policy-making of the European Union.
- Extended coverage of hot topics such as finance and the Eurocrisis, immigration, populism and xenophobia.
- Uses a wide range of pedagogical features including further readings and revision questions.
- Includes a fully updated companion website containing rich reference data, chapter summaries and weblinks.

Richly illustrated throughout, this work is an indispensable resource for all students and scholars of European politics.

José M. Magone is Professor in Regional and Global Governance at the Berlin School of Economics and Law, Germany. He was previously Reader in European Politics at the University of Hull, UK. Among his 16 books are the edited volumes *The Politics in Contemporary Portugal* (2014), *Routledge Handbook of European Politics* (2015), *Core-Periphery Relations in the European Union* (with Brigid Laffan and Christian Schweiger, 2016), *The Statecraft of Consensus Democracies* (2017) and *Contemporary Spanish Politics* (third edition, 2018).

Praise from the first edition

'Ambitious in scope, impressive in its mastery of historical detail and contemporary theory, bold in its methods – and highly readable. Magone's work is destined to become a classic reference for any student of European politics.'

David Hanley, Professor Emeritus of European Studies, Cardiff University, UK

'With a rare combination of encyclopaedic knowledge and analytical skills, this engaging textbook takes Europe back to where the action is. José Magone's pan-European approach offers a comprehensive and careful view of European politics since the fall of the Berlin Wall and provides a truly comparative basis for understanding the most recent dynamics of Europe at different levels. The result is a book which is an invaluable addition to the literature.'

José Ramón Montero, Universidad Autónoma de Madrid, Spain

Praise for this edition

'A sweeping buffet of facts and arguments analyzing change in Europe from the 17th century to 2018. A useful blend of theory and empirics for those who want an accessible introduction to a diverse region.'

Nancy Bermeo, Professor Emeritus, University of Oxford, UK

Contemporary European Politics

A Comparative Introduction

Second edition

José M. Magone

LONDON AND NEW YORK

Second edition published 2019
by Routledge
2 Park Square, Milton Park, Abingdon, Oxon OX14 4RN

and by Routledge
52 Vanderbilt Avenue, New York, NY 10017

Routledge is an imprint of the Taylor & Francis Group, an informa business

First edition published by Routledge 2011

British Library Cataloguing in Publication Data
A catalogue record for this book is available from the British Library

Library of Congress Cataloging in Publication Data
Names: Magone, Josâe M. (Josâe Marâia), 1962, author.
Title: Contemporary European politics : a comparative introduction / Josâe M. Magone.
Description: Second edition. | New York : Routledge, 2019. | "First edition published by Routledge 2011"—T.p. verso. | Includes bibliographical references and index.
Identifiers: LCCN 2018060073| ISBN 9781138894990 (hardback) | ISBN 9781138895027 (paperback) | ISBN 9781315179704 (master ebook) | ISBN 9781351717151 (web pdf) | ISBN 9781351717144 (ePub) | ISBN 9781351717137 (mobipocket/kindle)
Subjects: LCSH: Europe—Politics and government. | European Union countries—Politics and government.
Classification: LCC JN12 .M345 2019 | DDC 320.94—dc23
LC record available at https://lccn.loc.gov/2018060073

ISBN: 978-1-138-89499-0 (hbk)
ISBN: 978-1-138-89502-7 (pbk)
ISBN: 978-1-315-17970-4 (ebk)

Typeset in Sabon
by Swales & Willis Ltd, Exeter, Devon, UK

Visit the companion website: http://cw.routledge.com/textbooks/9780415418935/

For my dear nephew Leo
A great champion of life

A nation without the means of reform is without the means of survival.

Edmund Burke (1729–97)

La démocratie a donc deux excès à eviter: l'esprit d'inegalité, qui la mène à l'aristocratie, ou au gouvernement d'un seul; et l'esprit d'égalité extreme, qui la conduit au despotisme d'un seul, comme le despotisme d'un seul finit par la conquête.

Montesquieu (1689–1755)

Seele des Menschen,
Wie gleichst Du dem Wasser!
Schicksal des Menschen,
Wie gleichst Du Dem Wind!

Johan Wolfgang Goethe (1749–1832)
(Extract from *Gesang der Geister über den Wasser!*)

Contents

Figures

Tables

Boxes

Preface to the first edition

This book is based on my extensive research on European politics, both for comparative publications and for my fifteen years of teaching in this area. Two teaching modules that I delivered in the Department of Politics and International Studies, entitled 'Conflict and Consensus in European Politics' and 'Diversity and Convergence in European Politics', provide the basis for this book. Many of these topics were included in lectures and tutorials. I also had the opportunity to continue to teach aspects of European and European Union politics at my new position in Berlin. The two academic environments have enhanced my understanding of European politics. In Hull, I had the privilege of teaching students in a variety of different fields, such as Politics, European Studies, Business Studies, History, Law and Economics. Owing to the success of the two modules on which this book has been based, I also developed a lighter-weight free elective called 'Comparative European Politics' for students from other faculties in Hull. Many of these students' ideas have been included in this book. I was very privileged to gain such an insight from students in both Hull and Berlin. I want to thank all my students for contributing to exciting discussions about European politics, particularly in the dynamic tutorials.

This book profited immensely from the Brynmor Jones Library in Hull and the Staatsbibliothek at the Potsdamer Platz in Berlin. Both libraries have facilitated my work; for European politics it is essential that libraries are up to date because of the richness and diversity of the continent itself, a continent that is constantly reinventing itself and in which each country provides a wealth of different experiences. A pan-European academic community is contributing to our better knowledge of European countries, and this book attempts to give a comparative overview of European countries from a pan-European perspective. It takes into account the growing importance of the European Union, and that national sovereignty is being replaced by post-sovereign forms of cooperation and integration. This book can only be a modest introduction to the richness and diversity of European politics and I take full responsibility for any errors or omissions in the book. In spite of this, I hope it can offer an interesting and absorbing introduction to students of European politics and inspire further innovative research in this area.

I would like to thank my colleagues from my former Department of Politics and International Relations at the University of Hull. Special thanks go to Rudi Wurzel and Cristina Leston-Bandeira who belonged to the same teaching cluster of European politics and with whom I worked closely over fourteen years. I was also privileged to work with *eminence grise* Jack Hayward. His vast knowledge and passion for European politics was and will remain a source of inspiration that also had its impact on this book.

I also benefited from the various international research projects I took part in over the past fifteen years. These collective projects led to excellent edited monographs that I was able to use extensively when writing this book. I would like to thank all those who invited me to take part in these projects, in which I learned a great deal about other countries and regions. A special thank you goes to the many people I have worked with or with whom I have had academic exchanges, particularly Nancy Bermeo, José Ramón Montero, John Loughlin, Juliet Lodge, Jens Borchert, David Hanley, Peter Mair, my university teacher Wolfgang C. Muller, Patrick Dumont, Luca Verzichelli, Michael Edinger, Thomas Saalfeld, Tanja Börzel, Paul G. Lewis, Andris Runcis, Liewen de Winter, Ian Manners, Alasdair Young, Chad Damro and Feliciana Rajewska.

I particularly would like to thank Attila Ágh of the Centre for Democracy Studies at the Corvinus University in Budapest for the many books on Hungary, Central and Eastern Europe that he gave me at European and international conferences and that were used extensively in some chapters. Needless to say, these books form a cherished treasure in my library. Three sources of inspiration for this book are Gordon Smith, who died recently, Samuel E. Finer and Klaus von Beyme. I would like to thank all three for having published so many books based in excellent research and scholarship.

I especially would like to thank Senior Publisher Craig Fowlie for supporting this project and for so patiently waiting for the manuscript. I also extend my thanks to his assistant, Nicola Parkin, who has been very supportive during the writing and completion processes. Moreover, I am very grateful to copy-editor Jane Fieldsend who, in a very interactive dialogue, considerably improved the quality of the text. Furthermore, I would like to thank the production team at Florence Production, particularly Sue Leaper, Fiona Isaac and Julia Mitchell for their hard work and commitment. Their teamwork was instrumental in transforming the manuscript into what, I would say personally, is a beautiful book.

Last, but not least, I want to thank my Mom sincerely for her enthusiasm and support during the process of writing.

Berlin, June 2010

Preface to the second edition

After decades of stability, European politics has become quite considerably volatile. So many changes are happening at different levels in a more globalised politics, society and economy. The second edition builds easily on the previous one, because in terms of its theoretical framework, the so-called 'Great Transformation of the Late Twentieth Century', all these changes fit in well in explaining what is happening in Europe. Since the late 2000s, multiple crises (policrises as president of the European Commission Jean Claude Juncker characterised it) have led to more transnational political contestation and even a transnational space of debate in Europe. Crisis is certainly always a challenge for a country, even for a continent like the European Union; however, it also allows for a reflection of how one could develop better mechanisms to deal with such turbulent periods in the future.

The present edition of *Contemporary European Politics* was shortened in terms of chapters from 15 to 12 responding mainly to the request of the publishers, but also to several reviewers that took the time to reflect on the book. I tried as well as I could to respond to their critical input, which is always very much appreciated. Instead of three chapters on the European Union and the Common Foreign and Security Policy (CFSP), there is now just one chapter focusing on the relationship between the European Union and national politics. However, it is always the ambition of this work to highlight the growing intertwinedness and interdependence between national and supranational levels. We regard the European Union as being a multilevel governance system, in which the national level is integrated in a larger whole. Such a process of integration increased with the Treaty of Maastricht adopted in 1993 and has not stopped since then. Brexit, Czech Euroscepticism, growing discontent in Italy, illiberal tendencies in Poland and Hungary, are all signs of resistance against such ever closer union. The main focus of the book is therefore the national level, not the supranational level, so that the comparison between countries in the framework of EU multilevel governance becomes the main purpose of the book. By reducing the book's length, I acquired some space to include a new chapter on the political systems of wider Europe, namely Russia, Ukraine, Moldova, Georgia, Belarus and Turkey. These are political systems that are peripheral to core European politics, and I argue that they represent the borders of the regional democratic community and its values, in which the European Union and the Council of Europe are at its core.

As already mentioned in the first edition, the big difference with this textbook on European politics compared to other similar counterparts is the combination of general and more concrete comparative findings on the one hand, and a deep description of most countries, including the smaller ones, on the other. In this sense, the book looks to highlight the diversity of political systems and also their sustaining national political cultures. This is a difficult undertaking, maybe too ambitious, and certainly one that may also lead to mistakes. However, in my view this is the only way one can understand European politics, beyond an understanding of just mentioning the larger countries of the UK, Germany, France, Italy and sometimes Poland or Spain. None of the other countries are given any space in books on European politics. I am aware that mistakes may have occurred, and they are all mine. Nonetheless, I tried to reduce many of these mistakes compared to those in the first edition. I engaged in even more reading, and the internet facilitated access to many databases in parliaments and governments which contributed to a better understanding of what is happening in a particular country. I tended to watch live national television broadcasts from different countries in order to understand better their party systems. Although there are linguistic limits, the graphs explained on television allowed me to gauge an idea about the dynamics of electoral politics.

Meanwhile, I have been teaching in Berlin for a decade, and this has been a great privilege for someone who researches European politics. The Berlin School of Economics and Law has one of the most successful public Business schools in training people for the German and global economy. Therefore, my students forced me to research more on the political economy of the European Union. It is my belief that their queries about political economy contributed to a better book. I have tried to respond to their questions over the years, and I hope some of them have found their way into this book.

I take this opportunity to sincerely thank Andrew Taylor, Publisher at Routledge, for supporting the second edition of the book. Andrew has always been supportive of my projects and has provided me with quite considerable feedback from the academic community. A lot has found its way into this book. I want also to thank Senior Editorial Assistant, Sophie Iddamalgoda, for accompanying the whole writing process with good advice and patience in waiting for the final manuscript. Sophie has always been very helpful in responding to my queries about the manuscript. I want also to express my gratitude to production editor Emma Harder from Routledge, production manager Caroline Watson from Swales and Willis, and copyeditor Kay Hawkins for the splendid work they have done to the original manuscript. Kay Hawkins' copyediting input contributed to a substantially improved text.

Last but not least, I want to thank my beautiful mother who has always been a great source of inspiration for this book due to her veritable pan European biography.

Berlin, April, 2018

Abbreviations

ABVV/FGTB	Algemeen Vaksverbond – Fédération Général du Travail de Belgique – General Federation of Labour of Belgium
ACLVB/CGSLB	Algemene Centrale der Liberale Vakbonden van België/Centrale Générale des Syndicats Liberaux de Belgique – ACLVB/CGSLB
ACV	Algemeen Christenlijk Vaksverbond/Confédération des syndicats chrétiens en Belgique – ACV–CSC
AER	Association of European Regions
BDA	Bund der Deutschen Arbeitgeber – Association of German Employers
BDI	Bund der Deutschen Industrie – Association of German Industry
BNP	British National Party
BSP	Bălgarska Socialističeska Partija – Bulgarian Socialist Party
BUSINESSEUROPE	Union of Employers and Business Organisations in Europe
BZÖ	Bündnis für die Zukunft Österreichs – Union for the Future of Austria
CAP	Common Agricultural Policy
CBI	Confederation of British Industry
CCDR	Comissão de Coordenação de Desenvolvimento Regional – Commission of Regional Development
CCOO	Comisiones Obreras – Workers' Commissions
CDA	Christen Democratisch Appel – Christian Democratic Appeal
CDH	Centre Démocratie Humaniste – Democratic Humanist Centre
CDS-PP	Centro Democratico Social–Partido Popular – Democratic Social Centre – People's Party

CDU	Christlich-Demokratische Union – Christian Democratic Union
CD&V	Christen-Democratisch en Vlaams-Christian – Democratic and Flemish
CEAC/COSAC	Committee of European Affairs Committees
CEEP	Centre Européen des Entreprises à Participation Public d'Intérêt Économique Général – European Centre of Enterprises Providing Public Services
CEOE	Confederación Española de Organizaciones Empresariales – Spanish Confederation of Enterpreneurial Organisations
CEPYME	Confederación Española de Pequeñas y Medianas Empresas – Spanish Confederation of Small and Middle Sized Enterprises
CFDT	Confédération Française Démocratique du Travail – French Democratic Confederation of Work
CFTC	Confédération Française des Travailleurs Chrétiens – French Confederation of Christian Workers
CGE–CGC	Confédération Général de l'Encadrement – Confédération Generale de Cadres – General Confederation of Cadres
CGIL	Confederazione Generale Italiana del Lavoro – Italian General Confederation of Labour
CGPJ	Consejo General del Poder Judicial – General Council of the Judiciary Power
CGT	Confédération Générale du Travail – General Confederation of Labour
CGTP	Confederação Geral dos Trabalhadores Portugueses – General Confederation of Portuguese Workers
CGPME	Confédération Général des Petites et Moyennes Entreprises et du Patronat – General Confederation of Small and Middle Enterprises and Employers
CIP	Confederação da Industria Portuguesa – Confederation of Portuguese Industry
CISL	Confederazione dei Sindacati dei Lavoratori – Confederation of Trade Unions of the Workers
CiU	Convergencia i Unió – Convergence and Union
CNV	Christelijk Nationaal Vakverbond – Christian National Trade Unions
Comecon/CMEA	Council for Mutual Economic Assistance
Cominform	Communist Information Bureau
Comintern	Third Communist International
CONFINDUSTRIA	Confederazione di Industria – Confederation of Industry
COR	Committee of the Regions
COREPER	Committee of Permanent Representatives
CPI	Corruption Perception Index
CSCE	Conference for Security and Cooperation in Europe

CSF	Common Support Framework
CSFP	Common Foreign Security Policy
CSM	Conseil Superieur de la Magistrature – Higher Council of the Judiciary
CSM	Conselho Superior da Magistratura
CSM	Consiglio Superiore de la Magistratura – Higher Council of the Judiciary
ČSSD	Česká strana sociálně demokratická – Czech Social Democratic Party
CSU	Christlich Soziale Union – Christian Social Union
CSV	Chrëschtlech Social Vollekspartei – Christian Social People's Party
CVP	Christliche Volkspartei – Christian People's Party
CVP/PSC	Christen-Demokratisch Volkspartij – Parti Social Christien – Christian Democratic People's Party – Christian Social Party
DC	Democrazia Cristiana – Christian Democracy
DeSus	Demokratična Stranka Upokojencev Slovenije – Democratic Pensioners' Party of Slovenia
DF	Dansk Folkeparti – Danish People's Party
DGB	Deutsche Gewerkschaftsbund
DP	Darbo Partija – Labour Party
DPS	Dviženie za Prava i Svobodi – Movement for Rights and Freedoms
DUP	Democratic Unionist Party
DVU	Deutsche Volksunion – German People's Union
EAP	Environmental Action Plan
EAEU	Eurasian Economic Union
EC	European Community
ECHR	European Court of Human Rights
ECJ	European Court of Justice
ECOFIN	European Council of Finance Ministers of the European Union
ECSC	European Community for Steel and Coal
EDA	European Defence Agency
EEA	European Economic Area
EEC	European Economic Community
EFTA	European Free Trade Area
eGWG	e-Government Working Group
EIPA	European Institute for Public Administration
ELDR	European Liberal, Democratic and Reform Party
EMS	European Monetary System
EMU	European Monetary Union
ENP	European Neighbourhood Policy
EPP–ED	European People's Party – European Democrats
ER	Eestimaa Rohelised – Estonian Greens

ERC	Esquerra Republicana de Catalunya – Republican Left of Catalonia
ERDF	European Regional Development Fund
ERL	Eestimaa Rahvaliit – Estonian People's Union
ERM	Exchange Rate Mechanism
ERP	European Recovery Plan
ESDP	European Security and Defence Policy
ESF	European Social Fund
ETA	Euskadi ta Askatasuna – Basque Country and Freedom
ETUC	European Trade Union Confederation
EU	European Union
EUL–NGL	European United Left – Nordic Green Left Group
EUPAN	European Union Public Administration Network
Euratom	European Atomic Community
FDP	Freie Demokratische Partei – Free Democratic Party
FDP–PRD	Freisinnig-Demokratische Partei der Schweiz – Parti radical-démocratique suisse
Fidesz–MPS	Fidesz–Magyar Polgári Szövetség – Fidesz–Hungarian Citizen's Federation
FN	Front National – National Front
FNV	Federatie Nederlandse Vakbeweging – Dutch Federation of Trade Unions
FO	Force Ouvrière – Workers'Force
FPÖ	Freiheitliche Partei Österreichs – Freedom Party of Austria
GDP	Gross Domestic Product
GERB	Grajdani za evropeisko razvitie na Bulgarija – Citizens for the European Development of Bulgaria
GNI	Gross National Income
HMCTS	Her Majesty's Court and Tribunal Service
ICTU	Irish Congress of Trade Unions
IRL	Isamaa ja Res Publica Liit – Pro Patria and Res Publica
IU	Izquierda Unida – United Left
IV	Industriellenvereinigung – Industrial Association
JL	Jaunais Laiks – New Era
JKP	Jauna Konservativa Partija – New Conservative Party
JV	Jauna Vienotība – New Unity
K	Eesti Keskerakond – Estonian Centre Party
KD	Kristendemokraterna – Christian Democrats
KDH	Krest'ansdemokratické hnutie – Christian Democratic Union
KDNP	Kereszténydemokrata Néppárt – Christian Democratic People's Party
KDU–CSL	Křest'anska-demokratická unie – Československá strana lidová – Christian Democratic Union – Czechoslovak People's Party

KFP	Konservative Folkepartiet – Conservative People's Party
KFP	Kristellig Folkeparti – Christian People's Party
KPV LV	Kam Pieder Valsts – Who Owns the State
KKE	Kommunistiko Komma Ellada – Communist Party of Greece
KOK	Kansallinen Kokoomus – National Coalition Party
KSČM	Komunistická Strana Čech a Moravy – Communist Party of Bohemia and Moravia
LDS	Liberalna Demokracija Slovenije – Liberal Democracy of Slovenia
LiCS	Liberalų ir Centro Sąjunga – Liberal and Centre Union
LN	Lega Nord per l'independenza di Padania – Northern League for the independence of Padania
LO	Landesorganisationen – Trade Union Confederation in Sweden, Denmark and Norway
LPP–LC	Latvijas Pirmā Partija–Latvijas Ceļš
LPR	Liga Polskich Rodzin – League of Polish Families
LRLS	Lietuvos Respublikos Liberalų Sąjūdis – Lithuanian Republic Liberal Movement
LSDP	Lietuvos socialdemocratu partija – Lithuanian Social Democratic Party
LS–HZDS	L'udová strana–Hnutie za demokratické Slovensko
LVLS	Lietuvos Valstiečių Liaudininkų Sąjunga – Lithuanian Peasant Popular Union
LZS	Centriska Partija–Latvijas Zemnieku Savienība – Centre Party – Latvian Peasants Union
MDF	Hungarian Democratic Forum
MEDEF	Movement des Entrepreneurs Français – Movement of French Entrepreneurs
MoDem	Mouvement Democrat – Democratic Movement
MR	Mouvement Reformateur – Reforming Movement
MSI	Movimento Sociale Italiano – Italian Social Movement
MSZP	Magyar Szocialista Párt – Hungarian Socialist Party
NAF	Norges Arbeidsgiverforening – Norwegian Employers' Organisation
NATO	North Atlantic Treaty Organisation
NA	Nacionālā Apvienība – National Alliance
ND	Nea Dimokratia – New Democracy
NDSV	Nacionalno Dviženie za Stabilnost i Văzhod – National Movement for Stability and Progress
NGO	Non-Governmental Organisation
NHS	National Health Service
NKV	Nederlands Katholieke Vakverbond – Dutch Catholic Trade Union Confederation
NPD	Nationaldemokratische Partei Deutschlands – National Democratic Party of Germany

NPM	New Public Management
NS	Naujoji Sąjunga–Socialliberalai – New Union – Social Liberals
NSDAP	Nationalsozialististische Deutsche Arbeiterpartei – German National Socialist Workers' Party
NSI	Nova Slovenija–Krščanskih Democratov – New Slovenia – Christian Democrats
NVV	Nederlands Verbond van Vakbewegingen – Dutch Union of Trade Unions
ODS	Občanská demokratická strana – Democratic Civic Party
OECD	Organisation for Economic Cooperation and Development
OEEC	Organisation for European Economic Cooperation
ÖGB	Österreichischer Gewerkschaftsbund – Austrian Trade Union Confederation
OMC	Open Method of Coordination
OPEC	Organization of Petroleum Exporting Countries
OSCE	Organisation for Security and Cooperation in Europe
ÖVP	Österreichische Volkspartei – Austrian People's Party
PASOK	Panneliniko Sosialistiko Kinima – Panhellenic Socialist Movement
PCE	Partido Comunista Español – Spanish Communist Party
PCF	Parti Comuniste Français – French Communist Party
PCI	Partito Comunista Italiano – Italian Communist Party
PCP	Partido Comunista Português – Portuguese Communist Party
PCTVL	Par Cilvēka Tiesībām Vienotā Latvijā – For Human Rights in United Latvia
PD	Partidul Democrat – Democratic Party
PD	Partito Democratico – Democratic Party
PdL	Partito delle Libertá
PDS	Partei des Demokratischen Sozialismus – Party of Democratic Socialism
PDS	Partito Democratico della Sinistra – Democratic Party of the Left
PES	Party of European Socialists
PiS	Prawo i Sprawiedliwość – Law and Justice
PL	Popolo della Libertà – People of Freedom
PLD	Partidul Liberal Democrat – Liberal Democratic Party
PNF	Partito Nazionale Fascista – National Fascist Party
PNL	Partidul National Liberal – National Liberal Party
PNV	Partido Nacionalista Vasco – Basque Nationalist Party
PO	Platforma Obywatelska – Civic Platform
PP	Partido Popular – People's Party
PPI	Partito Populare Italiano – Italian People's Party
PRM	Partidul Romania Mare – Great Romania Party

PS	Partido Socialista – Socialist Party
PS	Parti Socialiste – Socialist Party
PSD	Partido Socialdemocrata – Social Democratic Party
PSD	Partidul Social Democrat – Social Democratic Party
PSI	Partito Socialista Italiano
PSL	Polskie Stronnictwo Ludowe – Polish People's Party
PSOE	Partido Socialista Obrero Español – Spanish Socialist Workers Party
PvdA	Partij van der Arbeid – Labour Party
RE	Eesti Reformierakond – Estonian Reform Party
RKSP	Roomisch Katholieke Staatspartij – Roman Catholic State Party
SAP	Sveriges Socialdemokratiska Arbetareparti – Swedish Social Democratic Workers' Party
SD	Socialni Demokrati – Social Democrats
SDE	Sotsiaaldemokraatlik Erakond – Social Democratic Party
SDKU–DS	Slovenská Demokratická a Krestanská Únia – Demokratická strana – Slovakian Democratic and Christian Union – Democratic Party
SDL	Sojusz Lewicy Demokratycznej – Democratic Left Alliance
SDLP	Social Democratic and Labour Party
SDPS	Sociāldemokrātiskā Partija 'Saskaņa' – Social Democratic Party 'Harmony'
SDS	Slovenska Demokratska Stranka – Slovenian Democratic Party
SDS	Săjuz na Demokratiăni Sili – Union of Democratic Forces
SEA	Single European Act
SEM	Single European Market
SF	Sinn Fein – We, Ourselves
SF/RK	Svenska folkspartiet/Ruotsalainen kansanpuolue – Swedish People's Party
SFP	Socialistisk Folkeparti – Socialist People's Party
SCP	Stability and Convergence Programme
SGP	Stability and Growth Pact
SIGMA	Support for Improvement and Governance and Management in Central and Eastern European Countries
SKL	Suomen Kristilinen Liitto – Finnish Christian Party
SLS	Slovenska Ljudska Stranka – Slovenian People's Party
SMER–SD	Smer–Sociálna Demokracia – Direction – Social Democracy
SMK	Strana madarskej koalície–Magyar Koalíció Pártja – Party of the Hungarian Coalition
SNP	Scottish National Party
SNS	Slovenska Nacionalna Stranka – Slovenian National Party (Nationalist)

SNS	Slovenská Národná Strana – Slovak National Party (Nationalist)
SP.A	Socialistische Partij – Anders – Socialist Party – Different
SPD	Sozialdemokratische Partei Deutschlands – Social Democratic Party of Germany
SPÖ	Sozialdemokratisches Partei Österreichs – Social Democratic Party of Austria
SRB	Samoobrona Rzeczpospolitei Polskiei – Self-defence of Republic of Poland
SV	Socialistisk Venstreparti – Socialist Left Party
SVP	Schweizerische Volkspartei – Swiss People's Party
SYN/SYRIZA	Synaspismos tis Rizospastikis Aristeras (SYRIZA) – Coalition of Radical Left
SzDSz	Szabad Demokraták Szövetsége – Union of Free Democrats
TA	Treaty of Amsterdam
TEU	Treaty of the European Union/Treaty of Maastricht
ToL	Treaty of Lisbon
TP	Tautas Partija – People's Party
TPP	Tautos Prisikėlimo Partija – National Revival Party
TS-LKD	Tėvynės Sąjunga–Lietuvos Krikščionys Demokratai – Homeland Union–Lithuanian Christian Democrats
TT	Tvarka ir Teisingumas – Order and Justice
TUC	Trade Union Congress
UDF	Union de la Democratie Française – Union of French Democracy
UDMR	Uniunea Democratică Maghiară din România – Hungarian Democratic Union in Romania
UEN	Union of European Nations
UGT	União Geral dos Trabalhadores – General Union of Workers
UGT	Union General de Trabajadores – General Union of Workers
UIL	Unione Italiana del Lavoro – Italian Union of Labour
UK	United Kingdom
UMP	Union pour le Mouvement Populaire – Union for the People's Movement
UN	United Nations
UNAPL	Union National des Professions Liberales – National Union of Liberal Professions
UPA	Union Professionelle Artisanale – Crafts Union
USA	United States of America
USSR	Union of Socialist Soviet Republics
UUP	Ulster Unionist Party
VB	Vlaams Belang – Flemish Interest

VBO-FEB	Verbond van Belgische Ondernemingen – Fédération des Employeurs de Belgique
VLD	Vlaamse Liberalen en Democraten – Flemish Liberals and Democrats
VVD	Volkspartij voor Vrijheid en Democratie – People's Party for Freedom and Democracy
WASG	Wahlgruppe für Arbeit und soziale Gerechtigkeit – Electoral Group for Work and Social Justice
Z	Zares – For Real
ZZS	Zaļo un Zemnieku Savienība (ZZS)

Chapter 1

Introduction to contemporary European politics

- The rationale of the book: the emergence of new European politics
- A comparative approach: cross-country differences, similarities and convergences
- Reducing complexity through the use of regional clusters
- The 'great transformation' of the late twentieth century
- The growing importance of the European integration process
- Constitutions and constitutionalism
- Suggested reading

The rationale of the book: the emergence of new European politics

The unification of the European continent since the fall of the Berlin Wall in 1989 and the collapse of communist regimes in Central and Eastern Europe has changed the nature of European politics. This book seeks to address the new European politics that emerged out of this coming together of West and East. Accordingly, a pan-European approach towards contemporary politics is used in order to understand better the political, social and economic dynamics of Europe.

Although we focus on comparing the national political systems across Europe, this is contextualised within the overarching and growing importance of European integration. The European Union (EU) multilevel governance system approach will be used to show the relationships and interactions between the supranational, national, regional and local levels. Some references will also be made to the relationship between the EU and global governance (see later and also Chapter 10).

In this book we argue that European politics has changed since the 1970s from modern politics, in which the nation-state was still in command of domestic politics, to what the sociologists Anthony Giddens and Ulrich Beck called reflexive global modern politics, in which the nation-state lost full control of domestic processes due to growing global interdependence. Among such processes one may mention deterritorialisation (e.g. the impact of globalised financial markets), denationalisation (e.g. the questioning of the nation-state by secessionist movements for example in Catalonia, Flanders or Scotland) and internationalisation (e.g. the need to cooperate in matters of global climate change), all of which have considerably altered the national politics of individual member-states (Beck, 2008; Giddens, 2016: 145–6).

A comparative approach: cross-country differences, similarities and convergences

Since Aristotle's book *Politics*, the comparative approach has been an excellent way to identify – out of the uniqueness of each political system, group or 'families' of countries – a method that clearly helps us to reduce the complexity of analysing all the political systems of Europe. The main aim of the comparative approach is not only to reduce complexity by showing similarities and differences but also to identify patterns of behaviour within institutions such as political parties, parliaments, governments and the judiciary (Aristotle, 2017 [1912]; Finer, 1970: 38–9).

If we take membership of the Council of Europe – the largest intergovernmental organisation in Europe, not to be confused with the EU, a much smaller supranational institution – there are forty-seven European member countries. This number includes Turkey, Russia, Ukraine, Moldova, Georgia, Armenia and Azerbaijan. Only Belarus, which is the only dictatorship in Europe and which does not comply with the minimum standards of democratic order, is not a member. A more restricted definition of Europe includes: the twenty-seven members of the EU (post Brexit) plus the UK; the seven Balkan states (expected to become members at some stage in the future) plus Kosovo; and the European Economic Area countries

Iceland, Norway and Liechtenstein. Iceland was also a potential candidate country for joining the EU, but after the finance crisis the more nationalist Independence party led government withdrew the candidacy. So far, a solid majority of Icelanders is opposed to the EU, and only two smaller parties in parliament after the October 2017 elections, namely the social democratic party and Reform, are pro-European. Therefore, a membership application has been put on hold for the immediate future (*Icelandic monitor*, 7 November 2017). This would lead to a total of thirty-seven countries if we do not include micro-states like Liechtenstein, Andorra and San Marino. Kosovo remains in a limbo situation due to the split in the international community about its recognition; slightly over 100 out of 192 countries have recognised Kosovo, including twenty-two of the EU member-states. Within the EU, Greece, Spain, Romania, Slovakia and Cyprus are against Kosovo becoming a member (*BBC News*, 17 February 2018), and only the future will tell whether there can be a solution to this problem. Although the present Serbian government is quite pragmatic in relation to EU membership, nevertheless it continues to use its diplomatic channels to either discourage countries to recognise or withdraw recognition. Tensions between Serbia and Kosovo emerge regularly. Presently, the issue of 'border corrections' in the north of Kosovo, suggested by the EU, where a Serbian minority live, have led again to the rise of tensions (*Euractiv*, 16 January 2017, 17 September 2018, 1 October 2018; *Balkan Insight*, 31 October 2017).

We have excluded an in-depth consideration of Russia, Ukraine, Moldova, Turkey, Georgia, Armenia and Azerbaijan. However, in some chapters we still make reference to those countries. One of the main reasons is that they represent different political traditions and 'families', more on the side lines of core European politics. However, Chapter 11 is dedicated to these political systems of wider Europe.

In this regard, the EU cannot expand forever. A more realistic approach about core and wider Europe would certainly be advisable. In this volume, I support former German chancellor Helmut Schmidt's wise advice that Russia, Ukraine, Belarus and Turkey do not belong to this core Europe, but rather to wider Europe. Good neighbouring relations and cooperation should be central to the relationship between the EU and the wider Europe, maybe a privileged partnership, but no membership should be offered (Schmidt, 2000). It is overstretching which countries belong to Europe, if I even consider the three Caucasus countries Georgia, Armenia and Azerbaijan. Moldova is the only post-Soviet state that clearly has a good chance of becoming part of the EU, mainly due to its close historical legacy to Romania. However, this is certainly disputable by supporters of an independent Moldovanist identity. Geostrategist George Friedman characterised Moldova as a state without a nation, due to a very divided national identity (Friedman, 2011: 44).

Box 1.1 Why compare European countries?

- In order to understand the main features of European politics it is important to reduce complexity.
- The main task is to group countries into 'families' and compare these families so that the comparison of thirty-seven European countries becomes manageable.

(continued)

(continued)

- The comparative method allows us to classify, describe and analyse not only individual countries but also 'families' of countries using a vast number of political variables.
- The comparison of different political systems contributes to a better understanding of how institutions and processes work and helps identify which similarities and differences one can find between the various 'families' of countries.

In order to gain broader insights into contemporary European politics, we focus on the thirty-seven countries, which clearly represent different patterns of European politics (Table 1.1). The least developed region in terms of democracy and human rights is the Balkans, which are scheduled to join the EU at the end of 2020s. Although we include some references to these countries, they will be rather neglected in comparison to the core EU countries (twenty-seven), the UK, Switzerland, Iceland and Norway.

In this book, we follow Samuel E. Finer's interpretation of the comparative approach. The main task is to group institutions, political systems or processes into 'families' or 'types' that are close to each other. Grouping countries that resemble each other into families and contrasting the countries both within the families and in relation to the countries within the other families helps us to understand why and how differences and similarities exist between countries (Box 1.1). The main questions in this book are: *why* European political systems, or at least families of countries, are different from or similar to each other; and *how* these differences and similarities are demonstrated (Finer, 1970: 38–9). In responding to these questions, we are able to learn a lot about some of the positive and negative aspects of institutions and processes, as well as understand why some political systems are performing better or worse than others. This process also allows the uniqueness of some political systems or ill-conceived institutional transfers from one country to another to be identified. Therefore, the book will mainly describe, classify and analyse comparatively the diverse political systems of Europe. In the end, comparing European politics depends very much on what the researcher believes is important to compare (Finer, 1970: 39)

One characteristic of this book is that it attempts to compare, at the least, all thirty-seven countries of Europe (although this is subject to how much information exists). In this sense, this reveals an ambition to overcome the bias of most comparative books on Europe that focus only on the larger countries plus, on occasion, the Netherlands. We have combined the comparative approach with detailed information about each of the European countries. Of course, such an enterprise will be stronger in some sections than others, but we considered it important to be distinctive from most comparative studies on European politics. In this book, both larger and smaller countries have been covered extensively in order to achieve a more balanced approach to the reality of European politics.

Reducing complexity through the use of regional clusters

In order to reduce the complexity of individually analysing all thirty-seven countries, we grouped them into regional clusters. This allowed us to simplify the comparison of countries (see Table 1.1), although we also kept some flexibility in using these regional clusters. Other categories at times superseded the importance of regional political cultures – for example, if countries clearly belong to a particular type such as majoritarian versus consensus democracies, weak or strong parliaments, federal or unitary states, then these regional clusters were only partially used or completely discarded. We differentiated at least twelve regions, some of them, such as France and Turkey, consisting of one country only.

The Benelux countries: Belgium, the Netherlands and Luxembourg have a common history. Belgium became independent from the Netherlands in 1830. Luxembourg became independent after the Vienna Congress, though it has strong historical links with both Belgium and the Netherlands. The union known as the Benelux was formed after 1944.

German-speaking/Drei-Sat Europe: This comprises Germany, Austria and Switzerland. 'German-speaking' is clearly a difficult label, but it refers to the common language of the three countries. In the case of Switzerland, there is also francophone Switzerland, influenced more by France; however, the vast majority of the population in Switzerland is German-speaking. There is a common television channel called 3Sat, established in 1984 by the public televisions of Austria (ORF), Switzerland (SRG) and Germany (ZDF, ARD) that broadcasts in all three countries.

Nordic Europe: This comprises the Scandinavian countries – Norway, Sweden and Denmark. Additionally Finland and Iceland are also included. The cooperation between the Nordic countries is intense, so this region has a strong common identity.

British Isles: This includes the United Kingdom and the Republic of Ireland. Although the UK is a monarchy and the Republic of Ireland is a republic, the historical legacy and the common language makes it sensible to group these two countries together. There is also the issue of Northern Ireland that has led to joint efforts by the two countries to achieve a peace settlement. There are considerable political institutionalised channels between the two countries.

Southern Europe: This comprises Portugal, Spain, Greece and Italy. They show many similar historical and structural features that allow us to speak of a regional cluster.

France: The uniqueness of France deserves a special place in the typology.

Mediterranean islands: The island status of Malta and Cyprus located in the Mediterranean is ideal for grouping them together.

Baltic Europe: The three former Soviet republics of Estonia, Latvia and Lithuania gained independence in 1992. They work together through Baltic institutions, and all of them were independent between 1918 and 1939. They are also small democracies with small populations, which is clearly a good reason to group them together.

(East) Central Europe: According to Attila Ágh, a Hungarian political scientist, there are considerable differences in both development and political culture between the east Central European countries and the Eastern European ones. The Central European countries are Hungary, the Czech Republic, Slovakia, Poland and Slovenia. Although Slovenia belongs geographically to the western Balkans, in terms of political culture and development it leans more towards East Central Europe.

Eastern Europe: This comprises Bulgaria, Romania and Croatia. In comparison to East Central Europe, they are less developed and their political systems are still being consolidated. Political corruption has been a major problem for all three countries. Just for analytical purposes, we decided to include Croatia in this group after they joined the EU in 2013. In reality, Croatia is geographically and culturally strongly associated with the western Balkans.

Balkan Europe: This comprises most of the republics of former Yugoslavia and Albania. The countries of former Yugoslavia are Serbia, Bosnia-Herzegovina, Macedonia, Montenegro and Kosovo. Slovenia and Croatia have been assigned to other clusters after joining the EU.

These different regional clusters comprise the thirty-seven countries which we will be comparing in this book.

Outside these regional clusters are the countries of wider Europe. We may differentiate between two clusters:

The post-Soviet countries: Here one has to locate Russia, Ukraine, Belarus, Moldova, Georgia, Armenia and Azerbaijan. They have a common heritage related to their past Soviet legacy. All these countries were republics within the Soviet Union and never had a period of sustained independence. They all are still characterised by divided populations that still partly support Russia.

Turkey: Some authors include Turkey as part of Southern Europe, others tend to exclude it (see Table 1.1 and Figure 1.1). Turkey seems to be heading towards a façade democracy or even dictatorship similar to many of the post-Soviet countries, so that it is in the process of abandoning the regional community of democratic states, if not dramatically changing its course.

Chapter 11 on the wider Europe and the neighbourhood policy of the EU will focus more on the political systems of these two regional clusters of wider Europe.

One particular issue is that the socioeconomic living standards of the different regional clusters still show many disparities (Figure 1.2). While Nordic countries, Benelux and German-speaking Europe have high living standards with the highest human development index of the world and a favourable structure of opportunities for the participation and empowerment of women, such standards are not reached in Southern Europe.

In order to gain a first quantitative overview of the differences between the regional clusters, we use here the well-established Human Development Index and the Gender Inequality Index developed by the United Nations. These two

Table 1.1 Data on territory and population of countries in Europe according to regional clusters

Regional clusters	*Countries*	*Area in square kilometres*	*Population in millions (2018) For Wider Europe (2017)*	*Urban population (2017)*	*Average birth rate of number of children per woman 2010–15*
Benelux	Belgium	32,545	11.4	98	1.8
	Luxembourg	2,586	0.6	90	1.6
	Netherlands	41,526	17.2	90	1.8
Germanic Europe	Austria	83,871	8.8	66	1.5
	Germany	357,093	82.8	85	1.4
	Switzerland	41,285	8.5	75	1.5
	Lichtenstein	0.160	0.038	nd	nd
Nordic Europe	Denmark	43,098	5.8	88	1.7
	Finland	338,144	5.5	84	1.7
	Iceland	103,000	0.3	94	2.0
	Norway	323,759	5.3	80	1.8
	Sweden	449,964	10.1	86	1.9
British Isles	Ireland	70,273	4.8	63	2.0
	UK	242,910	66.3	83	1.9
Southern Europe	Greece	131,957	10.7	78	1.3
	Italy	301,336	60.5	69	1.4
	Portugal	92,345	10.3	63	1.3
	Spain	504,645	46.7	80	1.3
	Andorra	0.467	0.1	nd	nd
	San Marino	0.061	0.033	nd	nd
France	France	543,965	66.9	80	2.0
Mediterranean islands	Cyprus	9,251	0.9	67	1.5
	Malta	316	0.475	95	1.4
Baltic Europe	Estonia	45,227	1.3	68	1.6
	Latvia	64,589	1.9	67	1.5
	Lithuania	65,301	2.8	67	1.6
Central Europe	Czech Republic	78,866	10.6	73	1.5
	Hungary	93,030	9.8	71	1.3
	Poland	312,685	38.0	61	1.4
	Slovakia	49,034	5.4	54	1.4
	Slovenia	20,253	2.1	50	1.6
Eastern Europe	Bulgaria	110,194	7.1	74	1.5
	Romania	238,391	19.5	55	1.5

(continued)

Table 1.1 *(continued)*

Regional clusters	*Countries*	*Area in square kilometres*	*Population in millions (2018) For Wider Europe (2017)*	*Urban population (2017)*	*Average birth rate of number of children per woman 2010–15*
Balkan Europe	Albania	28,748	2.9	57	1.8
	Bosnia-Herzegovina	51,129	3.8	40	1.3
	Croatia	56,542	4.1	59	1.5
	North Macedonia	25,713	2.1	57	1.5
	Serbia	88,361	7.0	56	1.6
	Montenegro	13,812	0.6	64	1.7
	Kosovo	10,887	1.8	nd	nd
WIDER EUROPE					
Post-Soviet states	Russia	17,075,400	144.5	74	1.7
	Ukraine	603,700	44.8	70	1.5
	Belarus	207,595	9.5	77	1.5
	Moldova	33,800	3.6	45	1.3
	Georgia	69,700	3.7	54	1.8
	Armenia	29,743	2.9	63	1.6
	Azerbaijan	86,600	9.9	55	2.3
Turkey	Turkey	779,452	80.8	73	2.1

Source: Data from Eurostat (2018e); Fischer (2018: 528–31); United Nations (2016: 222–5).

indexes are quite useful, owing to their universal acceptance, but also because the United Nations collects data from all countries of the world. Moreover, we also include the Global Gender Gap and the Gender Equality Indexes of the World Economic Forum and the EU respectively to make our comparison more robust. In spite of this, there are missing data for some countries in the Balkans such as Serbia, Montenegro, Albania and Bosnia-Herzegovina. The graph in Figure 1.3 shows that economic prosperity is highest in the Nordic countries, Benelux, the Drei-Sat countries, France and the British Isles. The lowest is to be found in the Balkans, Eastern Europe, Baltic Europe, the post-Soviet countries and Turkey (Table 1.2).

This leads to a similar differentiation in terms of human development, gender inequality and gender equality indexes (Figure 1.4). The latter measures gender equality. As a rule of thumb, one could dare to assert that the greater the gender equality in a country that exists, the more democratic society will be. The Nordic countries are known for a very lively participating civil society in a consensus-seeking and building political system. In contrast, the Balkans, Eastern Europe, the post-Soviet states and Turkey still have a long way to go in order to achieve greater gender equality and therefore a more democratic society. Such

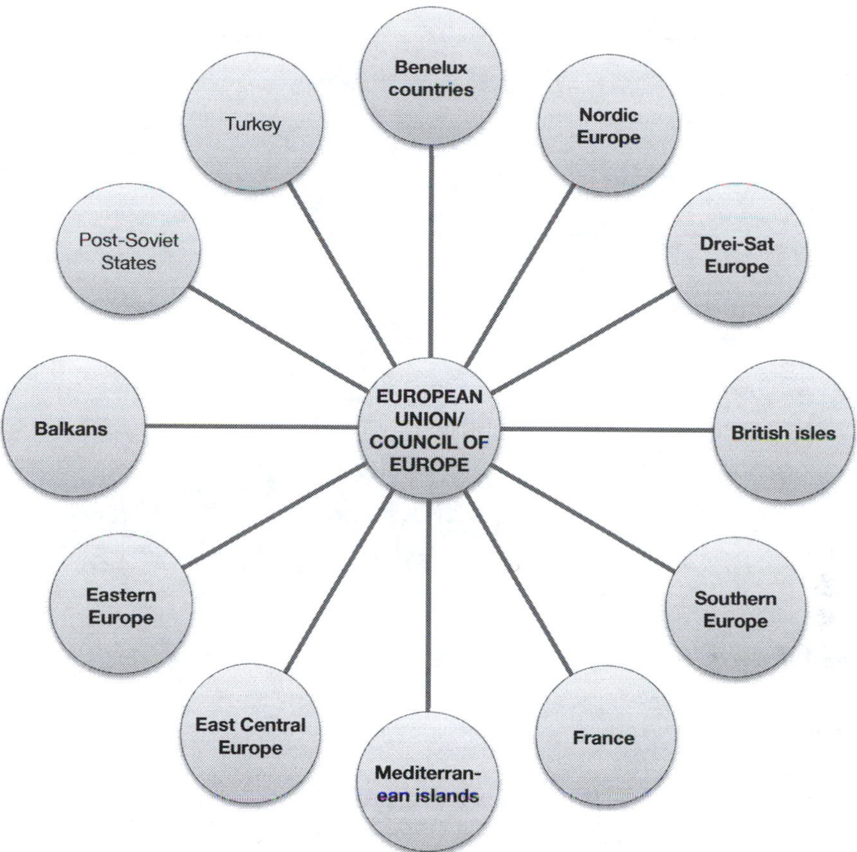

Figure 1.1 Regional clusters of Europe

Note: Wider Europe countries are not in bold

gender equality is still lagging behind in Southern, Central and Baltic Europe as well. Similar index levels to the Nordic countries can be found in the British Isles, France, the Drei-Sat countries and the Benelux.

In spite of these figures giving only a snapshot of the different regional clusters, they immediately show how diverse Europe still is. It is the aim of this book to look through all political aspects of European politics in order to compare the similarities, differences and tendencies towards convergence between the countries.

The 'great transformation' of the late twentieth century

Since the early 1970s European politics has changed considerably. Apart from the growing impact of globalisation and Europeanisation processes, one can observe change in the social structure of European societies in this major transformation.

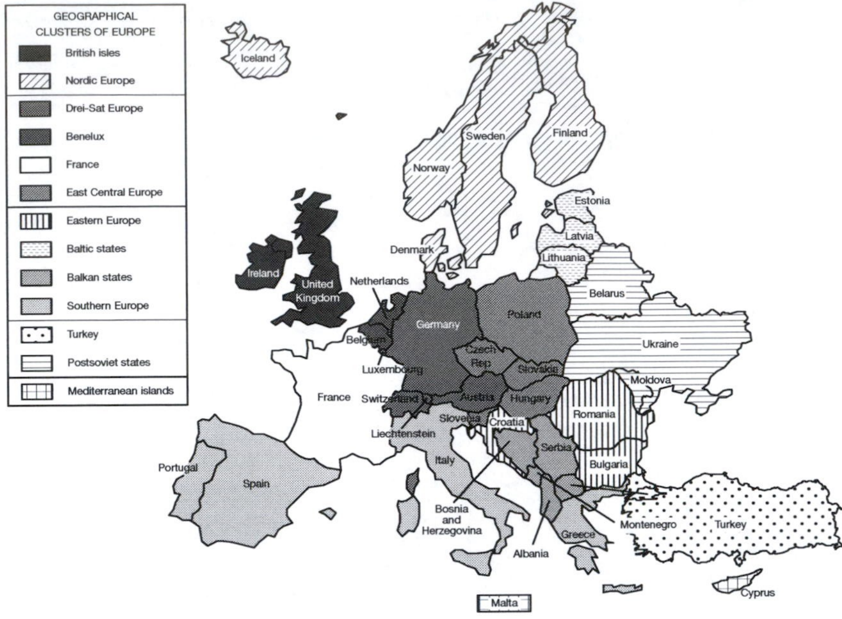

Figure 1.2 Geographical clusters of Europe

Table 1.2 Socioeconomic data on European countries

Regional clusters	*Countries*	*GNI/per capita (2016) US$ PPP*	*Human development index (HDI) inequality adjusted 2015 0 (Low) 1 (High)*	*Gender inequality index 2015 0 (equality), 1 (full inequality)*	*Gender gap index (World Economic Forum) 0 (Low) 1 (High)*	*Gender equality index (EU) 2012 0 (No equality) 100 (Full equality)*
Benelux	Belgium	46,383	0.821	0.073	0.745	58.2
	Luxembourg	105,882	0.827	0.075	0.734	55.2
	Netherlands	50,898	0.861	0.044	0.756	68.5
Germanic Europe	Austria	50,078	0.815	0.078	0.716	50.2
	Germany	48,730	0.859	0.066	0.766	55.3
	Switzerland	62,882	0.939	0.040	0.776	
Nordic Europe	Denmark	46,696	0.858	0.041	0.754	70.9
	Finland	43,053	0.843	0.056	0.845	72.7
	Iceland	52,490	0.868	0.051	0.874	

	Norway	59,302	0.851	0.053	0.842	
	Sweden	49,175	0.851	0.048	0.815	74.2
British Isles	Ireland	68,883	0.850	0.127	0.797	56.5
	UK	42,100	0.836	0.131	0.752	58.0
Southern Europe	Greece	26,783	0.758	0.119	0.680	38.3
	Italy	38,161	0.784	0.085	0.719	41.1
	Portugal	30,624	0.755	0.091	0.737	37.9
	Spain	36,310	0.791	0.081	0.738	53.6
France	France	41,466	0.813	0.102	0.755	55.7
Mediterranean islands	Cyprus	32,580	0.762	0.116	0.684	44.9
	Malta	37,899	0.786	0.217	0.664	46.8
Baltic Europe	Estonia	28,920	0.788	0.131	0.747	49.8
	Latvia	26,031	0.742	0.191	0.755	46.9
	Lithuania	29,966	0.759	0.121	0.744	40.2
Central Europe	Czech Republic	34,711	0.830	0.129	0.690	43.8
	Hungary	26,681	0.771	0.252	0.669	41.6
	Poland	27,711	0.774	0.137	0.727	43.7
	Slovakia	30,632	0.793	0.179	0.679	36.5
	Slovenia	32,885	0.838	0.053	0.786	57.3
Eastern Europe	Bulgaria	16,261	0.709	0.223	0.726	38.5
	Romania	23,626	0.714	0.339	0.690	33.7
Balkan Europe	Albania	10,252	0.661	0.267	0.704	
	Bosnia-Herzegovina	12,075	0.650 0.650	–	0.685	
	Croatia	20,291	0.752	0.141	0.700	39.8
	Macedonia	15,121	0.623	0.161	0.696	
	Serbia	14,512	0.689	0.185	0.720	
	Montenegro	17,854	0.736	0.146	0.681	
	Kosovo	10,200				
WIDER EUROPE						
Post-Soviet states	Russia	23,163	0.725	0.271	0.691	
	Ukraine	8,272	0.690	0.284	0.700	
	Belarus	18,060	0.745	0.144	0.737	
	Moldova	5,333	0.628	0.232	0.741	
	Georgia	9,997	0.672	0.361	0.681	
	Armenia	8,818	0.674	0.293	0.669	
	Azerbaijan	17,253	0.659	0.326	0.684	
Turkey	Turkey	24,244	0.645	0.328	0.623	

Source: EIGE (2015); UNDP (2016: 206–9, 214–17); WEF (2016: 10–11).

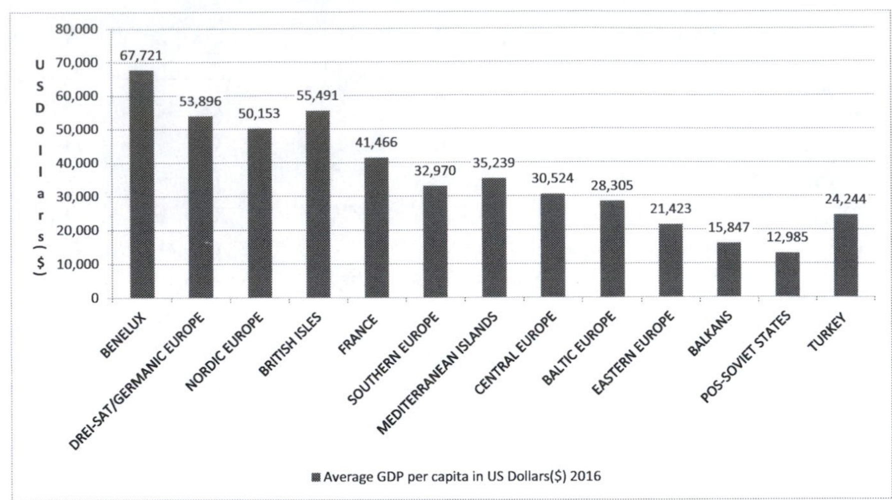

Figure 1.3 Gross domestic product per capita in 2016 in US$ in European and wider Europe regions according to PPP

Source: Author's graph based on data from World Bank (2017) database.

In the transition from the nineteenth to the twentieth centuries, the industrial revolution had already led to major changes and transformations in society, politics and the economy. Economic historian Karl Polanyi called this the 'great transformation' (Polanyi, 1944). Similarly, I would argue that in the late twentieth century, particularly since the 1970s, a major 'great transformation' has been taking place that has affected politics, the economy and society. As already mentioned, Anthony Giddens and Ulrich Beck call this is a continuing transition from a domestically nation-state-based modernity with a model of exponential growth to a globally based reflexive modernity, which is characterised by risk and a higher degree of uncertainty. Three logics are at play in global reflexive modernisation: a society more vulnerable to risk due to its complexity, individualisation and cosmopolitanisation (Beck, 2008: 37; Giddens, 2016: 145–6). The latter process has been emerging as a consequence of the denationalisation of the nation-state. More and more political, economic and social interactions cannot be controlled by the nation-state due to its globalisation. Chapter 3 deals more in detail with these transformations. In this first introductory chapter it suffices to describe superficially which main changes have taken place in European politics (see Figure 1.5).

State: One of the crucial features of the modern state is its internal and external sovereignty. Since the 1990s it has been experiencing a decline of both kinds of sovereignty, particularly as a result of the European integration process. Most European countries share sovereignty regimes in many policy areas, for example the environment, justice and home affairs, economic and monetary policy, and trade policy. Pooling sovereignty together at EU level allows for more leverage and influence globally (for further detail, see Chapter 10).

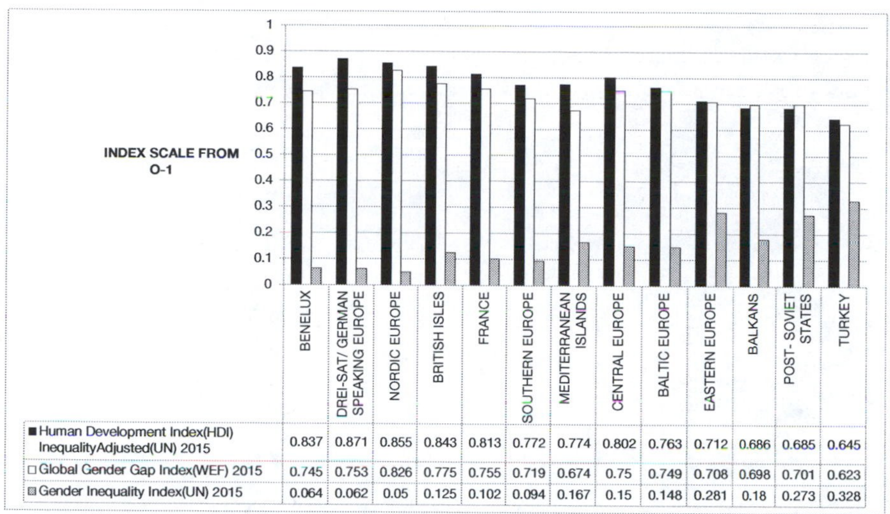

	BENELUX	DREI-SAT/ GERMAN SPEAKING EUROPE	NORDIC EUROPE	BRITISH ISLES	FRANCE	SOUTHERN EUROPE	MEDITERRANEAN ISLANDS	CENTRAL EUROPE	BALTIC EUROPE	EASTERN EUROPE	BALKANS	POST- SOVIET STATES	TURKEY
■ Human Development Index(HDI) InequalityAdjusted(UN) 2015	0.837	0.871	0.855	0.843	0.813	0.772	0.774	0.802	0.763	0.712	0.686	0.685	0.645
□ Global Gender Gap Index(WEF) 2015	0.745	0.753	0.826	0.775	0.755	0.719	0.674	0.75	0.749	0.708	0.698	0.701	0.623
▨ Gender Inequality Index(UN) 2015	0.064	0.062	0.05	0.125	0.102	0.094	0.167	0.15	0.148	0.281	0.18	0.273	0.328

Figure 1.4 Gender equality indexes for European regional clusters and wider Europe on a scale 0–1 in 2015

Source: Based on data from UNDP (2016: 206–9, 214–17); WEF (2016: 10–11).

Subnational government: Until the late 1960s most European countries were highly centralised, the exceptions being the federal states of West Germany, Switzerland and Austria. This changed considerably during the 1980s and 1990s. The regions became more self-conscious and practised their own paradiplomacy, bypassing the main gatekeeper of central government. Many countries such as the UK, Italy, Spain, Belgium, Poland, the Czech Republic and Slovakia moved to decentralised subnational government structures. Other countries such as Sweden, Finland, Denmark and the Netherlands adjusted to more flexible structures in order to deal with the emerging EU multilevel governance systems. Some 'stateless nations' such as Scotland, Catalonia, Basque country and Flanders want to go beyond a federal system within a larger whole, and become independent. Such movements have become more radical over the decades.

Welfare: In the 1970s, post-war economics stopped growing economically. Stagflation – stagnation of the economy mixed with high levels of inflation – created problems for the competitiveness of Western European economies (Scharpf, 2000; Schmidt, 2008). The state apparatus became too expensive due to an increasing welfare state. Since the 1980s, the former universalistic welfare state was transformed into a workfare one, in which flexibility of labour markets were at the centre supported by more or less strong social security systems. In the EU, this is called flexicurity, influenced by the Danish model. Social benefits are now linked to work and individual efforts towards employability. This shift of paradigm has also been labelled the 'social investment state' (Hemerijck, 2013, 2018).

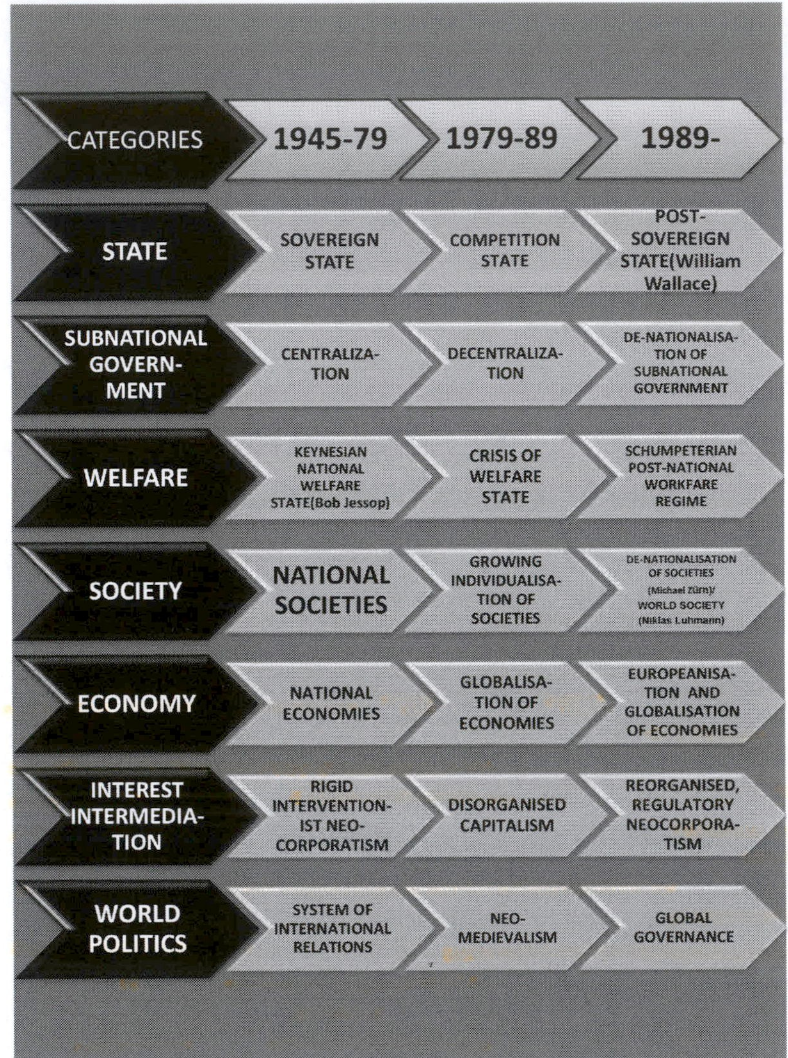

Figure 1.5 The 'great transformation' of the late twentieth century since the 1970s

Society: The fairly homogeneous national societies of the 1950s and 1960s have been replaced by more heterogeneous ones, where immigrants have integrated or live in European societies. 'Multicultural' societies have emerged in the UK, France, Spain, Belgium, the Netherlands and Germany. However, each country has developed different immigration policies. The European integration process is pushing countries to make an effort to integrate the immigrant population. This is important, because European societies are currently being affected by a major demographic change arising from a low birth rate and an ageing population. Immigration is the only way to sustain the economic development that these societies have enjoyed until now. Since 2015, Europe has had to deal with a refugee crisis due to the war in Syria, but also including illegal immigrants from other parts of the world, in the quest to find a better life.

Economy: The booming economies of Western Europe up to the late 1960s were replaced by a period of stagflation. Since the 1980s, liberalisation and privatisation have transformed the state into a competition state (Cerny, 1990: 220–31), which is efficient in ensuring the competitiveness of the national economy globally. Such transformations were initiated by Ronald Reagan in the United States (Reaganomics) and Prime Minister Margaret Thatcher in the UK (Thatcherism) and spread then to the European Community/EU through European Commissioner Lord Cockfield's Single Market Programme (SEM). Today, European integration constrains considerably the choices of EU countries, particularly those that are members of the Economic and Monetary Union (EMU). This became evident during the financial crisis 2008–13, in which the southern European countries had to struggle to keep their finances afloat (see Chapter 10).

Interest intermediation: After 1945 most Western European countries were very keen to integrate the social partners, employers' and workers' organisations in economic and social policy-making. The main aim was to achieve a high level of social peace and economic stability. However, when stagflation set in and the economy became inefficient, the new liberalisation thrusts led to a decline of such neo-corporatist arrangements. In the 1980s, one has to speak of 'disorganised capitalism', of which the UK example under Prime Minister Margaret Thatcher became the most radical expression. However, since the 1990s, there has been a return to cooperation with social partners in order to achieve support for regulatory policies in the economy (Schmitter and Grote, 1997). While until the 1970s, neo-corporatism was intrusive and interventionist, today's variant is rather regulatory and light. Moreover, it is multilevel, so that social partnership is also important in socioeconomic governance at supranational level through the European semester and national level through formal bodies or informal settings (see Chapter 8).

World politics: Since the 1980s there has also been a shift from a system of international relations in which states act according to their selfish interests, are the only actors and fight each other according to their national interest (the realist school), to a more complex global governance system in which other actors have emerged and been able to influence world politics. These include international non-governmental organisations (NGOs), supranational organisations such as the EU and also subnational actors such as the regions. The growing importance of transnational corporations and their corporate social responsibility policies has changed the role of the state in world politics.

The growing importance of the European integration process

Although European integration has many flaws and is incomplete, it has to be regarded as a great success of European politics. This project based on peace, the rule of law and tolerance of diversity changed the belligerent culture between countries, particularly between France and Germany. Today, most Europeans take this for granted, something that was achieved over centuries, at least since the peace of Westphalia in 1948. Concrete efforts towards European integration have been taking place since the second half of the 1940s. The Organisation for European Economic Cooperation (OEEC), founded in 1948 and sponsored by the United States as a means to coordinate the disbursements of the European Recovery Plan (the Marshall Plan) to Western European countries, may be regarded as a first important step towards trying to create a single European market. This was the idea of the US Truman administration but was blocked by many European countries (Milward, 1984). Therefore, the OEEC remained an intergovernmental organisation, similar to the Council of Europe, which was founded in 1949. It eventually became the international Organisation for Economic Cooperation and Development (OECD) in 1960, a global club of advanced democracies and economies.

The second attempt by the US administration to achieve a supranational institution was the Schuman plan proclaimed on 9 May 1950 (see Clemens et al., 2008: 95–100). It led to the European Coal and Steel Community (ECSC) after 1952, the origins of the EU as we know it today. In 1957, the Rome Treaties led to the establishment of the European Economic Community (EEC) and the Euratom. In 1967, all three communities were merged. Originally, there were just six members: France, West Germany, Belgium, Luxembourg, Netherlands and Italy. In the 1970s and early 1980s, European integration stagnated, only to be revived by president of the European Commission Jacques Delors during his incumbency between 1985 and 1995. Within a decade, Delors had transformed an almost invisible supranational organisation into a world economic and political power. This transformation was not easy, as there was a continuing resistance on the part of the member-states to transfer more powers to the EU. In spite of this, the achievements of European integration since 1985 have been remarkable. By 2013, the EU had expanded to twenty-eight members. Over the past thirty-two years, the EU has instituted a common currency, the euro, progressed considerably in the creation of a Single European Market (SEM), developed long-term strategies to gain more influence over the world economy, expanded its common foreign and security policy, has a common trade policy and is a world leader in the global climate change debate. The visionary strategic approach of Jacques Delors has transformed the EU into what it is today (on Delors strategy, see Ross, 1995). Although a lot has been achieved, in a time of re-emergence of super power politics, the EU needs now to position itself globally. The financial crisis 2008–13 and the refugee crisis of the summer 2015 has put the EU under considerable pressure and has also undermined its credibility as a potential superpower.

This book also intends to show that the national and supranational policy-making of the EU are increasingly interwoven . In reality, the member-states of the EU have become part of a new political system *sui generis* (Hix, 2005; Schmidt, 2005; Wessels, 2008). This means that member-states no longer have complete sovereignty over all their policies and politics. On the contrary, they increasingly work more closely together in order to move towards a European dimension of policy-making, such as the construction of the SEM or the EMU. They are increasingly locked in a regime of shared pooled sovereignty in many core policy areas, including economic and monetary policy (first mentioned by Wallace, 1999). Local, regional, national and supranational institutions interact with each other and with market and civil society actors in a multilevel governance system, which means that policy-making and politics have become fairly complex (see Hooghe and Marks, 2001; Marks et al., 1996).

In Chapter 10, the growing importance of Europeanisation processes leading up to a new multilevel governance system will be discussed thoroughly. More generally, most chapters also deal with this European dimension, demonstrating that the local, regional, national and supranational levels are becoming increasingly intertwined.

Constitutions and constitutionalism

The origins of European constitutions

The making of a European democratic constitutional space: the role of the Council of Europe and the EU

In spite of the European integration process, for each individual country the national constitution remains the most important document (Figure 1.6, Box 1.2). The failure to adopt a Constitutional Treaty in 2005, following negative referenda in both France and the Netherlands in May and June respectively, shows the reluctance of most populations to reduce the importance of their own national constitutions. In this section, we give some first comparative insights into constitutions and constitutionalism that will help the reader throughout the book to understand which principles, rights, duties and institutional orders are common to all European countries. The role of the Council of Europe and the EU in framing national constitutional orders cannot be emphasised enough.

The EU member-states as well as the countries outside it are embedded in a European constitutional democratic space that was built over time before and after the Second World War. Such processes started in the eighteenth century in the French Revolution of 1776, influenced by the American Revolution and US American constitution of 1776 and 1787 respectively, and culminated in the start of the European integration process on the foundation of the Council of Europe in 1949 and the European Coal and Steel Community (ECSC) in 1952. Therefore, myriad international intergovernmental and supranational institutions played a role in structuring legally and politically national constitutional orders. Probably the most relevant one is the intergovernmental Council of Europe, which comprises forty-seven countries and sets the standards for democratic governance in those countries. Central to the role of the Council of Europe is the Charter of Fundamental Rights and the European Court of Human Rights (for more detail on the historical development, see Chapter 2; additionally Magone, 2013). Paradoxically, the Council of Europe is a very respected institution, because it has no power to enforce any of its decisions. Their main instrument of achieving influence on a country that is taking a wrong direction in terms of democratic governance is to condemn, name and shame it, or in last case suspend its membership. Therefore, the Council of Europe is an important symbolic acknowledgment that a country belongs to the regional-continental community of democratic countries and shares its common values (on the concept, see Whitehead, 2001). Before a country can join the EU, it needs to be a member of the Council of Europe and follow its values and democratic governance codes of practice and conduct, otherwise it is difficult to be part of it. In this sense, the Council of Europe is an antechamber for joining the EU. This became quite evident after the fall of the Berlin Wall. All countries of Central and Eastern Europe joined the Council of Europe in the 1990s, before they were able to access the EU. The states emerging out of the disintegration of former Yugoslavia and wider Europe countries, with the exception of Belarus, became members in the second half of the 1990s or in the 2000s. In spite of this membership many democracies in wider Europe are still façade democracies; however, it is hoped that socialisation and cooperation processes will contribute to a change in their political cultures towards democratic governance over time. The Council of Europe remains the main producer and standard setter of democratic soft law (Kolb, 2013; Magone, 2009: 281, 2013: 49; Schuhmacher, 2012).

This makes sense, because the EU goes one step further. In contrast to the intergovernmental Council of Europe, it is a supranational organisation based on a now accumulated legal acquis communautaire of over sixty years of European law practice. Since a landmark ruling of the European Court of Justice (Costa vs. Enel) in 1963, European law overrides national law. Such a ruling strengthens the position of the EU as a supranational organisation. Since the 1950s, the EU has become a quite complex democratic multilevel governance system, in which consensual cooperation and decision-making is the central modus operandi among member-states, and its fundament is European law. However, the EU has no enforcement police forces. It relies mainly on the voluntary compliance of the member-states if a dispute is settled by the European Court of Justice.

The several enlargements of the EU have led to a quite sophisticated approach to democracy. Any country that wants to join the EU has now to adopt the Copenhagen criteria set up in the European Council during the Danish presidency in 1993. Such a stringent approach to democracy was necessary, because about ten Central and Eastern European countries were involved. The relevant passage states as follows:

> Membership requires that the candidate country has achieved stability of institutions guaranteeing democracy, the rule of law, human rights and respect for and protection of minorities, the existence of a functioning market

> economy as well as the capacity to cope with competitive pressure and market forces within the Union. Membership presupposes the candidate's ability to take on the obligations of membership including adherence to the aims of political, economic and monetary union.
>
> (European Council, 1993)

The major difference between the EU and the Council of Europe is that the supranational character of the former allows for a strong enforcement against any deviation from the stated values and codes of conduct and practice. It can lead to suspension of voting rights in the Council of the European Union through article 7 of the Treaty of the European Union (TEU). Therefore, member-states are obliged to comply with the provisions of the Treaty of Lisbon.

After the failed constitutionalisation of the EU in 2005, the Constitutional Treaty was watered down and became the Treaty of Lisbon, which was ratified by all member-states in 2009. The Treaty of Lisbon consists of two parts. The first part is the Treaty of the European Union (TEU), which is a general agreement on the values and structures of the EU. This is followed by a very detailed second part called Treaty on the Functioning of the European Union (TFEU), which explains all the policies as well as the decision-making structures and procedures of the EU. Moreover, article 6 of the TEU states that the Charter of Fundamental Rights of the European Union, negotiated and approved by a Convention in 2002–3, has the same legal value as the Treaties. In the same article, the EU adheres to the European Convention for the Protection of Human Rights and Fundamental Freedoms adopted by the Council of Europe. Moreover, it states that the Fundamental Rights 'result from the constitutional traditions common to the Member States' and 'shall constitute general principles of the Union's law' (European Union, 2012: TEU, art. 6). Moreover, article 2 of TEU states the values of this inner core of a regional-continental community of democratic states:

> The Union is founded on the values of respect for human dignity, freedom, democracy, equality, the rule of law and respect for human rights, including the rights of persons belonging to minorities. These values are common to the Member States in a society in which pluralism, non-discrimination, tolerance, justice, solidarity and equality between women and men prevail.
>
> (European Union, 2012: TEU, art. 2)

Article 3 of TEU further defines the political model of the EU and its relationship to society and economy in the member-states of the EU. It states the following:

1 The Union's aim is to promote peace, its values and the well-being of its peoples.
2 The Union shall offer its citizens an area of freedom, security and justice without internal frontiers, in which the free movement of persons is ensured in conjunction with appropriate measures with respect to external border controls, asylum, immigration and the prevention and combating of crime.

3 The Union shall establish an internal market. It shall work for the sustainable development of Europe based on balanced economic growth and price stability, a highly competitive social market economy, aiming at full employment and social progress, and a high level of protection and improvement of the quality of the environment . . . It shall combat social exclusion and discrimination, and shall promote social justice and protection, equality between women and men, solidarity between generations and protection of the rights of the child. It shall promote economic, social and territorial cohesion, and solidarity among Member States. It shall respect its rich cultural and linguistic diversity, and shall ensure that Europe's cultural heritage is safeguarded and enhanced.

(European Union, 2012: TEU, art. 3)

In sum, the member-states of the EU and the Council of Europe are embedded in an interdependent constitutional order which is being shaped more and more at international and supranational levels.

National constitutions and constitutional change: adjusting to a changing environment

Any modern democratic political system needs some kind of code of practice setting out the rules of the game for institutional interaction and for the involvement of the population. European constitutionalism emerged as a reaction to the arbitrary absolutist monarchies of the early modern period. Authors such as John Locke (*Two Treatises of Government*) and Montesquieu (*The Spirit of Laws*), who advocated a more accountable form of government, gave primacy to parliament or to a system of laws. Constitutionalism is a crucial part of democratic political systems and normally frames the way in which institutions are run in a particular country. In most countries the constitutional settlement in a Constituent Assembly is an important cross-party forum for drafting the laws. Such a constituent process goes back to the first constitution during the French Revolution. Since then, most European countries have experienced several processes taking them

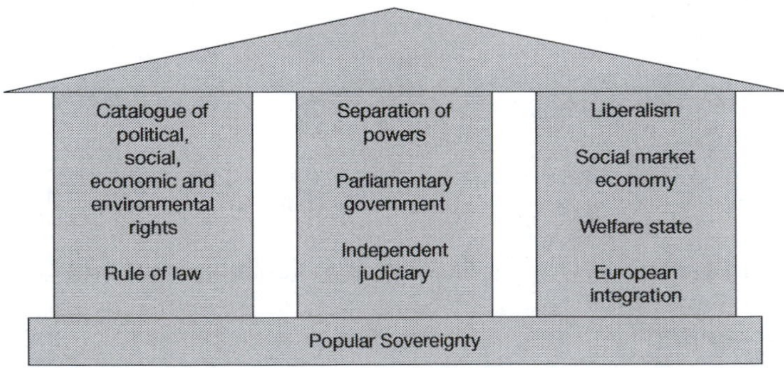

Figure 1.6 Constitutions in Europe

towards either creating or adjusting a constitutional order. It is very important that legislators get this founding document right, in order that the constitutional practice achieves political stability in the political system. Moreover, this genetic code will frame national life. The German Basic Law (*Grundgesetz*) of 1949 and the Spanish constitution of 1978 can be regarded as positive examples of such consensualism. In both cases, the historical legacy of Nazi Germany (1933–45) and the Francoist authoritarian regime (1939–75) played a role in moderating the positions of the different political parties and enhancing the propensity to consensualism. Originally, constitutions were very rigid and change was quite difficult, but the acceleration of international change and European integration has led to several amendments to European constitutions. The Finnish, Swiss and German constitutions are good examples in this respect.

Box 1.2 Constitutions and constitutionalism

- The constitution is the most important document in a democratic country.
- It is the source of the 'rule of law' of a country, so that arbitrariness in civil, political, economic, social and cultural life is prevented.
- First constitutions were drafted against arbitrary absolutist monarchies of the eighteenth century.
- In Europe almost all constitutions are 'written' codified documents.
- The UK has a partially written and partially 'unwritten' constitution that is based on several historical documents and political convention.
- Although the separation of powers – executive, legislative and judicial – is well enshrined in most constitutions, the reality in most European countries is one of close cooperation between executive and legislative power.

One factor that may determine a higher level of democratic culture in any one particular country is the longevity of the constitution. In the Nordic countries the longevity of the constitution is quite great, going back to the early nineteenth century, while other countries such as France, Spain, Portugal, Central and Eastern Europe and the eastern Balkans are characterised by a discontinuous history of constitutionalism. Probably, one of the oldest constitutions in Europe is the Norwegian Eidsvoll constitution of 17 May 1814, which became a symbol of collective resistance against the Swedish occupation. Norway was granted a quite considerable level of autonomy throughout the nineteenth century that allowed for the establishment of a strong nationalist movement leading to independence in 1905. Although the Swedish (1809), Norwegian (1814) and Dutch (1814–15) constitutions may be regarded as the oldest in Europe, they were subject to many revisions and amendments throughout their histories. The Swedish constitution was changed considerably in 1975 and consists now of several documents that perform different functions. The Instrument of Government is the actual constitution, but it is complemented by the Act of Succession, the Freedom of Press Act and, since 1991, the Fundamental Law on Freedom of Expression (Government of Sweden, 2017).

The Dutch Basic Law (*Grondwet*) was adopted in 1815 still under an absolutist regime and became democratic after several waves of constitutional reform in 1841 and 1848 during the nineteenth century. In the twentieth century it was changed in 1917, 1922, 1956 and 1983 (Voermans, 2013). Luxembourg's constitution was very much influenced by the Dutch one, and is presently being reviewed (Gerkrath, 2013). Belgium became independent from the Netherlands in 1830 and adopted one of the most liberal and modern constitutions of the time, which influenced many constitutions in south-eastern Europe. Meanwhile, the old unitary constitution was replaced by a federal one in 1993. Since the 1970s six state reforms in 1970, 1980, 1989, 1993, 2001 and 2012–14 took place that redesigned the constitutional architecture of Belgium. The continuing tensions between north and south may lead to even further decentralisation (Behrendt, 2013).

Similarly, Switzerland took quite a long time to modernise its constitution of 1848. A first major reform took place in 1874; however, in spite of innumerable amendments throughout the decades, a major modernisation of the constitution took place only in 1999 (Magone, 2017a: 72–4). This can also be said about the revision of the Finnish constitution of 1999. The Eduskunda undertook a major overhaul of the constitution of 1905 through several amendments in the 1990s. In this process, a rebalancing of the semi-presidential system took place, in which the president lost powers and parliament regained its centrality. The Eduskunda is one of the most efficient parliaments in scrutinising EU law and monitoring the work of their ministers in Europe (Raunio and Tiliikainen, 2004: 108–9, 151).

The Austrian constitution of 1920–29 was taken over by the Second Republic after 1945. In contrast to the First Republic, the new republic was characterised by the Allied occupation until 1955. The rise of Nikita Khrushchev in the Soviet Union during this period led to the state treaty (*Staastsvertrag*) that allowed Austria to become independent and simultaneously adopt neutrality. Although the constitution is the same for the two periods, the Second Republic is characterised by consensus and cooperation and is completely different from the First Republic in which paramilitary movements attached to the political parties dictated the polarised violent climate. This led to the emergence of Austrofascism (1934–38) and, later, the annexation by Nazi Germany (Magone, 2017a: 69–71; Stelzer, 2013).

In Germany, the Basic Law remained the main constitution of the land after reunification in 1989. Originally, the Basic Law was just a provisional constitution produced during the Cold War. However, the 'fathers' of the constitution took great care in creating a document that would last for what is now more than seventy years. However, changes were made in order to adjust to the new reality. Five new eastern Länder – Berlin, Brandenburg, Mecklenburg-Vorpommern, Sachsen, Sachsen-Anhalt and Thüringen – were integrated in the Federal Republic of Germany. According to Klaus von Beyme, eminence grise of German political science, constitutional change has been done consensually taking into account the position of all political parties. Such an approach was also used during the unification process, so that the revised Basic Law could gain the necessary majority. Von Beyme asserts that German political elites, but not necessarily all parts of the population, are guided by the idea of a constitutional patriotism (*Verfassungspatriotismus*) once developed by philosopher Jürgen Habermas. In this context, the loyalty to the constitution of all political parties allows for a peaceful consensus-seeking compromise when undertaking constitutional change.

Ultimately, the opposition can appeal to the Constitutional Court to rule on its constitutionality (Von Beyme, 2017: 46–58; on constitutional patriotism, see Müller, 2010).

Discontinuity of the constitutional order is a major aspect in France, which had five republican constitutions. Due to the fragmented party system of the Fourth Republic, the then president General Charles De Gaulle changed the constitution from a parliamentary to a semi-presidential one, giving more powers to the president. In 1962, direct elections to the presidency were introduced. Since then, the French political system has been more stable. Nevertheless, amendments and revisions of the constitution have been taking place quite frequently. One of the last major revisions was the change from one term of seven years to a maximum two-term presidency of five years in 2008 (for more detail, see Kempf, 2017: chapter 2; Cole, 2017).

Discontinuity of the constitutional order can also be found in the southern European countries. In Italy, after the fall of the fascist regime of Benito Mussolini on 25 April 1945, a referendum led to the abolition of the monarchy and the instalment of the republic. Furthermore, a new democratic constitution of 1948 was agreed consensually by the relevant political parties. It is a future-oriented constitution including quite a considerable catalogue of civil and social rights, including the right to housing and work. Between 1948 and 1992, several constitutional revisions failed due to the lack of a majority and the instability of the government. After the collapse of the previous party system due to the Clean Hands (*Mani Pulite*) operations of the judiciary in 1992, the Italian constitution had to be adjusted to the new reality. Finally, in 1999, a small constitutional change took place focusing mainly on giving more power to the regions, including the direct elections of regional presidents (Magone, 2003: 67).

The fall of the colonels' dictatorship in July 1974 led to a return to democracy in Greece. Before a new constitution was adopted, a referendum on the monarchy, which had supported the military junta, was held, leading to its abolition. Instead, Greece became a republic, but a proper constitutional settlement towards a new constitution never took place. New president of the republic Kostas Karamanlis revived the constitution of 1952 by introducing several changes. Karamanlis' party New Democracy had the two-thirds majority (208 votes out of 300) to impose the new constitution, but the opposition did not show up for the vote in protest. In 2001, a further revision of the constitution took place in order to adjust to the European integration process (Magone, 2003: 68).

The new democratic Spanish constitution of 1978, which has recently reached its fortieth anniversary, has also experienced very few minor amendments. There were just two small revisions in 1994 and 2011 respectively, both being required to adjust to EU processes. The consensually agreed constitution became a model of constitutional settlement for Latin America and Central and Eastern Europe (Poland, Hungary).

The constitutional settlement in Portugal was more turbulent than in Spain. The Revolution of Carnations on 25 April 1974 led to the toppling of the former rightwing authoritarian dictatorship by the military. After eighteen months of revolutionary process, finally Portugal moved towards a liberal democracy. An eclectic socialist-liberal constitution was adopted on 2 April 1976; however, several constitutional reforms in the 1980s eliminated any socialist inspired traces from the constitution. Meanwhile, the Portuguese constitution underwent seven revisions, partly to adjust to EU and international trends (Magone, 2014a: esp. 31–9).

Constitutional discontinuity can be found in all Central and Eastern European countries. The triple transition was quite complex and difficult. First, it was a transition from an authoritarian/totalitarian 'people's democracy' regime to liberal democracy. Second, it was a paradigmatic change from a planned economy to a market economy. Third, it was a cultural shift from an ideological egalitarianism in society to an achievement-oriented or meritocratic society. In this context, the role of the EU in shaping and consolidating the new constitutional orders cannot be emphasised enough. The Copenhagen criteria and screening processes helped to structure the long list of reforms that were necessary to overhaul the political systems. It took more than a decade until most countries became members of the EU. The basic criteria were the already-mentioned Copenhagen criteria (for more detail, see the excellent studies of Smith, 2004; Pridham, 2005). Depending on the nature of the constitutional settlement in the respective countries, some of these constitutions have been changed over time (for more detail on individual countries, see the excellent volume by Fruhstorfer and Hein, 2016). One overriding aspect is that many lessons were learned from the southern European democratic transitions and accessions to the EU in the 1980s. There has been a sociology of accumulated knowledge on a technology of democratisation and Europeanisation emerging since the 1980s (see Magone, 2006; on the impact of the EU on the constitutional order of central and Eastern European countries, see Karlsson and Galic, 2016). In Poland, in 1992, a round table led to a compromise between the communist elites and the new democratic opposition (called the 'small constitution'). Many negative aspects related to this constitution were changed in 1997, particularly by reducing the powers of the directly elected president in the political system. In Hungary, the old socialist constitution of 1949 was amended and restructured in 1989, so that it became compatible with liberal democracy. Both Hungarians and Poles adopted some devices from the German constitution, for example the constructive motion of censure, which ensures that before the opposition can challenge an incumbent government it has to provide an alternative candidate and a new programme. In a similar way to Germany and Austria, Hungary has been characterised as a chancellor's democracy (Schiemann, 2004: 131). However, both countries have been characterised by conflict around the constitution when conservative parties have alternated regularly in power like Viktor Orbán's Hungarian Civic Union and Christian Democratic People's Party (Fidesz-KDNP) coalition government in Hungary (1998–2002 and since 2010), and the Law and Justice Party (PiS) absolute majority government in Poland since 2015. In September 2013, Viktor Orbán's government was able to secure a major reform of the constitution of 1989, which included restrictions on the private media in electoral campaigning, a change in the balance of power towards the government in detriment of the Constitutional Court, a reduction in power of several public institutions including the Central Bank, and the inclusion of a conservative interpretation of the family. In September 2018, the European Parliament voted overwhelmingly to trigger article 7 against Hungary due to continuing illiberal legislation, mainly targeting NGOs and the higher education sector (Buzogány, 2017; *Euractiv*, 12 September 2018).

In Poland, the PiS absolute majority government with the support of president Andrzey Duda, who belongs to the same party, attempted to restructure the judiciary and curtail their independence. Particularly worrisome are changes made to the selection of judges on the Constitutional Court. In addition to the forced early retirement of about twenty-seven judges on the bench by lowering the age limit from seventy to sixty-five, they were subsequently replaced by new pro-government judges (*Euractiv*, 24 September 2018, 26 September 2018). However, at the end of 2018, after a ruling by the European Court of Justice, the judges were reinstated.

In both cases, the European Commission has been monitoring closely this democratic backsliding and has triggered article 7 of the Treaty of Lisbon that allows for suspension of voting rights in the Council of the European Union. In the case of Hungary, the European Parliament overwhelmingly condemned Hungary for ongoing continuing changes to the constitution and unconstitutional changes in the laws of the land (such as higher education law). Both countries may backslide into authoritarian illiberal façade democracies similar to Russia, Ukraine or Turkey (Schlipphak and Treib, 2017). Other countries, for example Bulgaria, Romania, Croatia, Czech Republic and Slovakia, have established new constitutions. After the 'velvet divorce' of Czechoslovakia, the original agreed constitution of 1992 was replaced by two different ones in the Czech Republic and Slovakia. However, Czech president Vaclav Havel clearly advised constitution-makers to use the first Czechoslovak constitution of 1920 as a template for the new constitution. In this sense, the historical legacy played a greater role in the Czech Republic than in Slovakia. For the then conservative pro-market Czech prime minister Vaclav Klaus, the 1920 constitution conferred too much power to the indirectly elected president, so that it focused on limiting these powers in the new constitution (Fruhstorfer and Moormann-Kimáková, 2016: 41–3).

In 2003, Romania adopted a considerable number of amendments to their 1991 constitution in order to adjust to European standards as preparation for its accession to the EU. This included the strengthening of the independence of judiciary, the separation of powers, protection of private property and the position of the ombudsman in the political system. Such a revision to the constitution was supported by a more than a two-thirds majority in both chambers as well as approved by a referendum in October 2003 with 89.7 per cent majority (Papadimitriou and Phinnemore, 2008: 83–4). There were attempts by president Traian Basescu (2004–14) to revise the constitution; however, the process was highly politicised so that no changes occurred (Gherghina and Hein, 2016: 181–5).

Some countries, for example Austria, Latvia and Estonia, have constitutions that, in spite of interruption by the Nazi and Soviet periods respectively, emphasise the continuity of historical legacy. In Latvia, the democratic constitution of 1922 was taken over, subject to some amendments and changes, when the country regained independence in 1992. The constitution and the political culture were very keen to emphasise the continuity of the regime, in spite of the long period of Soviet rule between 1940–5 and 1992. In contrast, the new constitutions of Estonia and Lithuania were adopted after independence in 1992. However, Estonia integrated parts of the three constitutions of 1920, 1934 and 1938, while the Lithuanian basic law is a new one.

Similar to Central and Eastern Europe, after the wars in the western Balkans of the 1990s, the new independent countries all produced new constitutions. They are clearly quite progressive and follow a template set up by the Council of Europe and the EU. Croatia had to adjust its constitution of 1990, which gave the president

Franjo Tudjman quite considerable powers until his death in 1999. This was probably necessary during the war period with former Yugoslavia and its involvement in the Bosnian war, but it became obsolete in times of peace. Two major constitutional reviews in 1997 and 2000 adjusted the constitution to European standards. In particular, the protection of minority rights was upgraded, a major issue during and after the Balkan wars (Zakošek and Maršić, 2010: 779–82) . In this respect, Bosnia-Herzegovina's constitution of 1995 is a good example of an internationally imposed document which tries to bring together all the three different ethnic groups: Serbian, Croat and Muslim Bosniaks. Therefore a shared executive structure was devised which is based on a rotating collective presidency influenced by the Swiss system. There are still major problems between the constitutions of the separated Serbian Republic (*Republica Srspka*) and the federated unit of Croats and Muslim Bosniaks in relation to the overarching constitution, particularly in terms of minority rights. An attempt to review the constitution failed in 2006, keeping the whole constitutional architecture in limbo (Richter and Gavrić, 2010: 844–6). After the Kosovo war in 1999 and end of the Milošević era, Serbia began to move towards a liberal democracy. The new constitution of 2006 follows closely the template of constitutional order suggested by the Council of Europe and the EU, and the same can also be said of those of the former Yugoslav Republic of Macedonia (FYROM) (1991), Montenegro (2007), Albania (1991/1997) and Kosovo (2008).

The former British colonies of Malta and Cyprus became independent in the 1960s and adopted new constitutions. Both islands had already acquired the right to self-rule when they still belonged to the British commonwealth. While the Maltese constitution (1962) is strongly influenced by the British Westminster model with a polarised two party system, the constitution of Cyprus (1960) was designed to give proportional representation to the two main ethnic groups, the Greek and Turkish Cypriots. This contrasts Cyprus to the European model of divided government which includes a more or less powerful Head of State (it may be a president or monarch) and a government led by a prime minister. The Cypriot model follows more the US model of a strong executive president which heads its government. The partition of the island clearly remains a problem for the confederal constitution giving rights to both ethnic groups according to their proportional size.

After more than 200 years of European constitutionalism, constitutions have become very similar to one another. Even the evolutionary 'unwritten' constitution of the UK is actually partly written, but not in a single codified structured document. Although the UK can be distinguished in this respect, there have been calls for a modernisation of the constitution in order to overcome uncertainties over some issues. The New Labour government that came to power in 1997 pushed forward an ambitious agenda of constitutional reform that was intended to bring the UK closer to other European countries. Among the changes was the creation of a Supreme Court. The successful referendum on the exit of the UK from the EU in June 2016 was also influenced by the argument that the UK should regain complete sovereignty over its internal affairs. In particular, the fact that European law superseded national law was perceived negatively by Brexiteers. The UK government subsequently triggered article 50 of the Treaty of Lisbon to withdraw from the EU. At the same time, the process of repatriation of competences that were once transferred to the EU has started. A so-called European

Table 1.3 Paths to constitutionalism in contemporary Europe

		Primary pressure	
		Internal	*External*
Tempo	*Gradual*	*Evolution* e.g. UK, Nordic countries,* Netherlands,* Belgium,* Luxembourg*	*Tutelage* e.g. benign empire, Malta, Cyprus
	Abrupt	*Discontinuity regime* Vacuum e.g. southern Europe, Fifth French Republic, western Balkans**	*Defeat and* *occupation* e.g. Germany, France after 1945, CEECs after 1989

Source: Adapted from Rose (1995: 74).

*Denmark, Norway, Belgium, Netherlands and Luxembourg were occupied by Nazi Germany during the Second World War (1940–5). Governments were in exile in London. Nevertheless, all countries fit more in the evolutionary model of constitutionalism.
**The new independent states in the western Balkans emerged out of the former Yugoslavia. They fit better in this category.

Union Withdrawal Bill was prepared by the UK parliament that will replace the 1972 European Communities Act. Its main purpose is to integrate about 80,000 pages of legal acquis communautaire of the EU into domestic law, in order to achieve a smooth transition after the Brexit date. Between 800 to 1,000 measures, named statutory instruments, will be used to achieve this daunting task (*BBC News*, 7 September 2017).

According to Richard Rose (1995), one can identify at least four roads taken by European countries towards today's constitutions: evolution (e.g. the UK, the Nordic countries), gradual independence from tutelage (e.g. Malta, Cyprus), discontinuous regime (e.g. France, southern European countries) and defeat/occupation/liberation (e.g. Germany, France and Central and Eastern European countries) (see Table 1.3). Some constitutions are characterised by evolution; others emerge after revolutionary periods or historical junctures. Moreover, some changes take place internally, while in other countries external factors play a major role in the emergence of a constitution.

The structure of European constitutions

European constitutions have similar structures. Most of them have adjusted the model of the US and French revolutionary constitutions to modern times. Most constitutions start with a preamble related to the historical legacy or the moment of the constitutional settlement and are then followed by different sections defining the 'rules of the game'. The first section normally includes the human and political rights of citizens or the definition of what constitutes a particular state and what its nature is. One of the best examples of a constitution in which human and political rights are particularly emphasised is probably Germany's Basic Law.

Nazi rule and its barbarism led to a strong emphasis on human dignity (article 1), in contrast to the constitution of the Weimar Republic, where civil and political rights were in the second main part, starting with article 109. Article 1 of Germany's Basic Law states:

Article 1 [Human dignity]

1 Human dignity shall be inviolable. To respect and protect it shall be the duty of all state authority.
2 The German people therefore acknowledge inviolable and inalienable human rights as the basis of every community, of peace and of justice in the world.
3 The following basic rights shall bind the legislature, the executive, and the judiciary as directly applicable law.

In many constitutions, for example the Italian constitution, the catalogue of rights is extended to the social sphere. In some countries, rights are also extended to quality of life and the environment, indicating that the catalogue of rights has been increased over time. This makes the protection of such rights and duties quite a complex task for any European state.

A further section of the constitution defines the main institutions and their relationships to one another. This is an important core aspect of constitutions, because members of a constituent assembly have to ensure this is right in order to prevent the failure of the constitution. Using historical legacy, as in the cases of Spain, Germany, France, Croatia, Hungary and Bosnia-Herzegovina, is a good way to avoid poorly designed institutions. This was particularly the case for Bosnia-Herzegovina. In order to accommodate the three different ethnic groups – Muslim Bosniaks, Croats and Serbs – Bosnia-Herzegovina had to create a rotating system at presidential level and provide equal representation for all ethnic groups in the bicameral parliament. However, today, Bosnia-Herzegovina is still split between the Bosnian-Croatian Federation and the Serbian Republic (Republika Srpska). Tensions between the ethnic groups still exist.

European constitutions also define the political structure of the territory. According to John Loughlin, four main forms of organising territory can be recognised in Europe: federal, regionalised unitary, decentralised unitary and centralised unitary systems (Loughlin, 2000: 26–7).

1 *The federal model* (Belgium, Germany and Austria) allows for a very decentralised political structure with elected subnational units.
2 *The regionalised unitary system* (France, Italy, Poland, the Czech Republic, the UK and Spain) has become closer to the federal model, but the centre still keeps many important decisions under its control. Within this form there are differences in the degree of decentralisation: Spain is quite decentralised, while in France, Poland and the Czech Republic the centre has a stronger position vis-à-vis the subnational units.
3 The third form of territorial organisation is the *decentralised unitary state* (for example, the Netherlands, Denmark, Sweden and Finland). Denmark has decentralised most of its public administration. Now, only about 20 per cent of all civil services are based in the centre and fulfil merely coordinating tasks.

4 The fourth form of political territorial organisation is the *centralised unitary state*. Here, there are also degrees of centralisation. Among the most centralised countries in the EU are Portugal and Greece, in spite of attempts by the EU and the political elites to change this tendency.

A constitution normally ends with the description of procedures for special situations, such as the institutional requirements for constitutional revision and the state of emergency and other important aspects related to individual institutions. A list of contents of an average European constitution is presented in Figure 1.7.

Constitutions and constitutional reality

Constitutions may be the most beautiful and perfect documents, but they only stand up to scrutiny if they work in real life over the long term. A fast snapshot using the multidimensional Democracy Index of *The Economist* shows that there are major differences in terms of democratic quality across Europe. While the Nordic countries, Drei-Sat Europe, the Benelux and Spain are among the top twenty democracies of the world, the Balkan countries, the post-Soviet states and

Figure 1.7 Longevity and discontinuity of European constitutions

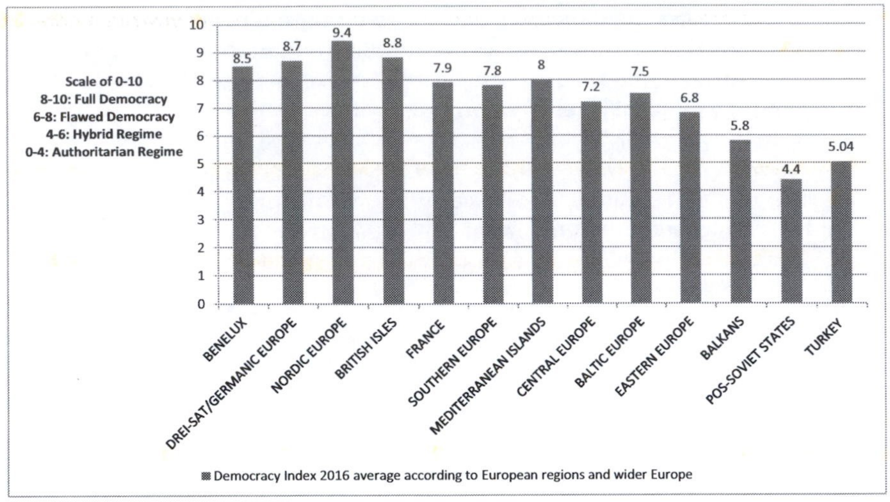

Figure 1.8 *The Economist* Democracy Index 2016 according to European regions and wider Europe

Source: EUI (2017).

Turkey are at the other end of the spectrum. In between are the southern, east central European and Baltic countries (see Figure 1.8).

This snapshot allows us to map the quality of democracy of our set of thirty-seven countries and beyond. In the remainder of the book we will compare more qualitatively and analyse more deeply the differences and similarities of political systems across Europe.

Suggested reading

Contiades, Xenophon (2013) (ed.), *Engineering Constitutional Change. A Comparative Perspective on Europe, USA and Canada*. London: Routledge.

Karlsson, Christer (2016), Explaining constitutional change: making sense of cross-national variation among European Union member states. *Journal of European Public Policy*, 23(2): 255–75.

Karlsson, Christer and Katarina Galic (2016), Constitutional change in light of European Union membership: trends and trajectories in the new member states. *East European Politics*, 32(4): 446–65.

QUESTIONS FOR REVISION

- What are the main principles of European constitutionalism?
- Compare the strengths and weaknesses of the German 'Basic Law' and the French constitution of the Fifth Republic.

- What are the main features of the UK partly written, partly unwritten constitution? Compare it with written constitutions in Europe.
- How successful has the constitutional settlement and consolidation in Central and Eastern Europe been so far?
- Explain constitutional developments in Spain and Belgium since the 1970s.

Chapter 2

The historical development of European politics

- The emergence of European politics in the Late Middle Ages
- The Reformation, wars of religion and the European state system
- The French Revolution and the emergence of the national state
- The democratic revolution of 1848 and the rise of liberal democracy
- Industrialisation, the proletariat and the social question
- The new imperialism, new militarism and the First World War (1914–18)
- The Russian Revolution and the expansion of communism (1917–89)
- The politics of totalitarianism: fascism, national socialism and Stalinism
- Reconstruction, consensus and the division of Europe after 1945
- Jean Monnet, Robert Schuman and the beginnings of European integration
- The 1970s: the end of the glorious thirty years
- The fall of the Berlin Wall and the emergence of a new European era
- The multiple crises of European politics: refugees, euro crisis and the transition to a low-carbon society and economy
- Conclusions: European politics as a kaleidoscope of experiment, innovation and tradition
- Suggested reading

The emergence of European politics in the Late Middle Ages

European politics emerged out of the Late Middle Ages in the thirteenth and fourteenth centuries. The Middle Ages that spans the period between the ninth and fourteenth centuries was a period of melancholy and intense sadness. It was also characterised by pessimism. This was a reflection of the life that people had to endure, which was marked by human insecurity, wars and the subsequent devastation they caused, and the very rapid spread of disease, including the plague. Moreover, political institutional development was ad hoc and without purpose, based on opportunistic use of existing structures and legal frameworks (Huizinga, 1955: 30, 36).

The political world of the Middle Ages was intrinsically linked to Christian religion and the powerful Church. The attitude of the population and elites was very much oriented towards the end of the world. The universal Christian Church provided the moral basis for the universal unity of mankind. The will of God permeated all aspects of life. Nevertheless, there was a general acknowledgement of the twofold nature of man, spiritual and temporal, that, according to interpretation, allowed for challenges against the hegemony of the Church to be made by powerful rulers. Indeed, one of the main disputes of the Middle Ages was between the Church and the German Emperor about the Church's hegemony over the temporal world. The climax was the non-recognition of Alexander III (1105–81) by Emperor Frederick I (Barbarossa, 1123–90) and the support of anti-popes to challenge him. Alexander III, who was elected in 1159 to succeed Adrian IV, was forced into exile by Frederick I in 1162 and had to live in France and then exile for most of the period of his pontificate. However, the northern Italian cities (organised in the Lombard League) rallied to the cause of Pope Alexander III and put an army together to fend off the incursions of Frederick I. In 1176, the army of Frederick I was defeated by the Lombard League in Legnano in Lombardy. Frederick I had to acknowledge Alexander III and sign the Peace Treaty of Venice (1177) (Davies, 1988: 303–17). In spite of this victory of the papacy, the conflict between spiritual and temporal power continued throughout the Middle Ages.

Feudalism was the main social structure during the Middle Ages, becoming an intrinsic part of the emerging nation-states of Europe. It was characterised by a hierarchical and static system of personal dependency relationships, and with a specialised military class occupying the higher levels of society with privileged rights. Moreover, political authority was dispersed among a hierarchy of persons who exercised in their own interest powers normally attributed to the State and which were often, in fact, derived from its break up (Ganshof, 1964: xv).

The last feature, related to the dispersal of political authority among a hierarchy of persons, had at its top the king or emperor. In most countries, the monarchy had to share power with its vassals, but in the Late Middle Ages France, Spain, Portugal and England were able to establish more advanced political structures that allowed the establishment of a fledgling nation-state. It is probable that the most centralised feudal system could be found in England, because at that time, following the Norman invasion by William the Conqueror in 1066, all land belonged to the king, and so all lords were vassals of the monarchy.

The establishment of assemblies that allowed the most important estates to be represented can be regarded as the origins of parliamentarianism in Europe.

The most developed such assembly was likely to have been the English parliament (Finer, 1999: 1336).

The system of justice was also ad hoc, fragmented and based on customary law. It was separated from the feudal structure, although the respective lords and vassals sat in these courts. The structures became more sophisticated at the end of the Middle Ages. The rediscovery of Roman law in Italy in the tenth century, which was derived from the Digest of Roman Law, developed under the auspices of the Roman Emperor Justinian (483–565) and was an important turning point for a more sophisticated approach to law. Its dissemination was very uneven across Europe, being more successful in Western Europe and slower in Germany and in the east of the continent (Gierke, 1996: xiii). The growing importance of law in Europe was a sign that government was becoming more complex with time, and both the respective rulers and the population desired a higher level of predictability and regularity (Koenigsberger, 1987: 232–3).

Towards the end of the Middle Ages, in the thirteenth and fourteenth centuries, most of Europe had reached a high level of stability. A first inter-state system began to emerge in Western Europe, while Central and Eastern Europe was still in flux. The emergence of the Ottoman empire after the fall of Constantinople in 1450 became a major threat to southeastern Europe. Pockets of feudalism and feudal structure survived until the eighteenth and nineteenth centuries, but at the end of the Middle Ages one could already see the emergence of pockets of capitalism in the urban centres, particularly in the northern city states of Italy and the Netherlands. A new, more self-confident, *Zeitgeist* was replacing the sad melancholic world of the Middle Ages.

The Reformation, wars of religion and the European state system

This new era is referred to as the Renaissance, in which a paradigm change took place from a society that was largely theocentric and geocentric, to one that was anthropocentric and heliocentric. This meant that the unity of the universal Church and the political world, which believed the planet Earth to be the centre of the universe, was replaced by a growing conflict between the two. A turning point was the scientific revolution, the centre of which was the discovery that the Earth rotates around the sun and not the other way round. The Renaissance is a celebration of individualism and individual contributions in culture, science and the arts (Huizinga, 1955: 217, 267–8).

This paradigm shift was certainly sustained by the expansion of capitalism as an alternative economic system. At the end of the Middle Ages, the bourgeoisie, in the form of businessmen who lived in the dynamic urban centres between the Netherlands and northern Italy, were an important social group undermining the previous feudal and stratified society. (Green, 1974: 21–2; Wallerstein, 1974). Several factors led to the formation of this new era.

First of all, the existing nation-states of Western Europe increased their ability to control and expand their territory. They created the principle of territorial sovereignty that is intrinsically the principle of the reason of state (*raison d'état*). This suggested that the rulers of the different national countries had to do everything in their power to further the interests of the state by whatever means (Meinecke, 1998).

Second, France, England, Spain and Portugal became absolutist states, meaning that the king was chosen by God and therefore became the direct divine intermediary in their own territory. The most developed form of such absolutism could be found in the sixteenth and seventeenth centuries in France during the reigns of Louis XIII and Louis XIV. The absolutist state had a future-oriented purpose to expand the territory and increase the power of the country in relation to other countries (Friedrich, 1952: 197–245).

Third, the rise of the nation-state was paralleled by the decline of the papacy. Corruption, the selling of offices and indulgence selling (which allowed sins to be forgiven in exchange for cash in order to finance the building of St Peter's) were major factors in undermining both the spiritual and temporal authority of the Church. The once united political and spiritual world of the Middle Ages became fragmented and divided. The rise of the nation-state and the *raison d'état* strengthened the position of monarchs in relation to the national churches (Meinecke, 1998). The growing importance of individualism contributed to the intellectual challenge and criticism of the Church. Already at the beginning of the fifteenth century, the Bohemian reformer Jan Hus (1370–1415) dared to criticise the Church and all negative aspects, and, in the Council of Constance, he was condemned and burned at the stake. It led to the Hussite Wars in Bohemia, a major event of Czech national history. One century later, Martin Luther (1483–1546) emerged as one of the first protagonists of the Reformation of the Church. He had been a professor of Theology at the University of Wittenberg since 1508 and spent most of his time studying, praying and teaching. Indeed, he was an ascetic friar until 1517. On All Saints' Eve he nailed up his Ninety-five Theses at the Castle Chapel of Wittenberg against indulgence selling. Luther's Ninety-five Theses were written in Latin, but the act itself gained such a good reputation that they were translated into German. After attempts to get Luther to change his views failed, he was banned from the empire by the Edict of Worms in 1521. He fled and hid in Wartburg Castle. There, he made the major contribution of translating the Bible from Greek into German, which became an important foundation of the modern German language. Luther remained a prolific writer throughout his life and an established figure in German history (Green, 1974: 109–25).

One of the consequences of Martin Luther's Reformation is that the different states and statelets of the German empire accepted either the Lutheran confession or the Catholic one. Each state would make a choice about confession to be adopted across its territory. In the end, the Augsburg Peace settled this issue in 1555. The adopted formula was *cuius regio, eius religio* (each region, the respective religion), meaning that each state and statelet had the right to choose a religious confession that was valid for the whole territory. This consensual formula and the mechanisms of reconciliation in Augsburg were characterised by Gerhard Lehmbruch as one of the sources of consociationalism in what he called West Central Europe, comprising Germany, Switzerland, Austria, the Netherlands and Belgium (Lehmbruch, 2002). The Reformation expanded to other parts of Europe through Ulrich Zwingli (1484–1531) in Zurich and John Calvin (1509–64) in Geneva, and through the Huguenots in France in the second half of the sixteenth century and to the Nordic countries. Among the most influential reformers was

John Calvin, who emphasised predestination theory, which acknowledged that, in spite of man's free will, man is not created equal, but is either granted eternal life or eternal damnation. For Max Weber this predestination theory became an important cultural frame of mind for the emergence of the bourgeoisie and capitalism, and was to become a major source of dispute between different academics. Indeed, even today, his theory is still a major source of discussion (Weber, 1934).

In France, the spread of Protestantism throughout the second half of the sixteenth and early seventeenth centuries led to a civil war that culminated in the St Bartholomew's Massacre of Huguenot leaders by King Charles IX and his mother Catherine de Médicis during August 1572. After a lengthy and bloody civil war between the two confessions, in 1598 King Henry IV finally declared the Edict of Nantes, which allowed Huguenots complete religious freedom. This was revoked in 1685 by Louis XIV. Between 400,000 and 1 million Huguenots fled the country to Prussia, England, the Swiss Confederation and other countries.

Throughout the first half of the seventeenth century these political-religious wars dominated the European continent. Religious adherence and nation-building became intrinsic processes. In England, Henry VIII (1491–1547) established the Anglican Church by proclaiming the First Act of Succession and the Act of Supremacy in 1534. The origins of the split with Rome were the divorce of Henry VIII from Catherine of Aragón and his marriage to his second wife, Anne Boleyn, a marriage that was condemned by Rome. The break with Rome was supported by Parliament.

The Thirty Years' War (1618–48) led to the intervention of all European powers and to several wars on German soil. It led to the devastation of the country and the continuing fragmentation of the German empire. The main powers – France, Austria, Sweden and the German states – aligned alongside the Catholic and Protestant confessions. In the end, the peace treaties of Westphalia in Münster and Osnabrück in 1648 established the first European interstate system and a central juncture of modern European politics (Friedrich, 1952: 161–97; Green, 1974: 293–313) (Box 2.1).

In the sixteenth and seventeenth centuries, only four years were without wars (1548, 1549, 1550, 1610) (Green, 1974: 386). The Thirty Years' War (1618–48) and subsequent peace treaties established the first interstate system, one that was to remain the main feature of modern European politics up to the present day, despite efforts towards European integration. The Seven Years' War (1756–63) between France and England could really be called 'the first world war', because it expanded as far as the extra-European colonial empires of these two powers. It led to overlapping wars in which European powers, such as the emerging Prussia, Russia, Austria, France and Sweden, became involved (Dorn, 1963: 318–64).

Box 2.1 Historical junctures of European politics

1648: the peace of Westphalia

- After the Thirty Years' War (1618–48) between Catholic and Protestant states in Germany and Bohemia, in which Denmark, Sweden and France intervened on behalf of one of the parties, a peace treaty was signed in the Westphalian city of Münster.

- One of the major consequences of the peace of Westphalia was the official establishment of a European interstate system, in which France emerged as the dominant power of the continent.
- The Thirty Years' War was conducted mainly in Germany, which lost one-fifth of its population and suffered the devastation of the country as a consequence.

Last but not least, the Enlightenment of the eighteenth century influenced some monarchs, for example Empress Maria Theresa and Emperor Joseph II of Austria, to introduce compulsory education for the population and regard this as a benefit for the overall economy (Anderson, 1963: 125–7; Williams, 1999: 411–12, 431–2).

The economic rationale became more important throughout the eighteenth century. Mercantilism tended to strengthen the economic power of a nation. Therefore, mercantilists postulated that such strength was to be achieved by protection of industry and trade. Moreover, a country should export more than it imports and hence be able to accumulate gold and silver reserves. Mercantilism was an important doctrine for the emerging nation-state, because it fitted within the framework of *raison d'état*. A major critic of mercantilism became François Quesnay who coined the liberal principles of laissez-faire and laissez-passer of economic processes. At the centre of the new doctrine was the belief that only agriculture was able to produce wealth. The so-called physiocrats can be regarded as the predecessors of the first theorists of capitalism as we know them today. Adam Smith (1723–90), in his book the *Wealth of Nations*, advocated the free market economy based on trade – the idea of an 'invisible hand' that regulated such economic processes – and based his theory on the anthropological benevolent nature of man (Anderson, 1963: 74–80).

The Dutch Republic of the United Provinces became established and could be considered the first 'superpower'. Such political, economic and military power had been established during the sixteenth century but became more visible in the seventeenth century. The power of the Netherlands was only eclipsed at the beginning of the eighteenth century when England formed a personal union with Scotland, creating the United Kingdom of Great Britain through the Act of Union in 1707, adopting the new principles of free market capitalism across the country and in relation to the colonies, something that had previously been denied to the Scottish population (Israel, 1998).

On the eve of the French Revolution, the European interstate system created by the Peace of Westphalia became less stable (see Figure 2.1). However, in south-eastern Europe, the Ottoman empire remained a major player until the end of seventeenth century, only to then decline in terms of power in the eighteenth and nineteenth centuries. In the northeast, the commonwealth of Poland and Lithuania was tragically partitioned by their neighbours Prussia, Austria and Russia in 1772, 1993 and 1995, and ceased to exist. One of the main reasons was the increasing corruption of the nobility in Poland's Sejm, who became manipulated by the interests of external powers.

The French Revolution and the emergence of the national state

After the Peace of Westphalia of 1648, the French Revolution of 1789 should probably be considered the most important event for modern European politics. The year 1789 represents a shift from the remnants of a feudal world towards a modern one. The revolutionary period lasted from 1789 to 1799. The main reason for the French Revolution was the deterioration in the finances of the French monarchy. Mismanagement, the heavy costs of wars in Europe and around the world, and the effects of systemic corruption led to a growing demand for convening the parliament of estates, the Estates-General (*États-Généraux*). They met on 5 May 1789 in Versailles. Nevertheless, the privileged estates' clergy and nobility were against the introduction of a simple majority vote, because the Third Estate (*Tiers État*) was the strongest group. The Third Estate consisted of members of the new bourgeoisie who wanted the introduction of constitutional government, including reform of the political system, press freedom and decisions over new taxes, so limiting the arbitrary powers of the King. This led eventually to the proclamation of a National Assembly by the Third Estate against the will of the king. On 27 June King Louis XVI capitulated and accepted the National Constituent Assembly and the drafting of a new constitution. The climax of the revolution was the storming of the Bastille, where political prisoners were held, on 14 July 1789, the present national holiday in France. (Rudé, 1980: 83–105) (Box 2.2).

The new constitution was only ratified in 1792 and was fairly radical. Also important was the Bill of Rights enshrined in the preamble of the constitution. Throughout this period new radical groups such as the Jacobins and the Cordeliers pushed the pace of the revolutionary process. The new Legislative Assembly, which consisted of 750 members, convened on 1 October 1791. Soon, it became evident that there were different opinions about what should happen to the king and the monarchy. For the first time in the history of European politics, different political parties began to emerge. They would sit in the Assembly from right to left. On the right, the Feuillants wanted to preserve the monarchy and the king, and were regarded as the conservatives of the Assembly. In the middle, the majority of MPs were moderate and without any concrete position in relation to the monarchy. Last but not least, on the left, one could find the Girondins and the Montagnards (Jacobins and Cordeliers). Both groups wanted a republic, the difference being only that the former advocated federalism and the latter a unitary state (Brinton, 1934: 88–116).

The radicalisation of the French Revolution and the hostility towards the king led to a growing alliance of other European monarchs, particularly Austria's Leopold II, against France. The 'French revolutionary wars', as they are often called, started in 1792 and lasted until 1815. A mass conscription of soldiers (levée en masse) took place to fight against the external powers. An army of 300,000 was created to fight against the European powers and increased to 750,000 a year later. (Brinton, 1934: 164–89; Thomson, 1972).

Box 2.2 Historical junctures of European politics

1789: the French Revolution

- The demand of the *Tiers État* (Third Estate of the emerging bourgeoisie) for proper representation in relation to the nobility and clergy in the *États Généraux* (General Estates, national parliament).
- Dependency of the king on the General Estates resulting from his catastrophic financial situation.
- The most famous event was the storming of the Bastille (the prison where political prisoners were held) on 14 July 1789.
- Some achievements:
  - the institutionalisation of written constitutions;
  - the roots of nationalism across Europe;
  - the establishment of modern political parties based on a left–right ideological spectrum;
  - the establishment of the Napoleonic Code, exported to other European countries such as Spain, Portugal, Italy and Belgium;
  - the establishment of national education systems.
- Some negative aspects:
  - the radicalisation of revolutionary processes leading to totalitarian regimes;
  - 'La Terreur': the persecution of all opponents to the regime in the climax of the radicalisation of the Revolution under Robespierre.

Furthermore, more radical elements pushed the boundaries of the revolutionary process. A Committee of Public Safety was established, a new more radical constitution adopted, a new religion called the 'Cult of Reason' created, and a new Republican calendar (based on the year that the Republic was proclaimed) replaced the Gregorian one. This was exacerbated by a reign of terror, from April 1793 to July 1794, in which potential enemies of the Revolution were identified and executed by the guillotine. The main protagonist of the policies of the Committee of Public Safety, which was in principle accountable to the National Assembly, but in reality became an arbitrary government, was Maximilien Robespierre. He used and abused his power to crush opposition in the name of potential counter-revolutionary coups. The re-emerging success of the French army against the Austrian Netherlands led to growing dissatisfaction with Robespierre and his supporters. They were imprisoned and condemned to death, by guillotine, on 27 July 1794 (also called the 9 Thermidor II after the Republican calendar) (Brinton, 1934: 142–63, 190–211; Rudé, 1980: 142–59).

The reign of terror is today regarded by political scientists as the origin of totalitarian democracy. Many comparisons to the Russian Revolution, Nazi Germany and other revolutions of the twentieth century were drawn by political scientists (Brinton, 1952; Talmon, 1955).

The fall of Robespierre and the radical Jacobins led to the establishment of a more moderate Committee of Public Safety, with the excesses of the Revolution being reversed. In October 1795, a new more moderate constitution was drafted giving power to the Directory of Five. This third constitution lasted until Napoleon imposed his own constitution in November 1799. Between 1795 and 1799, the new French political system was increasingly dominated by the external wars being conducted against several powers. This was the main source of the rising popularity of Napoleon Bonaparte, who became one of the main protagonists in these wars outside France. Despite these external warfare successes, the social and economic crisis deepened and the Directory became fairly unpopular, leading to the collapse of the radical majority in elections in 1797, 1798 and 1799. During an expedition in Egypt, Napoleon returned to France and, with Directors Paul de Barras and Emmanuel Joseph Sieyès, carried out a successful *coup d'état* on 9 November 1799 (18th Brumaire VII). He replaced the 1795 constitution with a new one, giving himself strong powers. He became the First Consul supported by two subordinate consuls. Moreover, the new constitution envisaged the establishment of a nominated state council and senate (Thomson, 1972: 42–8). Externally, France had also established seven satellite republics in the Netherlands (Batavian Republic), in Switzerland (Helvetic Republic) and in Italy (Cisalpine Republic, Roman Republic, Parthenopean Republic and Ligurian Republic). Belgium, the former Spanish Netherlands, became annexed (Thomson, 1972: 52–3).

Napoleon's new constitutional framework was in reality a military dictatorship. After declaring himself First Consul for life in 1803, he decided to transform France into an empire one year later. In 1804, Napoleon was crowned Emperor by Pope Pius VII in Paris. Despite this authoritarian streak in Napoleon, it should be acknowledged that he introduced major reforms that would continue for most of the European continent. The most important reform was probably the codification of French law based on the principles of Roman law. The French Napoleonic Code was designed to create greater security and stability in human relations in France. The Napoleonic Code, consisting of 2,287 articles, was completed in 1804. A further reform area was education, in which the creation of a centralised Ministry of Public Education, in turn leading to the first attempts to form a national education policy, was undertaken. Although primary education was neglected, a secondary school network was established to train future soldiers. Napoleon was also able to reform the finance and monetary system in order to create economic stability. Last, but not least, he strengthened and reformed public administration in order to have stronger control over public policies, taxation and the citizens. Napoleon's empire was controlled by a sophisticated police system, which removed opposition to his military dictatorship. After 1806, such repressive policies became tighter (Thomson, 1972: 56–63).

Although Napoleon controlled most of Europe, Great Britain and Russia were the two powers that were able to resist his incursions. At the end of 1813, following the severe defeat of Napoleon at Leipzig, France was invaded and finally capitulated on 7 April 1814, with Napoleon abdicating as Emperor of the French. He retired, as sovereign ruler, to Elba. Nevertheless, in March 1815, he returned to France and tried again to rally the troops against the other European powers. The defeat at the battle of Waterloo led to his second abdication in June 1815, and he was deported to the Atlantic island of St Helena (Thomson, 1972: 72–6).

The significance of the French Revolution and the Napoleonic Wars cannot be emphasised enough. First of all, it spread innovation and the modernisation of law and public administration through the adoption of the Napoleonic Code in many countries. Second, French nationalism led to reactive nationalism on the parts of the invaded countries and territories. Most of this nationalism then continued as a part of the national politics of each country (Hobsbawn, 2000; Thomson, 1972: 70–1). Third, it led to the spread of written constitutionalism, which was regarded as an important means of constraining arbitrary power. Such constitutionalism could be hijacked, in the same way as Napoleon's consulate, but it remained one of the founding stones of the new era of democratic politics. Such a democratisation process lasted right up to the 1990s, when most Central and Eastern European countries were finally able to establish definitive democratic regimes.

The democratic revolution of 1848 and the rise of liberal democracy

After the end of the Napoleonic Wars a period of restoration of the former absolutist monarchies took place. The Congress of Vienna of 1815 created a first system of coordination between the different emerging nation-states in order to prevent the return of revolutionary tendencies. The 'Concert of Europe' re-established a conservative monarchist Europe based on principles of absolutism. The re-established monarchies of the European continent wanted to preserve a balance of power between the different main countries (Holsti, 2000). This Concert of Europe was pushed through particularly strongly by the Austrian foreign minister, Prince Klemens von Metternich (1773–1859), who, after the revolutionary process, wanted to restore order in the European continent. He was able to gain hegemony in the German system of states and also attempted to do so in Italy but with mixed success. The domestic policies of the Austrian empire, established in 1808, were of a repressive nature relying on secret police and political stability (Vocelka, 2002: 174–8). In spite of the policies of the Concert of Europe the containment of the revolutionary spirit was only partly possible.

Therefore, after the Westphalian Peace of 1648 and the French Revolution of 1789, the third major juncture of European politics is the year 1848, when democratic revolutions took place in different European countries and started a pan-continental transition to mass politics. However, the process towards such revolutions had already started during the first half of the nineteenth century. Depending on the nature of the regime, democratisation processes were either evolutionary and peaceful or revolutionary.

The UK and the Nordic countries: early democratisation

In contrast to most continental European democracies, the UK and the Nordic countries evolved slowly by way of reform to full democracy.

In the UK, an evolutionary process towards democratisation started at the end of the seventeenth century after the 'Glorious Revolution' of 1688, which led to the forced abdication of the Catholic king, James II, and his replacement by the Dutch William of Orange. In 1832, the Reform Act was passed, following a conflict between the more conservative Tories and the more liberal Whigs under Lord Grey. In the end, the passing of the bill was only possible after William IV appointed a large number of Whigs (moderate liberals) to the House of Lords in order to offset the blocking Conservative majority. The reform itself got rid of the rotten and pocket (dominated by a single powerful landowner) boroughs that had lost population and importance during the ongoing industrial revolution, and enhanced the position of cities such as Manchester, Birmingham and Bradford. In the 1840s, the Chartist movement, based on a People's Charter signed by workers across England, clearly wanted to introduce universal male suffrage. However, this was rejected by parliament. In spite of this, further reform bills allowed the steady integration of the vast part of the population into democratic politics. Throughout the nineteenth century universal suffrage was extended and the constitutional monarchy responded to major social and economic changes. In the early twentieth century, male universal suffrage was introduced in 1918 and the female vote in 1928 (Harvey and Bather, 1982: 44–52).

Development towards democracy in Scandinavia evolved evolutionarily as well. Sweden moved to a liberal democracy at a very early stage. After defeat against Russia during the Napoleonic Wars, Gustav Adolph IV was deposed by the army and the Riksdag proclaimed a constitution that remained in force until 1975. After the Congress of Vienna, Sweden's king was a foreigner from the Bernadotte family, Charles XIV John (1818–44). Although the constitution of 1809 was the document of reference for politics in Sweden, in reality the king controlled both politics and policy. By mid century, Sweden had moved towards being one of the most democratic political systems in Europe. In 1865–66 a bicameral chamber was established, which abolished the representation by estates and introduced a directly elected lower chamber. Further reforms in 1907 and 1917 led to the granting of male and female universal suffrage respectively.

After 1848, Denmark became a constitutional monarchy and also started a process of evolutionary democratisation and social legislation. The emergence of a social democratic party in the 1880s contributed to the inclusion of the working class into the new democratic political system. Throughout the early twentieth century, particularly in 1901 and 1915, further reforms were undertaken to consolidate the parliamentary regime. Finally, in 1918, universal suffrage was introduced.

In 1814, Sweden attacked Norway and created a union between the two countries. In spite of Swedish control of Norway, domestic politics became increasingly influenced by a strong Norwegian nationalism. At the centre of this nationalism was the Storting, the unicameral parliament, that found itself in opposition to Sweden on several occasions. The 1814 Eidsvoll constitution gave strong powers to the Storting that allowed the assembly to resist Swedish attempts to curtail autonomy.

Finally, in 1905, the Norwegian government unilaterally declared independence from Sweden, later confirmed through negotiations and the signing of the Treaty of Karlstad. The democratisation process since 1914 reached its peak with the granting of the right to vote to women in 1913 (Arter, 1999: 30–6).

Finland was part of the Russian empire from 1815. Despite attempts by Russian nationalists to curtail such autonomy in the second half of the nineteenth century, Finnish nationalism and pragmatism prevailed. In terms of democratisation, in 1906 Finland made the transition from one of the most autocratic and undemocratic representative systems to being a fully fledged democracy based on universal suffrage (Kirby, 2006: 104–64). The Bolshevik Revolution in 1917 was an important catalyst for the independence of Finland, and one year later it became an independent country. In spite of a short civil war between communists and nationalists, the country was able to progress to a republican constitution.

France: discontinuous democratisation process

On the continent, after fifteen years of a return of absolutist rulers, new democratic movements began to emerge.

By 1830, a new revolution in France forced the ultra-conservative King Charles X to resign, and he was replaced by Louis Philippe, a member of the younger branch of the Bourbons. After 1815, France became a constitutional monarchy, but with a very restricted suffrage of 100,000 property owners. Nevertheless, the prospect that the revolutionary achievements could be reversed by an ultra-conservative monarch was a major worry for both the bourgeoisie and the wider population. Louis Philippe became known as the citizens' king. Economically, France profited from the newly found political stability, in spite of the fact that the regime was dominated by the well-to-do classes (Cobban, 1963: 123–5).

Discontent with King Louis Philippe and his prime minister, François Guizot, led to protests in France in February 1848. One of the main reasons for this was that France was facing an economic depression and King Louis Philippe resisted the new political demands being made. Repressive policies against the opposition led to the proclamation of the Second Republic. Nevertheless, it became clear in the autumn elections for the National Assembly that the radical Republicans were a minority in relation to the moderate forces. Moreover, the victory of the nephew of Napoleon Bonaparte, Louis Bonaparte, in the presidential elections led to a difficult coalition between the conservative monarchist government and the president. The continuing threat of radical revolution was used by Louis Bonaparte to undertake a *coup d'état* in early December 1851, establishing the Second Empire and his self-proclamation to Emperor Napoleon III, before the scheduled legitimate presidential elections of 1852. Despite that, the Second Empire, which lasted until 1871 (the year of defeat in the Franco-Prussian wars), was a period of economic growth, political reform and stability. Failure in foreign policy and several wars contributed to the establishment of the Third Republic that was to last until 1940, when France was occupied by German troops and a dictatorship was established in the southern part of France called Vichy France (Cobban, 1963: 196–210).

The emergence of Belgium and Luxembourg

In August 1830, the former Spanish Lowlands (which were an integral part of the kingdom of the Netherlands after the Congress of Vienna of 1815), influenced by events in France, staged an uprising that led to its independence and the foundation of the Belgian state. One of the main reasons for this uprising was the fact that Belgium was predominantly Catholic and resented being under the rule of a Protestant king, William I of the Netherlands. The new independent state created one of the most advanced constitutions in Europe. The new king, Leopold I, was astute about pushing forward Belgian interests and enhancing the position of the country within Europe (Witte et al., 2000: 18–23).

Luxembourg became an independent country after the Congress of Vienna 1815; however, it would remain in a personal union with the kingdom of the Netherlands through successive Dutch kings until the 1890s. However, in 1890 it got its own monarchical dynasty Orange-Nassau, ending the personal union with the Netherlands. Throughout the second half of the nineteenth century piecemeal reforms led to a considerable democratisation of the country.

The democratic revolution of 1848: Italy, Germany, the Austrian empire and Hungary

In 1848, several revolutions took place across Europe. In Italy, Germany and Hungary they became embryonic movements of nationalism and unification. In Italy, the two key figures were Giuseppe Mazzini and Giuseppe Garibaldi who were major protagonists of the Italian unification movement. The Kingdom of Piedmont, Sardinia and Savoy under King Charles Albert represented the Italian nation against the continuing dominance of the Austrian Hapsburgs in the north of Italy. The reawakening of Italian nationalism (*Risorgimento*) was to continue until 1870, when the Church state in the middle of Italy was reduced to the Vatican within the city of Rome. The main thrusts towards reunification came during the premiership of Count Camillo Cavour (1810–61) in the kingdom of Sardinia after 1852. He was to be instrumental in pushing forward the unification of the country through alliances with the superpowers, enabling increases in territory throughout the 1850s. In 1861, King Victor Emmanuel II was proclaimed king of Italy. Within a decade, the *Risorgimento* ('resurgence') led to the unification of Italy. The former Church state in the middle of Italy was annexed by the Italian state and reduced to just the Vatican city (Di Scala, 1995: 75–117).

In Germany, 1848 also led to early attempts to achieve national integration. The Constituent Assembly of Frankfurt am Main that convened in May and was to discuss a German constitution during the course of one year, led to a major rift between the supporters of a Germany under Prussian leadership (*Kleindeutsche Lösung*) and those who backed leadership under the Austrian empire (*Grossdeutsche Lösung*). The rift also brought to the fore the religious differences between Protestant states and representatives supporting leadership of Prussia and Catholic states under the leadership of the Austrian empire. In the end, 1848 sealed the hegemony of Prussia over a still very fragmented Germany (Behnen, 2002: 471) (Box 2.3).

When Emperor Franz-Joseph II of Austria came to power in 1848, after the resignation of Ferdinand I, he pursued repressive policies in order to crush the revolutionary movement in Austria. Nevertheless, by 1859, he had started a process of democratisation with a limited constitution and census electoral system. It evolved towards a fully fledged constitutional monarchy and the introduction of universal male suffrage in 1907 (Vocelka, 2002: 198–220).

Moreover, in other parts of the empire, particularly Hungary and northern Italy, there were strong nationalist developments. In Hungary, Lajos Kossuth (1802–94) became an important national figure, pushing for the independence of the country. Throughout 1848–49, a nationalist liberation and democratic movement emerged in Hungary. It was influenced by the democratic revolution in Paris in February 1848. The climax was Lajos Kossuth's dictatorship in the country during April and August 1849. In 1848, as a finance minister, Kossuth had already shown dictatorial tendencies combined with strong nationalism. After the intervention of the Russian army, which was part of the conservative alliance with Austria–Hungary, the latter again gained overall control over the country, and Kossuth went into exile (Molnár, 2001: 189–200).

Box 2.3 Historical junctures of European politics

1848: the democratic revolution

- A series of revolutions in different countries such as Germany, Italy, the Austrian empire and Hungary undertaken by elites and social groups excluded from power and wanting political liberalisation and democratisation.
- A first wave took place in 1830–32 in the Benelux countries and France.
- It was a reaction against the conservative 'Concert of Europe' orchestrated by the Holy Alliance, dominated by the Austrian foreign minister and later Chancellor Prince Metternich.
- It led to similar revolutionary processes throughout the second half of the nineteenth century, combined with an independence struggle as in Bulgaria and Romania in 1878.

Despite this setback, Hungary was later to gain equal status after the *Ausgleich* (compromise) of 1867 proclaimed by Emperor Franz-Joseph II. Hungary obtained its own constitution and had an almost independent status in the dual empire. Both concessions of Franz-Joseph II were consequences of defeats in Italy in 1859, when the kingdom of Piedmont was able to expel the Habsburgs from Italy, and in July 1866, when Austria lost in the decisive battle of Koniggrätz against the Prussian troops under general Helmuth von Moltke. In a similar way to the Italian case, Prussia achieved an end to the influence of the Austrian empire in Germany. In 1871, twenty-two principalities agreed to establish the second German empire under the leadership of Prussia. William I became German emperor and Otto von Bismarck became his chancellor. Although this German empire had a constitution, parliament and democracy were very limited. In order to counteract the growing socialist movement, Bismarck introduced the repressive anti-social democracy laws (*Sozialistengesetze*) between 1878 and 1890 and the first embryonic welfare state, which was to remain a major feature of the German political system up to the present day. The Second German empire ended after defeat in the First World War in 1918 (Behnen, 2002: 513–17; Düllfer, 2002: 546–7).

Ireland: the struggle for independence

In Ireland, a national movement against British rule was always present throughout the eighteenth and nineteenth centuries. In spite of the representation of Ireland in the House of Commons, the movement in Southern Ireland gained momentum shortly before the First World War, leading to the Anglo-Irish war between 1919 and 1921 and to independence in 1922 through the Anglo-Irish Act. The Anglo-Irish Act of 1922 allowed the establishment of the Irish Free State, which would be integrated into the Commonwealth. This was to end when a new constitution was proclaimed by President Eamon De Valera in 1937 establishing the independent Republic of Ireland (Coakley, 2000).

The Baltic states, Ukraine, Belarus and Russia

The dominance of the Russian empire prevented the Baltic states from becoming independent in the nineteenth century. Nevertheless, the February Revolution and the Bolshevik October Revolution of 1917 in Russia presented opportunities for all three Baltic states to become independent. All three Baltic states, Estonia, Latvia and Lithuania, were able to break away between 1918 and 1920 and move towards independent democracies. In contrast, in spite of attempts to achieve independence, Ukraine was not successful and was integrated into the Soviet Union as an autonomous socialist republic. The national movement in Belarus was always very weak, so that even lesser efforts were made to become independent from Russia.

Iberian democratisation: Spain and Portugal

In southern Europe, 1848 also had an impact when the cause of liberalism against the conservative forces of the different regimes was pushed forward. In the Iberian peninsula, both Portugal and Spain were characterised by a discontinuous process towards democracy. Periods of restricted democracy were either interrupted by military coup attempts or authoritarian periods of rule. Nevertheless, in both countries after 1871, liberal constitutional monarchies were established. Portuguese *rotativismo* and Spanish *turno pacifico* were based on the regular alternation of power of a two-party system. Owing to the small electorate, the two political parties were able to rig elections through clientelism and patronage. During the early twentieth century the whole political system degenerated into systemic corruption that was accompanied by a high level of political violence. In Portugal, the Republican movement was able to overthrow the monarchy in 1910, but this new regime also degenerated into systemic corruption in its quest to prevent the monarchists from returning to power. By mid 1926, the new republican regime was overthrown by a military *coup d'état*. In Spain, the high level of political violence, the growing anarchist movement and systemic corruption further undermined the regime. In 1923, General Miguel Primo de Rivera established a development dictatorship, based on the principle of creating law and order (Magone, 2003: 21–63).

The Ottoman empire and the independence of the Balkan countries

The Ottoman empire dominated southeastern Europe until the eighteenth century, but the inability of reform and the growing disintegration of the peripheral parts of the empire allowed for the emergence of nationalist movements in different parts of the western and eastern Balkans. The Ottoman empire became known as the 'sick man of Europe', particularly after the French Revolution of 1789 (Swallow, 1973).

In the western Balkans, Serbian nationalism became the major expression of this newly found self-confidence in relation to the Ottoman empire. The growing influence of Russia in this region protected Serbia from being dominated by the Ottoman empire. What was probably the most influential independence movement was undertaken by the Greek nationalist elites between 1807 and 1830. In the end, a constitutional monarchy was established during the nineteenth century and it continued until 1974, in spite of different constitutions. Similarly to Portugal and Spain, a two-party system based on a small electorate was established, although by the 1920s it had degenerated into corruption. In the same way as in the other southern European countries, periods of democracy were interrupted by attempts to establish authoritarian rule. Greece was also engaged in a policy of uniting (*einosis*) all Greek-speaking territories including Cyprus, which led to tension with its neighbours, in particular Turkey (Clogg, 1998).

In the eastern Balkans, Bulgaria and Romania were also influenced by the revolutions of 1848. Nationalist movements began to emerge at the end of the eighteenth century and continued throughout the nineteenth century. They led to national independence in Romania in 1859 and Bulgaria in 1878. In both cases, as already mentioned, Western European liberal constitutions, which closely followed that of Belgium in 1831, were adopted. In both countries, the British model of a two-party system of conservatives and liberals was established, but it soon degenerated into systemic corruption, alternating with periods of authoritarian rule. After the First World War, Romania was able to gain on territory in the Treaty of Versailles on 28 June 1919, while Bulgaria, which had joined the Central Powers, suffered a reduction of territory in the conference at Neuilly on 27 November 1919.

In conclusion, 1848 has directly or indirectly been a major juncture of European politics. The revolutions and social movements emerging before, during and after 1848 led to the expansion of universal suffrage and the establishment of a model of liberal democracy that was interpreted in each country in a different manner.

Industrialisation, the proletariat and the social question

The democratisation process was intrinsically linked to the industrial revolution, which was not just a point in time but a process that lasted for more than a century. The industrial revolution transformed European semi-feudal societies into modern dynamic ones. The economic historian Karl Polanyi (1944) called it the 'great transformation'. It emerged from the use of new technologies, for example the spinning wheel, steam engines applied to trains and ships, the blast furnaces in the steel industry, the railway and the telegraph. This was accompanied by new administrative management routines leading to predictability, reliability and rule of law (Finer, 1949: 710; Silberman, 1993).

Industrialisation led to a more complex society based on the market economy. It had a major impact on society due to the mass migration of rural workers to the cities. A detailed report by Friedrich Engels in 1844 of the working conditions of workers in England gave rise to the term 'Manchester capitalism', named after the city that was the centre of the textile industry in the UK. Among the negative aspects of 'Manchester capitalism' were unregulated labour leading to accidents, the exploitation of child labour in the textile industry, and both women and men having to work more than twelve hours a day. In addition, there was a 'truck system' set up by employers that allowed further exploitation of workers. This system provided workers with accommodation in overcrowded places and with the basic articles for survival through the employer's shop, with a consequence of debt dependency. Over time, workers accumulated debts that they were unable to repay within their lifetime. They became more or less slaves of the factory system (Engels, 1974). This was one of the conditions for the establishment of a rich bourgeoisie, who could make large profits from their various enterprises. Early industrialisation in Britain created a first national mass market, something that was emulated in other countries (Ferguson, 2007; Hobsbawn, 1984).

In the second half of the nineteenth century, there was a growing concern with the social conditions of the working classes leading to the emergence of new political parties that were keen to improve these conditions. Among the most important critical thinkers were Friedrich Engels and Karl Marx. Friedrich Engels wrote one of the first major criticisms of Manchester capitalism in his *The Condition of the Working Class in England* (1844) and proposed social reform in order to improve the situation of the working classes. He teamed with Karl Marx, and, during the 1848 revolutionary period they published the *Communist Manifesto*, which was to remain the founding document of social democracy and communism. When they wrote the *Communist Manifesto*, the working class was increasing but still small in terms of creating a political movement. Nevertheless, the social democratic and communist ideologies were able to mobilise a large part of the working class at the end of the nineteenth and beginning of the early twentieth centuries.

After Marx's death in 1883, social democratic parties emerged in most European countries. Marxism became the foundation of social democracy. Strategically, social democracy was split between those who wanted to use the democratic route through the institutions by taking part in elections based on an ever expanding electorate, and those that wanted to replace the bourgeois society and establish a socialist or communist society. Quite decisive for the split became the Bolshevik Revolution of October 1917 in Russia, which led to the victory of the radicals (Bolsheviks) and the establishment of a Communist International (Ulam, 1998: 493–514).

The emerging social democratic parties in Western Europe followed a reformist approach. Through this network of institutions (libraries, health centres, workers' clubs) they created a subculture that voted *en masse* for these social democratic parties. This encapsulation of the working class electorate remained an important factor for the stability of electorates after 1885 (Bartolini, 2000; Bartolini and Mair, 1990; see Chapter 3).

Pre-emptively, conservative governments tried to contain the perceived socialist threat by developing schemes to integrate the working class into the changing society. The best example was in the German empire under Chancellor Otto von Bismarck. After consultation, he introduced the first elements of a welfare state with initial measures of social protection for the working class. Although the Bismarckian welfare state was rudimentary, it nonetheless showed clear results. The main idea was to bind the working class to a benevolent state. The social legislation introduced health insurance (1883), accident insurance (1884), and old age and invalidity insurance (1889) for workers. In spite of some initial success, Bismarck's attempts to reduce the power of the social democratic movement was not realistic (Düllfer, 2002: 546–7). Although the social democratic party was forbidden in 1878, through the *Sozialistengesetze* (laws against socialist activity), after Bismarck's resignation in 1890, the party was able to operate freely and quite successfully (Düllfer, 2002: 543–7). Last but not least, political Catholicism emerged as a reaction to centralised nation-states and the social democratic parties. Christian democratic parties developed social policies after Pope Leo XIII published the encyclical *Rerum Novarum* (1891), which clearly allowed such parties to be more fully engaged in the social question and act politically in different countries. In the case of Germany, Bismarck was very keen to reduce the power of Catholicism in the German empire. The *Kulturkampf* was the fight of the lay state to gain complete supremacy over the powerful spiritual religious confessions, in particular Catholicism. *Kulturkampf* became less relevant after 1875 because Bismarck looked for conservative partners, among them the emerging Catholic-inspired party, which was against social democracy. The Zentrums Partei, which had close relations to the Vatican, became an important ally of Bismarck against what was perceived to be the main enemy of the empire: social democracy (Düllfer, 2002: 524–5). In the late nineteenth and early twentieth centuries Christian democratic parties emerged in Belgium, the Netherlands, Germany, Austria, Switzerland and Italy (after 1919).

In conclusion, industrialisation transformed European societies. A new large working class and the expansion of universal suffrage led to the emergence of mass politics. The social question became a permanent important issue of European politics, and even today it still remains an important part of the political agenda. Furthermore, the growing importance of the state and public bureaucracies in designing and implementing social and other public policies created a more intrusive state, which also began to develop the first statistical databases (Finer, 1949: 48).

The new imperialism, new militarism and the First World War (1914–18)

The industrial revolution further increased the integration of regional markets into one large one. This had consequences for the categories of world politics and geography. The best example of this was the acceptance of Greenwich time in an interstate conference of twenty-five countries that convened on 22 October 1884 in Washington, DC. The supremacy of the British empire on the world political stage was reflected in the fact that, by 1883, 65 per cent of the world's shipping used charts drawn to the Greenwich meridian, 10 per cent to the Parisian meridian, 5 per cent to the Cadiz meridian and the other 20 per cent to over nine other meridians (Black et al., 1984: 385).

This was relevant because, at the end of the nineteenth century, the new-found belief in progress led to a race to create large colonial empires outside Europe. Several European powers such as Belgium, France, Italy and Germany emulated Britain in establishing colonies that sustained the demand for manufactured products.

In contrast, former colonial powers such as Portugal and Spain became extremely vulnerable to the economic strength of the other powers. In Spain, the catastrophic year of 1898 led to the loss of Cuba, the Philippines and Puerto Rico in the Spanish-American war, leading to a major identity and cultural crisis in the country (Carr, 1999). In 1890, Portugal tried to create a corridor between Mozambique and Angola, situated on the southeastern and southwestern African coasts, respectively, which led to an ultimatum by the British government to refrain from this. The main reason for the ultimatum was that the corridor would interrupt the ambitions of the British empire to have a vertical corridor between Cairo and Cape Town. Owing to the military and economic weakness of the country, the Portuguese government had to back down to the British demands (Oliveira Marques, 1983: 206–11).

This new imperialism was supported by a new militarism that, during the early twentieth century, was to spill over into the First World War. Although the murder of Crown Prince Ferdinand in Sarajevo in July 1914 is regarded as the trigger leading up to the First World War, there was a general atmosphere that was somehow conducive to this belligerent attitude. The network of alliances between the different superpowers was set in motion after the Austro-Hungarian ultimatum on Serbia ran out (Tuchman, 1962). After a long peaceful nineteenth century with only small regional wars outside or on the periphery of Europe, most armies went into war believing that they would be home within a couple months. Instead, the First World War lasted for four years until November 1918. The war led to major transformations in Europe. Apart from the fact that the Austrian, German, Russian and Ottoman empires collapsed and led to the emergence of new nation-states, the Russian Bolshevik Revolution transformed European politics completely. The establishment of a communist country in Russia was to shape the order of Europe until the fall of the Berlin Wall in 1989.

In 1919–20, as a consequence of the Peace Treaties in Versailles, Trianon and Neuilly, Europe consisted of a lot of new states in the east. Apart from the present configuration in the western Balkans, most Central and Eastern countries gained their independence and some of them also territory and population.

The Russian Revolution and the expansion of communism (1917–89)

The Russian Bolshevik Revolution of October 1917 was certainly one of the most important junctures of European politics (Box 2.4). Originally, main revolutionary Vladimir Ilyich Lenin did not believe that the revolution in Russia, the weakest link in the chain of capitalism, would be able to survive without a simultaneous revolution in Germany. During the Spartacus revolt in Munich in 1919, Russian troops were stationed in Poland, so that they could help the Germans to stage the revolution. However, this did not happen. In the end the Russian Revolution remained restricted to Russia. One of the reasons for the Russian Revolution was that Czar Nicholas II had conducted a disastrous campaign in the First World War. Apart from defeat on various fronts, the economic and social situation was extremely precarious. A *coup d'état* organised by Lenin and the Bolsheviks on 26 October (7 November, according to the Gregorian calendar) 1917 led to the establishment of a communist regime. A civil war (1918–21) broke out between the Bolsheviks (who created a Red Army) and the anti-communist monarchists (also known as the Whites). The Bolsheviks were able to prevail and established the Union of Soviet Socialist Republics (USSR) on 30 December 1922. The death of Lenin in 1924, following three strokes, led to internal infighting. In the course of this internal infighting, the Georgian Josef Stalin prevailed and further reinforced the existing repressive policies of the Soviet regime. What became known as Stalinism was labelled by political scientists as belonging to the totalitarian pattern of regimes. Apart from a forced restructuring of society through an accelerated industrialisation and collectivisation of farmers, Stalin established a regime of terror, in which adversaries and enemies would be killed or sent to labour camps (gulags).

Box 2.4 Historical junctures of European politics

1917: the Russian Revolution

- The catastrophic running of the First World War, combined with a disastrous economic and social situation, led to the Russian Revolution in 1917.
- A first revolution took place in March 1917 owing to shortages of bread. The revolutionary situation led to the abdication from the throne by Czar Nicholas II. A provisional government introduced democratic institutions and liberalisation, but was not willing to give up the war effort.
- A second revolution undertaken by Ivan Ilyich Lenin and the Bolsheviks (in reality a successful *coup d'état*) took place on 26 October (Gregorian calendar 7 November). The 'October Revolution' led to the establishment of the first Communist regime, which became quite influential in European politics.
- The October Revolution led to the establishment of the Third Communist International, which became an extended arm of Russian foreign policy. This became clear under Josef Stalin, who contributed with his expansionary policies in Central and Eastern Europe to the division of Europe between 1947 and 1989.

One of the most important instruments of communist expansion was the Communist International (*Comintern*), founded in 1920 and based on twenty-one principles – principles that Moscow forced all parties to adhere to, which included total discipline and complete allegiance to the Soviet leadership. During Stalin's time the *Comintern* was used to protect the first socialist nation, the Soviet Union. It became an integral part of Soviet foreign policy. The new Communist parties across Europe became instruments of Soviet foreign policy. Western powers tried to contain the expansion of communism through a *cordon sanitaire* consisting of the countries of central and southeastern Europe, but their efforts failed when the Second World War broke out. After the war, Stalin's Soviet Union was able to control most of Central and Eastern Europe by establishing people's democracies dominated by communist parties. It led to the division of Europe and the beginning of the Cold War that was to last until the fall of the Berlin Wall in 1989.

The politics of totalitarianism: fascism, national socialism and Stalinism

After the First World War, Europe consisted of many new democracies. Universal suffrage was becoming a reality in many countries, but overall the picture was quite uneven from country to country. As already mentioned, many Western European countries moved to universal suffrage by the end of the 1920s, among them the UK, Ireland, the Nordic countries, Belgium, the Netherlands, France, Germany and Austria. However, the picture in the rest of Europe was more uneven. Southern, central and southeastern Europe still had restricted or manipulated electoral systems. In some cases, countries just introduced authoritarian dictatorships like for example in Poland under general Pilsudski after 1926 and the Baltic states in the 1930s, in order to deal with the political and economic instability of emerging democratisation. The interwar period was characterised by many economic problems that, after a golden period in the 1920s, were exacerbated by an economic depression in 1929. The crash of the Stock Exchange in New York and other countries had devastating consequences for these newly emerging democracies. Authoritarian regimes were regarded as a third way, avoiding the dangers of communist revolution and the instability of liberal democracy.

Italian fascism was regarded as the prototype of such regimes. After the war, Italy was affected by a severe economic and social crisis. Although universal male suffrage was granted in 1919, the phenomenon of mass politics was too new, and new political parties too inexperienced, to achieve a stability of the political system. In Turin, the main factories became centres of socialist revolution. The 'Red Biennium' of 1918–20 was influenced by events in the Soviet Union.

New moderate mass parties, such as the new Christian democratic Italian People's Party (Partito Popolare Italiano, PPI) and the Italian Socialist Party (Partito Socialista Italiano, PSI) emerged in post-war Italy. Nevertheless the National Fascist Party (Partito Nazionale Fascista, PNF), which derived its ideology from the Italian nationalism of the pre-war and revolutionary politics of the socialist parties, pushed for an authoritarian solution in order to not only restore law and order but also to restore the glory of the Roman empire. Romanness (*Romanitá*) was part of the liturgy of the Italian Fascist Party and fulfilled the function of a substitute religion, a so-called civil religion (Polanyi, 1944: 241). The strategy of the Fascist party under the leadership of Benito Mussolini was to destabilise further the vulnerable post-war Italian party system and seize power by presenting itself as the only alternative to liberal democracy. Mussolini could rely on a vast number of people who were discontented with the existing liberal democratic political system. He created the *Fasci di Combattimento* (fighting bands) consisting of former soldiers who had difficulties returning to normal life in Italy after the First World War. They intended to achieve a change of regime. Fascist squads terrorised the left-wing politicians and local government authorities. After issuing an ultimatum, Benito Mussolini marched on Rome on 31 October 1922 and was then invited by King Vittorio Emmanuele III to form a government. In 1924, after successful legislative elections in which an electoral coalition led by the PNF was able to get over 60 per cent of votes and seats, Mussolini began to restructure the liberal democratic political system into a dictatorship. New laws led to the establishment of an authoritarian state based on a new corporatist organisation of the economy. Corporatism drew some inspiration from the social doctrine of Catholicism and was presented as a third way between capitalism and communism. In essence, corporatism wanted to restore an idealised harmony between labour and employers' organisations, which was perceived to have existed in the Middle Ages, and avoid both the negative aspects of competition and the restrictions of a planned economy. At the centre of the ideology of fascism were three principles – the glorification of the nation, the paternalist family and harmony with the Church. Mussolini was able to settle the longstanding conflict between the Italian state and the Catholic Church through the signing of the Lateran Treaty, which stipulated that the Vatican recognise the sovereignty of Italy and vice versa. Moreover, it regulated state–Catholic Church relations.

Although it was Mussolini who developed the idea of the *stato totalitario* (totalitarian state) geared towards fulfilling the destiny of the Italian nation, fascism never managed to fully indoctrinate and control the population. In the late 1930s, Mussolini became an increasingly junior partner of the Berlin–Rome axis. Italy's entrance into the Second World War led to catastrophic results and ultimately to the downfall of the regime after 1943.

More ruthless than Mussolini's semi-totalitarian regime was the national socialist state in Germany. One of the main distinctive characteristics was the xenophobic thrust in the overall ideology of national socialism. In the same way as in Italy, the national socialist strategy was based on destabilisation of the liberal democratic regime of the Weimar Republic. The economic depression of 1929 badly affected the German economy. Unemployment was quite high. Adolf Hitler and the German National Socialist Workers Party (Nationalsozialistische Deutsche Arbeiterpartei, NSDAP) used political violence and scare tactics to come to power. The NSDAP came to power in 1933, because no party was able to achieve the absolute majority needed in the elections to the Reichstag. Franz von Papen, an ultra-conservative leader of the Catholic Centre Party, a successor of the Zentrumspartei of the nineteenth century, supported Adolf Hitler in his bid to become German chancellor, in order to undermine the efforts of his own rival, Kurt von Schleicher, to come to power. In the end, this mistake by von Papen led to the establishment of a totalitarian dictatorship. The institutions enshrined in the constitution were suspended and replaced by new national socialist bodies. The militaristic indoctrination through the total mobilisation of the population created a totalitarian state, which in turn led to the Second World War. Moreover, a new militaristic liturgy of mass rallies and other devices created a civil religion around the glorification of the German nation and its reconstructed past and future. At the centre of the system was the leader (Führer) Adolf Hitler, and the rule of law was replaced by the arbitrary principle of the leader (Führerprinzip) (Michalka, 2002: 694–715; see also the excellent detailed study by Neumann, 1942).

Among the most perfidious aspects of national socialism was the xenophobic racist theory attached to it. The glorification of the German nation was interpreted in racist terms, meaning that only Aryan Germans belonged to it. It meant that any other groups that were not able to produce proof through blood of their 'aryan-ness', were excluded from society. Although the main targeted group was the German Jewish population, other groups, such as gypsies, homosexuals and mentally ill or physically handicapped people, were also excluded from society. These groups were sent to concentration camps. In 1941, such exclusion turned into policies of extermination, the so-called final solution (*Endlösung*). The holocaust, the systematic killing of an estimated six million Jews in the 1940s by the national socialist regime, became a major tragedy for European politics. Even today, the holocaust and the consequences of it are felt deeply in the way Europeans conduct politics. Although the German and Austrian governments have established funds to compensate victims of the holocaust, the tragedy remains a reminder of how human beings can easily fall into barbarianism (Michalka, 2002: 715–19, 750–4).

National socialism was also characterised by a very aggressive foreign policy, which finally led to the Second World War. The trigger for the Second World War was the invasion of Poland on 1 September 1939; nevertheless, before that, Hitler had invaded Czechoslovakia and Austria. One of the driving forces for the expansionist policies was *Lebensraumpolitik* (the policy of living space) (Michalka, 2002: 720–5).

Fascism, national socialism and Stalinism are regarded as three forms of totalitarian rule that became widespread in the twentieth century. As already mentioned, the origins of totalitarian rule could be found in the French Revolution and became more sophisticated in the early decades of mass politics. The complete control of all activities within a regime by the state is referred to as totalitarianism. Fascist Italy, Nazi Germany and Stalin's Soviet Union were characterised by several common features such as:

1. a one-party system;
2. the blurring of the state and party bureaucracies;
3. the total indoctrination of the population through an ideology (communism, national socialism, fascism);
4. the creation of social and political structures for the total mobilisation of the population;
5. the use of secret police to control the population;
6. an expansionist and aggressive foreign policy.

(Friedrich, 1966)

During the interwar period, only a few countries were able to resist the totalitarian or authoritarian temptation. Regimes emulating fascism were established in most countries in Europe. Some of them could count on the support of national socialist Germany, particularly during the Second World War (for example, the Croatian Ustaša regime or Josef Tiso's Slovak People's Party in Slovakia). Many of these regimes crumbled during the Second World War. Some of them, particularly in Central and Eastern Europe, became totalitarian people's democracies between 1944 and 1989. In Western Europe, in Portugal and Spain, authoritarian regimes survived until 1974 and 1975, respectively. Only a few democracies survived the totalitarian/authoritarian temptation of the 1920s and 1930s, among them the UK, France, Belgium, the Netherlands and the Scandinavian countries.

The Second World War changed all this; the aggressive policies of the Third Reich led to the division of Europe into two large blocks, the Allies, comprising the UK, the United States and the Soviet Union, and the Axis powers comprising Nazi Germany, Italy and Japan. Many countries in Central and Eastern Europe, Nordic Europe and western Central Europe became annexed by Germany; and friendly regimes such as the Quisling government in Norway, the Vichy regime in southern France and the Ustaša regime in Croatia were established to run day-to-day business. The collapse of the Third Reich and, later on, the Japanese empire in 1945 created the conditions for a more democratic and united Europe.

Reconstruction, consensus and the division of Europe after 1945

After the victory of the Allied forces over the Axis powers, the devastated economies of Europe were the starting point for what has now been a period of more than seventy years of peace. The dark history of the holocaust should remind us forever of the way Europeans could behave towards each other and minorities within their countries. The end of 'Europe's Civil War' (this term describes the First and Second World Wars and the interwar period) was an important turning point in the social organisation of society (Mazower, 1998). The post Second World War period was one of Christian/social democratic consensus. On the one hand, conservative or Christian democratic parties and, on the other, social democratic parties, converged towards consensus in terms of social and economic policies. The reconstruction of the economies of these countries was paralleled by the establishment of a generous welfare system that expanded considerably up to the mid 1970s. In the case of West Germany, social policies were regarded as an important bulwark against a return of populism and national socialism (movements that were able to profit from the large armies of unemployed in the early 1930s). Of all the OECD countries, West Germany spent the most in social expenditure in the 1960s. In 1942, during the Second World War, Sir William Beveridge chaired a UK commission in charge of dealing with the reform of social legislation. The outcome was a comprehensive social policy plan based on principles of social citizenship that comprised health care, an unemployment scheme, social benefits and a pension system. The difficult social situation in the interwar period, during which unemployment was extremely high, led to the wish of the political elites to improve conditions after the Second World War. In the 1945 legislative elections, Labour won against the Conservatives under Winston Churchill. This demonstrated the general support of the population for the introduction of welfare policies. The Clement Attlee cabinet introduced major social reforms, among them the introduction of the National Health Service (NHS) under the leadership of the state secretary for health, Aneurin Bevan, in 1948. Today, the NHS still represents a symbolic foundation stone of Labour politics, and it was also embraced by the Conservatives as part of the social democratic consensus. By the 1960s, all Western European democracies had thriving economies; even the economies of the last two authoritarian dictatorships, Spain and Portugal, were able to profit from accelerated economic growth.

The economic recovery of Western Europe was not possible without US help. The destroyed economies of Europe were a major problem for the United States. This was the largest market for their goods and therefore there was a need to support reconstruction efforts in order to recreate demand in Europe. The European Recovery Programme (ERP, or Marshall Plan) was devised by US State Secretary George Catlett Marshall in order to help reconstruct the economies of Europe. Originally, the Central and Eastern European countries including the Soviet Union were invited to take part in the ERP. Nevertheless, the growing tensions between the United States and the Soviet Union, arising from the satellisation of most Central and Eastern European countries by the latter, led to the rejection to take part in such invitation. Therefore, the Marshall Plan became caught up in the ideological war between the United States and the Soviet Union, and was used in its later phases to boost the defence policies of West Germany and the other Allies. Between 1947 and 1952, the Marshall Plan disbursed about US$13 billion, most of which went to the UK (24.3 per cent), France (20.2 per cent), Italy (11 per cent), West Germany (10 per cent) and the Netherlands (8.5 per cent). In total fifteen countries profited from the US funds, including Turkey and the authoritarian dictatorship of Portugal. The funding was spent through the Organisation for European Economic Cooperation (OEEC). The overall idea of the US administration was to push for a single European market, because this would be much easier and cheaper for US firms to distribute their goods. Instead, European rivalries and concerns about sovereignty prevented such innovative integration of Europe from taking place (Milward, 1984).

The ideologisation of the Marshall Plan was inevitable. The growing hold of the Soviet Union on the countries of Central and Eastern Europe between 1945 and 1949 led to the emergence of the Cold War. It became an important instrument among others of the overall doctrine of President Harry S. Truman on 12 March 1947. Similarly, the Soviet Union presented their own doctrine of the inevitable war between the imperialist camp (the United States and its allies) and the anti-imperialist camp (the Soviet Union and the new people's democracies) by Foreign Minister Andrej Zhdanov. At the end of September 1947, in Szklarska Poreba, Poland, the Communist Information Bureau (*Cominform*) was founded by seven communist parties of Central and Eastern Europe (Poland, Czechoslovakia, Hungary, Romania, Bulgaria, Yugoslavia and the Soviet Union) plus France and Italy. Although the Cominform was just a network of information exchanges, the Western allies regarded this as a possible resurrection of the *Comintern* of the 1920s and 1930s. Throughout this period, the Soviet Union was trying to rein in the Yugoslav Communist Party to no avail. The successful liberation of the western Balkans from Nazi Germany by the communist partisans under the leadership of Josip Broz Tito, without the help of the Soviet Union, gave them enough self-confidence to resist Soviet control of the country. Between March 1948 and September 1949 there was a growing tension between the two countries until finally there was a break in the relationship. In response to this defiance of Soviet dominance, the United States was generous in providing 'aid without strings', which was used to finance the entire Yugoslav budget until the death of Stalin in 1953, when, finally, normal relations between the two countries resumed (Halperin, 1957: 178). Similarly, the *Cominform* was an important mechanism to control the communist parties in France and Italy, whose leadership had been in exile in the Soviet Union. From the point of view of the allies, the closeness of the French and Italian communist parties to Stalin's Soviet Union was regarded as a threat to these democracies.

The division of Europe goes back to the Yalta (4–11 February 1945) and Potsdam conferences (17 July and 2 August 1945). In particular, Yalta had allegedly led to a secret agreement, scribbled on a piece of scrap paper, to divide Europe into spheres of influence. The division of Europe led to a nuclear arms race that was used as a deterrent by both the West and the East against each other. The result was a 'Cold War' that led to thousands of troops being deployed permanently along the Iron Curtain. The military North Atlantic Treaty Organisation (NATO) was founded in 1949, comprising Western European countries, Greece, Turkey and the two Iberian dictatorships. And the Warsaw Pact was established in 1955, comprising the Central and Eastern European communist countries.

The occupation of most Central and Eastern European countries (apart from Yugoslavia) led to the establishment of popular front governments, in which the Communist party gained the upper hand, step by step. This process became known as 'salami tactics', referring to the fact that, little by little, members of the popular government and the opposition were either absorbed by the communist-led coalition or got rid of. Despite the success of the communist parties in Central and Eastern Europe, to achieve control over the respective countries, the Stalin–Tito controversy led to major purges of alleged nationalists or supporters of Tito. These show trials conducted in all people's democracies reinforced the image of totalitarianism in these countries (Crampton, 2002: 26–37). Among the most famous show trials were: Laszlo Rajk in Hungary (sentenced to death); Wladislaw Gomulka in Poland (condemned to house arrest); and Traicho Kostov in Bulgaria (sentenced to death) (Brzezinski, 1965: 91–7). The people's democracies established during the second half of the 1940s emulated the Soviet model but were considered to be less advanced than the mother land of socialism. To counteract the Marshall Plan, the Soviet Union and the Central and Eastern European countries founded the Council for Mutual Economic Assistance (*Comecon*, CMEA) in January 1949 in Moscow. Its main intention was to assist and coordinate the economic development of its members (Bideleux and Jeffries, 2007a: 463).

By 1949, the division of Europe was a fait accompli. After the Basic Law of Germany was proclaimed on 8 May 1949, the German Democratic Republic (GDR) established itself as a Soviet satellite state on 7 October 1949. The two Germanies remained at the forefront of the Cold War, as the West Berlin blockade of 1948–49 showed. The Allies supplied the western part of the city through an airlift that lasted for eleven months. Moreover, an embargo on strategic goods of the Soviet Union and Central and Eastern European countries contributed to the lifting of the blockade on 30 May 1949 (Wegs and Ladrech, 2006: 17–19).

After Stalin's death in March 1953, there were signs of rebellion and opposition in most people's democracies. In Moscow, a *trojka* took over; however, it was afraid of allowing a new dictator like Stalin to emerge. Slowly, Nikita Khrushchev was able to introduce policies of de-Stalinisation that culminated in the condemnation of Stalin and his abuses in a secret report to the twentieth party conference of the Communist party on 25 February 1956. The new leadership also replaced Zhdanov's doctrine of inevitable war between the imperialist and anti-imperialist camp by the doctrine of 'peaceful coexistence', which envisaged a competitiveness between the communist and capitalist model. The transition period in Moscow was used by the opposition in some Central European countries to rebel against the totalitarian regimes in their countries. On 17 June 1953, an uprising of workers in East Berlin, the capital of the GDR, was crushed with brutal force leading to the deaths of twenty-one people and the arrest of over 1,000 insurgents. Moreover, many people made efforts to leave the GDR for West Germany, in spite of the closed border. By 1961, 3 million had left the country, so that the East German leadership decided to build a concrete wall between West and East Berlin. The GDR became known as one of the most orthodox communist countries (Bideleux and Jeffries, 2007a: 490–1).

Similarly, in Poland, the workers' strike in Poznan in June 1956 led to a major crisis in the relationship between Poland and the Soviet Union. The rehabilitation of the national communist Vladislav Gomulka and his diplomatic skills prevented the intervention of the Soviet troops, which would have intended to crush resistance in Poland. Gomulka promised to remain loyal to the Soviet Union but introduced reforms towards a Polish way to socialism (Bideleux and Jeffries, 2007a: 476–7).

In July 1953, the Communist party in Hungary deposed the unpopular leader Mátyás Rákosi and replaced him with Imre Nagy. Despite pressure from Moscow to reinstate Rákosi, and later on his deputy Erno Gerö, Imre Nagy was able to return to power. In 1956, he proclaimed that Hungary was leaving the Warsaw Pact, the intergovernmental military organisation that functioned as a counterpart to NATO. As a response, Soviet troops crushed the Nagy regime and put János Kádár in its place. This ended the honeymoon with Soviet leader Nikita Khrushchev. Kádár became a symbol of betrayal of the Hungarian uprising, but at the same time he introduced major reforms that led to a so-called 'Goulash communism', meaning that the communist leadership allowed some private enterprise in the economy. The result was that, over time, Hungary became one of the less orthodox communist regimes in the Central and Eastern bloc (Bideleux and Jeffries, 2007a: 477–8).

Soviet leader Leonid Brezhnev emerged as the successor of Khrushchev after 1966. The 'Prague Spring' of 1968 under the leadership of national communist Alexander Dubček was intended to introduce major economic reforms in order to activate the Czechoslovak economy. Several economists supported Dubček. He was also supported by a large number of people in the party. In the end, troops from the Warsaw Pact invaded the country and replaced the leadership. The intervention of the Warsaw Pact was based on the principle of socialist brotherhood and the new Brezhnev doctrine that regarded such action as legitimate, if there was sufficient evidence to believe that capitalism would be restored in a socialist country (Bideleux and Jeffries, 2007a: 491–3). Czechoslovakia turned out to be one of the most orthodox regimes on the eve of the 1989 Central and Eastern European revolutions.

By the mid 1970s the Iron Curtain was quite entrenched in the minds of Europe on both sides of the fence. Despite the tensions between the two superpowers, a form of coexistence, based on peaceful tolerance, was established between West and East. It led to the Conference of Security and Cooperation in Europe in Helsinki in the summer 1975 and the beginnings of a unification process between the West and East of Europe.

Jean Monnet, Robert Schuman and the beginnings of European integration

After the Second World War, peace was the main item on the agenda of all countries (Box 2.5). After two devastating world wars, Europe wanted to ensure that such a calamity would not happen again. In the post-war period several plans emerged aimed at achieving a political unification of Europe. The intergovernmental Council of Europe was founded on 5 May 1949 by ten Western European countries. Its role remained confined to the development of pan-European legal frameworks, among them the European Convention of Human Rights (1950) and the Convention for the Protection of National Minorities (1995). The institution remained dormant until the 1970s, but in the 1980s and 1990s regained new prominence as an antechamber for EU membership. The rulings of the European Court of Human Rights (ECtHR) are of considerable importance for national judicial systems, because they contribute to changes in legislation for particularly difficult issues.

Disappointment with the Council of Europe led to further projects of European integration. Apart from the US-driven OEEC, the reconciliation between France and Germany through the initiative of French foreign minister Robert Schuman was devised by the head of the French Planning Agency, Jean Monnet. It started by creating a European Community of Steel and Coal (ECSC) through the Treaty of Paris in 1951. The ECSC became the first economic supranational organisation consisting of six member states – France, West Germany, the Benelux countries and Italy. At the centre stood the High Authority, presided over by Jean Monnet. This modest approach of one step after another had the ambitious aim of achieving the 'United States of Europe' in the long term. The successful integration of those two major essential areas of industrial society led, in 1958, to the Treaty of Rome (which founded Euratom, related to atomic energy and the European Economic Community) (Dinan, 2004: 46–82).

Box 2.5 Historical junctures of European politics

1952/1958/1993: the European integration process

- In spite of the continuing resistance of the UK, French Foreign Minister Robert Schuman, advised by civil servant Jean Monnet, created with West Germany and other European countries (Benelux and Italy) the supranational ECSC. The main objective was to share the coal resources of the Ruhr, which, in the past, had been a source of political conflict. The United States was an important supporter and promoter of the idea.

(continued)

(continued)

- This became known as the 'Schuman Plan' proclaimed by French Foreign Minister Robert Schuman on 9 May 1950.
- After lengthy negotiations in the Messina conference of 1956, two further communities were created in 1958:
  - The European Economic Community;
  - Euratom [related to nuclear energy].
- A further milestone was the Treaty of the European Union (TEU), signed in Maastricht and ratified in 1993. It created the legal foundations for Economic and Monetary Union (EMU), Justice and Home Affairs (JHA) and Common Foreign and Security Policy (CFSP).

Despite its ambition to be a supranational organisation, the European Economic Community was very much dominated by the member states. During the 1960s, the Commission tried to push forward the agreed plan of a single European market. It was instrumental in completing a wide range of legislation in order to achieve the completion of the common market. Between 1959 and 1968 all internal tariffs were removed. Furthermore, on 1 July 1967, the three communities were merged into one, receiving the name of 'European Community'. This accelerated integration was mainly the merit of first president of the EEC Commission the German law professor Walter Hallstein (1958–67). However, in 1965–66, through an empty chair policy, Hallstein was blocked by President Charles de Gaulle who was afraid of the growing powers of the EEC. The pendulum of integration swung from supranationalism to intergovernmentalism (Dinan, 2004: 101–19). The Luxembourg Compromise of 1966 is known for having slowed down or even halted the ambitions of the supranational institutions. Indeed, the period between 1966 and 1985 is known as 'Eurosclerosis' (Dinan, 2004: 177–8). A milestone of European integration was the introduction of direct elections to the European Parliament in 1979, ending decades of just elite-driven integration. Meanwhile, the European Parliament has co-decision powers in legislative acts through the ordinary legislative procedure. Moreover, in 1973, the UK, Ireland and Denmark joined the EEC, increasing its members from six to nine (Nugent, 2004: 22–7).

In sum, despite all setbacks the western part of the continent was moving slowly but steadily towards economic integration.

The 1970s: the end of the glorious thirty years

One of the major events of the 1970s in Europe was the almost simultaneous collapse of three authoritarian regimes in southern Europe: the Carnation Revolution on 25 April 1974 in Portugal; the evolutionary transition to democracy in Spain after the death of dictator General Francisco Franco on 20 November 1975; and, last but not least, the collapse of the military dictatorship of the colonels in Greece in July 1974. This became known as the beginning of the third wave of democratisation, which also expanded to Latin America, Africa and Asia in the 1980s and 1990s. All three democratic transitions were successful, so that after this point no more authoritarian dictatorships existed in Western Europe. Throughout the 1970s and 1980s these new democracies consolidated and became quite stable politically and economically. One important factor was their integration into the EC in the 1980s, Greece in 1981 and the Iberian countries in 1986. Apart from the consolidation of democracy and stabilisation of the southern flank of NATO in the context of the Cold War, the structural funds of the EC were important in strengthening the weak infrastructures of these countries (Huntington, 1991; Pridham, 1985, 1999).

In the context of the Cold War, the Helsinki Conference for Security and Cooperation in Europe (CSCE) took place in the summer of 1975 and should be regarded as a milestone in the process of European unification. The Helsinki accords signed on 1 August 1975 started a structured dialogue between West and East in order to improve the protection of human rights in Europe. The highly significant CSCE became an important forum to discuss issues of a pan-European dimension. The dialogue concentrated on four main areas: (1) European security; (2) scientific and economic cooperation; (3) humanitarian and cultural cooperation; and (4) follow-up to the conference. In 1994, the CSCE was transformed from a conference into an organisation with headquarters based in Vienna.

After decades of sustainable, uninterrupted economic growth, most European countries began to slow down and even stagnate economically in the mid 1970s. And after decades of an ever increasing expensive welfare state, the whole economic system was becoming less and less competitive. The growing importance of other economic powers such as Japan, the United States and new emerging economies in Southeast Asia were a major factor in the loss of competitiveness of European economies (Wegs and Ladrech, 2006: 262–4). In many cases, public enterprises accumulated huge losses that had to be financed from the state budget. This crisis is best symbolised by Austria during the late period of the chancellorship of Bruno Kreisky, who tried to keep ailing public enterprises afloat with state subsidies financed from the national budget.. Kreisky was extremely influenced by the dangers of unemployment during the 1920s and 1930s (Pelinka and Rosenberger, 2003: 41–3; Vocelka, 2002). Similar neo-corporatist strategies were followed across Western Europe, particularly in Germany, Benelux and the Nordic countries.

Moreover, the Organization of Oil Producing Countries (OPEC) reacted to the Yom Kippur War of October 1973 in which Israel was attacked by Egypt and Syria. The six-day war led to a complete victory of the Israeli army over the powers of the region leading later to peace agreements. During the Yom Kippur War, OPEC, dominated mainly by Arab states, increased its price by 70 per cent, and two months later it further raised its prices by 130 per cent. The United States and the Netherlands, which both supported Israel, were punished with oil embargos. Until the different countries were able to find alternative oil and energy supplies, they were exposed to continuous price rises until end of the decade.

One of the main consequences of higher oil prices was growing inflation that hit consumers hard. The overall macroeconomic policy mix of failing Keynesianism and rising inflation undermined the prospects of a recovery.

In this context, the neo-monetarist policies of British Prime Minister Margaret Thatcher after her election in 1979 became an important model for most European countries. It entailed the control of monetary circulation and major reforms in the public sector and the state, including welfare policies. The policies, known as Thatcherism, aimed at reactivating Britain's market economy after a long period of stagnation caused by social unrest that itself stemmed from intensive trade union activity. Thatcherism in the 1980s led to major changes in order to make the UK more competitive worldwide. One of the major policies of Thatcherism was privatisation, which led to the restructuring of major public enterprises and resulted in lay-offs on a mass scale in order to make companies not only profitable again but also attractive for potential foreign and domestic investors. This also included the privatisation of public utilities, such as the national railway system, other public transport, telecommunications, water, gas and electricity, allowing the state to become lighter and more competitive in international terms. Thatcherism successfully propagated the idea of 'people's capitalism' by advocating the idea of share ownership. Thatcherism also introduced major reforms in the public administration by allowing new public management thinking to modernise the relationship between civil servants and citizens. Nonetheless, other countries, including the European Communities, took on many of these ideas (Overbeek, 1991).

Apart from Germany, most countries engaged in major reforms. In France, François Mitterrand's victory in the presidential elections of 1981 and that of the Socialist party in the legislative elections, provided a great opportunity to push through a social democratic agenda. Nevertheless, after failed experiments, they had to change from Keynesian towards neo-monetarist policies, keeping inflation low in order to stop the vicious circle of hyperinflation (Elgie, 2003: 25–6). Other countries such as the Netherlands, Austria, Belgium and Luxembourg were able to negotiate with social partners a more or less radical reform programme. After German reunification, Germany became known as the sick man of Europe due to a low growth economy and the heavy burden of restructuring the East German Länder. Piecemeal reforms took place before and after reunification, but it was chancellor Gerhard Schröder's social democratic-green government that introduced the most radical but unpopular reforms between 1998 and 2005, leading to a major alienation on the part of the electorate from the Social Democratic party (Fleckenstein, 2012: 858–63).

In the 1980s and 1990s, European countries experienced a transformation of welfare states based on the principles of social redistribution towards a competitive workfare state that has to survive in an increasingly globalised world. The restructuring of the state towards lighter structures and the drive to make policies more efficient changed the socioeconomic dynamics of most European countries (Cerny, 1990; Jessop, 2002: 138–40).

The appointment of Jacques Delors to the presidency of the Commission of the European Communities in 1985 was a crucial turning point for the dynamics of European politics and the economy. His dynamism led to the transformation of the European Communities into the EU. One of the most important objectives was to push forward the SEM and make Europe the most competitive regional economy of the world. The main competitors were the United States and Japan/Southeast Asia. The report of economist Paolo Cecchini in 1988 showed that the creation of an SEM would considerably reduce production costs through the establishment of economies of scale and, in the long term, lead to an increase in employment. Although Delors was interested in preserving some aspects of the inherited social market economy, he was advocating softer Thatcherite policies at a European level. Moreover, the White Paper on the Single European Market, elaborated by Lord Cockfield in 1985, envisaged its basic implementation by the end of 1992. Another major achievement of Jacques Delors was to integrate the new member states (Greece (1981), Portugal (1986) and Spain (1986)) by achieving a doubling of the EU budget – of which 35 per cent was destined for structural funding in order for them to catch up with the rest of the developed economies and thus create a level playing field (Cecchini et al., 1988; Dinan, 2004).

One of the major consequences of these economic transformations was that society became more post-industrial and individualised. New technologies allowed for a personalisation of consumer goods and also the luxury of nomadism. This had implications for politics. The new information age is more value oriented than ideology oriented. Loyalty to social cleavages, which led to translation into political votes for particular parties, became replaced by a dealigned individualised electorate that voted for parties instrumentally and on a value basis (see Chapter 3).

The fall of the Berlin Wall and the emergence of a new European era

Throughout the 1970s and 1980s the economies of the Soviet Union and the Central and Eastern European countries were stagnating. They were not able to meet the demand for most consumer goods. The planned economy was too oriented towards heavy industry goods in order to keep up the arms race with the West. In the Soviet Union, the emergence of leader Mikhail Gorbachev was regarded as a possibility for achieving reform. Gorbachev wanted to introduce *perestrojka* (reform) and *glasnost* (transparency) to the Soviet system. He tried to reactivate political institutions and civil society after decades of totalitarian rule. Nevertheless, this led to an explosion of demands and the final demise of the Soviet Union on 25 December 1991. Although Gorbachev did not have a high reputation in Russia during this late period, he is hailed in the West, because he was instrumental in dismantling the Iron Curtain and paving the way for democratic transition throughout the whole of Central and Eastern Europe (Wegs and Ladrech, 2006: 220–4).

This process began with the withdrawal of support for the repressive policies of Erich Honecker in the GDR. Many East Germans fled to West Germany through Hungary and Austria during the summer and early autumn 1989. The protests continued throughout October until negotiations had to be undertaken to start a process of German reunification. Finally, on 9 November 1989, the Berlin Wall was dismantled by the people themselves (Box 2.6). The process of German reunification ended on 3 October 1990, after lengthy negotiations between the West and East German elites and the four allied powers (the US, the UK, France and the Soviet Union). The speedy reunification was mainly owing to the efforts of West German chancellor Helmut Kohl, who clearly feared a change of mind in Moscow. This is also one of the reasons why the West German Basic Law, after a lengthy discussion and adjustments in a parliamentary committee, was extended to the territory of the former GDR (Vogt, 2002: 920–41; Von Beyme, 2017: 48–58).

Between May 1988 and December 1989, other Central and Eastern European countries moved towards democracy. The only country that had opened up considerably and made possible regular exchange with the West was Hungary. Following the 1956 uprising, the reforms of János Kádár had led to tolerance of a private enterprise culture that was able to provide the market with the necessary consumer goods. 'Goulash communism' was also successful in pushing the boundaries of freedom. In May 1988, János Kádár was forced to resign and was replaced by a collective leadership. The Communist party was dissolved and replaced by the Hungarian Socialist party. In a round table of government and opposition representatives, the Hungarian constitution was amended to allow democratic transition. After the first free legislative elections, the Hungarian Democratic Forum (MDF), an umbrella party, won the elections while the re-formed communists got only 10 per cent. In subsequent elections, the re-formed communists were able to recover. A stable two-party system emerged, allowing for alternation between left and right (Montgomery, 2006: 412–14; Wegs and Ladrech, 2006: 228–31).

Box 2.6 Historical junctures of European politics

1989: the fall of the Berlin Wall

- Between 1947 and 1989 Europe was divided by the 'Iron Curtain'.
- On 9 November 1989, after the mounting discontent of the East German people, the Berlin Wall dividing Germany and the city was opened, leading to the collapse of communist rule in Central and Eastern Europe.
- After lengthy negotiations, it led to the reunification of Germany on 3 October 1990, a major holiday in the country.
- From November to December, one after another, the communist regimes in Central and Eastern Europe were toppled.
- 1989 can be regarded as the start of a new era of European politics.

In Poland, a dialogue between General Jaruzelski and the main opposition group, Solidarnošč, led to restricted legislative elections on 4 June 1989. The elections resulted in a considerable victory for the latter in the free elected seats of the Sejm and all seats of the Senate. The establishment of an all-party government under the leadership of Christian democrat Tadeusz Mazowiecki led to major reforms, directed at the establishment of a liberal democracy and a free market economy. In 1990, finance minister Leszek Balcerowicz introduced a shock therapy approach to economic reform which was intended to achieve transition to a market economy within a very short period of time (Balcerowicz plan). Such democratic transition ended with the adoption of a new constitution in 1997, after the Small constitution of 1993 was regarded as having many flaws (Sanford, 2001:

54–83; Taras, 2006: 358–60). Since 2015, the conservative Justice and Law party has been engaged in changing core provisions of the constitution, particularly in the judiciary sector, leading to negative reactions from EU institutions.

In November 1989, several demonstrations for democratic reform took place in Czechoslovakia, the country with the most orthodox and rigid regime. This led to the establishment of a 'government of national understanding' and the election of Václav Havel as president in December. In the first legislative elections on 10 June 1990, the umbrella Citizens' Forum (OF) won 53 per cent in the Czech Republic and Public against Violence (VPN) won 32 per cent in Slovakia. However, contestation of the Slovak nationalists over the federal nature of Czechoslovakia led to the 'velvet divorce' and the creation of two independent states (Vodička, 2005: 43–54; Wegs and Ladrech, 2006: 203–6).

In Bulgaria, several demonstrations during 1989 led to the resignation of leader Todor Zhivkov from all offices. A national round table in January to March 1990 started the process towards democratic transition. However, the elections of June 1990 led to the victory of the Bulgarian Socialist party, the former Communist party under a new name. The opposition renewed its demonstrations during summer and autumn 1990, forcing a renewed round table in January 1991. On 12 July 1991, a new constitution was approved that led to the first legislative elections in October 1991, leading to the victory of the Union of Democratic Forces (SDS) (Crampton, 2002: 308–14). Although on the left the Socialist party remained a stable piece of the new party system, on the right several parties have emerged and disappeared since the 1990s. Meanwhile, Bulgaria has been dominated by the Citizens for a European Development of Bulgaria (GERB) party and their leader, Boyko Borisov, since 2009.

The bloodiest revolution was in Romania, leading to the fall of former dictator Nicolaj Ceausescu and his family on 22 December 1989. It was a *coup d'état* of a part of the Communist party against Ceausescu. Soon after, Ceausescu's entire family was executed, and Ion Iliescu and the Front of National Salvation took over on 26 December. Ion Iliescu was elected as president in 1990 and also in 1992 and 2000. The re-formed communists in the renamed Party of Social Democracy in Romania remain an influential party on the left in the new political system (Crampton, 2002: 324–31; Gallagher, 2009).

The failed coup attempt in the Soviet Union in August 1991 also strengthened the independence movements in the Baltic countries which had been annexed by the Soviet Union in 1941/43 during the Second World War. All three countries proclaimed independence in 1990, but Moscow delayed her acknowledgement of independence. There were interventions in Lithuania and Latvia in early 1991. Nevertheless, by the autumn, the independence of all three Baltic states was recognised (Lane, 2002: 87–131; Pabriks and Purs, 2002: 45–66; Smith, 2002: 65–93). Similarly, Ukraine, Belarus and Moldova also became independent.

The recent democratisation processes in Central and Eastern Europe were a major boost for the European integration process. Negotiations between *Comecon* and the European Communities had started in 1988 (Smith, 2004: 29–35). The 1989 events forced the European Communities to develop a common strategy for all the countries. This process took place between 1989 and 1993. One of the reasons for the delay was that the EU was dealing with the process of accession of Austria, Sweden, Finland and possibly Norway, due to take place in 1995. After a rejection of EU membership in Norway, only Sweden, Finland and Austria joined the EU. Only afterwards did the EU devote more attention to the Central and Eastern European democratisation processes.

Box 2.7 Historical junctures of European politics

2004–13: united Europe

- After a decade of negotiations between 1993 and 2002, finally most Central and Eastern European countries joined the EU on 1 May 2004.
- This was followed by the accession of Bulgaria and Romania on 1 January 2007 and Croatia on 1 July 2013.
- There are now twenty-eight member states in the EU, being the vast majority of European states, although the UK will leave in 2019.
- It is expected that the Balkan countries will join the EU during the 2020s.
- Turkey's candidature was put on hold due to the authoritarian and repressive tendencies since 2013, but more concretely after the military *coup d'état* on 15–16 July 2016.

Apart from financial and logistical support, major reforms had to be undertaken to comply with what has been labelled the 'Copenhagen criteria', comprising political, economic and administrative issues (Box 2.7). These criteria were agreed during the Danish presidency of the EU in 1993. Almost a decade later, during the Danish presidency of 2002, most Central and Eastern European countries apart from Bulgaria and Romania (plus the Mediterranean islands of Cyprus and Malta) were allowed to join the EU (Lippert, 2003). By 1 May 2004, the EU had enlarged to twenty-five members; Romania and Bulgaria joined on 1 January 2007 and Croatia's accession was on 1 July 2013, increasing the number to twenty-eight (see Figure 2.1), but will reduce to twenty-seven when the UK leaves in 2019.

In spite of this success, the European continent was struck by tragedy. The fratricide wars in former Yugoslavia in the 1990s showed how weak European institutions were in dealing with such conflicts. The nationalist policies of Serbian leader Slobodan Milošević were a major factor in leading to the complete disintegration of Yugoslavia. In 1992, Slovenia was already able to free itself from the federation in spite of threats coming from Belgrade. Afterwards, Croatia followed the path of independence leading to a short war between the two sides. Then the main focus of conflict became the multi-ethnic Bosnia-Herzegovina, consisting of Muslim Bosniaks, Croats and Serbs. Ethnic cleansing between the different groups, in particular by Serbs and Croats, led to war crimes. The conflict was only stopped after mediation of the international community leading up to the Dayton agreement, which was also signed by Slobodan Milošević in 1995. Despite this agreement, a reintegration of Bosnia-Herzegovina has been quite a difficult process and only possible because of the presence of both the peacekeeping forces and civilian officers deployed by the international community. In spite

Figure 2.1 Political Europe, 2018

of these defeats, Milošević's war against the Kosovo Liberation Army (KLA) in Kosovo led to a further attempt at ethnic cleansing of the Albanian population in 1999. Milošević's policies were very much a response to the attempt by the KLA to intimidate the small Serbian minority in the region. The intervention of NATO under the leadership of Secretary-General Javier Solana, which consisted of bombarding key strategic positions in Serbia, led to the surrender of Milošević. The independence of Macedonia (or correctly Former Republic of Yugoslavia Macedonia) in 1993, did not spare the country from ethnic tensions. Indeed, in July 2001, ethnic tensions led to a major insurgency on the part of the large Albanian minority. This was only diffused when NATO and, later on, EU peacekeeping troops were deployed (Bideleux and Jeffries, 2007b: 451–2; Crampton, 2002: 239–98).

The independence of Montenegro from Serbia after the referendum of 21 May 2006 led to the definite end of Yugoslavia. Montenegro has only 650,000 inhabitants, who are extremely divided in their loyalties to Serbia (*Neue Zürcher Zeitung*, 14 July 2006). Last, but not least, the unilateral declaration of independence of Kosovo from Serbia on 17 February 2008 has led to further tensions and a nationalist backlash in the region (*El Pais*, 23 February 2008, 28 February 2008). Many countries with similar problems, such as Russia, China and Spain, refrained from acknowledging the independence of Kosovo, for fear that this may set a precedent for their own territories. Meanwhile, Kosovo is recognised by 113 countries and 23 EU member-states.

The multiple crises of European politics: refugees, euro crisis and the transition to a low-carbon society and economy

Since the late 1990s the EU has become an important actor in the continent. After several Treaty revisions, the EU's main guiding document is the Treaty of Lisbon ratified in November 2009. One of the innovations of the Treaty was to include article 50 to leave the EU, as happened with the UK's EU membership vote (the so-called Brexit Referendum) in June 2016.

At the core of the European project is now the EMU. By 2002, twelve countries had introduced the single European currency, the euro, in their countries; by 2017, the Eurozone had increased to nineteen EU member-states. Slovenia joined in 2007, Malta and Cyprus in 2008, Slovakia in 2009, Estonia in 2011, Latvia in 2014 and Lithuania in 2015; other countries of Central and Eastern Europe may join as soon as they have fulfilled the Maastricht criteria or feel that the economic conditions are right (i.e. government budget deficit should not be more than 3 per cent of GDP; public debt should be limited to 60 per cent of GDP). Poland, the Czech Republic and Hungary have delayed any accession to the euro because of possible negative repercussions upon their economies and the high level of Euroscepticism in all three countries. However, Bulgaria, Romania and Croatia are possible candidates if the economic conditions and fulfilment of the economic criteria are achieved, at least according to a speech given by president of the European Commission, Jean-Claude Juncker, on 17 September 2018 (Juncker, 2017; *Financial Times*, 13 September 2017). Even before the Brexit Referendum in June 2016, the UK was reluctant to join the euro, and the same applies to Denmark and Sweden with populations rejecting it in referendums in 2000 and 2003 respectively. On 23 June 2016, the referendum on the UK's exit from the EU led to a slight majority of 51.9 per cent of the eligible voters voting 'yes' and 48.1 per cent voting 'no' in a high turnout of 72.2 per cent. In all three cases, the population voted against the established parties and interest groups, showing a high level of Euroscepticism on this core project of the EU.

A major factor affecting the reluctance to join the Eurozone was the way the EU has managed the euro and sovereign debt crisis. Particularly in Poland and Hungary, there are fears that they could face the same fate as Greece.

As a consequence of the financial crisis in the United States in 2008–09, many governments in Eurozone countries, including France, Germany and Belgium, had to bail out their banks. However, in Ireland and the southern European countries, the bailouts increased their public debt considerably. Due to declining ratings by the credit agencies, they then had problems securing funding from the markets. Therefore, these countries, particularly Greece, Ireland, Portugal and Cyprus, hoped for assistance from the EU. However, due to the fact that the Treaty of Lisbon has a no bailout clause of member-states by the EU (art. 125), the Eurozone countries decided to create an intergovernmental bailout fund to which all would contribute a share based on their GDP. The final design of the intergovernmental bailout fund was negotiated by German chancellor Angela Merkel, and French president, Nicholas Sarkozy, which became known as 'Merkozy' due to the chemistry between the two leaders (Crespy and Schmidt, 2014; Hinz, 2013; Schwarzer, 2013). The bailout fund was at first provisional, and after October 2012 it became permanent. The so-called European Stability Mechanism (ESM) comprised €750 billion in credit guarantees in order to help member-states with difficulties obtaining funding from the markets. Due to its intergovernmental character, creditor member-states had to ask their parliaments for permission to support debtor countries. This clearly led to a major cleavage between creditor and debtor countries within the Eurogroup, which contributed to unequal power relations. Between 2008 and 2014, very rigid austerity policies were imposed on Greece, Ireland, Portugal and Cyprus, which contributed substantially to the pauperisation of these societies (Laffan, 2016). The main symbol of this policy was the so-called troika consisting of representatives of the European Commission, the European Central Bank and the International Monetary Fund, whose main task was to monitor the economic adjustment programme that crisis countries had agreed to implement (for more detail on individual countries, see Pisani-Ferry, 2013; for individual chapters on countries, see Magone et al. 2016; Magone, 2016; *BBC News*, 14 August 2015; *Cyprus Mail*, 7 March 2016).

The UK Brexit is certainly a good example of a growing politicisation and contestation of the European integration process. Such politicisation and contestation has been happening at different levels of the EU's multilevel governance system. It has become a major cleavage in most societies leading to the emergence of Eurosceptic, rightwing and leftwing populist parties. These new parties are challenging the established parties and contributing to an accelerated party change in most European countries. Also Central and Eastern Europe and the Balkans have seen the rise of extreme right populist parties, but not in all countries. In Slovakia and Romania extreme rightwing parties have lost considerable support. It seems that the European integration process has become a catalyst for the emergence of a socioeconomic and identity split between exclusive nationalists emphasising on repatriation of powers transferred to Brussels, and the cosmopolitan Europeans including many people with an inclusive national identity (Haller, 2009; Hooghe and Marks, 2018; Risse, 2010).

Clearly, the refugee crisis of August 2015, during which an estimated 1.3 million asylum seekers and illegal immigrants were able to come mainly to Germany, Austria and Sweden, exacerbated the feelings of loss of control and fears of losing national identity. Moreover, the difficulty in accommodating the exceptional wave of refugees in Austria, Germany and Sweden led to fears among the native population of losing out in terms of social benefits to the newcomers. In all three countries, rightwing populist parties – the Freedom Party (FPÖ), Alternative for Germany (AfD) and the Swedish Democrats (SD) – were able to profit electorally or in opinion polls from the refugee crises in their countries. Moreover, at the European level, the European Commission has had major difficulties developing a burden-sharing system that would be accepted by all member-states. Particularly, the so-called Visegrad group (Poland, Czech Republic, Slovakia and Hungary) formed a block against any distribution of refugees to their countries. In spite of an agreement with Turkey to keep refugees out of Europe, and the closing down of the Balkan route, the refugee crisis led to restrictions in the Schengen space. Most refugees now remain in their main arrival countries of Italy and Greece (on Germany, see Jäckle and König, 2017; Trauner, 2016; *Reuters*, 1 June 2016; *Die Zeit*, 29 September 2017).

Apart from the refugee crisis, plus the finance, sovereign debt and euro crisis, Europe has been shattered by a continuing wave of terrorism since the attacks on the twin towers in New York on 11 September 2001 (known as '9/11' events). In a first wave, Al Qaida was the main culprit, organising terrorist attacks in Madrid in 2004 and London in 2005. However, since 2015, the terrorist organisation Islamic State of Syria and Iraq (ISIS) has committed a considerable number of attacks across the world, but particularly in Europe. It started with the killing of twelve people mostly of the satirical magazine *Charlie Hebdo* on 7 January 2015. Since then, at least seventeen attacks have been perpetrated in Paris (November 2015, twice in 2017), Brussels (twice in 2014, 22 March 2017), London (three times on 22 March 2017, 3 June 2017, 19 June 2017), Normandy (26 July 2016), Nice (14 July 2016), Manchester (22 May 2017), Berlin (19 December 2017), Munich (22 July 2016), Stockholm (7 April 2017) and Barcelona (17 August 2017) (*Express*, 18 August 2017). Meanwhile, ISIS is considerably weakened due to the war conducted by a coalition of the willing in Iraq and Syria. According to estimates there were over 30,000 foreign fighters from the whole world fighting for ISIS in Syria, out of them 5,000 are from Western Europe, particularly France, the UK, Germany, Belgium and Bosnia-Herzegovina (Soufan Group, 2015: 8–10). The political Islamist threat, which is a mal interpretation of the religion of Islam, and based on hate against the West, is certainly a major challenge for all Western European countries. In contrast, the Central and Eastern European countries are still quite homogenous countries with very few Muslim communities. The big exception is Bulgaria with a Turkish minority group of roughly 600,000 people (9 per cent) of the population, but not known for being seduced by ISIS propaganda. However, the successful fight against ISIS in Syria and Iraq throughout 2017 has also led to an exodus of foreign fighters from the region, and their return to Europe, so that the basis for potential terrorist perpetrators has been on the increase (*The Guardian*, 26 April 2017). This will certainly remain one of the major challenges for the future of European politics, which is linked to the fight against racism and the upgrading of sensible integration policies. In the past decades, integration efforts have been characterised by rather repressive liberal measures, particularly in France and Belgium. The secular religiously non-denominational state is having a major problem in framing integration policies without perceived Islamophobic tendencies (Joppke, 2017).

Last but not least, a major challenge for European countries will be to keep their joint action in the management of global climate change. The Kyoto protocol of 1998 was a major milestone towards it, but finally, in Paris (COP 21), 195 states signed up to the Climate Change Agreement in December 2015. This clearly is a non-binding agreement, but nevertheless it is an acknowledgment that the climate is changing and affecting considerably current ways of life. The hope is to decrease the temperature of the earth by 2 degrees Celsius. So far 181 countries (as at October 2018) have signed up to the agreement. Moreover, cities and regions can sign up to the agreement independently of the national government (United Nations, 2017). Although President Donald Trump has announced the intention of the United States to withdraw from the agreement (*The Guardian*, 31 May 2017), the EU has become even more supportive of this development.

Conclusions: European politics as a kaleidoscope of experiment, innovation and tradition

This chapter gave an overview of European politics since the Late Middle Ages. In the past 500 years, European politics has been evolving towards emancipation and self-expressive values (Inglehart and Welzel, 2005). The complexity and diversity of national political systems and political cultures are intrinsically linked to processes of convergence and cooperation. The common heritage in both good and bad times has transformed national histories as part of what we call here 'interconnected European politics'. All parts of Europe have contributed to the richness and diversity of the political systems that we experience today.

Suggested reading

Davies, Norman (1997), *Europe: A History*. London: Pimlico.

Dinan, Desmond (2004), *History of the European Union*. Basingstoke: Palgrave.

Mason, David S. (2019), *A Concise History of Modern Europe. Liberty, Equality, Solidarity*. Lanham: Rowman and Littlefield.

Wegs, Robert J. and Robert Ladrech (2006), *Europe Since 1945: A Concise History*. Basingstoke: Palgrave.

QUESTIONS FOR REVISION

- Which main historical events shaped European politics?
- What is the main legacy of the French Revolution?
- What is understood by the 'Cold War' after 1945, and what were the implications for Europe?
- Explain the importance of the fall of the Berlin Wall in 1989.
- What were the main achievements of the European integration process?

Chapter 3

The transformation of European politics

- Towards a new understanding of European politics
- Stein Rokkan's theory of European politics
- The postmodernisation of European politics: the society of individuals and the impact of the new media
- Conclusions: the great transformation of the late twentieth century
- Suggested reading

Towards a new understanding of European politics

During the past fifty years European politics has undergone major transformations that we are able to recognise only now, with the benefit of hindsight. Throughout these decades the new transformations were analysed using theoretical instruments of the past. In this sense, students of European politics were confronted with a constant mismatch between theory and reality. The main theoretical edifice for understanding European politics was developed by Stein Rokkan. Many scholars took inspiration from his writings and developed different interpretations that are still important but which no longer reflect the fast changing reality of European politics today.

One of the main problems of Rokkan's theory is that it is embedded in the period 1945–67, which was characterised by a high level of political and economic stability. This does not help us to explain the period following 1967, which is characterised by high levels of political, social and economic change. However, this is not the place to criticise the huge and pioneering work of Stein Rokkan on nation-building, democratisation of national politics and the making of European party systems.

On the contrary, the work of this eminent Norwegian can only be an inspiration for us all. It should be acknowledged that Rokkan's theories have limited validity up to the 1970s, though mainly for Western Europe. His studies were concentrated on specific regions and countries where academic literature and data were available. In this sense, the Iberian countries, the Balkans, Central and Eastern Europe and even France (Guillorel, 1981: 390) are either completely neglected or scarcely covered. In spite of this, Rokkan left us an enormous legacy, a huge data collection and a host of ideas for renewed thinking about European politics. This includes a rethinking about processes of change, the hollowing out of the nation-state as a power container due to European Union(EU)-isation and globalisation.

This chapter is divided into three main parts. The first part deals with the main aspects of Stein Rokkan's theoretical contribution. The second part is dedicated to the criticisms to which Rokkan has been subjected since the 1970s. And the third part discusses the main catalysts for change since the 1960s.

Stein Rokkan's theory of European politics

Although there is diversity in Europe and one has to speak of different Europes, the trend towards convergence is largely inevitable. Comparative European politics does still matter, but convergence trends have been more important than actual conflict. Nonetheless, it is argued that, in spite of the tendencies towards convergence, national politics still matter and will not go away in the foreseeable future.

Stein Rokkan is therefore important, because he argued that such a trend from conflict towards consensus and non-violent decision-making of modern societies had been manifesting itself since the Middle Ages.

Rokkan was interested in three main issues:

1 *The nation-building process and the emergence of national politics.* This also includes the process towards inclusive citizenship.
2 *How different subcultures are accommodated through national party systems.* Here, he focused predominantly on studying the different cleavages that emerged through historical legacy.
3 *The centre-periphery cleavage.* Rokkan's Norwegian background and particularly his origins in the northern part of the country (Lofoten) led to a strong interest in comparing centre-periphery relations across Europe. If we look at the EU membership referendums held in Norway in 1973 and 1994, we can observe some continuity of opposition to the EU in the northern rural and coastal areas, which can be compared with the pro-European southern urbanised Norway, especially around the capital city of Oslo (Heidar, 1995: 446–7).

Nation-building and the formation of cleavages

It is not Rokkan's studies on nation-building and the emergence of national politics that stirred controversy among scholars. On the contrary, his historical-theoretical work on how citizenship emerged in European countries is well recognised. Today it forms the foundations for many studies on democratisation in Europe and other continents. Indeed, Rokkan's work allowed for differentiation within Europe, for example early democratisation, late democratisation, continuous democratisation and discontinuous democratisation (see Chapter 1). While Rokkan concentrated his studies on Western European countries and was very strong on the analysis of such processes in Northern Europe, the recent democratisation of Southern, Central and Eastern Europe allows us to finally map out the asymmetrical democratisation among European countries (Box 3.1).

Rokkan thoroughly studied transformations related to nation-building and the establishment of national politics in the nineteenth and early twentieth centuries. He was particularly interested in understanding the making and spreading of citizenship in the different European countries. His main aim was to map out the process of democratisation in Europe. Indeed, his ambition was to create a conceptual map of Europe.

Box 3.1 Stein Rokkan (1921–79)

Stein Rokkan was probably the greatest and most influential political scientist in European politics in the post-war period from 1945 until his death.

He was born on 7 July 1921 in the small village of Vågan, in the Lofoten in the northern province of Nordland in Norway. He studied philosophy in Oslo; however, he had a broad range of interests, particularly in the social sciences.

His main work is his conceptual map of Europe, which is based on historical path-dependency in the explanation of state- and nation-building. Furthermore, he was a pioneer in the development of longitudinal and synchronic empirical databases for several European countries for comparative purposes.

Appreciated by his fellow colleagues, his dynamism and hard work made him an invaluable leader in the profession. He took the first steps towards global comparative studies under the auspices of the United Nations. He was also a cofounder of the European Consortium for Political Research in 1970, which comprises over 350 institutional members coming from 50 countries.

He died on 22 July 1979 in the city of Bergen.

His Norwegian background also gave him the insight that nation-building can be a process that takes place simultaneously with the democratisation process. This, of course, makes the whole process towards national politics in different countries more diverse.

One particular aspect of his studies was that one cannot conceptualise a democratising nation-state as a homogeneous unit. On the contrary, he emphasised that societies are heterogeneous and characterised by cleavages. In spite of using the concept of cleavages, Rokkan never defined it; he clearly had difficulty in reaching a final definition. Nevertheless, he was very keen to emphasise that cleavage structures already existed before party systems emerged (Flora, 1999: 34). He was extremely influenced by a book written by Eugen Weber, called *Making Peasants into Frenchmen*, which showed this process of nationalisation of the masses and the creation of citizenship. Weber's historical masterpiece shows how rural France became increasingly integrated into mass politics between 1860 and 1914 and hence how the social fabric in the countryside became less stable, more porous and dominated by the rhythm coming from the urban centres (Weber, 1977).

Stefano Bartolini and Peter Mair endeavoured to come to a workable definition of the concept of cleavage. According to them, a cleavage is created through a process of closure that includes several factors. This closure is organised through marriage, common educational institutions, the spatial setting of the population, religious practices and social customs. In this cultural distinctiveness there is a high level of social homogeneity. This cultural distinctiveness leads to the establishment of social and political institutions in order to defend the way of life of the community. Cultural distinctiveness, social homogeneity and the establishment of dense organisational structures contribute to long-term stable sociopolitical membership of a subculture and allows for the translation of this membership into party and electoral politics (Bartolini and Mair, 1990: 225). According to Bartolini and Mair, these three factors lead to the stability of electorates in the long run. They represent them as a three-dimensional cube (Figure 3.1).

One of the big achievements of Rokkan was to make a connection between the sociopolitical processes and critical junctures of European politics. By critical junctures, he meant crucial European events that had a greater or smaller impact on all European countries (see Chapter 2). The three main junctures leading to cleavages were:

1 first, during the *Reformation* – the struggle for the control of the ecclesiastical organisations within the national territory;

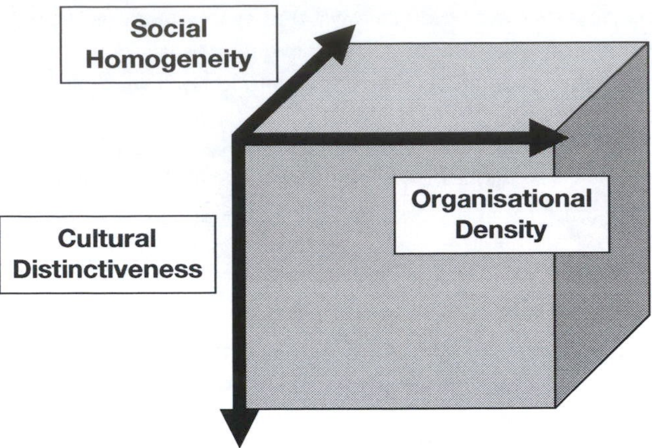

Figure 3.1 The dimensions of Rokkan's cleavage, according to Stefano Bartolini and Peter Mair

Source: Bartolini and Mair (1990: 225). Reproduced by permission of Cambridge University Press.

> 2 second, in the wake of the *'Democratic Revolution' after 1789* – the conflict over the control of the vast machineries of mass education to be built up by the mobilising nation-states;
>
> 3 finally, during the early phases of the *Industrial Revolution* – the opposition between landed interests and claims of the rising commercial and industrial leadership in cities and towns.
>
> (Lipset and Rokkan, 1967: 36–7)

In a more reflective way, with the hindsight of having read through all the manuscripts of Stein Rokkan, Peter Flora identified four cleavages:

- **Cleavage I:** Opposition against centralisation after the French Revolution in 1789;
- **Cleavage II:** State–Church conflicts over control over education since the eighteenth century;
- **Cleavage III:** The rural–urban conflict since the late eighteenth century that emerged during the Industrial Revolution;
- **Cleavage IV:** The workers–employers conflict since the late eighteenth century that emerged as a consequence of the Industrial Revolution: the so-called 'class cleavage'.

(The above is the author's summary, taken from Rokkan, 1980: 121; Flora, 1999: 37–8; Bartolini, 2000. See also Figure 3.2.)

Rokkan did not exclude the emergence of new cleavages after these three crucial events, but his theoretical framework was organised around the three critical junctures that produced the four cleavages. He certainly acknowledged that the Russian Revolution of 1917 was a major critical juncture, but he was

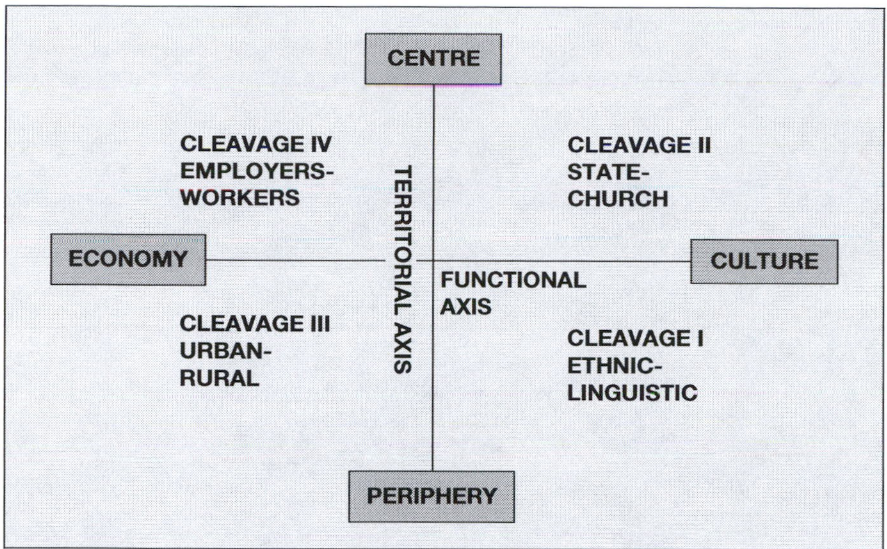

Figure 3.2 The four cleavages of European politics, according to Stein Rokkan

Source: Rokkan (1980: 121).

not sure whether the emergence of new communist parties that followed should be considered to be a new cleavage, distinct from that established earlier by the employers–workers during the nineteenth century (Rokkan, 1999: 305, 310).

The translation of cleavages into stable party systems

Rokkan was extremely interested in using these identified cleavages to study the development towards universal suffrage in a comparative perspective (Rokkan in Flora et al., 1999: 252–3) (see Figure 3.3). In this sense, he was interested in the incorporation of the masses into national politics. The likely instruments/ institutions to achieve this were political parties. The translation of cleavage structures into party systems became the central part of his theoretical work. He was very keen to reduce this process of creating party systems in the different European countries to a model of development. He identified four thresholds for the emergence of a functioning party system that have to be overcome over time, although not necessarily in sequence or in a particular time span:

Legitimation: This should be considered as an important threshold because, without legitimation, a political system will be dealing with an increasing number of protest movements. Opening up the political system for political activism will, of course, strengthen the establishment of political parties that channel the protests of their constituencies into mainstream politics and therefore help to legitimise the political system through its participation.

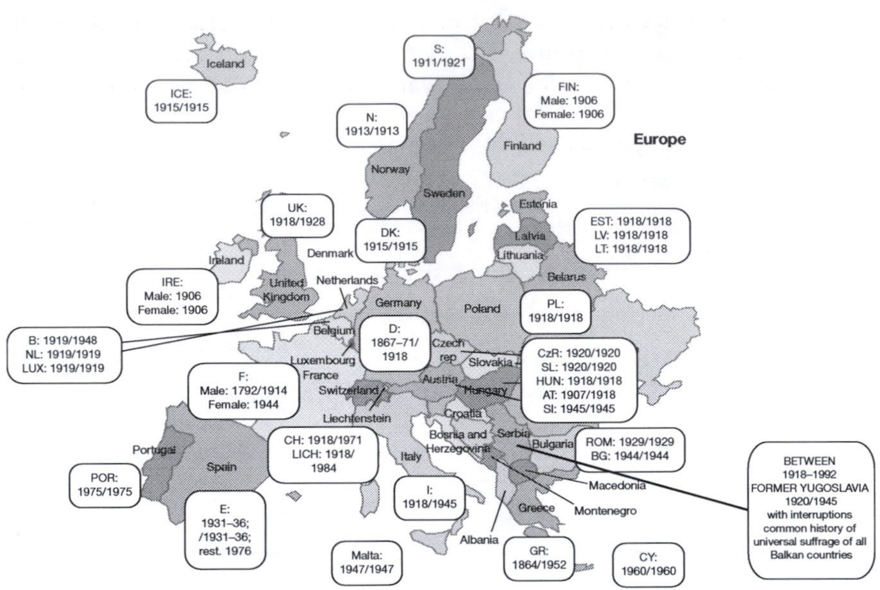

Figure 3.3 Universal suffrage in Europe

Incorporation: This refers to the acknowledgement of political rights for a vast majority of the population. The denial of political citizenship may put the political system under pressure. The extension of universal suffrage in stages allowed for an ordered process towards democracy as experienced in the UK and Scandinavia. In many continental countries, such as in Southern, Central and Eastern Europe, the process of incorporation was quite conflictive.

Representation: Another major aspect is the ability to achieve representation in the political system. This threshold is important because it further legitimises the political system and translates incorporation into concrete influence. The emergence of working-class parties in the late nineteenth and early twentieth centuries and their representation in national parties can be regarded as an important process in overcoming this threshold. The manipulation of the representative system, for example through the rigging of elections, as in Spain from 1870 until 1923, may lead to the emergence of political violence and even terrorist activity.

Majority power: The definition of the rules of the game in electoral politics is essential for the successful integration of political cleavages in the political system. It is important that all relevant social groups feel properly represented through their parties. A positive example of this is the Dutch policy of pacification during and after the First World War. This allowed the establishment of a proportional representation system, in which all relevant political groups could find a place in the new political system. Other issues that were important to different cleavages, such as the funding of faith-based private schools, were solved through this settlement (This is the author's summary, taken from Lipset and Rokkan, 1967: 27–32; Lijphart, 1975: 70–2.)

According to Rokkan there is an interconnection between these four thresholds. They all put each other under pressure, not necessarily in a sequential order, but nevertheless in some kind of relationship. These interrelated pressures will lead to political parties that are able to structure the cleavages and contribute to the integration of the political system. The political party is a crucial agent of conflict but also one of integration. Political parties fulfil three main functions:

- **Expressive function:** Parties express and structure the way of thinking and the demands of a particular cleavage or subculture inside a country.
- **Instrumental function:** The use of party structures for the achievement of the demands of a particular cleavage or subculture. This may include participation in elections, representative institutions or other forms of participation in which the party functions as a channel.
- **Representative function:** The participation in institutions such as parliament. The representative function allows also for incorporation into the political system and the achievement of the demands of a particular constituency through peaceful means.

As Rokkan emphasises, the main role for political parties is to provide channels of integration in order that the democratic state is able to remain stable over time. Competition between parties allows a legitimate system for implementing the demands of different cleavages of society, either through single or coalition government. Lipset and Rokkan summarise as follows:

> A competitive party system protects the nation against the discontents of its citizens: grievances and attacks are deflected from the overall system and directed toward the current set of powerholders . . . The establishment of regular channels for the expression of conflicting interests has helped to stabilize the structure of a great number of nation-states. The effective equalization of the status of different denominations has helped to take much of the brunt off the earlier conflicts over religious issues.
>
> The extension of suffrage and the enforcement of the freedom of political expression also helped to strengthen the legitimacy of the nation-state.
>
> The opening up of channels of expression of manifest or latent conflicts between the established and the underprivileged classes may have brought many systems out of equilibrium in the earlier phase but tended to strengthen the body politic over time.
>
> This conflict–integration dialectic is of central concern in current research on the comparative sociology of political parties.
>
> (Lipset and Rokkan, 1967: 4–5)

One of the most controversial of Stein Rokkan's theses, which he presented with Seymour Martin Lipset, was that most European party systems froze in the interwar period of the twentieth century (Box 3.2). This meant that in the late 1960s citizens were able to choose from the same number of mass parties that existed in the interwar period. Indeed, his 'freezing hypothesis' generated major criticisms soon after it was published. Party system change in some European countries led to a very high level of volatility in many European countries, in particular

Denmark and the Netherlands. Lipset and Rokkan argued that the majority of citizens in Western Europe had been acquainted with the existing parties since their childhood, or at least when they were allowed to vote for the first time. In this sense, they were socialised into particular subcultures that reinforced these cleavages (Lipset and Rokkan, 1967: 50). For the moment it suffices to present Rokkan's freezing hypothesis. We will look at the criticisms of this highly controversial thesis in the next section.

Box 3.2 The freezing hypothesis

Seymour Martin Lipset and Stein Rokkan edited a volume together with the title *Party Systems and Voter Alignments: Cross National Perspectives* (New York: The Free Press, 1967). In the introductory chapter called 'Cleavage structures, party systems and voter alignments: an introduction' (pp. 1–67), they presented a theory about the consolidation and institutionalisation of parties and party systems in Europe. The main thesis was that the party systems of 1967 had not changed particularly since the 1920s. They presented the thesis that the then contemporary party systems in different countries had been frozen since the 1920s. This meant that electorates had tended to vote for the same parties since the 1920s.

This was a daring thesis because, not long after the chapter was published, many countries (for example, the Netherlands and Denmark) had to deal with considerable party change. Supporters of this thesis, such as Peter Mair, argue that it is still valid owing to the low level of volatility from election to election. However, there are also critics of the thesis, for example Stephen Wolinetz and Mogens Pedersen.

Rokkan's interest in centre-periphery cleavages

Although Rokkan was interested in centre-periphery relations and the process of nation-building throughout his life, it is only in the later phase of his distinguished career that we find a more systematic work in relation to it. He teamed up with Derek W. Urwin to present a more organised view of his centre-periphery cleavage research. This work starts with a dominant interest in the periphery or peripherality of regions in relation to the centre. He recognised three features that characterised the periphery in relation to one or more centres:

- First, the periphery was dependent on one or more centres and had insufficient resources to overcome this dependency. The best examples of such peripheries are, of course, Galicia in Spain, Wales in the UK, and the regions in southern Italy.
- Second, the periphery had a marginal culture without a proper identity. It may be fragmented and divided.
- Third, its economy was normally quite weak and extremely dependent on the centre. Here again the southern Italian regions, the German Eastern *Länder*,

> Spanish Andalucia or the Austrian Burgenland can be named as examples. The extreme case is when this periphery is dependent on the exchange of just one commodity. In any case, peripheral economies always have to pay more for any services offered within a territory owing to the distance from the centres. In short, Rokkan counts three features for the ideal type of periphery: distance, political and economic dependency, and difference.
>
> (The above is the author's summary, taken from Rokkan and Urwin, 1983: 2–3.)

Rokkan became interested in the periphery owing to the fact that he himself came from the periphery in Norway (he was born in Vågan in the Lofoten, an island off the northern coast of Norway). This interest was reinforced by the fact that regionalism experienced a revival in the late 1960s and early 1970s. He spoke of the 'silent regionalist revolution'. In some ways he regarded this as a revolt of the regions with a stronger subnational identity than with the respective centralised national states. This revived consciousness could be witnessed in many Western European countries, in particular in Italy after the introduction of regionalisation, in France, in the UK and, understandably, in the then authoritarian Spain.

This renaissance of regions could take different forms. For example: the revival of the regional language; the right to use the minority language in education; the establishment of mass media structures; in dealings with government agencies (as could be found in Austria among the Slovenes and Croats in Carinthia); and claims for self-determination (as presented by the Basque and Catalan nationalists in Spain or the Scottish nationalists in the UK). This revivalism undermined the reified reality of the nation-state, which was very much taken for granted, and which itself was a social construction sustained by national socialisation systems and other ideological devices (for example, a nationalist civil religion) (Rokkan and Urwin, 1983: 118).

In particular, the revival of languages was an important factor in recreating regional peripheral identities. Since the Renaissance, nation-states across Europe had made huge efforts to impose a national language across a circumscribed territory, and language is an important factor in fostering a national identity. (The above is the author's summary, taken from Schröder, 1993: 28–39; Hobsbawn, 2000: 54–63.)

Throughout the nineteenth and twentieth centuries the larger nation-states pursued language policies nationally and internationally to achieve even more influence. The era of imperialism led to the expansion of the languages of superpowers, for example English, French, German and Russian, across the globe. Smaller, less viable languages and cultures were simply absorbed into the dominant culture (Schröder, 1993: 45). In some cases, new nation-states tried to impose new national languages but without very much success. This was the case of Nynorsk in Norway, which was created for the purpose of overcoming differences across the territory. In spite of this attempt, the more popular Danicised Norwegian (Bokmål) was a major impediment for its dissemination. In 2012, only about 11 per cent of municipalities spoke predominantly Nynorsk (the peak was 34 per cent in 1944). While 49.5 per cent speak Bokmål, the remaining 39.5 per cent use predominantly Bokmål but also Nynorsk as a minority language (they are referred to as neutral) (Språkrådet, 2017; Statistics Norway, 2017). Another attempt was the creation of the artificial Serbo-Croat language in former Yugoslavia. Apart from Slovenian, all languages in the western Balkans are quite similar, in many ways dialects of Shtokavian. Standardisation goes back to the efforts of Serbian language scholar Vuk Stefanović Karadzić between 1814 and 1864. It became known as the Serbo-Croat language and was used in the interwar kingdom of the Croats, Serbs and Slovenes, later known as Yugoslavia. Although former Yugoslavia allowed the different languages, it soon also adopted 'Serbo-Croat' as a major language. However, after the collapse of the former Yugoslavia, Serbo-Croat was soon replaced by the different languages of the new, independent countries during the 1990s. These examples show that artificial languages implemented at a late stage in the nation-building process may not have the desired success. In the case of the western Balkans, the dialect versions of the same language were soon upgraded to different languages related to the different political cultural contexts (Browne, 2017).

In this sense, it is possible to recognise the development of the centre-periphery cleavage in four main phases, with asymmetrical, synchronic development in different countries:

First phase (1780–1918): national elites created aspirations for national integration in respective countries. Some countries such as France and Spain had already created strong states that were engaged in constructing the nation. Germany and Italy created such nation-states only after the 1870s.

Second phase (1918–45): nationalisation of the masses. This was a period where mass politics began to emerge in most European countries. Different countries developed different approaches to integration. Successful evolutionary integration could be witnessed in the northern countries, while in Germany, Italy, Portugal, Spain and most Central and Eastern European countries authoritarian and/or totalitarian regimes emerged as a consequence.

Third phase(1945–79): social democratic consensus. There was a growing cooperation within a European integration framework, but the nation-state remained the main centre of decision-making. The introduction of welfare states further led to the nationalisation and centralisation of the nation-state. Periphery movements were perceived as negative and a threat to the unity of the state.

Fourth phase (1979–): erosion of national sovereignty owing to globalisation. The difficulty of steering public policy in a globalised accelerated economy has led to the establishment of regimes of shared sovereignty. Simultaneously, the region has become a more flexible unit in the political economy. At the same time, the nation-state has become decentralised, giving greater autonomy to the region (e.g. France in 1983, the UK in 1997, Spain in 1978 and Belgium in 1993; exceptions are Portugal, Greece, Romania and Bulgaria). There is also a growing process of denationalisation towards supranational and intergovernmental forms of integration, such as the case of the EU (these four phases are influenced by Hobsbawn, 2000; for fourth phase see Leibfried and Zürn, 2005).

One of the findings of Rokkan was that Europe was characterised by two kinds of periphery, which define the incomplete process of nationalisation: the interface peripheries and the external peripheries.

Interface peripheries are located between two countries and can produce a culture that encompasses both languages and cultures. The best example is Alsace-Lorraine, which has been a field of conflict between Germany and France since the sixteenth century. Other examples are Wallonia and Flanders in Belgium, and Schleswig-Holstein between Germany and Denmark.

The external peripheries had the opportunities to become national centres themselves owing to their economic prosperity and cultural awareness, but they failed to achieve this. Examples are the Basque Country and Catalonia in Spain, Occitania in France, Scotland in the UK, and Bavaria in Germany. They remain today regions with a strong cultural awareness, but firmly embedded in national states. In some of them we can find strong political movements demanding independence such as Scotland, Catalonia, the Basque Country and Flanders.

This growing erosion of the nation-state from above and below (Christiansen and Jørgensen, 2000) is one of the features of the great transition of the late twentieth century that demands a reconsideration of the theories of Stein Rokkan. The European nation-states are no longer the main decision-making units, and they are interdependently integrated with other European and non-European countries. As a contrast to the rigid structures of government of the nation-state, today there is emerging a more flexible multilevel governance system which has eroded the boundaries between the public sphere (a monopoly of the state up to the mid-1970s) and the private sphere. The Anglo-Saxon neo-liberal thrusts of Reaganomics and Thatcherism (1979–89) can be regarded as a major factor leading to the restructuring of the state towards more competitive structures (Cerny, 1990; Jessop, 2002; R.A.W. Rhodes, 1996: 659–65; 1997) (see Chapter 10 for EU multilevel governance and Chapter 4 for the emergence of the governance concept in public administration).

Reviewing the criticisms of Stein Rokkan's theory

According to Stein Kuhnle, Stein Rokkan's contribution remained restricted to certain aspects of the development of democratic politics. Kuhnle distinguishes between four main phases in the emergence of the modern democratic state:

- *the state-building process*, which took place during and since the fifteenth and sixteenth centuries (policies geared towards establishment of a tax-collecting bureaucracy, the establishment of an army, and the protection of the country from a monopoly of violence by establishing a police force);
- *the nation-building process*, which took place in the period following the French Revolution of 1789 (policies geared towards homogenisation of the country);
- *the democratisation and participation process*, which took place between 1789 and 1945 (the emergence of mass democracy);
- *the redistribution process*, which took place mainly after 1945 (welfare state).

According to Kuhnle, Rokkan concentrated most of his work on the third phase, relating to the emergence of mass democracy. Rokkan's interest focused on the emergence of mass politics and how political parties were able to structure this new phenomenon (Kuhnle, 1981: 502; see also Ferrera, 2005).

For this reason Charles Tilly, one of the former most important scholars of the European state-building process, criticised Stein Rokkan, because Rokkan studied history from the present time back to the past. This is regarded by Tilly as a problematic approach, owing to the fact that it tends to simplify a much more complicated process that is characterised by contingencies. According to Tilly, Rokkan's political development studies were embedded in the booming literature of the 1960s and 1970s that tended to ignore war in the whole process of state-building. In this sense, Rokkan's studies would discuss political developments through the lenses of the present, instead of being committed to serious historical research. His retrospective approach does not account for the 'powerful constraints in which all choices operate' and 'obscures the multiple, systematic, unanticipated consequences of the choices made' (Tilly, 1981: 123).

Although Rokkan collected large amounts of data and information, his reading of historical development was very much constrained by his training as a philosopher and social scientist. His hypotheses are very appealing and have some heuristic importance, but it is important to be aware of his limitations as a scholar.

Criticisms of the freezing hypothesis

In spite of this benevolent critique of Charles Tilly, the fiercest criticism came from political scientists. Stein Rokkan and Seymour Martin Lipset's 'freezing hypothesis' became the main target for criticism. One of the foremost reasons for the criticisms was that, shortly after the hypothesis was published, major changes began to occur in most Western European party systems. The fragmentation of the Dutch and the Danish party systems, where there was a high level of volatility and therefore party system change, were probably the best examples of these changes. The fragmentation of the Danish party system in the 1970s led to the establishment of over ten parties. Among them were parties that were Eurosceptic, anti-immigration and anti-taxation (for example, the Progress Party). They reacted against the Danish membership of the EC in 1973 and against the growing migrant population in the country. In the Netherlands, the main Catholic and Protestant parties experienced a decline in support, although in the end, after long negotiations, the Christian-Democratic Appeal (Christen-Democratisch Appél, CDA) was established in 1980 leading to a reversal of fortunes.

The criticisms and qualifications of the 'freezing hypothesis' can be categorised in at least five groups:

1 *Increased volatility after 1966.* Among the critics, Mogens Pedersen pointed out that Rokkan's agenda of tracking down the development of mass parties and its emphasis on stability was now being replaced by a new agenda, which emerged in the 1970s and was concerned with the growing party system change in some countries in relation to others. He identified two groups of countries.

   - Group one countries were those that registered a low level of inter-block, intra-block and general volatility, meaning the transfer of votes from one ideological block to another and/or between parties of the same ideological family, for example Austria, Sweden and Switzerland.

- Group two countries were those of high general volatility, for example France, Italy, Belgium, the Netherlands, the UK, Finland and Ireland. This growing volatility was evidence that the 'freezing hypothesis' should be questioned (Pedersen, 1979).

As a response, Peter Mair, one of the most prominent supporters of the 'freezing hypothesis' in the 1990s, drew attention to the fact that, in contrast to the interwar period, the average general volatility of Western European party systems was quite low. He presented a figure of 8.1 per cent for the post-1945 period, with inter-block volatility being even lower at around 2.1 per cent (Mair, 1993).

2 *The emergence of new parties*. One major criticism presented by Kitschelt (1995a; see also Ignazi, 1997) was that, in the 1980s and 1990s, new political parties emerged which were able to capture a share of the electorate. The best examples are the Green parties, which emerged as social and political environmental movements against, for example, nuclear energy plants, the destruction of natural habitats and the deployment of nuclear warheads (Ignazi, 1997; Kitschelt, 1995a). One important and influential international document was the report of the Club of Rome called *The Limits of Growth*. In this document, it was predicted that the main natural energy resources would come to an end within the next sixty years (Meadows, 1972). Today, scientists are more critical of this report, but at the time it had a major impact on the research community. In terms of values, we see the emergence of a new post-materialist worldwide culture. The main scholar who has drawn attention to the emergence of a post-materialist society is Ronald Inglehart. His studies are now globally acknowledged and have become part of the regularly held International Social Sciences Survey, which tries to assess the development of individual countries towards this post-materialist society (Inglehart, 1968, 1977; Inglehart and Welzel, 2005).

As well as the green parties, other parties emerged to challenge the established political parties. Among them were what Paul Taggart labelled the 'new populist' parties, which address several aspects of new politics. New populism emerged in the 1980s in some of the most established democracies, including France, Germany, Belgium, the Netherlands, Germany, Austria and Denmark. Most of these new populist parties could be summed up as 'new right' political groups, because they addressed topics that the established centre-right parties would not dare to put at the top of the agenda, for example, limits on immigration and issues of law and order. However, there also are leftwing populist parties such as the Block of the Left (Bloco da Esquerda) in Portugal, Podemos in Spain or The Left Party (Die Linke) in Germany. The new 'right' populist parties blur the boundaries with rightwing extreme parties. Among the most successful parties are the Freedom Party (FPÖ) in Austria, Alternative für Deutschland (Germany), Freedom Party (PVV) in the Netherlands and the Swiss People's Party (SVP) in Switzerland. Some far-right parties try to moderate their discourse and become similar to new 'populist' parties such as the Swedish Democrats (SD) in Sweden and Rassemblement National (Front National) in France or Jobbik in Hungary. Most recently, the Eurosceptic parties in the UK (UK Independence Party) and Scandinavia (Danish People's Party) further add to this expression of new populism, which appeals to a wide section of the population (Pirro, 2014; Taggart, 1998, 2000, 2004).

3 *The emergence of civil society organisations.* Another criticism is that in the last sixty years political parties have lost their monopoly in terms of representation of the interests of the population. The emergence of national civil societies, with thousands of interest groups, and non-governmental organisations have created new forms of policy influence. The role of civil liberties organisations, environmental associations, consumer groups and think-tanks has made the interaction between parties and the population much more complex. The expansion of education allows citizens to be much better informed about all policy areas. New technologies, such as the internet and television, allow citizens access to a large amount of information and hence form a more balanced view. Moreover, the role of newspapers and investigative journalism increases the level of transparency and accountability, if we exclude the more sensationalist and less serious representatives of the profession. While these social movements were able to increase their participation since the late 1980s, the membership of political parties has been declining (Katz and Mair, 1992; Mair and Van Biezen, 2001; Van Biezen et al., 2012; Van Biezen and Poguntke, 2014).

4 *The emergence of cartel parties.* A result of these changes was that political parties therefore had to change considerably in order to adapt to these new realities. According to Richard Katz and Peter Mair, a major transformation of political parties is taking place in all European countries. The catch-all party of the 1960s and 1970s is being replaced by the cartel party, which no longer represents an encapsulated 'frozen' subculture/constituency, but is interested in preserving its position of power in the political system. This twenty-first-century political party is electoralist in its nature and prioritises the winning of elections, in order that the majority of its party in office is re-elected. Apart from the UK and Switzerland, all other European countries introduced systems of public party funding (some more generous than others), which contribute to electoral expenditure according to the number of votes obtained, a subsidy to the parliamentary group over the legislature period and funding for the central party. Such systems are fairly generous in Germany, Belgium, Portugal, Spain and Austria. The cartel party has become an electoral machine with a lightweight structure. The late appearance of modern parties in the new democracies that emerged in the 1970s in Southern Europe (Portugal, Spain and Greece) and in the 1990s in Central and Eastern Europe and the Baltic states prevented an early encapsulation of parts of the electorate, so that they became cartel parties from the outset, highly dependent on state funding and with access to the media, but with low levels of membership (Van Biezen, 2003: 36, 40–1) (see also Chapter 6).

5 *The 'Americanisation' of European politics.* Last, but not least, political parties are now acting in complex electoral markets that require knowledge of political marketing, permanent management of election changes, and optimal use of new technologies, new media and focus groups (Mair et al., 2004; Newman, 1999). According to Manuel Castells, national politics in all European politics has become Americanised (Castells, 2000: 317–18). Such Americanisation of European politics is leading to the bipolarisation of party systems, similar to

the US and UK systems, in many countries (for example, Portugal, Spain, Italy, Greece, Austria, Germany and, naturally, France (Von Beyme, 1996: 140)). This Americanisation also expresses itself in the transformation of former encapsulated ideologically and socially segmented cleavages, which were reproduced election after election, into a volatile, individualised electoral market. This means that people vote instrumentally for the party that is able to offer them the better deal. This electoral market behaviour of both the political parties and the electorate has also changed attitudes towards politics. According to Richard Katz and Peter Mair, 'The leaders become the party, the party becomes the leaders' (Katz and Mair, 2002: 126). The personalisation of politics has its extreme expression in the presidentialisation of the prime ministerial office in some countries (good examples are the Prime Minister Tony Blair (1997–2007) in the UK and Prime Minister Sebastian Kurz in Austria) (Poguntke and Webb, 2005) (see Chapter 5 for presidentialisation of government).

European integration as a new development of political restructuring

Stein Rokkan was a Eurosceptic scholar who was not convinced that European integration would substantially change the development of European politics. However, Stefano Bartolini tried to develop Rokkan's theory, taking into account the recent thrust of European integration since 1985.

Today we have to include a new phase related to the growing transnationalisation of national politics through the policies of the EU. According to the excellent work of Stefano Bartolini, we may be in a process of reconfiguration of centre formation, system-building and political structuring between the nation-state and the EU. This means that many Eurosceptic parties are already sensing this transformation that Bartolini characterises as the sixth developmental trend in European history since the sixteenth century (see Figure 3.4). According to him, we are experiencing a further restructuring of European politics, following:

1 the processes of state building;
2 capitalist development since the sixteenth century;
3 nation-building since the nineteenth century;
4 democratisation;
5 welfare state development since the twentieth century.

He analyses the sixth process, related to European integration, as follows:

> Integration, as a sixth powerful phase in the development of the European system of states, economies, nations, democracies, and welfares necessarily relates to each of the five preceding phases. This process of European integration was triggered by two main problem-pressures. On the one hand, it was driven by the unbearable costs of rivalries of the state systems in an era of war technologies whose destructive power had become disproportionate to the stake of the rivalries themselves. On the other, it was driven by the growing pressure deriving from the slow but significant economic peripheralisation of Europe in the post-Second World War world economy and the

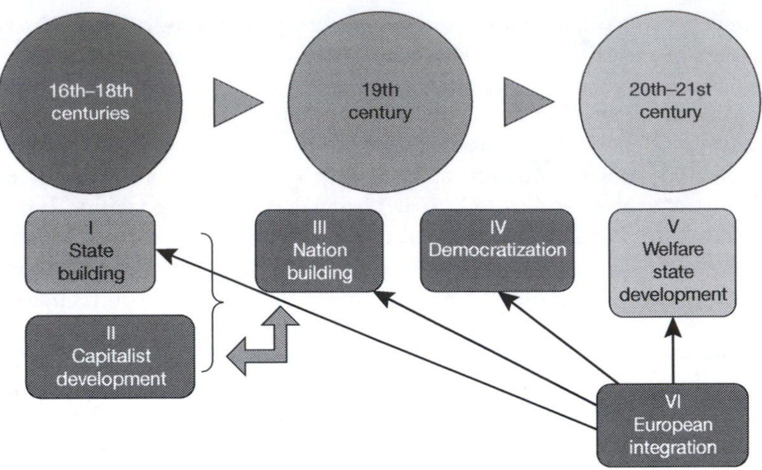

Figure 3.4 The six phases of development of European politics, according to Stefano Bartolini

Source: Based on a figure by Bartolini (2005: 366).

> corresponding perception of the inadequacy of the European state as a unit of economic organisation in world competition. European integration can therefore be historically interpreted as a response by national elites to the weakening of the European state system and to the new pressures brought to bear by capitalist world development.
>
> (Bartolini, 2005: 366)

A linkage between national and EU politics is becoming more visible. Recent studies use the cleavage theory to analyse the restructuring of European and national identities (Börzel and Risse, 2018; Hooghe and Marks, 2018; Risse, 2010).

In sum, the contribution of Stein Rokkan to the theory of European politics is invaluable and a good basis for research. Nevertheless, the transformations that have taken place since the late 1960s have created a new reality that can only be understood if we use Rokkan's ideas in a less rigid and doctrinal way, but flexibly and as an inspiration to understanding present European politics. In the following pages we will delineate some of the changes that lie behind the transformation of European politics since the late 1960s.

The postmodernisation of European politics: the society of individuals and the impact of the new media

From the industrial to the post-industrial society

Since the 1960s major changes have taken place in national societies in Europe. Among these changes are: the growth of the welfare states after 1945; the technical progress achieved in the last seventy years; different waves of immigration both within and from outside Europe; the decline of religion and religiously based cleavages; the end of class politics as we knew it until the late 1970s; the emergence of civil society; and the rise of subnational consciousness and identity in some European countries.

The European integration process played an important role in increasing the networks between national economies, societies and political systems. This process of transformation has strong similarities to what Karl Polanyi identified as the 'great transformation' from the nineteenth to the twentieth century that led to the industrialisation and modernisation of national societies. One of the consequences was the migration of the rural population to the larger cities and the emergence of an industrial working class (Polanyi, 1944). Modernisation can be characterised as a transition from simple agrarian societies to complex differentiated industrial societies (Wolfgang Zapf, quoted in Immerfall, 1995: 41). This process started in England, Belgium and Germany and later expanded to other countries. One of the consequences was the need to integrate the new citizens into the new political system through the extension of suffrage and the creation of political parties, this to include large parts of the electorate. In some cases, integration led to the emergence of totalitarian regimes (for example, Nazi Germany and Italy as well as in many other European countries) (see earlier and Chapter 2).

Since the 1970s another great transformation, similar to that of the nineteenth century, has been taking place. The great transformation of the late twentieth century is the transition from a modern class-based society to a postmodern knowledge-based one (see Table 3.1). Classes still exist, but they are less visible today and are determined not only by profession but also by additional factors, such as marriage, number of children and education. One of the characteristics is the increase in the new middle classes who are employed in the services sector (Esping-Andersen, 1995). Moreover, since 1970, there has been a growing need for governments to control expenditure of welfare policies. The transformation of the welfare state into a workfare state, which links any benefits to employability, allows most of the funding to be shifted to socially excluded people (Jessop, 2002; Hemerijck 2013, 2018).

While modern society was characterised by a homogeneous national population, since 1945 waves of immigration from other European countries, and also from outside Europe, to the more advanced European economies have made present postmodern societies more heterogeneous and multicultural. Demographic developments, in which the birth rate is too low to sustain population levels in most European countries, has increased the need for ordered immigration policies, otherwise there would be an imbalance between the older generations (who, as a result of both medical progress and better living conditions, are living much longer), and the younger cohorts working in the labour market and supporting the pension system. Most European countries are reforming their pension systems such that the solidarity linkage between older and newer cohorts is preserved. Such reforms entail the expansion of the working age, incentives for more savings and adherence to supplementary private pension schemes. Budgetary policies need to be designed from a long-term perspective in order to preserve their sustainability in the future. The European integration process through economic and monetary union puts constant pressure on national governments to take into account the demographic changes and their long-term effects on pensions (see

Table 3.1 The great transformation of the late twentieth century

	Dimensions	*Industrial age (1945–79)*	*Information age (1980s–)*
Politics	State	Government, welfare state	Governance, workfare state
	Parties	Catch-all parties and mass parties	Cartel party
	Participation	Monopoly of political parties through encapsulation of cleavages	Pluralisation of participation forms – conventional and unconventional
	Territorial structure	Tendency towards centralised, hierarchical structures	Tendency towards decentralisation and subnationalisation of politics
Economy	Economy	Economy centred around industrial sector	Economy centred around tertiary sector
	Structure of economy	• Fordism • dominance of huge factories • synchronisation of space and time through assembly line	• post-Fordism • lean production • dominance of small enterprises, • decentralisation and relocation of production to labour-intensive countries • Digitalisation and automation of workplace
	Labour market objective	Full employment	Employability
	Interest intermediation	Interventionist social democratic neo-corporatism	Regulatory liberal neo-corporatism
Society	Nature of society	Homogeneous national society	Heterogeneous multicultural society
	Social structure	Class-based society; dominant working class	Knowledge-based society New middle classes dominant
	Social mobility	Increase of upward mobility through redistributive welfare policies	Increase of both upward and downward mobility owing to reduction of redistributive welfare policies
	Civil society	Emergence of civil society organised within collective official organisations	Increase in complexity of civil society, non-governmental organisations

Source: Author.

Chapter 10, section 'Economic and monetary policy'). The necessary increased immigration, reinforcing the heterogeneous multicultural societies, creates more tensions if there are no integration policies to allow immigrants and their families to become part of the society. Such debates and tensions have been quite intense in many countries, for example in Germany, Austria, Switzerland, the Netherlands, Belgium, France, Sweden, Denmark, Norway and the UK.

Religion and religiosity have declined considerably since the late 1980s, and modern class-based cleavages have been substantially eroded, being replaced by a society of individuals who act either politically, based on values, or instrumentally, according to the principle of the best deal.

According to Ronald Inglehart and Christian Welzel, most European countries are moving towards a post-materialist society. They conceptualise human development as a transition from modern societies integrated into collective structures (parties, factories, the Church) with materialist survival values of consumption, to postmodern societies integrated into flexible tailored structures (e.g. non-governmental organisations) with post-materialist values emphasising human emancipation, gender equality and self-expression (Inglehart and Welzel, 2005: 262). The development is, not surprisingly, quite uneven across Europe. The most developed post-material societies are in Nordic Europe, the Netherlands and Germany, while Southern Europe (particularly Portugal and Greece) and the Central and Eastern European countries lag behind in this process (see Box 3.3 and Figure 3.5).

Box 3.3 Materialism vs post-materialism

- According to Ronald Inglehart and Christian Welzel in their book *Modernization, Cultural Change and Democracy: The Human Development Sequence* (2005), a world development is taking place, moving from a materialist society, based on survival values, to a post-materialist society, based on self-expressive values.
- The materialist society is usually linked to the process of industrialisation and industrial society, but not always.
- The post-industrial society is usually linked to the information and services society, but not always.
- Some European countries have a tendency towards post-materialist values, for example the Nordic countries, the Netherlands, Belgium, Luxembourg, Germany, Austria, Switzerland and the UK.
- Some European countries still have a tendency towards materialist values, for example the Southern, Central and Eastern European countries.

In spite of these cross-regional differences, the European integration process is a major factor in pushing all other parts of Europe towards the Nordic pattern. For example, until the 1970s Portugal and Greece were emigration countries. Most emigrants went to richer northern countries, such as Germany, Belgium, the Netherlands, the UK and France. After 1974, most of these richer countries began

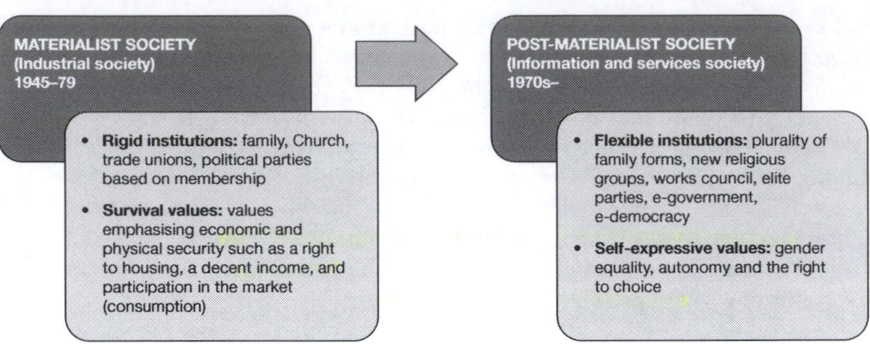

Figure 3.5 From materialist to post-materialist society in Europe

to have major economic problems. And after joining the EC/EU, Southern Europe became an immigration target for people from Africa, Asia and Eastern Europe. One of the main reasons that Southern Europe became an attractive destination for immigration is the fact that their border controls are less stringent and, also, that since the 1980s, Southern European countries have become wealthier.

Although over three-quarters of Europeans support the institution of marriage, postmodern society has seen the rise of a pluralisation of living styles that has had an impact on politics. While in the modern industrial society the nuclear family of two to three children was the dominant family form, today the number of single households has increased considerably. Moreover, there are more varieties of families, for example single-mother or single-father families, bi-nuclear families, two-career families, same-sex families and working parents. This naturally makes politics and policy-making more complex. Family and marriage can be expressed in different ways and politicians have to be aware of it. The social organisation of society has become more fragmented and more complex, not least because the number of divorces has increased considerably – in the UK as well as certain countries in Nordic Europe it has actually overtaken the number of marriages per year. These developments are uneven across Europe, with the Southern European countries and Ireland (owing to their Catholic traditions) lagging behind in this respect. Apart from cultural constraints, another main reason is the late economic development of these societies (Castells, 2000: 223; Eurostat, 2018a; Hopflinger, 1997; Immerfall, 1997: 143; Mau and Verwiebe, 2009: 101–4).

All these transformations have led to what Zygmunt Bauman calls the 'individualised society', meaning that former encapsulated social and political cleavages are being replaced by a looser, less rigid and fluid organisation of society, based on individual freedom, self-expression and choice. It contrasts heavily with the rigid modernity based on heavy industrialisation and rigid institutions, due to its liquidity and fluidity (Bauman, 2001). This individualised society has major consequences for politics. Political parties can no longer count on the automatic support of political subcultures, but have to compete with other parties for each vote in a very volatile electoral market. As already mentioned, parties act in complex electoral markets in which focus groups, opinion polls, political marketing and use of the media become crucial for electoral success (Mair et al., 2004: 3–9) (see also Chapter 7 for a fuller discussion on political parties, party systems and elections).

From a welfare to a workfare state

Another major change in many advanced European societies, which is being emulated by the periphery, is the gradual replacement of the welfare state that existed until the 1970s, by workfare systems (Figure 3.6). The industrial society achieved a high level of stability, because generous welfare states were established that gave way to social peace between the employees' representatives, employers' representatives and the state. One of the main policies of the welfare state was to achieve full employment (meaning unemployment levels at less than 3 per cent of the working population). This meant that in many cases (e.g. in Austria during the Bruno Kreisky premiership in the 1970s) the state would subsidise public sector working places at a loss just to preserve a high level of employment. Most countries had large public sectors that provided employment to a large part of the population. Bob Jessop characterised this as the 'Keynesian welfare national state' (KWNS). He refers to John Maynard Keynes (1883–1946), an eminent British economist, who proposed expansive public works policies to achieve a relaunching of an internal market which may be in recession. So the full employment demands in most Western European countries of the 1970s was a major aspect of the KWNS.

Some of these policies were conducted in periods of expansion, so they then had a negative impact in periods of recession. One important aspect was the fact that KWNS was possible because the level of national autonomy was much higher than in the present post-industrial society. Furthermore, the 'mixed economy', in Germany called the *soziale Marktwirtschaft* (social market economy), was the predominant economic organisation. The state intervened regularly in the economy. This meant that the huge public sector in most Western European countries played a role in steering the strategy of the national economy and 'compensating for market failures' (Jessop, 2002: 58–9). The KWNS was particularly expansive in the Scandinavian countries, Belgium, Luxembourg, the Netherlands, Germany and Austria. Indeed, Gösta Esping-Andersen developed a typology of three welfare state models: (i) the social democratic Nordic model, which was the most generous one and was geared towards reducing inequalities in society; (ii) the conservative model prominent in Belgium, Austria and Germany, which was more geared towards stability of economic and social relations; and (iii) last, but not least, the liberal welfare state, which was minimalist in its provision (the best example of this being the US welfare system). In Europe the UK is probably the country that comes closest to this third type (Esping-Andersen, 1990). It is necessary to be cautious about generalisations because some countries may be hybrid systems – in-between types. Probably Belgium could be more properly placed between the social democratic and the conservative model. The Swiss case is very much influenced by the conservative models of Austria and Germany, but its development is more akin to the liberal model (Bonoli and Häusermann, 2011: 196–7).

Martin Rhodes and Maurizio Ferrera have added the 'Southern' model of the welfare state: it is narrower in scope than the other welfare states in terms of provision and is dominated by elements of clientelism and patronage. The Southern European type comprises Portugal, Spain, Greece and Italy. Furthermore, there is now discussion of the Central and Eastern European welfare state model created after 1989. As a result of the recession at the beginning of the 1990s, the welfare provision that existed in the former socialist people's republics declined considerably after the transition from a planned to a liberal market economy, leading to an increase in poverty and unemployment. The new welfare systems in Central and Eastern Europe are too weak to provide adequate support for the population. Aspects of micro-corruption, clientelism and patronage may affect a fair redistribution of social benefits (Ferrera et al., 2000) (Box 3.4; see also Chapter 10).

The KWNS model began to be replaced at the end of the 1970s by what Jessop calls the 'Schumpeterian workfare post-national regime' (SWPR). Joseph Schumpeter (1883–1950) was an Austro-American political economist who was based for most of his academic life at Harvard University. He developed economic theories based on the importance of innovation and competitiveness. Schumpeterianism emphasises the importance of innovation characteristics, particularly of the knowledge-based economy. SWPR emphasises aspects of employability, and there is a clear dominance of economic priorities over the more efficient way of using social policy. The erosion of national autonomy and the adjustment of state structures towards globalisation processes is a further feature of this regime. Furthermore, the role of government is replaced by a self-organising and regulatory governance system to correct market and state failures (Jessop, 2002: 252–3). Governance emerged out of the growing retreat of the state throughout the 1980s and 1990s. It is a non-hierarchical, horizontal complex set of policy networks and is regarded as being differentiated from hierarchies, such as government and markets.

The state has an overarching 'meta-governance' supervisory capacity to ensure that partial policy regimes of governance are working properly. This transformation from government to governance took place in the 1980s and 1990s, led by the Thatcher governments in the UK between 1979 and 1990 and the Reagan government in the United States between 1981 and 1992. The reduction of the state, the privatisation of many public services and the huge public sector led to the introduction of market principles in UK public administration. Following this, similar public service reforms were introduced in most European countries (Rhodes, 1996, 1997) (see Chapter 4 for more on governance in public administration). Once again, the UK was at the forefront of such principles.

Box 3.4 From three to five worlds of welfare

In 1990, political sociologist Gösta Esping-Andersen wrote his book *Three Worlds of Welfare* in which he presented a typology of three welfare states:

- the *liberal welfare state* – based on universalistic minimalist coverage funded through the national taxation system (UK, Switzerland, United States, New Zealand, Australia);
- the *social democratic–Nordic welfare state* – based on universal, extensive coverage funded through the national taxation system (Sweden, Norway, Denmark, Finland and Iceland);
- the *conservative–continental welfare state* – based on universal, extensive coverage funded originally through employers' and employees' contributions and increasingly through additional state funding (Germany, Austria, Belgium, the Netherlands and France).

In 2000, political scientists Maurizio Ferrera, Anton Hemerijk and Martin Rhodes wrote a book, in Portuguese, entitled *The Future of Social Europe: Recasting Work and Welfare in the New Economy* in which they added two more welfare state types to the typology:

- the *Southern European welfare state* with pretensions of universal coverage but, in reality, characterised by particularist–clientelist regimes mixed with a minimal, universal coverage; it combines elements of the liberal and the conservative–continental welfare states (Italy, Portugal, Spain and Greece);
- the *Central and Eastern European welfare state* with pretensions of universal coverage but, in reality, also characterised by micro-corruption and low benefits; depending on the country, a mix of liberal and continental welfare states is also the rule (Hungary, the Czech Republic, Slovakia, Poland, Slovenia, Bulgaria and Romania).

One of the main intentions of workfare states is to reduce the number of people dependent on social benefits. Social policy in the workfare/flexicurity state concentrates particularly on bringing people back to work, and social exclusion is regarded as an issue that has to be addressed by a positive social policy. This means mainly policies to facilitate inclusion into the labour market.

Labour markets become more flexible but jobs become less secure and, instead of secure employment, employability and mobility are encouraged. The EU policies relating to the creation of the Single European Market are a major factor in reshaping the national economies and labour markets in European societies. A buzz word used in the EU is 'flexicurity', meaning flexible labour markets supported by strong welfare states. The model was developed in Denmark and

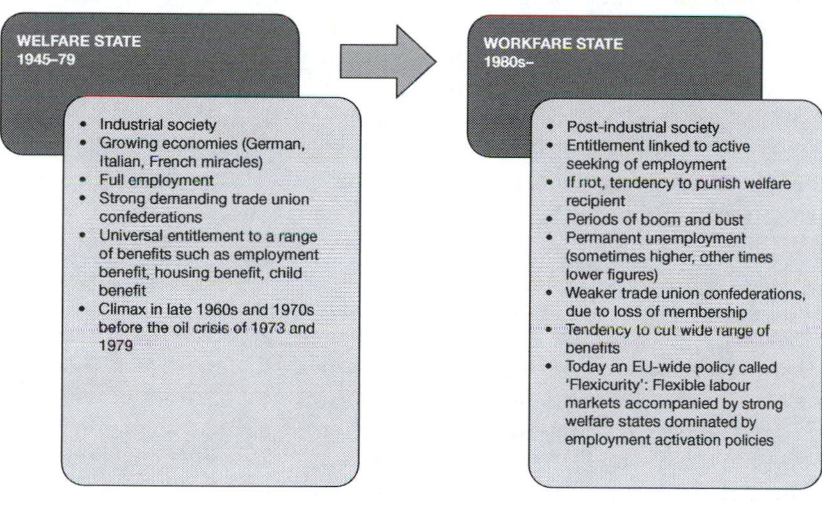

Figure 3.6 From welfare to workfare state

other Nordic countries. Certainly, it will be quite difficult to transfer the model to the less wealthy economies in Southern, Central and Eastern Europe (Table 3.2).

Towards the post-industrial economy: the end of traditional class politics

Until the 1960s, social democratic and communist parties were able to mobilise large constituencies in the working class. It was the climax of the industrial Fordist age in which the working class in the industrial sector was the dominant social group. However, since the 1970s and 1980s, such support of the working class for social democratic and communist countries has been declining (for an excellent account of the class cleavage, see Bartolini, 2000 and Kitschelt, 1995b). The main reason is the transition from the modern industrial to the new knowledge-based liquid society.

One of the main features of the new knowledge-based liquid society is the steady decline both of the industrial sector as the largest in terms of Gross Domestic Product (GDP) and in the employment of the majority of the working population. The decline of the industrial and the agricultural sectors has been replaced by an increase in the services sector. The vast majority of the population is now employed in the services sector and this has major consequences for society. The services sector is quite dynamic and volatile. It allows for the emergence of what has been dubbed the 'new middle classes', with high levels of educational attainment, working in knowledge-based sectors. It means that the traditional industrial society in which the working class was the dominant group, is being replaced by a new class system based on knowledge-based skills. Educational attainment becomes an important element in establishing such a new class system (Haller, 1997: 391–402; Immerfall, 1995: 67–72). Gösta Esping-Andersen labelled this 'changing classes'. In this process there is an emergence of a new, unskilled underclass, at the bottom of the new class pyramid, which performs all possible jobs. At the top of the pyramid, there are knowledge producers, such as scientists and professionals. All the other groups fall between these two extremes (Esping-Andersen, 1995b; Esping-Andersen et al., 1995).

Such de-industrialisation is asymmetrical across Europe. The poorer Southern European countries of Portugal and Greece may be able to attract some of the jobs lost in the more advanced economies. Nevertheless a growing challenge comes from cheap labour within the emerging economies (for example, China, India and other developing countries), giving Southern, Central and Eastern Europe only a midterm advantage. Most of these industries have been reallocated to developing countries, which were able to produce labour-intensive products at a lower cost, with the result that the role of knowledge-based investment has become crucial for the survival of European countries. However, innovation has been quite uneven across the EU. While Sweden, Denmark, Finland, Germany, the UK and the Netherlands are innovation leaders in terms of research and development, Southern, Central and Eastern European countries are rather less innovative (European Commission, 2017a).

This means the traditional class cleavage – based on a more or less homogeneous working class which worked in large factories over the same period of time

Table 3.2 The industrial sector in selected European countries

Country	*Period of industrial dominance*	*Climax share of employment in industrial sector*	*Year*	*Population in employment in millions in third quarter of 2018 (employment rate in % 2017)*	*Structure of employment 2016 in %*		
					Agriculture	*Industry*	*Services*
Austria	1951–66	42.8	1973	4.288 (75.4)	4.3	25.6	70.1
Belgium	1880–1965	49.1	1947	4.737 (73.2)	1.3	21.3	77.4
Bulgaria				3.115 (71.3)	6.3	29.7	64.0
Croatia				1.662 (63.6)	7.5	27.1	65.4
Cyprus				0.395 (70.8)	3.5	17.1	79.4
Czech Republic				5.155 (78.5)	2.9	37.9	59.2
Denmark	Never	37.8	1970	2.800 (76.9)	2.6	18.8	78.6
Estonia				0.631 (78.7)	3.9	29.9	66.2
Finland	Never	36.1	1975	2.498 (74.2)	3.9	22.3	73.8
France	1954–59	39.5	1973	26.883 (70.6)	2.8	20.2	77.0
Germany	1907–75	48.5	1970	40.894 (79.2)	1.3	27.3	71.4
Greece	Never	30.2	1980	3.816 (57.8)	11.7	21.1	67.2
Hungary				4.425 (73.3)	3.3	26.4	54.9
Ireland	Never	32.6	1974	2.197 (73)	5.4	19.2	75.4
Italy	1960–5	39.7	1971	22.704 (67)	3.7	26.3	70.0
Latvia				0.884 (74.8)	7.5	24.0	68.5
Lithuania				1.330 (76)	7.7	34.5	57.8
Luxembourg	1947–69	46.9	1966	0.277 (71.5)	1	11.9	87.1
Malta				0.235 (73)	1.3	20.1	78.6
Netherlands	Never	41.1	1965	8.598 (78)	2	15.3	82.7
Poland				16.251 (70.9)	10.6	31.3	58.1
Portugal	1982	37.5	1982	4.664 (73.4)	6.8	24.8	68.4
Romania				8.527 (68.8)	22.9	29.1	48.0
Slovenia				0.970 (73.4)	4.9	32.6	62.5
Slovakia				2.546 (71.1)	2.9	36.3	60.8
Spain	Never	38.4	1975	19.330 (65.5)	4.2	19.7	76.1
Sweden	1940–59	42.8	1965	4.994 (81.8)	1.9	18.1	80.0
UK	1821–1959	52.2	1911	31.123 (78.2)	1.0	18.5	80.5
EU				225.929 (72.2)	4	24.2	71.8

Source: Immerfall (1995: 69); figures on employment based on Eurostat (2019a, 2019b); World Bank (2019).

and which was protected by strong social legislation and agreed wages through regular negotiations between employers' and employees' organisations – was eroded after the 1980s (Ebbinghaus and Visser, 1997; Traxler, 2004) (see Chapter 8 on neo-corporatism).

The emergence of new technologies, the rise of the new middle classes and the erosion of the traditional working class led to changes in the parties that relied on the political support of such constituencies. In the 1990s, most social democratic or reformed communist parties had to move strategically to the centre and begin to appeal to the new middle classes. In some ways these parties became victims of their own success, particularly as a result of the redistribution policies introduced by generous welfare states. The New Labour party during Tony Blair's premiership (1997–2007) became the model of a Third Way of social democracy influenced by the policies of the US president Bill Clinton's administration (Giddens, 1998).

This 'bourgeoisification' of the working class forced many social democratic parties to move to the centre and abandon class-based, socially heterogeneous politics. Herbert Kitschelt spoke then of a 'transformation of social democracy', resulting from the growing importance of the new middle classes, new politics and post-materialist values. As a consequence, social democratic parties had to develop socially heterogeneous politics in order to appeal to different constituencies simultaneously, which led to less ideological but more pragmatic party strategies (Kitschelt, 1995b: 295–301). One could say that class voting continues to be relevant in many countries, but traditional class politics, based on encapsulated subcultures, is declining fast. Class voting has also become much more complicated owing to the differentiation of the services sector. There is considerable cultural heterogeneity between groups within the services sector; also the working class has lost its homogeneity and is no longer embedded in a synchronic spatio-temporal context.

According to the index developed by Robert Alford in the 1960s, which measures the level of support of manual workers for left-wing parties by subtracting the share of votes of non-manual workers from all voters to those parties, class voting has been declining (Alford, 1964: 73–86). Paul Nieuwbeerta and Nan Dirk

Table 3.3 A typology of class voting in Western Europe, 1945–90

Low level of class voting	*Intermediate level of class voting*	*High level of class voting*
France	Austria	UK
Greece	Belgium	Denmark
Ireland	Germany	Finland
Italy	Luxembourg	Norway
Netherlands	Sweden	
Portugal		
Spain		
Switzerland		

Source: Based on Nieuwbeerta and De Graaf (1999: 31).

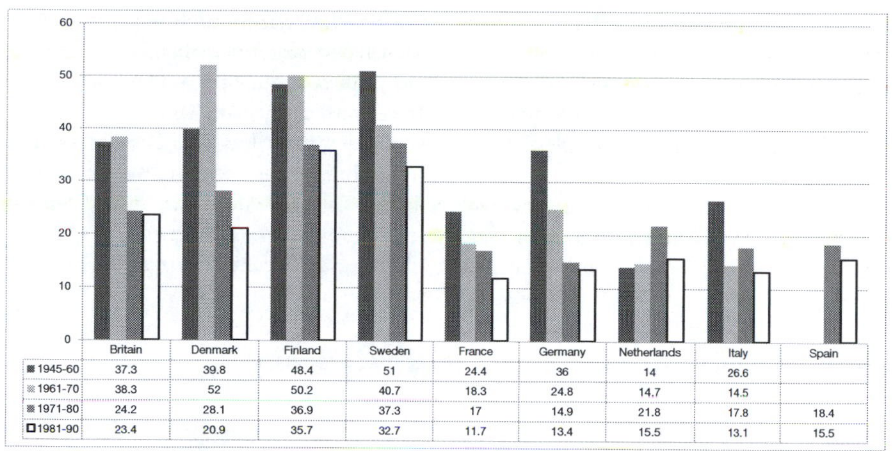

	Britain	Denmark	Finland	Sweden	France	Germany	Netherlands	Italy	Spain
1945-60	37.3	39.8	48.4	51	24.4	36	14	26.6	
1961-70	38.3	52	50.2	40.7	18.3	24.8	14.7	14.5	
1971-80	24.2	28.1	36.9	37.3	17	14.9	21.8	17.8	18.4
1981-90	23.4	20.9	35.7	32.7	11.7	13.4	15.5	13.1	15.5

Figure 3.7 Decline of class voting for selected European countries, 1945–90

Source: Author's own graph based on data from Nieuwbeerta and De Graf (1999: 32).

De Graaf have identified three groups of countries in Western Europe in terms of their level of class voting. In spite of the differences, the countries with the highest level of class voting since 1961 also had the steepest declines according to the Alford Index – in the UK from 38.3 per cent in the decade of 1961–70 to 23.4 per cent in the decade of 1981–90. For the same period in Denmark, the decline was from 52 to 20 per cent; in Finland, from 50.2 to 35.7 per cent; in Norway, from 32 to 20.5 per cent; and in Sweden, from 40.7 to 32.7 per cent (Nieuwbeerta and De Graaf, 1999: 32). The process of erosion has been quite asymmetrical (Table 3.3 and Figure 3.7). Class voting is still partly relevant in the UK, Germany, the Benelux, Austria, Switzerland and the Nordic countries.

While in Western Europe traditional class voting is declining, new party systems of Central and Eastern Europe have emerged which were already competing in the volatile individualised electoral market. Class voting has lost its importance, although a class society has established itself in the past forty years. The Czech Republic party system seemed to show elements of such a cleavage linked to Social Democrats (ČSSD) and the Communist Party (KPČM) against the pro-liberal Civic Forum (ODS) party. However, in the new millennium anti-corruption and anti-establishment parties have emerged which have opportunistically profited from volatile individualised electoral markets (Mateju et al., 1999: 240–9). Overall, it seems 'class' was negatively connoted with the previous communist regime, so that political parties avoided using it in the public discourse. Furthermore, the new capitalist society was presented in bright lights by the new liberal-conservative parties like ODS in the Czech Republic or the Union of Democratic Forces (UDF) in Bulgaria. The use of a centrist middle class in the discourse of political parties, which was based on the ideas of a functionalist theory of society influenced by the idea that economic growth will lead to economic wealth and subsequently to the emergence of a middle class (the model presented by Lipset, 1959), became a major principle of politics (see the excellent introduction and special issue on class in Eastern Europe by Ost, 2015).

In sum, traditional class voting and class politics, with which we were familiar until the 1960s, have waned, because of the erosion of collective identities around the working class and established middle classes. Instead, a new class structure has emerged that is fragmented and differentiated in terms of categories and is not attached to large collective identities. Parties now have to devise socially heterogeneous catch-all strategies to appeal to different constituencies with different lifestyles. This means that the way in which people vote depends on short-term factors and the offers presented by parties in the competitive electoral market. A similar trend has eroded religious collective identities, as the following pages show.

The decline of religious cleavages and religiosity

One of the consequences of the transition from a materialist to post-materialist society is the fact that it leads to reinforced secularisation, meaning there is a decline in participation in traditional religious rites and growing emancipation of the population from the tutelage of Church organisations (see Box 3.5 and Figure 3.8). The religiosity index shows that the northern parts of Europe are more secularised than the south. Moreover, Greek Orthodox and Catholic countries as well as countries with large Muslim populations are more religious than Protestant Christian countries (see Figure 3.8).

Box 3.5 The secularisation of society

The word 'secular' is concerned with the affairs of this world. 'Secularise' means to transfer something from a religious to a non-religious use, or from control by a religious body to control by the state or a lay body. It may also mean the removal of the religious dimension or religious element from something.

Secularisation characterises a societal process in which the role of religion is replaced by the principles of the 'non-denominational' state. This means particularly the laicisation of civil life and the reduction of the influence of the Church in society. Central to this secularisation is the emergence of the modern state, based on the principle of strict separation of state and Church. Such a process was undertaken by all European countries in the nineteenth and first half of the twentieth centuries.

Probably, the most advanced secularisation processes can be observed in Nordic Europe, Germany, the Netherlands, the UK and France. Less advanced secularisation can be found in the Catholic countries of Southern Europe and Ireland.

Among the different trends towards secularisation are the decline of church attendance among religious groups and the decline in the belief in God and life after death. The trend has been downwards across Europe, in some regions steeper than others. While secularisation progressed considerably in the Nordic countries and Central and Eastern Europe, apart from Poland, Southern Europe lags behind in this trend. Nevertheless, even in Southern Europe we

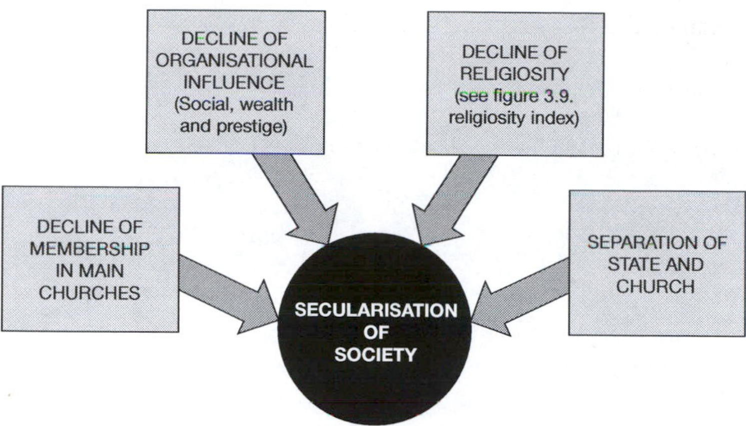

Figure 3.8 The secularisation of society

Source: Adapted, simplified and amended from Giddens (1992: 486–7).

can recognise a stronger trend of secularisation in Spain while there is greater resistance to it in Italy, Portugal and Greece. Religious voting has been strongest in areas where relations between the Church and the liberal state were tense. This was quite marked before the First World War and during the interwar period. After the Second World War most Christian democratic parties became catch-all parties in order to counteract the declining subcultural religious voting. Nevertheless, not all countries have the same religious make-up. It is sensible to differentiate between homogeneous Catholic countries (Portugal, Spain, Italy), homogeneous Protestant countries (Sweden, Denmark, Norway), homogeneous Christian Orthodox countries (Greece) and confessionally mixed countries (the Netherlands, Germany and Switzerland). In the Balkans one can find some confessionally mixed countries, for example Bosnia-Herzegovina, which consists of three ethnic minorities: the Bosniak-Muslims, the Catholic Croats and the Greek Orthodox Serbs

The cleavage based on religion emphasised particularly policy tensions between the Church and the state (for an excellent review on this cleavage, see Kalyvas and Van Kersbergen, 2010). Strong subcultural cleavages that translated into electoral voting could be found in countries with strong Catholic minorities, such as the Netherlands and Germany. However, after the war the secularisation of society led to the merging of Christian parties representing different religious denominations. Today represented by mainly the Christian Democratic Appeal (CDA) (2017 elections: 12.5 per cent) in the Netherlands and the Christian Democratic Union/ Christian Social Union (CDU/CSU) (2017 elections: 33 per cent in Germany). In the Netherlands, it is also important to count the Calvinist minority religious parties Christian Union (CU) and the Reformed Political Party (SGP), which have few seats but can be the king maker in coalition building (Roberts, 2000: 65–9; Van Holsteyn and Irwin, 2000: 82–5) (Figure 3.10). Apart from the Netherlands and Germany, we can find this cleavage in Belgium (Christian-Democratic and Flemish – Cd&V; Democratic Humanist Centre – CDH), Luxembourg (Christian-Social

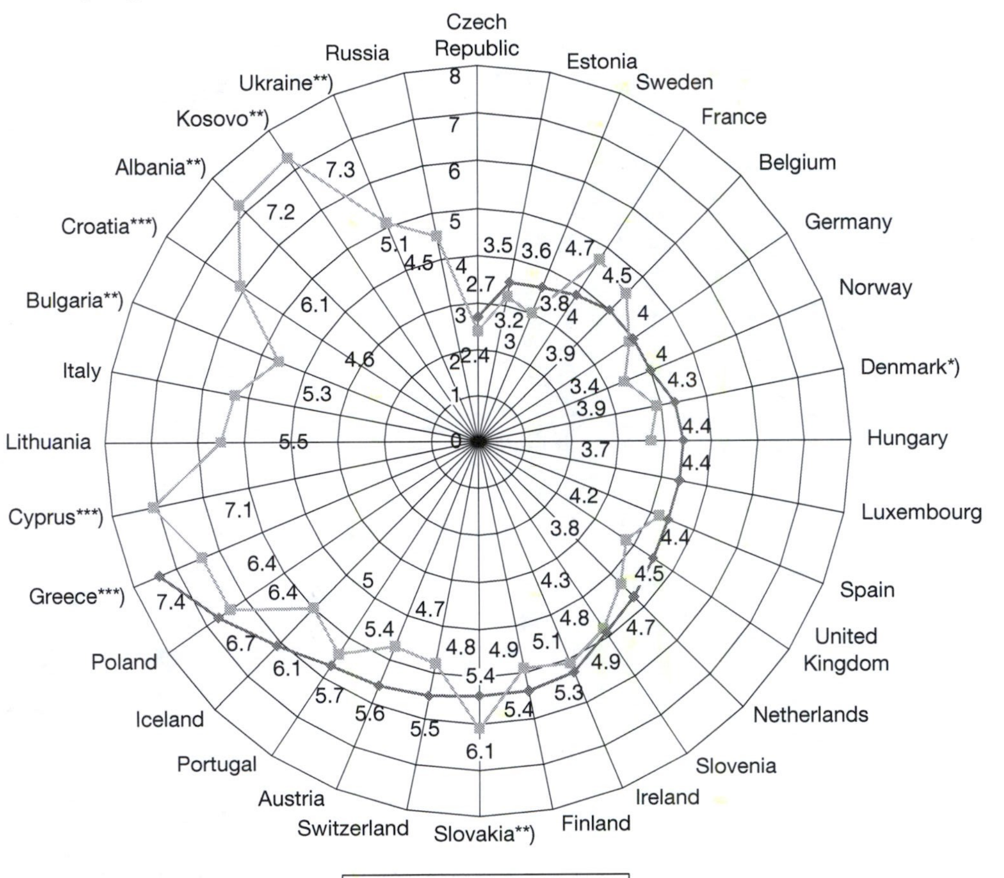

Figure 3.9 Religiosity index in Europe, 2004 and 2016

Notes: *) figure for 2014; **) figure for 2012; ***) figure for 2010.
Source: ESS 2004–16.

Party – CSP), Austria (Austrian People's Party – ÖVP) and Switzerland (Christian People's Party – CVP).

In the new democracies of Southern, Central and Eastern Europe the new party systems lack the historical continuity of cleavage-building that is common in the more established democracies. Therefore, most Christian democratic parties cannot relate to clear subculture. Nevertheless, today, religious voting can still be found in Central and Eastern Europe in Hungary (Fidesz-Hungarian Civic Union and Christian Democratic People's Party – KDNP), Poland (Justice and Law Party – PiS), Slovakia (Christian Democratic Movement – KDH; Slovak Democratic and Christian Union-People's Party – SDKU-DS) and Slovenia (New Slovenia-Christian Democrats – NSI). In Southern Europe such voting can be found in all four countries among the electorate of conservative parties. Italy has also had a quite long tradition of Christian democracy going back to the Italian People's Party in the interwar period and Christian Democracy (DC) between 1945 and 1992, but after the collapse of the Italian party system due to widespread systemic corruption practised mainly by that party, no Christian democratic party has emerged to replace it. Presently, Silvio Berlusconi's Forza Italia is the party that has inherited at least part of the electorate of DC. In Portugal, the Democratic Social Centre-People's Party – CDS) was and remains traditionally the party for the more conservative Catholic voters. In Spain and Greece, the conservative People's Party (PP) and New Democracy (ND) are the parties with the highest levels of religious vote.

In the Nordic countries, traditionally the most secularised societies, we can still find small Christian democratic parties in Denmark (Christian People's Party – KrF), Norway (Christian People's Party – KrF), Finland (Christian Democrats of Finland – KD) and Sweden (Christian Democrats – KD). Apart from Denmark, all of them are in parliament achieving 4 to 6 per cent in general elections. The religious voting seems to be concentrated in certain peripheral regions of the countries and directed against the centre. In Norway, it is this 'Bible Belt' concentrated in the south and west, in Finland the rural parts of the south, in Sweden most of the votes are located in Jonköping in the south, while in Denmark they are concentrated in northern Jutland (Madeley, 2000: 34–8) (see Figure 3.10).

In both the UK and France religious voting is quite tenuous, but still exists. Neither the UK nor France has Christian democratic parties, but religious voting may go to the main parties in the political system. In France, it is normally the centre-right parties that attract religiously motivated votes from practising Catholics. The non-practising Catholics may tend towards the leftwing parties, in particular the Socialist Party. The National Front (Front National, FN) is not able to attract the vote of the practising Catholics and most of its votes come from non-religious people.

Similarly, the electoral system leads to a split of the religious vote between the two main parties in the UK. Catholics tend to vote for the Labour Party, while practising Protestants are strong supporters of the Conservative Party. The religious vote is stronger and more salient in Scotland. Secularisation has progressed considerably in both countries, which are closer to the Scandinavian pattern (Bréchon, 2000; Seawright, 2000). The conflict in Northern Ireland has perpetuated the cleavage between Catholics, who tend to support nationalism by voting for either Sinn Fein or the Social Democratic Liberal Party, and Protestants,

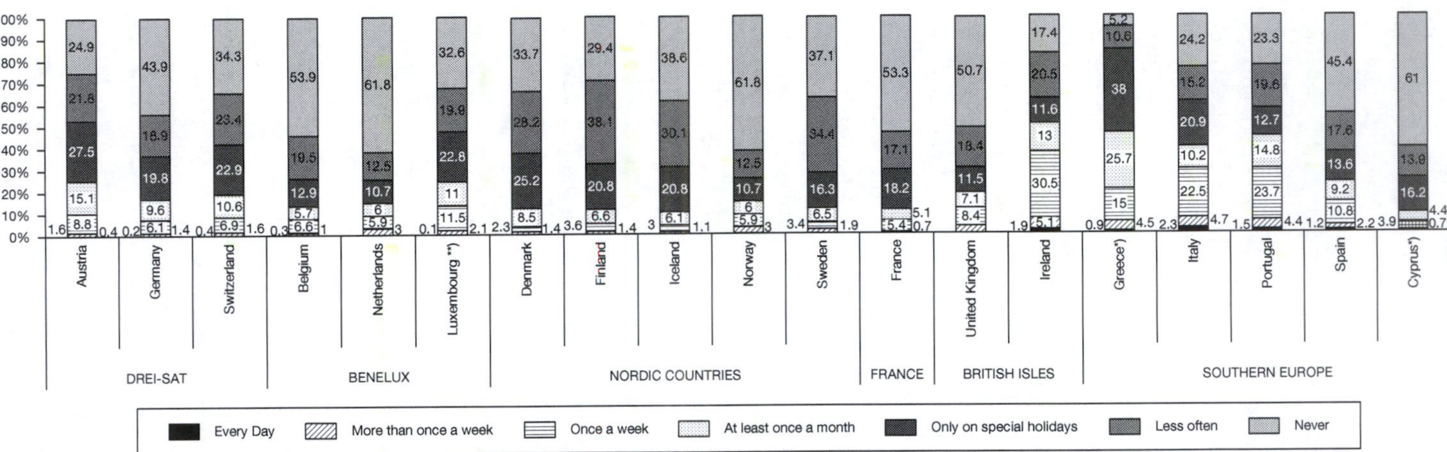

Figure 3.10 Church attendance in Western, Southern and Nordic Europe, 2016

Notes: *) figure for 2014; **) figure for 2012.
Source: ESS 2004–16.

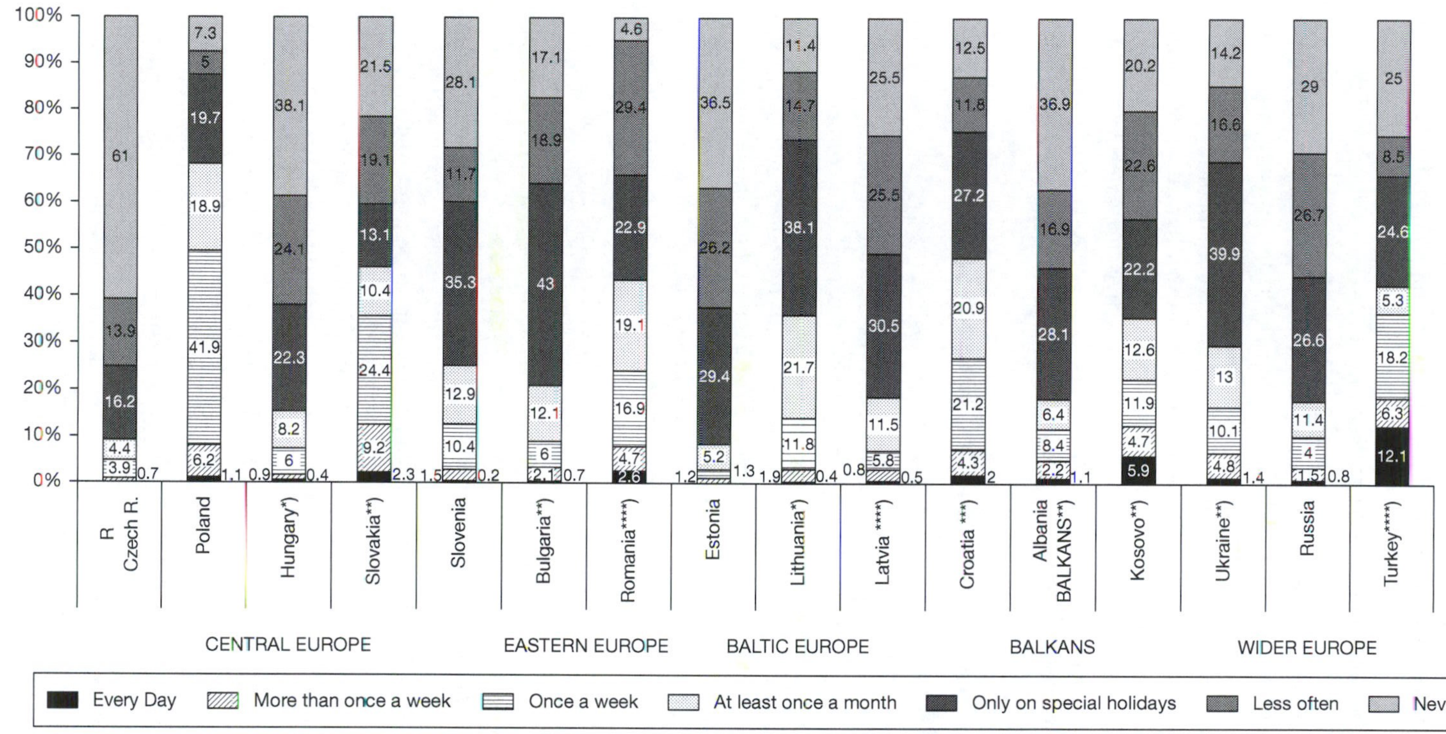

Figure 3.11 Church attendance in Central, Eastern, Baltic, Balkan and wider Europe, 2016

Notes: *) figure for 2014; **) figure for 2012; ***) figure for 2010; ****) figure for 2008.
Source: ESS 2004–16.

who support the Union with the rest of the UK by voting for the Ulster Unionists and the Democratic Unionist Party. Religion plays a major role in the Republic of Ireland, although it is not used for party politics (Caramani, 2004: 260–1; Farrell, 2000: 30–6).

Religion combined with nationalism played a major role in the Balkan wars and the constitution of the new states. The Catholic Croats, Christian Orthodox Serbians and Bosniak-Muslims conducted war campaigns based on their different ethnic and religious identities. Ethnic cleansing of territory became a well-known tactic to get rid of minorities. Today, Macedonia, Kosovo and Montenegro have still to integrate their large minorities of Albanians and Serbians.

In sum, religious voting still exists across Europe, but historical traditions, continuity of party systems and the nature of democratic transitions play a major role in sustaining such a vote. The role of post-materialist values, which do not necessarily undermine religiosity, certainly tends to support the movement away from organised religion and towards its privatisation.

The rise of regional identity and the impact on national political cultures

The original starting point of Stein Rokkan's research on European politics was the centre-periphery cleavage. As already mentioned, at the end of his life he concentrated his research on the regional awakening of many regions across Europe. In the 1970s the first signs of increased regional awareness and consciousness began to emerge. Three countries in particular led to the strengthening of regional identity in Europe: Spain, Belgium and the UK.

The Spanish constitution of 1978 allowed the re-emergence of regional identities after a long dictatorship in which they were oppressed. Although the autonomy granted in the constitution was originally only intended for the historic regions of Catalonia, the Basque Country and Galicia, other regions were soon able to profit from one of the articles that allowed for a slower route towards autonomy. Between 1979 and 1983, seventeen autonomous communities emerged across Spain, each one with its own political system and some with strong regionalist parties. Since the late 1970s, more and more competences were expanded to all regions, particularly Catalonia and the Basque country. Nevertheless, in the new millennium, demands for independence began to be expressed by leaders of regionalist-nationalist parties in both Catalonia and the Basque Country. In the latter, such demands were made between 2004 and 2008 by the regional president (lehendakari) Juan José Ibarretxe but rejected by the national parliament (Cortes). Ibarretxe tried to get a referendum on independence approved but was rejected twice by Madrid. Such independence demands were always present in Catalonia but erupted during the financial crisis. Although the socialist Zapatero government successfully negotiated a revision of the Catalan statute, the conservative People's Party complained to the Spanish Constitutional Court about the inclusion of several articles that would conflict with the Spanish constitution. In 2010, the Constitutional Court rejected several articles that were in the Catalan statute, including the very important one that Catalonia is a nation. This contradicted the Spanish constitution which saw the nation as an indissoluble entity. Since 2010, a major independence movement pushed by the Catalan regional government dominated by nationalist-regionalist parties tried to force the issue of a referendum onto the agenda, leading to two illegal referenda on 9 November 2014 and 1 October 2017. In both cases, an overwhelming majority voted 'yes' for independence, but the turnout was low. It meant that the pro-Spanish half of Catalonia boycotted the vote. The conflict remains a major problem for Spanish politics and is still characterised by a high level of tension.

While Spain remains a regionalised unitary state, Belgium became a federal state after 1993. The regional cleavage between the Francophone Walloons and the Dutch-speaking Flemish has existed since the nineteenth century, but it became particularly acute in the 1960s. Ethnic conflict between the two communities led to a complete separation of administration. The most difficult issue was Brussels itself, which was mixed. Moreover, about 100,000 German-speaking Belgians live close to the German border in Eupen and St Vinth. Several regionalist-nationalist parties in Flanders have been representatives of this ethnonationalist cleavage. Between 1954 and 2001, The People's Union (VU) played a major role in keeping the demands of the Flemish population alive. Since the 1990s, a more radical party emerged called Flemish Block, later changing its name to Flemish Interest (Vlaamse Belang – VB). The party grew quite considerably until 2010, when it was replaced by a more moderate, but populist party, namely New Flemish Alliance (N-VA). Their ultimate aim is to become independent. The party cooperates with all other parties and is part of the government. Although N-VA is the largest party in Flanders and Belgium (2014: 20.3 per cent), the majority of the population is rather inclined to keep Belgium together, which is also expressed in the votes for the traditional parties of the Christian Democrats, Liberals, Socialists and Greens in both parts of the country (2014: all parties together 65.1 per cent). Due to the emergence of N-VA, the rather anti-immigration and rightwing extreme VB declined to 3.7 per cent of the vote. This is also due to a successful political cordon sanitaire of moderate Belgian parties not cooperating with VB.

Following calls for devolution made by Welsh and Scottish nationalists since the 1970s, in 1997 the UK started a devolution process which led to a transfer of competences to the Scottish Parliament and the Welsh Assembly. The successful peace process in Northern Ireland has also led to the re-establishment of its Assembly, although this was suspended in January 2017 (and remains so at the time of writing) due to policy disagreements within the leadership and a failed renewable energy incentive scheme. The UK has completed a decade of devolution and it is to be acknowledged that it has led to a democratic revitalisation in these parts of the country. However, the failure of former Deputy Prime Minister John Prescott to get through a second wave of devolution in England in 2005 has led to an abrupt halt to such constitutional reform. There is also a growing uneasiness among English MPs that Scottish, Welsh and Irish MPs can block legislation that relates solely to England, while they are not allowed to do so in relation to Scottish, Irish and Welsh matters. This 'West Lothian question' continues to be part of the discussion related to devolution. Since the 1970s, Scottish nationalism has been growing, so that the Scottish Nationalist Party (SNP) is now the main government party in Edinburgh. After negotiations with the central government under prime minister David Cameron in London, it was agreed to conduct a referendum on Scottish independence. On 18 September 2014, 55 per cent of Scots rejected independence; just 45 per cent were for it. This clearly was a major blow for the Scottish independence movement, leading to the resignation of long-standing charismatic leader Alex Salmond as first minister in Scotland (*BBC News*, 19 September 2014). However, his successor Nicola Sturgeon put a new referendum on the agenda. This became particularly relevant, because on 23 June 2016, in a referendum on the UK's membership of the EU, 51.9 per cent voted to leave the supranational organisation and 48.1 per cent voted to stay. However, in Scotland and Northern Ireland, 62 per cent and 55.8 per cent respectively voted to remain in the EU. Therefore, Sturgeon revived again the need for a second referendum, because she believed that after the Brexit referendum things have changed, and therefore another Scottish independence referendum was necessary. This was rejected by the government of David Cameron and later on Theresa May, as they were now dealing with the major issue of Brexit as their main priority (*The Guardian*, 11 September 2017; *The Independent*, 24 June 2016).

Probably, the most civilised separation of a country is the former Czechoslovakia. The so-called velvet divorce of 1992 led to the creation of two new countries, the Czech Republic and the Slovak Republic. Such a model of separation has often been suggested by the separatist extreme rightwing VB in order to break up Belgium (Magone, 2017: 117–18).

Independence or separatist tendencies do not exist in Central and Eastern Europe, in spite of large ethnic minorities such as Hungarians in Slovakia and Romania, or the Turkish-speaking population in Bulgaria. Also, in the Baltic states, the large Russian population is not fully integrated. In all these countries, one condition of joining the EU was to provide minority representation in parliament and a protection of their rights, which is part of the so-called Copenhagen criteria.

The most dramatic realignment of sovereignty happened in the Balkans. While Slovenia was able to escape the fratricide civil war within the former Yugoslavia, the same cannot be said for Croatia, Bosnia-Herzegovina, Serbia and Kosovo. Nationalism and separatism dominated all these countries and the wounds related to war will only heal with time. Probably the most problematic cases are Bosnia-Herzegovina, which is still far from being a properly functioning state, and the question of Kosovo, which still has a small Serbian minority closer to the Serbian border. Also in Macedonia, there are regular tensions between the Albanian minority parties, which represent about a third of the population, and the more nationalist Macedonian groups. Montenegro is a rather homogenous population which speaks overwhelmingly Serbian. One factor undermining exalted nationalism and extremism is the hope to join the EU, which means that successive governments have to show high levels of moderation and democratic behaviour (*Euractiv*, 16 October 2017).

In sum, regional cleavages and even national secession became important in the 1980s and 1990s. This shows that the regional-ethnic cleavage is still an important aspect of European politics, in some, though not all, of the countries. One particular consequence is that there are now many more countries in Europe, some of them quite small (for example, Montenegro). This adds to the diversity and complexity of European politics and also to the difficulties faced in decision-making processes at EU level. The current president of the European Commission, Jean-Claude Juncker, stated succinctly during the Catalonia unilateral declaration of independence crisis what would be the major problem for the

EU: 'I would not like an EU that in 15 years consisted of 98 states' (*The Telegraph*, 13 October 2017).

From a homogeneous national to a heterogeneous multicultural society

The immigration waves to different European countries since 1945 have led to less homogeneous national societies. Today, most European societies are heterogeneous and multicultural. There may be some resistance by segments of national populations to this, but the decline or stagnation of growth in most endogenous populations, as well as the parallel process of higher birth rates of immigrant populations, has created new, more ethnically diverse, societies. In this respect, the UK, Belgium, the Netherlands, Germany, Spain, Luxembourg, Switzerland and France are probably among the best examples of truly multicultural societies (Figure 3.12). The discussion of multiculturalism follows at least two different strands. One is, basically, the Republican 'melting pot', assimilationist model, in which ethnic diversity is acknowledged, but overridden by the principles of republican citizenship based on equal rights for all groups. Religious differences are a private matter and should remain separated from the affairs of the state. This model is common in most European countries, even in the constitutional monarchies of the Netherlands and Belgium. Integration into national society based on egalitarian principles and respect for diversity is central (Figure 3.12).

The other model is the acknowledgment of diversity and its expression. In this model, there is strong autonomy of ethnic groups, which are invited to integrate into society, but there is no overarching ideology of citizenry. Citizenry can be expressed in different ways, without forcing all groups to follow a set of principles. The separation between the private and the public is less clear. This second model is followed in the UK, where it is not only applied to non-European ethnic groups coming from the Caribbean, India, Pakistan and Africa but also to the different endogenous groups, such as the Welsh, Scottish and Irish. The principle of tolerance of cultural diversity is central to this model of multiculturalism.

However, the best model probably lies between assimilation and multiculturalism. It is labelled today as integrationism. It is also the emerging model for European countries (Box 3.6).

Most European societies are either at one end or the other of the spectrum but are moving towards the middle, with levels of tolerance higher in some societies than in others. The European Social Survey conducted in most countries every two years since 2002–3 gives us a good snapshot of how far each different society is from a multicultural society. In some cases, the high level of ethnic homogeneity makes a society insensitive to calls for a multicultural society, and these societies do not need to face any problems of integration. In this sense, we have an asymmetrical picture of multiculturalism in Europe. Some societies overwhelmingly advocate an assimilationist approach, like Greece, Cyprus, the Czech Republic and Austria. Assimilationism is also strong in the Central and Eastern European countries, which may be related to the fact that all these countries had a late development towards nationhood. At the other end of the spectrum are the more industrialised Nordic countries and those of Western Central Europe.

Switzerland, Germany, the Netherlands, Sweden, Finland and Iceland are the most tolerant towards diversity. Albania is clearly an outlier here, as it is normally an emigration country. It probably therefore looks at immigration in a more positive way (Table 3.4). Switzerland can be regarded as the model of multiculturalism par excellence. As well as the linguistic cleavages between the French-speaking, German-speaking, Italian-speaking and Raetoroman-speaking groups, Switzerland has had to deal with a large immigrant population (about 24.2 per cent in 2015) coming mainly from Southern European countries, such as Portugal, Spain, Italy and Greece. This is confirmed by the multiculturalism indicator that raises questions about tolerance of immigration (see Figure 3.12).

Box 3.6 Assimilationism, multiculturalism and integrationism

European societies are no longer homogeneous nation-states. On the contrary, they have become heterogeneous, incorporating many integrated as well as non-integrated immigrants. Today and in the future, because of the demographic changes of ageing populations and low birth rates, proper integration of immigrants will be a crucially important aspect of government policy. There are different forms of integrating immigrants into society:

- **Assimilationism**: Immigrants have to adjust to the culture of the host country and become part of it, in extreme cases giving up their home culture.
- **Multiculturalism**: Immigrants and other groups in society are able to live according to their cultural values. The danger is that multiculturalism may lead to segregationism and to 'parallel societies', which do not interact with mainstream society. Such examples of 'parallel societies' can be found in the Netherlands, Germany and the UK, for example, among the Muslim community.
- **Integrationism**: This is the middle way between assimilationism and multiculturalism. The EU is pushing for a common active policy of integration of immigrants that includes introductory language and citizenry courses. More active engagement in integrating immigrants into the labour market is also required. The Dutch model has been copied across the EU.

In the post-war period after 1945, most North and Central Western European countries needed quite a considerable immigration from particularly Southern European and Southern Mediterranean countries, which then decided to stay in these countries. This clearly led to the emergence of a multicultural society. Immigration remained an important factor for the growing economies of these north-western countries. The UK recruited a considerable number of immigrants from the Commonwealth countries until the late 1960s. In the vast majority of cases, integration has been quite successful. However, some groups had more difficulty than others, particularly among parts of the Muslim population in countries such as the UK, France, Germany, the Netherlands, Belgium, Austria, Denmark and Sweden, which created parallel societies that were major obstacles to integration. After the terrorist attacks on the Twin Towers in New York on 11 September 2001 by Al Qaeda-affiliated perpetrators, the atmosphere changed considerably for non-integrated Muslims in particular. This led to an increase in potentially Islamophobic laws, like the prohibition of the burka and niqab in public life in France (2011), Belgium (2011), Bulgaria (2016), Austria (2017) and Denmark (2018) (*Süddeutsche Zeitung*, 31 May 2018).

In spite of the bombings on 14 March 2004 in Madrid perpetrated by Al Qaeda, Spain kept a rather positive cooperative approach towards the Muslim population in the country. In the Netherlands, the UK, Germany and France, policies of terrorism containment or prevention have created a negative atmosphere. In the UK, one year after the London bombings on 7 July 2005, Prime Minister Tony Blair blamed the Muslim community for not being more proactive in helping the authorities to find potential terrorist plots. The general feeling was that there was still a serious lack of dialogue and cooperation between government authorities and the ethnic communities. The indiscriminate shooting of the Brazilian, Jean Charles de Menezes, on 21 July 2005 and the lack of accountability and culpability in this respect was compounded by the police raid on a house in north-east London in which two Muslim brothers lived, one of whom was shot without prior warning. These were major factors that undermined confidence in the police force in the UK (*The Economist*, 17 June 2006: 32–7; 8 July 2006: 29–30; *The Independent*, 18 July 2006: 6) and led, in 2008, to the resignation of Metropolitan Police Chief Ian Blair. Finally, in December 2008, after a trial in which the Metropolitan Police was found guilty of the incident, the new police chief had to apologise. Moreover, the greatest shock was that the atrocious London bombings of 2005, which claimed fifty-two victims, were perpetrated by young Muslim men who lived in the north of England and were of British citizenship. This threw a sharp light on the failures of integration by first- and second-generation Muslims in the UK.

Nonetheless, despite the many failures of integration in the UK, the awareness of racism has been raised and the advantages of multiculturalism have been recognised. There is also recognition that some assimilation and integration has to accompany such multiculturalism and diversity. The ideal is to strike a balance between assimilation and multiculturalism.

The case of France highlights that republican assimilation policies have failed in relation to second-generation Muslim immigrants, especially for those living in suburban areas of major towns. The urban riots of November 2005 and 2007, in which cars and businesses were vandalised, showed that the poorest sectors of the population were not able to become part of French society. On the contrary, the high levels of unemployment in France – between 9 and 10 per cent – have particularly affected the young Muslim population, without proper qualifications, living in the suburban areas of the cities. The negative language of former Interior Minister Nicolas Sarkozy against these sectors only served to inflame the situation. The use of the internet helped to sustain the riots across France over several days, which in turn led to the intervention of the army to prevent an escalation of the situation. Although the French national football team is a symbol of multiculturalism, having a high percentage of players with non-French cultural backgrounds, the concrete reality showed that most second-generation Muslim youths were living with little hope. This strengthened the Front National of Jean Marie Le Pen, which was able to gain support based on a simplistic racist discourse (*The Economist*, 17 November 2005, 14 December 2005, 29 November 2007). According to Christian Joppke, since the early 1990s the French have moved towards a less assimilationist and more integrationist approach, in which aspects of citizenship, language learning and understanding of French culture have been central to the socialisation of new immigrants into the country (Joppke, 2007: 9–12; 2017).

The model for such an integrationist approach to immigration is the Netherlands. The Netherlands is well known for its extremely tolerant policies towards immigrants and the multicultural approach was dominant there. However, since the 1990s, there has been a movement towards integrationist policies because of the lack of integration of some groups in the major cities of the country, particularly Amsterdam and Rotterdam. The formation of the political party Pim Fortuyn List (Lijst Pim Fortuyn, LPF) in 2002 and the murder of Pim Fortuyn himself, a sociology professor and politician, shortly before the elections by an environmentalist who disagreed with Fortuyn's negative campaign against the Muslim population, brought these issues of immigration and integration to the fore. The murder of film director Theo van Gogh by Islamic fundamentalists, after the making of a controversial film on women in Islam, further showed the growing tensions in the population. Moreover, the extreme rightwing Freedom Party (PVV) of Geert Wilders has been a major factor in pushing the debate on immigration, particularly of Muslims in keeping the issue on the agenda (Magone, 2017: 116–17). The policies of the Dutch government have become less liberal and tolerant, and today any legal immigrant has to follow successfully a process of civic integration in which they are required to learn the language, have a knowledge of Dutch culture and be aware of the rights and duties of citizens (Joppke, 2007: 6–9).

While the UK and France have been the main target for attacks of Islamist terrorist organisation Islamic State of Iraq and Syria (ISIS) since 2015, Belgium, Germany and Spain have also become victims of such attacks. At least fifteen major terrorist attacks have been perpetrated since the editors of the satirical magazine *Charlie Hebdo* were killed on 7 January 2015. Meanwhile, ISIS is severely weakened and there is a fear that the return of many of these fighters to their home countries may contribute to increase the terrorist danger.

As already mentioned, a high level of assimilation tendencies can be found in the Southern and Central and Eastern European countries. In particular, the homogeneous societies of Portugal and Greece have encountered difficulties in coping with the new situation, whereby they are no longer emigration countries but have become immigration countries.

Meanwhile, the Dutch model has become the benchmark and is regarded as best practice. The EU is moving towards such a common framework of integration. According to Joppke, five aspects are highlighted in integrationist policies:

1. Integration is a dynamic, two-way process of mutual accommodation by all immigrants and residents of the member states.
2. There are concrete expectations on immigrants: 'Integration implies respect for the basic values of the European Union, the principles of liberty, democracy, respect for human rights and fundamental freedoms, and the rule of law'.
3. Employment is a key part of the integration process: important to provide jobs for the immigration community, so that 'parallel societies' may not emerge which undermine integration.

4 Basic knowledge of the host society's language, history, and institutions is indispensable to integration (compulsory). This was pioneered by the Netherlands in 1990s and has been emulated by Finland, Denmark, Austria, Germany, France and the UK.
5 Access for immigrants to institutions, as well as to public and private goods and services, on a basis equal to national citizens and in a non-discriminatory way, is a critical foundation for better integration.

(Joppke, 2007: 2–5)

Joppke labels this as 'repressive liberalism' owing to the shift from more tolerant to stricter immigration and integration policies. The slow convergence of immigration policy across the EU will certainly contribute increasingly to the consolidation of this common framework, even though different countries may apply these principles to different degrees. It still remains a broad framework that depends on the configuration of political, economic and social forces in each individual country (Joppke, 2007: 14–18; on discourses on Islam and Islamism in society, see Joppke, 2014).

According to Jeremy Rifkin in his bestseller *The European Dream* (2004), Europe will need 50 million immigrants by 2050 in order to compensate for the negative growth of the population. This means that European countries will have to continue the trend towards multicultural integration strategies if national societies are to rejuvenate and continue to exist. He proposed the integration of Turkey as a solution to the problem, because it has a growing population and is quite young in comparison to most European countries (Rifkin, 2004: 252–7). The possible integration of Turkey into the EU has become a reason for mobilisation by many new right or extreme right parties, such as the Alternative for Germany (AFD) in Germany, The Parties of Freedom (PVV and FPÖ) in the Netherlands and Austria, the Swiss People's Party (SVP) in Switzerland, the National Front (FN) in France, the Flemish Interest (VB) in Flanders, the Danish People's Party (DF) in Denmark, and the Swedish Democrats (SD) in Sweden, which speak of the danger of Islamisation, leading also to growing Islamophobia in the countries with large Muslim communities (Kallis, 2014).

A multicultural index shows that Southern, Central and Eastern European countries are still far from the model of a multicultural society. In contrast, Switzerland, Austria, Germany, the UK, Ireland, Sweden, Denmark, Finland and the Benelux countries have all moved towards being multicultural societies. Apart from Finland, most of these countries have been targets for immigration from other European countries or non-European ones for a long time, and so they have had a long period to adjust and develop positive attitudes towards multiculturalism. However, immigration is new in Southern, Central and Eastern Europe. The late creation of nation-states in the eastern part of the European continent is a further factor for strong racist and xenophobic tendencies in these countries.

Multiculturalism implies not only the acceptance of ethnic otherness but also other lifestyles and sexual inclinations, such as homosexuality. Tolerance of diversity has become an important issue in present European societies. Indeed, according to the studies of Ronald Inglehart and Christian Welzel, tolerance of homosexual behaviour is regarded as one of the indicators of a society moving towards post-material self-expression values. In this sense, the most permissive societies are in Nordic Europe, Western Central Europe or Spain.

Among the most recent issues related to the emancipation of the gay community has been the issue of same-sex marriages, which has led to major splits in many societies. The legalisation of same-sex marriages in the Netherlands, Germany, Canada, France, Spain, and England, Wales and Scotland, but not in Northern Ireland, is contributing to a more permissive, but also more tolerant, society (Inglehart and Welzel, 2005: 126–9; Masci et al., 2015) In Central and Eastern European countries and the Baltic there is still a strong prejudice against homosexuality. While the summer love parade has become a symbol of gay pride and also an important tourism event in Germany, the situation in Central and Eastern Europe and Russia is still very difficult for gay people. However, the Czech Republic, Poland, Bulgaria and Estonia are more tolerant towards homosexuality (ESS, 2016). This criterion can be used as an indicator of the level of development of a society towards post-materialist values of self-expression and tolerance towards multiculturalism. Multiculturalism and post-materialist values of emancipation will continue to shape politics and the political culture of most European countries.

In sum, the growing diversity of European societies can only be ordered through the use of well-structured, positive immigration policies, which should be

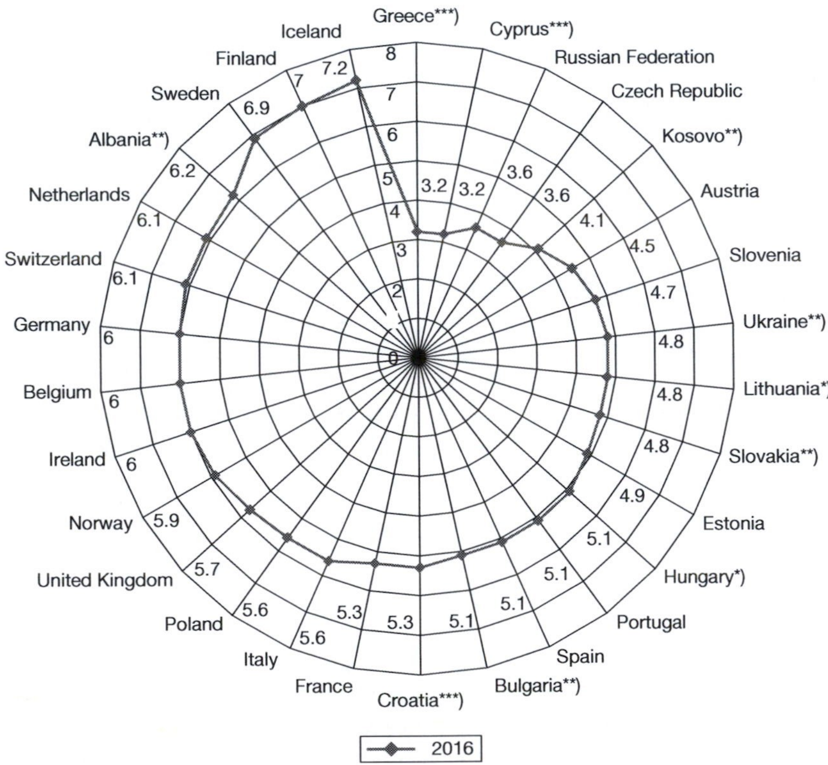

Figure 3.12 Multiculturalism index, 2016
Answering question: Country's cultural life undermined (0) or enriched by immigrants (10)

Notes: *) Figure for 2014; **) Figure for 2012; ***) Figure for 2010.

Source: ESS 2004–16.

Table 3.4 Populations and ethnic groups in the EU, Norway, Iceland and Switzerland, 2018

Regional clusters	*Countries*	*Total population in the country (national population in %) 2018*	*Foreign nationals (EU citizens) in % 2018*	*Muslim population (percentage of population) 2016*
Benelux	Belgium	11,398,589 (87.9) 59% Flemish, 40% Walloon, 1% German	11.9 (7.9)	7.6
	Luxembourg	602,005 (52.1)	47.8 (40.6)	3.2
	Netherlands	17,181,084 (95.2)	5.7 (3.1)	7.1
Germanic Europe	Austria	8,822,287 (84.2)	15.6 (7.9)	6.9
	Germany	82,792,151 (88.3)	11.7 (5.1)	6.1
	Switzerland	8,484,130 (74.9)	25 (16.5)	6.1
Nordic Europe	Denmark	5,781,190 (91.3)	8.6 (3.7)	5.4
	Finland	5,513,130 (95.5)	4.5 (1.8)	2.7
	Iceland	348,450 (89.1)	10.8 (9.2)	
	Norway	5,295,619 (89.3)	10.7 (6.7)	5.7
	Sweden	10,120,242 (91.1)	7.2 (3.0)	8.5
British Isles	Ireland	4,830,392 (88.1)	12 ((9)	1.4
	United Kingdom	66,273,576 (90.5) 80% English, 10% Scottish, 4% Northern Irish, 2% Welsh, 4% Other	9.5 (5.8)	6.3
France	France	66,926,166 (93)	7 (2.3)	8.8
Southern Europe	Greece	10,741,165 (92.4)	7.6 (2)	5.7
	Italy	60,483,973 (91.5)	8.5 (2.6)	4.8
	Portugal	10,291,027 (95.9)	4.1 (1.3)	0.4
	Spain	46,658,447 (90.2)	9.7 (4.1)	2.6

(continued)

Table 3.4 *(continued)*

Regional clusters	*Countries*	*Total population in the country (national population in %) 2018*	*Foreign nationals (EU citizens) in % 2018*	*Muslim population (percentage of population) 2016*
Mediterranean Islands	Cyprus	864,236 (82.6)	17.3 (13.3)	25.4
	Malta	475,701 (85.9)	14.1 (8.1)	2.6
Baltic Europe	Estonia	1,319,133 (85) 70% Estonians, 25% Russians, 5% Other	15 (1.4)	0.2
	Latvia	1,934,379 (87%) 62.1% Latvians, 26.9% Russians, 11% Other	14.2 (0.3)	0.3
	Lithuania	2,808,901 (85.9) 84.2% Lithuanians, 6.6% Poles, 5.8% Russians, 3.4% Other	0.933 (0.2)	0.1
Central Europe	Czech Republic	10,610,055 (95.1)	4.5 (2.1)	0.2
	Hungary	9,778,371 (98.3)	1.7 (0.8)	0.4
	Poland	37,976,687 (99.4)	0.6 (0.1)	Less than 0.1
	Slovakia	5,443,120 (98.7) 80.7% Slovaks, 8.5% Slovaks, 2% Roma, 8.8% Other	1.3 (1)	0.1
	Slovenia	2,066,880 (95.3) 83.1% Slovenes, 16.9% Other	5.9 (1)	3.8
Eastern Europe/ Balkan Europe	Bulgaria	7,050,034 (98.7) 85% Bulgarians, 9% Turks, 5% Roma	1.2 (0.2)	11.1
	Romania	19,530,631 (99.4) 88.9% Romania, 6.5% Hungarians, 3.3% Roma	0.6 (0.3)	0.4
	Croatia	4,105,493 (99.2)	1.2 (0.4)	1.6

Source: Eurostat (2018e); Pew Research (2017); Fischer Almanach (2018).

combined with an integration policy based on a good mix of assimilationist and multiculturalist measures. Indeed, such a mix strategy may well make European societies richer and stronger in the context of globalisation.

Conclusions: the great transformation of the late twentieth century

Since the late 1970s, politics in Europe have been subject to major transformations, which are still ongoing. We started this chapter with a review of Stein Rokkan's theory on European politics and we continued with the main criticisms of Rokkan's theory expressed by several scholars. Among these transformations, in Western Europe, is the erosion of traditional collective identities (working class, religion-based subculture) and replacement by more individualised pluralistic society in terms of life style, while in Central and Eastern Europe, the collapse of communism led to embracement of a new society based on capitalism and liberal democracy. A further major transformation was that many European societies are no longer nationally culturally homogenous and have become multicultural, leading to major challenges of integration and rebuilding identity.

Suggested reading

Caramani, Daniele (2004), *The Nationalization of Politics: The Formation of National Electorates and Party Systems in Western Europe*. Cambridge: Cambridge University Press.

Caramani, Daniele (2015), *The Europeanization of Politics: The Formation of a European Electorate and Party System in Historical Perspective*. Cambridge: Cambridge University Press.

Joppke, Christian (2017), Civic integration in Western Europe: three debates. *West European Politics*, 40(6): 1153–76.

Lipset, Seymour Martin and Stein Rokkan (1967), Cleavage structures, party systems and voter alignments: an introduction. In: Seymour Martin Lipset and Stein Rokkan (eds), *Party Systems and Voter Alignments: Cross-National Perspectives*. New York: The Free Press, pp. 1–64.

Seiler, Daniel Louis (2015), The legacy of Stein Rokkan for European polities: a short tribute. In: José M. Magone (ed.), *Routledge Handbook of European Politics*. London: Routledge, pp. 41–51.

QUESTIONS FOR REVISION

- Explain what is meant by the 'freezing hypothesis' of party systems and outline the main criticisms.
- Compare the main political cleavages between the Netherlands, Germany and Italy.

(continued)

(continued)

- How relevant are historically grown political cleavages in contemporary Europe? Discuss using examples from at least two different regions of Europe.
- Explain what is understood by 'post-materialism' and what impact, if any, it has on European societies.
- Is support and opposition to European integration becoming a new political cleavage?

Chapter 4

Government in multilevel Europe

- A two-headed executive: the European model
- The head of state: moderating party politics
- The government: the centre of executive power
- The exception to the rule of divided European governments: presidentialism in Cyprus and the directoire in Switzerland and Bosnia-Herzegovina
- Diversity in the quality of democratic governance
- Conclusions: government in Europe – majoritarian versus consensus politics
- Suggested reading

A two-headed executive: the European model

Traditionally, European politics is characterised by a two-headed executive. The head of state and the government share executive power in most European countries. However, although in most countries the role of the head of state is simply a formality, the exceptions are the semi-presidential systems in Europe, among which the French model is the most well known. In most Central and Eastern European political systems, the French model was adopted and adjusted to the needs of each country. The only two exceptions to the two-headed executive are Cyprus and Switzerland. The former adopted a presidential system and the latter can be referred to as the 'directoire model' similar to the 1795 French constitution, in which the presidency rotates yearly between the seven members of the federal council (government).

In this chapter we discuss first, the head of state both in parliamentary and semi-presidential systems, and then the core government as the centre of executive power. A third section will also discuss briefly central public administration, the major instrument of policy formulation and implementation of governments.

The head of state: moderating party politics

While the head of state (president/monarch) has merely formal functions and represents the country at international forums, the prime minister, sometimes called the president of the council of ministers (Spain or Italy), concentrates most of the executive powers of a particular country. This two-headed executive differs from the US and Latin American models, where the president is directly elected and concentrates the executive powers (Table 4.1, Figure 4.1).

The European model created the formal head of state as a moderating force of national politics. Normally, the head of state is a prestigious elderly statesmen or stateswoman who commands respect from all sectors of society. A good example in this respect was the president of Germany, Richard von Weizsäcker, between 1984 and 1994. He was perceived to be a strong moral figure by most of the population, mainly because of his critical position in relation to the political class, in particular Chancellor Helmut Kohl. This outstanding president did not fit in the traditional role of a president in Germany, which was one of formal powers and low profile. Václav Havel had a similar high standing when he became president of the Czech Republic after the collapse of the authoritarian regime. His opposition to the former regime and involvement in the Charter 77 human rights movement gave him strong moral authority in the political system.

The moderating influence of the head of state goes back to the practice of the constitutional monarchies in nineteenth-century Europe, when, in some constitutions (for example, those in Portugal and Spain), the monarch would be regarded as the moderating force of the political system. Such a moderating role is more likely to be fulfilled in countries in which there is still a monarchy (for example, the Netherlands or Sweden), or a president who is elected by legislature (for example, Germany and Italy). In contrast, in countries where presidents are directly elected, so-called 'semi-presidential' systems, such offices can gain greater prominence and interference in national politics than is provided in the constitution.

Table 4.1 Political forms of democracy in Europe

	Presidential	*Semi-presidential*	*Parliamentary*	*Parliamentary monarchy*
Unicameral	Cyprus	Portugal	Greece	Denmark
		Finland	Latvia	Sweden
		Bulgaria	Estonia	Norway
		Slovakia	Albania	Luxembourg
		Lithuania	Malta	
		Serbia	Kosovo	
		Croatia		
		Macedonia		
		Montenegro		
Bicameral		France	Germany	UK
		Austria	Italy	Belgium
		Ireland	Switzerland	Netherlands
		Poland	Malta	Spain
		Romania	Bosnia-Herzegovina	
		Slovenia		
		Czech Republic		
		Ukraine		

Semi-presidentialism: a popular model in Central and Eastern Europe

The best example of semi-presidentialism is France, where, in spite of the fact that the president has limited powers in the constitution, in practice he/she is an important veto player in the political system. The French model of semi-presidentialism is related to France's specific national political culture, which is still shaped and framed by the French Revolution. Jack Hayward argues that, in the French case, semi-presidentialism symbolises the re-emergence of Bonapartism (Hayward, 1987: 4), however the main intention was to overcome the instability of the Fourth French Republic, which was established after 1946. In 1958, Charles de Gaulle asked constitutionalists to draft a new constitution that would ensure greater stability. As a result, the position of the president was strengthened in relation to parliament and within the executive (Knapp and Wright, 2001: 50–7). The original constitution of the Fifth Republic did not provide for the direct election of the president – this was only introduced after a revision in 1962. The first elections took place in 1965 (Elgie, 2003: 112–13). The original constitution provided for a seven-year term, which could be renewed. However, after a referendum in 2000, this term was reduced to five years, but without any limitation of terms (Knapp and Wright, 2001: 63). The particular conventions of French semi-presidentialism allow the president to have strong powers in foreign policy. This is also the reason

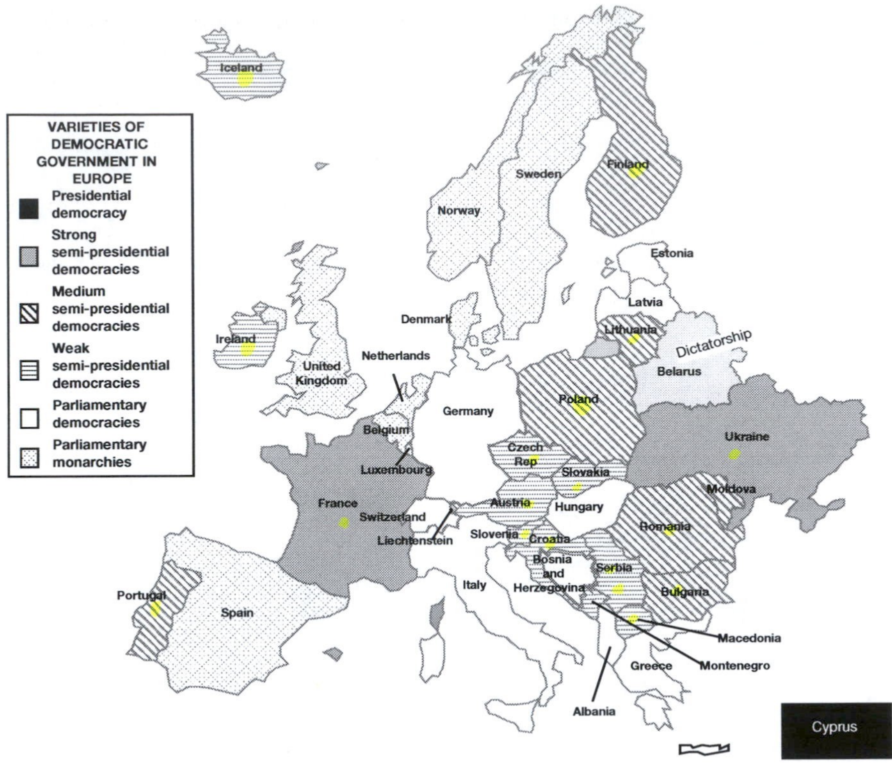

Figure 4.1 Varieties of democratic regimes in Europe

why French presidents are always present at European summits or at other international gatherings, such as the G8 or G20. The French president also has some input in domestic policy. S/he is allowed to chair and take an active part in the cabinet of ministers. However, in practice there is normally a division of labour between the two heads of the executive, with the president focusing on foreign policy and the prime minister on domestic policies and the day-to-day running of the country. Semi-presidentialism is particularly weakened when the party closest to the president has no overall absolute majority in the National Assembly, and sometimes the president may have to cooperate with an adversary party – as with Jacques Chirac and the socialist-led coalition of Lionel Jospin between 1997 and 2002. Similarly, there was a *cohabitation* between President François Mitterrand and Edouard Balladur between 1994 and 1997 (Knapp and Wright, 2001: 113–20).

Today, France still has the strongest semi-presidential model, particularly with respect to its practice. Direct election of presidents in other countries has led to semi-presidential tendencies, but in recent years scholars have been more cautious in setting those systems at the same level as the French model. Maurice Duverger was the first to coin the expression 'semi-presidentialism' (*régime semipresidentiel*), but even his work on Western European semi-presidential systems shows that there have been major changes since 1958 (Bahro et al., 1998; Duverger, 1970; Elgie, 2001, 2008).

One factor to consider is that the political culture of a country may contribute to the moderation of the role of its president. This can be seen in the case of Ireland and Austria. Although both countries have directly elected presidents, they have a rather formal role and therefore they are at the other side of the spectrum in comparison to the French case. In spite of this, I dare to call it weak semi-presidential systems with some potential for a stronger role for the president, like happens now in the Czech Republic, Slovakia and Slovenia. For example, there was an attempt by Austrian president Thomas Klestil (1992–2004), a former internationally recognised diplomat, to gain greater foreign powers during his term as president, but his country's conventions prevented him from doing so. Klestil was also very opposed to the highly contested coalition government between the ÖVP and the populist FPÖ in 2000, but he had to accept it after both parties signed a statement that they would endorse European integration and repudiate the Nazi regime and also that Jörg Haider would not be part of the coalition government (Welan, 2000: 26–31). During the presidential elections of 2016 and 2017 in Austria, a major discussion took place between the two main candidates: the rightwing Norbert Hofer from the Freedom Party (FPÖ) and the moderate Alexander Van der Bellen from the Green Party (VGÖ) on how they would interpret the constitutional powers of the presidency. Hofer tended to present a more proactive semi-presidential style, while Van der Bellen emphasised the need to follow the traditional interpretation of just having a formal role in the political system (*Zeitonline*, 4 December 2016). In Ireland, presidents have taken the role of moral authority but have had a very low profile in national politics. They fulfil a formal role similar to those presidents in parliamentary regimes. This means that semi-presidentialism in this context is almost non-existent, owing to the fact that the Irish president only has formal powers (Gallagher, 2010a).

In Southern Europe only Portugal has adopted the semi-presidential system. In the original constitution of 2 April 1976, the president was allocated substantial powers. The constitution itself was a product of a revolutionary process that was dominated by a military junta. The first president was General Antonio Ramalho Eanes, who clearly was sympathetic to the left and wanted to protect the achievements of the revolution. The constitution included a revolutionary council, whose main function was to oversee the democratic process and protect the revolutionary achievements. Therefore, it functioned as a constitutional court through a constitutional commission. However, after 1982, the political parties started a civilianisation process (the withdrawal of the military from political institutions that had existed since the revolutionary transition of 1974–5) that led to a reduction of the powers of the president, the abolition of the Council of the Revolution and the establishment of a constitutional court. Since then, presidents have been an important check on governments, because of their power to veto or delay legislation by sending it to the constitutional court in order to check legislative bills for its constitutionality. In particular, Presidents Mário Soares (1986–95) and Anibal Cavaco Silva (2006–15) were quite active in using vetoes or referring legislation to the constitutional court when the prime minister was from another party (Frain, 1995; Pinto and Freire, 2005; Magone, 2014a).

In Finland, a semi-presidential system was introduced in 1919. During the interwar and Cold War periods it fulfilled an important function of stability. No political party was able to achieve a strong or absolute majority and therefore the parties had to form a coalition government. The closeness of the country to the former Soviet Union meant that a strong president, able to talk to the Soviet leadership, was required. The long incumbencies of Juho Kusti Paasikivi (1946–54), Urho Kekkonen (1956–82) and later Mauno Koivisto (1982–94) are symptomatic of this aspect of the Finnish political culture. However, the most important postwar president was certainly Urho Kekkonen who completely controlled the political system. His long incumbency of almost three decades led to control of all aspects of political life. Governments were quite weak and characterised by instability. After his retirement in the early 1980s, new president Mauno Koivisto introduced a new phase of self-limitation of the presidency, evolving over time towards a parliamentarian system. All these changes bore fruit, so that more government stability began to emerge (Karvonen, 2014: 83–7).

After 1995, a revision of the constitution led to a limitation of the term of office by any incumbent and his/her powers. These changes can be seen as part of the processes of Europeanisation that the country has been subject to since the early 1990s, especially after 1995. In 2000, the four constitutional acts were integrated into one constitution, which led to the strengthening of parliament within the parliamentarisation of the political system (Raunio and Tiilikainen, 2004: 101–2). The legislative veto powers of the president almost completely disappeared and the government formation process is now entirely controlled by the political parties. Semi-presidentialism in Finland was reduced to a formal role and is now weak (Karvonen, 2014: 86). Since then, presidents can only be elected to a two-term period. So far only Tarja Halonen (2000–12) has held office for two terms, the first woman to hold the office in Finland. She was replaced by the former president of the national parliament Sauli Ninistö.

After 1989, many countries in Central and Eastern Europe adopted a semi-presidential system, but the standing of the president in each political system has differed considerably. As a rule of thumb, because of its stabilising moderating role, semi-presidentialism in Central and Eastern Europe has been more important than in Western Europe. The unstable period of democratic transition and consolidation allowed for a strong role for directly elected presidents. The best examples in this respect are probably Poland and Romania.

A seminal comparative study by Philip Köker gives us some insights into the differences in the activism and use of veto power in the Central and Eastern European countries. According to his study, between 1990 and 2010, most presidents of Bulgaria, Poland, Lithuania and Poland used their veto power wisely, on average vetoing 2.1 per cent of all legislative proposals (Köker, 2017: 59). Vetoing increases if the government is neutral or from another party to that of the president (Köker, 2017: 60).

In Poland, after the round table, provisional President General Wojciech Jaruzelski was replaced by the charismatic Lech Walesa, who won the elections in 1989. The small constitution of 1992 gave strong powers to the president, and with his own party in parliament, Lech Walesa attempted to further extend his powers; however, in the elections of 1995 Aleksandr Kwaniewski, the representative of the Social Democratic Alliance (SLD), became the new president. Soon after, in the constitution of 1997, the powers of the president had limitations placed on them. However, the Polish president still has a strong suspensive veto in relation to legislation, and it can only be overridden by a two-thirds majority in parliament. Normally, in the same way as in Portugal, contested legislation is sent to the constitutional court for a ruling on its constitutionality (McMenamin, 2008: 123; Taras, 2006: 362). Kwaśniewski remained in office until 2005. In 2006, the Law and Justice (PiS) party candidate Lech Kaczyński became the new president and was quite supportive of the coalition government led by his brother Jaroslaw (McMenamin, 2008: 128). He clearly used his full powers, particularly during the cohabitation with the absolute majority government of Civic Platform (PO) under Prime Minister Donald Tusk after 2007. He could also count on the support of his twin brother who was the leader of the PiS. Kaczyński was quite critical of the EU, as became clear by his delaying the signing and ratification of the Treaty of Lisbon, after the second Irish referendum was positive. Moreover, President Kaczyński pursued a quite hard anti-Russian position. On 10 April 2010, Lech Kaczyński died after a plane crash nearby Smolensk, while he was going to take part in the seventieth anniversary of the Katyn massacre of Polish officers by Soviet troops in 1940. About 96 people died, including almost half of the Polish political leadership. Since then, his brother Jaroslaw Kaczyński has kept the former president's memory alive, presenting regularly unfounded conspiracy theories about the accident of Smolensk and linking it to Russian activism (*The Guardian*, 10 April 2010).

He was followed by the more moderate and uncharismatic Bronislaw Komorowski (2010–15) who was close to the PO under the then leadership of Donald Tusk. Komorowski was replaced by the charismatic and popular president Andrzej Duda in 2015. He has been quite supportive of the conservative policies of the PiS's absolute government which came to power that year. The recent controversial restructuring of Poland's judiciary was only partly criticised in Poland. The EU, however, deemed this restructuring to be in contravention of article 7 of the Treaty of Lisbon, a judgment that was also upheld by the European Court of Justice. This clearly shows the danger of having a president and a prime minister in charge from the same party, as there is a lack of checks and balances (Jasiewicz and Jasiewicz-Betkiewicz, 2016, 2017; *Politico*, 2 December 2017, 19 December 2017).

After independence in 1992, Lithuania drafted a new constitution that envisaged a strong semi-presidential system that was strongly influenced by the French system. However, in a referendum, the population rejected such a strong semi-presidential system, so a weaker version was adopted which allows the president to share competences with the government in foreign policy but not in other matters (Tauber, 2010: 176–7). Meanwhile, several presidents have been elected to this position since 1992. Clearly, the first president was the communist leader Algirdas Brazaukas who had conducted the country towards independence. He was succeeded by Valdas Adamkus (1998–2003), who was then re-elected in 2004 for a second time to serve until 2009, after a brief period of Roland Paksas who had had to resign after allegations of collusion with some rather dubious businessmen. Paksas warned one of these businessmen about investigations that were taking place by the Lithuanian secret services. He tried to remain in power, but impeachment proceedings introduced by parliament and the constitutional court led him to resign shortly before the process was almost finished (Tauber, 2010: 178). Adamkus was an expatriate living in the United States, but he was quite popular in Lithuania. He was moderate and stayed above politics (for more detail on Lithuania, see Krupavicius, 2008). He was replaced by the first Lithuanian female president, Dalya Grybauskaite (2009–). She is quite a charismatic president and uses her foreign policy powers to the full. Grybauskaite has particularly gained a reputation in Europe due to her hawkish attitude towards Russia, particularly after the Ukraine crisis (*BBC News*, 30 August 2014). Moreover, she was also very critical of a bailout to the Southern European countries, particularly to Greece. During the third bailout negotiated with Greece, Grybauskaite spoke about the 'mañana' approach of the Greek government, which was perceived as delaying reforms forever (*The Guardian*, 12 July 2015). Domestically, the relationship between presidency and government has been quite calm and constructive. There was some tension in 2015 between President Grybauskaite and parliament due to her appointees to the office of the General Prosecutor. The appointees have to be confirmed by parliament (Jastramskis and Ramonaitė, 2016: 173).

A similar process of democratic consolidation and limitation of powers took place in Romania. However, here the president may enhance their role in constitutional practice (including the dissolution of parliament if no party is able to present a viable government). Moreover, the president has the power to mobilise the armed forces. Tensions between the presidency and the government were quite frequent in the 1990s, especially under the presidency of former communist Ion Iliescu between 1990 and 1996. Between 1996 and 2000, his successor, Emil Constantinescu, fulfilled a more traditional formal head-of-state role and kept closely to the powers assigned to him in the constitution (Gabanyi, 2010: 638–9). Iliescu returned again in 2000 and fulfilled a further term. He was replaced by Traian Băsescu, the former mayor of Bucharest. Băsescu was able to keep his office for two consecutive terms between 2004 and 2014. He was quite a controversial leader and twice was able to fend off impeachment proceedings. The second attempt was undertaken by Prime Minister Victor Ponta in 2012, but failed again (Bucur 2012a, 2012b, 2012c; *Euractiv*, 14 August 2012, 28 August 2012; Gallagher and Andrievici, 2008). Băsescu was allegedly involved in several corruption scandals which involved his son Mircea, who had dealings with a Romanian crime boss, and his son-in-law Radu Pricop, who speculated with property seized by the former communist regime. In spite of attempts to oust him by parliament, he was able to complete his second term (*Euractiv*, 26 June 2014).

In the elections of 16 November 2014, Klaus Iohannis became the new president, defeating Prime Minister Victor Ponta in the second round, receiving 54.8 per cent against the 45.2 per cent of his rival. Iohannis belongs to the German ethnic minority concentrated in Transylvania and was a former mayor of Sibiu. He ran his campaign on an anti-corruption ticket. One of the main aims of Iohannis was to oust Prime Minister Victor Ponta, which he achieved in 2015 (*Euractiv*, 19 November 2014, 11 February 2016). Since January 2017, Iohannis has had to deal with a major crisis of the Romanian political system. The dominance of the social democrats (PSD) in the parliament led to attempts to introduce amnesty for politicians who were convicted due to corruption charges, particularly leader Liviu Dragnea. Civil society protested against attempts to help convicted corrupt politicians. Daily demonstrations in front of the government building in January and February led to the withdrawal of the decree and the resignation of the minister responsible for it. President Iohannis sided with this 'democratic revolution' led by civil society organisations. They were also supported by the Ombudsman. Street protests continued throughout the year and were quite pro-European (*Euractiv*,

8 February 2017, 9 February 2017; Zbytniewska, 2017). After all bar one of its twenty-six ministers had resigned, Prime Minister Gridneanu still tried to hang onto power, but his own party PSD and its ally Alliance of Liberals and Democrats in Europe (ALDE) ousted him through a motion of censure, which was successful with 241 votes, 7 more than was necessary. On 29 June 2017, the president appointed Mihai Tudose from the PSD as the new prime minister (*The Guardian*, 21 June 2017). However, he had to resign six months later due to the loss of support from the PSD. Meanwhile, he was replaced by Prime Minister Vlorica Dancila, who is the first woman to be appointed to the job. Successive Romanian governments and presidents have been under considerable pressure from the EU because of a still very incipient judiciary and the lack of political and economic reforms, particularly in the fight against political corruption.

In Bulgaria, the relationship between prime minister and president was also characterised by tensions. The alternation in the power of presidents nominated by different parties, but mainly by the Bulgarian Socialist Party, has been quite successful. Probably, out of the six presidents after 1989, the most successful one has been Georgi Parvanov between 2002 and 2012 (Andreev, 2008). However, since 2009, the populist Prime Minister Boyko Borisov and his party Citizens for the European Development of Bulgaria (GERB) have been dominating politics, and tensions with the presidency have always been there. He has been prime minister for almost eight years with a couple of interruptions (2009–13, 2014–17, 2018–). According to the assessment of Cristina Bucur (2017), incumbent President Rumen Radev regards himself as an independent candidate, so it is not correct to talk of a cohabitation with the rightwing government under Prime Minister Borisov. However, Bucur expects that the ongoing debate on electoral reform introducing elements of majoritarian voting may lead to conflict in the long term.

In Croatia, Slovenia, Slovakia, the Czech Republic Serbia, Macedonia and Montenegro, the powers of the president are quite limited and the incumbents follow a low-profile approach to their offices.

This is especially true for Croatia after the dominance of the nationalist Franjo Tudjman. Tudjman's successor Stjepan Mesić (2000–10) tried to keep a balance between his overwhelming formal powers and his more substantial ones. His successors followed this tradition, keeping a moderate low profile (Kasapović, 2008). Diplomat Kolinda Grabar-Kitarović (2015–) continued this moderate approach to politics. In her short period of incumbency, she has already had to deal with three prime ministers and has called three times for early elections. Therefore, her role as honest broker has enhanced the role of the presidency.

In Slovenia, the directly elected president has only formal ceremonial powers. It is a rather weak semi-presidentialism similar to Ireland, Austria, the Czech Republic and Slovakia (Krašovec and Lajh, 2008). However, some conflict has emerged during the ten years of incumbency of Janez Drnovšek (1992–2002) who tried to have a stronger international profile during his second term. However, in 2005, considerable disagreements and conflicts began to emerge between the president and the centre-right government of Prime Minister Janez Janša. During July 2006, President Janez Drnovšek had to deal with the consequences of his office's budget being frozen by the government (one such consequence was the cancellation of his visit to Spain owing to a lack of funds) (Fink-Hafner, 2007; Lukšic 2010: 734–6). Borut Pahor (president since 2012) keeps a low profile according to the demands of the job. He is known as being an avid user of social media, and his nickname is 'King of Instagram'. On 12 November 2017, he was re-elected for a second five-year term (*Euractiv*, 14 November 2017).

In the original post-communist constitutions, both the Czech Republic and Slovakia had presidents that were elected by parliament, in the former by both houses. However, political conflicts and difficulties in building the necessary majorities led to a change towards direct elections of the president (Kipke, 2010: 320; Wintr et al., 2016: 150–1). This happened in 1998–9 in Slovakia after difficulties electing a successor to Michal Kovač (1993–8), and in 2008 in the Czech Republic due to the difficult re-election of President Vaclav Klaus. In spite of these changes, presidents in both countries are rather formal head figures. In 2013, Miloš Zeman was the first Czech president to be directly elected (on the election, see Kaniouk and Hloušek, 2013), and he was re-elected in 2018.

In Slovakia and internationally, President Michal Kovač will be remembered for being a fierce opponent of the nationalist Vladimir Mečiar who was prime minister between 1993 and 1998. In particular, Mečiar's policies against the Hungarian minority were condemned by the EU. In spite of having very limited powers, Kovač was able to be a symbol of integration in a period of nation-state formation (Kipke, 2010: 320–3). In the first direct elections on 15 and 29 May 1999, Rudolf Schuster was able to beat the charismatic Mečiar. He was succeeded by Ivan Gasparovič who also beat Mečiar in the presidential elections of 2004 and achieved re-election in 2009. Since 2014, the businessman Andrej Kiska has been president of Slovakia, and he clearly stated from the outset that he would keep a low profile and be independent of the political parties. In 2015, he was able to defeat the charismatic Robert Fico from the ruling social democratic party (Baboš and Malová, 2015: 261–2; *Euractiv*, 8 March 2015).

Table 4.2 Semi-presidential systems in Europe

Semi-presidential systems			
Presidential–parliamentary	*Parliamentary–presidential*		
	Strong	*Medium*	*Weak*
Russia	France	Poland	Ireland
Ukraine		Romania	Austria
		Portugal	Iceland
		Finland	Slovenia
		Bulgaria	Slovakia
		Lithuania	Croatia
			Serbia
			Czech Republic
			Macedonia
			Montenegro

The three Balkan countries of Serbia, Macedonia and Montenegro adopted the model of direct elections of the president, but they conferred only limited powers to the office.

According to Wolfgang Merkel, it is important to create a typology of semi-presidential systems according to the powers exerted by the president in each country. He differentiates between presidential–parliamentary, which is characterised by a strong president and a weak prime minister (for example, as in Russia and Ukraine), and parliamentary–presidential (found in most European countries) (Merkel, 1996: 80). I would add to Merkel's type of parliamentary–presidential the qualifications of strong, medium and weak (see Table 4.2, Box 4.1).

Box 4.1 The semi-presidential government

The term 'semi-presidential government' (*régime semi-presidentiel*) was coined by the eminent French political scientist Maurice Duverger who wrote *Political Institutions and Constitutional Law* (*Institutions politiques et droit constitutionel*, 1970 [1958]). It means a government that is neither clearly parliamentary nor clearly presidential. Features of a semi-presidential government are:

- direct election of the president (subsequently an alternative source of legitimacy to parliament);
- the president has considerable constitutional powers;
- the president shares power with the government;
- the government depends on parliamentary confidence, in contrast to the president who has a direct legitimacy from elections.

Duverger used this label to characterise the nature of the French political system of the Fifth Republic, which was established after 1958. It is worth noting that, long before this, Finland's political system had been semi-presidential, and that this had been the case since 1919.

Today, apart from France, semi-presidential governments can be found across Europe: Finland, Portugal, Poland, Romania, Bulgaria and Lithuania

In the past decades, it has been the hard work of Robert Elgie that has put the study of semi-presidential regimes on the map. Instead of just looking at semi-presidentialism in Europe, he also undertook the challenge to study such regimes in other parts of the world, particularly in the Caucasus and Central Asia (Elgie, 1999, 2001, 2008, 2011; Elgie and Moestrup, 2016).

Heads of state in parliamentary systems

The spread of semi-presidentialism in Europe led to a considerable reduction of presidents elected by parliament. In 2018, just Germany, Italy, Latvia, Estonia, Greece and Albania had presidents elected by parliament. In all cases, presidents have a rather formal role.

The presidents elected by parliament normally have fewer powers than presidents in most of the other semi-presidential systems, fulfilling more of a formal role. However, they have the very important rights to suspensive veto of legislation and the right to send such legislation to a constitutional court to rule on its constitutionality. Former President Václav Havel (1993–2003) in the Czech Republic and President Árpád Göncz (1990–2000) in Hungary have both used the suspensive veto fairly often, whereas the suspensive veto has been used in a more conciliatory form by Guntis Ulmanis (1993–9) in Latvia and Lennart Meri (1992–2001) in Estonia, particularly in relation to citizenship law (Ismayr, 2010: 24).

Although the Italian president has only formal powers, the long term of office of seven years allows him/her not only to be a strong moral authority but also to shape national politics. The main reason for this is that postwar governments in Italy were, as a rule, very unstable. Before 1992, Italian governments lasted an average of only ten months, so that the president was instrumental in leading the negotiation process towards a new government (Pasquino, 1995: 162). In many cases, the president would appoint a technocratic government under a prime minister who would come from the private sector or some other Italian institution, such as the Central Bank. After 1992, the Italian governments became more stable, although in 2000 President Carlo Azeglio Ciampi had to intervene after the collapse of the centre-left coalition and appoint a technocratic government under experienced politician Giuliano D'Amato (Magone, 2003: 75; Pasquino, 2015a).

As already mentioned, presidents in Germany have just a formal role, but they can play a major role if there are problems during government formation. After the elections of September 2017, the major party of the Christian Democratic Union/Christian Social Union (CDU-CSU) had major difficulties finding a coalition partner. In this context, president Frank-Walter Steinmeier was pivotal in bringing together the two main parties CDU/CSU and the Social Democratic Party (SPD) by appealing to their sense of duty to the country in creating a stable government beyond party interests. This was clearly a very difficult decision for the junior partner, the SPD, which had suffered a heavy defeat in the general elections. The election of the president is done by the federal assembly (*Bundesversammlung*), which consists of members of the Bundestag and a coopted number of people coming from society at large appointed by the regional parliaments. The coopted delegates are normally linked to the respective political parties according to their proportional representation in parliament. One major reason for this parliamentary-civil society approach to the election of the German president is that the Weimar Republic had a directly elected president. The second and last president of the Weimar Republic, Paul von Hindenburg, contributed through his actions to the rise of the totalitarian national socialist regime imposed by Adolf Hitler in 1932. Since 1945, the political elite has a strong distrust of plebiscitary democratic instruments, particularly related to the incumbency of top positions. Parliament should be the only legitimate source of power, so preventing the establishment of an independent directly elected legitimated president who may act as a counter power (Von Beyme, 2017: 341–2).

In Europe, there are still eight constitutional monarchies. The institutional convention for all these constitutional monarchies has led to the delegation of most governmental competences to the prime minister. In all constitutional monarchies, the monarch is a formal head of state with representative duties. In the Nordic countries, the Swedish, Danish and Norwegian monarchies have become fairly democratic. In the Netherlands, the formation of a coalition government allows the monarch to play a more active role. According to article 42, formally the king and the ministers comprise the government, but only the ministers are responsible for acts of government (article 47). Meanwhile, new King Willem-Alexander from the Netherlands succeeded Queen Beatrix on 30 April 2013. So far, he has been assessed as a very popular king well supported by his glamorous Argentinian wife Maxima and their children. This can also be asserted for Belgium and Luxembourg, of which monarchs King Albert II (1993–2013) and Grand Duke Jean (1964–2000) abdicated in favour of their sons King Philippe and Grand Duke Henri, respectively. In contrast to the Scandinavian countries, the Dutch, Belgian and to a limited extent the Luxembourg monarch may play a pivotal role in managing the process of coalition government formation by appointing *informateurs* and a *formateur* (see later in Box 4.5).

The strongest constitutional monarchy is the British one. This is largely because of the wealth and resources that Queen Elizabeth II commands. Moreover, although the royal prerogative has been delegated to the prime minister, in the UK it is still an institutional convention to consult the monarch on major issues. This practice is important, because Queen Elizabeth II is a source of political experience from which prime ministers can draw support in order to reach a decision. The climax of political life in the UK is the Queen's Speech, which is read at the end of the year in the House of Lords and outlines the programme of the government of the day for the coming year. According to Dennis Kavanagh, good timing has been an essential method of survival for the British monarchy: 'The key to the monarchy's survival in Britain has been its willingness over the last three centuries to concede power in good time to head off demands for its abolition' (Kavanagh, 2001: 54) As Philip Norton asserts, the monarchy preceded the representative democracy that we know today, so that the historical legacy still shapes many of the structures of the British political system. Both government and courts are Her Majesty's courts and governments; also parliament 'is summoned and prorogued by royal decree' and civil servants are crown appointees (Norton, 2014: 274). The formal powers of the British monarch are not codified in a written constitution. They are by and large conventions which are adhered to. In this sense, an unelected hereditary head of state is the main guarantor of democratic institutions, which is quite a paradox (Norton, 2014: 284).

One should not forget that the British monarch is the head of the Anglican Church and as such is the defender of the faith. This clearly is a major challenge in one of the most secularised societies and also due to its multiculturalism, including a very diverse population adhering to different faiths (Norton, 2014: 283).

A more modern monarchy is the Spanish one, which was reinstalled after the death of dictator Francisco Franco in 1978. King Juan Carlos (1975–2014) became a symbol of reconciliation and unity of the new Spain. However, at the end of his reign, he made many erratic decisions leading to calls for his abdication. In this context, King Juan Carlos abdicated from the throne in favour of Crown Prince Felipe in May 2014. Since then, the rating of the institutional monarchy has again reached high levels of support. However, this may also be related to the excellent performance of new King Felipe VI. Spain remains the only monarchy that was reinstalled after a republican period (for more detail, see Magone, 2018: 67–71).

In sum, the role of the head of state varies from country to country. However, in the vast majority it has purely representative functions alongside some competences in relation to the appointment of ministers or delaying legislation. Some exceptions can be found in semi-presidential systems, particularly in France, Finland, Portugal, Poland, Romania and Bulgaria, where constitutional practice and political culture allow for a stronger, more assertive role of the president.

The government: the centre of executive power

Majoritarian and consensual patterns of government

One of the best ways to categorise governments in Europe is the typology introduced by Arend Lijphart of majoritarian and consensual patterns of government. According to Lijphart, the UK's 'Westminster model' comes closest to the majoritarian type of government. In the UK, the prime minister holds a strong position and the government can be characterised as an 'elective dictatorship' if the prime minister is backed by a strong absolute majority, as in the heydays of Margaret Thatcher (1979–90) and Tony Blair (1997–2007). In contrast, the Dutch consociational democracy is the closest to a consensual government. Here, the prime minister is always dependent on the support of several parties. Representatives of these parties are part of a working coalition, which is based on consensus in order to keep stability in the cabinet. Lijphart defines majoritarian democracy as 'majority rule' that is responsible to a minority (Lijphart, 1984: 4–5). Such majoritarian government is elected by an electoral system that tends to create a bipolarised two-party system, such as in the UK, France, Spain or Greece. For Lijphart, such majority rule becomes less viable in plural segmented societies, such as in the Netherlands. Therefore, a different pattern of government emerges, which is characterised by consensus. Lijphart argues as follows:

> In plural societies, therefore, majority rule spells majority dictatorship and civil strife rather than democracy. What these societies need is a democratic regime that emphasises consensus instead of opposition, that includes rather than excludes, and that tries to maximise the size of the ruling majority instead of being satisfied with a bare majority: consensus democracy.
>
> (Lijphart, 1984: 21)

The importance of Lijphart's typology is that most European countries (for example, the Benelux countries, the Nordic countries, Germany and Austria) tend more towards the consensual pattern of government. However, there is also an increasing tendency towards majoritarian government, despite proportional representation systems, in France, in all Southern European countries and in many Central and Eastern European countries. Majoritarian or consensual patterns of government are not only created by electoral systems but also by the respective political cultures. They are essentially related to the ways national political elites resolve the relationship between majority and minority, between government and opposition.

In order to achieve a better differentiation between the two patterns of government, Lijphart introduced ten elements to pinpoint the differences between them, as summarised in Table 4.3.

These ten elements are structured along two axes. One is the executive-parties dimension and the other is the territorial federal-unitary dimension. In the executive-parties dimension, five elements allow us to differentiate between the two types. While majoritarian democracies are characterised by a concentration of

Table 4.3 Majoritarian versus consensus democracy

Categories	*Majoritarian democracy*	*Consensus democracy*
Executive-parties dimension		
Nature of executive power	Concentration of executive power in single party	Executive power-sharing in broad multi-party coalitions
Executive-legislative relations	Dominant executive	Balance between executive and legislative
Party system	Two-party system	Multi-party system
Electoral system	Majoritarian, disproportional electoral system	Proportional representation electoral system
System of interest intermediation	Pluralism	Neo-corporatism
Federal-unitary dimension		
Nature of territorial organisation	Unitary centralised	Federal, decentralised
Organisation of legislative power	Unicameral system	Bicameral balanced system
Constitutions	Flexible constitution, easy to amend	Rigid constitution, difficult to amend
Judicial review	Judicial review lies in parliament	Judicial review lies in constitutional court or supreme court
Central bank	Central banks that are dependent on executive	Central banks that are independent of the executive

Source: Author's own compilation based on Lijphart (1999, 2009).

executive power in a single party and a strong prime minister, achieved by a majoritarian or at least a highly disproportional electoral system, consensus democracies are characterised by a power-sharing government that works consensually with the legislature and that consists of several parties without an overall majority, mainly as a result of elections based on a highly democratic proportional representation. It is important that the executive-legislative relations based on majoritarianism or consensualism are also reflected in the system of socioeconomic interest intermediation of the respective country. The UK is closest to a model of pluralism, while the Netherlands, Belgium and Austria are closer to a neo-corporatist system of interest intermediation (see Chapter 8). Similarly, the federal-unitary dimension comprises five elements. The Westminster model (see Box 4.2), at least until 1997, was characterised by a unicameral system (the dominance of the House of Commons) and a flexible constitution with parliamentary judicial review. However, in the ideal type of Lijphart, consensus democracies are federal and decentralised, and they are characterised by a balanced bicameralism (equal power in two chambers of parliament), a rigid constitution that is difficult to amend, and judicial review allocated to a constitutional court or supreme court. Moreover, the national central bank is dependent on the executive in majoritarian democracies, but independent in consensus democracies. This typology of Lijphart is still influenced by the period before 1997, when, in the UK, the central bank was dependent on the executive. After 1997, Gordon Brown, the former chancellor and then prime minister, introduced an independent statute for the central bank similar to other governments across the EU, because of the requirements of economic and monetary union. Independence of the central bank has become the rule in all European countries. In the EU, the European Central Bank and national central banks are now independent entities that shape economic and monetary policy independently from government

Box 4.2 The Westminster model

The Westminster model refers to the political system of the UK. The Palace of Westminster houses the two chambers of the British parliament – the House of Commons (the lower house) and the House of Lords (the upper house). The British parliament is regarded as the mother of all modern parliaments, having a long history that reaches back to the thirteenth century. The place where parliament met was the Palace of Westminster, which was a royal residence and which later became the parliamentary building. In 1836 a major fire destroyed the Palace of Westminster and a new building was reconstructed with the famous watchtower known as Big Ben.

This long parliamentary tradition and the evolutionary development of the British political system, which is still characterised by an unwritten constitution, became an attractive model of democracy around the world. The Westminster model was exported to many Commonwealth countries including Canada and Australia, and just adjusted to meet local needs.

The UK is still a unitary country, but after the referenda in Scotland and Wales in autumn 1997, when devolution was introduced by New Labour, it became more regionalised and decentralised. Another feature is that most European countries, in contrast to Lijphart's typology, now have a more flexible approach to constitutional revision. This is achieved through consensual politics and cooperation between the main parties. Globalisation and Europeanisation are pressurising political elites in all European countries to adjust their constitutions accordingly. As already mentioned in Chapter 1, Finland and Switzerland in 1999–2000 are good examples of constitutions that had to be adjusted to take account of Europeanisation and globalisation. An important qualification for this typology is naturally the fact that most countries have both majoritarian and consensual elements in their constitutions. They may tend to one side or the other.

Pippa Norris undertook a major study to operationalise the two ideal types along two axes. Based on her results and my own amendments one can categorise European democracies according to a simplified four-field table (see Table 4.4, Box 4.3). Norris clearly emphasises the impact of the electoral system as a major factor leading to consensus or majoritarian governments (Norris, 2001: 879).

Any categorisation makes it quite difficult to assess the new democracies in Central and Eastern Europe. Most of them have fragmented party systems that have only slowly been transformed into stable ones. One of the reasons for categorising most of them as majoritarian is that the cleavage between the former communists and the centre-right parties seems to structure most of these new democracies. In time, these countries, depending on their national political cultures, may move towards more consensual or majoritarian politics. Therefore, our assessment on these countries is rather tentative and based on the reading of the country-specific literature over a lengthier period, particularly since the early 1990s (see Figure 4.2).

Box 4.3 Majoritarian versus consensus government

Dutch-American political scientist Arend Lijphart developed a typology in order to understand government in Europe better, particularly in his own country, the Netherlands. He contrasted the British Westminster model and the Dutch model of democracy. He wrote two highly influential books – *Democracies: Patterns of Majoritarian and Consensus Government in Twenty One Countries* (1984) and *Patterns of Democracy: Government Forms and Performance in Thirty-Six Countries* (1999; second updated edition in 2009).

Table 4.4 Majoritarian and consensus government in Europe

	Executive parties	
	Majoritarian/ majoritarian consensual	*Consensual/consensual majoritarian*
Federal or regionalised	UK	Germany
	Spain	Austria
	Italy	Belgium
	Poland	Switzerland
	France	Czech Republic
Unitary	Ireland	Netherlands
	Malta	Norway
	Greece	Sweden
	Croatia	Denmark
	Hungary	Finland
	Bulgaria	Iceland
	Romania	Portugal
	Lithuania	Estonia
		Latvia
		Slovakia
		Slovenia

Source: Adapted and amended from Norris (2001: 989).

Figure 4.2 Consensus and majoritarian democracies in Europe, 2018

The most stable majoritarian governments are in Western Europe. The longevity of the political systems and accumulated government traditions are an important factor in this respect. According to Jean Blondel, all countries, with the exception of Switzerland, are led by working 'cabinet governments'. The origins of such governments go back to the early models set up in Britain and Sweden in the eighteenth and nineteenth centuries (Blondel, 1995: 71–2). Across Europe, there are similarities (as well as differences) in how these governments are structured and how they operate. According to Blondel, one can differentiate between three types of cabinet government: the collegial, the team and the prime-ministerial (presidentialised).

The collegial style is where the prime minister cooperates with the ministers and formulates policy with them. This can be found in many European consensus democracies (for example, Sweden, Denmark and the Netherlands). The team style is common in the Commonwealth countries across the world and especially in the UK, although the governments of Margaret Thatcher and Tony Blair showed strong presidentialisation traits. The prime ministerial style has become relevant in the information age due to the erosion of encapsulated cleavages attached to political parties and the rise of the internet allowing for a direct relationship with the voters through social media. The personalisation of politics has led to the prominence of the prime minister, who will normally have strong charismatic traits. Normally, governments include all these styles but can be characterised according to how strong one particular style is in relation to the others (Blondel, 1995: 276, 278; see Figure 4.3).

The presidentialisation of the prime minister

One interesting aspect of European politics is that there is a tendency for both majoritarian and consensual democracies to personalise politics around the prime minister. The prime minister has to have a good relationship with the electorate. The increasing importance of electoral marketing in political campaigns has transformed the prime minister into a multifaceted politician with several skills. This is a consequence of the growing 'cartelisation of politics' by political parties (see Chapter 7 on political parties). Additionally, the Americanisation of European politics has led to the strengthening of the importance of the political leader, who is supported by political parties. Furthermore, social media like Twitter, Tumblr, Instagram, Facebook and Snapchat have become important devices for a direct link between leaders and followers.

Normally the prime minister presides over the council of ministers, and in some countries he or she is called the 'president of the council of ministers', as, for example, in Spain and Italy. Indeed, political campaigns in these two countries use the word 'president' when referring to the prime minister. The charismatic Silvio Berlusconi used this analogy to the US president, in spite of the fact that Italy has a seven-year formal president who is head of state. In the UK, Tony Blair (1997–2007) used his charismatic personality to the full in order to push forward his message. Very often he was referred to in the press as 'President Blair' in analogy to the President of the United States. Since the 1980s, similar trends can be found in Spain under José Maria Aznar and in Sweden under Göran Persson, and even in consensus democracies (for example, in the Netherlands under Jan Peter Balkenende, in Belgium under Guy Verhofstadt (1999–2008) and in Austria under Franz Vranitzky (1988–97)). One of the most successful electoral campaigners was German Chancellor Gerhard Schröder (1998–2005), who emulated the Blairite model and was able to win two consecutive elections for the Social Democratic Party (SPD) and was close to winning a third one in 2005.

According to Thomas Poguntke and Paul Webb, such presidentialisation has three faces: the executive face, the party face and the electoral face:

- *executive face*: shift of intra-executive power to the benefit of the head of government;
- *party face*: shift of intra-party power to the benefit of the leader;
- *electoral face*: growing emphasis on leadership appeals in election campaigning.

The more strongly the prime minister is able to deal with these three pillars of her or his power, the greater the influence and power s/he has. According to Poguntke and Webb, prime ministers have a larger margin of autonomy towards presidentialisation in majoritarian democracies than in consensus democracies (Poguntke and Webb, 2005: 8–12) (see Box 4.4).

Majoritarian patterns of government

As already mentioned, the strongest majoritarian government is that of the UK. As a result of the simple plurality electoral system, political parties tend to receive an absolute majority in seats, in spite of a low proportional share of the votes. This naturally leads to a disproportional result, in which a government can command a strong majority. The best example is probably the strong majority of Prime Minister Tony Blair after 1997, 2001 and 2005 in the House of Commons. Such an absolute majority of seats strengthens the position of the prime minister, because the success in elections is linked directly to him or her. Charismatic leaders such as Margaret Thatcher or Tony Blair are nearly able to fulfil the conditions for an 'elective dictatorship'. One of the main characteristics of the UK's prime ministerial government is that there is a fusion between legislative and executive powers. The government consists entirely of elected MPs and peers. According to November 2017 figures, out the 106 senior and junior ministers, 85 were MPs, 19 were Lords and 2 came from the judiciary sector (among them the Attorney General who also attends the cabinet). The core cabinet comprises twenty-three MPs (Government of the United Kingdom, 2017) The government is predominant in relation to parliament, despite occasional problems for the party in government (for example, under Prime Minister Tony Blair there were several rebellions within the parliamentary group about education and National Health Service reform bills, and under John Major in 1993 there was a rebellion against the ratification of the Maastricht Treaty). Also David Cameron (2010–16) and Theresa May (2016–) have had to deal with opposition within their party. After the unsuccessful snap parliamentary election of 2017, the latter could only manage to get a very thin majority, which was achieved after a deal with the Democratic Unionist Party (DUP), the more extreme unionist party in Northern Ireland. Certainly, Prime Minister Theresa May is rather the opposite of the more charismatic 'presidential prime ministers' such as Margaret Thatcher and Tony Blair. The difficult negotiations around Brexit do not help her to strengthen her position. According to a poll commissioned by *Sky News*, 52 per cent thought Theresa May was a weak leader and 44 per cent a strong leader (*Sky News*, 6 October 2017).

Box 4.4 The presidentialisation of government

Thomas Poguntke and Paul Webb edited an important book, *The Presidentialisation of Politics: A Comparative Study of Modern Democracies* (2005), which described the tendency towards the centralisation of power around the prime minister. Several factors play a major role in this process, but the growing importance of the personalisation of politics around the top candidates of political parties, and ultimately the elected prime minister, is a key factor. Their definition is:

> [the] presidentialisation of politics can be understood as the development of
>
> (a) increasing leadership power resources and autonomy within party and political executive respectively, and
> (b) increasingly leadership-centred electoral processes.
>
> (Poguntke and Webb, 2005: 5)

One of the reasons why the UK government still has an incomplete modernised separation of powers is that the overall political structure has evolved over centuries and is still characterised by many medieval, traditional features. One such feature was the former position of the Lord High Chancellor, responsible for the administration of the judiciary in the UK. The Lord High Chancellor had to fulfil three roles: state secretary of constitutional affairs in the Council of Ministers, the Speaker of the House of Lords and the chief of the judiciary. Such a position was quite unheard of in the rest of Europe (Kavanagh, 2001: 344). In 2004–5, a major reform took place and separated the functions, although the Secretary of State for Justice has retained the medieval title of Lord Chancellor (on the judiciary in the UK, see Chapter 6).

Although the prime minister is at the centre of decision-making, everything depends on how charismatic and dominant s/he is in relation to the other ministers. The cabinet principle, which binds all the ministers to decide matters collectively, is a powerful instrument that can reinforce the position of the prime minister. However, it can also undermine that position, if prominent members decide to resign (Massari, 2005: 112). The prime minister can also use a cabinet reshuffle either to renew the team or to overcome difficult crises relating to particular policy areas and ministers. Most decision-making takes place in committees attached to the prime minister's office. This means that the prime minister centralises a considerable degree of power and can reduce the time spent with the cabinet, which meets weekly on Thursdays. In her period of office, Margaret Thatcher considerably reduced the time spent in cabinet meetings. And the cabinet meetings under Tony Blair were less than an hour in duration. In comparison with the Clement Attlee government of 1945–51, which spent ninety hours per year in cabinet meetings, the Blair government spent just thirty hours per year. Successor Prime Minister Gordon Brown was known as having a more cooperative style than Tony Blair (Burch, 1988: 21; Massari, 2005: 122).

The British prime minister also has a power of patronage. Every year s/he drafts an Honours List (scrutinised by the Queen) of people in public life who have honours conferred on them as a result of their contribution to society. The Labour government introduced a committee to scrutinise such applications, but this led to allegations that peerages were given in return for interest-free loans to the Labour Party, resulting in an investigation by the police. The 'cash for honours' scandal damaged Prime Minister Tony Blair considerably, because he was interviewed three times by the London Metropolitan police (Grant, 2009: 52–3). Although such practices were common among all parties, the scandal erupted during the

Labour government. Also David Cameron's honours list of 2016 was regarded as cronyism, because most of the people were either Tory fundraisers or important allies of himself (*The Guardian*, 5 August 2016).

Some aspects of the British tradition entered the Irish political system, however the majoritarian tendencies of the Taoiseach (chief of government) have been moderate. Even so, the Taoiseach system has been categorised as being the strongest prime ministerial system after the British one, along with the Greek, Spanish, Portuguese and German systems (Elgie, 2000: 237). Overall, the growing importance of coalition government since 1989 has constrained the Taoiseach. According to Robert Elgie, quoting Brian Farrell, the Taoiseachs tend to be either chiefs (meaning dominant) or chairmen (consensual) in their governments (Elgie, 2000: 245–6; O'Malley and Martin, 2010: 313). However, it seems that a combination of the two roles and their use according to context is the best way for the Taoiseach to remain in power. Prime Minister Bertie Ahern (1997–2008) was referred to as Bertie Teflon Ahern, because of his ability to switch from one role to another according to the situation, and he was hailed for having exceptionally strong diplomatic skills as a result of the successful completion of the Intergovernmental Conference related to the Constitutional Treaty in the first half of 2004 (Giannetti, 2005: 133). The Taoiseach has an important role to play in coordinating and negotiating neo-corporatist agreements, which have become more important in Ireland in recent decades. A major challenge for the Irish prime minister as a chief was clearly the Irish banking crisis around the several Irish banks, among them the Anglo-Irish Bank and the Nationwide Irish bank, which contributed to a major sovereign debt crisis as a consequence in 2010. In the end, Prime Minister Brian Cowan and his coalition government had to ask for a bailout of €85 billion from the EU and International Monetary Fund. In this context of national crisis, political parties from left and right tend to work together. However, Cowan had to deal with an erosion of cohesion within his coalition government between his party Fianna Fail, the Greens and the Progressive Democrats. After the bailout agreement, he was reduced just to a minority government of his party until the next elections on 28 February 2011. New elections led to the replacement of Cowan by new leader Enda Kenny who continued a tough austerity policy. He could rely on a majority, however, due to the coalition with the Labour Party. In these situations the combination of being a 'chief' and 'chairman' becomes of utmost importance (for an account of the management of the crisis, see Connaughton, 2016).

Moreover, the Taoiseach has certain patronage rights in relation to the second chamber in the Senate, being allowed to appoint eleven members to the sixty-seat second chamber. An important constraint for the Taoiseach is the Supreme Court, which emulates the US model and has, in the past, led to important decisions, particularly in relation to divorce (1995), abortion (2002) and EU treaty referenda (2003). The most important decision was probably that the Taoiseach and the government should not use public funds to promote their official position. They have to use party political funding or raise private funding for this purpose. This decision in 1995, known as the McKenna decision, was important for non-governmental campaigners (Giannetti, 2005: 146). The Taoiseach is supported by a vice-prime minister (Tanaiste) and the department of the Taoiseach, consisting of over 300 people, which includes the very important Office of the

Chief Whip, the Northern Ireland Office, the Government Information Office and the Press Secretary Office (Connolly and O'Halpin, 2000: 259–61; Giannetti, 2005: 143).

As already mentioned, the French semi-presidential system leads to divided government. The prime minister is subaltern to the president, who uses his/her position in a dominant, Bonapartist way, leaving the prime minister the onerous task of coordinating all aspects of domestic and foreign policy. However, the prime minister is fairly strong in relation to parliament (Di Virgilio, 2005: 44). In the case where the prime minister is in a situation of *cohabitation* with the president, as with Edouard Balladur (1993–95) during the presidency of François Mitterrand, s/he has more autonomy. However, between 1958 and 2007, subaltern prime ministers existed for forty years out of forty-nine. This shows the weakness of the prime minister in relation to the president. There is a constant cooperation between the prime minister's office and the general secretariat of the government (Secretariat General du Gouvernement – SGG). This is the official bureaucratic structure supporting the prime minister, which possesses a quite considerable number of material and human resources to do the work of coordination and management of policy-making. This clearly is very similar to the Cabinet Office in the UK. The General Secretary is a quite powerful position in terms of knowledge of the processes of government and institutional memory. Therefore, they tend to remain in office in spite of changes in government. According to Elgie, the SGG does clearly do the daily administrative and managerial work of the core executive. Moreover, there is also a General Secretariat of Defense and National Security (Secretariat General de la Defence et Securité Nationale – SGDSN) that deals just with this area, and General Secretariat of European Affairs (Secretariat General des Affaires Europeénnes – SGAE). The latter consists of 175 members of staff (SGAE, 2018). Quite crucial is the more informal private office of the prime minister which consists of people who are political appointees and who engage in informal coordination and negotiation, as well as assisting the work of the prime minister (Di Virgilio, 2005: 45; Elgie 1991, 2003) (Figure 4.1). According to Alistair Cole, the roles of the prime minister 'are those of political leader, of government manager and of presidential lieutenant'. As political leader it needs to push through its agenda, sometimes using all instruments at its disposal, including restrictive constitutional measures (Cole, 2017: 9). However, presidents may try to take over government responsibility. According to Alastair Cole, Nicolás Sarkozy tended to organise meetings with just seven ministers (the so-called G7), thereby bypassing the prime minister during the François Fillon incumbency (Cole, 2017: 79–80). The prime minister, as a government manager, implements the policies of the government. Last but not least, the prime minister is also the presidential lieutenant, a difficult role, because s/he has to protect the president from any bad publicity or poor policies. S/he takes the blame for anything that goes wrong. Therefore, prime ministers have a difficult stand to then move on to become presidents. None of the incumbent prime ministers has ever been able to become president. Only Georges Pompidou and François Mitterrand have ever become president after being prime minister, but only after several attempts each. This was also clear in the presidential elections in May 2017, in which three prime ministers tried to become president – the then incumbent prime minister Manuel Valls from the Socialist party, and the former prime ministers Alain Juppé and

François Fillon who served under Jacques Chirac and Nicolás Sarkozy, respectively. But they were all either eliminated in the primaries (Juppé, Valls) or in the first presidential round (*Politico*, 11 January 2017).

In Spain and Greece prime ministers hold a strong position. In Spain, until the general elections of November 2015, the proportional representation system reinforced the bipolarisation of the two parties. This had to do with the small size of most of the fifty-two constituencies. The system led to a high level of disproportionality, similar to that in the French and UK systems. Because of the constructive motion of censure, single-party minority governments could continue for four legislative periods if they were able to count on a working majority in parliament. This meant that a minority government could survive as long as the prime minister (called *El Presidente*) commanded strong authority within the government. Prime ministers were protected by the constructive motion of censure, similar to Germany. It meant the opposition could only topple the government if it had an alternative programme and candidate. Therefore, minority governments looked for a so-called pact of investiture (*pacto de investidura*) and/or a pact of legislature (*pacto de legislatura*) with key parties represented in parliament, in order to have a stable majority. However, during the Zapatero governments (2004–11), a variable majority with different parties according to particular policies became the rule. This was quite successful during the first government until 2008. But in the second government, which took place during the financial crisis, such majorities became more difficult, particularly when the budget had to be approved (Field, 2016: 111–18).

Like in the UK system, the Spanish government is ruled by the presidential principle, the cabinet principle of collective responsibility and the ministerial principle. Although the cabinet principle of collective responsibility is important, in periods of absolute majority the presidential principle tends to gain the upper hand. There is wide autonomy for the ministries, in spite of a coordinating ministry of the presidency (*Ministerio de la presidencia*). Several delegated committees are used for coordination of relevant policies. In the Zapatero governments they comprised crisis situations, economic matters, scientific and technological policy, policies on regional autonomy, immigration policy, climate change, equality policy, international cooperation and development, and secret services (Colino and Olmeda, 2012; López Calvo, 1996: 48). Reform of the core executive and public administration has always been on the agenda, but during the financial crisis Prime Minister Mariano Rajoy introduced a major programme supervised by a committee and supported by the OECD in order to increase the transparency and efficiency of government (OECD, 2014a).

In Greece, the reinforced electoral system created a bipolarised two-party system and two smaller left-wing parties until 2012. Until the sovereign debt crisis broke out in 2010, prime ministers usually came from the two main parties – New Democracy (Nea Dimokratia – ND) or the social democratic Panhellenic Socialist Movement (Panneliniko Sosialistiko Kinima – PASOK). They were able to rely on a strong majority in parliament (*Vouli*), which has many of the characteristics of the French National Assembly. Although cabinet meetings are held, most decision-making is taken in smaller 'mini-cabinets' (permanent committees) related to specific policy areas of the general government council (KYSIM), the foreign and defence policy council (KYSEA), the council for economic and monetary policy (ASOP) as well as the council to implement the programme of the government.

This means that the cabinet principle is always undermined by these less formal settings of decision-making. During the Andreas Papandreou period (1981–9, 1993–6) and the Kostas Simitis period (1996–2004) the collegiality disappeared completely and was replaced by a presidential approach. Decision-making was done mainly by the prime minister. Kostas Karamanlis (2004–9) reintroduced a more collegial approach, with the result that cabinets met at least once a week (Zervakis and Auernheimer, 2009: 834). Clientelism, corruption and institutional inertia have been continuous features in Greek government since at least the 1980s under prime minister Andreas Papandreou. The successive austerity packages during the financial crisis have certainly contributed to a decline in government capacity under the still presidential leadership of the prime minister (Visvizi, 2014, 2016). A seminal study by Kevin Featherstone and Dimitris Papadimitriou shows that actually one has to understand the role of the 'powerful' prime minister as being more of a solitary centre in segmented government, similar to the governments of Central and Eastern Europe, particularly Bulgaria and Romania (see Goetz and Margetts, 1999). So government itself plays a more lowly function, in part due to the fact that ministers have ministerial autonomy and are able to create personal fiefdoms over time. This is possible because most governments are unicolour absolute majority governments and remain in place for long periods of time. Moreover, the prime minister has a very inefficient office. In this regard, one can understand why Greece has so far been demonstrating the strong features of a 'failed state' (for more detail, see Featherstone and Papadimitriou, 2013, 2015; on the failed state, see Featherstone, 2011).

In the case of Italy one has to differentiate between the First and Second Republics. In the First Republic (1948–92) a consensual style of politics prevailed with a so-called 'imperfect bipartyism', because the communist party was excluded from power due to the Cold War. However, in the Second Republic since 1992, several changes to the electoral system and the emergence of a new party system have led to a tendency towards bipolar majoritarian politics between the left and the right. The UK model has been the main template for the new Italian politics, but a lack of discipline within political parties, defections and personalities have led to very fragmented parliaments.

In the Italian First Republic (1948–92) the prime minister was just *primus inter pares* and a mediator between the parties. Moreover, well into the 1980s, it had almost no own material and human resources and was in a worse position than most ministries. Coordination was achieved mainly through interministerial committees. A process of incremental reform of the prime minister's office and government started in the late 1980s. In 1988, the government of Ciriaco de Mita approved Law 400, which is a long document defining very exactly the roles of the prime minister and government. Also a general secretariat of the presidency with a general secretary is attached to the prime ministers' office. This was an important law which triggered further reforms throughout the 1990s and into the new millennium, particularly after the collapse of the First Republic due to the network of systemic corruption affecting most parties that were in government between 1948 and 1992. The Second Republic after 1993 was under considerable pressure to improve government capacity due to the impact of European integration, particularly during the second Berlusconi (2001–6) and the second Prodi (2006–8) governments (Cotta and Verzichelli, 2007: 119–20). The prime minister and government are supported by a well-resourced general secretariat with a staff of around 4,500 staff. Within the general secretariat the prime minister and vice-prime ministers have their own office. In 2014, the budget allocated to the secretariat was about €3.1 million (Cotta and Marangoni, 2015: 185; Cotta and Verzichelli, 2007: 127–9; 2015: 138–42). Since the 1980s, the finance and treasury ministers have become quite important actors in the government. The permanent crisis of the finances in Italy was the major reason for this upgrade. The priorities of the Italian government became quite visible when the fourth government of Berlusconi (2007–12) had to step down and give way to a technocratic government led by former European Commissioner Mario Monti from 1995 to 2004 (Culpepper, 2014: 1276–8).

Prime minister Matteo Renzi (2014–16) tried very hard to reform the political system, but a failed referendum in 2016 halted his attempt. This example shows the difficulty in showing leadership in the Italian context, as it may backfire, particularly if the prime minister is not able to convince civil society at large (Pasquino, 2016; Pasquino and Valbruzzi, 2017). After the general elections of April 2018, a coalition government of the rightwing populist Lega Nord (Northern League) and the citizens' movement Cinque Stelle (Five Star) was formed under prime minister Giuseppe Conte on 1 June 2018. The coalition government has a stable majority in both houses, but its programme is rather difficult to implement in the context of Economic and Monetary Union, which is a major constraint on government policy which has a debt level of 130 per cent of GDP, far away from the 60 per cent threshold prescribed by the Maastricht criteria.

In Central and Eastern Europe, democratic consolidation and Europeanisation were two faces of the same coin. The EU was the major agent in transforming post-communist governments into Western-style ones. Much has already been mentioned in the section on semi-presidentialism, so here we will focus more on the prime minister and government.

All Central and Eastern European countries had to undertake a major cultural transition in the way they perceived the role of government. In all countries, the Soviet model of the Council of Ministers meant that it was subordinated to the politburo of the communist party or similar entity. Basically, the council of ministers just implemented policies decided by the politburo and had barely any autonomy. It was not a political body but was in charge of technical and administrative tasks. In this context, adopting the Western European style of liberal democracy, partly imposed by the EU, led to rebuilding of the Council of Ministers into a truly autonomous political body. Moreover, cabinet formation and governance became important aspects in moving to efficient democratic party government (Blondel et al., 2007: 3–4). Here is not the place to delve too deeply into this. The excellent studies by Jean Blondel, Ferdinand Müller Rommel and Darina Malová (2001, 2007) as well as Vesselin Dimitrov, Klaus H. Goetz and Hellmut Wollmann (2006) have traced these transformations. When analysing governments in Central and Eastern Europe we should be aware about this transition from a more autocratic non-transparent culture of decision-making to a democratic transparent one. Traces of autocratic non-transparent culture will persist but erode over time. Meanwhile, Central and Eastern European countries have had a period of almost thirty years of democracy to get used to the new culture of cabinet governance (Blondel et al., 2007: 16–17). The OECD is an important

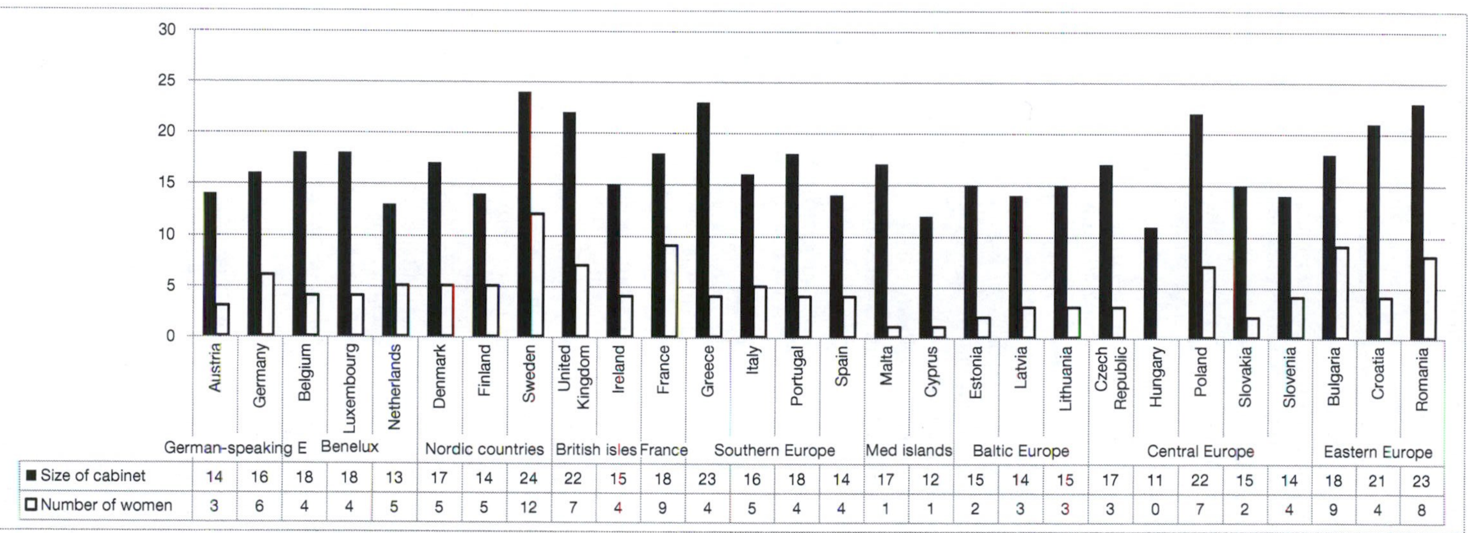

	Austria	Germany	Belgium	Luxembourg	Netherlands	Denmark	Finland	Sweden	United Kingdom	Ireland	France	Greece	Italy	Portugal	Spain	Malta	Cyprus	Estonia	Latvia	Lithuania	Czech Republic	Hungary	Poland	Slovakia	Slovenia	Bulgaria	Croatia	Romania
■ Size of cabinet	14	16	18	18	13	17	14	24	22	15	18	23	16	18	14	17	12	15	14	15	17	11	22	15	14	18	21	23
□ Number of women	3	6	4	4	5	5	5	12	7	4	9	4	5	4	4	1	1	2	3	3	3	0	7	2	4	9	4	8

Figure 4.3 Cabinet sizes in EU member-states, 2016

Source: Bågenholm and Weeks (2017: 9).

support in this respect, but also peers in Western Europe (Blondel et al. 2007: 15). There are learning processes that have taken place that have contributed to the efficiency of governments in most Central and Eastern European countries. However, negative cases persist with the cases of Hungary and Romania.

In the first phase of democratic consolidation between 1990 and 2003, in most Central and Eastern European countries it was difficult for a party to gain an absolute majority and sustain it over two terms, therefore four-fifths of all governments were coalition governments, and just two-thirds of governments had an outright majority (Blondel et al., 2007: 46). Only in Poland, the Czech Republic, Estonia, Slovakia, Romania and Bulgaria were there single party governments (Blondel et al., 2007: 47). Therefore, governmental instability and poor cabinet governance were a major feature during this period. Cabinet governance improved only over time and with differences across countries. The European integration process was an important factor in pushing governments to be stable and efficient.

For a long time the Polish party system showed difficulties in achieving consolidation. After the legislative elections of 2007, Donald Tusk's Civic Platform (PO), a liberal democratic party, contributed to a bipolar majoritarian party system configuration. Since then Poland has moved to a two-party system alternating between the centre-right liberal Civic Platform (PO) and the conservative rightwing Law and Justice party (PiS). In the early years, divided government led to conflicts between the president and the prime minister. Moreover, the lack of experience of coalition governance contributed to the collapse of governments up to 1997 (Taras, 2006: 364–5). According to Jean Blondel and Ferdinand Müller-Rommel, between 1991 and 1997 there were six prime ministers and seven governments, most of them coalition governments. Moreover, there was a large turnover of personnel. In an eight-year period, there were 107 ministers who had an average incumbency of 1.48 years (Blondel and Müller-Rommel, 2001: 58). There was also a tendency towards a majoritarian two-alliance system, induced by the proportional electoral system introduced in 1993. After 1997, the majoritarian system led to greater longevity of government. Between 1997 and 2007 there were four prime ministers and four governments. Also, during the period from 2007 to 2017, there have so far been just four prime ministers: Donald Tusk (2007–14), Ewa Kopacz (2014–16), Beate Szydlo (2016–7) and Mateusz Marowiecki (since December 2017), and four governments with absolute majorities. The cabinet is normally quite large with between seventeen and twenty-three ministers, and cabinet meetings are prepared by the chancellery of the cabinet. The chancellery can be regarded as an important resource for the prime minister to which different departments are attached. According to the excellent research of Radoslaw Zubek, the Polish government was subject to considerable transformation since its transition to democracy. Originally, the communist politburo of the Polish United Workers' Party (PZPR) dominated government decisions. A prime minister and government did exist, but it was merely an executive arm of the politburo, quite a common model across Central and Eastern Europe. It also had an incipient prime minister's office. European integration played a major role in shifting government structures to more Western-style ones. Between 1990 and 1997, a major shift was undertaken to a moderate semi-presidential regime (Zubek, 2001: 912–14). In this process, the prime minister and government were strengthened considerably. Apart from the shift in power from presidency and parliament to the government, the constitution of 1997 introduced a constructive motion of censure which acted as a protective shield against ill-designed challenges to the government. It increased considerably the political stability of the government. In September 1997 a reform of the core executive was undertaken by the Cimoswiecicz government (Ziemer, 2013: 93). The former prime minister's office was transformed into a large chancellery with several departments, including one for policy analysis and legislation (created in 2000) (Zubek, 2001: 920–5). Moreover, a permanent committee of the council of ministers was established in order to achieve inner cabinet coordination (Blondel and Müller-Rommel, 2001: 58–9; Ziemer, 2013: 102–3). During the premiership of Jaroslaw Kaczyński he was able to count on the support of his brother Lech Kaczyński, who was president until his tragic death in a plane crash in 2010. Donald Tusk and Ewa Kopacz were able to count on the support of president Bronislaw Komorowski who was from the same party, and this facilitated policy-making considerably. Also prime ministers Beate Szydlo and Mateusz Marowiecki have been able to count on a president of the same party, namely Andrzej Duda. The president can convene meetings of the council of ministers in order to emphasise specific aspects of policy-making that should be given attention. This approach was also taken frequently by Lech Kaczyński during his term in office (Ziemer, 2013: 103).

The Hungarian core political system has taken many devices from the German model. However, in contrast to the German system, it follows a majoritarian style. The prime minister's position in relation to the cabinet and parliament is stronger. Between 1990 and 2018 there were eight prime ministers, which indicates that it is a reasonably stable system, certainly when compared with Poland.

The Hungarian government orientates itself considerably towards the German and Austrian chancellor model of government, indicating that government stability is an important factor in Hungarian politics. This is ensured by the constructive motion of censure copied from German Basic Law (Schiemann, 2004: 130). This also means that, over time, the Hungarian government has gained more resources and power in order to implement its policies. At the centre of this 'chancellorisation' is the prime minister's office, which was substantially reinforced in 1998 (Schiemann, 2004: 131, 137–9). Between 1998 and 2002, the first Viktor Orbán government structures increased quite substantially. According to Attila Ágh, staff increased from 316 in 1997 to 536 in 2002 and a centre for strategic analysis was brought in, to coordinate the processes of European integration (Ágh, 2003: 100–8). After 2010, Viktor Orbán returned to power and further reinforced centralisation. However, the centralisation of power did not contribute to a stronger state and better governance (Brusis, 2017; Zubek, 2008)

Although Lithuania has had sixteen governments since its transition to democracy, it has been far more stable than Estonia and Latvia. The party system has been, if compared to the other Baltic republics, quite stable, being dominated by the leftwing Lithuanian Social Democratic Party (LSDP) on the one hand, and the Homeland Union on the other. None of these political parties is able to achieve absolute majorities so that it has to coalesce with smaller parties. Between 1990 and 2000, governmental consolidation was quite difficult leading to eleven governments with nine different prime ministers. However, between 2000 and 2017, there were just five governments and four prime ministers. The longest period was served by prime minister Algirdas Brazauskas who headed two governments

(2001–4, 2004–6). He was the first president of Lithuania between 1993 and 1998. The two governments were clearly very important, because they completed the process of the accession of Lithuania to the EU. However, Brazauskas was also involved in a number of corruption scandals, a problem that affects many politicians, like the former president Roland Paksas who was impeached, or even members of the parliament in Lithuania (*The Independent*, 29 June 2010). In terms of the core government executive structures, the OECD has been instrumental in contributing to more efficient governance structures, including strategic planning. Government shares resources with the presidency, which clearly has a mandate by the constitution to act in foreign affairs. At the centre of core executive government is the office of government, but also the ministry of finance. A commission for the improvement of public administration (the so-called Sunset Commission) was set up in 1999 and was attached to the government office. Public finance processes are coordinated and led by the ministry of finance (OECD, 2015: 43–6).

Bulgaria and Romania are the two countries in the EU with the lowest level of government capacity. One major factor is that political corruption and a lack of transparency are still major problems in these two countries. As already mentioned, semi-presidentialism is sometimes abused by the president, so that in the end prime ministers and governments are rather weak.

In the case of Bulgaria, government consolidation began to take place only after 1997. Before 1997, political parties were not consolidated, and defections of members of parliament were rather usual. Moreover, governments did not last very long. Between 1990 and 1997, there were six prime ministers and six governments, none of them completing the legislature period and none lasting longer than two years (Dimitrov, 2005: 189). Between 1997 and 2009, there were three governments led by Ivan Kostov from the Union of Democratic Forces (UDF), Simeon Sakskoburski from National Movement Simeon II), and the grand coalition of Sergei Stanishev from the Bulgarian Socialist Party, respectively. In spite of all the problems within and outside government, they contributed to increasing stability in anticipation of joining the EU. However, after the grand coalition, the National Movement Simeon II was heavily punished by the electorate, and a new party called Citizens for the European Development of Bulgaria (GERB) led by the former bodyguard Boyko Borisov emerged on the right. Borisov had been a very popular mayor of Sofia beforehand. Since then, if we exclude the caretaker governments in between, he has dominated Bulgarian politics. The core government in Bulgaria consists of an administration of the council of ministers headed by a secretary general. Moreover, the prime minister has his or her own office with a chief of staff. The Economic Policy directorate located in the administration of the council of ministers is also quite important. However, the governance of policy-making and coordination has been lacking in efficiency and transparency, leading to regular disagreements between the prime minister and individual ministers, particularly in quite sensitive issues such as the judiciary sector, appointment of the head of secret services, or major reforms undermining fiefdoms of clientelism for certain parties (Dimitrov, 2006).

A similar assessment can be made about Romania. Government has been weak and quite unstable. Until the end of 2000, government instability and collapse were more the rule than the exception. Between 1990 and 2000 there were five prime ministers, without counting the two acting ones, and eight governments.

Clearly, the government of Adrian Nastaše (2000–4) was a major milestone in achieving more consolidation in the executive. Moreover, the conservative-liberal governments of Călin Popescu-Tăriceanu (December 2004–December 2008) and Emil Boc (December 2008–February 2012) further contributed to a strengthening of government. However, Victor Ponta's three governments between 2012 and 2015 were rather destabilising due to conflicts with the president Basescu and then Klaus Iohannis. In the end, the EU had to intervene to resolve the conflict between the political parties by introducing a road map. Ponta was replaced by the independent Dacian Cioloş (2015–17), a former European Commissioner in charge of agriculture. However, instability due to the dominance of the social democratic party (PSD) in the political system has prevailed, clearly being a major factor blocking reform in the political system and the economy. According to Neculai-Christian Surubaru, Romania may be characterised as a dysfunctional state, which is dominated by politicians that try to prevent any change to the political system. Surubaru speaks of a 'negative' politicisation of politicians that try to prevent transparent and accountable government from emerging (Surubaru, 2015). Moreover, the original 1991 constitution was rather badly designed, putting the judiciary under considerable executive control (Gallagher and Andrievici, 2008: 148–9). Also the constitutional reform of 2003 did not improve this situation very much either. Moreover, the job of prime minister is quite a thankless task, similar to that in France. Although the prime minister and government undertake all the jobs, it is normally the president that receives all the attention and credit (Gallagher and Andrievici, 2008: 143–6). Victor Ponta tried to become president in the 2015 presidential elections, but lost to the outsider Klaus Iohannis who was supported by the opposition parties. Similar to Bulgaria, there are still problems in the professionalisation of the core executive. A secretariat-general of government with several departments supports the prime minister and the government.

One should also add Malta as a typical majoritarian system. In spite of a single transferable voting system (STV) which clearly allows for better proportional representation of political parties, in Malta it has a majoritarian effect. Due to the dominance of the two political parties, the Nationalist Party and the Labour Party, Malta has a reputation for high levels of clientelism, patronage and even political corruption. Allegedly, but not proven, the present prime minister Joseph Muscat's wife was mentioned in the Panama papers. Due to growing opposition to his government and criticisms from the media, he called for early elections, which he won (*Deutsche Welle*, 1 May 2017, 4 June 2017). The killing of journalist Daphne Caruana Galizia by a car bomb on 16 October 2017, who was allegedly investigating the business dealings of the government with the Russian mafia, clearly put prime minister Muscat in the spotlight again (*BBC News*, 17 October 2017).

Consensual patterns of government

The traditional consensus democracies can be found in central Western Europe – consisting of Belgium, the Netherlands, Luxembourg, Switzerland, Austria and Germany – and the Nordic countries. The main characteristic of consensual government is coalition government alongside strong cooperation between the main parties in most areas of politics (Box 4.5). In these countries, such coalition governments are necessary because the party systems are so fragmented that no one party is able to achieve an absolute majority. The political culture established since the beginning of the twentieth century has adjusted to this fact and accommodates diversity through compromise. One of the factors that allows diversity to be expressed in elections is the proportional representation system. The Netherlands is the country with the most favourable conditions for representation, because MPs are elected in one constituency, which matches the Dutch territory, and the threshold is 0.67 per cent. In some countries, for example Belgium and the Netherlands, a coalition government has become a way of life.

Box 4.5 Coalition government as central to consensus democracies

The traditional consensus democracies in continental Europe and the Nordic countries are characterised by a high level of fragmentation of the party system. Since the nineteenth century, these divided societies have developed their own technology of government building in order to achieve political stability. Due to the fact that no one party is able to achieve an absolute majority, coalition government between different parties is the normal outcome. The winning party tries to find parties that it is able to coalesce with (in German, *Koalitionsfähigkeit*). Sometimes ideological differences prevent such coalition-making, e.g. a coalition between a centre-right party and a radical left party, or a social democratic party and a rightwing populist party. After the electoral results which no party is able to win outright, there is a formalised process to select a new government. This ritual of coalition formation entails the use of an *informateur* (appointed by the king in the cases of the Netherlands and Belgium). The main task of the *informateur* is to find out what the different parties seek to achieve within the coalition. The process may take quite a long time, in some cases months. This is followed by a second phase, when a *formateur* is appointed. The *formateur* is in charge of putting the new government together and writing down an extensive coalition agreement in which all the rules of the game are set out. The whole process of *informateur* and *formateur* together may last between three and four months, depending on the difficulty of the negotiations; however, fragmentation of the party system may contribute to even more lengthier negotiations as cases in Belgium and the Netherlands have shown. The four main questions that a *formateur* has to deal with are:

1 Which parties will form the new cabinet?
2 What will be the content of the new government's programme?
3 How will ministerial portfolios be distributed among governing parties?
4 Who will be nominated as ministers?

(adapted from De Winter et al., 2000: 309)

Out of these negotiations, the ideal is to get an absolute majority of votes in parliament, in some cases in both houses of parliament, such as in the

Netherlands. This means sometimes coalition comprises several parties to achieve this absolute majority. The main aim is to have a stable cohesive coalition. The more parties there are and the more the ideology is different, the more difficult it will be to keep the government together over the four-year/five-year period.

The following coalition types can emerge after negotiations (Table 4.6):

1 **A minimum winning coalition**: this normally consisting of two parties that are able to achieve the absolute majority threshold; however, in very fragmented party systems like the Belgian system it can include more parties. Minimum winning coalition is the dominant form across Europe.
2 **An oversized coalition**: this consists of more parties than are necessary for an absolute majority. They frequently occur in Finland and were also present in the French Fourth Republic until 1959 and in the Italian First Republic. Oversized coalitions are also used in moments of national crisis or technocratic governments.
3 **The minority coalition government**: this is very common in the Nordic countries. The coalition government has no majority in parliament but is tolerated by the other parties. Normally, minority coalition governments try to get majorities for individual or packages of bills among parties in parliament. Such practice has been perfected in Denmark, which clearly relies on a national culture of consensual politics.

After deciding on the parties that should form the coalition, a lengthy coalition agreement of 80–200 pages is agreed defining the rules of the game within the coalition governance, and in the different external arenas, particularly parliament. A legislative programme is included in the coalition agreement. The coalition agreement is a compromise of what is possible.

Coalition governance then becomes a major challenge for the government parties due to the fact that they always have to coordinate policy statements with their partners. Moreover, parties may face opposition in their constituencies. One crucial skill that a prime minister has to have is the ability for conflict management and direction towards a compromise. Normally, a coalition committee of the party chiefs tries to sort out the major problems in order to keep the coalition going.

Last but not least, coalition termination is also very important. In many cases, compromise may lead to losses for some government parties at the following elections. In this regard, there is always a tension between government responsibility and party politics, and in many cases it may lead to divisions within political parties.

The Austrian Wolfgang C. Müller, the Norwegian-American Kaare Strøm and Swede Torbjörn Bergman pioneered a more systematic research on coalition government in Western Europe. They were able to bring together a team of excellent researchers who were able to give us more insight into the secrets of coalition government (Müller and Strøm, 2000a; Strøm et al., 2008).

Table 4.5 Government and public administration in Europe

Regional clusters	*Countries*	*Core executive administration*		*Total public employment (different years) 2014–2016*	*Share of public employment(%) 2014–2016*	*Share of general government spending in terms of GDP(2017)*
		Name of coordinating unit at core executive administration	*Size of staff (2010s)*			
				Total		
Drei-SAT	Austria	Staatskanzleramt	1,528	683,900	15.9	49.2
	Germany	Bundeskanzleramt	620	4,549,000	10.6	43.9
	Switzerland	Bundeskanzlei	270	500,900	9.9	34.2
Benelux	Belgium	Chancellerie Federale	143	848,800	18.5	52.2
	Luxembourg	Ministére d´État	100	50,320	12.4	43.1
	Netherlands	Ministerium van algemene Zaken	74	1,171,000	12.8	42.5
Nordic Europe	Denmark	Statsministeriet	74	824,000	29.13	51.2
	Finland	Valtioneuvoston kanslia	550	621,000	24.3	54.0
	Iceland	Stjórnarrad	41	46,110	14.26	42.5
	Norway	Statsministeren kontor	70	825,000	30.0	49.9
	Sweden	Regeringskansliet	4,600	1,375,000	28.6	40.9
British Isles	UK	Prime Minister Office Cabinet Office	2,050	5,139,000	16.4	42.4
	Ireland	Department of the Taoiseach	190	298,200	15.0	26.3
France	France	Sécretariat General Du Gouvernement	2,100	5,886,000	21.4	56.5

Southern Europe	Greece	General Secretariat of Government	80	722,920	18.0	47.3
	Italy	Segreteria Generale della Presidenza del Consiglio di Ministri	1,246	3,337,800	13.6	48.7
	Portugal	Secretaria Geral da Presidencia do Conselho de Ministros	133	683,950	15.2	45.7
	Spain	Presidencia del Gobierno	549	2,904,000	15.7	41.0
Mediterranean Islands	Malta	Office of the prime minister	n.d.	30,645	25.8	36.2
	Cyprus	Secretariat of the Council of Ministers	n.d.	50,715	14.0	37.5
Central Europe	Czech Rep.	Urad vlady	104	838,000	16.2	41.6
	Hungary	Miniszterelnökség	n.d.	942,510	21.9	49.6
	Poland	State chancellery	628	975,150	n.d.	41.5
	Slovakia	Úrad vlády	484	439,190	19.4	45.4
	Slovenia	Generalni Sekretariat Vlade	153	163,670	17.4	47.8
Baltic Europe	Estonia	Riigikantselei	160	143,200	23.0	40.1
	Latvia	Valsts kanceleja	122	178,250	20.1	37.0
	Lithuania	Vyriausbès kanceliarija	n.d.	349,900	22.8	35.1
Eastern Europe	Bulgaria	Administration of Council of Ministers	n.d.	480,000	16.0	35.1
	Romania	Secretariatul General al Guvernului	n.d.	532,350	13.0	33.6

Source: Author's compilation based on OECD (2015b: 93, 2017a, 2017b); OECD websites of core government websites; for Greece estimated figures based on Featherstone and Papadimitriou (2015: 226).

Table 4.6 Types of government in Europe, 1945–2017

	Nr. of governments	*Nr. of governments*	*Number of years*	*SPMA*		*SPMI %*		*OC %*		*MWC %*		*MC %*		*Technocratic governments / Caretaker governments / non-partisan*	
				%	*Time*	*Nr.*	*Time*	*Nr.*	*Time*	*Nr.*	*Time*	*Nr.*	*Time*		
Drei-Sat	Austria	29	72	4 (5.6)	17 (13.8)	1 (3.5)	0.6 (0.8)	2 (6.9)	4.6 (6.4)	22 (75.8)	61 (84.7)				
	Germany	25	68					4 (16)	12 (17.7)	21 (84)	56 (82.5)				
	Switzerland	19	70					16 (84.2)	58 (82.8)	3 (15.8)	12 (17.1)				
Benelux	Belgium	43	71	3 (6.9)	4 (5.6)	2 (0.43)	0.1 (0.1)	9 (20.9)	13.5 (19)	28 (65.1)	53.1 (74.8)	0		1 (2.3)	0.3 (0.4)
x	Luxembourg	20	72					12 (60)	50.8 (70.6)	8 (40)	21.2 (29.4)				
	Netherlands	30	72					10 (32.3)	25.2 (35)	14 (45.2)	42 (58.3)	1 (3.3)	1.5 (2.1)	5 (16.1)	2.6 (3.6)
Nordic Europe	Denmark	34	72			12 (34.3)	22.7 (31.5)	1 (2.9)	0.3 (0.4)	3 (8.6)	5.5 (7.6)	18 (51.4)	43.5 (60.4)		
	Finland	45	72			3 (8.3)	4.6 (6.4)	28 (62.2)	52 (72.5)	4 (11.1)	6.4 (5.6)	3 (8.3)	1.8 (2.5)	7 (19.5)	3 (4.2)
	Iceland	35	71			4 (12.5)		2 (6.2)		24 (75)		3 (9.4)		2 (6.2)	
	Norway	31	72	6 (19.4)	16 (22.2)	13 (41.9)	26 (36.1)			6 (19.4)	16 (22.2)	6 (19.4)	14 (19.5)		
	Sweden	30	72	4 (13.3)	5 (7)	16 (53.3)	49.2 (68.3)			5 (16.7)	17.2 (23.8)	5 (16.7)	0.5 (0.7)		
British Isles	UK	26	72	23 (92)	63.5 (88.2)	2 (8)	3.5 (14)			1 (4)	5 (6.9)				
	Ireland	26	69	7 (26.9)	19 (27.5)	4 (15.4)	9 (13)	1 (3.8)	5 (7.2)	6 (23.1)	30.2 (43.8)	8 (30.8)	5.8 (8.4)		
France	France IV	24	12					21 (80.8)	8.8 (73.3)	2 (7.7)	1.2 (10)	1 (3.9)	2 (16.7)		
	France V	33	58	8 (24.2)	12.6 (13.2)	9 (27.3)	10 (17.2)	2 (6.1)	7 (12.1)	14 (42.4)	28.4 (49)				
	France IV+V	57	70	8 (13.5)	12.6 (18)	9 (15.3)	10 (14.3)	23 (39)	15.8 (22.6)	16 (27.1)	29.6 (42.3)	1 (1.7)	2 (2.9)		

Southern Europe	Greece	23	71	14 (60.9)	35.3 (86.1)			2 (8.7)	2 (5)	3 (13)	2.9 (7.1)			4 (17.4)	0.8 (2)
	Italy I	48	48			11 (22.9)	8.3 (17.3)	23 (47,9)	39 (81.3)	2 (4,2)	1.8 ((3.8)	8 (16.7)	6.3 (13.1)	48 (16.7)	1.6 (3.3)
	Italy II	14	23					1 (7.1)	0.6 (2.6)	10 (71.4)	19.8 (86.1)			3 (21.4)	2.6 (11.3)
	Italy I+II	62	71			11 (17.7)	8.3 (11.7)	24 (38.7)	39.6 (55.8)	12 (19.4)		8 (12.9)	6.3 (8.9)	11 (17.7)	4.2 (5.9)
	Portugal	20	41	3 (15)	12.6 (31.5)	6 (30)	7.4 (18.5)	1 (5)	2.4 (6)	7 (35)	16.3 (40.8)			3 (15)	1.34 (3.4)
	Spain	14	40	5 (35.7)	18.8 (47)	8 (57.1)	20.3 (50.7)							1 (7.1)	0.9 (2.3)
Mediterranean Islands	Malta	12	43	12 (100)	43 (100)										
	Cyprus	13	57					2 (15.4)	10 (23.3)			5 (38.5)	25 (58.1)	6 (46.2)	22 (38.6)
Central Europe	Czech Republic	13	27							5 (38.5)	10 (37)	4 (30.8)	10.8 (40)	4 (30.8)	6.2 (23)
	Hungary	9	27					5 (55.6)	14.6 (54.1)	4 (44.4)	12.4 (45.9)				
	Poland	19	27	2 (10.5)	2.2 (8.1)	3 (15.8)	2 (7.4)	6 (31.6)	6.7 (24.8)	4 (21.5)	8.3 (30.7)	4 (21.5)	3.8 (14.1)		
	Slovakia	16	25	1 (11.2)	4 (16)			6 (66.7)	13 (52)	2 (22.3)	8 (32)				
	Slovenia	12	27					11 (91.7)	26 (96.3)			1 (8.3)	1 (3.7)		
Baltic Europe	Estonia	16	27					7 (37.5)	10.5 (39)	6 (31.3)	8 (29.6)	3 (31.3)	8.5 (31.5)		
	Latvia	21	27	1 (4.8)	3 (11.1)			7 (23.8)	8 (29.6)	10 (57.1)	13.5 (50)	3 (14.3)	2.5 (9.3)		
	Lithuania	17	27	4 (23.5)	4 (14.7)					8 (47.1)	18.5 (80.4)	3 (17.6)	3 (11.1)	2 (11.8)	1.5 (5.6)
Eastern Europe	Bulgaria	15	27	2 (12.5)	6 (22.2)	2 (12.5)	5 (18.5)	2 (12.5)	8 (29.6)			1 (6.2)	3 (11.1)	8 (56.2)	4 (14.8)
	Croatia	14	27	5 (35.7)	8.6 (31.1)			1 (7.1)	1.1 (4)	4 (28.6)	9.5 (34.4)	4 (28.6)	8.4 (30.5)		
	Romania	23	27			2 (8.7)	8 (29.6)			11 (47.8)	15.5 (57.4)			10 (43.8)	3.5 (13)
		769	52.4	104 (13.5)		98 (12.7)		182 (23.6)		237 (31)		82 (11)		64 (8.3)	

Source: own compilation by author based on data from individual chapters by different authors in Müller and Strøm (2000a); Pasquino (2015b: 301); Caramani (2015: 237); individual chapters of Ismayr (2009, 2010); Nordsieck (2017).

Notes: SPMA – Single party majority (absolute majority); SPMI – Single party minority; OC – Oversized coalition; MWC – Minimum winning coalition; MC – Minority coalition.

In Belgium, coalition government formation is fairly complicated because of the federalisation of the country. Federalisation has led to a considerable devolution of policies, including foreign policy, and the national government has now only a *primus inter pares* position in relation to the other subnational units, with its main function being that of coordination. This means that the coalition government requires a high level of consultation and coordination in different cabinet committees. One important protecting factor in relation to parliament is the constructive motion of censure, which makes it quite difficult for the opposition to topple the government (Fiers and Krouwel, 2005: 130). Another important aspect of Belgian politics is that it is dominated by parties. Since 1945, this 'party-ocracy' has developed a patronage system, which is still relevant across different parts of the political system. However, European integration, federalisation and new social movements asking for greater transparency are undermining its viability and financial sustainability in view of the poor financial record of the Belgian state (De Winter et al., 1996; 2000: 342). Due to the fragmentation of the party system which competes in two separate arenas at national level, coalition formation has become quite complex and more difficult. Normally, several parties are needed for government formation. The second Yves Leterme government (2009–11) and the Elio Di Rupio government (2011–14) needed five and six coalition partners respectively. However, the Charles Michel government consisted of just four coalition partners. Prime minister Charles Michel is also a good example of the top government job not needing to be allocated to the largest party, but it is based on a compromise. The liberal party of Charles Michel was only fourth in Belgian elections and the second largest in Wallonia (for more, see Magone, 2017: chapter six).

In the Netherlands, because of the need to accommodate the interests of the different coalition partners and factions inside the party, the position of the prime minister is formally one of *primus inter pares*. However, as in Belgium, the position of the prime minister has gained a greater reputation because it is central to the cohesion of the cabinet. The importance of coordination in order to have a successful government has become crucial. There is also an increasing longevity of government, which is helping to strengthen the executive. The prime minister's office has gained more resources over time. In both countries, the prime ministers are required to be actively involved in foreign relations, particularly the Belgian prime minister, because Brussels is host to so many international organisations (Fiers and Krouwel, 2005: 135–6). According to Peter Mair, the Netherlands has been at the forefront in terms of innovative coalition formation, allowing for a wide range of coalition possibilities. This became even more important due to the growing fragmentation of the party system. Only the Party of Freedom (PVV) of Geert Wilders is shunned by all the other political parties (Mair, 2008a: 243–4). However, majorities have become more difficult in both houses of parliament in the past decades. Although a majority in the Tweede Kamer, the lower house, is possible, the changing composition of the Senate after the provincial elections may not produce a congruent majority. In this case, the prime minister needs to negotiate each policy with different parties. The small religion-based parties and the Animal party, in particular, may play an important role in this respect (Magone, 2017: 192; Thomassen et al., 2014).

Informateurs and *formateurs* are also used in the Nordic countries, particularly in Finland and Denmark, while in Norway, Sweden, Germany and Austria coalition bargaining is more freestyle.

Last, but not least, Luxembourg also belongs to this pattern of government. Since 1945, all governments in Luxembourg have been coalition governments and, in the same way as in Belgium, a highly sophisticated model of coalition governance has been created, which requires the coalition partners to be extremely loyal to the government. This has created a stable government in the country (Dumont and De Winter, 2000: 424–5).

Although, since 1945, the Benelux countries have almost always had coalition governments, other countries have also had periods of single-minority government. An updated version of coalition governments in Europe would largely confirm the findings of Wolfgang C. Müller and Kaare Strøm that, between 1945 and 2017, Germany, the Netherlands and Luxembourg were the countries with the longest periods of coalition governments, while Belgium, Finland, France, Italy, Austria and Denmark followed close behind (Müller and Strøm, 2000b: 2) (see Table 4.5).

It is important to note that, over time, coalitions have become more stable in all these countries. Until the 1960s, the collapse of coalitions before the end of their legislatures was quite common. However, since the 1970s, most countries have been able to achieve a more stable coalition governance. The role of extensive coalition agreements stipulating the rules of the game has been important in achieving this, but the practice of creating smaller core government cabinets has proved to be the best way to deal with conflictive issues.

In Germany, the chancellor's office plays a major role in controlling the way government runs. Several interdepartmental cabinets work together to solve most of the problems of the government. According to Thomas Saalfeld, it was common practice to reject cabinet agenda items if they were not previously agreed between the ministers (Saalfeld, 2000: 60–3). The constitutional position of the chancellor is fairly strong, leading to a position of strength in the cabinet. Moreover, the chancellor will usually also be the head of the strongest party, and this strengthens the position even more. In spite of coalition governments, there are presidentialising tendencies in chancellorships that allow very stable governments to be created. However, because of the practice of consultation with interest groups and other important social and political actors, German political culture does not lead to majoritarian rule. The federal system, through the changing Bundesrat composition, is an important suspensive veto player, which contributes to a more consensual style of leadership despite the presidentialising tendencies of the political system (Poguntke, 2005: 65–7). Helmut Kohl (1982–98) and Gerhard Schröder (1998–2005) represent these presidentialising tendencies of the German government, but chancellor Angela Merkel (from 2005) shows that for a grand coalition between the CDU/CSU and the SPD (in 2005–9 and 2013–17) there is a need for a consensual approach and strong managerial and coordinating abilities. Governments are quite constrained by the Constitutional Court as well, which may rule against policies of the government if they are unconstitutional. Therefore, Peter Katzenstein characterised Germany as semi-sovereign due to this quite complex system of checks and balances (Katzenstein, 1987).

Similarly, in Austria, the chancellor democracy creates stability, and most decision-making is taken outside the formal cabinet structure, which leads to an increasing lack of transparency in decision-making (Müller, 2000: 104–5; Müller, 2006b: 104–5; Pallaver, 2005: 26). In coalition governments, which have been more frequent since the long absolute majority period under Chancellor Bruno Kreisky (1970–83), a coalition committee was an important factor in coordinating and deciding policy. Despite the existence of presidentialisation tendencies resulting from the mediatisation of politics, the Austrian chancellor's democracy is embedded in a political culture emphasising consensualism (Pallaver, 2005: 33–9). After 1983, the decline in the electoral share of the two main political parties was a major factor leading to greater competition. In particular, the rise of new parties, such as the Greens and the transformed Freedom Party (FPÖ) under Jörg Haider, led to greater polarisation between left and right. European integration led to a decline of the social partnership (*Sozialpartnerschaft*) of the main economic interest groups (Pelinka and Rosenberger, 2003: 64–9, 192–8). The rise of the populist FPÖ since the mid-1980s changed considerably consensus democracy in Austria. However, so far, the FPÖ has been a reliable coalition partner of the conservative People's Party (ÖVP). Meanwhile, they have been in government twice, between 2000–6 under prime minister Wolfgang Schüssel (ÖVP) and since 2018 under prime minister Sebastian Kurz (ÖVP). In spite of all the criticisms, coalition governance has been quite stable in the Kurz government. Moreover, it is a refreshing change to an almost permanent period of grand coalition between the ÖVP and the social democratic party (SPÖ), which since 1945, has represented 63.9 per cent of all governments (updated from Magone, 2017: 158).

The Nordic countries are also characterised by a high level of consensual politics. The main reason is that today, in all countries, no party can achieve an absolute majority, so that coalition government has been the rule. In particular, Denmark, Finland and Norway always look for a stable government, sometimes even as a minority government.

In the case of Finland, the semi-presidential system was weakened by the revised constitution, adopted in 2000 (see earlier), which had the purpose of increasing the parliamentarisation of the political system. Consensualism is an important feature of the Finnish political system, and consultation with civil society groups and the main economic groups is an important aspect of national politics. Similar to Belgium and the Netherlands, the council of ministers is fairly egalitarian. However, until the constitution reform, Finland had a strong semi-presidential system in which the president was the strongest actor and the government was confined to the implementation of the president's policies. Finland is among the countries with the highest number of governments since 1945, due to a high level of instability partly caused by the then dominance of the president. After the retirement of long-standing president Kekkonen, coalition government became more stable. A characteristic of Finnish coalition government formation is the tendency towards an oversized pattern. Clearly, this allows for a quite stable government, even if small parties leave the coalition. This has been a pattern which has also strengthened the cooperation between government and opposition (Karvonen, 2014: 79–82). Following the constitutional reform of 1999, the president's strong position was weakened and that of the government was strengthened. In spite of this, the president and the government still share some power. Many of the important policies are decided in smaller, formalised committees. There are four important standing committees that make important policy decisions and are prescribed by law: the economic policy committee (since 1977), the financial committee (since 1917), the foreign policy committee (since 1923) and the committee for the

European Union (since the 1990s) (Karvonen, 2017: 94). This is complemented by an informal 'evening school' (*iltakoulu*) at the prime minister's residence on the evening before the meeting of the council of ministers. At this evening school, government ministers and officials discuss policy and make informal decisions, which are then decided formally in the council of ministers (the state council) on Thursday mornings. The evening school goes back to the period 1937–9, when it was created to improve the relationship between agrarians and social democrats. It lost some of its importance in the 1990s and, more recently, such meetings have become less regular. It is called the 'evening school' more as an internal joke among government staff. In recent decades party leaders have been invited to the evening school, so that its character has changed quite considerably (Auffermann, 2009: 232–3; Karvonen, 2014: 98; Nousiainen, 1988: 221–2). Overall, ministers have a high level of autonomy in relation to their policy area. Indeed, the decentralisation of decision-making to the ministries has been a tendency in Finnish government. Just the central issues comprising more than one ministry or the whole government are on the agenda at cabinet meetings. This has reduced considerably the agenda of cabinet meetings. One day later, on Fridays, the president takes part in the council of ministers to decide on issues that are within his competence or shared with the government. Although the presidency works cooperatively with the government in foreign policy, the constitution has reduced considerably the powers of the president, and strengthened those of the prime minister and prime minister's office (Karvonen, 2014: 99). In a seminal article written by Karl Magnus Johansson and Tapio Raunio, European integration played a major role in strengthening the prime minister's office, which now has control over EU policy coordination. One of the main reasons for the transfer of EU coordination from the foreign ministry to the prime minister's office was the fact that, since the Treaty of Maastricht, EU policy has become domestic policy. In this sense, after the Finnish presidency of the EU in 1999, the prime minister's office was substantially upgraded with a government secretariat for EU affairs which was previously part of the ministry of foreign affairs in 2000. Therefore, the prime minister and its office have gained additional resources. While in 1970, 70 members of staff belonged to the prime minister's office, by late 2007 it had increased to 243 members of staff, 23 belonging to the EU secretariat (Johansson and Raunio, 2010: 656). This transfer of coordination of EU affairs allowed the prime minister to increase efficiency in coordination. Finland emulates in many ways the Danish model of core government executive, particularly in terms of EU coordination.

In Sweden, coalition governments had been more seldom due to the dominance of the social democrats (SDAP) in the party system. However, after 2006, even the SDAP had difficulties gaining clear majorities and had to coalesce with other leftwing parties like the Greens (Miljöpartiet) and gain support from the Radical left (Vänsterpartiet). In this regard, ideological intra-block consensus has become the main pattern for coalition building. The pragmatic style of Nordic governments also adjusted rapidly to the demands of European integration. It triggered processes of institutional transfer and learning (Bäck and Bergman, 2015; Johansson and Raunio, 2010: 650).

Similar to other political systems, there was an increase in the presidentialisation of the prime minister during 1996 and 2006 when Göran Persson was able to rule with a large majority. His strong electoral performance led to his holding a good position in relation to both the party and parliament, which are normally major constraints for a prime minister. In spite of this, the whole political culture in Sweden remains consensual. This presidentialisation has also led to a considerable increase of resources for the prime minister since the 1970s, especially since the mid-2000s (Aylott, 2005: 179–84). The consultation of interest groups in the over 300 royal committees before policies are decided is an important feature of the system. There are lots of meetings in the main government building, which leads to the characterisation of Sweden being labelled as the 'democracy of Harpsund', after the name of the building. In this sense, the social partners are still very important, although less so than they were in the 1970s (Poli, 2005: 299–305). Similarly to Sweden, during the Göran Persson governments (1996–2006), a major reform of the core government executive took place which also involved considerations on how best to coordinate EU policy. Originally, Sweden looked to the UK for a model, but later it shifted its attention to neighbouring Finland. This became clear after several reports on coordination efficiency in the Swedish core executive. In comparison to Finland, there was more resistance from stakeholders in the ministry of foreign affairs, and foreign minister Anna Lindh was a strong charismatic figure protecting the interests of that ministry. Until the EU presidency of 2001 no major changes took place, but after the death of Anna Lindh in 2003, the EU coordination secretariat was transferred to the prime minister's office. This was against the path-dependent tradition that the prime minister's office should just be slim and not a super ministry. However, the growing importance of European integration in domestic politics led to the upgrading of the prime minister's office. In 2007, the prime minister's office had 135 members of staff, out of which 30 worked in the new EU coordination secretariat (Johansson and Raunio, 2010: 656–60).

In Denmark, there is ministerial autonomy and responsibility, and the position of the prime minister is one of a coordinator who seeks compromise and flexibility, avoiding confrontation (Pedersen and Knudsen, 2005: 160). There are six cabinet committees for specific policy areas, including economic policy and EU affairs. The role of the prime minister in monitoring the ministers has increased over time, and s/he is responsible for the good performance of ministers, being obliged to intervene if necessary. A court of impeachment was established in 1910, with the power to force a prime minister to resign. The impact of Europeanisation and internationalisation has increased the responsibilities of the prime minister in foreign policy. Poul Nyrup Rasmussen (1993–2001) and Anders Føgh Rasmussen (2001–9) both increased their involvement in international affairs. Anders Føgh Rasmussen resigned from office to become the new NATO secretary-general. Since the 1960s, there has also been a substantial increase in the resources of the prime minister's office, which clearly led to a stronger centralisation of power in his/her hands (Pedersen and Knudsen, 2005: 163–6). Consensualism through the consultation of interest groups is similar to that in other Nordic countries. Since the late 2000s, the Danish government has been characterised by minority government. The difficulty in creating stable majorities in government has led to pragmatic cooperation between parties in parliament. One of the reasons for such successful cooperation is that a consensual approach to politics is ingrained in the mentality of Danish politicians. Normally, eight to nine parties are represented in parliament, so that pragmatism prevails and minority government is tolerated by everyone. It means also that polarisation of policy-making is replaced by the search for compromises, including the opposition parties. In a seminal article Christiansen and Seeberg state that one of the main purposes for negotiating a compromise with the opposition is that they become co-responsible for the legislation. This seems to be happening in 80 per cent of the cases that they studied (Christiansen and Seeberg, 2016). In 2011, Helle Thornig-Schmidt became the first woman to be elected to the prime minister's office. She clearly was not able to form an absolute majority coalition government. Instead, she formed a government with parties with ideological affinity, the Social Liberal Party (Radikale Venstre) and the Socialist People's Party (Socialist Folkeparti). However, by the end of 2011, the latter had left the coalition. It meant that prime minister Thornig-Schmidt's majority declined from seventy-three to sixty-one, in both cases below the ninety required for an absolute majority. In spite of this weakening of her government, she was able to remain in power and almost complete her term. Throughout the period, she has had to deal with the economic crisis that also affected Denmark quite considerably, particularly leading to a rise in unemployment. She called for a snap election on 18 June 2015 and lost to the conservatives under previous prime minister Lars Løkke Rasmussen. Prime minister Rasmussen then formed a one-party government with his Liberal party (Venstre) with thirty-seven seats and only seventeen months afterwards did he also include the Liberal Alliance and the Konservative People's Party (Konservative Folksparti – KF) comprising fifty-three seats altogether and looking for majorities in parliament in order to achieve the required majority of ninety votes for approval of legislation. Among the most controversial laws introduced by the single minority government was to limit immigrants and refugees coming to the country, but this was supported by the social democrats in parliament, which clearly indicates the consensual politics based on negotiations and compromise in the Danish parliament. Among the new measures was the search for valuables among refugees and their confiscation if the value was above 10,000 kroner (€1,340), leading to widespread criticisms in the EU and the UN (*BBC News*, 27 May 2015; *Deutsche Welle*, 26 January 2016, 27 November 2016; Kosiara-Pedersen, 2016).

The position of the prime minister in the Norwegian political system can be considered weak. Until the late 1980s, prime ministers tended to resign before the end of the legislation, usually because of problems with coalition partners or other ministers (Eriksen, 1988: 193). The prime minister is not hierarchically superior to the ministers, s/he only has the right of information about what is happening in other ministries. The overall pattern is one of collegiality. Although a coalition government is typically formed along the left–right spectrum, consensualism prevails in the way policy-making is undertaken. However, owing to the fragmentation of the party system, governments may be able to survive, even without a majority in parliament. The lack of an alternative majority among the opposition parties may allow for what has been labelled 'negative parliamentarianism', a typical approach of opposition in Nordic parliaments (coined by Bergman, 1993; quoted from Narud and Strøm, 2000: 166–7). Moreover, Norwegian governments have been under considerable pressure from a growing judicialisation of political issues due to a considerable amount of judicial review and Europeanisation. The latter is quite a paradox, because Norway is not a member of the EU. However, being a member of the European Economic Area (EEA) obliges Norway to apply all the legislation of the European internal market, which, like in the member-states, has become domestic politics (Strøm et al., 2005: 786–7). Moreover, it seems that incumbent parties are being punished severely by the voters. According to Narud and Strøm (2000), there has been an increase in the average loss in terms of percentage of the vote from decade to decade (Strøm et al., 2005: 801–2). Similar to other Nordic countries, minority government has become the norm. In 2013, a minority coalition government was formed between the Right Party (Høyre) and the Progress Party (Fremskrittsparti – FRP) under prime minister Erna Solberg, and she was able to repeat a narrow victory in September 2017 (*The Independent*, 12 September 2017). The latter is rather a Eurosceptic and anti-immigration party. However, together they have just 72 seats out of 169, so that similar to other Nordic countries they have to pragmatically look for ad hoc majorities with the eight or nine parties that regularly get representation in parliament.

In Iceland, ministerial autonomy is also one of the features of government. Individual ministers are required to take charge of several ministries, making the Icelandic government one of the smallest in Europe (Eythórsson and Jahn, 2009: 202–3). In addition, coalition government has become the norm due to the fragmentation of the party system. The economic and banking crisis in 2008 onwards has clearly created more instability in the political system, with governments not completing their four-year period.

Between 1976 and 1985, after democratic transition, there were nine Portuguese governments, most of which were coalition governments. None of these succeeded in completing a legislature period. Between 1976 and 1979 they lasted on average seven months, and between 1979 and 1985, sixteen months (Magone, 1997: 46). Cavaco Silva's charismatic style allowed a consolidation of government in Portugal, and this benchmark was then followed by other leaders (Lobo, 2005: 215–38). Charismatic leadership has become an important factor to achieve absolute majorities in Portugal, but so far just the second and third Cavaco Silva governments (1987–95) and the first José Socrates government have been able to rely on an absolute majority. In 2015, socialist prime minister Antonio Costa was only able to form a minority government with the parliamentary support of the leftwing parties – the communists (PCP) and Block of the Left, a governmental innovation. So far this has been a successful experiment and clearly indicates the possibility for a more consensual approach to politics in Portugal.

At the core of the Portuguese government is the general secretariat of the council of ministers' presidency (SGPCM). It is part of the prime minister's office created in 1976, but was quite inefficient until 1985. Prime minister Cavaco Silva transformed the SGPCM into an efficient machinery, highly influenced by new public management philosophy. Such improvement has been achieved incrementally (Lobo, 2005; Magone, 2014a). In 2017, the budget of the core executive was €18.5 million and consisted of 141 staff, of which 11 are higher or intermediary ranking positions. Such a machinery was crucial in supporting the management of the bailout programme imposed by the EU Troika during the financial crisis (see Magone, 2018).

In comparative terms, both the Czech Republic and Slovakia have become the best cases for democratic consolidation in Central and Eastern Europe.

In the Czech Republic, the Václav Klaus government of the Civic Forum (ODS) was instrumental in undertaking major reforms towards the liberalisation of the political economy. The Klaus government allowed a smooth transition after the 'velvet divorce'; however, the economic scandals that began to emerge in 1998 led to a change of government to the social democrats (ČSSD). The scandals also led to the creation of a more moderate party system, with the ČSSD minority government (1998–2002) of Miloš Zeman supported by the ODS through an agreement with the opposition that divided these two parties. In spite of the difficulties in building coalitions, Czech governments have developed important rules of engagement that allow for stable governments. This has also led to ideological inter-block cooperation between left and right parties. In particular, the ČSSD formed coalition governments with smaller centre-right parties like the Christian democrats (KDL-CSU)between 2002 and 2005. Such coalition behaviour has been increasing over time due to the highly fragmented party system. None of the nine parties represented in parliament is able to achieve an absolute majority. Everything became more complicated with the rise of new anti-corruption and populist parties directed against the political elite. Among them one has to mention the conservative Tradition, Responsibility and Prosperity (Top 09) founded by aristocrat Karel Schwarzenberg and Ja 11 (Ano 11) by billionaire Andris Babiš. The old established parties have been able to work with these new anti-corruption parties, forming coalitions with them since 2010. Since 2017, Andris Babiš of Ano 11 has been the prime minister of a coalition government of his party with the ČSSD. This shows that Czech party politics is quite pragmatic in terms of looking for working majorities. The role of the prime minister is one of *primus inter pares* like in coalition governments in the Benelux countries. One of the main reasons for this position of the prime minister is that ministers have a high degree of ministerial autonomy (Vodička, 2005: 249–51). In comparison with Poland and Hungary, the prime minister does not have a vast amount of resources. Czech prime ministers need considerable skills in consensual politics, negotiation, compromise and coordination, and less in terms of presidentialisation. The prime minister is supported by a government office (created in 2002) with over 100 members of staff and comprising several departments. Among them there is also a legislative office and one on EU policy coordination. As Radoslaw Zubek asserts, there are constitutional limitations to the creation of a strong supportive structure, due to the fact that Czech governments allow for a substantial ministerial autonomy, thus preventing too much concentration of human and material resources in the hands of the prime minister. The latter was quite important during the country's accession to the EU, particularly in making sure that the *acquis communautaire* was transposed, but after accession such efforts have been relaxed and have become less of a priority (Zubek, 2011: 443–4, 447).

Similarly, Slovakia has moved over time towards a more consensual style of politics, mainly due to the fact that it has been difficult for one party to achieve absolute majority after the velvet divorce in 1992. Slovakia was dominated by the Movement for a Democratic Slovakia (HZDŠ) under the nationalist populist Vladimir Mečiar, who contributed to a polarisation of the party system between the left and the right. However, after pressure from the EU, a new moderate coalition government under Mikulas Džurinda was elected in 1998, allowing for a transition to more European-friendly adjustment policies. Since 2006, the populist Social Democratic Party-Direction (SMER) under prime minister Robert Fico has been the dominant player in Slovak politics. Meanwhile, he has led two coalition

(2006–10 and 2016–18) and one minority government (2010–12). Robert Fico's SMER is quite pro-European and his government adopted the euro in 2009. Since 2016, he has formed an oversized coalition government with the smaller Slovak Nationalist Party (SNS), the new centre-right Network (Siet) and the Hungarian minority party Bridge (Most) with an absolute majority of 85 seats out of 150. Although he had to resign in March 2018 over the murder of Czech journalist Jan Kuciak and his fiancée, allegedly by the Italian mafia, he remains a powerful leader behind SMER. He tried also to become president in 2016, but failed. In comparison to the Czech Republic, there is a stronger role for the prime minister, particularly during the Robert Fico governments (*Politico*, 15 March 2018). Similarly to the Czech Republic, the prime minister is supported by a government office with several departments. At the end of 2015, 550 people were working for the government office, out of which 331 were civil servants. This core civil service is highly qualified, with two-thirds having higher education degrees, and also relatively young, with 61 per cent aged between 21 and 50 years old (Úrad Vlády Slovenskey Republiku, 2016: 7).

Slovenia also belongs to the consensual type of democracy. The weak semi-presidentialism clearly gives more space to the prime minister and his/her government. Nevertheless, the fragmentation of the party system has contributed to coalition governments with several small parties. In this regard, Slovenia from early on has had to deal with a fragmented parliament and look for compromise. Such consensual approach seems also to be ingrained in the Slovenian political culture. Quite important for the consolidation of government in Slovenia were the four Janez Drnovšek (1992–2000; 2000–2) governments. He also later became president of Slovenia between 2002 and 2007. The first two Drvovšek governments were grand coalitions including both the social democrats as well as the liberals, setting a standard for coalition building in the country. During the past decades, new parties have emerged and disappeared, so that just the social democrats, liberals, the Christian democrats and the Pensioners Party have emerged as representing the continuity of the party system.

Like many other Central and Eastern European countries, the prime minister has his/her own office which coordinates policy across ministries. Moreover, an office of government manages the council of minister's business and also all other inter-ministerial committees. Furthermore, an office for development and European integration, and an office for government legislation are also at the core of government. Slovenia has been very keen to streamline and strengthen the core of its government by reducing ministries and government agencies and making the government machinery more efficient. The OECD recommended a more integrated and efficient central office which would be less rules based and more management based, adhering to principles of cooperation and coordination (OECD, 2012: 166–9). In spite of the OECD's report, the structure seems to have remained intact.

Croatia tends to moderate polarisation between the two main parties: the Croatian Democratic Union (HDZ) and the Social Democratic Party (SDP). However, none of them is able to achieve an absolute majority, so they need to form coalitions with smaller parties. This is a complex enterprise because the Croatian party system is quite fragmented. In this regard, some coalition governments have included parties from left and right in order to achieve a stable majority. While before 2003 most of the nine governments were single majority governments led by the HDZ, after 2003 all five were minority coalition governments. In this context, the larger parties had to coalesce with more than one small party, some of them from ideologically different camps. Croatia is a latecomer to the EU, so that its core government is still adjusting to the new reality. Similar to Slovenia, the prime minister is supported by his/her own office, which clearly is in charge of policy coordination, while the secretariat-general of the government deals with the management of the council of ministers and government committees.

The Baltic states may also be increasingly regarded as consensus democracies. The highly fragmented party systems, and the ongoing ostracism of parties supported by the Russian population in Estonia and Latvia, reduce the possibilities for the formation of governments. In this context, such consensual approach to politics is strongest in Estonia and probably weakest in Lithuania. Like Slovakia, all three Baltic countries are members of the Eurozone.

Estonia is probably the most successful of the Baltic countries in terms of achieving government stability. Similar to the Benelux countries and Scandinavian countries, successive Estonian governments have been able to create a consensual approach towards government formation and also governance. The highly fragmented party system allows for ideological inter-block coalitions, particularly including the social democratic party. Since 2007, the largest party has been the liberal Reform Party (ER) with about 27–28 per cent of the vote. Between 2007 and 2014, ER's leader Andrus Ansip headed several coalition governments, which allowed for considerable stability in the country. He was also able to guide the country towards Eurozone membership. Before and after the exceptional long period in office by Ansip, prime ministers would stay in power for one or two years and then be replaced by another one. Coalition governance is quite collegial. The prime minister is just *primus inter pares* and informal connections have been a major factor in making Estonian governments quite effective. The prime minister's office consists of advisers and experts that help the prime minister to harmonise policy-making. However, policy coordination is done at cabinet meetings or in specific committees attached to the government. Very important is the state chancellery founded in 1918, which was in place during the period of independence in the interwar period (1918–41). It was abolished during the Soviet period, to then be reinstated after 1990. It comprises several departments supporting the government's work.

More problematic has been the consolidation of government and the party system in Latvia. Between 1990 and 2017, there have been twenty governments, none of which has lasted for more than one and two years. Coalition government has dominated Latvian politics, consisting normally of several smaller parties due to the highly fragmented and volatile party system. One major problem has been that the electoral law allowed for many parties to gain representation. This was only changed by raising the threshold to 5 per cent in 1995. Another peculiarity is that most Latvian political parties that were in government have been rightwing, centre-right or liberal, and predominantly anti-Russian. Latvia remains a highly divided society between the Latvian population and the Russophones, who are partly Latvian and partly denizens. In the elections of 2011, 2014 and 2018, the largest party became the social democratic party Harmony (Saskana), which is the only party on the left and supported overwhelmingly by the Latvian Russophone population, but not only them. The Harmony Party has strong relations with

Vladimir Putin's supporting party Our Russia in Russia. However, so far it has been ostracised from power due to the negatively perceived Soviet legacy. This clearly is a dangerous approach to democratic politics, as it may lead to high levels of corruption of the other parties to remain in power, like happened in pre-tangentopoli Italy. Party organisation consolidation seems to also be a major problem in Latvia, contributing to a permanent change in the party landscape. The longest serving prime minister was the charismatic Valdis Dombrovskis who headed three governments between March 2009 and 22 January 2014 (Cianetti, 2013, 2014; Ikstens, 2014: 198–9). Since then, several quite unstable governments consisting of several parties have been in power. In 2014, Latvia adopted the euro and conducted a highly successful EU presidency in the first half of 2015 (Ikstens, 2016: 167). Coalition governance needs to increase its efficiency in order to prevent the breakdown of government within a one- or two-year period. The prime minister is supported by the state chancellery, similar to Estonia. European integration and the OECD have been instrumental in building transparent structures in the country. Quite an important event was the accession of Latvia to the OECD on 1 July 2016 after a three-year process of adjustment to the standards of governance set out by the organisation (OECD, 2016).

The consolidation of government in the Balkans

The Balkan countries have governments that are still consolidating. Many of them are characterised by multi-ethnic communities that are still dealing with the scars of the Balkan wars. The processes of normalisation and democratisation are advancing slowly, and the European integration process may contribute to further stabilisation of the region. Thus far, the Bosnia-Herzegovina experiment has been important in transforming the region; however, divisions still prevail and undermine a proper transition to a consociational society. In this respect, Macedonia has been more successful in changing patterns of behaviour and strengthening the position of the Albanian minority in government since a major inter-ethnic conflict in 2001. Albania, Serbia, Macedonia and Montenegro are now all candidate countries for EU accession. It means that European standards devised by the Council of Europe and the EU are contributing to a transformation of government through the screening process. As already mentioned, the EU was quite active in Macedonia during the crisis between the political parties in 2015. Just Kosovo remains an unresolved issue along with Bosnia-Herzegovina.

The exception to the rule of divided European governments: presidentialism in Cyprus and the directoire in Switzerland and Bosnia-Herzegovina

So far we have written about patterns of government in Europe. However, there are three exceptions to the rule: Cyprus, Switzerland and its copy-cat Bosnia-Herzegovina.

In contrast to all other European countries, Cyprus is the only country that has adopted a presidential constitution. It means that there is no divided government in the country. In principle, the Cypriot constitution envisaged shared government between the Greek and Turkish population, but in the end just the Greek Cypriots have been represented by the constitution, while the Turkish Cypriot population has stayed away from the system. In July 1974 it formed its own republic in the northern part of the island after a Turkish invasion. It means that today only Greeks and other smaller minorities are represented in the institutions of the Republic of Cyprus. The president is elected every five years and forms a government consisting of eleven ministers. The president chairs the government. S/he has a veto right in questions of security and foreign policy in relation to parliament, and a suspensive one in other matters. The Republic of Cyprus follows a clear separation of powers between executive and legislative. This means that members of parliament cannot be members of government like, for example, in the UK. The presidential system provides for a fairly stable government, preventing too much fragmentation (Zervakis and Costeas, 2010: 1105–12).

Switzerland has also to be regarded as the exception to the rule. It clearly is a consensus-based democracy, and government is permanently shared through a kind of *directoire* of seven members elected after the legislative elections by the national assembly consisting of the two chambers of parliament, the National Council (lower house) and the Council of States (upper house). The *directoire* goes back to the French model established in 1795, consisting of five people who ruled the country after the totalitarian period of Maximilien Robespierre and La Terreur. Robespierre's rule led to the mass killings of several opponents that were against his regime. The *directoire* made sure that no one of the five members would be able to achieve the same level of power as Robespierre (Fleiner 2013: 350; Kriesi and Trechsel, 2008: 75). Such a model reminds us of the period of collective leadership after Stalin's death in 1953, from which Nikita Khrushchev was able to emerge as its leader. In Switzerland, the largest parties in parliament are automatically entitled to proportional representation in government. Such composition has been changing over time according to the strength of the political parties. Originally, all seats were allocated to the liberal party which clearly was able to win the most seats in the original majoritarian system in the nineteenth century. However, with the introduction of proportional representation and universal suffrage, other parties were able to secure representation in the *directoire*. This was the case for the Christian People's Party (CVP), the social democrats (SP) and the Citizens, Shopowners party and Farmers (BGB). In 1958, a compromise between all relevant political parties was reached which became known as the 'magical formula' (*Zauberformel*). The compromise allocated two seats to each of the liberals, social democrats and Christian People's Party respectively, and one to the BGB. Such formula remained in place until 2003. However, the rise of the populist Swiss People's Party (SVP, a rebranding of the former BGB) and the decline of the Christian People's Party led to a shift of seats from the latter to the former. Nevertheless, this has been quite a conflictive process since 2007, leading to a splinter party of SVP, the Democratic Citizens' Party (BGP), keeping the second seat of the SVP with the tolerance of the other parties. Only in 2015 did the situation normalise when a more conciliatory SVP was able to get its second councillor elected. The government of Switzerland, the so-called Federal Council (*Bundesrat*), decides everything by consensus and submits their legislative bills to both houses of parliament. This is then discussed by the political parties, which tend to decide by consensus in order to avoid the call for a referendum on an issue. It is better for the parties to achieve consensus, even if this is a bad compromise, then to go for a referendum, which is quite costly and may lead to undesired outcomes. The policy approach of the SVP has been to threaten referenda on particular issues, such as on the free movement of people or controls over immigration, undermining partly the consensual culture of Swiss democracy. The *Bundesrat* is a collective body without a prime minister and is not accountable to parliament. It has an annually rotating president who represents the country inside the country and abroad but with minimal support staff. So far, calls for reforms of the *Bundesrat* have been not very successful. The number of members is rather small, but the work burden has been increasing over time (see Magone, 2017: 155–6, 167–70).

The constitution of Bosnia-Herzegovina imposed by the international community follows the Swiss model. However, joint shared government has been rather difficult. The division of the country into a Serbian Republic (Republika Srspka) and a Bosnian Republic comprising Croats and Bosniak Muslims has not facilitated cooperation. The president rotates annually according to the three ethnic groups, and s/he chairs the council of ministers consisting of nine ministers. Parliamentarianism remains rather incipient (Richter and Gavrić, 2010: 852–5, 855–61).

Diversity in the quality of democratic governance

Governments rely on their public administrations to formulate, decide and implement their policies. Efficiency and transparency in which these processes are undertaken have become quite central to democratic governance. The quality of democratic governance is a crucial variable in understanding how efficient governments are able to deliver on public goods. In spite of all convergence processes in terms of the nature of government, there are still major differences between the countries. The sustainable governance indicators of the Bertelsmann Foundation allow us to map these differences. Although Figure 4.4 is just a snapshot, it clearly shows that there are three patterns of democratic governance in Europe. The highest level of good governance can be found in the Nordic countries, apart from Iceland, in Benelux, German-speaking Europe and the British Isles. Satisfactory democratic governance can be found in France, Iceland, southern Europe, Poland, the Czech Republic, Slovakia, Slovenia and Croatia. Poor democratic governance characterised by high levels of corruption and poor administrative services can be found in Hungary, Romania, Bulgaria and most countries of wider Europe. This is also confirmed by the World Bank Governance Indicators and the Global Corruption Barometer of Transparency International (TI, 2017; World Bank, 2018).

From the Weberian bureaucratic state to new public management

In most European countries there has been a substantial transformation of the state. The original Weberian state, based on a neutral civil service, had become less and less viable by the end of the twentieth century (see Box 4.6).

The huge welfare states in most advanced countries were absorbing funds and creating stagnation in national economies. The problem became evident during the 1970s with the oil shocks (resulting from the war of the Arab states against Israel and the 1979 Iranian revolution), when all advanced democracies had to deal with oil shortages. This meant that, by the mid-1970s, the growth of state and public administration had reached its limits and become financially unsustainable (Scharpf, 2000).

From the 1970s, the OECD developed benchmarking and best practices for public administration based on the principles of new public management. At the forefront was a transition from a Weberian model of civil service and public administration to the new public management model (Peters, 2003). The whole process had already started in the 1970s, as a result of the increasing crisis caused by the growth of the welfare states and the stagnation of most OECD economies (Scharpf, 2000). According to Sabino Cassese, such reforms were started in the late 1970s in Germany (1978) and the UK (1979), followed by France (1989), Spain (1992) and then various other countries (Cassese, 2003: 131; Pollitt and Bouckaert, 2004).

Box 4.6 Max Weber and modern state bureaucracy

The German sociologist Max Weber (1864–1920) is one of the founding fathers of modern political sociology. His main work was a very thorough volume entitled *Economy and Society* (*Wirtschaft und Gesellschaft*) published posthumously in 1922. Weber used a historical-sociological method to understand the emergence of modernity in the West in general, and the modern democratic state in particular. He differentiated between the pre-modern (feudalism, patrimonial, absolutist monarchy), in which arbitrary rule dominated, and the modern state based on the rule of law and a specialised civil service implementing it. This 'rational-legal state' was based on six bureaucratic principles:

1 There is the **principle of fixed and official jurisdictional areas**, which is generally ordered by rules, that is, by laws or administrative regulations.
2 The **principles of office hierarchy and of levels of graded authority** mean a firmly ordered system of super- and subordination in which there is a supervision of the lower offices by the higher ones.
3 The **management of the modern office is based upon written documents** ('the files'), which are preserved in their original or draft form. There is, therefore, a staff of subaltern officials and scribes of all sorts.
4 **Office management**, at least all specialised office management, which is anyway distinctly modern, usually presupposes thorough and expert training. This increasingly holds for modern executives and employees of private enterprises, in the same manner as it holds for state officials.
5 **When the office is fully developed, official activity demands the full working capacity of the official, irrespective of the fact that his obligatory time in the bureau may be firmly delimited**. In the normal case, this is only

(continued)

(continued)

the product of a long development, in the public as well as in the private office. Formerly, in all cases, the normal state of affairs was reversed: official business was discharged as a secondary activity.

6 **The management of the office follows general rules, which are more or less stable, more or less exhaustive, and which can be learned**. Knowledge of these rules represents a special technical learning, which the officials possess. It involves jurisprudence, or administrative or business management.

(Max Weber quoted from Gerth and Mills, 1946: 196–8)

Today we take all these principles of public administration for granted, but during Weber's time at the turn of the nineteenth to the twentieth centuries, most public administrations in Europe were engaged in moving towards a rational-legal state. He analysed and described something that was happening between 1850 and 1945 in most European countries. Some countries are still struggling to establish the basic principles of a Weberian state.

One could characterise this transformation as one from government to governance, meaning that the separation between the public and private sector is not clear any more. This also means that the state has introduced more and more administrative devices taken from the private sector, such as evaluation, competition and flexibility, in order to make their organisational structures more efficient.

Although government and governance share similarities, both refer to purposive behaviour, goal-oriented activities and to systems of rule. However, while government undertakes activities that are backed by 'formal authority and by police powers that ensure the implementation of duly implemented policies', governance comprises activities that are backed 'by shared goals that may or may not derive from legal and formally prescribed responsibilities and that do not necessarily rely on police powers to overcome defiance and attain compliance'. Briefly, government is quite formalised, while governance includes both formal and informal elements (Rosenau, 2000: 4). Moreover, governance implies cooperation of public institutions with economic actors and civil society organisations, so that governance becomes quite a complex myriad of interactions between these three actors.

According to Cassese, seven main elements of this new rationale can be identified:

1 **'Agencification'**: the establishment of special independent bodies to either regulate or perform duties once performed by the state. In the UK, good examples are agencies such as Ofcom (for control of the communication sector) and the Rail and Road Authority (for the railway system). In Germany, one can mention the huge *Bundesnetzagentur* responsible for many utilities.
2 **'Process re-engineering'**: the revision of procedures inside the public administration in order to reduce the administrative burden on citizens.

Figure 4.4 Quality of democratic governance in Europe based on Sustainable Governance Indicators 2018 of Bertelsmann Foundation

Source: Assessment based on composite of the three indices of Sustainable Governance Indicators – democracy, governance and policy performance, Bertelsmann Stiftung (2018a; 2018b: 15, 27, 41).

3 **'Value for money'**: the reduction of costs by introducing commercial principles and increasing the productivity of services.
4 **'Result-oriented budget'**: enhanced accountability of public accounts accompanied by measurement of performance of expenditure.
5 **'Public-private partnerships'**: the contracting out of public services to the private and voluntary sectors and/or seeking financial support for certain services, such as education or transport.
6 **'Marketisation'**: opening up public services to private competition.
7 **'Customer orientation'**: the identification of quality indicators and productivity standards, and the measurement of user satisfaction.

(Author's summary from Cassese, 2003: 131–2)

This growing marketisation of public administration raises questions about its neutrality and the possibilities for interest groups to control policy-making processes of the state as a result of the state's dependence on their expertise. Today the state is losing its monopoly in the delivery of public services. It has to compete in the market, based on principles of 'value for money'. It becomes *primus inter pares* (first among equals) and works through public-private partnerships (PPP) with private economic actors and civil society actors in the delivery of public services and other state-related activities (Jessop, 2002: 243). This means that governance seeks to overcome the rigidity and strong separation that existed between the public and private sectors until at least the 1970s. In this sense, governance in a particular policy field can be interpreted as greater than the sum of interactions between the governmental institutions, the private sector actors and the civil society actors.

All member-states of the EU are engaged in this *OECD-isation* or transformation process from government to governance, which is also the basis for transnational Europeanisation and the integration of public administrations, particularly through the European Public Administration Network (EUPAN) founded in the late 1990s and which is quite active in disseminating administrative good practice, innovation and setting benchmarking rules.

Conclusions: government in Europe – majoritarian versus consensus politics

Government in Europe expresses itself differently in each European country. According to the typology of Arend Lijphart, it can be categorised as either majoritarian or consensual government types. Majoritarian government is characterised by polarisation between two main parties, which are regularly able to achieve absolute majorities and form a single-party government, while consensual government is characterised by cooperation between political parties, because none of the parties is able to achieve an absolute majority and therefore parties have to form coalition governments. The European integration process is creating the beginnings of a European administrative space. This means mainly that the European Commission and national public administration are increasingly acting interdependently as an integrated whole. Such a process began in 1988 and has been accelerating in recent years.

Suggested reading

Blondel, Jean and Ferdinand Müller-Rommel (eds) (1997), *Cabinets in Western Europe*. 2nd edition. Basingstoke: Palgrave.

Blondel, Jean, Ferdinand Müller-Rommel and Darina Malová (2007), *Governing New European Democracies*. Basingstoke: Palgrave.

Colino, César and Eloisa del Pino (2015) National and European patterns of public administration and governance. In: José M. Magone (ed.) *Routledge Handbook of European Politics*. Abingdon: Routledge, pp. 611–39.

Elgie, Robert and Sophie Moestrup (eds) (2008) *Semi-Presidentialism in Central and Eastern Europe*. Oxford: Oxford University Press.

Keman, Hans and Ferdinand Müller-Rommel (eds) (2012), *Party Government in the New Europe*. Abingdon: Routledge.

Lijphart, Arend (2009 [1999]), *Patterns of Democracy: Government Forms and Performance in Thirty-Six Countries*. New Haven, CT: Yale University Press.

Müller, Wolfgang and Kaare Strøm (eds) (2001, 2003), *Coalition Governments in Western Europe*. Oxford: Oxford University Press.

Pasquino, Gianfranco (2015) Governments in European politics. In: José M. Magone (ed.), *Routledge Handbook of European Politics*. Abingdon: Routledge, pp. 295–310.

QUESTIONS FOR REVISION

- Compare the main features of majoritarian and consensus governments. Use examples of at least two different countries.
- What are the main differences between governments in the UK and Germany?
- What is understood under a 'semi-presidential' political system and how widespread is it in Europe? Discuss, using examples of at least two different countries.
- Is 'presidentialisation' of government in Europe an old or a new phenomenon? Discuss, using two different countries as examples.
- Explain the main steps in the formation of coalition government in the Netherlands and/or Belgium.
- What are common features of public administrations in Europe? Discuss using examples from at least two countries.

Chapter 5

The diversity of parliamentarianism in multilevel Europe

The main functions of parliament in postmodern European political systems: patterns of parliamentarianism in Europe

Symbolically, one can characterise parliament as the centre of democracy of the modern European political system (Figure 5.1, Box 5.1).

The symbolic importance of national parliaments has been challenged by the growing dominance of the work of governments and public administrations in Europe. Moreover, globalisation, internationalisation and Europeanisation have played a major role in transposing many international legal acts into national legislation, reducing further the power of parliaments.

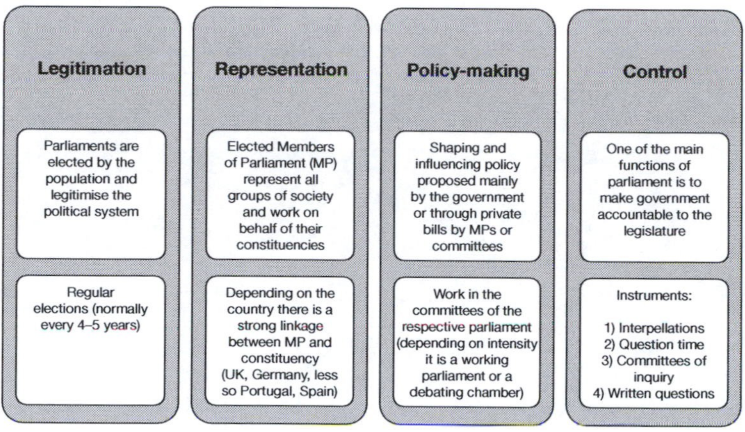

Figure 5.1 The functions of democratic parliaments

Box 5.1 The origins of European parliamentarianism

The origins of modern European parliaments go back to more oligarchical assemblies in the Middle Ages, the main function of which was to approve funding for enterprises of the monarch. Such assemblies can be traced back to the thirteenth century in England, leading up to the Magna Carta in 1215, to the early fourteenth century in France, to the twelfth century in Spain at the regional level, and the oldest known European parliament, the Althingi founded in 930.

According to Samuel E. Finer, parliamentarianism as we know it today owes a great deal to the developments that took place in England in the seventeenth century, where parliament was able to push the monarchy away from its absolutist form of government and towards limited government. Although parliamentarianism and assemblies existed in other countries during the seventeenth and eighteenth

(continued)

(continued)

centuries (e.g. États Généraux (General Estates) in France, Cortes in Spain), it is only in England that it became part of the way of life of government and politics. In England it was an oligarchical parliamentarianism, which was steadily democratised in the nineteenth century. For Finer, parliamentarianism is a major distinctive feature in the development of European politics (Finer, 1999: 1335–6, 1372–4).

The best characterisation for categorising parliaments is probably that developed by Philip Norton, who was inspired by Michael Mezey's typology of legislatures (Mezey, 1979: part II; The book by Blondel (1973) influenced Mezey) (see Box 5.2). Norton developed two categories for legislatures: policy-making and policy-influencing legislatures. The former is appropriate for the US bicameral Congress because of its independence from the White House and because of the human and material resources that it commands. In contrast, the policy-influencing legislatures are all *reactive* legislatures, not active ones. All European legislatures can be characterised as policy-influencing and therefore reactive. However, European legislatures differ in the strength with which they can influence the proposed legislatures (Norton, 1998a: 3).

Box 5.2 Michael L. Mezey's typology of legislatures

Political scientist Michael L. Mezey developed a typology for the analysis and classification of legislatures in his book *Comparative Legislatures* (1979). There are three clusters of functions: policy-making, system-maintenance and representation activities.

Several internal and external factors help us to determine to which category a legislature belongs. Among the external factors Norton speaks of are the political culture, the constitutional constraints and the position of parliament in the political process, while among the internal factors he closely follows Nelson Polsby's institutionalisation thesis (Polsby, 1968) that emphasises the level of specialisation, the agenda control, the rules and organisation, and the resources (Norton, 1998a: 8–13; Table 5.1, Figures 5.2 and 5.3, Boxes 5.3 and 5.4).

If we follow Norton's typology for policy-influencing legislatures, then we have to acknowledge that most European legislatures are weak reactive ones. The most specialised and institutionalised are in the Nordic countries, the Netherlands, Austria, the UK, Germany and Italy. All the countries of Southern, Central and Eastern Europe are weak reactive because of their low level of institutionalisation. Most of these countries are still taking part in a process moving towards qualitative democratisation. Moreover, because of the low salaries and the value of the MPs' position in the political system, the professionalisation of parliamentarians may take a long time.

Table 5.1 A typology of parliaments in Europe

Policy-influencing legislatures	*Countries*
Strong reactive	Sweden, Finland, Denmark, Netherlands
Medium-term reactive	Germany, Austria, Norway, Italy, Switzerland, the UK
Weak reactive	Belgium, Luxembourg, France, Ireland, Portugal, Spain, Greece, Hungary, Poland, Latvia, Lithuania, Estonia
Extremely weak reactive legislatures	Bulgaria, Romania and Croatia
Consolidating democratic parliaments	Serbia, Montenegro, Macedonia, Bosnia-Herzegovina, Albania, Kosovo, Ukraine, Moldova
Dictatorship	Belarus

Source: Author's own categorisation based on Norton (1998a).

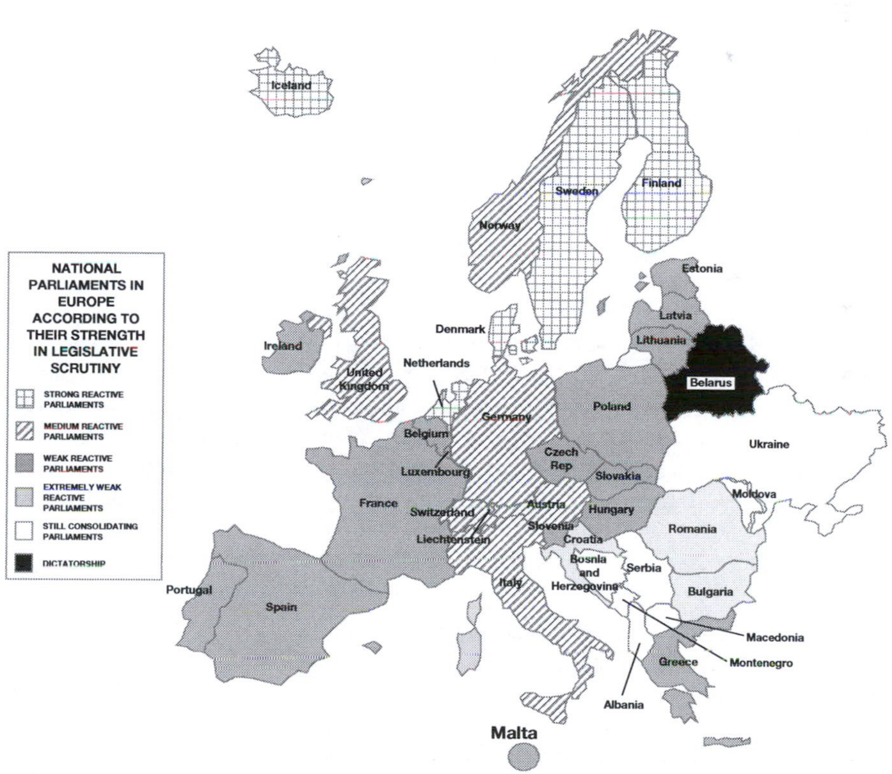

Figure 5.2 Mapping parliaments in Europe according to the level of policy influencing

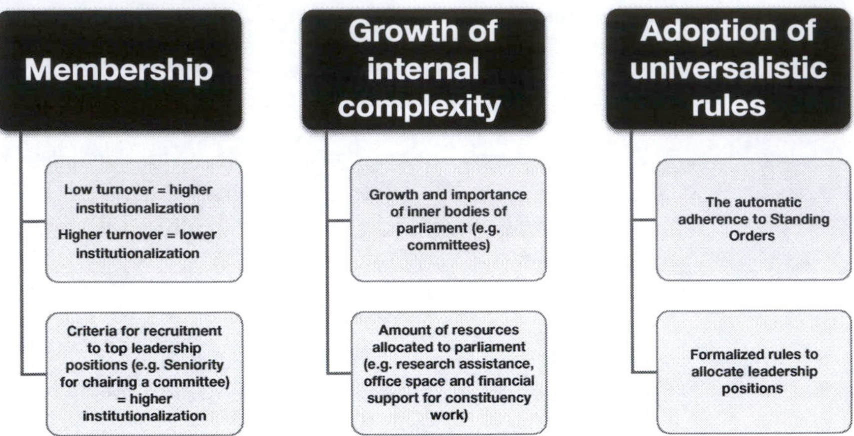

Figure 5.3 Institutionalisation indicators of legislatures, according to Polsby (1968)

Box 5.3 Philip Norton's typology of European legislatures

In 1998, Philip Norton edited a comparative book entitled *Parliaments and Governments in Western Europe*. He presented there a typology of policy-making and policy-influencing legislatures. While the US legislature is characterised as policy-making because it commands so many resources and was devised as a check and balance power to the presidency, all European legislatures are characterised as reactive policy-influencing. In some cases, they are very weak, in others fairly strong.

Heidi Z'Graggen has written an excellent PhD dissertation on the topic that highly influences issues of professionalisation of parliaments in this chapter (Z'Graggen, 2009). Although her figures are now outdated and refer just to Western Europe and to the early 2000s, they still give us a good idea of the level of professionalisation of national parliaments. Higher professionalisation does not mean that automatically parliaments are strong. She uses three indicators to measure professionalisation: income of MPs, costs of parliament and workload in 2004 (see also Figure 5.3).

Strong reactive policy-influencing legislatures: the Nordic countries and the Netherlands

The legislatures of the Nordic countries and the Netherlands may be regarded as the strongest in Europe. Apart from the fact that they already have a long tradition of democracy, there is a constant preoccupation with improving the quality of parliamentarianism at the centre of each country's political life. One important aspect is that all these countries are consensus democracies in which coalition government has become the norm rather than the exception (see Chapter 4).

The Swedish Parliament (Riksdag) consists of 349 MPs elected for four years by a proportional representation electoral system.

Box 5.4 Nelson W. Polsby's institutionalisation process of legislatures

One of the most quoted articles on parliaments is from US political scientist Nelson W. Polsby under the title 'The Institutionalization of the US House of Representatives', which was published in the prestigious *American Political Science Review* in 1968. His main focus is on how an organisation, in his case a legislature, is able to gain autonomy in the overall systemic context (political system). Such autonomy is established through a long-term internal institutionalisation process. Polsby identifies three different ways of analysing such institutionalisation:

- lower turnover of membership means higher institutionalisation
- growth of internal organisational complexity means higher institutionalisation (e.g. differentiation of committees)
- adoption of universalistic rules (e.g. following the Standing Orders, clear rules of selection to leadership positions).

Since the constitutional reform of 1975, Sweden has moved towards a full parliamentary system. The role of the king has been substantially reduced, while that of the president of the Riksdag has been strengthened. It is the president who appoints the prime minister, not the king. Moreover, the new government has to be approved by parliament. The king is still important as a formal head, but parliament has become the centre of political life in Sweden. The Instrument of Government, the institutional part of the Swedish constitution, states that the 'Riksdag is the foremost representative of the people'.

According to Torbjörn Bergman and Thomas Larue, this was an adjustment of the constitution to the practice in the political system (Bergman and Larue, 2004: 232). In 1971, the second chamber of parliament was abolished and the Riksdag became unicameral.

The general rationale of the reform was to formalise the existing practice and consolidate the five-party system that existed in Sweden up till then. The 4 per cent threshold was designed to prevent fragmentation of the vote. However, like in many other countries, electoral volatility led to the emergence of new parties, presently eight parties, making it more difficult to achieve stable government. It took some time for political parties to deal with the new institutional framework. Since 1958, one can characterise Sweden as a moderate two-block party system, which may lead to different constellations in terms of government, from coalition to parliamentary investiture and/or legislature pacts. In order to prevent abuse by governments, in 2011 a rule was introduced by the then conservative majority which makes it obligatory that after the election, the new prime minister must secure an absolute majority in parliament, thus hardening the principle of 'negative parliamentarianism' based on tolerated government if there is no formal opposition (Möller, 2015: 127).

In terms of legislation, the government proposes laws which are checked *ex ante* on their constitutionality by the Council of Legislation (*Lagrådet*). Although parliament has the right to ignore the advice, the opinion of the *Lagrådet* has to be attached to the law. Moreover, *post facto*, if the law is against the constitution, any sector of public administration can refuse to apply the law. Between 2012 and 2017, the *Lagrådet* scrutinised on average annually 121 laws sent by civil servants from government ministries or parliamentary committees. This enhances democracy and accountability (Bergman and Larue, 2004: 233; *Lagrådet*, 2018). The committee system within the Riksdag is well institutionalised. The Swedish parliament is a working parliament (*Arbeitsparlament*) in which the fifteen committees are central to the whole process. Internationally, Swedish parliamentary committees are quite strong measured on drafting authority and agenda control. Its main task is to amend legislation presented mainly by the government. Very important legislation is already discussed in the pre-parliamentary phase in the Royal Commissions by most political parties, with the exception of the populist anti-immigration Swedish democrats (Mattson, 2015: 684). In this regard, political parties are key players in shaping legislation. Party discipline is extremely high in the Swedish parliament. Nevertheless, committees remain the arena to create consensus. According to Ingvar Mattson, normally only minor amendments are made to government bills. Unanimous voting for government bills was common until the 1980s, but then parliament became more fragmented and also more conflictive. According to Mattson, based on several studies, the number of opposition minority reports attached to bills has increased in the past decades (Mattson, 2015: 687). The number of private bills has been increasing, but the success rate is less than 1 per cent (Mattson, 2015: 686–7). Professionalisation is quite high in the Swedish parliament. Seniority and experience matter in order to allocate the chair of a particular committee (Mattson, 2015: 681). The Swedish parliament has strong powers in the budget law process. However, its powers are used moderately and they tend to be more salient during minority governments (Mattson, 2015: 685–6). In 2003, a restructuring of the audit role of government by parliament took place, leading to the establishment of a specialised National Audit Agency (Riksrevisionen), which now fulfils this role (Bergman and Larue, 2004: 242; Riksrevisionen, 2018).

All the other Nordic parliaments have similar structures. The Danish unicameral Folketing consists of 179 MPs elected for four years by a proportional representation electoral system. Similar to the Swedish Riksdag, it is an extremely well-resourced parliament. Although over 90 per cent of legislation approved was initiated by the government, the whole approach has been one of cooperation and consensus. There are very few occasions when the government has not won a vote. While between 1982 and 1993 the government lost, on average, 6.9 per cent of a total 2,147 votes, between 1993 and 2000 this decreased to almost zero, which is similar to the period between 1971 and 1982 (Nannestad, 2009: 84). A quite sophisticated study on executive-legislative relations by Flemming Juul Christiansen and Henrik Bech Seeberg, based on a database of 325 legislative agreements between 1973 and 2003, shows that apart from the fact that most government legislation is up to 80 per cent approved with the votes of the opposition, about 20 per cent is achieved through quite sophisticated legislative agreements between the government and opposition parties. This strategy of coalition government, mostly minority coalition governments, prevents the opposition parties from being able to hurt government parties in the next election. Legislative agreements are a kind of shelter against opposition criticism, thus contributing to more peaceful policy-making and implementation. Clearly, legislative agreements not only require the opposition to silence their criticism but also that government has to give in and be attentive to the concerns of the opposition. In this regard, the quite fragmented parliamentary party system contributes to avoiding absolute claims and negotiating legislation consensually, which ensures the long-term guarantee of implementation. In this kind of political culture the opposition parties are committed to constructive criticism, while government behaviour tends to be inclusive and respectful of serious opposition proposals (Christiansen and Seeberg, 2016).

Between 1988 and 2017, the Folketing approved on average 182 laws per legislative period. Although these were mainly a result of government initiatives, they were nonetheless also negotiated with the opposition in committees. In the legislative year 2016–17, 97.3 per cent of adopted bills came from the government (Folketing, 2017: 41; Nannestad, 2009: 71). This means that consensus on legislative acts is achieved at committee level. In Table 5.2 we can see that in spite of widespread minority government, the executive has quite a high level of success rate in passing laws. Many of these laws are passed unanimously. This is clearly an indicator that legislation is quite negotiated to achieve the broadest level of support.

In terms of parliamentary control, parliament can express its censure to an individual minister and press charges against him or her in a special court (Rigsretten). Since its foundation in 1849, there have been just five cases in 1856, two in 1877, 1910 and in 1995, but just two ministers were impeached and sentenced to prison time (1910, 1995). The last case in 1995 was about justice minister Erik Ninn Hansen, who prevented family reunification of Tamil refugees. He was sentenced to four months in prison and one probationary year (Folketing, 2018a). This clearly is an important deterrent for abuse of power by ministers. Normally, a minister tends to resign before such proceedings can really start. Therefore, it is just a last chance court for ministers who refuse to resign (Folketing, 2018a).

The Finnish unicameral Eduskunda consists of 200 MPs elected by proportional representation for a four-year period. In Finland, the main objective of the

Table 5.2 Legislative output of the Danish Folketing, 2001–17

	2001–05		*2005–07*		*2007–11*		*2011–15*		*2015–17*)*	
	Submitted	*Adopted (%)*	*Submitted*	*Adopted (%)*	*Submitted*	*Adopted (%)*	*Submitted*	*Adopted (%)*	*Submitted*	*Adopted (%)*
Government bills	970	86.5	427	99.8	855	96.8	831	98.3	396	101.8
Government bills adopted unanimously							299	36	146	37
Other bills	107	5.6	40	15	21	14.2	18	33.3	15	53.3

Source: Folketing (2018c).

*) data for just two legislative sessions available.

constitution of 2000 was to achieve a parliamentarisation of the political system. Tapio Raunio and Teja Tiilikainen characterise it as a *working* parliament in contrast to a *debating* parliament, as most of the work takes place in the committees. The number of committees may vary according to the number of government departments, but there are certain committees that are constitutionally enshrined. Probably, the most important is the grand committee (*Suuri valiokunta*), which comprises twenty-five members and deals with EU legislation (it has similar powers to the Swedish Committee of European Affairs). Similar to other Nordic parliaments, the fragmentation of the party system contributed to the institutionalisation of a consensual style of politics in parliament, because no party is able to achieve a working majority alone. Most governments are oversized coalitions, so there is a good chance that a party will be part of government at some stage (Karvonen, 2014: 79–82; Raunio and Tiilikainen, 2003: 76–7). According to the 2016 annual report, the running of the Finnish parliament costs €129.5 million, or about €23.50 per citizen, and is referred to as the cost of democracy. About 25 per cent of funding is allocated to pay the MPs, their assistants and the parliamentary groups; another 25 per cent pays for the administrative staff; the rest is used for maintenance of the infrastructure of parliament. Similar to the other Nordic parliaments, MPs are quite well paid at €6,407 per month and the salary of the Speaker is up to €11,792 per month (Eduskunta, 2017: 5). As already mentioned for Sweden and Denmark, one of the strengths of Nordic parliaments is that they are well resourced. At the end of 2016, the Finnish parliament had 553 full-time employees, out of whom 122 were personal assistants to MPs, and a further 67 were employed by the parliamentary groups (Eduskunta, 2017: 5).

The Norwegian Storting is considered to be one of the oldest parliamentary assemblies of Europe. It was established by the constitution of 1814 during the Napoleonic Wars and was fully democratised after 1884. Norway became an independent country in 1905. Until then the kingdom was in personal union with Sweden (for more detail on the history, see Storting, 2015: 3–8; for a thorough jubilee research volume, see Narud et al., 2014). Until 2009, it was a semi two-chamber parliament, consisting of an upper house called Lagting, to which one-quarter of the 169 MPs belong, and Odelsting, which the vast majority of the MPs are part of. The Lagting members were elected by the Storting. In reality, the Storting acted as one chamber – only 20 per cent of business was dealt with through the two-chamber system, while 80 per cent was dealt with by the whole chamber. Just formal acts were dealt with through the Lagting (Gross and Rothholz, 2009: 155; Rommetvedt, 2015: 3). Two of the main reasons for establishing a two-chamber system was to create a proper impeachment procedure and a thorough legislative process scrutinised by both houses (Narud, 2003: 301). However, in 2007, the constitution was amended, and the Storting became a unicameral parliament like all the other Nordic countries (Rommetvedt, 2015: 3). The Storting is elected for a four-year period and there is no possibility of having early elections; this diverges completely from the practice in other European countries. In this sense, the Norwegian Storting is not a debating parliament, but rather a working parliament, like the other Nordic ones (Narud, 2003: 301; Rommetvedt, 2015: 4; see also Strøm et al., 2005). Although Norway can be considered a consensus democracy, it seems that the number of conflicts over legislation has been increasing since 1973. According to Hilmar Rommetvedt, this can be observed in the rise of private members' bills from 15 in the 1984–5 legislative session to 180 in 2009–10, then a drop to 138 in 2012–13. This could also be seen in the number of oral and written questions (Rommetvedt, 2015: 4). While between 2001 and 2016 in terms of oral questions one can observe a decrease from 467 to 211, written questions remained at a high level with on average 1,500–1,700 per legislative session (Storting, 2017: 14). Consensualism in the legislative procedure has also been affected. According to Rommetvedt, between 1945 and 1973, 84 per cent of all the committee recommendations were unanimous. This declined substantially in the period between 1973 and 2013, to 38 per cent (Rommetvedt, 2015: 5). In spite of this, most legislation is agreed consensually and by very disciplined parliamentary groups (Gross and Rothholz, 2009: 159). The decline of the traditional corporatist boards and committees, including most interest groups in the governmental legislative and policy-making process, has been declining over the past decades, leading to a considerable increase in lobbying, which is appreciated by MPs as it secures counter expertise (Rommetvedt et al., 2013; Rommetvedt and Veggeland, 2017). In 2016, the Storting was supported by 493 administrative and research staff (Storting, 2016: 39).

The Icelandic Parliament (Althingi) is considered to be the one of the oldest parliaments in the world. Today's Althingi follows the Nordic model by investing a lot in committee work. It consists of sixty-three MPs elected for four years by a proportional representation system. Before the financial crisis, Icelandic parliamentary politics was based on consensus similar to the other Nordic countries; however, Table 5.3 shows that consensualism was much stronger before the banking and sovereign debt crisis than after it. Before the crisis, over 80 per cent of government bills were adopted, and more than 50 per cent unanimously. After the crisis, government bill pass rate declined to about 69.4 per cent on average for the three legislatures between 2009 and 2017. Moreover, unanimity reaches only 23.4 per cent.

Table 5.3 Legislative output of the Althingi, 2003–17

	2003–7		*2007–9*		*2009–13*		*2013–16*		*2016–17*	
	Submitted	*Adopted (%)*	*Submitted*	*Adopted (%)*	*Submitted*	*Adopted (%)*	*Submitted*	*Adopted (%)*	*Submitted*	*Adopted (%)*
Government bills	494	85	245	81.2	448	66.4	331	75	60	66.7
Adopted unanimously	214	51	112	56.3	74	25	46	18.4	11	26.7
Private bills	344	7.6	241	12	297	9.4	221	5.4	61	6.6
Committee bills	26	92	23	87	61	85.3	51	84.3	10	90
Committee bills adopted unanimously	21	88.5	17	83	28	54.1	16	37.3	4	40

Source: Yearly reports posted in Althingi (2018) and data provided by Hildur Gróa Gunnarsdóttir from Althingi upon request on 23 January 2018 via email.

In 2010, there were 123 members of staff, with an average age of 49 years, of whom 60 per cent are women (Althingi, 2011: 29). In comparison to most other Nordic parliaments, in 2015 the Althingi spent just €23.6 million, most of it for the running of parliament. Only €414,451 (1.8 per cent) was direct support for the parliamentary groups (Althingi, 2016: 42). MPs receive a reasonable salary of €8,000 per month before tax, and the Speaker about €13,000 (information provided by Hildur Gróa Gunnarsdóttir from Icelandic parliament via email, 11 January 2018).

The place of the bicameral Dutch parliament in the political system is very important. It consists of a lower house, called the Second Chamber (Tweede Kamer), which consists of 150 MPs elected by a generous proportional representation system for four years, and an upper house, the First Chamber or Senate (Eerste Kamer), which consists of 75 members who are elected by the members of the twelve provincial assemblies after they themselves have been elected by the population. The nature of the proportional representation electoral system, which creates a fragmented party system, compels the main parliamentary groups to work together consensually and with the government. Instead of an adversary style of politics, the Dutch parliament is an important arena where the amendments of the opposition parties to proposed government legislation are normally included. The Dutch States-General is a strong parliament, in spite of being dominated by government legislation. The strong system of twenty committees and the existing resources attached to it strengthen its position in relation to the government. Instead of conflict, consensus tends to dominate the legislative process with about half of all government bills being amended with proposals from the opposition parties. Overall, 90 per cent of all bills of government are supported by the opposition parties before they are approved (Andeweg and Irwin, 2014: 180–1). The low number of private bills is therefore the consequence of this pragmatic consensual approach to politics, i.e. the art of the possible (Tweede Kamer, 2014: 8). Interestingly, in contrast to the UK system, there is limited dualism between government and parliament, which is evident in the fact that members of the government cannot be members of parliament (Andeweg and Irwin, 2014: 163–4). The government and the coalition parties in parliament are the main actors in charge of the decision-making process.

The relationship between the two chambers is important. The upper chamber, known as the First Chamber as well as, unofficially, the 'Senate', consists of the seventy-five elected members from the twelve provincial legislatures after subnational provincial elections have been conducted. In the past, elections for the provincial legislatures were staggered; however, today, they take place on the same day, leading to the election of the members of the First Chamber in each individual assembly. The First Chamber has an important right of absolute veto that has been used sparingly, but not of amendment. This means bills can only be approved or rejected when they come to the Senate. Although there have been proposals to reduce this absolute veto to a suspensive one, the First Chamber has been able to resist. The king also has the right of veto, but has avoided using it and has allowed the First Chamber to fulfil this task. The centre of parliamentary work is the Tweede Kamer, which concentrates all the human and financial resources. Dutch MPs are highly professionalised. The Senate is a deliberating chamber which consists of part-time members who normally have a full-time job in another sphere of life. Senators cannot count on human or financial resources; they lack even their own office space. However, since the late 2000s, due to the difficulties of successive governments to secure majorities in both houses, small parties in the Senate have gained a considerable power as kingmakers. This became quite visible during the second Mark Rutte coalition government (2012–17) between the liberals (VVD) and the social democrats (PvdA), which had an absolute majority in the lower chamber, but not in the upper chamber. A pragmatic approach of variable geometry in terms of majorities had to be adopted in order to achieve support for legislation. Such an approach includes informal negotiation of government parties of the lower chamber with the respective representatives of the smaller parties in the upper house, so that amendments are then included in the bill of the lower house, before it comes to the Senate. The main reason, as already mentioned, is that the Senate has no power of amendment, just of veto, so that input of the First Chamber can only be informal, before it goes through the formal channels. Such parliamentary behaviour has increased over time due to the growing incongruence between Senate and Tweede Kamer majorities (Magone, 2017: 192; Thomassen et al., 2014: 193). The Senate vetoes legislation rather seldomly, because the government will withdraw the bill if there is no possibility to gaining approval there. Between 1952 and 1971, eleven laws were vetoed, but between 1972 and 1991 and 1982 and 2011 this increased to twenty-one in each period. Moreover, the government has been forced to withdraw more legislative bills over time due to the lack of a majority in the Senate (Andeweg and Irwin, 2014: 166; Thomassen et al., 2014: 193). All this has contributed to greater instability of coalition governments since the 1980s (Thomassen et al., 2014: 191).

In sum, although these six strong national parliaments are considerably constrained by the activity of each government, they are nonetheless central to the political system.

Medium reactive policy-influencing legislatures: UK, Germany, Austria, Belgium, Ireland and Italy

The early development of parliamentarianism in the UK was an important factor in developing well-established procedures and practices, which led to a high level of institutionalisation. Even today, the parliament located in the Palace of Westminster is probably the most famous and is considered as the mother of modern parliamentarianism. It is a two-chamber parliament consisting of a lower house, the House of Commons comprising 650 MPs, and an upper house, the House of Lords comprising (in 2017) 795 members (679 life peers, 91 hereditary peers and 25 bishops). Constitutional reform is needed to make the House of Lords a more representative chamber by making it a hybrid chamber with hereditary, life and *elected* peers. The new composition of the House of Lords is a consequence of a reform introduced by the Tony Blair government in 1997, which was never finished. Moreover, in spite of the introduction of a committee to appoint life peers based on merit and contribution to public life, the 'Cash for Honours' scandal of 2006–7 severely damaged the labour government and the image of the House of Lords (*The Economist*, 1 February 2007, 26 June 2007; Grant, 2009: 52). Also the David Cameron coalition government between the conservatives and liberals stopped a reform attempt due to considerable resistance from the establishment. The different parties still cannot agree on a final formula to reform the House of Lords.

Although the right of suspensive veto of the House of Lords has been eroding since the beginning of the twentieth century, today it still plays an important role in deliberating on important bills of the government. This right allows the House of Lords to delay legislation by up to one year by a continuing amending process, although the House of Commons can override it with an absolute majority. Before 2011, the House of Lords had an absolute veto on the right of government to prolong the parliamentary term indefinitely. However, in 2011, a fixed term of a maximum five years was agreed. This is quite important in order to prevent the potential of an 'elective dictatorship' (Grant, 2009: 55; Jones and Norton 2014: 377). In this sense, it remains a significant chamber, where party political differences can be overcome for the common good. Indeed, members of the House of Lords have a less adversarial approach to the work of the committees than the House of Commons (information provided by Philip Norton, who is a member of the House of Lords).

The centre of UK parliamentarianism is the directly elected House of Commons. It is dominated by the government agenda, which is presented in the Queen's speech at the beginning of the one-year legislative period. Apart from very important bills, MPs usually vote completely along party lines; according to Richard Rose, MPs vote along party lines for nine out of ten bills (Rose, 2006: 102) (see Table 5.4).

The House of Commons has a very well-established committee system as a result of its long evolutionary tradition. Since 1979, the most important committees have been the nineteen select committees that are organised to match the government departments, consisting of eleven, in some cases up to twelve, thirteen or fourteen members (UK Parliament, 2018). The chairing of such committees is assigned to the most experienced MPs and can be a very good position to hold in terms of the career of an MP (Norton, 1998b: 32). Central to UK parliamentarianism are the prime minister's questions on Wednesdays, early afternoon, for thirty minutes. Prime minister's question time is an important aspect of UK parliamentarianism, during which the leader of the opposition is able to challenge the prime minister on major policy decisions. The style is quite adversarial. This is important, because all members of the government are also members of parliament. However, since 1945, prime ministers have been spending less and less time in parliament. Prime minister Tony Blair's record of participation in voting sessions was one of the worst of modern prime ministers (Dorey, 2004: 111). Prime minister's question clearly are an important symbol of the House of Commons as a debating chamber, in contrast to most Nordic and Dutch parliaments. A prime minister's success will depend on her or his ability for well-crafted rhetorical speeches and good responses to questions.

While prime minister Tony Blair (1997–2007) and after him Gordon Brown (2007–10) could command a strong absolute majority in the House of Commons, their successors David Cameron (2010–15) and Theresa May (2015–17, 2017–) from the Conservative party were more constrained by either coalition government or smaller majorities in the legislature. In this sense, parliament gained more prominence after Tony Blair left office in 2007.

Table 5.4 Legislative output of the UK parliament, 2001–17

	Second government of Tony Blair (2001–5)			*Third government of Tony Blair (2005–7) and government of Gordon Brown (2007–10)*			*First government of David Cameron (2010–15)*			*Second government of David Cameron 2015–6) and first government of Theresa May (2016–17)*		
	Total submitted	*Total receiving royal assent (absolute numbers and percentage)*	*Total amended in House of Lords*	*Total submitted*	*Total receiving royal assent (absolute numbers and percentage)*	*Total amended in House of Lords*	*Total submitted*	*Total receiving royal assent (absolute numbers and percentage)*	*Total amended in House of Lords*	*Total submitted*	*Total receiving royal assent (absolute numbers and percentage)*	*Total amended in House of Lords*
Total bills brought from House of Commons	116	110 (95)	55 (47)	134	126 (94)	63 (47)	121	120 (99)	61 (50)	49	48 (98)	19 (39)
Government bills	90	85 (94)	53 (59)	102	101 (99)	62 (61)	91	91 (100)	48 (53)	25	34 (97)	19 (54)
Private bills	26	25 (96)	2 (8)	22	18 (82)	2 (9)	30	29 (96.7)	1 (3)	14	14 (58)	0
Total bills introduced in House of Lords	95	42 (44)	51 (54)	98	50 (51)	53 (55)	140	40 (29)	36 (26)	113	14 (12)	20 (18)
Government bills	43	40 (93)	34 (79)	48	44 (92)	43 (90)	31	30 (97)	25 (81)	14	14 (100)	13 (93)
Private members' bills	52	2 (4)	18 (35)	86	4 (5)	11 (13)	129	10 (8)	11 (9)	99	0	7 (7)
Total	211	142 (73)	106 (55)	232	176 (79)	105 (46.9)	261	160 (61)	72 (28)	162	62 (38)	39 (24)

Source: authors' compilation based on UK parliament (2001–17).

The UK parliament is regarded as a 'debating parliament' in which the opposition has major difficulty getting through its initiatives. Indeed, private bills are normally amended and discussed in the House of Lords instead of the House of Commons, and the vast majority are rejected (see Table 5.4; Grant, 2009: 55).

In contrast to the UK parliament as a debating parliament (*Redeparlament*), the bicameral German parliament has often been characterised as a working parliament (*Arbeitsparlament*). It consists of the Bundestag (Federal Chamber), the lower chamber comprising 598 directly elected MPs, and the Bundesrat (Federal Council), the upper chamber with 69 nominated representatives of the regional governments. However, the German Bundestag makes sure that all the parties represented in parliament get the right share of seats according to their share of the vote. The German electoral system is probably one of the fairest in the EU, if we do not take the 5 per cent threshold into account. Half of MPs are elected in 299 constituencies and the other half by proportional representation. Voters have two votes, one for the constituency and the other for the wider regional proportional representation list. However, sometimes it happens that one party, normally the larger parties of CDU/CSU or SPD, does well in terms of constituency seats, so that there is no exact match in terms of the proportional representation results. These surplus seats (*Überhangmandate*) distort therefore the proportional representation result, and therefore since 2013 a new electoral reform allows for compensatory seats (*Ausgleichsmandate*) for other parties in order to match the surplus seats. The representation of new political parties in parliament further complicated this arithmetic, so that after the 2017 elections the Bundestag comprised 709 seats, being the second largest chamber of parliament after the European Parliament with 750 seats (*Augsburger Allgemeine*, 25 September 2017). A central role is assigned to the standing committees in the lower house, the Bundestag, which consist of between fifteen and forty members, each according to the strength of the political parties in the legislative assembly. Most of the work is undertaken in these committees and is usually conducted consensually between government and opposition. This means that the high rate of approved legislation proposed by the government is the result of compromises and the inclusion of amendments from the opposition parties. In this sense, parliamentarianism in Germany is less adversarial and is dominated by a consensual style of cooperation between the parties (see Table 5.5).

Germany as a whole can be characterised as a consensus democracy, similar to its Western and Southern neighbours, Belgium, Luxembourg, Netherlands, Austria and Switzerland. One factor that makes the German Bundestag so effective is the level of resources that it has at its disposal. According to Thomas Saalfeld, quoting Werner J. Patzelt, the number of research assistants per MP increased by a factor of 8 from 0.7 to 6.05 between 1969 and 1991. Originally most of the staff were placed in the Bundestag, but since the 1970s most of them have been placed in the constituency. Saalfeld gives a ratio of 3:2 in favour of the constituency (Saalfeld, 1998: 53). In early 2017, each MP had his or her own office space, earned about €9,500 monthly and had an additional €4,440 monthly to cover housing in Berlin and the constituency office. They had the right to hire personal assistants up to €20,870 per month, which had to be done through the personnel office of the Bundestag. This personal staff of MPs could be placed in the Bundestag or in the constituency. It is estimated that about 4,500 assistants

are directly supporting the MPs. MPs can also be engaged in jobs related to the wider society or even enterprises, as long they declare it publicly on the website (Bundestag, 2018b). All this is independent of the funding that parliamentary groups receive, which allow them to hire further support staff. This, of course, strengthens the position of parliament in relation to the government. In spite of this strength, the constitutional framework has created a system of checks and balances in which the Bundestag is embedded. One of these is the upper house of Parliament, the Bundesrat, which consists of sixty-nine representatives, appointed by the regional governments in the *Länder*, following their elections. The representatives are bound by the instructions of their respective regional governments. The votes of the respective regional governments cannot be divided. The majority in the Bundesrat is always changing as a result of the staggered elections in the sixteen *Länder*. The number of votes in the Bundesrat is related to the population in each Land. The whole legislation process starts in the ministries of the government, and legislation needs to be submitted to the Bundesrat in order to secure their comments before it is sent to the Bundestag. From then on, most of the work is done in the Bundestag, which adopts legislation after going to the committees and undergoing three readings. Then, at the end, it goes to the Bundesrat for approval (Rudzio, 2015: 240–1). However, the Bundesrat is quite constrained in terms of time and any deliberation can only last for three to six weeks (Rudzio, 2015: 248).

For most important consent laws (*Zustimmungsgesetze*) the Bundesrat has absolute veto. This sometimes leads to conflict between government and the Bundesrat. In order to overcome differences a Joint Mediation Committee (*Vermittlungsausschuss*) of the two houses can be appointed. Originally it was quite a small committee, but, with unification, there are currently thirty-two members, sixteen from each chamber. Therefore, before being discussed in the Joint Mediation Committee, there is a small round of negotiations. Until 1972, 100 per cent of all such vetoes were overcome in the Joint Mediation Committee, between 1972 and 1990 over 90 per cent of such conflicts were overcome, between 1990 and 1998 (Kohl governments) 88 per cent, between 1998 and 2005 (Gerhard Schröder governments) 90 per cent, and last but not least, between the grand coalition governments under chancellor Angela Merkel (2005–9 and 2013–17 almost 100 per cent solution of conflicts were resolved. During the CDU/CSU and FDP coalition (2009–13) under chancellor Angela Merkel just 77 per cent were resolved (Bundesrat, 2018a: 6; Rudzio, 2015: 246, 293–8). Moreover, the Bundesrat has a suspensive veto (*suspensives Einspruchsrecht*) over simple laws, which can only be overcome by the Bundestag with an absolute majority of MPs.

A second factor that constrains the powers of the Bundestag is the fact that Germany is a federal state. In this sense, detailed negotiation of legislation is an important factor in the committees. This 'cooperative federalism' (*Politikverflechtung*) is strengthened by the watchful eye of the Bundesrat. However, different or changing majorities in both houses may lead to blockades and stagnation in policy-making (Benz, 2009: 117).

Last, but not least, the strong position of the chancellor in the political system compels the German parliament to cooperate and negotiate with the government in order to achieve a broader majority for the bill. The experience of the Weimar Republic, where seventeen cabinets each lasted on average 287 days (less than a year) and which for 58 per cent of this period had no majority, contrasts

Table 5.5 Legislative output of the German Bundestag, 1994–2017

Legislature/ chancellor	*13th legislature 1994–98 Helmut Kohl*			*14th legislature 1998–2002 Gerhard Schröder*			*15th legislature 2002–5 Gerhard Schröder*		
	Submitted	*Approved*	*Percentage of submitted*	*Submitted*	*Approved*	*Percentage of submitted*	*Submitted*	*Approved*	*Percentage of submitted*
Government bills	443	403	91	443	394	89	320	281	88
Private bills	329	102	31	328	108	33	211	85	40.3
Bundesrat bills	151	36	24	93	22	23	112	17	15.2
Total bills	923	566		864	559		643	400	

Legislature/ chancellor	*16th legislature 2005–9 Angela Merkel*			*17th legislature 2009–13 Angela Merkel*			*18th legislature 2013–17 Angela Merkel*		
	Submitted	*Approved*	*Percentage of submitted*	*Submitted*	*Approved*	*Percentage of submitted*	*Submitted*	*Approved*	*Percentage of submitted*
Government bills	537	488	91	484	433	90	526	488	93
Private bills	264	89	34	278	88	32	148	52	35
Bundesrat Bills	104	19	18.3	82	17	21	57	10	18
Total bills	905	616		844	553		731	555	

Note: The difference in the totals is related to the fact that some bills are split or merged so that in the end the totals differ from the sum.

Source: author's compilation Bundestag (2018b).

heavily with the stable majority-seeking system of the present German system. The constructive motion of censure is an important instrument in preventing the early downfall of a government. This means that the opposition has to present an alternative candidate for the position of chancellor and eventually an alternative programme before it can submit a constructive motion of censure. This is an understandably difficult task, because such attempts may fail and damage considerably the main leader of the opposition (Rudzio, 2015: 230–4). Several forms of scrutiny and control of the government are used by the Bundestag, particularly interpellations such as big questions (*Grosse Anfrage*) and question time (*aktuelle Stunden*) (Saalfeld, 1998: 65). In the past three Angela Merkel governments (2005–17) there were on average 112 such *Aktuelle Stunden*, lower in the grand coalition and higher in the coalition between CDU/CSU and the Liberals (FDP) (Bundestag, 2018b).

In terms of human and material resources, the German parliament is quite well resourced. Overall, there are about 2,600 staff working for parliament and each committee is well-resourced in terms of human resources. A quite important department is the scientific support service (*Wissenschaftliche Hilfsdienst*), which provides MPs with excellent research work, giving them an edge in relation to the government (Bundestag, 2018a). In contrast, in the Bundesrat, the secretariat consists just of 200 civil servants and has fewer resources (Bundesrat, 2018b).

There are strong similarities between the German and Austrian parliaments, as both have a chancellor democracy and are federal states. However, the German parliament is probably better resourced than the Austrian one. In a study by the Austrian parliament in 2000, it was established that the Austrian parliament receives just 0.12 per cent of the state budget, and in 2005 this declined to 0.10 per cent (Schefbeck, 2006: 150). This means that, in terms of financial resources, it is at the lowest level among Western European parliaments. This also leads to the joint administration of both the lower house, Nationalrat (National Council), and the upper house, Bundesrat (Federal Council). In spite of this fact, the Nationalrat has been able to gain more human and financial resources since 1992. In a similar way to Germany, most of the work is done in the standing committees (*ständige Auschüsse*), and there is a culture of consensualism allowing the opposition to make amendments to the bill. The vast majority of the legislation is proposed by the government. About 60 to 70 per cent of bills are from the government, while only 20 to 30 per cent are from the opposition (Schefbeck, 2006: 152).

The upper house in Austria, the Bundesrat, has a suspensive veto only. It consists of appointed representatives of the regional parliaments, the *Landtage*, and not the regional governments as in Germany. However, both the annual rotation of the presidency among the *Bundesländer* and the changing composition of the assembly resulting from the staggered elections bear strong similarities to the German system. The use of written questions (*schriftliche Anfragen*) is the most common instrument used by the opposition parties to control the government. This is complemented by oral question time, which is highly regulated and formalised. Moreover, there has also been a growing quantity of urgent questions through *aktuelle Stunden* (topical question time) and *dringlichen Anfragen* (urgent questions) (Schefbeck, 2006: 158–60).

The lack of an absolute majority by one party since 1979 has contributed to a strong connection between government and parliament. The need to keep a

Table 5.6 Legislative output of the Austrian parliament, 1996–2013

	1996–9		*1999–2002*		*2002–6*		*2006–8*		*2008–13*	
	Submitted	*Adopted %*	*Submitted*	*Adopted %*	*Submitted*	*Adopted %*	*Submitted*	*Adopted %*	*Submitted*	*Adopted %*
Government bills	423	71	257	66	365	70	161	69	478	74
Government bills adopted unanimously		25.7		41.9		50.8		37.1		37.4
Private bills	116	19	85	22	115	22	49	21	120	19
Other bills	57	10	49	13	44	8	22	9	49	8

Source: Figures kindly supplied by Günther Schefbeck from the Austrian Parliament upon request.

broad absolute majority through a coalition of parties leads to a culture of compromise and consensus. Between 1983 and 2017, 79.4 per cent of the period was coalition government. Only between 2000 and 2006, and since 2018, has there been two coalition governments just between two parties, the ÖVP and FPÖ. The consequence is that parliament has been used by the grand coalition parties to just rubber stamp most of the legislation agreed in the coalition government and they have only informally consulted with their social partners (trade union confederations, economy chamber, labour chamber and the agriculture chamber), However, it seems that the culture of consensual unanimity has been declining considerably. As Table 5.6 shows, while between 1945 and 1986 on average 80 per cent of government bills were adopted unanimously, between 1986 and 2013, the figure had declined to 37 per cent (Magone, 2017: 200).

This may be a sign of a still consensual approach to the legislative work, but with more opposition. There has been a fragmentation of the party system taking place. The new parliament after 2017 includes five parliamentary groups in the lower house and a Green parliamentary group in the upper house. This is a quite a change in comparison to the period before 1986, when there were just the ÖVP, SPÖ and the FPÖ.

The Swiss case is probably the most difficult to categorise. As already mentioned in Chapters 1 and 4, the Swiss political system gets inspiration from the French constitution of 1795, in which a *directoire* was installed to overcome the period of la Terreur of Maximilien de Robespierre. In this context, parliament is the core of the political system of Switzerland and all other branches emanate from it. It is the parliament that selects the members of government (Bundesrat) and the judges on the Supreme Court. The constitution of 1848 conceptualises the government of Switzerland rather as a committee of parliament (*gouvernement d'assemblée*); however, over time they have become separated. Nevertheless, the seven members of the Bundesrat are still elected by the federal assembly (*Bundesversammlung*), comprising the members of the two houses (Vatter, 2014: 262). In comparison to other countries, no laws of national parliament can be examined on its constitutionality, because a constitutional court does not exist. It means that legislation adopted in Swiss parliament is then the law of the land (Lüthi, 2014: 170). Another feature of the Swiss political system is that it shows

many similarities to the United States in terms of a complete separation of powers between legislative and executive. Although the Bundesrat submits most of the bills (on average 80 per cent), parliament has been able to improve its legislative initiative possibilities. Neither parliament nor government can be dismissed during the four-year legislative period. It means that no government can call early elections. Parliament has no right to submit motions of censure to government (Lüthi, 2014: 170).

The Swiss parliament is a symmetrical bicameral parliament. The lower house, the National Council (Nationalrat, Conseil Nationale, Consiglio Nazionale), consists of 200 MPs elected by proportional representation. The upper house, the Council of States (Ständerat, Conseil d'Etats, Consiglio di Stati), consists of forty-six MPs (twelve from each of the twenty cantons and six from the half cantons) elected for four years by a simple majority system. The Council of States comprises mainly established politicians with a long career, and they sit according to their names, not political parties. This means that there is a strong parliamentary culture of consensus in the upper chamber, fulfilling its role as a chamber of reflection. Parliament is the centre of the Swiss political system. Bills can be initiated through either of the houses. Government bills normally are initiated in one of the houses according to the topic. Topics related to federalism and regional policy are usually submitted in the upper house, whereas more general bills go to the lower house. The Speakers of both houses also have a say, and if no agreement can be achieved, sometimes a simple raffle system may be used to allocate the bills (information from Swiss parliament).

Probably a very important factor was the upgrading of the ad hoc committees to standing committees in 1992 (Lüthi, 2014: 174). The new constitution of 1999 and the subsequent law on parliament (*Bundesgesetz über die Bundesversammlung*) on 13 February 2002 further strengthened parliament (Lüthi, 2014: 187). In this regard, most of the work happens in the standing committees, allowing parties opposed to the government bill to amend it (Lüthi, 2014: 174). Differences between the two houses of parliament are solved through a conciliation committee (*Einigungsausschuss*). However, it seems that the Council of States is more successful in pushing its case. In the past decades, the number of cases dealt with by the conciliation committee have been between sixteen and thirty, but very few failed to be agreed upon. One of the reasons for disagreement is that the two chambers have different majorities. In the lower chamber, there is a rightwing majority consisting of the Swiss People's Party (SVP), the Liberal Party (FDP) and sometimes the Christian People's Party (CVP), while in the upper house there is a centre-left consisting of the Socialist Party (SPS) and the CVP. It seems that the councillors of the upper house are more skilled and better prepared when negotiating a deal, so that they have been more successful in shaping the final bill.

Its status as a militia parliament disguises to some extent how much MPs work in the two houses. MPs are not paid a salary for their work and only receive reimbursement for expenses. However, these reimbursements are quite generous and may amount to a salary if the payments for committee work are added to it. Quite a lot of MPs work full time, but there are also a number who are just part time. According to the website of the Swiss parliament, an MP may be able to earn between €92,000 and €138,000 if s/he takes part in the four three-week sessions and is engaged in one or two committees in between periods. Although this is referred to as reimbursement, in reality MPs get a generous lump sum for every day spent in parliament, which can be used as they see fit. They do not need to show any receipts for it. The quite high reimbursement lump sums are necessary because Switzerland is a relatively expensive country. In additional, they are entitled to research support of €16,500 a year, which they can use as they like. However, Swiss MPs have no office space of their own (Magone, 2017: 194; see also, Vatter, 2014: 269–70).There have been calls for a reform in the direction of professionalisation, but this has been resisted so far by the vast majority. The Swiss parliament is a semi-professionalised parliament in which elected representatives of interest groups are also present. One can probably identify three main groups: the militia parliamentarians (*Milizpolitiker*) who are in the main lawyers, entrepreneurs and some rich farmers who work full time in addition to their job in parliament and represent a minority of about 10 to 13 per cent in the lower house (they have almost vanished from the upper house); the part-time politicians are those that are presidents, vice-presidents or high-ranking representatives of interest groups who clearly are acting mainly on behalf of their constituencies and can rely on human and material resources from their respective institutions and comprise about 60 per cent of all MPs in both houses; and the professional full-time politicians who are dedicated full time to the job and represent 28 to 30 per cent of councillors (Vatter, 2014: 268–9). The growing complexity of the policy process is creating problems for MPs in keeping up with new developments, so that the militia parliament is just a myth among the population. In reality some professionalisation has to take place in order to keep parliamentary business afloat. There is a real danger that parliament is slowly being captured by special interests due to the fact that political parties need lots of funding for elections in a multilevel system and therefore become dependent on funding coming from these groups. As already mentioned, interest groups may not only gain control over MPs but also get their own representatives elected. All this is possible because there is no state funding for political parties and campaign funding has to be raised. It means that Switzerland is the only country in which there are no mechanisms of transparency of party funding. These issues have been highlighted by the Group of States Against Corruption (GRECO) of the Council of Europe, but have been more or less ignored by the Swiss institutions (Greco, 2015: 6).

The consensual culture of parliamentarianism forces political parties to achieve a viable compromise in legislation, so that it is not challenged by referendums, which can overturn the hard work done in parliament. Moreover, the pre-parliamentary legislative process (*Vernehmungslassungsrecht*) is a specific constitutionally enshrined right that allows relevant interest groups to comment on the preparation of new bills that should be approved in parliament. In this regard, lobbying is structured by a wide range of committees attached to the Bundesrat (Federal Council, the government). It means that parliament is just the last stage of a long process of decision-making on legislation. Therefore, all the big parties represented in the Bundesrat are very keen to achieve a consensual formula for the bills to ensure legislation is 'referendum-secure' (*referendumssicher*) (Lüthi, 2014: 171).

According to a study commissioned by the Swiss Parliament, only Spain is less professionalised based on income, parliamentary costs and workload (Z'Graggen, 2009: 100).

Probably, the strongest Southern European parliament is in Italy. It has had to deal with major transformations leading from the First (1948–92) to the Second Republic (since 1993). In this regard, scholars speak of a second transition to democracy after 1992. The Italian parliament is bicameral with a Senate (upper house) consisting of 322 members, and a Chamber of Deputies with 630 members. Both chambers are directly elected and have the same significance in the legislative process. A lot of legislation is done together through the so-called 'shuttle' approach, which allows both houses to work on government legislation until both are happy with the result. Coordination mechanisms and skills in this process have been developed since 1948 (Newell, 2006: 388).

Until the collapse of the First Republic in Italy in 1992, the balanced symmetrical bicameral Italian parliament was central to the political system. One of the main reasons was the instability of government. The lack of absolute majorities by a single party strengthened the positions, as individuals, of MPs of any party. Maurizio Cotta called it the 'centrality of parliament', because of this dependency of government on the majority in parliament (Cotta, 1994). The collapse of the former political elite and parties due to the uncovering of a web of systemic corruption – tangentopoli – in 1992 led to a major reshuffle of the MPs, resulting in the vast majority of MPs having no real experience. In 1994, 70 per cent of members were elected for the first time, with only a small minority having had experience in the First Republic (Verzichelli, 1995: 118).

However, by 2001, 70 to 80 per cent of MPs had had previous experience in parliament, showing a low level of rotation and a high degree of professionalisation. Additionally, the number of senior members of the Chamber of Deputies increased to 30 per cent. Moreover, the number of MPs renewed in the same committees reached 67 per cent in 2001 (Verzichelli, 2003, 2004: 143–5). In spite of this growth in professionalisation, until 2006 the average legislative turnover was still 49 per cent, and excluding the first election of the Second Republic in 1994, about 40 per cent (Cotta and Verzichelli, 2008: 85). This means that, in a very short period of time, parliament regained its position in the political system but still needed to strengthen its level of professionalisation.

In the Second Republic, Italian parliamentarianism has been rationalised, in particular by reducing the powers of the committees as decision-making bodies, especially the clientelistic use of 'small laws' (*leggine*) which were purposefully adopted to help specific constituency groups. There has also been a shift of final decision-making from the committees to the plenary in order to avoid such a proliferation of laws. The scrutiny of government decrees and legislation has become more important than the approval of micro-sectional legislation (Della Sala, 1998: 87–8). As a rule of thumb, one can state that committee-adopted legislation represents about 20 per cent, while those adopted in the plenary represent 80 per cent. According to James Newell, in spite of the traumatic transformation of the Italian party system, the political culture of parliamentarianism did not change very much. He asserts that a culture of consensually bargaining, so-called *consociativismo*, dominated the work before tangentopoli. Even the Communist Party (PCI) was included in this process through its committee work. The overall level of consensus was not as high as in the lofty days of *consociativismo*. Nevertheless it clearly showed a path dependency in terms of the legislative process (Newell, 2006: 394–7). The switching of individual MPs from one party to another has always been present in Italian politics. However, the collapse of the previous party system strengthened the statute of the individual MP in parliament. Due to the emergence of new parties after 1993, party discipline has been quite weak, leading to more party switching. An excellent study by Luca Pinto shows that weak party institutionalisation is one of the major factors allowing for extensive individual MP party switching. The main reasons for party switching seem to be policy based, and they happen during policy and budgetary debates or government formation. Individual party switching was quite high in the thirteenth legislature (1996–2001) and sixteenth legislatures (2006–11), with 221 and 185 such cases, respectively (Pinto, 2015: 328, 337–8).

There is a general concern that successive Italian governments have tended to use government decrees to bring through legislation, which is a chaotic approach to legislation (Gianniti and Lupo, 2004: 233–7; see also Capano and Giuliani, 2003: 27–8). The use of decree laws has been a constant feature of the governmental legislative pattern. As Table 5.7 shows, about 20 to 40 per cent of all laws are decree laws. Clearly, this has partly been due to the cumbersome approval of laws in the Italian parliament. In terms of crisis, which has been always present in Italy, governments rely heavily on this form of legislation to bypass parliament. The economic and financial crisis between 2008 and 2013 is a good example of this kind of legislative behaviour by governments. The replacement of the Berlusconi IV government (2008–11) by the electorally non-legitimised technocratic of Mario Monti's government (2011–12), but supported by parliament, shows the still ambiguous relationship of executive-legislative relations towards democracy (Culpepper, 2014; Marangoni and Verzichelli, 2015). Attempts such as that of prime minister Matteo Renzi to reform parliamentarianism have so far ended in failure (Ceccarini and Bordignon, 2017).

Weak reactive policy-influencing legislatures

In contrast to strong and medium policy-influencing legislatures, weak legislatures have greater difficulty in making government accountable to parliament. Apart from the limited availability of resources, the overall structure of parliament is only partly fit for purpose.

The French unbalanced bicameral parliament, consisting of the National Assembly (Assemblée Nationale) with 577 MPs and the Senate (Sénat) with 348 Senators, was considerably weakened after the introduction of the constitution of the Fifth Republic in 1958. It was one of the main objectives of Charles de Gaulle to weaken the position of parliament in relation to the executive. This meant that the scrutiny of legislation is overwhelmingly dominated by the executive (see Table 5.8).

One major problem is the lack of a strong committee system. There are only eight standing committees, which are normally too large to be effective. Such committees are overcrowded, with seventy to eighty MPs in each – almost small parliaments in their own right. The annual legislative period is also quite restricted (120 days, article 28), creating problems in dealing with the ever-growing legislative work (Elgie, 2003: 164–5). A major factor that weakens parliamentarianism is that senators and MPs are allowed to accumulate mandates. Most senators are

Table 5.7 Legislative output of the Italian parliament, 1996–2017

13th Legislature (1996–2001) Lamberto Dini (1995–6) Romano Prodi I (1996–8) Massimo D'Alema I (1998–9) Massino D'Alema II (1999–2000)			*14th Legislature (2001–6) Giuliano Amato I (2000–1) Silvio Berlusconi I (2001–5) Silvio Berlusconi II (2005–6)*			*15th Legislature (2006–8) Silvio Berlusconi III (2006–8) Romano Prodi II (2006–8)*			*16th Legislature (2008–13) Prodi II (2006–8) Silvio Berlusconi IV (2008–11) Mario Monti (2011–13)*			*17th Legislature (2013–17) Mario Monti (2011–13) Enrico Letta (2013–14) Matteo Renzi (2014–16) Paolo Gentiloni-Silveri (2016–17)*		
Number of laws (decree–laws)	Governmental laws (%)	Parliamentary laws (%)	Number of laws (decree–laws)	Governmental laws (%)	Parliamentary laws (%)	Number of laws (decree–laws)	Governmental bills (%)	Parliamentary bills (%)	Number of laws (decree–laws)	Governmental bills (%)	Parliamentary bills (%)	Number of laws (decree–laws)	Governmental bills (%) (decree–laws %)	Parliamentary bills (%)
927 (174)	79 (19)	21	692 (200)	79 (29)	21	112 (32)	88 (29)	12	395 (106)	77 (37)	23	366 (83)	77 (23)	23

Source: own compilation based on database of the Senato (2018) of the Italian Parliament.

Table 5.8 Legislative output of the French parliament, 2002–18

	12th Legislature (2002–7)			*13th Legislature (2007–12)*			*14th Legislature (2012–17)*			*15th Legislature (2017–)*		
	Submitted	*Approved*	*%*	*Submitted*	*Approved*	*%*	*Submitted*	*Approved*	*%*	*Submitted*	*Approved*	*%*
Government bills	1,035	411	40	643	368	57	409	339	82	86	31	36
Private bills	5,676	60	1.1	4,986	71	1.4	1,837	110	6	294	15	5
Amendments	243,380	17,113	7	68,962	11,050	16	115,200	18,821	16	10,490	1,530	15

Source: database of Assemblée Nationale (2018).

elected out of the local constituencies and therefore are important local councillors or even mayors. It means that both houses of parliament have high levels of absenteeism. After the constitutional reform of 2008, MPs and Senators could just accumulate one additional public position, mainly at local level. In this regard, quite a lot of MPs were also mayors, presidents of a regional council, or members of governments at any of these levels. This was changed during the François Hollande presidency in 2014. Law 125 (Incompatibilities for Members of Parliament and Senators) and Law 126 (Incompatibilities for Members of the European Parliament) forbid MPs and Senators from being able to accumulate an executive position, but positions in legislative bodies at subnational level are still possible. The new laws entered in force on 31 March 2017, shortly before the end of the legislature period. In terms of figures, at the end of 2013 there were 228 MP-mayors (41 per cent) and 107 Senator-mayors (31 per cent), while in January 2017 there were 175 MP-mayors (30 per cent) and 108 Senator-mayors (31 per cent) (*La Libération*, 31 March 2017; *Le Monde*, 18 October 2016). In a seminal study on the relationship between national and local office, it was found that there has always been a quite large preference for constituency work. Clearly, this preference for constituency work over national parliamentary work has contributed to a vicious circle of perpetuating the weakness of national parliament in the political system (Brouard et al., 2013: 157). In spite of this fact, 69.6 per cent of MPs regard the national parliamentary work as the more important, with just 30.4 per cent thinking that local constituency work is more important. The main reason for this attitude is that the vast majority are worried about the asymmetrical balance of power between the executive and the legislative institutions (Brouard et al., 2013: 145). The 2014 reform may contribute to a shift of attention to the national level.

However, according to Eric Kerrouche, individual French MPs are still able to play a strong role in shaping the legislative process. Both in terms of private bills and amendments, MPs are active, particularly among the centre-right parties. It seems that amendments are a way of integrating most of the concerns of the opposition and the majority parties. According to Kerrouche, MPs have a better strategic chance of submitting amendments at the committee level than at the floor level (Kerrouche, 2006: 357). Moreover, there has been a shift towards more active and conflictive behaviour since 1981. Amendments are placed strategically to delay controversial government legislation. This strategy of the opposition has clearly more success if the bill is also controversial within the political parties forming the government (Knapp and Wright, 2001: 156). The processes of socialisation have been important in enhancing the role of parliament, in spite of the dominance of the executive (Kerrouche, 2006: 362). Cécile Vigour found out that MPs regard the invisible work in committees and parliamentary groups as quite important. MPs consider their first task in parliamentary work to be law-making. As already mentioned, the amendment procedure is regarded as quite crucial to influencing the final outcome of bills. Coordination of the position in the parliamentary group also seems to be quite important. According to Vigour, 50 per cent of time spent in committees is dedicated to the legislative process (examination of government and private bills, hearings, reports and decrees), a further 25 per cent is spent on non-legislative work and a further 15 per cent on administrative matters within the committee (Vigour, 2013: 225–7). Overall, MPs are split over their influence on the legislative process. A slight majority of 37 per cent thinks that they have a moderate influence, 36 per cent a strong or very strong influence, and 27 per cent no or a very limited influence (Vigour, 2013: 227–8).

The federalisation of Belgium, after approval of the constitution of 1993, led to the major devolution of competencies to the subnational parliaments. Meanwhile, there have been six state reforms since the 1970s. The Belgian parliament consists of two houses, the Chamber of Deputies (Chambre des Deputés) and the Senate (Sénat) comprising 150 MPs and 60 Senators respectively. The new constitution allowed for a major reform of national parliament in which the Senate was transformed into a chamber representing the interests of the subnational units. Belgian bicameralism is asymmetrical. In the sixth state reform in 2014, the Senate was finally designed as a chamber consisting of delegates coming from the subregional parliaments. The main forum of policy-making is the Chamber of Deputies. This is evident from the number of committees. While the lower house has eleven committees, the Senate has just three (institutional, community and regional affairs), clearly indicating that the lower house is now the dominant chamber, and the Senate concentrates more on issues related to central-regional relations. Although Senators are delegates from the subnational parliaments, according to article 42 of the constitution they are supposed to represent the whole country (Goossens and Cannoot, 2015: 38–41). Like in Germany, Austria and Switzerland, there is a conciliation committee dealing with divergences in terms of legislation between the two chambers, particularly in matters that are dealt with through the compulsory or facultative bicameral procedure. However, the number of bills discussed in the Senate coming from the lower house has been on average just 6.2 per cent, indicating the peripheral importance of the upper house in the legislative process (Magone, 2017: 195, 197).

The reform strengthened the position of the government in relation to parliament by introducing a constructive motion of censure, similar to Germany, Spain, Poland and Hungary. This may indeed work both ways, because it makes the opposition better able to express its discontent with government policy without calling for a resignation. The number of MPs and Senators respectively in the two houses was substantially reduced. Moreover, MPs are not allowed to be part of the government, thus ensuring a separation of powers (De Winter, 1998: 115–18). The Belgian parliament has been provided with increased human and material resources since the 1980s, including research assistance and office space for individual MPs (De Winter, 1998: 105–6). According to Paul Magnette, there has been a considerable quantitative use of instruments of control by the government, such as interpellations, written questions and oral questions. However, it is difficult to assess whether this has had any impact on government behaviour (Magnette, 2004: 99–103). In reality, the coalition government consisting of several parties constrains considerably MPs in terms of developing their own initiatives. The very strict party discipline of the government parties makes the lower house a kind of rubber stamping chamber for government work. On average, between 1991–2014, 93 per cent of all government bills were adopted and just 10 per cent of private bills (Magone, 2017: 197; Moury, 2013: 63).

The House of Deputies (*Chambre des Deputés*) is the unicameral parliament of Luxembourg consisting of 60 MPs. Similar to Belgium, it is a rather weak parliament, because MPs are quite overwhelmed in terms of workload. One of the main reasons is that parliament allows for a *cumul de mandats*. In 2013, about two-thirds of MPs were also local mayors or councillors and clearly this reduces their time spent in national parliament (*L'essentiel*, 24 September 2013). MPs are under considerable pressure because they have to work in several of the twenty-four committees and be experts in different matters. In 2013, almost half (47 per cent) of the budget of parliament was generously allocated to the individual MPs and parliamentary groups (Magone, 2017: 195). One feature of the House of Deputies is that it relies strongly on the Council of State, an advisory institution that serves both the government as well as parliament, in order to screen first the constitutionality and legal feasibility of bills. In this regard the Council of State acts as an informal upper chamber (Magone, 2017: 182).

The Irish unbalanced bicameral Oireach, consisting of the lower house (Daíl) and the Senate (Seanad), was structured along the lines of the Westminster model, although, as Michael Gallagher asserts, it has features of both this model and of consensus democracy. The Oireach consists of the lower house with 158 members representing 40 constituencies of about 20,000 to 30,000 people elected by a single-transferable vote (STV) and the Senate with 60 seats appointed by corporatist panels from the economy, society and also government. In principle, the members of the Senate should be independent from political parties and represent wider social and economic interests; however, in reality, many of them are also contributing to the majority of the government. The originality of the Senate in Ireland is only emulated by Slovenia, which has a similar bicameral system. Forty-three of the sixty Senators are elected in five panels representing vocational interests, namely culture and education, agriculture, labour, industry and commerce, and public administration. A further six Senators are elected by the graduates of two prestigious Irish universities, namely National University of Ireland and University of Dublin (Trinity College). Eleven are nominated by the prime minister (Taoiseach) (Oireachtas, 2018). The centre of parliamentary business is the lower house (the Daíl). Legislation is initiated in the lower house and revised in the Senate. However the Senate may also initiate legislation proposed by the government, but such bills should not involve any funding. This has been happening more recently (Oireachtas, 2018). The Irish parliament is considered to be weak. In 1983, it tried to create more effective standing committees, emulating the UK ones after 1979, but, despite several attempts, the committee system has been inadequate in making the executive accountable to parliament (Gallagher, 2010a: 217). One of the consequences is a politicisation of the other control instruments, in particular question time, which takes place over one hour three times a week (Gallagher, 2010a: 219). The Senate is also weak, because the government of the day is very keen to have a majority through the eleven appointees of the government.

All three Southern European parliaments in Portugal, Spain and Greece are quite weak. The increasing importance of strong minority or absolute majority governments has undermined the position of parliament even more. In spite of forty years of democratisation, the three parliaments are still engaged in a process of institutionalisation and professionalisation. The role of committees, which have high levels of rotation in all three countries, can lead to some amendments from the opposition, but overall their role is quite weak. One of the major problems is that all three parliaments have limited human and material resources, and MPs are poorly paid. These parliaments tend to be debating parliaments (*Redeparlamente*) rather than working parliaments (*Arbeitsparlamente*). Research on Southern European parliamentarianism has been rather scarce, particularly in the case of Greece.

Probably, the weakest of the three is the Greek Vouli, consisting of 300 MPs, which has large committees (inspired by the French model) and is dominated by government legislation. Normally, the respective permanent committees have only five to eight days to discuss a bill and prepare a non-binding report. Most of the work is done in the plenary session, which also works over the summer with a smaller parliament of 100 MPs. Between 90 and 95 per cent of legislation is initiated by the government and, because of the majoritarian nature of the political system, there is only minimal involvement of the opposition in the legislative process. Indeed, the low quality of legislation of the Greek parliament, resulting from the low level of scrutiny by MPs, is a major problem for the country. One growing problem is the fact that the government often reverts to passing laws by decree, which is only intended to be used in exceptional circumstances, bypassing the scrutiny of parliament. After the adoption of the revised constitution in 2001, the incompatibility of the position of MP with other activities was enshrined in the constitution. As a tradeoff, MPs were allocated increased resources in terms of living expenses, benefits, an increase in salary, plus office space and research assistants. Each MP has, on average, five assistants (three civil servants, one of whom will be an academic, a personal assistant and a security officer) (Zervakis and Auernheimer, 2009: 826, 837). This has also meant the end of what has been called 'part-time parliamentarianism'. However, it will take some time to change a culture that has existed since 1952 (Zervakis and Auernheimer, 2009: 853). In a similar way to the UK, the government is selected from the elected MPs. Governments in Greece are large (forty-eight to fifty members), with ministers and junior ministers, meaning that all MPs belonging to the dominant party have a good chance of being part of the cabinet. This strengthens the political patronage opportunities for the government (Foundethakis, 2003: 97–9).

The financial crisis has contributed to a deterioration of the position of parliament in relation to government. This phase has been catastrophic for Greek parliamentarianism because Greece was subject to a strict supervisory regime related to the conditions imposed on the country by the three loan packages they received during the financial crisis. It meant parliament had to approve a considerable number of pieces of legislation indicating their will to reform the political system by making major cuts in crucial areas such as pensions and the healthcare system. Legislative packages were rubber stamped by parliament in a very short period of time, in order to be able to receive a further tranche of funding from the EU and the IMF (Gemenis and Nezi, 2015: 26). The paradox is that a communist party like Syriza is carrying out the implementation of the austerity packages, which it opposed vehemently, and it is using the same rubber stamping parliamentary procedures that it criticised when ND and PASOK were in power.

The Spanish parliament is characterised by an unbalanced bicameral system consisting of the lower house, the Congress of Deputies (Congreso de Deputados) with 350 MPs, and the upper house, the Senate (Senado) with presently 265 Senators. While MPs are elected in fifty-two mainly small multi-member constituencies by a D'Hondt proportional representation system, the Senate is partly elected and partly nominated. The vast majority of 208 Senators are elected by a non-transferable voting system (NTV) at provincial level as well as in Ceuta and Melilla; the rest are nominated by the assemblies of the sixteen autonomous communities according to the strength of the political parties in each. The allocation of seats to each region is based on the size of population. It means that allocations can vary over time depending on demographic changes. Another aspect is that regional elections take place in different years from general elections, leading to political party changes during the legislature. The Congreso is the main policy-making forum, while the Senate can just delay legislation, but not veto it. Today the Senate is still awaiting reform – something that Elisa Roller has called 'an impossible mission', because of the diversity of opinions on how to achieve it. The main aim is to make it more compatible with the existing state of autonomies consisting of seventeen regional governments, but the main parties and regionalist parties cannot agree on a final model (Cidoncha Martín, 2011; Roller, 2002). At the end of October 2017, the Senate gained a new momentum during the Catalan crisis which was related to the quest for independence by the regional independentist coalition government under the leadership of Carles Puigdemont. The Rajoy government activated article 155 of the constitution after this was discussed and approved by the Senate, suspending the Catalan autonomy after their unilateral declaration of independence (Declaración unilateral de independencia) was declared by the independentist parties in the Catalan parliament. This clearly shows the importance of the Senate for issues related to the regional autonomies in Spain. The activation of article 155 to deal with the Catalan independentist challenge was approved with 214 votes for and 47 against (mainly the Catalan independentist parties and the Basque nationalist party (PNV) and one abstention (*El Pais*, 27 October 2017). The Spanish parliament tends to be more active and dynamic when a party does not achieve an absolute majority and needs support from some of the parliamentary parties. A variable geometry of majorities has to be negotiated with parliamentary groups in order to get its legislative packages approved. Governing is rather difficult during periods of crisis, like in the recent financial and sovereign debt crisis, which forced prime minister Zapatero during his second term to make major concessions to opposition parties in order to get successive austerity packages approved (Capo Giol, 2003; Field, 2016; Oubiña, 2012). After the turbulent experiences of instability in the Second Republic, and a long dictatorship under general Francisco Franco, 'stability' is highly prized by the political elite and population. This became evident when the old two-party system consisting of socialists and the People's Party (PP) began to falter in the European Parliament elections of 2014, and then in the subsequent regional and general elections of 2015, leading to a four-party system, which now includes a radical leftwing party called Podemos and a moderate centre-right party Ciudadanos. The first contributed to the collapse of the vote of the PSOE, while the latter became a major challenge to PP.

Once in power, the prime minister is in a strong position, because the constructive motion of censure requires the presentation of an alternative candidate. There were four motions of censure in four decades, and just one of them was successful. This was the challenge by the leader of the socialist party Pedro Sanchez against prime minister Mariano Rajoy on 1 June 2018, since when he has become the new prime minister (*El Pais*, 1 June 2018).

The strong position of the executive, even it is a minority government, leads to dominance of the legislative process. The vast majority of bills adopted are government bills, and just a small number are private bills (Table 5.9). In spite of this strong position of the executive, it is up to the craftsmanship of prime ministers, ministers and the governing party in parliament to achieve viable majorities, particularly at committee level, that have some ability to approve the legislative process (*competencia legislativa plena*). However, the committees of the Spanish system are still characterised by a high level of rotation, making it difficult for professionalisation and institutionalisation (Maurer, 2008a, 2008b: 100). Both minority and majority governments are keen to strike a deal at committee level, as this comprises about 30 to 40 per cent of all legislation (Field, 2009: 423). One of the main reasons seems to be the fact that MPs are poorly paid and have very scarce human and material resources. In past decades, parliamentary groups have been generously funded, allowing them to hire a considerable number of assistants, and this has been improving over the years. In 2017, there were 271 assistants, which represent a ratio of 0.8 to each MP. The salary of an MP is probably one of the lowest in Western Europe at about €3,000 per month (£2,600, $3,700) before tax (Congreso de Diputados, 2017). Just for comparison, a German MP receives over €9,000 and additional generous allowances (see earlier).

The unicameral Portuguese Assembly of the Republic consists of 230 MPs and has become a more efficient legislature over time. In spite of a low level of human and financial resources, Portuguese parliamentarianism has improved its professionalisation and institutionalisation. The decade during which Cavaco Silva dominated Portuguese politics was crucial. Although the absolute majority government used its position to bring about a reform programme, the high level of political and economic stability allowed restructuring and, as Cristina Leston-Bandeira asserts, the maturation of democracy in Portugal (Leston-Bandeira, 2004: 25). One of the reasons for this is that some MPs and parliamentary staff have become more professionalised and are able to build long-term careers within parliament. Although there are reasons for optimism, the Portuguese parliament continues to be weaker than other Western European parliaments. Nonetheless

Table 5.9 Legislative output of the Spanish parliament, 2000–16

	Seventh Legislature (2000–4) Aznar absolute majority government (PP)		*Eighth Legislature (2004–8) Zapatero minority government (PSOE)*		*Ninth Legislature (2008–11) Zapatero minority government (PSOE)*		*Tenth Legislature (2011–15) Rajoy absolute majority government (PP)*		*Eleventh Legislature (2015–16) Rajoy caretaker government (hung parliament)*	
	P	*A (%)*	*P*	*A (%)*	*P*	*A (%)*	*P*	*A (%)*	*P*	*A (%)*
Government bills (Proyectos de Ley)	175	99	152	92	147	83.7	163	98.2	0	0
Private bills (Proposiciones de Ley)	322	5	230	8.3	292	5.5	216	2.8	43	0
Other bills	47	6.4	65	3.1	64	6.3	62	4.8		

Source: based on database of Congreso de Diputados (2018).

the institutional structuring process has created stronger committees which are able to scrutinise the government and play a role in shaping legislation. In a recent seminal study Jorge Fernandes asserts that committee work has improved considerably since major reforms were undertaken in the 1990s. Similar to other Western European countries, the twelve standing committees with on average twenty-one to twenty-three members are organised to match government ministries (Fernandes, 2016a: 115). He also shows that there is such a thing as a parliamentary career for higher ranking party representatives. In his analysis of the assignment of committee chairs by political parties at the beginning of three legislature periods (2005–11), it seems to indicate that some low level of seniority and professionalisation is emerging, although still not statistically significant (Fernandes, 2016: 122).

Table 5.10 shows that the success rate of legislative initiatives of the Portuguese government has improved over time, showing that a more rationalised approach to the opposition is emerging. Similar to Spain, parliamentarianism has a stronger say during minority governments and less so during absolute majority governments.

Similar to the Spanish and Greek cases, the salary of a Portuguese MP is quite low when compared to other Western European countries. A full-time MP without any other jobs gets about €4,000 per month before tax, but an MP with additional jobs receives €3,600 before tax. This clearly is not the best way to attract full-time MPs (Assembleia da Republica, 2018a). This clearly leads to a high level of legislative turnover and a high level of substitutions of elected members by non-elected ones for a certain period of time. This may be regarded as a negative practice of the Portuguese parliament.

The Maltese and Cypriot legislatures are categorised as weak. Both countries emerged out of the decolonisation process undertaken by the UK governments in the 1960s. As such, both follow many elements of the Westminster model, although their constitutions comprise many differences, and particularly more constraints on the executive. While Cyprus is the only presidential democracy in the EU, Malta is still quite close to the Westminster model. It is referred to as the constitutionalised Westminster model (Hazell, 2008, quoted by Bulmer, 2014: 236). The unicameral Maltese House of Representatives closely follows the UK model. Although the 65 MPs are elected by the proportional single transferable vote for a five-year period, only two parties are represented in parliament: the conservative Nationalist Party and the leftist Labour Party. Sometimes other parties emerge, but they have major difficulties getting representation. The Maltese parliament is dominated by the government because, in the same way as in the Swiss parliament, most MPs only work part time (Bestler and Waschkuhn, 2009: 875). They meet three times a week in the evening. There is a strong parliamentary group discipline in the two parties, so that legislation is normally adopted in a second reading, instead of the prescribed three readings (Bestler and Waschkuhn, 2009: 879–80). In many ways, the Maltese parliament shows many similarities to the UK parliament. The overdominance of the executive and strict party discipline thwarts any initiatives of parliament (Bulmer, 2014: 237–9).

Cyprus has two legislatures, one in the Greek Republic of Cyprus and the other in the northern Turkish Republic of Cyprus. Internationally, only the Greek Republic of Cyprus is recognised, so we will concentrate on this one. The

Table 5.10 Legislative output of the Portuguese Assembly of the Republic, 1976–2016

	1976–80	*1980*	*1980–3*	*1983–5*	*1985–7*	*1987–91*	*1991–5*	*1995–9*	*1999–2002*	*2002–5*	*2005–9*	*2009–11*	*2011–15*	*2015–*
Government bills	248	85	134	106	47	176	118	262	85	201	359	80	336	93
Adopted government bills %	43	36.5	54.4	72.6	63.8	96.6	92.4	88.5	84.7	56.2	58.7	37.5	94	35.5
Private bills	459	87	251	305	344	460	433	506	182	645	1209	746	1020	585
Adopted private bills %	26.8	6.8	11.2	9.5	22.4	20.4	19.6	38.1	29.6	27.5	18.6	17.6	20.1	20.2

Source: Magone, 2014a: 53–4; Assembleia da Republica (2018b).

Greek Cypriot House of Representatives (Vouli Ton Antiprosopon) consists of eighty members, of which fifty-six are Greek Cypriot representatives and twenty-four Turkish Cypriot representatives. Nevertheless, the Turkish representatives have boycotted the assembly since 1963–4. Until 1985, the Vouli was insignificant in the presidential system of Cyprus; however, since then, it has stepped up its engagement (Zervakis and Costeas 2010: 1113–4). During the presidency of Archbishop Makarios (1960–74), there was a tendency to get former underground independence movement (EOKA) members elected to parliament so that he could control it. Therefore, only in the 1980s was parliament able to gain more independence from the executive. The first standing orders were adopted in the fourth legislature (1981–5) after almost twenty years (Zervakis and Costeas, 2010: 1113–4). Constitutionally, the Cypriot parliament is completely separate from the executive. Members of parliament are not allowed to be members of the executive and vice versa. Since the mid-1970s, the human and material resources of the Vouli have been substantially upgraded so that they are no longer part-time MPs, but full time (Zervakis and Costeas, 2010: 1113). Committees can rewrite legislation in their jurisdiction before it comes to the plenary session for approval. Such strong powers are facilitated by a culture of consensus, which is due to the lack of absolute majorities of most governments. In this regard, the opposition is granted quite an important role in the legislative process. Parliament also gains an important role when the president is out of the country, because in that case the Speaker of the House, the Deputy Speaker, or in the last case scenario the oldest MP represents him or her within the country. Overall, 71 per cent of the people trust in the work of the Vouli, well above the EU average of 57 per cent and certainly well above Malta with only 30 per cent in May 2017 (Eurobarometer Interactive, 2018).

New democratic parliaments in Central and Eastern Europe

The new liberal democratic parliaments in Central and Eastern Europe are characterised by different historical legacies and transitions to democracy. David Olson and Philip Norton differentiate between legislatures that followed their national traditions and even practices during the communist period, and those that decided to break with the past and search for models from Western Europe. The more established legislatures decided for continuity, while those that had to establish new legislatures every time a new regime was established usually chose to create new parliaments (Olson and Norton, 1996: 4–5). Research on these small parliaments has been scarce, with the exception of Hungary and Poland. It means that there are a lot of knowledge constraints on the way we can discuss individual parliaments. However, it certainly suffices for a good overview.

In spite of historical legacies, all these new parliaments were operating during a period of political and economic instability. The process of professionalisation and institutionalisation is still continuing. The European integration process has been an important factor in shaping parliamentarianism in Central, Eastern, and wider Europe.

Central and Eastern European parliaments: Hungary, the Czech Republic, Slovakia, Poland and Slovenia

Probably the most researched parliament in Central and Eastern Europe is Hungary, which, since its inception after 1989, has been monitored by a research team led by Professor Attila Ágh, Gabriela Ilonski and Sandor Kurtán from Corvinus University, Budapest. This research has led to four excellent volumes on the Hungarian parliament covering the first two legislature periods between 1990 and 1998 (Ágh, 1994; Ágh and Ilonski, 1996; Ágh and Kurtán, 1995, 2001). The Hungarian National Assembly (Országgyülés) originally consisted of 386 MPs: 176 (45 per cent) were elected by a French-style two-ballot majority system, while the rest were elected by a reinforced proportional representation electoral system using the Hagenbach-Bischoff method. It is an unconnected mixed electoral system. However, a new electoral law in 2011 during the second Viktor Orbán government (2010–14) reduced the number of MPs to 199, which came into force in the elections of 2014. In this new configuration, 106 MPs (53 per cent) are elected in the single member constituencies, but in a single round, and 93 in national lists (47 per cent) (Országgyülés, 2018a; for a review of the electoral law, see Ilonski, 2017). From the very start, the National Assembly had the ambition of becoming a parliament that would represent a new democratic political culture. Therefore, it was characterised as a working parliament (*Arbeitsparlament*) in the first two legislature periods between 1990 and 1998. In this context, the German parliament was a powerful model for the new Hungarian political elite. One characteristic of the Hungarian parliament was that committee work was central. The role of parliament as a controlling institution lost influence after Viktor Orbán came to power in 2010. The new electoral law is creating a disproportionate allocation of seats and runs against all principles of electoral integrity (Ilonski, 2017). In 2010, Orbán's Fidesz Party and its electoral coalition partner the Christian Democratic People's Party (KDNP) got 44.9 per cent of the vote but 68 per cent (two-thirds) of the seats. In 2014, such disproportional allocation remained when Fidesz-KDNP got 44.7 per cent of the votes and 68 per cent of seats. Also in 2018 they received 49.3 per cent of the votes and 68 per cent of the seats. This is clearly a major problem for opposition parties in their quest to alternate in government, particularly because important laws need a two-thirds majority, like changing the constitution. Orbán has been using and abusing this majority to change the constitution, central bank laws, press laws and the composition of the constitutional court. This led to clashes with the European Commission, which ended with the Orbán government backing down (see Chapter 4; Ágh, 2016; Batory, 2016).

About 55 to 60 per cent of legislation is initiated by the government and 80 to 90 per cent of laws passed are initiated by the government (see Table 5.11). This is reinforced by a six-month legislative programme of the government, which has priority over other legislation. According to Gabriella Ilonski, the Hungarian parliament was assessed as a working parliament, but during its third term it declined considerably in output. The government was able to dominate parliament and impose a strict legislative programme. Moreover, instruments of scrutiny and parliamentary control were not used to compensate for the loss of power (Ilonski, 2007: 53–4; Table 5.11; see also the Hungarian parliament website). Since 2010, the position of the parliament has deteriorated considerably, becoming just a mere

Table 5.11 Legislative output of the Hungarian parliament, 1990–2014

Bills by	*1990–4*		*1994–8*		*1998–2002*		*2002–6*		*2006–10*		*2010–14*	
	Init. %	*Pass %*	*Init. %*	*Pass. %*	*Init. %*	*Pass %.*	*Init. %*	*Pass. %*	*Init. %*	*Pass. %*	*Init. %*	*Pass %*
Government	54.3	80.9	62.3	87	51.5	85.9	53.7	82	53.8	81	39.3	66.3
MPs	38.6	13	35.6	10.8	44.6	9.6	43.9	15.7	42.4	15.1	59.2	31.4
Committee	7.1	6.1	2.1	2.2	4	4.5	2.4	2.3	3.8	3.9	1.5	2.3
Total	788	430	755	499	858	464	968	573	963	587	1521	859

Source: author's own calculations based on database of Országgyülés (2018b).

Note: Init. = bill proposal, Pass. = approved bills.

rubber stamping legislature of the government. Many private bills are actually disguised government bills presented by members of parliament of the governing party (see Table 5.11). It is the opposition that uses extensively its control instruments of interpellations, oral and written questions. Moreover, the constituency-based MPs are quite active in submitting interpellations, oral and written questions to the government on behalf of their government (Sebök et al., 2017: 478). The Hungarian parliament is characterised by a high level of MP turnover. In the sixth legislature (2010–14) the turnover was 46.7 per cent (Hungarian Parliament, 2018b). This has undermined attempts for further professionalisation and institutionalisation of parliament. Moreover, the number of people with an academic education increased considerably to 92 per cent in 2006, while the number of employees and working-class representatives was reduced to zero (Körösényi et al., 2010: 367).

Overall, the Hungarian parliament has lost considerable power, and therefore Gabriella Ilonski compares it to the same processes that happened in Southern Europe. Indeed, the parliamentary groups are quite selective in keeping to the rules of the standing orders. Party political interests may lead to exceptions, such as the number required for the formation of a political parliamentary group, which is fifteen, but has been lowered to accommodate junior coalition partners which were not able to achieve the required number of MPs. Ilonski calls this 'formal institutionalisation' meaning that the rules are there, but political parties may choose to circumvent them (Ilonski, 2007: 56–7).

The bicameral Czech parliament emerged after the 'velvet divorce'. It consists of a lower chamber called the Chamber of Deputies (Poslanecká Sněmovna), with 200 MPs elected by proportional representation, and has staggered electoral thresholds for parties and coalitions of parties depending on size. The upper chamber, the Senate, consists of eighty-one Senators elected for six years by a plurality electoral system, normally involving two rounds. Czech bicameralism is asymmetrical, meaning that the lower chamber is the dominant one, while the Senate is simply a chamber to reflect on proposed legislation. The adoption and/or change of constitutional laws needs a majority of three-fifths in both houses. After two years, one-third of Senators have to stand for re-election. The Senate was only established in 1998, four years after the velvet divorce. Initially, the lower house considered that there was no need for a second chamber. Although there was some tradition of bicameralism in the inter-war period, and after 1968 in the communist period, the experiences were not very positive. Therefore, the Senate had difficulty in finding a place in the new political system (Kysela, n.d.). The lower house has the right to scrutinise and control the government. However, the Senate has the right to start impeachment procedures against the president and to evaluate his or her appointees to the constitutional court.

Since the early 1990s, the Czech parliament has been able to evolve towards a Western model of parliamentarianism, but major problems remain. The role of coalition government in Czech politics is crucial, and negotiated bargains of coalition partners with the opposition take place in the Chamber of Deputies. Moreover, government ministers are allowed to be members of parliament simultaneously, something that encourages greater cooperation between executive and legislative. However, minority governments have considerable difficulty in imposing themselves – governments need a majority in parliament to bring through some of the legislation. The relationship between the Chamber of Deputies and Senate

Table 5.12 Legislative output of the Czech parliament, 1992–2017

Bills by	*1992–6*		*1996–8*		*1998–2002*		*2002–6*		*2006–10*		*2010–13*		*2013–17*	
	Init.	*Pass. (%)*	*Init.*	*Pass. (%)*	*Init.*	*Pass. (%)*	*Init.*	*Pass. (%)*	*Init.*	*Pass. (%)*	*Init.*	*Pass.*		
Government	251	78	115	77	431	72	457	86.4	314	81.2	347	78.1	380	n.d.
MPs	185	35	103	26	285	40	231	40	246	34	214	24.2	232	n.d.
Senate (%)			2	50	19	47	17	29	28	21.4	34	38	23	n.d.
Regions (%)					10	30	36	19.5	25	24	26	11.5	13	n.d.
Absolute numbers of bills	436	260	221	116	785	465	740	252	613	351	621	339	648	n.d.

Note: Init. = bill proposal, Pass. = approved bills.

Source: Simplified from Linek and Mansfeldová (2007: 33); statistical data for period 2002 to 2017 kindly supplied by Stanislaw Caletka from the Parliamentary Institute attached to the Czech Parliament via email on 5 February 2018 upon request.

has become settled over time. While in the early years, until 2002, the Senate was fairly confrontational towards the minority government of the Social Democratic Party (ČSSD), it then became more cooperative. In the early period it tended to seek major changes and amendments to bills that, finally, failed to achieve a majority in the Chamber of Deputies; however, it changed its pattern of behaviour by concentrating on minor changes that were more easily accepted by the Chamber of Deputies (Linek and Mansfeldová, 2007: 20–1, 34) (see Table 5.12).

In a similar way to other countries, the legislative process has been dominated by the government (see Table 5.12). Between 75 and 85 per cent of approved legislation was initiated by the government. The period between 1998 and 2002 led to a considerable number of laws being approved, largely because of the Czech government's need to absorb the EU *acquis communautaire* into national law. A growing institutionalisation of the Czech parliament has taken place since 1990 that can be measured by the increased number of plenary sessions and the increased complexity of its system of eighteen committees (including the creation of subcommittees to discuss bills in more detail) consisting of between seventeen and twenty-four MPs. Over time, the Czech parliament has introduced the requirement for three readings in order to ensure that legislation is properly scrutinised before being approved.

Such institutionalisation can be seen in the decreasing turnover in both chambers. At the end of 2006, new MPs with no previous experience comprised 41 per cent (Linek and Mansfeldová, 2007: 21). In spite of this positive development of Czech parliamentarianism, there is still scope for improvement through a major constitutional reform. According to Miloš Brunclik and Michal Kubak, there is a need for some constitutional engineering in order to improve and rationalise executive-legislative relations. According to the authors between 1996 and 2014 there were eleven governments and ten prime ministers (Brunclik and Kubak, 2016: 17). The fact that the Czech Republic is a new democracy with new parties is one of the reasons for this fragmentation and government instability (Van Biezen, 2003). The introduction of direct elections for presidential elections since 2013 has further weakened government versus parliament. Strong charismatic presidents such as Milos Žeman may undermine even further the authority of the government. Some rationalisation of parliamentarianism will be necessary, so that government is more protected against a highly fragmented parliament, maybe through a constructive motion of censure like in Germany, Spain and Poland (Brunclik and Kubak, 2016: 17–22).

The Slovakian parliament was designed during a period of 'revolutionary democratism' (Malová and Sivaková, 1996b: 344). Indeed, the first decade was characterised by weak governments and a weak party discipline, both of which helped parliament to establish itself. The constitution provides for parliament to be reasonably independent from government. The National Council (Narodna rada) consists of 150 MPs, who are directly elected by a proportional representation system, and has staggered thresholds for parties and coalitions of parties depending on size. Although Slovakia has a directly elected president, the constitutional framework really emphasised the centrality of parliament in the political system. According to Darina Malová and Danica Sivaková, it has vast powers over government, including the dismissal of ministers subject to presidential approval. Moreover, government has to seek parliament's approval to deploy troops abroad (Malová and Sivaková,

Table 5.13 Legislative output of the Slovak parliament, 2006–16

	Fourth legislature (2006–10) Government: Robert Fico I		*Fifth legislature (2010–12) Government: Robert Fico II*		*Sixth legislature (2012–16) Government: Robert Fico III*	
	Submitted (N)	*Passed N (%)*	*Submitted (N)*	*Passed N (%)*	*Submitted (N)*	*Passed (%)*
Government bills	478	442 (92.5)	229	178 (77.7)	411	382 (92.9)
Private bills	478	84 (17.5)	130	26 (20.0)	957	69 (87.2)
Committee bills	7	4 (57.1)	5	4 (80.0)	4	4 (100.0)
Total	963	530 (55.0)	364	208 (57.1)	1,372	455 (33.2)
Out of which laws of fast-track legislative procedure (%)		54 (9.8)		25 (12.0)		24 (5.3)

Source: Narodna rada slovenskey republiku (2018).

1996a: 108). This became evident during the Vladimir Mečiar government of autumn 1993. Several ministers resigned, were dismissed by government or were voted down by parliament (Malová and Sivaková, 1996b: 343).

As Table 5.13 shows, the legislative process is dominated by government. During the three Robert Fico governments between 2006 and 2016, the rate of adoption of government bills was 90 per cent.

The Polish parliament is an asymmetrical bicameral system, based on a lower house (Sejm), with 460 MPs elected by proportional representation for four years, and an upper house (Senate), with 100 MPs elected in forty pluri-nominal constituencies by single majority voting. The Sejm is the central chamber of the political system. The Senate is a revising chamber, although during and shortly after transition, it tried to take a more important role. Such ambitions settled down over time, and today, the Sejm dominates the parliamentary system and is the main chamber to which the governments are accountable. After adoption of the constitution of 1997, the powers of the president in relation to the Sejm declined. The Sejm now needs only three-fifths of the votes in order to override the presidential suspensive veto, as opposed to the two-thirds of votes required before adoption. Moreover, the president cannot use the constitutional court *before* using the veto: now s/he has to approve a bill, veto it, or send it to the constitutional court, which ruling will be binding (Sanford, 2001: 119–20).

The Polish parliament is considered to be a working parliament, focusing most of its work on the committees. The use of subcommittees is widespread and designed to draft pending legislative bills with more care. According to Ewa Nalewajko and Wlodzimierz Wesołowski, the quality of legislation has been poor, despite three readings and a considerable amount of work in the committees (Table 5.14).

Table 5.14 Legislative output of the Polish Sejm, 1989–2015

	10th Sejm (transition) 1989–91		*1st Sejm 1991–3*		*2nd Sejm 1993–7*		*3rd Sejm 1997–2001*		*4th Sejm 2001–5*		*5th Sejm 2005–7*		*6th Sejm 2007–11*		*7th Sejm 2011–15*	
	Submitted	*Passed (%)*	*Submitted*	*Passed (%)*	*Submitted*	*Passed (%)*	*Submitted*	*Passed (%)*	*Submitted*	*Passed (%)*	*Submitted*	*Passed (%)*	*Submitted*	*Passed (%)*	*Submitted*	*Passed (%)*
President's bills			10	40	30	53.3	16	12.5	21	71.4	23	73.9	28	50	22	86.4
Senate's bills			9	44.5	19	36.8	27	44.5	25	64	16	18.8	114	68	101	73.3
Government bills			91	52	346	89	553	82.5	808	92	377	66	674	96.7	463	97.2
Private bills			199	16.6	363	53.7	469	45	358	50.6	273	44.3	493	42.6	644	37.4
Committee bills			26	54	68	85.3	82	79.3	40	82.5	11	18.2	183	68.9	42	83.3
Bills initiated by citizens							5	60	13	30.7	8	12.5	19	10.5	28	7.1
Total in absolute numbers (%)	250	247 (98.8)	335	94 (38.1)	826	473 (57.3)	1152	640 (55.6)	1265	894 (70.7)	708	384 (54.2)	1511	952 (63)	1300	752 (57.8)

Source: Data kindly provided by Magdalena Baszkowska, senior specialist at the Communication Office of the Sejm via email 14 February 2018 upon request.

One of the main reasons for this can be related to the high turnover of MPs without experience and a lack of training in the legislative process. This is reinforced by the fact that first-time MPs are required to chair committees and yet are extremely faithful to their parties, thus creating a tense adversarial culture (Nalewajko and Wesołowski, 2007: 80). According to the website of the Sejm, in the seventh Sejm (2011–15) the legislative turnover was 30 per cent, but in the eighth Sejm (2015–) with the change of government from the PO-led coalition to PiS, the figure increased to 44 per cent (Sejm, 2018). Moreover, at least until 2007, parliamentary party groups were not stable and party discipline was not strong, so MPs defected or, more likely, created rival parties. In the fourth term, at the beginning of 2001, eight parliamentary groups and one group of non-affiliated MPs were created; by the end of the legislature, however, there were fourteen parliamentary groups and one of non-affiliated members, which had increased from seven to thirty-two members (Nalewajko and Wesołowski, 2007: 75). In some ways, the Polish parliament shows similarities to certain features of Southern European parliamentarianism, which clearly was and still is dominated by the personalisation of politics. However, since the sixth Sejm (2007–11) a two-party system has emerged which allows for more consolidation. Nevertheless, a high level of volatility persists leading to the emergence of new parties and the disappearance of others, like in the last two elections in 2011 and 2015.

In this sense, the Senate was able to play an important role in scrutinising legislative bills and looking for erroneous wording and logic. It thus became an important reflective chamber for dealing with the growing adversarial culture in the Sejm (Nalewajko and Wesołowski, 2007: 80). As Table 5.14 shows, until 1997 MPs and committees were able to achieve a high level of approved legislation. Government legislation dominated, although it was counteracted by a strong input from the Sejm. This pattern changed considerably in the third and fourth Sejm, after 1997, in which government legislation dominated completely – the main reason being the huge amount of EU legislation that had to be transposed into national law. Such pattern has consolidated since the late 2000s due to the strong majorities on which the governments of Donald Tusk, Ewa Kopacs, Beate Szydło and Mateusz Marowiecki have been based since 2007.

In an excellent seminal article combining qualitative and quantitative methods, Monika Nalepa analysed the relationship between party institutionalisation and legislative organisation in Poland. According to her findings, Poland as a new liberal democracy was characterised by weak institutionalised parties that lacked internal cohesion (Nalepa, 2016: 358). Due to the oppressive structures of parliamentarianism during the communist regime, new parliaments designed constitutions that allowed for strong rights for individual MPs. Therefore, opposition parties were quite strong in the first legislatures of the new Sejm, undermining very often the attempts of government to control the agenda (Nalepa, 2016: 356). Such processes went on until 1997, but began to change when the centre-right Solidarity Electoral Action and Freedom Union (AWS-UW) coalition came to power. They changed the standing orders and strengthened the role of the Speaker (Marshall) as gatekeeper for government and opposition legislation. It was the Speaker that had the full power as 'emissary' of the government to structure the legislative process. Also in government there were several committees coordinating policy. However, the lack of institutionalisation of the government parties led to its collapse. They were replaced by the Democratic Left Alliance-Labour Union (SLD-UP), which reduced coordination structures in cabinet to just one committee and was more efficient in using the Speaker of the House to block legislation by the opposition (negative agenda control) and get government bills approved (positive agenda control). This approach increased in efficiency in the next governments of the Law and Justice Party (PiS) and Samobroona (SRP) coalitions (2005–7) and the Civic Platform (PO) and Polish People's Party (PSL) coalition (2005–15) (Nalepa, 2016: 359–62). According to Nalepa, this explains very well why the PiS absolute majority government is now able to rush quite controversial legislation through parliament, in spite of the protests of the opposition. It is a pattern around the Speaker and more consolidated government coordinating mechanisms that have been in the making since at least 2005 (Nalepa, 2016: 366).

The Slovenian parliament is also a bicameral parliament, although the second chamber is elected by different interest groups. At the centre is the lower house, the National Assembly (Državni Zbor), which consists of ninety MPs, eighty-eight of whom are directly elected by proportional representation. Two MPs are non-elected representatives of the Italian and Hungarian minorities. The upper house, the State Council (Državni Svet), consists of representatives of interest groups that are normally closely linked to the political parties. It consists of forty members – twenty-two representatives of local interests, six representatives of non-commercial activities, four representatives of employers, four representatives of employees, and four representatives of farmers, crafts and trades, and independent professionals. The design of the second chamber was influenced by the Senate of the Bavarian state. The second chamber of the regional parliament (as it was between 1946 and 1999) was abolished after a positive referendum with over 69 per cent of votes. At the national level within Europe only Ireland has a similar system. The Slovenian second chamber draws also from the legacy of the socialist Yugoslav period (1945–92), in which a three-chamber parliament was in place. Apart from a political chamber, there was also a chamber in which municipalities were represented and another chamber with interest group representatives. Such a model also existed in Croatia.

The second chamber has predominantly a consultative corrective role, but it can also initiate legislation and has a right to a suspensive veto (Lukšič, 2010: 743).

In terms of performance, the Slovenian National Assembly has developed a functioning committee system and has an impressive legislative output for its size. However, as in other Central and Eastern European countries, government is the dominant initiator of legislation and most of its laws are passed. Table 5.15 shows between 1996 and 2014, an average of 89 per cent of government bills were adopted. This became quite clear in the third term (2000–4) when EU-related backlogged bills were approved shortly before accession to the EU (see Zajc, 2007: 94). Once again the need for the transposition of EU law should be emphasised here. However, as Zajc points out, the quality of legislation has been poor at times, particularly when the government has used fast-track procedures (almost half of legislation being declared urgent) to bring through many legislative bills which were not of a high standard. Furthermore, the high level of turnover of between 51 per cent (third term 2000–4) and 59 per cent (sixth term 2011–14) have not been conducive to the professionalisation of parliament (legislature reports posted at Državni Zbor, 2000–14).

Table 5.15 Legislative output of the Slovenian parliament, 1996–2014

Legislatures	*2nd Legislature (1996–2000)*		*3rd Legislature (2000–4)*		*4th Legislature (2004–8)*		*5th Legislature 2008–11)*		*6th Legislature (2011–14)*	
Governments	*Janez Drnovšek (1996–2000)*		*Janez Drnovšek (2000–2) Anton Rop (2002–4)*		*Janez Janša (2004–8)*		*Borut Pahor (2008–11)*		*Borut Pahor (2011–12) Janez Janša (2011–13) Alenka Bratušek (2013–14)*	
	Submitted	*Passed (%)*	*Submitted*	*Passed (%)*	*Submitted*	*Passed (%)*	*Submitted*	*Passed (%)*	*Submitted*	*Passed (%)*
Government bills	586	570 (97)	502	642 (128)*)	710	614 (86.5)	562	427 (76)	386	322 (83.4)
Private bills	232	59 (25)	97	37 (38)	125	18 (14.4)	166	39 (23.5)	77	22 (28.6)
National Council (Senate)	10	2 (20)	3	0	13		7	2 (28.6)	4	1 (25)
Voters					2	1	1	0	7	0
Total	828	631 (76)	602	679 (113)	850	633 (74.4)	736	468 (63.6)	474	348 (73.4)
Out of which fast-track procedure or shortened procedure		240 (38)		288 (42)		259 (41)		217 (46)		185 (53.2)

Source: Držani Zbor (2000–14): 2000: 23, 25; 2004: 29, 31; 2008: 26, 28; 2011: 28–9; 2014: 25–7.

*)The number of approved legislation exceeds the number of submitted bills, because quite a considerable number of submitted bills of the previous legislative term were adopted. This is certainly also due to the large amount of legislation related to the EU *acquis communautaire* which had to be approved before accession to the EU on 1 January 2004.

The Baltic parliaments: Lithuania, Estonia and Latvia

The three Baltic unicameral parliaments have also achieved stabilisation and institutionalisation; however, their different political systems have led to different dynamics in each case. According to Vello Pettai and Ulle Madise, the Estonian Riigikogu, consisting of 101 MPs, is the strongest parliament largely because of the autonomy of its MPs and the centrality of the assembly in the political system, while the Latvian Saeima, consisting of 100 MPs, is the weakest because of the dominance of the executive in the political system. This dominance exists mainly because the executive is able to pass emergency laws or important regulations through a fast-track procedure. Between these two lies the Lithuanian Seimas, consisting of 141 MPs, which is embedded in a weak semi-presidential system. The president does not interfere in domestic policies and concentrates his/her activities on foreign policy (Pettai and Madise, 2006: 291). The greater autonomy of Estonian and Lithuanian MPs is partly because of the different electoral systems, proportional representation with preferential voting in the former, and first-past-the-post system for half of the constituencies in Lithuania. In spite of thresholds, all three parliaments have had to deal with the fragmentation of parliamentary groups; this was worse in Latvia and Estonia, and, in particular, the Latvian Parliament has had to deal with very weak unstable governments. New rules had to be devised in order to prevent party switching after elections. According to the excellent comparative study of Daunis Auers, Estonia and Latvia introduced a ban on party switching during the lifetime of a parliamentary term. It means that the only option for an MP is to join the mixed groups, however s/he has to pay the price in terms of reduced resources. This clearly has helped to achieve some cohesion of parliamentary groups (Auers, 2015: 47–8). However, Latvia had to deal with a major restructuring of the party system during the financial crisis. In 2011, a new party system with new poorly institutionalised parties emerged. New parties emerged out of the old ones, which had been charged with corruption and illegal financing, therefore the parties were abolished to avoid the negative publicity of judicial trials. This clearly prevents a strengthening of party organisation, including the parliamentary groups, following Ingrid van Biezen's thesis of new political parties in new democracies (Biezen, 2003) (see Chapters 4 and 7).

Similar to Poland and other Central and Eastern European legislatures, MPs have quite strong rights. However, the differences between the three parliaments are also evident in the rights that MPs and committees have in each parliament. Individual MPs are fairly strong (in terms of their power and influence in shaping legislation) in Estonia, but less so in Latvia and Lithuania. In all three countries there has been an increasing share of success of legislation passed by the government. The Estonian example may illustrate the growing ability of the government to get its legislation approved. While until the accession to the EU approved governmental legislation was about 83.3 per cent, already quite high, after accession it increased to 94 to 95 per cent, at least until 2015. This may be related to the lengthy nine-year premiership of Andrus Ansip, who certainly contributed to some executive stability and a more stable executive-legislative relationship. Also, committee bills achieved success rates of 70 and 90 per cent indicating a strong culture of consensus dominated by the main liberal centrist parties (see Table 5.16). The same applies to Lithuania. Semi-presidentialism seems to be an important factor in

Table 5.16 Legislative acts according to sponsor in Estonia, 1992–2015

Government	*7th Riigikogu (1992–5)*		*8th Riigikogu (1995–9)*		*9th Riigikogu (1999–2003)*		*10th Riigikogu (2003–7)*		*11th Riigikogu 2007–11)*		*12th Riigikogu (2011–15)*	
	Mart Laar (1992–4) Andres Tarand (1994–5)		*Tiit Vähi (1995–7) Mart Siiman (1997–9)*		*Mart Laar (1999–2002) Siim Kallas (2002–3)*		*Juhan Parts (2003–5) Andrus Ansip (2005–7)*		*Andrus Ansip (2007–11)*		*Andrus Ansip (2011–14) Taavi Roivas (2014–15)*	
	Initiated	*Adopted (%)*	*Initiated*	*Adopted (%)*	*Initiated*	*Adopted (%)*	*Initiated*	*Adopted (%)*	*Initiated*	*Adopted (%)*	*Initiated*	*Adopted (%)*
Government bills	345	285 (82.6)	513	435 (84.8)	646	555 (83.3)	561	531 (94.7)	489	461 (94.3)	432	412 (95.4)
Private bills	248	79 (31.9)	219	91 (41.6)	234	96 (41)	106	33 (31)	25	5 (20)	34	7 (20.6)
Committee bills	74	52 (70.2)	88	69 (78.4)	106	96 (90.6)	48	38 (79.2)	69	59 (85.5)	43	39 (90.7)
Parliamentary group	52	88 15.4)	189	60 (31.7)	137	41 (30)	217	62 (28.6)	216	37 (17.1)	159	22 (13.8)
Riigikogu Board	21	18 (85.7)										
President of Republic					1	0	1	1 (100)				
Elected citizens	1	0										
Total	741	542 (73.1)	1009	655 (65)	1124	788 (70)	932	664 (71)	799	562 (70.3)	668	480 (72)

Source: Riigikogu (2015: 111).

Table 5.17 Legislative acts initiated and adopted by sponsor in Lithuania, 1992–2016

	6th Seimas (1992–6)		*7th Seimas (1996–2000)*		*8th Seimas (2000–4)*		*9th Seimas (2004–8)*		*10th Seimas (2008–12)*		*11th Seimas (2012–16)*	
	Initiated	*Adopted*	*Initiated*	*Adopted*	*Initiated*	*Adopted (%)*	*Initiated*	*Adopted (%)*	*Initiated*	*Adopted (%)*	*Initiated*	*Adopted (%)*
President of the Republic	116	–	80	–	110	77.3	84	71.4	106	93	128	92.2
President of the Republic (government). Draft laws on ratification	98	–	225	–	258	104.5	133	96.2	97	91.8	80	101.3
Government	1082	–	1157	–	1304	84.9	1039	69.6	1752	67.8	1525	91.2
Members of the Seimas	1477	–	1541	–	2275	51.3	2243	44.1	3097	36.1	3145	38.6
Total	2,773	1,690	3,003	2,141	3,947	2,631	3,499	1,901	5,052	2,487	4,878	2,804

Source: Data kindly provided by Mr Valdas Sinkevicius, Acting Head of the Public Relations Unit per email on 6 February 2018 upon request.

strengthening the executive in relation to parliament. The legislative programme is shared between the president and the government (see Table 5.17).

Committee work is important, yet human and financial resources are modest. Estonia remains the most developed country in terms of Baltic parliamentarianism where MPs have better human and material resources than the parliaments of Latvia and Lithuania (Auers, 2015: 48–9). Information provided by the Lithuanian parliament states that every MP has an office in parliament and may have one in the constituency. Moreover, three assistants are allocated to each MP, and those with special needs may request a fourth one. Overall, the Lithuanian Seimas has a budget of €30 million. About 960 people work for the parliament, although half of them are political civil servants, probably attached to the political parties (Letter of Mr Valdas Sinkevicius, 6 February 2018).

With growing rationalisation, all three parliaments are likely to move towards similar patterns shown in other European countries. There is a strong affinity with the Baltic states and the Nordic countries, so that the long-term perspective may offer the possibility of learning from the latter.

Eastern European parliaments: Bulgaria, Romania and Croatia

Both Bulgaria and Romania are characterised by weaker parliamentarianism than Central European and Baltic legislatures.

The Bulgarian unicameral National Assembly (Narodno Sabranie) consists of 240 MPs, who are elected for four years by proportional representation. The Bulgarian Parliament is embedded in a semi-presidential system that has been rationalised over time, particularly since the constitutional reform of 2005. Indeed, the president has a limited right of veto that can be overridden by parliament with a simple majority. During the 1990s, conflict between the presidency and parliament dominated political life to the extent that it became known as the 'war of institutions'. The polarisation between the Bulgarian Socialist Party and the conservative anti-communist Union of Democratic Forces was a major factor fuelling this conflict (Karasimeonov, 1996: 46–7). In the 1990s, parliament was quite unstable, and it is only since 1997 that parliament has begun to be able to complete the four-year legislature period. There was considerable use of the motion of censure in order to topple coalition governments; however, only the Dimitrov government of 1992 resigned after a failed motion of confidence (Riedel, 2010: 684). This was reinforced by control of the standing committees by the government, which allocated only a few to the opposition. It took some time until the opposition was assigned the chairmanship of some committees. Such a practice seems to have started during the Sergei Stanishev government between 2005 and 2009. Out of the twenty-five committees, only four were chaired by the opposition (Riedel, 2010: 686). Such new practices are rather related to pressure from the EU to make the government more accountable.

Over time, the government has gained control over the legislative process. This became crucial after 2000, when EU legislation had to be transposed into national law within a very short period of time, which undermined the position of parliament in relation to the government. In general terms, parliament does not have the human and financial resources to undertake a critical review of EU legislation (Stoykova, 2007: 264–8).

Table 5.18 Legislative output of the Bulgarian parliament, 1990–2017

	36th National Assembly (4.11.1990–17.10.1994)		*37th National Assembly (12.1.1995–13.2.1997)*		*38th National Assembly 7.5.1994–19.4.2001)*		*39th National Assembly (5.7.2001–17.6.2005)*		*40th National Assembly (11.7.2005–25.6.2009)*		*41st National Assembly (14.7.2009–14.3.2013)*		*42nd National Assembly (21.5.2013–5.8.2014)*		*43rd National Assembly (27.10.2014–26.1.2017)*	
	Initiated	*Adopted (%)*	*Initiated*	*Adopted (%)*	*Initiated*	*Adopted (%)*	*Initiated*	*Adopted (%)*	*Initiated*	*Adopted (%)*	*Initiated*	*Adopted (%)*	*Initiated*	*Adopted (%)*	*Initiated*	*Adopted (%)*
Government bills			251	86.8	557	91.3	652	81.9	597	91.9	515	83.1	138	61.6	302	77.2
Private bills			261	21	534	22.8	551	17.4	681	24.	425	31.5	190	27.9	407	25.3
Total		221	512	273	1091	631	1203	630	1278	718	940	562	328	138	709	336

Source: Data kindly supplied by the Secretary General of the National Assembly of Bulgaria, Stefana Karaslavova on 23 February 2018 via email.

Table 5.18 shows that the Bulgarian executive dominates the legislative process like in most countries. However, so far, the Boyko Borisov government has been less efficient in doing this. One of the main reasons seems to be that they are a minority government and the overall relationship between the political parties is quite conflictive.

The Romanian parliament is characterised by a symmetrical bicameralism. The lower chamber, the Chamber of Deputies (Camera Deputatilor), consists of 332 MPs, who are elected for four years by a mixed member system (but before 2008, this was by a proportional representation system). The upper chamber (Senatul) consists of 137 Senators, elected directly for four years. The communist legacy is still present in many aspects of the standing orders. Parliament is a hybrid between the legacy of the interwar period and the communist regime (Crowther and Roper, 1996: 149). Like Bulgaria, parliamentarianism is embedded in a 'rationalised parliamentarianism' following the constitutional reform of 2000. This meant that a kind of distribution of work between the two chambers according to legislative areas was undertaken. According to Ute Gabanyi, the government initiates legislation related to international treaties and institutional laws (e.g. the nomination of judges, government members, the Higher Council for national defence, laws related to public administration and the school system) in the lower house, which is then adopted in the Senate. Vice versa, legislation on electoral and party systems, national minorities, industrial relations and social security are initiated in the Senate and adopted in a second reading in the Chamber of Deputies. All ordinary laws are initiated in the Senate and finally approved in the Chamber of Deputies. This has clearly reduced the complexity of the process, particularly the mechanisms of reconciliation of legislation of both houses (Gabanyi, 2010: 640). The president can veto bills, but this veto can be overridden by parliament with a simple majority. Moreover, the president has the option to send a bill to the constitutional court in order to be examined on its constitutionality. As in Bulgaria, there is a tendency for successive governments to rush through legislation using emergency procedures; and this has been highlighted as putting parliamentarianism in danger by the legislative council, which oversees and examines the content of legislation. The use of emergency law has been a regular feature of legislative behaviour of successive governments. The Nicolae Vacaroiu government (1992–6) introduced twenty such emergency laws, most of them related to the economy. However, the government of Petre Roman (1996–2000) adopted 679 emergency laws. This was continued in the governments of Adrian Năstase (2001–4) and Călin Popescu Tăriceanu (2005–8), which adopted 773 and 631 emergency laws respectively (Gabanyi, 2010: 650). Problems of parliamentarianism in Romania have been highlighted before and after accession to the EU. The abuse of emergency law was mentioned in the screening reports of the EU up to the date of accession (Papadimitriou and Phinnemore, 2008: 81). According to the latest report of the cooperation and verification mechanism on Romania of 2017, parliament is protecting several MPs from being prosecuted for corruption charges by refusing to lift their immunity, consequently not following judicial orders and clashing inevitably with the judiciary sector. Quite worrying was the attempt by the government to decriminalise corruption charges against twenty-five politicians, which led to major demonstrations across the country in 2016 and 2017 (European Commission, 2017b: 2–3) However, the quality of parliamentarianism remains low. Similarly to Bulgaria, the European integration process has further reinforced this trend towards an overwhelming dominance by the government.

Croatia joined the EU in 2013, and it is clear that parliamentarianism is moving towards achieving higher standards. Today, however, it is still characterised by the same problems as Romania and Bulgaria. The Croatian parliament (Hrvatski Sabor) is fragmented and divided in terms of parliamentary groups. The fluid situation of party membership is a major feature that it shares with other Balkan countries. After the death of President Franjo Tuđman in March 2000, the constitution was revised from a semi-presidential to a purely parliamentary system. Moreover, it changed from being a bicameral to a unicameral parliament by abolishing the upper house, the Chamber of Counties. The Croatian Parliament consists of between 100 and 160 directly elected members for four years by proportional representation. Five members are elected by ethnic minorities in Croatia. The composition number has been changing from legislature to legislature (Zakošek and Maršić, 2010: 788). Since 2016, it has had 151 members. The Croatian parliament cannot rely on a strong democratic tradition, so it will take some time until it achieves a higher standard. It is basically a debating parliament (*Redeparlament*) (Zakošek and Maršić, 2010: 789). Also, emergency law is used frequently. According to figures by Nenad Zakošek and Tomislav Maršić, over 75 per cent of legislation in the first decade of the millennium was through the fast-track procedure, reaching 89 per cent in 2009 (Zakošek and Maršić, 2010: 799). In terms of democratisation, one has to discount the Tuđman period, so a genuine democratic parliamentarianism has only existed for less than two decades.

The parliaments in the Balkans: Croatia, Serbia, Bosnia-Herzegovina, Macedonia, Montenegro and Albania

An efficient and professional parliamentarianism is still in the making in the Balkans. National parliaments are embedded in political systems with high levels of political corruption, patrimonial networks between criminal organisations and political parties, and ideological polarisation between the different political parties. Parliamentary behaviour is still a long way away from having high levels of professionalism. A lack of respect for the opposition and vice versa for the government often leads to stalemates that can only be resolved by the intervention of the EU, the major agent pushing for professionalisation and institutionalisation of parliament, due to the fact that Serbia, Macedonia, Montenegro and Albania are candidate countries due to join the EU in the late 2020s or early 2030s.

Conclusions: parliament as a moderating institution

European parliamentarianism is not characterised by adversarial politics (as in the United States). Parliament in Europe is closer to government and tends to act as a force of moderation in terms of legislation. Unlike the United States, parliamentarianism in Europe is not a policy-making legislature, but policy-influencing. It means that the government initiates legislation and the parliamentary groups inside parliament will usually review, amend or change it.

Suggested reading

Arter, David (ed.) (2007), *Comparing and Classifying Legislatures*. London: Frank Cass. (Also available electronically as a special issue of *Journal of Legislative Studies*, 12(3/4)).

Norton, Philip (ed.) (1998), *Parliaments and Governments in Western Europe*. London: Frank Cass.

Norton, Philip and David M. Olson (eds) (2007), *Post-Communist and Post-Soviet Legislatures*. London: Frank Cass (also in special issue of *Journal of Legislative Studies*, 13(1)).

Journal of Legislative Studies is an important electronic journal, excellent for research studies on European parliaments.

See also *West European Politics* and *East European Politics and Societies*.

QUESTIONS FOR REVISION

- What are the main functions of legislatures in contemporary European politics? Discuss, using examples from at least two countries.
- What are the main features of executive-legislative relations in Germany and France?
- How consolidated are Central and Eastern European parliaments?
- Compare Nordic and Southern European legislatures. Discuss, using at least one country from each region.
- Compare the influence of parliamentary opposition on policy-making in the Netherlands and the UK.

Chapter 6

Judicial power in multilevel Europe

- Introduction
- Patterns of judicial power in Europe
- The judicialisation of politics and the politicisation of the judiciary: a constitutional review, European style
- The European dimension: the growing impact on national legislation
- Conclusions: the Europeanisation of judicial power
- Suggested reading

Introduction

The separation of powers, as advocated by the French philosopher and political scientist Montesquieu (1973) in his *L'Esprit des Lois* (*Spirit of Laws*) in 1748 and formulated in the chapter on the Constitution of England (book eleven, chapter six) has remained a central doctrine of European politics.

Although executives are able to dominate legislative politics, the independence of the judiciary has always been an important issue in European politics. Political pressure on the judiciary is usually regarded as negative by a country's citizens. The politicisation of the judiciary can lead to corruption of judicial activity and, in the end, erode the legitimacy of the political system.

Box 6.1 The judiciary and the rule of law

Throughout the eighteenth and nineteenth centuries, the bourgeoisie in Europe fought against the absolutist state in order to achieve a modern state based on the rule of law. The absolutist state was characterised by some judicial order, for example as in France; however, the monarch held absolute power and could decide arbitrarily about any subject. The 'Glorious Revolution' in England in 1688–9 and the French Revolution of 1789 led to the emergence of the rule of law based on a written constitution.

The idea of the rule of law was first mentioned by English philosopher James Harrington in his book *The Commonwealth of Oceana* (1656) in which he proposed an ideal republic during Oliver Cromwell's Republican intermezzo (1650–8). He called it the 'empire of laws' and equalled it to 'government'.

There are, of course, different traditions of the rule of law. In England, the rule of law is based on individual freedom and is about citizens' rights in relation to the state. On the continent, rule of law means mainly *Rechtsstaat* (the legal state), meaning that public administrations are confined by the legal framework, thus preventing arbitrariness of decision-making. In France, in particular, the significance of the rule of law means administrative law (*droit administratif*) in relation to public administration. In this context, the Weberian 'rational state' is an essential part of the independence of the judiciary as we understand it today (see Chapter 4). The judiciary is probably the most important check and balance to government.

Although some convergence has occurred between these three interpretations of the rule of law, the diversity of traditions still persists. The dogmatic approach of Napoleonic and Germanic law based on codes is quite different from the more flexible common law traditions. The Nordic countries show a mix of the two approaches, characterised less by dogmatic rigid codes but by a more pragmatic approach.

This chapter tries to assess the importance of judicial power in Europe. It begins by looking at several dimensions of judicial power in Europe. Afterwards, the role of the constitutional courts, which grew in importance in Europe after the Second World War, is discussed. This is followed by a brief section on the European dimension of judicial politics and the emergence of an area of freedom, security and justice (AFSJ).

Patterns of judicial power in Europe

One of the characteristics of European politics is that there are different legal traditions shaping judicial power across Europe. One can identify at least five such legal traditions:

1. the *common law tradition* in the British Isles, based mainly on precedent and case law;
2. the *Napoleonic law tradition* which emerged in France during Napoleon's rule between 1804 and 1811 and expanded to all Western European countries and the Benelux;
3. the *Germanic law tradition* mainly influenced by Roman law discovered in the tenth century and combined with customary law in the German states of the Holy Roman Empire of the German Nation (962–1804). It expanded to Austria and Switzerland and influenced most countries in Central and Eastern Europe and Greece;
4. the *Scandinavian/Nordic law* tradition is based mainly on customary law practised in Northern Europe with a rather weak influence of Roman law. It can be found in Sweden, Denmark, Norway, Finland and Iceland (Bell, 2006: 234).
5. the *Central and Eastern European law* tradition which clearly includes different legal traditions and has to deal with the socialist law legacy which was in force between 1947 and 1989 (Manko, 2007: 89–103). Apart from the Germanic tradition, the legal-bureaucratic tradition of the Austro-Hungarian monarchy after 1867 has also to be taken into account for a wide range of countries (Kommisrud, 2009: 126,152). Furthermore, the influence of the Soviet legal philosophy on the Baltic countries during the annexation period (1944–92) should also be included. (Figure 6.1)

Table 6.1 gives an overview of the quality of the judiciary systems according to the regions. There are major differences in terms of allocated budget to the judicial system, per capita spending and staff per 100,000 inhabitants. This is based on the regular research of the European Commission for the Efficiency of Justice (CEPEJ) of the Council of Europe. The rule of law index 2018–9 world justice project gives a good picture of the differences in quality of the judicial system. According to their score, we can locate the Nordic countries at the very top. These countries are closely followed by the Benelux and the Drei-Sat/Germanic Europe (however, there is no score for Switzerland). At more distance we can find the Southern European countries and Central and Eastern Europe. At the bottom are the judicial systems of the Balkans, wider Europe and Turkey, which clearly give us a further indicator of the quality of the countries in Europe (see Figure 6.2, Box 6.1).

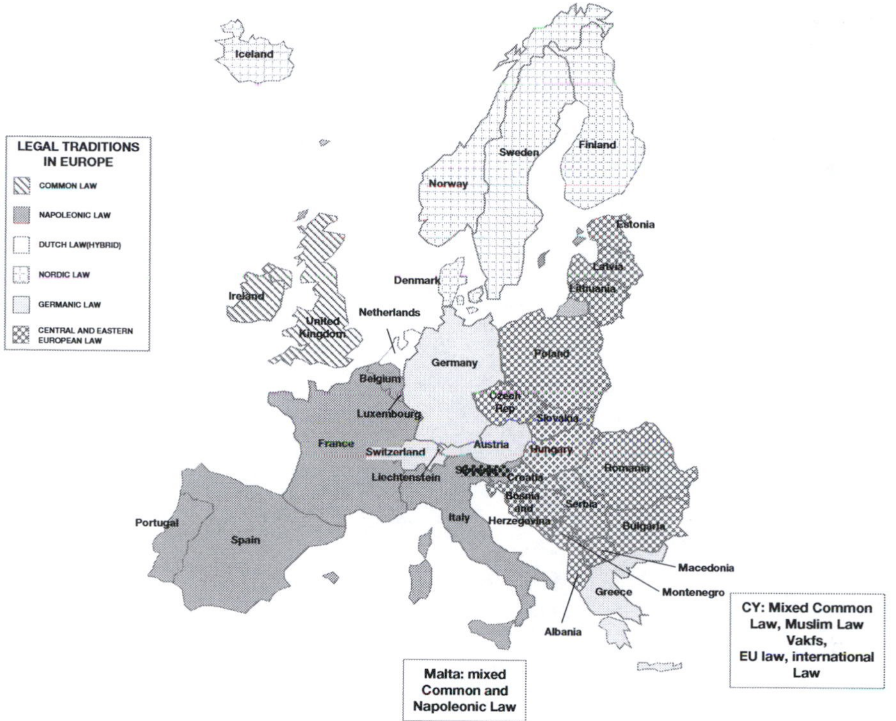

Figure 6.1 Legal traditions in Europe

The common law countries: the UK, Ireland, Malta and Cyprus

In the common law tradition, the judiciary is very keen to defend its independence from political pressure. One major problem for the UK government was that, until 2005, the Lord High Chancellor was the chair of the judiciary, but was also in charge of ensuring that the courts were working properly and that the independence of the judges was protected. However, he was also the Speaker of the House of Lords and sat in the cabinet. The position of Lord High Chancellor clearly contradicted the principle of the separation of powers. A major reform by the Tony Blair government, introduced in 2004 and adopted in 2005, the so-called Constitutional Reform Act, limited the role of the Lord High Chancellor by transferring some powers to other incumbents. The role of the presiding officer of the House of Lords was taken over by the Lord Speaker and the administration of the judiciary became the competence of the Lord Chief Justice. The position of the Lord High Chancellor was merged with the position of State Secretary of Justice, the first incumbent being Jack Straw. The modernisation of the judiciary in the UK also required the introduction of more transparent procedures for judicial appointments. Since the reform, there are now three Judicial Appointments boards for England and Wales, Scotland

Table 6.1 Some indicators on the judicial systems in Europe, 2016

		Budget in €m 2016	*Expenditure per capita 2016*	*Number of judges 2016*	*Judges per 100,000 inhabitants*	*Prosecutors per 100,000 inhabitants*	*Number of non-judge staff per 100,000*	*Rule of Law index 2018–9 0 Low 1 High /ranking worldwide out of 113*
Germanic speaking Europe	**Austria**	937.5	107.3	2,397	27	4.1	63.4	0.81/8
	Switzerland	1,808.9	214.1	1,251	15	10.4	53.5	n.d.
	Germany	10,015.5	122.0	19,867	24	6.7	64.7	0.83/6
Benelux	**Belgium**	931.8	82.3	1,600	14	7.6	44.6	0.77/15
	Luxembourg	92.9	157.3	187	32	8	33.9	n.d.
	Netherlands	2,036.6	119.2	2,331	14	5.4	42.8	0.85/5
Nordic countries	**Denmark**	481.4	83.8	372	6	12.1	28.6	0.89/1
	Finland	421.1	76.5	1,068	19	6.8	39.4	0.87/3
	Iceland	37.6	111.0	53	16	20.7	17.5	n.d.
	Norway	424	80.6	559	11	13.8	17.1	0.89/2
	Sweden	1,185.3	118.6	1,179	12	9.6	48.6	0.86/4
British Isles	**UK**	5,020.2	78.9	1,960	4	4.8	27.1	0.81/11
	Ireland	234.5	50.2	162	3	2.2	20.9	n.d.
France	**France**	4,413.3	65.9	6,995	10	2.9	33.9	0.74/18
Southern Europe	**Greece**	445.5	41.3	2,780	26	5.5	39.3	0.6/39
	Italy	4,544.4	75.0	6,395	11	3.5	35	0.65/31
	Portugal	583.3	56.6	1,986	19	14.5	54.8	0.72/21
	Spain	3,678.3	79.1	5,367	12	5.3	105.7	0.7/23

Mediterranean Islands	**Malta**	16.2	36.7	45	10	4.1	87	n.d.
	Cyprus	52.1	61	111	13	13.7	51.5	n.d.
Baltic Europe	**Estonia**	56.7	43.1	232	18	13	66.7	0.8/12
	Latvia	78.4	39.8	503	26	22.9	80.3	n.d.
	Lithuania	114.7	40.3	778	27	24.4	96.2	n.d.
Central Europe	**Czech Republic**	504.2	47.7	3,005	28	11.7	91.8	0.81/8
	Hungary	429.6	43.8	2,811	29	19.2	81.7	0.55/50
	Poland	1,991.6	51.8	9,980	26	15.2	112.3	0.67/25
	Slovakia	269.7	49.6	1,311	24	17.1	82.5	n.d.
	Slovenia	185.3	89.7	880	43	10.5	161.2	0.67/26
Eastern Europe	**Bulgaria**	262.7	37.0	2,255	32	21.3	86.9	0.53/55
	Croatia	222.5	53.6	1,797	43	14.6	140.3	0.61/35
	Romania	597.7	30.4			13.4	52.4	0.65/29
Balkans	**Albania**	28.9	10.0	363	13	11.2	31.6	0.51/68
	Bosnia-Herzegovina		33.7	1,014	29	10.9	89.9	0.53/56
	Macedonia	41.9	20.2	566	27	8.3	107.3	0.52/57
	Serbia	n.d.	n.d.	2,707	38	8.8	132.7	0.5/76
Turkey	**Turkey**	1,453.5	18.2	11,218	14	6		0.42/101
Wider Europe	**Russia**	3,552.4	24	26,443	18	25.2	66.8	0.47/89
	Ukraine	343.7	8.1	6,203	15	23.8	55.2	0.5/77
	Moldova	29.6	8.0	418	12	19.2	51.9	0.49/78
	Georgia	36.2	9.7	278	7	11.8	37.8	0.61/38

Source: CEPEJ (2018: 21, 26, 103, 131, 160); WJP (2018).

Figure 6.2 Quality of the rule of law in Europe, 2018–19

Source: based on WJP (2018).

and Northern Ireland respectively, and the respective Lord Chief Justices (Lord Chancellor in Scotland) are appointed by these committees. According to John Bell, until the 1970s, the judicial community was quite small and most appointments were made informally, partly according to merit, but also partly through patronage and clientelism. However, from the 1970s, the judiciary became a more complex, diversified system that needed reform, meaning that more transparent procedures of appointment had to be developed in order to make the judicial class more accountable. The recent reforms are the culmination of this evolutionary transformation of the UK judiciary (Bell, 2006: 312). Probably, the most important innovation was the introduction of a supreme court, which has functioned as the final appeals court for all law cases in the UK since 2009. It replaced the so-called five law lords, eminent judges of the country, who were appointed to the House of Lords to fulfil the function as the final appeals court. It means that since 2005, the UK institutional structure has been considerably modernised.

The 2005 reform also led to the unification of the administration of the court system under one agency, Her Majesty's Court and Tribunals Service (HMCTS), which is in charge of the governance of the complex judicial system in England and Wales. This is an important stepping stone towards the modernisation of the court system. The judicial structure includes different instances. At the bottom, there are the magistrates' courts and the county courts in smaller places. Above them are the High Courts with about 100 judges and above them is the Appeals Court. At the very top of the hierarchy is the supreme court as the last place for appeals. Specialised courts complete the system. In contrast to other European countries, the jury system is central to the UK system, allowing the population to be involved to some degree in the management of justice. This is probably the most democratic aspect of the UK judicial system. On 1 April 2017, there were 3,134 judges working for the judicial system of England and Wales. The vast majority are male (62 per cent) and women remain underrepresented (38 per cent). Even worse is the representation of Black, Asian or other ethnic minorities (so-called BAME) with about 7 per cent. However, in the tribunals 45 per cent are women and 10 per cent are BAME. This clearly has been a wake-up call for the HMCTS, which now conducts annual judiciary diversity statistical reviews in order to bring more women and minorities into the judiciary (Ministry of Justice, 2017: 1–2, 5).

Although the Republic of Ireland is a common law country, its judiciary is more accountable than that of the UK. The Republican written constitution ensures a considerable independence for Irish judges, who are appointed by a governmental committee. Once appointed, the Irish judges can only be removed from office if they misbehave or show incapacity. Such removal can only be achieved by a majority in both houses of parliament (Oireachtas) – the Daíl and the Seanad. Ordinary Irish judges interact with the political system because they can shape the constitution through the interpretation of its text. Any Irish judge has judicial review powers when interpreting the constitutional articles. This brings the Irish judicial system closer to the US model. In the same way as the United States, the Irish system also has a supreme court with similar powers of judicial review (Gallagher, 2010a: 84–95). Apart from this, the Irish structure is similar to that of the UK. In 2016, it employed 131 judges, 976 court and administrative staff employees, and a had a budget of €1.676 billion (Courts Service, 2017: 4).

Both Malta and Cyprus also belong to the common law tradition, due to the fact that they were former colonies of the UK. However, similar to Ireland, their legal systems are more structured and framed by a written constitution. Similar to Ireland also, the UK legacy of accumulated precedent decisions is also used in their legal systems. However, since independence in the 1960s, law has become more nationally oriented, translating UK law into more Cypriot or Maltese law. Some aspects of Cypriot law are strongly influenced by Greek law, particularly public and family law. Therefore, Cypriot law is rather hybrid comprising elements of the UK common law and the continental European tradition (Filos, 2009: 172–3, 180).

The Napoleonic Code countries: France, Italy, Spain, Portugal, Belgium and Luxembourg

In contrast to the common law countries, law is codified in all the other European countries. In France, the Napoleonic Code (with updates) is still central to the legal system. The civil and criminal courts are interpreted rigidly and there is less room for judges in the Napoleonic legal tradition to be creative in the interpretation of the law. According to Alec Stone Sweet, such canonisation of the law has become the pattern for dealing with constitutional law; indeed there is also a *code constitutionel*, which is studied almost dogmatically by law students (Stone Sweet, 2000: 138). In spite of the number of constitutions that have existed in France since the French Revolution, the different legal codes have remained central to the French judiciary. There is a territorially organised court system for criminal and civil matters. At the top there are the courts of appeal and, as last instance, the Court of Cassation, which becomes involved when all legal means have been exhausted. In 2018, the French judiciary consisted of 36 appeal courts at regional and national levels, 164 high courts (*tribunaux de grand instance*), 307 district courts (*tribunaux de instance*), 210 labour courts (*conseils de prud'hommes*), 134 commercial courts (*tribunaux de commerce*) and 155 children's courts (*tribunaux pour enfants*) (Ministère de Justice, 2018).

In 2017, 83,216 people were working in the justice department. In 2014, there were 8,023 judges, a figure that has stagnated or is decreasing . In 2017, the overall budget for the justice department was €8.5 billion; however, this also included the administration of the prison service (Conseil Superieur de la Magistrature, 2017: 31; Ministère de Justice, 2018). Judges normally follow a career pattern that starts with a specialised course in the National School of the Judiciary (École Nationale de Magistrature – ENM), from which a successful graduation will lead to a judiciary career. The administrative body of the courts system and the judiciary is the Higher Council of the Judiciary (Conseil Superieur de la Magistrature – CSM), which was established in 1958. It emulates the Italian Consiglio Superiore della Magistratura (CSM), which has the same name and was founded in 1948 after the Italian constitution was adopted. Also Portugal and Spain adopted similar magisterial councils. In France, as well as the other countries in this group, these administrative agencies are responsible for the good governance of the judiciary in terms of the good functioning of the courts, resource allocation, and the appointment, promotion and conduct of disciplinary processes of judges (Magalhães et al., 2006: 156).

The dual French court system of criminal/civil and administrative courts was emulated in all three Southern European countries in this group. On the whole, Italian, Spanish and Portuguese courts are not very efficient, largely because, particularly in the cases of Portugal and Spain, the judiciary is under-resourced. In Spain there has been an effort to take on more judges and improve the human and material resources of the court system. This has been supported by the main parties PSOE and PP since they signed the two pacts of justice in 2002 and 2008. In 2016, the overall budget for running the justice system in Spain was €3.6 billion, of which 58.4 per cent was allocated to the court system, particularly to the autonomous communities, 40.1 per cent went to the Ministry of Justice, and 1.5 per cent to the CGPJ (Consejo General del Poder Judicial, 2016: 13, 28). Due to the lack of human and material resources, the Spanish judiciary is quite slow. Moreover, the population still does not trust the judiciary system, with over 50 per cent in 2016 saying that is politicised. The regular political conflict in the CGPJ over the appointment of its members, or that of the constitutional court, are some of the examples. The Catalan crisis has shown that the Spanish judiciary is strongly committed to the constitution, which defines Spain as an indissoluble nation. This became evident when Catalan independence leaders tried to manipulate the Catalan regional judicial system against Madrid, but failed (*La Vanguardia*, 26 August 2018). Similar to other EU member-states, Spain is engaged in a process of change management; however, management seems to failing to give ownership to the judges. It seems also that decentralisation has created a more differentiated justice system with variations in its quality. A positive aspect is certainly that after forty years of democracy (since the late 1970s), a new younger cohort is taking the top positions and a little more than half are female judges (for more, see CGPJ and TI, 2015).

Portugal has also been engaged in change management with mixed results. Such process started around 2008 and comprised mainly the implementation of a new judicial map, a process that is still ongoing. Reform of the judiciary was part of the package of measures promised to the Troika during the bailout implementation period between 2011 and 2014. However, no serious costings were attached to the reform, so that many buildings of the new judicial map were not ready when the deadline arrived. Therefore, similar to Spain, the Portuguese judiciary has a quite negative reputation in society (for more, see Magone, 2014a: chapter 7; Santos and Gomes, 2011; one of the best studies is Santos, 1996; Eurobarometer Interactive, 2018).

The geographical proximity of Belgium and Luxembourg to France has also led to the establishment of similar judicial systems. The overall structures match the French model in many ways. Both countries have a cassation court (Cour de Cassation), an appeals court and, depending on the territorial organisation, local and regional courts. In the same way as in the Southern European countries, there is also a constitutional court adjudicating in constitutional matters. In Belgium, in spite of federalisation, there is still a nationally organised judicial system in Belgium. A federal public service for the judiciary, which has existed since 1830, was reformed in 2002 in order to adjust to the new system. Overall, in 2016, the Service Publique Federal Justice (SFPJ) had 21,281 full-time staff, out of which were about 1,600 full-time judges, and it had an overall budget of €1.9 billion (SFPJ, 2017a: 10). Belgium has been engaged in a continuous process of reform, which now includes a quite ambitious plan to move towards an e-justice system, meaning the use of new technologies to make it easier for citizens to gain access to the judiciary (SFPJ, 2017b). In the 1990s, the Belgian judiciary system was in a major crisis due to the corruption scandals related to partyocracy, but mainly due to the Dutroux case related to an alleged paedophile ring comprising many members of the political, economic and judicial elites (Els Witte, et al., 2009: 323–8). Therefore, trust in the judiciary is still low achieving just 58 per cent in May 2017. In the other Benelux countries, Luxembourg has a 71 per cent trust rating and the Netherlands 79 per cent (Eurobarometer Interactive, 2018).

Luxembourg belongs also to the Napoleonic French legal tradition. The main official administrative language is French. Most of the judicial activity is spent in the capital Luxembourg, but also in the small town of Diekirch, the two regional high courts (*tribunaux d'arrondissements*). The budget is €4.7 million, out of which 85 per cent is just for wages. There are 183 judges, of which 61 per cent are women. Additionally, there are 33 justices of the peace (La Justice du Grand Duché du Luxembourg, 2017: 9–11).

The Germanic Law tradition: Germany, Austria and Switzerland

Typologies can tend to simplify the complex historical legacy of different countries. In spite of many similarities between Germany, Austria and Switzerland, their historical backgrounds are quite different. There has been a borrowing of institutions from each other, so that the similarities have been achieved over a long period of time.

Historically, the Germanic legal tradition is linked to the German Holy Roman Empire which existed between 962 and 1806. Originally, the legal tradition was based on customary German law established at the local level. However, the rediscovery of Roman law based on the collection of laws of the Code of Justinian (Justinianus Codex) was a major contribution to its codification. This collection of laws was ordered by Justinian, the Emperor of the East Roman Empire, and compiled by commissions of legal scholars between 529 and 565. There were several subsequent waves in order to adjust the law to new situations. The Code of Justinian was rediscovered in the eleventh century, mainly by the Southern European universities and led to its dissemination across the continent (Wieacker, 1981: 272). Roman law became a quite important source for organising customary law. In this regard, the German legal tradition is strongly influenced by Roman law, but also takes into account customary legal traditions. For the Emperors of the Holy Roman Empire of the German Nation, Roman law was an important instrument to emphasise the continuity to the previous ancient polity. Therefore, Roman-Germanic law gained in importance over the centuries.

The German legal and judiciary system was established in the nineteenth century. The Prussian judiciary was the core model, which was then emulated by or transferred to the other German states. In comparison to other countries, it took a long time for Germany to have a unified codified legal system, mainly due to the fact that unification only happened after 1871. Probably, the Prussian General Law of the Country (*Allgemeines Landesrecht*) of 1794 started the process towards such national codification. In spite of this beginning, each statelet of the German confederation after 1806 had several legal systems running in parallel. It was quite a confusing situation (Krüger, 1914: 124–5). Nevertheless, the customs union (*Zollverein*) established in 1834 led slowly to common legal frameworks. One of them was the commercial code of 1859 and the code of Bills of Exchange in 1847 (Krüger, 1914: 125–6). Unification after 1871 made it imperative to create a unified national legal system. However, a civil code (*Bürgerliches Gesetzbuch*) was only adopted in 1896 and entered into force on 1 January 1900. In spite of the time spent drafting the civil code, it became a juridical masterpiece and was admired by the legal community. Essentially, it is based on the old Roman-Germanic organisation and principles of law that most legal scholars were accustomed to at that time (Krüger, 1914: 126–30). In contrast, a criminal law code was already in place in May 1870 (Krüger, 1914: 130–2). Nevertheless, the bureaucratic-legal model achieved its completion at the end of the nineteenth century, and many features of the model remained important until today. Max Weber's rational-legal state is strongly influenced by the German model. The 1949 *Grundgesetz* (Basic Law) clearly strengthened the judiciary as a reaction to the traumatic experience of the national socialist period. Apart from the fact that the catalogue of rights became central to the constitution, particularly the protection of human dignity, a constitutional court, which is separate from the ordinary judiciary system, was established to adjudicate on all constitutional issues. The fact that judges can only be removed by a two-thirds majority in both houses of parliament, the Bundestag and Bundesrat, is also important. Judges are probably the most important civil servants of the country in terms of pay and status. On the one hand, this strong position of the judges allows for a strong autonomy and independence, but, on the other, it may cause problems of inertia under the bureaucratic-legal organisation of the courts (Bell, 2006: 144–5).

The reputation of the judiciary suffered a lot during and after the collapse of national socialist rule. In the same way as in Italy, the Allies decided not to prosecute any judges that worked during the nationalist period. This meant that many middle- and lower-ranking judges were brought over from the previous totalitarian regime without charge. The older judges have retired and younger generations have replaced them. There was also some solidarity of judges, which allowed for this continuity (Conradt, 2001: 210–11).

The German judicial system is federalised, meaning that there are sixteen different regional judiciaries as well as the federal level. Although most of these regional legal systems need to be compatible with federal law, there may be differences in handling minor offences in different parts of the country. In 2017, there were 638 local courts (*Amtsgerichte*), 115 regional courts (*Landesgerichte*) and 24 higher regional courts (*Oberlandesgerichte*). Besides these, there were 51 administrative courts and 15 higher administrative courts (*Oberverwaltungsgerichte*), 18 tax courts (*Finanzgerichte*), 110 labour courts (*Arbeitsgerichte*) and 18 higher labour courts (*Landesarbeitsgerichte*), as well as 67 social courts (*Sozialgerichte*) and 14 higher social courts (*Landessozialgerichte*). At the federal level, the different federal high courts were placed in different German cities (Bundesamt für Justiz, 2017a). This reinforced federal solidarity and also enhanced loyalty between the *Länder* (*Bundestreue*). The constitutional court (*Bundesverfassungsgericht*) and the federal court (*Bundesgerichthof*) are both located in Karlsruhe, the federal administrative court (*Bundesverwaltungsgericht*) is in Leipzig, the federal tax court (*Bundesfinanzhof*) and federal patent court (*Bundespatentgericht*) are based in Munich, the federal labour court (*Bundesarbeitsgericht*) in Erfurt and the federal social court (*Bundessozialgericht*) in Kassel.

At the end of 2016, there were 20,739 judges, of which 44.5 per cent were women. The vast majority work in the regional judicial system (98 per cent), whereas only very few judges work in the federal court system (2 per cent). Moreover, 7 per cent work in the ordinary criminal and civil court system, while the rest are distributed among the other specialised courts (Bundesamt für Justiz, 2017b).

Institutionally, German unification in 1989 particularly affected the judiciary in the eastern *Länder*. The tradition of the German Democratic Republic (GDR) was to have a partisan judiciary that would adhere to the ideology of the Socialist Unity Party (Sozialistische Einheitspartei – SED). In this sense, many judges were party members and supportive of the regime. After 1989, the whole East German judiciary had to be restructured. According to Hellmut Wollmann, this process took place between 1990 and 1995. About 62 per cent of the 1,625 GDR judges applied to be taken on within the new system; however, only 650 (40 per cent) were successful. The implementation of the complex new judiciary system consisting of the ordinary and specialised courts led to an increase in the number of positions to 3,331. However, these new positions were filled by West German judges, who were either reallocated or were newly recruited. This meant that the proportion of East German judges declined even further to 18 per cent by 1992 (Wollmann, 1996: 103–4).

The Austrian system is similar to the German one. However, the legacy of the Austro-Hungarian monarchy has to be added to the Germanic-Roman law tradition. There is some continuity of the legal acquis from the Austro-Hungarian monarchy, which was modernised over time. There is a stronger centralising tendency because of the nature of Austrian executive federalism. However, in terms of structure, there are many similarities. As in Germany, in 2014 there were 116 district courts (*Amtsgerichte*) at the local level, 20 regional courts of justice (*Landesgerichte*) and 4 regional courts of appeal (*Oberlandesgerichte*). At the head of the whole system is the supreme court (*Oberster Gerichtshof*). In July 2017 there were 1,731 judges working in the Austrian judicial system, and they were supported by a staff of 4,713 people (Bundesministerium für Justiz, 2014).

Although Switzerland has many similarities to Germany and Austria, the highly decentralised federal system gives a strong position to the twenty-six cantons. Historically, Switzerland is intertwined with the legal traditions of the Holy Roman Empire of the German Nation. In this regard, the Roman-Germanic tradition had a quite considerable impact on the Swiss confederation. However, simultaneously, the cantons and cities developed their own decentralised customary law traditions. Resistance against a centralised government has prevented a full harmonisation of law between the cantons even today. The loose confederation has produced a large pool of documents which clearly still shape the constitutional and legal history of Switzerland (for a review, see Peyer, 1978). However, the invasion of Switzerland by Napoleonic troops in 1798 led to the establishment of the first centralised government of the Helvetic Republic. The Napoleonic code was imposed on Switzerland. Nevertheless, after the defeat of Napoleon, the confederation returned to their old ways. It was just after the constitution of 1848 and 1874 that the process towards a unified Swiss legal system began to emerge. A kind of 'soft federalisation' of the legal system took place in 1898. Until 1874, the federal dimension was almost non-existent and parliament was both a legislature and the last instance of the judiciary. A civil code was only established in 1912 and a criminal code in 1937 (Kälin, 2002: 189). Today, each canton still has its civil and criminal process, and in spite of attempts to standardise to a national one, such efforts have only been partially successful (Rothmayr Allison and Varone, 2014: 234–5).

The supreme court has limited constitutional review at federal level. parliament is the source of all laws and also the principal of the supreme court. More important than rulings of the supreme court, are decisions taken in direct democratic referendums. in this regard, the supreme court cannot reject constitutionally contravening laws. Nevertheless, as already mentioned, European and international law have strengthened the position of the supreme court (Rothmayr Allison and Varone, 2014: 220–2, 229, 231; Vatter, 2014: 477–502).

Federalism reform is an ongoing process in Switzerland and has also affected the judiciary. The constitutional reform created new federal courts in order to ease the workload of the supreme court (*Bundesgericht*) in Lausanne. Therefore, since 2005 there has been the federal administrative court (*Bundesverwaltungsgericht*) based in St Gallen, a federal criminal court (*Bundestrafgericht*) based in Bellinzona and since 2012 a federal patent court in St Gallen (*Bundespatentgericht*) (Rothmayr Allison and Varone, 2014: 220–1).

Another peculiarity of the system is that the judicial system of the Francophone part of Switzerland has been influenced by the French model. The cantons of Geneva, Waadt and Neuenburg use, for example, justices of the peace (*justices de paix*) at the lowest level of the judiciary system and labour courts. In contrast, German-speaking Switzerland (for example, Zürich, Bern, St Gallen and Aargau, more closely follow the German model, particularly in the use of commercial courts) (Kälin, 2002: 190).

The Netherlands: a hybrid system

Historically, Dutch legal history was highly influenced by the legal tradition of the Holy Roman Empire of the German Nation, particularly after the rediscovery of Roman law by Southern European universities, particularly Bologna in the eleventh century. During the seventeenth century, in the Dutch Republic several law scholars, particularly Hugo Grotius, contributed to the establishment of a Hollandic Roman Law which integrated Roman, Catholic Church canon and customary law. Also natural law, very prominent in the Holy Roman Empire of the German nation, played a major role in shaping a distinct Dutch legal tradition (Lesaffer, 2004: 46–7). In spite of this, myriad legal orders at different levels existed until the late eighteenth century. The Napoleonic wars contributed to a strong French influence over the legal system. While the Dutch Republic, similar to Switzerland, was based on a loose federation in which no unification of law and the judicial system was undertaken, the French invasion was a major factor in centralising the country and providing a codified legal system through the introduction of the Napoleonic codes. Such process took quite a long time because of the difficulty of including Dutch customary law. However, after the annexation of the Netherlands as part of France, the French Napoleonic codes were imposed on the country (Lesaffer, 2004: 50–3). In 1814, after the establishment of the Kingdom of the Netherlands, several attempts were made to create a Dutch civil code; however, in the end, the simplicity, transparency and clarity of the French codes prevailed (Lesaffer, 2004: 56–7). In 1947, law scholar E.M. Meijers from Leyden University began to rework the civil code, a task that was only completed in 1992. It is a different code, taking into account changes in Dutch society, and also the importance of European integration. In this sense, it is open to other sources of law, including European law and the rulings of the European Court of Human Rights (Lesaffer, 2004: 58).

Although located on the continent of Europe, the Netherlands has a legal system closer to that of the UK. The constitution upholds the principle of parliamentary sovereignty and therefore forbids any review by the judiciary. This is denied by article 120 of the constitution. This also means that there is no constitutional court in the Netherlands (Andeweg and Irwin, 2014: 152). There is a supreme court (Hoge Raad), four appeal courts for criminal, civil, administrative and tax law (*Gerechtshoven*), eleven district courts and thirty-two first instance courts. Since 1998, the Netherlands has been engaged in new public management reforms to create a more value for money and citizen-oriented judicial system (Van Dijk, 2014: 2). The Council of State (*Raade van der Staat*) not only advises the government on legal matters but is also the highest appeal court for administrative issues. Although the Netherlands has a civil and criminal code that has supremacy, it also allows case law to shape the legal system.

The Nordic model: Sweden, Denmark, Norway, Finland and Iceland

The geographical proximity of these five countries has led to the institutional transfer and convergence of judicial models during the last 200 years. Historically, we can differentiate between a Western and Eastern Scandinavian/Nordic transfer of legal systems. In the Western part is Danish law that clearly plays a major role. Denmark controlled Norway until 1814 and Iceland until independence in 1918 (independent but in personal union with Denmark until 1944, after which it became an independent Republic), and therefore Danish law was used in the two countries. After 1814, Norway was in personal union with Sweden but was able to keep its institutions, so that Danish law continued to be used. In the Eastern Scandinavian/ Nordic legal tradition, Finland was part of Sweden, so that Swedish law was used throughout the country until 1809. Between 1809 and 1918, Finland became part of the Russian Empire, but it kept all its institutions including Swedish law. After independence in 1918, Finland kept Swedish law. Moreover, Swedish became an official language enshrined in the constitution, so that the proximity of both countries allowed the creation of a Swedish law community (Bernitz, 2007: 16). Nordic cooperation played a major role in sustaining this larger Nordic legal culture (Bernitz, 2007: 23–5). Therefore, these countries are part of a legal family that clearly has distinct elements to the Romanic-French and Germanic approach to law.

According to Ulf Bernitz, the Nordic legal family is characterised by the lack of a codified civil code, in spite of having some affinity to the civil law tradition in Europe. Moreover, the influence of Roman law has been much weaker or non-existent than in most other European countries. Furthermore, the lack of over-arching almost perfect rational legal systems like Napoleonic or Germanic law are absent in the Nordic tradition. Rather more important is a realist approach closer to the citizens' reform-oriented law that puts the economy and welfare at its core. It is a support for the existing social market economy (Bernitz, 2007: 19). However, since the 1970s and 1980s, international law, European law and the European Convention of Human Rights has been eroding the coherence and consistency of such Nordic legal culture (Bernitz, 2007: 26–8).

The Swedish court system consists of, on the one hand, civil and criminal courts and, on the other, administrative courts. The civil and criminal courts are organised in forty-eight district courts (*Tingsrätt*), six regional courts of appeal (*Hövrätt*) and the supreme court (*Högsta Domstol*). The administrative courts have twelve county administrative courts (*Lansrätt*), four courts of appeal (*Kammarrätt*) and a supreme administrative court (*Regeringsrätt*) (Regeringskansliet, 2015: 19–21). The court system is managed by a National Courts Administration Agency (*Domstolsverket*), founded in 1975 and based in Jönköping in order to ensure independence from the government. It employs over 5,500 staff and has an annual expenditure of €574.1 million (£526 million, US$725 million). Since 2008, the National Courts Administration (*Domstolverket*) has had an advisory board under a director-general. It consists of nine members, most of them from the judiciary system, but also two members from the Rijksdag.

In the same way as the Swedish system, the Danish judicial and legal system has its roots in its own evolutionary development towards democracy. A key date is 1849, when a democratic Danish constitution enshrined the separation of powers. According to John Bell, Swedish judges are particularly impressed by the management of the court system in Denmark, which is undertaken by the Danish Court Administration Agency (*Domstolsstyrelsen*) and is run solely by judges. This was introduced in 1999 after a unanimous vote in the Folketing, making the agency independent of the Ministry of Justice (Bell, 2006: 243). The reform also allowed for the independent appointment of judges through a Judicial Appointments

Council. Apart from this difference, the Danish judiciary system is very similar to the Swedish system and has adjusted to the needs of the country. In 2006, the Folketing decided to undertake a major reform to improve the efficiency and management of the courts. The supreme court (*Hojesteret*) is the final instance of appeal for the civil and criminal courts and for the maritime and commercial courts. Moreover, there are also the high courts in Greenland and the Faroe Islands. Like many other European countries, the new court system is the result of reforms that started to come into force in 2007. Among these reforms, there was a considerable reduction in the number of district courts and the introduction of more efficiency in terms of court system management. District courts also function as appeals courts. Only fundamental issues can be referred to the supreme court, if permission is granted by the Appeal Permission Board (*Processbevillingsnaevnet*). In 2014, there were 2,800 staff working for the judiciary, of whom 380 were judges. In 2016, the overall budget for Denmark's Court Administration Agency was about €215 million, of which one-third was for wages, and the rest for equipment, training and education, and administration (Domstolsstyrelsen, 2015, 2017: 10).

Although Danish law influenced considerably Norwegian law, historically there was a previous history that goes back to the ancient traditions of the Vikings in the tenth and eleventh centuries. The peak of this development was the codification of a National Law (*Landsloven*) under king Magnus VI, the 'Lawmender' in 1274. Between 1390 and 1814, Norway was in personal union with Denmark and Danish became quite dominant in the country. In 1687, the *Landsloven* was updated leading to Norwegian Law (*Den Norske Lov*); however, it was strongly framed by the Danish code of 1683 (Domstol Administrasjonen, n.d., 13–15). The Norwegian judiciary system shows the same features as the Swedish and Danish systems. In the same way, there is a supreme court (*Høyesterett*) as the final instance of appeal. As in Sweden and Denmark, there is an agency for the administration of courts (*Domstoladministrasjonen*), which was founded in 2002 (Domstol administrasjonen, n.d.). In 2014, the Norwegian judiciary had 558 judges.

Iceland follows this model, but it has no appeals court, so that only two tiers exist – eight district courts and the supreme court. The court managing authority is the judicial council (*Dómstolrad*) responsible mainly for the running of the district courts. Moreover, there is a labour court and an impeachment court, the latter adjudging in cases of criminal misconduct in office by government ministers.

Finland has a similar three-tier judicial with the supreme court (*Korkein oikeus*) at the top. The high court deals with charges against a member of government, the Chancellor of Justice, the Parliamentary Ombudsman, a member of the Supreme or the Supreme Administrative Court. It is chaired by the president of the supreme court and consists of five members (Oikeus, 2018). In contrast to the other Nordic countries, the ministry of justice is directly in charge of the management of the court system. Quite important is the figure of the Chancellor of Justice and his/her deputy who are in charge of the supervision of the courts and the quality of law throughout the government (Sarvilinna, 2007). In 2014, the Finnish judiciary comprised 988 judges and spent about €389 million.

The Nordic countries have probably the best judicial systems of the EU, because they are so oriented towards the citizen. Easy access to justice is important in the most egalitarian societies of the world. All five countries spend a quite considerable amount on their judiciary systems.

The Central and Eastern European countries: continuities and discontinuities

After decades of a socialist judiciary system, most Central and Eastern European countries had to restructure their judiciary systems. The rule of law based on liberal principles became a central aspect of the restructuring of the judiciary in these countries. The transformation of the judiciary has been difficult, partly because of the need for new personnel trained in liberal democratic legal systems and partly because of the difficulty of rewriting complete civil and criminal codes. Some aspects of the period of socialist law had to be taken over by the new regimes. The EU, the Council of Europe and the OECD have been instrumental in monitoring and supporting judicial reform in all Central and Eastern European countries. In spite of this, partisan politics still plays a major role in shaping judicial reforms as the cases of Hungary, Poland and Romania document. Martin Mendelski differentiates between two large groups of countries, Central Europe and the Baltics (CEB) on the one hand, and southeastern Europe (SEE) on the other. The former has a strong (Estonia, Slovenia) or moderate system of rule of law (Poland, Hungary, Czech Republic and Slovakia, Lithuania and Latvia), while the latter has a rather weak system of rule of law (Bulgaria, Romania, Serbia, Macedonia, Bosnia-Herzegovina as well as Russia). Albania has a very weak system of rule of law like the countries of wider Europe (Mendelski, 2017: 114).

Central Europe and the Baltics: the making of a democratic rule of law system

The most pragmatic country is probably Hungary, which simply revised the socialist constitution and adjusted to the new liberal order. The historical legacy of the nineteenth century and the interwar period allowed some continuity with previous regimes to be achieved. The present Hungarian model is strongly influenced by German and Austrian law. The Austro-Hungarian monarchy, even after the Ausgleich of 1867, has remained an important reference of the Hungarian legal system. The unification process of the courts began in 1872 and continued until the end of the nineteenth century (Hoensch, 1989: 49). This Austro-Hungarian codification of law remained in place until the end of the Second World War, to be replaced at that point by the new socialist civil and criminal codes. In spite of its transition to democracy in 1989, Hungary simply adjusted these socialist codes to meet the demands of the European Convention on Human Rights. There have been no major revisions of the codes since 1990, although there were some further adjustments in 1997. The highly polarised political arena prevented a strong cooperation between the left and the right, so that when one party came to power, it tried to impose their reforms without proper consultation and cooperation with the other side. Throughout the 1990s until accession to the EU, the Hungarian judiciary was struggling in terms of the workload, poor infrastructure, lack of support staff, and particularly the lack of a training system for new judges (Badó, 2014: 17–25). Meanwhile , between 2010 and 2014, the second Viktor Orbán government (2010–14), with a super majority of more than two-thirds in parliament, was able to introduce a second major reform of the judiciary, which was quite controversial leading to criticisms by the Council of Europe and the EU, among others. A quite ambitious package of changes to the judiciary was introduced parallel to the changes in the constitution. One rather controversial change was the restructuring of the management governance system of the courts which was done by the National Council of the Judiciary in 2011. However, the Orbán government reduced the power of the National Council of Judiciary by just giving a control function to the judiciary system. The operational work was assigned to a nominated president of the National Office of the Judiciary. S/he would have almost full powers to manage the day-to-day running of the courts. The president of the National Office of the Judiciary and the National Council of the Judiciary would now be appointed by parliament. However, the modes of appointment were criticised by the European institutions, because it allowed for the possibility for absolute majority governments to just dominate the selection process to their advantage. In this sense, there were fears of an undue politicisation of the judiciary. Changes had to be made in order to gain the approval of the EU and the Council of Europe, although flaws in the system remain (Badó, 2014: 48–51; Council of Europe/Venice Commission, 2012).

The Hungarian judicial system consists of four tiers: the 111 local courts (*JárásBíróságok*), the 20 county courts (*Törvényszék*), 5 regional appeals courts (*Itélötáblák*) and the supreme court (*Curia*). Such a model, in one form or another, was largely implemented in all the new democracies of Central and Eastern Europe (Birósag, 2018).

The Polish case shows many similarities to Hungary. The politicisation of the judiciary is a recurrent theme, particularly when the conservative Justice and Law party is in power, which was the case in the period of 2005–7 as well as after 2015. In spite of this, there was and still is strong consensus among the political parties that an independent judiciary is an important element of the new third Polish Republic, particularly as a contrast to the previous socialist regime. Indeed, even the socialist regime spoke of a 'technocratically interpreted need to restore a socialist rule of law' in 1982, after decades of mismanagement of the economy leading to considerable levels of debt. In 1982, a constitutional court and a state court were established to prosecute politicians who abuse their power while in office. All this experience then became part of the negotiations of the round table of 1989, so that the independence of the judiciary became a major priority. Like in Hungary, this was achieved by a continuous step-by-step approach, and was also part of the process of accession to the EU. Between 2000 and 2015, several legal aspects of the old system were updated and modernised such as the selection process of judges, the training of young judges, the relationship between the institutions and the modernisation of the civil code in 1997, despite many building blocks remaining unchanged (Bodnar and Bojarski, 2012: 681, 685–6, 693–4; Ziemer, 2013: 133–4, 141). The importance of the rule of law for Poland is clear. It is a strategic necessity not only for strengthening democracy but above all to attract foreign direct investment. Judicial independence and legal certainly are important aspects of a booming economy. Quite crucial to this process was the creation of the National Council of the Judiciary (*Krajowa Rada Sądownictwa*), which is in charge of the internal management of the judiciary and works closely with the ministry of justice, which is in charge of external management, including a shared competence related to budgetary matters (Bodnar and Bojarski, 2012: 670–3). The composition of the National Council of the Judiciary includes a majority of fifteen judges and also the minister of justice and members of parliament).

Similar to Hungary, the PiS absolute majority government elected in 2015 began to introduce a major programme to restructure the judiciary in Poland. Among the changes was an increase in the number of judges and the replacement of existing ones by pro-government members in the constitutional court. The retirement age for judges was decreased from 70 to 65 years, so many judges could be removed. In October 2018, the European Court of Justice suspended temporarily the removal of the judges and ruled that they should be reinstated until a final ruling could be issued (*Euractiv*, 23 October 2018; *Politico*, 24 September 2018; Venice Commission, 2017: 8–11).

The structure of the judiciary during the socialist period had just two tiers; however, the new judiciary moved towards a four-tier system with 321 district (*sądy rejonowe*), 45 regional (*sądy okręgowe*), 11 appeals courts (*sądy apelacyjne*) and the supreme court (*sądy najwyższy*). Parallel to this are the administrative courts (*sądy administracyjne*) and a large military court (*sądy wojskowe*) system, taken over from the previous socialist system and which is losing in importance. One important court is the tribunal of state to which the acts of office holders are accountable in terms of their constitutionality should incumbents become involved in criminal activities or abuse their power (Taras, 2006: 365–6). As already mentioned, the Polish legal system has many continuities from the old socialist system. The Polish civil code of 1964 is part of this communist legacy, in spite of major changes in past decades. Moreover, Polish civil law procedure is also based on the previous socialist legacy. Furthermore, the interwar period of civil law was strongly influenced by the Napoleonic code and found its way into the socialist version (Jaremba, 2014: 142–4; Manko, 2007: 90, 92). Moreover, the criminal code remains a source of conflict. A new code was established in 1997 replacing the socialist one. This was clearly a milestone towards a new legal system and was strongly influenced by the latest developments internationally. In this regard, globalisation was a major factor affecting the code. However, many offences and crimes were not properly defined leading to problems of interpretation. In this regard, legislation may be rather weak and lacking in legal certainty (Nowak, 2013: 152).

The Czech judiciary system shows that institution-building was a difficult and long process. The best example of this was the late establishment of the supreme administrative court in 2003, ten years after the 'velvet divorce'. In 2010, the court system had eighty-six district courts (*okresní soudy*), eight regional courts (*krajské soudy*), two high courts (*vrchní soudy*) and the supreme court (*nejvyšší soudy*). In contrast to Hungary, Poland, Slovakia, Romania and Bulgaria, the Czech judiciary is still administered directly by the ministry of justice. The main reason seems to be a kind of almost sacrosanct historical legacy and preservation of continuity to the interwar state, which clearly had no special council to administer the judicial system (Kühn, 2011: 33). The potential for politicisation is quite high, particularly in view of political corruption cases, and also the emergence of populist leaders like Andris Babiš, the present prime minister. According to Karel Vodička, the Czech judiciary system is quite slow and inefficient and has lost many good judges to the private sector because of the low pay (Vodička, 2005: 228–30). Indeed, the lowering of judges' salaries was contemplated, which clearly undermined the morale of this important profession (Kühn, 2011: 31). Quite positive is that both a new civil code and a new criminal code were adopted in 2014 (until then the 1964 code of the socialist period was still valid) and 2010, respectively. In spite of all these critical comments, the Czech judicial system is among the better ones among the SEEs due to a strong liberal political culture within the country and the role of consensus in a country of small parties.

In comparison to the Czech Republic, Slovakia has been affected by the rule of populist leaders. Until 1998, the nationalist tendencies of the Vladimir Mečiar government had a negative impact on the political and judiciary institutions, particularly in a crucial period of nation- and state-building. The creation of a Judiciary Council in 2002 was very much a response to pressure from the EU to enhance the independence of the judicial system. In spite of this, the politicisation of the judiciary is still a major issue, particularly in view of the dominance of Robert Fico's social democrats in the political system. Political corruption remains a major issue, which also allegedly affects the judiciary. The murder of a Czech journalist, Ján Kuciak, who was investigating alleged links between government members, mainly the prime minister's personal assistant Maria Trosková, to the Italian mafia organization N'dranghetta, shows clearly the problems the judiciary has to face (*The Guardian*, 28 February 2018; for a more detailed study comparing Czech and Slovak judicial reform, see Kosař, 2016).

Quite a good example of compliance with EU and international conditionality is the case of the small country of Slovenia, which was part of the former Yugoslavia. After independence, the political and economic elites were able to achieve quite early consensus about the strategic merits to join the EU. It means that Slovenia adopted all the measures proposed by the EU in order to create a strong functioning state, including an independent judiciary. In 1994, the Slovenian parliament adopted three crucial laws, the Constitutional Court Act, the Judicial Service Act and the Courts Act. In the Courts Act, a judicial council (*Sodni Svet*) was created which follows very closely the Southern European model, particularly the Italian one. It is a model of shared governance between the judicial council and the ministry of justice (Dallara, 2014: 37–8). Conflict within government over the independence of the judiciary has been rare or non-existent. However, major conflicts have been over the poor pay of judges and the inefficiency of the court system due to backlogs (Dallara, 2014: 39–40). As a small country, the Slovenian court system is a quite simple three-tier system with forty-four local/eleven district, four higher appellate courts and a supreme court.

In contrast to Slovenia, in 1992 Croatia established an ethno-authoritarian façade democracy under the leadership of Franjo Tuđman. Although the new Croatian constitution included separation of powers and the principle of independence of the judiciary, the constitutional reality was one of continuing interference of the government controlled by Tuđman. The participation of Croatia in the war in Bosnia-Herzegovina further undermined any developments towards European integration. The death of Franjo Tuđman in December 1999 opened the way for a more democratic organisation of the judiciary. It seems that similar to Slovenia the political elites were able to achieve consensus over the merits of striving for European integration. The semi-presidential political system was quite important to achieve democratic stability and implement necessary reforms. President Stjepan Mesić, who was incumbent between 2000 and 2010, played a major role in changing the negative image of Croatia abroad (Dallara, 2014: 41).

Among the conditions for accession to the EU, Croatia had to cooperate with the International Criminal Tribunal for the Former Yugoslavia (ICTY), including the release of military leaders who were suspected of crimes against humanity, and allow Serbs to return to Krajina (Dallara, 2014: 42).

Already in 1994, Croatia had established a State Judiciary Council, but without the independence necessary for its work (Dallara, 2014: 46). Only during the new millennium have the necessary safeguards been established, so that independence of the judiciary could be guaranteed. After 2004, the EU conditionality became quite important in ensuring more independence for the judiciary. One major problem remained the high level of political corruption, so that commentators tended to speak of 'Potemkin harmonisation', meaning just cosmetic changes, but without any real concrete change management (Dallara, 2014: 49). In both Slovenia and Croatia, the national judges' associations were instrumental in mobilising their international networks to achieve more judicial independence (Dallara, 2014: 50).

In the Baltics, it is Estonia that has advanced most towards a strong rule of law and respective judiciary. Particularly, the use of new technologies to facilitate e-government has become a trade mark of the Estonian model. This has also had its impact on the management of the judiciary, which uses the new technologies to create a more efficient judiciary. The Estonian model consists of a three-tier court system. The so-called Council for the Administration of the Courts (*Kohtute haldamise nõukojas*) consists of eleven members, of which five are judges who are elected by the profession. It advises and works closely with the ministry of justice (Eesti Kohtud, 2018).

We can find similar court systems in Lithuania and Latvia. In Lithuania, the National Courts Administration (*Nacionaline Teismu Administracija*) was established in 2002, which governs the court system independently of political influence. The executive board is the Judicial Council (*Teisėju Taryba*) consisting of twenty-three judges. They are elected by a general meeting of judges. In contrast to Estonia and Lithuania, Latvia had more difficulties moving to a functioning judiciary. One reason was the fact that government instability prevented a more strategic approach to judiciary reform. However, an overriding element is historical legacy. Similar to the Czech Republic, Latvia stuck to a model of judiciary and rule of law that emphasised continuity of the interwar period (Lazdins, 2016: 70–4; Osipova, 2014). It took therefore until 2010 to establish an independent council of judiciary (*Tieslietu padome*), which consists of fifteen members, most of them judges and members of the top judiciary hierarchy, but also members of the legal profession. It is an important self-governance institution of the judges that works closely with the ministry of justice, which is in charge of the operational governance of the three-tier court system – thirty-four district, six regional courts and the supreme court – through the Court Administration Agency as well other attached agencies (Tiesu Administracija, 2018: 6). Like the cooperation between the Nordic countries, in spite of their differences, the three countries have clearly created well-functioning judiciary systems. Political corruption continues to still be a major problem in Lithuania and Latvia, but there is a growing awareness of the problem by policy-makers and judges and a will to find a solution. The EU, the Council of Europe and the OECD have been instrumental in helping these three countries to improve the quality of their judiciaries.

The Balkan syndrome: political corruption, inefficiency and lack of reform

The judiciary reforms in Romania and Bulgaria have been quite difficult. This is also one of the main reasons why both countries are still kept outside the Schengen area. Political corruption and high levels of inefficiency still characterise the judiciary, as does the political culture of the politicians. Although a higher council of the magistrature (*Consiliul Superior al Magistraturii*) exists in Romania, several amendments had to be made shortly before joining the EU, so that judiciary independence is properly ensured. However, it seems that the council consists almost entirely of judges, which may lead potentially to the defence of corporatist interests. Moreover, the ministry of justice is still very much involved in the operational running of the court system, particularly in budgetary terms. In spite of a cooperation and verification system closely monitoring reform processes in the country, the independence and quality of the judiciary remains a major problem. The recent attempt by the minister of justice to pardon twenty-five politicians barred from politics in 2016–17 led to mass protests over several months in Romania (European Commission, 2017b; Parau, 2012: 639–65).

Bulgaria is also far from having a well-functioning judiciary. It has had a supreme judicial council since 1991, consisting of twenty-five members. It includes both judges and MPs, as well as ex officio members. However, the main problem seems to be the relationship to the ministry of justice and high level corruption (European Commission, 2017c). Meanwhile, the cooperation and verification mechanism monitoring the progress undertaken in the two countries, particularly in the judicial sector, has lasted for more than a decade. This is certainly not a very good sign of a positive development, and it seems the forces of reform are still too weak in both member-states.

The restructuring of the judiciary is of central importance in the countries of the western Balkans, the successor states of the former Yugoslavia. The ethnic wars between the countries have led to the dominance of nationalism, which has prevented the establishment of a democratic judiciary. The EU has been at the forefront in building new judiciary institutions. The ICTY helped to bring justice to the millions of victims of the senseless wars of the 1990s (UN, 2018). The European Commission has presented a road map allowing for accession to the EU in the late 2020s or early 2030. Nevertheless, the examples of Bulgaria and Romania are certainly a reminder that judiciary reforms are among the most important if these countries want to join the EU. Serbia seems to be the most advanced country in this respect, while Macedonia, Bosnia-Herzegovina and Albania still have a long way to go. However, state capture by criminal organisations and their linkages to politicians and political parties are still a major obstacle to an independent judiciary (Heinrich Böll Stiftung, 2017).

All these Balkan countries show a remarkable similarity to the case of Greece, which belonged to the cluster of countries of the capitalist West during the Cold War, but was still characterised by a quite inefficient judiciary. The economic and sovereign debt crisis further deteriorated the condition and quality of the Greek judiciary. Political corruption of the institutions by politicians is a constant aspect of Greek politics, as the Papandreou governments have shown (1981–9, 1993–6). In spite of a package of major reforms, the Greek judiciary is characterised by slowness and inefficiency. This has been a major problem for foreign investors, who struggle with legal certainty and important aspects of the rule of law. One major problem seems to be the abuse of the adjournment of trials, the poor preparation of judges in specialised matters, a lack of support personnel, and outdated formal forms in the court system. Moreover, the politicisation of the judiciary by ruling parties is also a characteristic of the Greek judicial system. Unfortunately, not only have ND and PASOK been unable to reform the judicial system but so too have Alexis Tsipras's Syriza-led governments. The latter have shown more continuity with previous governments, being embedded in networks of clientelism and political corruption, rather than bringing about a new transformational start (Papaioannou, 2011; Papaioannou and Karatza, 2018).

The judicialisation of politics and the politicisation of the judiciary: a constitutional review, European style

One of the innovations of European constitutions following the Second World War was the introduction of constitutional courts that would adjudicate on the constitutionality of laws and, sometimes, procedures (Table 6.2). One of the reasons for the wish to strengthen constitutional law in European democracies was the negative experience recently undergone with authoritarian and totalitarian regimes. The theoretical foundations were laid down by the Austrian legal scholar, Hans Kelsen (1881–1973), who was central to the drafting of the Austrian constitution of 1920. In 1929, he developed the idea of a constitutional court, which would be separate from ordinary law, in order to adjudicate the constitutionality of laws. Kelsen's overall idea was based on a self-contained legal architecture in which all legal norms of a particular polity could be referred back to a single fundamental document, the constitution. The constitutional court would be intended to act as a negative legislator, reviewing the laws accepted by parliament in order that they should be compatible with the constitution. One of his strongest opponents was the highly controversial German scholar, Carl Schmitt (1888–1985), who regarded the Kelsenian model of a constitutional court as a 'super legislature' and, as such, one to be rejected (Stone Sweet, 2000: 34–47). In the second half of the nineteenth century, the Austro-Hungarian monarchy already had an imperial court (*Reichsgericht*), which was established through the constitution of 1867. Citizens were able to file complaints against the state relating to the violation of political rights. There was a state court (*Staatsgerichtshof*) that dealt with trials against MPs or ministers. After

Table 6.2 Constitutional courts and supreme courts in Europe

Country	*Foundation*	*Number of judges*	*Term (years)*	*Renewable*	*Citizen's complaints*
Genuine constitutional courts					
Albania	1992	9	9	No	Yes
Andorra	1993	4	8	No	No
Austria	1920–9	14	Lifetime	–	Yes
Belgium	1980/2007	12	Lifetime	–	Yes

Bosnia-Herzegovina	1995	9	9	No	Yes
Bulgaria	1991	12	9	No	No
Croatia	1963/1990	13	8	No	Yes
Czech Republic	1992	15	10	Yes	Yes
France	1958	9	9	No	No
Germany	1949	16	12	No	Yes
Hungary	1990	11	9	Yes (once)	Yes
Italy	1948/1956	15	9	No	No
Latvia	1949	16	12	No	Yes
Liechtenstein	1926	5	Lifetime	–	Yes
Lithuania	1993	9	8	No	
Luxembourg		9			No
Macedonia	1964	9	9	No	Yes
Malta	1964	5	Lifetime	–	Yes
Montenegro	1963/1992	4	Lifetime	–	Yes
Poland	1985–6/1992	15	9	No	Yes
Portugal	1982	13	9	No	Yes
Romania	1992	9	9	No	No
Serbia	1963/1990	10	15	No	No
Slovakia	1992	13	12	No	Yes
Slovenia	1992	9	9	No	Yes
Spain	1978	12	9	Conditional	Yes
Supreme courts with limited constitutionality function					
Cyprus	1966	13	Lifetime (68)	–	No
Denmark	1661	18	Lifetime (70)	–	No
Estonia	1919	19	Lifetime	–	No
Finland	1918	18	Lifetime	–	No
Ireland		7+2 ex officio	Lifetime (70)	–	No
Iceland	1920	8	Lifetime	–	No
Norway	1815	20	Lifetime	–	No
Sweden	1614/1809	15	Lifetime	–	No
Switzerland	1917	38	Lifetime	–	No
Wider Europe					
Belarus	1994	12	11	Yes	No
Moldova	1995	6	6	Yes	Yes
Russia	1993	19	Lifetime	–	No
Ukraine	1996	18	9	No	Yes

Source: Websites of constitutional and supreme courts.

Figure 6.3 Constitutional courts in Europe

the collapse of the Austro-Hungarian monarchy, Austria adopted the new constitution of 1920, which established the constitutional court as we know it today. The Austrian constitutional court became a model for other countries, particularly Germany after the Second World War (Verfassungsgerichtshof, 2018).

Following the end of the Second World War, several countries had to adopt new constitutions as a result of the ending of the authoritarian and totalitarian period, and also decided to introduce constitutional safeguards in order to prevent such undermining of democratic rule from happening again. Meanwhile, this has become a global phenomenon and is gaining more recognition as an important safeguard to strengthen democracy. According to Andrew Harding, such bodies exist in eighty-five countries worldwide (Harding, 2017: 1; for Europe, see Rehder, 2015). Apart from Austria (*Verfassungsgerichtshof*), other countries such as Germany (*Bundesverfassungsgericht*) and Italy (*Tribunale constituzionale*) included constitutional courts in their constitutions. Later, the constitution of the French Fifth Republic of 1958 introduced a constitutional council (*Conseil constitutionel*), which was designed to strengthen the government in relation to parliament. The model of constitutional review became important in the new democracies of Southern Europe, such as Portugal (*Tribunal constitucional*) in 1982 and Spain (*Tribunal constitucional*) in 1978, and later in those of Central and Eastern Europe, such as Hungary, Poland, the Czech Republic, Slovakia, Lithuania, Latvia, Romania, Bulgaria, Slovenia and Croatia in the 1990s. This meant that the constitutional courts became a highly respected means for the solution of legislative and competence disputes in most European countries (Figure 6.3).

The German federal constitutional court has been regarded as a model for many Southern and Central and Eastern European countries. It allows constraints to be put on politicians and also on certain controversial legislative programmes. The decriminalisation of abortion has been a key issue in many European countries. The constitutional courts needed to find a legal-ethical answer that would satisfy both the pro-life and pro-choice parties. This became crucial in West Germany in 1975, in unified Germany in 1992 and in Catholic Spain in 1985. The constitutional courts did not endorse abortion but allowed it under certain extreme circumstances. In Germany, politicians frequently try to anticipate rulings by the constitutional court and act accordingly, and this was the case with regard to the law on abortion. Governments generally tend to take over the precise guidelines set by the constitutional court (Landfried, 1992: 54–5). The German constitutional court has a strong reputation not only in Germany but worldwide. Their rulings are carefully studied and emulated in other countries. In spite of this the constitutional court has had to deal with major challenges of German constitutional interpretation related to EU issues. Therefore, constitutional court judges are carefully selected and appointed by parliament, taking into account a consensual approach in relation to European integration. Most rulings tend to uphold the constitution and also further moves towards integration, due to the fact that article 22 of the Basic Law stresses the importance of the EU to Germany. In this regard, they are pro-European rulings, like for example the Lisbon ruling of 2010 in which the role of parliament was strengthened as a participating actor in the European integration process, so safeguarding the democratic rights of citizens in this respect (for more detail, see Lhotta et al., 2013). During the financial crisis, key politicians complained to the constitutional court about the transfer of funds for a bailout to Greece and other ailing Southern European countries. However, the ruling of the constitutional court was rather supportive of government action, establishing just a few conditions by which these transfers could be done (Wood, 2016). The complaints by politicians against quantitative easing of the European Central Bank under the chairmanship of Mario Monti were also made very clear. The German constitutional court decided to refer this issue to the European Court of Justice, acknowledging quite clearly the supremacy of European law and also the European Court of Justice over national law (*Spiegelonline*, 21 June 2016).

Constitutional courts are particularly important to the process of democratic consolidation in new democracies. In the case of Spain, the constitutional court adjudicated and shaped the emerging state of autonomies and also decided on disputes over competencies between central and regional governments. The important work of the constitutional court in Spain took place between 1979 and 1989, after which such disputes became less relevant. Since 2010, the Spanish constitutional court has been under considerable pressure due to the ongoing conflict between the central and regional governments in Madrid and Catalonia respectively.

Until 1971, the French constitutional council was a dormant institution. That year represented a turning point, because the constitutional court judged the preamble of the 1958 constitution, which took over from the constitution of 1946, as part of constitutional law. This meant that several other legal documents had to be included in the constitution; for example, the 1789 Declaration of the Rights of Man, the Fundamental Principles Recognised by the Laws of the Republic, and additional rights mentioned in the 1946 preamble, such as:

> [e]quality of sexes; the right to work, to join a union, to strike and to obtain social security; and the responsibility of the state to guarantee a secular school system and to nationalise all industries that have taken on the character of a monopoly or public service.
>
> (Stone, 1992: 33–4)

Since then, the constitutional council has almost come to resemble a third chamber of the legislature, because of the weak nature of parliamentarianism in France (see Chapter 5). In the 1980s, the increased activity of the Council of State led to changes in the law of nationalisation proposed by the socialist government in 1982. It increased the level of compensation payments, which were originally presented by the government in its bill (Stone, 1992: 36).

In spite of the fact that the Italian constitutional court was enshrined in the 1948 Italian constitution, it was only established in 1956. Between 1948 and 1956, the regional high court in Sicily had many competencies of the Italian constitutional court, which was founded later. The constitutional court was quite cautious initially, but then aggressively began to annul many legislative acts of the fascist period. Moreover, the constitutional court was instrumental in changing the legal relationship between the Catholic Church and the Italian state. Last, but not least, the constitutional court, in a similar way to the Spanish case, now adjudicates on disputes between the central and regional governments. According to Maria Elisabetta de Franciscis and Rosella Zannini, the constitutional court lost credibility at the end of the First Republic as a result of a string of bad rulings (Franciscis and Zannini, 1992: 71–8).

According to Alec Stone Sweet, we can differentiate between the more restrictive Italian constitutional court and the French constitutional council, which both write very short declaratory opinions and rulings, and the longer opinions and rulings of the German and Spanish constitutional courts (Stone Sweet, 2000: 145). There is also better direct access to the constitutional court for German and Spanish citizens than for Italian and French citizens. In Germany, there is the instrument of the *Verfassungsbeschwerde* (constitutional complaint), which citizens can call on if they feel that rights are being violated. In Spain the same procedure is called *amparo*. In both cases, the constitutional court considers such complaints and whether they should proceed to be discussed.

Also, according to Alec Stone Sweet, constitutional courts increased their repertoire of instruments over time. In many respects, they have almost become a legislating body when asked about the constitutionality of certain laws. This became especially relevant in the legislation on abortion in Germany and Spain. The constitutional courts also developed the instrument of corrective revision (Stone Sweet, 2000: 83).

The constitutional courts are also engaged in the protection of rights enshrined in the constitution or that are incompatible with the European Convention of Human Rights. The importance of the rights of citizens before the interest of state institutions has been particularly important in Germany, Italy and Spain, but also in the Central and Eastern European countries. All these countries have undergone periods of authoritarian-totalitarian rule, so this provision is a safeguard against the return of such regimes (Stone Sweet, 2000: 95).

This means that today, European politics must take into account a triad of relationships between government, parliament and the constitutional court (in those countries where the constitutional court exists). However, as mentioned before, other countries, for example Switzerland, the UK and the Netherlands, are finding ways of allowing constitutional review to take place, even if forbidden by the constitution.

In sum, constitutional review through constitutional courts or similar institutions has become an integral part of European politics since the Second World War. Most European countries, apart from the Republic of Ireland, have avoided following the US model of judicial review, adopting rather the Kelsenian model of separate constitutional review. This again is a distinctive feature of what constitutes European politics.

The European dimension: the growing impact on national legislation

Today's European judicial architecture is not complete without mentioning the developments at supranational level. Although there is supremacy of the EU over national law, there is still resistance against major principles of European judicial politics. Apart from the European Court of Justice as a crucial institution of the EU (for more, see Chapter 10), the European Court of Human Rights (ECHR) of the Council of Europe, founded in 1959, has become a last instance for appeals after the national route has been exhausted. It bases its mandate on the European Convention of Human Rights and Fundamental Rights adopted in 1953 (Harmsen and McAuliffe, 2015: 269–73; Storey, 1995: 141–2).

The internal market programme of the EU has become an important factor in creating a transnational justice and home affairs space, dealing with international criminality, cyber-crime and terrorism among other threats to the European economy, society and politics. Since the Treaty of the European Union (1993) there is a pillar related to this area. It is labelled the Area of Freedom, Security and Justice (AFSJ) and has become more integrated since the early 1990s. A crucial turning point was the decision of the Tampere European Council in 1999. The Schengen area that was agreed on in 1985 in the Luxembourg town of the same name is also important. Twenty-two countries are part of the Schengen space; only the UK, Ireland, Bulgaria, Romania, Croatia and Cyprus are not part of it. The UK and Ireland decided to remain outside the Schengen area due to their geographical position as islands and the desire to control their borders. Bulgaria, Romania, Croatia and Cyprus have been barred for joining the Schengen area due to remaining problems with an incipient judiciary sector and a lack of control over criminal organisations. Probably the most important network in the AFSJ is Eurojust, comprising the national public prosecutors. However, several transnational bodies were created to coordinate the activities of police enforcement forces and the judiciary. In 2017, it was agreed to establish a European Public Prosecution Office (EPPO) based in Luxembourg and with decentralised structures in each member-state to fight transnational crime and fraud cases related to funding coming from the EU budget. It functions as a coordinator of the EU and national judiciary activities (*Euractiv*, 6 October 2017; Giuffrida, 2017). Probably, the most salient one is Europol, founded in 1998 and based in The Hague. In the area of asylum and migration, the European Asylum Support Office (EASO), founded in February 2011, gained special importance during and after the migration crisis in the summer of 2015. Since then, we have seen a reinforcement of the European Border and Coast Guard Agency (Frontex), which was founded in 2004 (for more detail on aspects of AFSJ, see European Union, 2016: 14; Lavenex, 2015, 2016; Léonard and Kaunert, 2016; Trauner, 2016).

Overall, it means that the EU has become more realistic about internal and external security, and is potentially becoming what critics call 'Fortress Europe' (Finotelli and Sciortino, 2014).

Conclusions: the Europeanisation of judicial power

In this chapter, we have argued that judicial power has gained greater prominence since 1945. The creation of a constitutional review through constitutional courts has become an important aspect of this increased judicial power, which has evolved in the different European political systems. The European judicial architecture is increasingly multilevel. However, the integration between national and European structures is still a work in progress and may last a considerable time until it has become more efficient in combatting criminality and terrorism in the European internal market.

Suggested reading

Bell, John (2006), *Judiciaries within Europe: A Comparative Review*. Cambridge: Cambridge University Press.

Harmsen, Robert and Karen McAuliffe (2015), The European courts. In: José M. Magone (ed.), *Routledge Handbook of European Politics*. Abingdon: Routledge, pp. 280–91.

Pernice, Ingolf (2015), The EU as a citizens' joint venture: multilevel constitutionalism and open democracy in Europe. In: José M. Magone (ed.), *Routledge Handbook of European Politics*. Abingdon: Routledge, pp. 184–201.

Stone-Sweet, Alec (2004), *The Judicial Construction of Europe*. Oxford: Oxford University Press.

QUESTIONS FOR REVISION

- What are the main judicial traditions in Europe? Discuss, using examples from countries from each region.
- Compare the executive-judiciary relations in Italy and Germany.
- Assess what kind of problems judiciaries have in the new democracies of Central and Eastern Europe.
- Explain the role of constitutional courts in Europe. Discuss, using examples from at least two countries.
- Is European integration eroding national judicial traditions? Discuss, using examples from at least two countries.

Chapter 7

Political parties, party systems and elections in Europe

- The Americanisation of European parties and party systems
- The transformation of political parties: from cadre to cartel parties
- The main party families
- The decline of party membership
- The importance of public funding for political parties
- The impact of electoral systems on party systems
- Party systems in Europe
- The European Parliament: towards Americanisation of politics?
- Conclusions: party politics in Americanised electoral markets
- Suggested reading

The Americanisation of European parties and party systems

European party systems are undergoing considerable change owing to the changing social structures in most European countries. The encapsulation of the electorates that existed until the 1950s, which allowed for the establishment of strong linkages between political parties and particular social classes or groups in society, have been replaced by a more socially volatile society in which class is still relevant but no longer the main determining factor in elections (for more see Chapter 3).

Today, all party systems are more volatile, and traditional political parties, such as the social democrats, Christian democrats, liberals and communists cannot rely any more on returning the same results, election after election. The cultural and social group cohesion has eroded over time. Traditional party systems based on mass parties such those in Austria, Belgium, the Netherlands and the Scandinavian countries have experienced major transformations, and fragmentation of the electorate has forced parties to use new technologies to appeal to the voters. Today 'mediatisation of politics' through a vast range of instruments, including continuing opinion polling, focus groups, targeted media campaigns and social media (including its manipulation as in the case of Facebook/Cambridge Analytica in the US elections, see the study by Hoffstetter, 2016) has become an integral part of electoral politics. Parties appeal to a fragmented electorate with different interests and requirements, and they therefore need to use new approaches. The strategies of parties have to take into account which kind of electorate they want to address. The larger parties have to address a very diverse electorate and are beginning to resemble assembly line 'supermarket parties' more and more, while the smaller parties, sometimes known as 'boutique parties', specialise and target particular groups on the left or right (Kitschelt, 1997: 149).

Parties compete today in electoral markets. Political marketing has become essential for political parties. This also means that, similar to the United States, European political parties are becoming less ideological and more pragmatic. This can be observed in the growing tendency of the main parties on the left and right to move towards the centre. Because of this growing pragmatism and de-ideologisation, political parties require other means to make themselves heard. Among them is the growing importance of personalisation in politics. Charismatic leaders have become an important factor in postmodern politics. There are now lots of examples, confirming this trend – formidable politicians such as Margaret Thatcher, Tony Blair, Gerhard Schröder, José Maria Aznar, Silvio Berlusconi, Nicolas Sarkozy, Emmanuel Macron, Andris Babiš, Robert Fico and Boyko Borisov were able to take advantage of this new structure of opportunities by using the media. According to Pippa Norris, there has been a transformation from pre-modern to postmodern electoral campaigns. According to her, electoral campaigns have become more expensive and more media-oriented (Norris, 1997: 3).

The mediatisation of politics has become a major aspect of current European politics. Such practice has always been common in the United States, so that there is a general trend among political scientists to call it 'Americanisation of electoral politics'. However, such processes of diffusion from the United States to other parts of the world, particularly Europe, may have different effects and impacts in different countries. According to Alexander Geisler and Ulrich Sarcinelli, one can interpret 'Americanisation' in three ways. First, it can be interpreted as 'diffusion', which is a selective integration of US patterns that are regarded as the models and objectives of modernisation. Second, one may regard this as a process of 'global standardisation', which would be conceptualised as an interactive exchange of new forms of electoral politics between the United States and Europe. Finally, it can be seen as modernisation leading to universal convergence processes in media democracies. In this last interpretation, the United States would be the pioneer of such social modernisation (Geisler and Sarcinelli, 2002: 51).

In this chapter, Americanisation is understood primarily in the latter sense. It means that there has been a convergence of electoral politics of European countries to the US model. Hans Georg Soeffner and Dirk Tänzler summarised the most important features of this Americanisation in electoral campaigns as follows:

1 *Personalisation*: concentration on the candidate, neglect of campaign issues.
2 *Electoral campaign as 'horse race'*: competition as in sport events.
3 *Use of negative campaigning*: in order to destabilise the opponent or even destroy his/her credibility.
4 *Professionalisation of electoral campaigns*: electoral campaign experts, sometimes independent from the party, run the campaign.
5 *Marketing approach of political advertisements*: use of well-known and successful means of the marketing industry to promote a candidate.
6 *Events and issues management*: choreographed and controlled organisation of events and presentation of issues.

(Soeffner and Tänzler, 2002: 130)

Political marketing has become an important aspect of contemporary European politics. The citizen has become an individualised political consumer and as such looks at the products of political parties, their policies and politics. They are now political consumers in all fields of public life, particularly when using public services or using their purchasing power to change policies, nationally or abroad (Føllesdal, 2006; Micheletti et al., 2006). Therefore, political parties are now acting in electoral markets and need to apply either product- or market-oriented marketing strategies. While political parties, mostly smaller parties, that use product-oriented marketing strategies are quite specialised in a specific issue and target particular groups in society, those that apply market-oriented marketing strategies are always concerned with adjusting to the changing expectations of the political consumer (Lees-Marshment, 2004: 9–11; Newman, 1999).

The transformation of political parties: from cadre to cartel parties

Both the present party systems and the political parties are quite different from those of the past. The main typology for Europe is the transformation of the cadre party into the mass party and later into the catch-all party. Finally, today, we are experiencing the transformation of the catch-all party into a cartel party.

Table 7.1 summarises the main features of these transformations. The cadre party of the nineteenth century consisted of notables who were recruited through patronage networks. They did not live off politics; on the contrary they were normally wealthy people who chose to take part in the politics of the day. In the twentieth century, we can observe the rise of the mass parties related to social democracy, Christian democracy and communism. This is the consequence of industrialisation and urbanisation due to a growing number of people working in factories in the cities. The working class emerged as a major factor for mass politics. Both social democracy as well as Christian democracy tried to gain influence over the masses. As a consequence a more professionalised political party emerged with professional politicians that lived off politics. This was possible because many countries, particularly in Western Europe, expanded suffrage continuously to the male population, and later to the female population. Encapsulated subcultures allowed political parties to reappear to the same electorate at every election. However, in the late 1960s, such subcultures began to erode and parties began to look for other voters beyond the subculture leading to the catch-all party. The label of Volkspartei (People's Party) emerged particularly in West Germany. Such parties like the Christian democrats (CDU/CSU) and the social democrats (SPD) would regularly receive 38 to 45 per cent of the vote (for the concept, see Kirchheimer, 1965; Mair, 1997: 37). However, since the 1990s, the catch-all party has slowly been replaced by the cartel party. This new form of party is interested in staying in power and is more detached from the electorate. It functions like an organisation that needs to survive in a hostile competitive environment. The main rationale is to be office-seeking and to gain access to the spoils of the state, particularly generous public funding. The almost complete erosion of the ideological subcultures, volatile electoral markets and the increasing mediatisation are major factors driving political parties towards cartelisation, sometimes with other traditional parties. One can observe this particularly in Germany, Austria, Portugal, Spain and Belgium (Katz and Mair, 1995: 17–21; see also Mair, 2013).

Owing to the marketisation of electoral politics, most parties are becoming cartel parties. The decline of membership across Europe has been a major factor leading up to this situation. Parties cannot rely anymore on membership fees, and electoral campaigns are so expensive that apart from public funding, they have to engage in fundraising. Katz and Mair, therefore, differentiate between the party in office, the party on the ground and the party in central office. According to them, the party on the ground was quite important during the phase of the mass party up until the late 1950s, but has lost importance nowadays. The party in the central office was quite important during the catch-all phase but has more difficulties in imposing itself today. It is now the party in office that dominates decision-making processes within the party. Although all three party faces are important, in the end office-seeking has become central to the aims of the party. Owing to the interdependence of all three party faces and the structures of the parties for success at the next elections, present parties are creating 'stratarchies', meaning that there is lots of autonomy for each party face (Katz and Mair, 1995: 21; an empirical update can be found in Van Biezen and Kopecký, 2014; Kopecký et al., 2012; Kopecký and Mair, 2012) (see Table 7.1).

While the older democracies went through this process, the new democracies of Southern, Central and Eastern Europe established cartel parties from the onset due to the fact that they could rely on quite generous public funding systems. However, the fierce competition over these spoils led to a quite high level

Table 7.1 The transformation of parties

	Pre-modern	*Modern*		*Postmodern*
	nineteenth century	*1880–1960*	*1960s–80s*	*1980s–*
Type of party	**Cadre party**	**Mass party**	**Catch-all party**	**Cartel party**
Social-political inclusion	Restricted suffrage	Mass suffrage	Mass suffrage	Mass suffrage
Principal source of party's resources	Personal contacts	Members' fees and contributions	Contributions from a wide variety of sources	State subventions
Relations between party elite and membership	Small and elitist	Bottom-up; elites accountable to members	Top-down; elites dominate membership	Stratarchy, mutual autonomy
Membership	Small and elitist	Large homogeneous subcultural membership	Large heterogeneous inter-classistic membership	Declining or small membership
Party channels of communication	Inter-personal networks	Party provides its own channels of communication	Party competes for access to non-party channels of communication	Party gains privileged access to state-regulated channels of communication
Position of party between civil society and state	Unclear boundary between state and politically relevant civil society	Party belongs to civil society, particularly as representative of particular subculture	Parties as competing brokers between state and civil society	Party becomes part of state
Representative style	Trustee	Delegate	Entrepreneur	Agent of the state

Source: Simplified from Katz and Mair (1995: 18).

of party instability in many Central and Eastern European countries, in particular Latvia and Bulgaria. The main reason is that parties in the new democracies in Central and Eastern Europe cannot rely on strong party structures and a committed membership.

According to Ingrid van Biezen these parties had no time to encapsulate an electorate. Competitive pressures led to the use of the media to address potential voters. She states:

> Parties in new democracies lack the stable constituencies with relatively durable political identities that enable them, like their Western European counterparts, to encapsulate the electorate and to narrow down the electoral market. While, as Sartori (1968, 2005) has emphasised, the mass party played a crucial role in the structural consolidation of West European party systems, parties in new democracies lack the organisational capacities ultimately to stabilise the party system.
>
> (Van Biezen, 2003: 36)

This is confirmed by Paul G. Lewis who emphasises that the Lipset–Rokkan freezing hypothesis does not apply to the new democracies, because 'Central and Eastern Europe is (an) unstructured political field and conditions for party system formation are open rather than tightly constraining' (see Chapter 3; Lewis, 2003: 143; Lewis, Paul 2015: 513–15).

Klaus von Beyme calls it 'Americanisation', because the approach towards the electoral market is similar to that of political parties in the United States. Parties in new democracies are more or less electoral machines (Von Beyme, 1996: 140).

According to Attila Ágh, there has been what he calls 'overpartycisation' in Central and Eastern Europe. Many parties emerged in the early 1990s, but few survived over time owing to lack of linkages to civil society and resources. Slowly, the surviving parties had to build strong party organisations with a disciplined membership. However, these parties, sometimes supported by international democracy assistance institutions such as the German foundations attached to the political parties, remained just cartel parties (Ágh, 1998: 88). Owing to weak party organisation, political parties in Southern, Central and Eastern Europe had to spend considerable amounts of money on the media in order to reach their potential voters. In their very interesting study on consolidation in Central and Eastern Europe, Jon Elster, Claus Offe und Jürgen Preuss assert that it was easier for political parties in Central and Eastern Europe to play the electoral game than to dedicate more resources to building a party organisation. Television played a major role in attracting supporters. Therefore, without a local, regional or national grass-roots organisation, parties became even more dependent on the media to mobilise voters (Elster et al., 1998: 134–5).

Similarly, processes of consolidation of parties took place fifteen years earlier in Portugal, Spain and Greece. In Spain, 579 parties registered before the Constituent Assembly elections of 1977, but only a few were able to achieve representation. Some of them were called taxi parties, because they had no membership and all possible members fitted into a car (Montero, 1998: 76–8).

In this sense, it is a good idea to differentiate between continuous, discontinuous and new democracies when discussing the development of political parties. The continuous democracies have experienced all these party models since the nineteenth century and the process has not been interrupted. The discontinuous democracies had a major interruption during the authoritarian/totalitarian age of the 1920s and 1930s, but experienced more or less all party models. Last, but not least, the new democracies had quite long interruptions of around forty years, which led to complete disruption of such party development. These new democracies experienced very corrupt cadre parties in the nineteenth century, but did not, with the exception of Spain, experience the development of mass parties. Such typology of countries is summarised in Table 7.2.

Table 7.2 Party development in different parts of Europe

	Continuous democracies	*Discontinuous democracies*	*New democracies after 1974 (Southern Europe) and 1989 (Central and Eastern Europe)*
Description of typology	No interruption of democratic regime, apart from German Nazi occupation of many European countries (1939–45)	Interruption of democratic regime (authoritarian, totalitarian period 1920, 1930, but democratic after 1945)	Over four decades of interruption of democratic regime and phases of democracy characterised by manipulation and corruption. Genuine democracies after 1974 as representatives of the third wave of democratisation
Countries	• UK • France* • Belgium* • Netherlands* • Luxembourg* • Switzerland • Norway* • Sweden • Finland • Denmark*	• Germany • Italy • Austria	• Greece • Spain • Portugal • Hungary • Czech Republic • Slovakia • Poland • Slovenia • Bulgaria • Romania • Moldavia • Croatia • Serbia • Bosnia-Herzegovina • Montenegro • Macedonia • Kosovo • Albania
Colonies that acquired independence	• Iceland (from Denmark), Malta and Cyprus (from the UK)		

*Countries under German occupation during the Second World War (1939–45).

Source: Author.

The main party families

In spite of the differences between them, most European countries have political parties with similar ideologies and common origins. The origins of the political parties are related to the junctures of European politics (see Chapters 2 and 3). In the mid-1980s, Klaus von Beyme wrote an excellent study on political parties in Western Europe, and he identified several party families (Von Beyme, 1984). There has been change since then, so it is necessary to update his classification. Any typology simplifies the reality considerably, but we may differentiate between at least eight party families:

- liberals
- Christian democrats and conservatives
- social democrats
- greens
- communists and extreme-left-wing parties
- regionalists and independentist parties
- new populism (the Eurosceptics, the new right and the new left)
- neo-fascist and extreme right parties.

Many of these parties, particularly those of the new right, may combine elements of Euroscepticism and populism with topics of the extreme right. Therefore we will discuss these new parties under the label of 'new populism parties' at the end of this section.

The liberal party family

The liberals can be considered as the oldest party family. They emerged in the nineteenth century as part of the democratisation movement. They responded to arbitrary absolutist monarchies and became important in the 1848 democratic revolution. The word 'liberal' is Spanish and was used to characterise the liberals in 1807 when the Cadiz constitution was adopted (Von Beyme, 1984: 45). Liberals were instrumental in democratising education, and in many countries such as the Netherlands, Belgium and Germany they were very keen to reduce the power of the Catholic Church. Liberals can be found in the UK, Scandinavia, Germany, Italy, Austria, Switzerland, Hungary, Poland, and other Central and Eastern European countries. The ideology of liberalism emphasises freedom and individualism; however, depending on the country the social dimension through an efficient welfare state may be part of the model (see Figure 7.1).

The Christian democrats and conservatives

The Christian democrats have their origins in the Reformation of the sixteenth century. The growing importance of the state and the reduced influence of the Catholic Church in the nineteenth century finally led to the emergence of Christian democratic parties. Christian democratic parties were linked to

Figure 7.1 The liberal parties in Europe

the Catholic Church and were supported by the Church hierarchy. Strong parties could be found in Italy, Austria, Switzerland, Belgium, Germany and the Netherlands. Pope Leo XIII was instrumental in providing the ideological framework for such social engagement through the 1891 *Rerum Novarum* encyclical and later through the 1901 *Crucis de communi* encyclical. The latter introduced the concept of Christian democracy (Democratia Christiana, DC). Also Pius XI's *Quadragesimo Anno* encyclical (1931) is part of this doctrine and is strongly influenced by the Church.

In terms of ideology, Christian democracy is not easy to define. David Hanley characterises Christian democracy as 'an elusive and shifting phenomenon' but still easier to study and define than the conservative sister parties (Hanley, 1996: 2). In spite of the transformation of traditional Christian democratic parties to catch-all parties (*Volksparteien*), there are some characteristics that make them distinctive from other party families. First, the view of an individual as a person, who is directed towards solidaristic communities, summarised under the label of 'personalism', is an important feature. The dignity of the person is an important aspect of Christian democracy. The emphasis on the social dimension of capitalism is, therefore, important. Social capitalism or social market economy are integral parts of the ideology, especially so until the early 1980s. Since then, there has been a liberal shift towards reducing the welfare state, however inconsequently implemented (Keesbergen, 1996: 35–42; for more on Christian democracy, see Kalyvas and Van Kersbergen, 2010; Van der Hecke, 2004; see Figure 7.2).

Figure 7.2 The Christian democratic parties in Europe

The conservative parties are very close to the Christian democratic parties. In both cases the parties are ideologically centre-right parties. In general, the conservative parties are considered to be very pragmatic and, in contrast to the Christian democrats, strongly nationally oriented. They are strong in the UK and in the Scandinavian countries. Probably, the best example is the Conservative and Unionist Party in the UK, which was founded in 1832 and evolved into a modern, pragmatic political formation defending the British way of life and its traditions. Therefore, Euroscepticism has become a major feature of the party since at least the Treaty of Maastricht of 1993 due to its provisions encroaching on the parliamentary sovereignty of the country (for more detail, see Bale, 2011).

Conservative parties exist also in the Nordic countries, France, the Czech Republic, Greece, Poland, Hungary, Bulgaria and the Baltic states (Figure 7.3).

The social democratic party family

Social democracy can be considered as the third major party family. It was a response to the industrial revolution and the very bad conditions that the working class were subjected to in the nineteenth and twentieth centuries. The First (1864–76) and the Second (1889–1919) Internationals were important here. Although social democracy started as a radical movement seeking to achieve a classless society, after the death of Karl Marx its members became increasingly

Figure 7.3 The conservative parties in Europe

interested in achieving results through the democratic institutions. This moderation of social democracy led to success in elections during this period of expanding suffrage. Strong parties emerged in Italy, Austria, Germany, Switzerland, Belgium, the Netherlands, France and Sweden (Sassoon, 1997: 4–26). After the Second World War, social democratic parties were quite dominant in Western European democracies, becoming a catch-all party in the late 1960s along with Christian democratic and Conservative parties.

The erosion of modern industrial society and the decline of the working class forced social democratic parties to broaden their appeal. The transformation of European social democracy took place between the 1970s and the mid-1990s. This transformation particularly saw a change from the traditional mass party to catch-all or cartel parties. Most of this change took place in the 1980s and 1990s. Some parties were quick to recognise the need to change strategies, but others had difficulties in adjusting to the national electoral markets (Kitschelt, 1995b: 232–52). However, an Americanisation of social democracy set in during the second half of the 1990s. The influence of the more pragmatic policies of the Democratic Party and the Clinton administration led to major transformations in the British Labour Party and the German SPD. The Third Way between traditional social democracy and neo-liberalism became a new framework for change among social democratic parties (Giddens, 1998). However, this alienated the traditional followers of the party, so that many of these parties are presently divided and in an identity crisis (particularly the German SPD , Dutch PvdA and the British Labour Party) (Figure 7.4).

Figure 7.4 The social democratic parties in Europe

The communist party family and other left-wing parties

After the Bolshevik Revolution of 1917 in Russia, particularly after the foundation of the Third Communist International (Comintern) in 1920, the more radical factions of the social democratic parties split to form communist parties in most countries. They became an important rival party to social democracy. In some cases, communist parties tried to destroy social democratic parties, for example during the Spanish Civil War and the Weimar Republic in Germany.

The Stalinist experience, the persecution and murder of Leon Trotsky in Mexico in 1941 and the emergence of communist regimes in China and Albania were reasons for some left-wing intellectuals to create new smaller political parties which opposed the official communist parties. These parties emerged particularly in France and Southern European countries in the 1960s and 1970s, and some of them have survived until the twenty-first century (see Figure 7.5).

Three decades after the fall of the Berlin Wall, there are few electorally significant parties in Europe, and they are mostly small. Radical and extreme left parties had a revival during the financial crisis (2008–13) as main critical voice against austerity. Probably the most successful in achieving success were Syriza under the charismatic Alexis Tsipras in Greece, which is now the largest party since the 2015 elections, and Podemos in Spain under the charismatic Pablo Iglesias, which has contributed along with Ciudadanos to transforming the long-standing

Figure 7.5 The communist and new left parties in Europe

two-party system of Social democrats and Populares into a four-party system of political groups of almost equal size. Probably the most important party is the German Left Party (Die Linke), which is quite active in building a European party at supranational level.

Extreme rightwing and populist new right

The legacy of authoritarianism and totalitarianism in Italy, Germany and many other countries led to the establishment of an extreme right-wing party family that led to the emergence of neo-fascist parties after the Second World War. These parties have a nationalist ideology, are against the EU and are xenophobic. Apart from that, they are partly anti-systemic and want to establish an authoritarian regime. In Germany, the National Democratic Party of Germany (National Demokratisch Partei Deutschlands – NPD), in the UK, the British National Party (BNP) and in France the National Front/National Assembly (Front National/Rassemblement National – FN/RN) are all representatives of this party family. The latter is in the process of transformation towards a new right party; however, its legacy clearly is still a major obstacle towards that. These are all small parties, and many of them have retained an extreme right-wing ideology. In Germany, the NPD was founded in 1964 and regards itself as a successor party to the National Socialist Party. The party works closely with the German People's Union (Deutsche Volksunion – DVU) that was founded in 1971. The ideology of both parties is xenophobic, nationalist and authoritarian. Both parties are regarded as extreme rightwing and are being monitored by the Verfassungsschutz (protection of the constitution) authorities. Several attempts to ban the NPD through the constitutional court have failed. In the 2017 general elections, the NPD received just over 0.4 per cent of the votes and no seats.

In Britain, the British National Party, founded in 1982, pursues a nationalist, xenophobic policy. Central issues for the party are also law and order and opposition to immigration, with a strong undercurrent against the Muslim population. In the 2017 general elections the party received just 4,642 votes and is not represented in parliament.

In France, Marine Le Pen's FN/RN was founded in 1972. It shares a xenophobic, nationalist and anti-immigration ideology with the extreme right in other countries. Former leader Jean-Marie Le Pen is a charismatic figure and was able to achieve second place in the 2002 presidential elections with over 17 per cent of the vote. In 2011, his daughter Marine Le Pen took over the leadership and started changing the profile of the party towards a national conservative party against the will of her father. She became a candidate for the presidency in the presidential elections of 2017, and became the main challenger to Emmanuel Macron in the second round, but lost by a considerable margin. Marine Le Pen also lost badly in the subsequent legislative elections. Since then, she has been trying to further change the profile of the party towards a centre-right party and abandoning completely the image of an extreme rightwing party. The model is that of a 'new right populist party'. In 2018, the party was relabelled National Rally (Rassemblement National – RN).

The victory in the US presidential elections by Donald Trump was a major boost to the 'new right' parties which clearly use populism to bring their message of overt nationalism to the population. Among the more successful parties are the Alternative for Germany (AfD) in Germany, the Party of Freedom (PVV) under leader Geert Wilders in the Netherlands, the UK Independence Party in the UK, Lega Nord in Italy, Swedish Democrats in Sweden, the Freedom Party (FPÖ) in Austria, the Danish People's Party (DF) and the Swiss People's Party (SVP). Many of them target the EU directly (Figure 7.6).

New populist parties have a less well-defined ideology. In some cases, there is no clear distinction between extreme right and new right. In some parties, extreme right splinter groups may still be present, in spite of the fact that the leadership tries to move away from this legacy (they can be on the left or right, although the vast majority of them are on the right). The parties tend to emphasise a world that is being lost because of European integration or globalisation, and they propose nationalist policies to deal with the new realities, appealing directly to the people through charismatic leaders (for example, Jörg Haider in Austria and Pim Fortuyn in the Netherlands). This period of transformation from the industrial to the post-industrial society creates zones of insecurity, particularly for those who are not able to cope with rapid social and economic change. Therefore, Cas Mudde characterises contemporary Europe as being in a 'populist Zeitgeist' that he defines as follows:

> I define populism as *an ideology that considers society to be ultimately separated into two homogeneous and antagonistic groups, 'the pure people' versus 'the corrupt elite', and which argues that politics should be an expression of the* volonté générale *(general will) of the people*. Populism,

Figure 7.6 New right and new populist parties

> so defined, has two opposites: elitism and pluralism. Elitism is populism's mirror-image: it shares its Manichean worldview, but wants politics to be an expression of the views of the moral elite, instead of the amoral people. Pluralism, on the other hand, rejects the homogeneity of both populism and elitism, seeing society as a heterogenous collection of groups and individuals with often fundamentally different views and wishes.
>
> (Mudde, 2004: 543–4; italics in original)

According to Paul Taggart, there are five characteristics of new populist parties that should be taken into account.

1 *New populist parties are hostile to representative politics*: they seek a direct relationship with the people in the political system. They are characterised by anti-elitism and pluralism.
2 *Identification with an idealised 'heartland'*: this is an imagined community that is under threat from contemporary processes such as European integration (losing national sovereignty and national identity) or globalisation.
3 *Lack of core values*: there is no clear ideology. They may change ideological suppositions in order to increase their electoral support or take part in government.
4 *Reaction to a period of extreme crisis*: the present transformation from industrial to post-industrial society creates zones of insecurity that include unemployment, change of welfare to workfare state or waves of immigration.

5 *Use of short-term appeal using new politics and charismatic leaders*: a charismatic leader can be a very easy way to catapult a new populist party into the mainstream discussion. Pim Fortuyn in the Netherlands, Jörg Haider in Austria until 2008 or Christoph Blocher in Switzerland until 2007 are good examples.

(adapted from Taggart, 2004: 273–6; see also Taggart, 2000: 91–114)

Last, but not least, the Eurosceptic parties had already emerged in the 1970s, particularly in the Nordic countries and later on in the UK. The Treaty of the European Union, which was signed in Maastricht and came into force in 1993, led to a considerable rise of these parties in electoral terms. Some parties are hard Eurosceptic by rejecting the EU, while others were rather soft Eurosceptic, being against only certain policies of the EU, such as the move towards economic monetary union and eventually political union. Particular concerns of the Eurosceptics are the lack of democratic accountability at European level and the loss of sovereignty of the individual country. The strongest parties can be found in the UK, Scandinavia and Central and Eastern Europe, particularly the Czech Republic and Poland. However, Euroscepticism had almost no expression in Southern Europe until the financial crisis, but austerity policies led to the emergence of a temporary instrumental Euroscepticism (Magone, 2014b; Verney, 2011). Eurosceptic parties can be found on the left or on the right, sometimes for the same common reasons. Taggart differentiates the different Eurosceptic movements as follows:

1 Complete opposition to the EU because parties oppose its ideals.
2 Not opposed to the EU in principle, but are not convinced that this is the best way to achieve inclusion, owing to the diversity of countries. These parties emphasise the rights of states and want to prevent the EU becoming a gateway for immigration.
3 Not opposed to the EU in principle, but are convinced that the present model is too exclusive. The majority of leftwing Eurosceptic parties fear that the EU will lead to more inequalities in a global perspective.

(adapted from Taggart, 1998: 365–6)

The green party family

The crisis of the exponential model of growth in most industrialised Western European democracies and a growing dissatisfaction of the younger generation with the established parties led to the emergence of green parties across Europe in the early 1980s. They formed a new party family that is quite established nowadays. The findings of the Club of Rome in its report (organised by Dennis Meadows, called *The Limits of Growth*), in which the scarcity of major raw materials, especially oil, was predicted, contributed to the emergence of the model of sustainable development. This was reinforced by a UN conference in Stockholm in 1972. A milestone was the report of former Norwegian prime minister Harlem Grø Brundtland to the United Nations in 1987, in which sustainable growth and sustainable development were recommended for the way economic policy should be undertaken. Another factor was the slow emergence of a new set of cultural values in industrialised countries that also included concerns over the deterioration of the environment. These post-materialist values, carried predominantly by younger generations, were identified by Ronald Inglehart as the 'silent revolution' (see Chapters 3 and 10) (Inglehart, 1977, 2008; Inglehart and Welzel, 2005).

The most important green parties can be found in Germany, Austria (until 2017), Sweden, Finland, Switzerland, the Netherlands, Belgium, Luxembourg, Hungary and the Baltic states (Figure 7.7).

The regionalist and ethnic minority party family

Stein Rokkan had already recognised in the 1970s that regionalism as a political movement was becoming more important. Since then, many European countries have formed strong regionalist parties that have been able to shape politics at national level (Rokkan and Urwin, 1983: 118) (see also Chapter 9; Figure 7.8).

It is important to differentiate between genuine regionalist and regionalist-independentist parties. This is a quite important differentiation particularly for the cases of the UK, Spain and Belgium. In the UK, the Scottish National Party (SNP) in Scotland, Sinn Fein (SF), the Democratic Unionist Party (DUP), the Ulster Unionist Party (UUP) and the Social Democratic Liberal Party (SDLP) in Ireland, and the Party of Wales (Plaid Cymru) are regionalist parties. Just the SNP and Sinn Fein want independence of their regions from the UK. In Spain, there

Figure 7.7 The green parties in Europe

are myriad regionalist-nationalist and regionalist parties. Regionalist-nationalist parties can be found in Catalonia and the Basque Country. In Catalonia, there is The European and Catalan Democratic Party (Partit Demòcrata Europeu i Catalá – PdeCAT) founded in July 2016 as a successor party to Convergence and Union (Convergencia i Unió – CiU), the long-standing main party of Catalonia. Furthermore, there is the Catalan Republican Left (Esquerra Republicana de Catalunya – ERC), which was founded in 1931 at the beginning of the Second Spanish Republic (1931–6). Similarly, in the Basque country, the Basque Nationalist Party (Partido Nacionalista Vasco – PNV), founded in 1894, is a regionalist-nationalist party. Since 2008, the PNV, without giving up on the ultimate goal of independence, became more moderate in their political approach, playing a major role in defeating Basque terrorism perpetrated by Basque Country and Freedom (Euskadi ta Askatasuma – ETA), which finally stopped their activities in 2014. The political arm of ETA, Basque Country Rally (Euskal Herria Bildu – EH Bildu), a radical national left party (*esquerra abertzale*), also has quite strong support in the population, achieving 21.26 per cent of the votes in the 2016 Basque elections. The party is also represented in the Navarre region. In contrast, regionalist parties in other regions are quite small (for more, see Magone, 2018: chapter 5).

In Belgium, there are no longer national parties, just regional ones. In the 1980s, the party system split into two main electoral arenas, Wallonia and Flanders. Less known is that the German community has its own party system. In the myriad regional parties, just the xenophobic extreme right Vlaams Belang and the more moderate New Flemish Alliance (Nieuwe Vlaamse Alliantie – NV-A) may be considered as regionalist-independentist, the latter has since 2010 become the largest party in Belgium with between 17 and 21 per cent of the vote.

The Northern League (Lega Nord) in Italy started as a regionalist-separatist party in Lombardy, but since the general elections of 2018 it has become a national party with 17.4 per cent of the vote and part of the coalition government with Five Star movement (Cinque Stelle Movimento). Lega Nord is a rather xenophobic, anti-immigration and soft Eurosceptic party. In Germany, the Christian Social Union (Christlich-Soziale Union – CSU) in Bavaria works closely with its sister party the Christian-Democratic Union (Christlich-Demokratische Union – CDU).

In Central and Eastern Europe, there are also quite a lot of parties representing minorities and playing a major role as kingmakers in coalition governments. These are the Bridge (Most) and the Democratic Union of Hungarians in Romania (UDMR), both representing Hungarians in Slovakia and Romania respectively. The Movement of Rights and Freedoms (DPS) represents the Turkish population in Bulgaria, and four Albanian minority parties (Democratic Union for Integration, Movement BESA, Alliance for Albanians, Democratic Party of Albania) play an important kingmaker role in the party system of Macedonia (Figure 7.8).

In sum, political parties have been evolving since the nineteenth century to build today this diversity on ideological points of view. In spite of a growing marketisation of politics, these differences still remain important as the main characteristic of European pluralist societies.

Figure 7.8 The regionalist and ethnic minorities parties in Europe

The decline of party membership

The transformation from the mass party to the catch-all and cartel parties led to the decline of mass membership. According to Ronald Inglehart and Christian Welzel, there has been a departure from the traditional institutions of modern society, such as political parties, trade unions and church organisations, to more postmodern, flexible organisational types such as non-governmental organisations (NGOs) (Inglehart and Welzel, 2005: 262). Citizens as political consumers are much better informed and critical when looking at institutions, and particularly political parties. This cognitive (knowledge-based) mobilisation has contributed to the development of electoral market behaviour of citizens and political parties. The traditional parties relied on the fees of its members, but today public funding for political parties and the impact of the media have made having large memberships obsolete. According to Ingrid van Biezen and Thomas Poguntke, there has been a decline of membership across Europe from on average 10 per cent of the electorate in the 1980s, to 5 per cent in the first decade of the millennium. However, one has to qualify these figures, because before 1989 only the countries of Western Europe were included, and data for Central and Eastern Europe are only for the period after 1990. The data collected by Mair, van Biezen and Poguntke also show that the ratio between membership and electorate is on average much lower in Central and Eastern Europe than in Western Europe (Mair and Van Biezen, 2001: 6–7; Van Biezen et al., 2012; Van Biezen and Poguntke, 2014: 206–7).

The importance of public funding for political parties

Today, only two countries in Europe still have no system of public funding for political parties: the UK and Switzerland. The Netherlands also belonged to this exclusive group, but since 1998 public funding has been upgraded over time in order to support the party organisation, the youth organisation, the party research institute and any international work undertaken by the respective political group. The main criterium for support is not the electoral share of the vote, but the number of members of the respective party (Magone, 2017: 123–4).

At the moment, Switzerland is the only country with a substandard regulatory framework in relation to private funding. A part of the party funding for the parliamentary groups, Swiss MPs and parties is extremely dependent on private funding. However, this private funding remains opaque and without any strict regulations, allowing loopholes for political corruption. Therefore, the Council of Europe through its Commission of States Against Corruption (GRECO) has highlighted these problems of Swiss democracy on several occasions. Indeed, the Swiss parliament is strongly dominated by high-ranking members of Swiss interest groups that were directly elected to parliament, partly due to their strong financial backing, thus undermining a level playing field at elections (GRECO, 2015; Magone, 2017: 122–3).

In the UK, since the 1990s, there have been legislative acts streamlining and limiting party funding, but the turning point was the Political Parties and Elections Act of 2000, which, as a reaction to the 'cash for honours' scandal, was upgraded in terms of limitations to private funding and electoral campaigns in 2009. Private donations over £200 have to be declared, and donations from foreign donors are forbidden (Legislation UK, 2009; Piccio, 2012: 87–8).

All other countries have introduced generous public funding systems that include not only annual grants to the parties represented in parliament according to their share of the vote at the last election, but also coverage of national, regional, local and European elections. In spite of this, many parties are dependent on private donors in order to fund the expensive use of the media in politics in the 'permanent campaign' during and between elections (for an overview, see Casal-Bértoa and Ingrid van Biezen, 2014b; IDEA, 2014; Piccio, 2012). Enforcement mechanisms in Southern, East Central, Baltic and Eastern Europe are still very weak (Casal-Bértoa and Van Biezen, 2014a, 2014b).

Internationally, the OECD, the Institute of Democracy and Electoral Assistance (IDEA) and GRECO have been putting governments under pressure due to the fact that unaccounted soft money may lead to corruption (IDEA, 2014; GRECO, 2018; OECD, 2016b).

A summary of this important aspect of party and electoral politics is shown in Table 7.3, which shows the three main systems of public funding in Europe. One group of countries receives funding for the political party in parliament through the parliamentary group, and for the party organisation and their adjacents, and for electoral campaigns (e.g. Portugal, Spain, Germany, Belgium, Luxembourg, Hungary). A second group comprises countries that receive just funding for the parliamentary group and the party organisation (the Netherlands), and a third group receives funding just for the parliamentary group (Switzerland).

Table 7.3 Three models of public funding of political parties

	Party organisation, electoral campaigns and parliamentary group	*Party organisation and parliamentary group*	*Parliamentary group only*
Countries	Portugal Spain Slovak Republic Czech Republic Luxembourg Italy Hungary Greece Slovakia Bulgaria Romania Latvia Lithuania Estonia Belgium Austria Germany	UK Ireland Sweden Norway Denmark Finland Netherlands	Switzerland

Source: Based on OECD (2016b: 39); IDEA (2014, 2018); Piccio (2012); own research on individual countries.

Probably, the most sensitive issue related to party funding is the influence of large private donors. Table 7.4 shows the estimated ratio between public and private funding of political parties in selected countries. The UK, the Netherlands and Switzerland are outliers in the main model of Europe, which is based mainly on public funding.

The impact of electoral systems on party systems

Before we turn to an analysis of the party systems in Europe (Table 7.5, Figure 7.9), it is important to review the main aspects of the relationship between party and electoral systems. The selection of an electoral system during the constitutional settlement is probably one of the most important tasks of a political elite. It has to take into account whether it wants political stability or whether to emphasise representation of all political forces. It is important that the rules of the game leading to access to power are accepted by all political parties by consensus, otherwise it

Table 7.4 Public and private funding of political parties in Europe, 2007–19

	Share of overall funding			*Private donations limits (€)*	*Ban on anonymous private donations*	*Ban on foreign donors (€)*
	Public funding	*Private funding*	*Fees*			
Austria	80	6	14	No limit	Yes, above threshold €7,600	No
Belgium	85	15*)		500	Yes, above threshold	No
Czech Republic	75	25*)		Yes	Yes	Yes
Denmark	75	25*)		No limit	No	No
Estonia	78.8	0.2	1.9	Yes, 1,200	Yes	Yes
Finland	75	25*)		30,000	Yes	Yes
France	72	14	14	7,500	Yes	Yes
Germany	45	18	25	No limit	Yes, above threshold	No, 1,000
Greece	90	10*)		15,000	Yes	Yes
Hungary	60	40*)		No limit	Yes	Yes
Iceland	75	25*)		2,720	Yes	Yes
Ireland	75	8	8	2,750	Yes, above threshold	Yes
Italy	82	18*)		Yes, 10,000	Yes, above threshold	No
Luxembourg	80	20*)		No	Yes	No
Netherlands	35	65*)		No limit	No	No
Norway	67.4	32.6*)		No limit	Yes	Yes
Poland	54–90	10–46*)		Yes	Yes	Yes
Portugal	80	20*)		Yes	Yes	Yes
Slovak Republic	87.5	12.5*)		No	Yes	Yes
Slovenia	90	10		Yes	Yes, above threshold	Yes
Spain	87.5	12.5*)		10,000	Yes	Yes
Sweden	75	25*)		No limit	No	Yes
Switzerland	30**)	70		No limit	No	No
Turkey	90	10*)		Yes	Yes	No
UK	35	65*)		No limit	Yes, above threshold	Yes

Source: OECD (2016b: 38–39, 47–48, 51, 148); reports of GRECO (2018) third round; Sickinger (2009) for Austria; Bundeszentrale für politische Bildung (2014) for Germany; IDEA (2018a).

*)comprises membership fees and private donations; unable to find breakdown.
**)indirect through parliamentary lump sums to parliamentary groups and the contributions of MPs and judges.
Figures are all estimates and do not add due to other income sources such as party assets.

may lead to attempts to change the electoral system unilaterally, like has happened after Viktor Orbán's Fidesz party came to power in 2010. The UK case differs from most other European countries due to the legacy of the first-past-the-post system, which is quite simple but unfair towards smaller parties, particularly the liberal democrats. Similarly, during the Spanish constitutional settlement, the political elite opted for political stability by creating small constituencies with a threshold of 3 per cent, while preserving some proportionality through the adoption of the D'Hondt electoral system with closed lists (Magone, 2018: 108–15). Here is not the place to discuss the impact of all electoral systems, but just to highlight certain important properties that may contribute to a certain party system. Nevertheless, the German electoral system merits some discussion, because it is a relatively fair system. The threshold was devised to contribute to stability of the party system. In 1949 the Federal Republic of Germany opted for political stability, although it tried to balance this with a high level of proportional representation, meaning that half the seats are elected by a plurality system (first-past-the-post) and half by proportional representation. There is a 5 per cent threshold, so that fragmentation of the party system is avoided. In each election, the citizen has two votes, one for the constituency seats and one for the proportional representation section. In this sense, the Germans may act strategically by splitting the vote among two parties in order to achieve a coalition government on the right or on the left. The German system also shows that, after adopting the basic aspects of the electoral system, it can take some time before an electoral system becomes permanent and finetuning will often be necessary. For example, it took until 1956 to finally finetune the German electoral system to ensure it was valid at both national and *Länder* level (Scarrow, 2003: 62).

The Hungarian model emulated the German system and was able to create one of the most stable party systems in Central and Eastern Europe. However, in 2012, the Victor Orbán government changed the electoral system. One of the main reasons for the change was the fact that constituencies were very uneven in terms of size. The main changes to the electoral system were the reduction of seats from 386 to 199. About 53 per cent of seats are now elected in 106 single constituencies by a first-past-the-post system, and the other 47 per cent by a proportional representation system. Both parts are unconnected. It means that the three-tier system was changed to a two-tier system. While the remaining votes for the other parties can be used in the national proportional representation list, the surplus votes of the successful candidates in the single member constituencies can also be added to the tally, which clearly favours even further the winning party. Due to the changes, Fidesz-KDNP was able to win 44.0 and 49.4 per cent of the vote and receive 117 (59 per cent) and 133 seats (66.8 per cent) in the 2014 and 2018 elections respectively. As a consequence, other parties are substantially under-represented. A major issue is that probably there was a lot of gerrymandering of the constituencies, so that it led to this disproportionate result. Therefore, Hungary has the lowest Perception of Electoral Integrity index (PEI) value of the EU, in particular due to its electoral law, boundaries, campaign funding and campaign media. The PEI was developed by Pippa Norris and her team and clearly monitors how elections are carried out and if they fulfil international standards. According to the PEI and other reports, it seems that the opposition parties are considerably disadvantaged in the way the public and private media landscape is owned and organised (Fomarola, 2018; Norris et al., 2015; OSCE, 2014: 6–8; Figure 7.12).

In Lithuania, the electoral system is similar to the Hungarian system, but uses the two-ballot system for single constituencies. It does not allocate compensatory seats. This means that the two systems are disconnected, so it is known as a parallel system.

The two-ballot system in France was introduced in 1958 and forces political parties to join either the right or the left coalition in order to have a chance in the second round. A candidate is elected if s/he wins the election with at least 25 per cent of the vote in the first ballot and only candidates who pass the 12.5 per cent threshold are allowed to take part in the second round (however, if there is only one candidate who achieves this threshold, the runner-up can also take part). The French electoral system is one of the most disproportional in Europe (Knapp and Wright, 2001: 252–5).

Meanwhile, Italy has had four different electoral systems since 1948 and three in the Second Republic after 1993. Originally, the idea was to move from proportional representation to a majoritarian system, but this proved difficult because the legacy of proportional representation political culture still shaped the way the new system was in force. After several experiments, the present system was agreed in 2016. In October 2017, the new law used a parallel system with 37 per cent being elected by simple majority and 63 per cent by proportional representation (the so-called *Rosatellum*, named after the head of the Democratic Party Ettore Rosato (*La Reppublica*, 26 October 2017; Regalia, 2018).

Table 7.5 Electoral systems for national elections, lower chamber

Electoral systems	*Country (number of seats)*	*Method of election and threshold for political parties*
Majoritarian systems	UK (650)	Plurality, simple majority, first-past-the-post system
	France (577)	Two-ballot system, 12.5% threshold in first round, 50% of votes to win constituency, if not two strongest candidate proceeds to second round
Parallel systems	Lithuania (141)	Two ballot system in uninominal constituencies (71) and proportional representation in single national constituency (70)
	Italy (630)	Simple majority, uninominal (37% of 630 seats), proportional representation (63% of 630 seats)
Mixed systems	Germany (598)	Simple majority/proportional representation – Sainte-Laguë Half elected in uninominal constituencies and half elected by proportional representation, surplus and compensatory seats allocated may lead to enlarged assembly, 5% threshold
	Hungary (199)	Simple majority/Hagenbach-Bischoff, 5% threshold for parties, 10% for two parties, 15% for three or more parties

Proportional representation	Bulgaria (240)	31 elected in multi-member constituencies by PR, closed list, Hare-Niemeyer, 4% threshold
	Switzerland (200)	Hagenbach-Bischoff, Panachage, 5 seats (in two cantons, and three half cantons) out of 200 elected by simple majority It is referred to as a 'mixed system', but it is rather a proportional representation system
	Greece (300)	Hagenbach-Bischoff at constituency and simple quotient for national constituency
	Slovakia (150)	Hagenbach-Bischoff, Hare-Niemeyer for leftover seats, 3% threshold
	Luxembourg (60)	Hagenbach-Bischoff/Panachage
	Portugal (230)	D'Hondt, closed lists
	Spain (350)	D'Hondt, closed lists, 3% threshold at constituency level
	Belgium (150)	D'Hondt, preferential voting
	Netherlands (150)	D'Hondt, preferential voting, threshold of 0.67 %
	Czech Republic (200)	D'Hondt, preferential voting, threshold of 5% for parties, 10% for two parties, 15% for three parties, 20% for four parties or more
	Romania (329)	D'Hondt, closed lists, threshold of 5% for parties, 10% for two-party coalitions, 15% for three-party coalitions or more
	Iceland (63)	D'Hondt
	Austria (183)	Three levels 43 regional districts by Hare quota system, at Länder and national level allocation through D'Hondt , threshold of 4% or one seat won in one of the 43 regional districts
	Slovenia (90)	Droop method (simple quotient) at constituency level, D'Hondt (largest remainder) at national level, preferential voting, 4% threshold
	Croatia (153)	D'Hondt, 5% threshold
	Serbia (250)	D'Hondt, 5% threshold
	Montenegro (81)	D'Hondt, 3% threshold
	Macedonia (120)	D'Hondt
	Albania (140)	D'Hondt, 3% threshold for parties, 5% threshold for pre-electoral coalitions
	Denmark (179)	Modified Saint-Laguë, Hare quota and largest remainders
	Sweden (349)	Modified Saint Laguë, closed list, preferential voting, 4% nationally or 12% in one constituency

(continued)

Table 7.5 *(continued)*

Electoral systems	*Country (number of seats)*	*Method of election and threshold for political parties*
	Norway (169)	Modified Saint Laguë
	Poland (460)	Modified Saint-Laguë, threshold of 5% for parties and 8% for pre-electoral coalitions
	Latvia (100)	Modified Saint-Laguë, preferential voting, 5% threshold
	Bosnia-Herzegovina (42)	Simple quotient (Droop method), largest remainder (Hare-Niemeyer), need to win at least one seat at constituency level
	Ireland (166)	Single transferable vote
	Malta (65)	Single transferable vote Compensatory seats may lead to more MPs
	Estonia (101)	Modified single transferable vote (constituency level) and modified D'Hondt (compensatory seats), 5% threshold for compensatory 26 seats at national level

Source: IPU (2018) Parline Database; IDEA (2018b).

The fairest electoral systems in terms of proportional representation are probably those found in the Netherlands and the Nordic countries, all of which use some form of proportional representation and also have quite fragmented party systems. In the Dutch parliament there are regularly ten or more parties, and the same is true for Denmark, Norway and Finland. In the Netherlands, there is only one national constituency, although candidates are allocated to eighteen sub-constituencies. Parties need only to overcome the low threshold of 0.67 per cent to secure representation in the lower chamber, the Tweede Kamer. The Nordic countries have proportional representation systems using quite fair electoral methods. In Southern, Central and Eastern Europe proportional representation is the most common electoral system, just Lithuania and Hungary have a disproportional parallel system.

In terms of proportional representation electoral systems, it is important to differentiate between different methods: the D'Hondt system, the Saint-Lagüe, the Hare system and the single transferable vote. The difference is that the D'Hondt and Saint-Laguë systems use a division quotient, whereas the Hare system is calculated based on a subtraction quotient.

- *D'Hondt system*: This system was developed by the Belgian mathematician Victor D'Hondt at the end of the nineteenth century. It was adopted in 1899 in Belgium and in 1906 in Finland. The D'Hondt system divides the quotient by 1, 2, 3 until it has allocated all the seats. The steep division is favourable to larger parties.
- *Saint-Lagüe system*: This system was developed by the French mathematician André Saint-Laguë and is based on the largest average, so that the quotient is divided by 1, 2, 3, 4 and so on. It is more moderate and helps smaller parties.

Figure 7.9 Electoral systems for national general elections, lower chamber

- *Modified Saint-Laguë system*: This system lies between the D'Hondt and the pure Saint-Laguë system. It uses a quotient of 1.4, 3 and 5. It is used in most Nordic countries with the exception of Finland, which uses the D'Hondt system. It is also used in Latvia and Bosnia-Herzegovina.
- *Hagenbach-Bischoff'sche system*: This also uses a quotient that is based on the total number of votes received by the parties divided by the number of seats plus one. Afterwards the votes of each party are divided by the quotient to see how many seats can be allocated. Remaining seats are allocated based on who gets the highest quotient when divided by the already allocated seats plus one. This electoral method is used in Greece, but also at first level in Austria. It is a system that favours larger parties, something which is evident in Greece.
- *Single transferable system (STV or Hare-Clark system)*: This uses a subtraction quotient based on the division of the total sum of votes by the number of seats. STV also includes the opportunity to rank candidates according to preference, so there is a lengthy electoral process before the results can be announced. Indeed, it may take several days until the exact results are known. It is used in Ireland, as well as in Northern Ireland and in Malta.

- *Panachage*: Normally, the voter chooses political parties from the existing lists. However, many electoral systems allow for preferential voting by choosing candidates within the list. Panachage goes one step further by allowing voters to rank candidates from different lists for the particular constituency. This is a quite complex system and is used in Luxembourg and Switzerland (adapted from Farrell, 2000).

The variety of electoral systems in Europe has allowed for the creation of different party systems and also for different styles of politics, contributing to the establishment of majoritarian or consensus democracies (see Chapter 4). According to Douglas Rae, all electoral systems favour the larger parties, the only question that remains is about the extent of such disadvantage. Electoral engineering plays a major role in shaping such relationships between larger and smaller parties (Rae, 1967), and once the electoral system has been agreed on, it is difficult to change the rules of the game.

As already mentioned, there are at least three devices that can shape the electoral system towards more stability with a reduced number of parties or more proportional representation with a large number of parties.

First, the creation of an electoral threshold contributes to a reduction of small parties being represented in parliament. Many countries use a threshold at national level to reduce party fragmentation, for example Germany (5 per cent), the Czech Republic (5 per cent) and Sweden (4 per cent). On the other hand, Spain uses a threshold of 3 per cent at the constituency level, while some countries, such as France (12.5 per cent), use thresholds for candidates in single-constituency elections to advance to the second round.

Second, some countries use the direct mandate (*Grundmandat*), which means that a party is able to achieve a seat in a constituency and is therefore eligible to take part in the second round of allocation of seats. This is the case in Austria and Bosnia-Herzegovina. Germany has a similar system for parties that do not achieve the 5 per cent threshold but are able to get seats in their electoral strongholds.

Third, inclusion or exclusion of parties can be achieved through the size of the constituency. A very large multi-member constituency with a low threshold is favourable to small parties, whereas a small multi-member constituency contributes to the exclusion of small parties. General elections in the Netherlands are conducted in a very large constituency that actually comprises the whole country, meaning that the threshold is very low at 0.67 per cent. The result is a high level of representation of small parties. In contrast, Spain is divided into fifty-two constituencies, most of which are quite small. This is reinforced by a threshold of 3 per cent, which means that only the larger parties achieve representation.

All this shows that electoral systems produce different levels of disproportionality. Even if countries have the same electoral system, the particular characteristics of the individual system may lead to different levels of disproportionality. In this context, the UK and France have probably the most disproportionate systems because they use plurality/majoritarian systems (see Figure 7.10). Although high levels of disproportionality can also be found in the Greek and Spanish electoral systems, which considerably favour the larger parties and are disadvantageous for the smaller parties, these electoral systems still have lower levels of disproportionality than the UK and France.

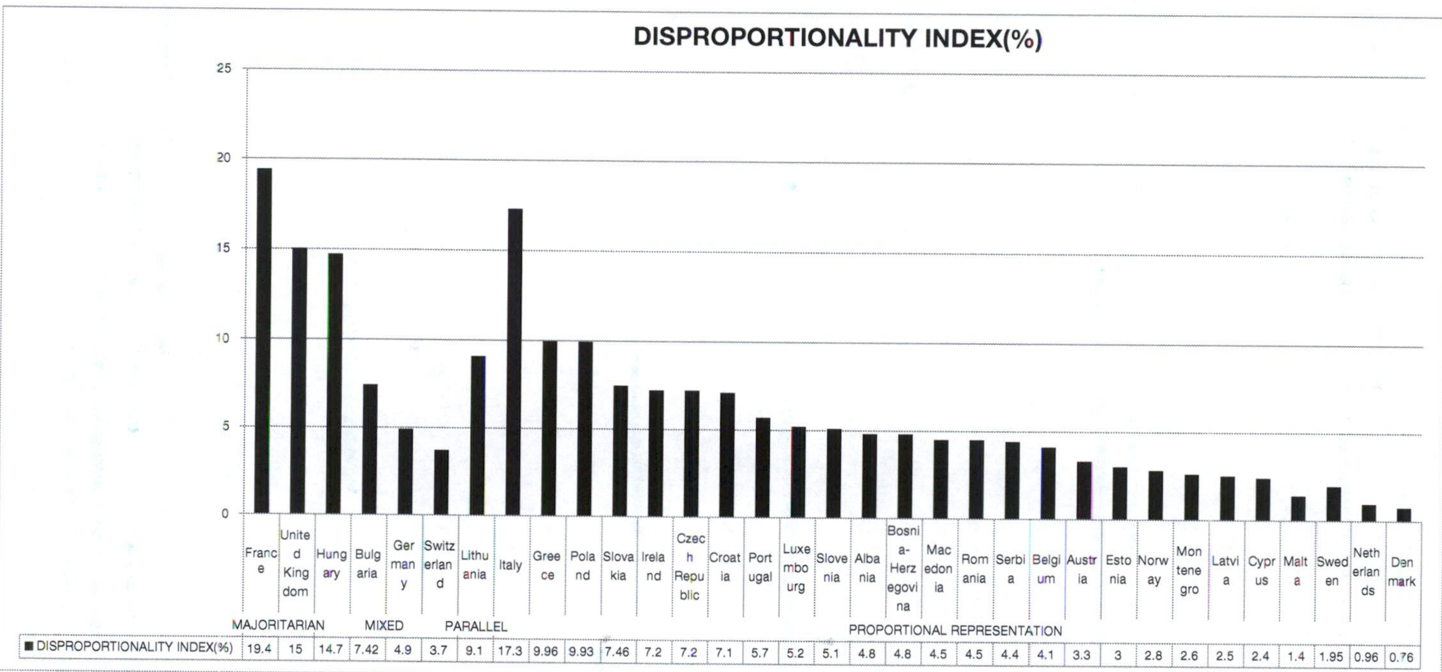

Figure 7.10 Disproportionality of electoral systems (difference between share of votes and allocation of seats), 2010–18

Source: based on data of least squares index developed by Gallagher (1991, 2018).

In sum, the design of electoral systems matters. Sometimes, political systems may be characterised by high levels of political instability because of an ill-designed electoral system. In this sense, there is a close relationship between electoral and party systems. However, the best electoral design cannot prevent a potential corruption of elections and electoral process. Several international organisations such as the Council of Europe, Organisation for Security and Cooperation in Europe (OSCE), but also the EU monitor electoral processes worldwide. Probably, the most ambitious project in this field is the electoral integrity index led by the prominent Pippa Norris and her team to develop a functioning electoral integrity index. Meanwhile the team has undertaken several waves of electoral integrity worldwide. The so-called Perception of Electoral Integrity (PEI) index tells us about the quality and integrity of the electoral process based on the expertise of country specialists. It includes information about electoral laws, electoral procedures, electoral boundaries, voter registration, party registration, media coverage, campaign finance, voting process, vote count, results and electoral authorities. As Figure 7.11 shows, most European countries have a quite excellent standard in terms of electoral integrity, but there are also countries such as Hungary, Bulgaria, Romania, Montenegro, Albania, Moldova and Ukraine with flawed electoral systems. At the very bottom are Serbia, Macedonia, Belarus and Russia (Norris et al., 2018: 7).

Before we turn to a description and analysis of national party systems, it is important to just make a note on turnout in general elections. As Figure 7.12 shows, turnout is quite diverse among European countries. On average, turnout is quite high in the Nordic countries, the Netherlands, Belgium, Luxembourg, Italy, Malta and Cyprus. In contrast, it is quite low in Central and Eastern European countries. Germany, Austria, Greece, Portugal, Spain, France, the UK and Ireland fall in between the Nordic and Central and Eastern European countries. Turnout is important, because, if low, it can open up a range of opportunities for more radical parties.

Party systems in Europe

Each national party system in Europe is unique considering all the factors that contribute to electoral engineering. Unfortunately, in this general book on European politics, it is not possible to analyse each one in depth. Therefore, some comparative notes suffice to show the differences of party systems in the different regional clusters with basic data on electoral results.

The Nordic model

Scandinavian parties were characterised by considerable stability until the 1960s. A freezing of party systems occurred during the interwar period, and in the post-1945 period, five parties regularly gained electoral representation in the different parliaments: the social democrats, the conservatives, the liberals, the communists and the centre party. In all the party systems in Scandinavia, the social democrats were the

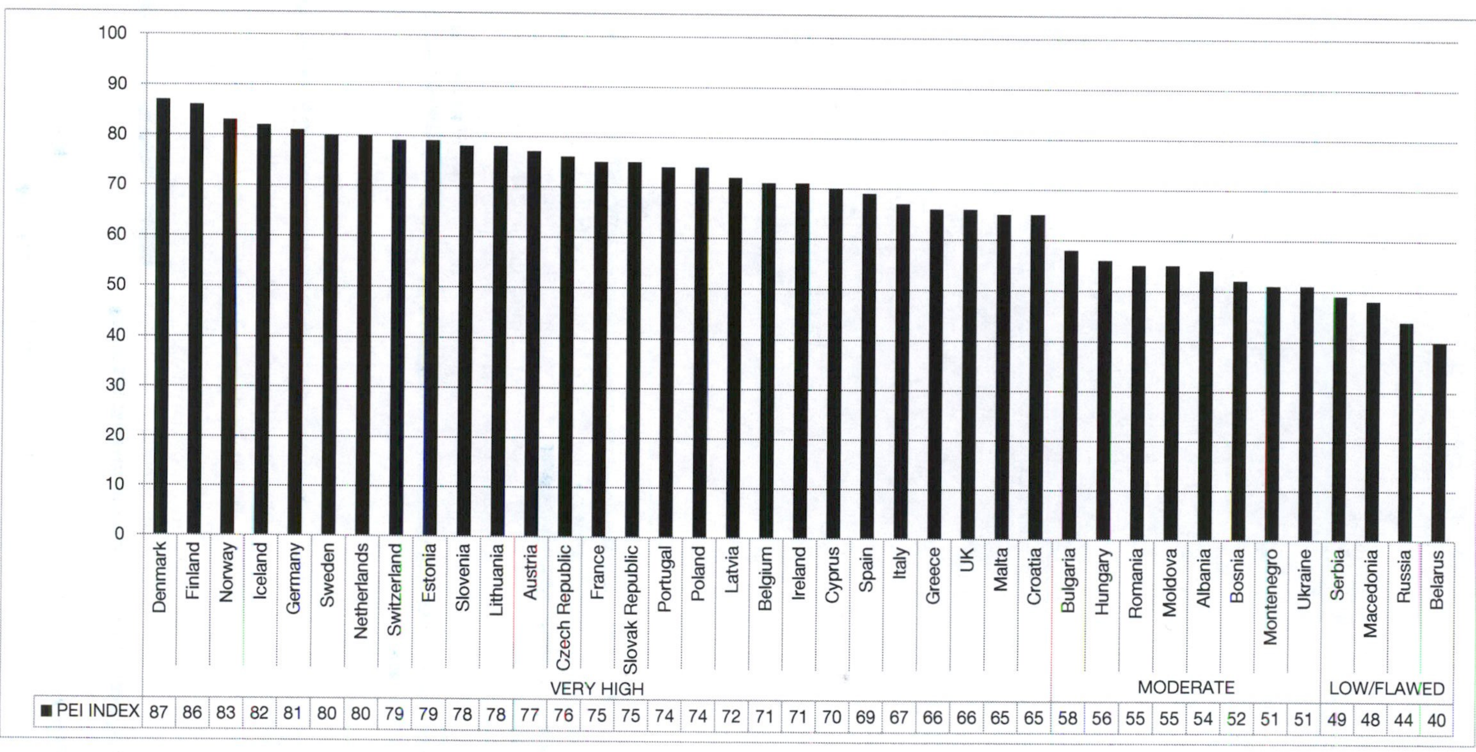

Figure 7.11 Perception of electoral integrity (PEI) index in Europe, 2012–17

Source: Norris et al. (2018: 7).

Figure 7.12 Turnout at general elections in European countries on average, between 2000 and 2018 in percentage

strongest party and were able to implement strong welfare policies in coalition with other parties. In the 1970s and 1980s, a high level of electoral volatility led to the emergence of new political parties (for example, the greens and the Christian democrats), including Eurosceptic parties (for example, the Progress Party in Norway and the Danish People's Party in Denmark). This fragmentation of the electoral vote also led to considerable volatility between the main parties (Table 7.6).

One particular aspect of party system change has been the declining electoral support for social democratic parties, but also liberals and conservatives across the regions. Some of the parties achieved over 40 per cent of the vote in the 1950s and 1960s, but this has declined considerably since the 1970s (Hansen and Kosiara-Pedersen, 2017: 116).

In most Nordic countries, a polarisation between left and right takes place during elections. It means that coalition partners are already partly defined before the elections. In spite of this, there is always some flexibility in working with parties from the opposing ideological families. Minority government requires a prime minister and a government that is able to pragmatically find solutions to specific policy problems. In this sense, polarisation and consensus are intertwined aspects in most Nordic countries (Hansen and Kosiara-Pedersen, 2017: 118–19).

Finland is probably the exception, because political stability through grand or oversized coalitions has been the major pattern. There, three main

Table 7.6 Main political parties in the Nordic countries

Party systems until 1970s		*Party system after 1970*						
	Social democrats	*Conservatives*	*Centre*	*Liberals*	*Communists/ radical left*	*Greens*	*Christian-democrats*	*Eurosceptic/ xenophobic parties*
Sweden	Sveriges socialdemokratiska arbetareparti (SAP)	Moderata samlingspartiet (M)	Centerpartiet (C)	Folkpartiet liberalerna	Vänsterpartiet (Left Party)	Miljöpartiet (Green Party)	Krist demokraterna	Sverigedemokraterna (Swedish Democrats)
Finland	Suomen Sosialidemokraattinen Puolue (SDP) Social Democratic Party	Kansallinen Kokoomus, KOK (National Coalition Party)	Suomen Keskusta, KESK (Centre of Finland)	Svenska folkpartiet (SFP) (Swedish People's Party)	Vasemmis Toliitto (VAS) (Left Alliance)	Vihreä Litto, (Vihr) (Green Alliance)	Kristillis demokraatit	Perussuomalaiset (True Finns)
Denmark	Socialdemokraterne	Det Konservative Folkeparti		Venstre Danmarks Liberale Venstre (Liberal left) Radikale Venstre (Radical left)	Socialistisk Folkeparti (Socialist People's Party)	Enhedslisten (Unity list)	Kristen demokraterne	Dansk Folkeparti (Danish People's Party)
Norway	Det norske Arbeiderparti	Høyre (Right)	Senterpartiet (Centre)	Venstre (Left)	Sosialistisk Venstreparti (Socialist left)	Miliøpartiet De Grønne (Greens)	Kristelig Folkeparti	Fremskrittspartiet (Progress Party)
Iceland	Samfylkingin (Socialdemocratic Alliance)	SjálfstæÐis flokkurinn (Independence Party)	Ramsóknar flokkurinn (Progressive Party)	Frjálslyndi flokkurinn (Liberal Party)		Vinstrigraen (Green Party)		

parties dominate: the social democrats, the conservatives and the centre party. Since the late 2000s, the centre party has been successful in dominating the political system. In spite of the rise of the Eurosceptic True Finns to become the second largest and third largest party in 2011 and 2015 respectively, the pattern of Finnish politics based on consensus did not change (Arter, 2011, 2015; Karvonen, 2014: 79–82; Vainikka, 2016) (Figure 7.13).

In Sweden, the Social Democratic Party was the dominant party until the late 1970s; however, since then, its electoral share has declined and it has been successfully challenged by its rival the conservative moderates. They are also the two pivotal parties forming government coalitions on the left and right. Quite problematic has been the government formation after the September 2018 elections in which neither right nor left was able to achieve an absolute majority. The extreme right Swedish Democrats (SD) are rather shunned by all political parties due to their xenophobic anti-immigration rhetoric (Figure 7.14).

Since the elections of 1973, the Danish party system has been considerably fragmented, which has also led to polarisation between left and right. In the 2015 elections nine parties achieved representation in the Folketing. The Social Democrats declined considerably electorally, whereas centre-right parties have been able to improve their electoral position since the late 2000s. The Liberals (Venstre) have become a pivotal party in gathering together the centre-right parties. In the 2015 elections the centre-right coalition under Lars Løkke Rasmussen was able to build a viable minority coalition government and return to power, in spite of the fact the social democrats were the largest party (Figure 7.15; Kosiara-Pedersen, 2016).

In Norway, the Labour Party has declined considerably, as have the conservatives. The conservatives (Høyre) usually join with the liberals, Christian democrats and Centre Party to form a government coalition; however, the prime minister formed a coalition with the populist Progress Party after the elections of 2013 and 2017 (Figure 7.16).

In Iceland, the Independence Party has been dominant throughout the postwar history of Iceland. The Social Democrats were rather a distant second. Between 2009 and 2017 several new parties emerged that created more political instability and volatility, a sign of the considerable discontent of the population. Among them, since 2013 are the Pirate party and the Left Green Movement (VG), which is clearly popular with the younger parts of the population. One major factor leading to this change was the financial crisis and the impact on the Icelandic economy. After the elections of 2017, it included also the left-green movement in the coalition government (Figure 7.17).

One common feature of all countries, with the exception of Iceland, is the rise of rightwing populist parties emphasising the imagined heartland that is being lost due to increased immigration. Most of these parties are new right populist parties such as the Danish People's Party (DF) in Denmark, the True Finns in Finland, the Progress Party (FP) in Norway and the Swedish Democrats (SD) in Sweden. The refugee crisis in 2015 was a major catalyst for the increase in their vote (Jungar, 2017).

In spite of the volatility, the Nordic countries still have the highest levels of turnout of 80 per cent (with the exception of Norway which is at 70 per cent and Finland which is above 65 per cent) and trust in the political system.

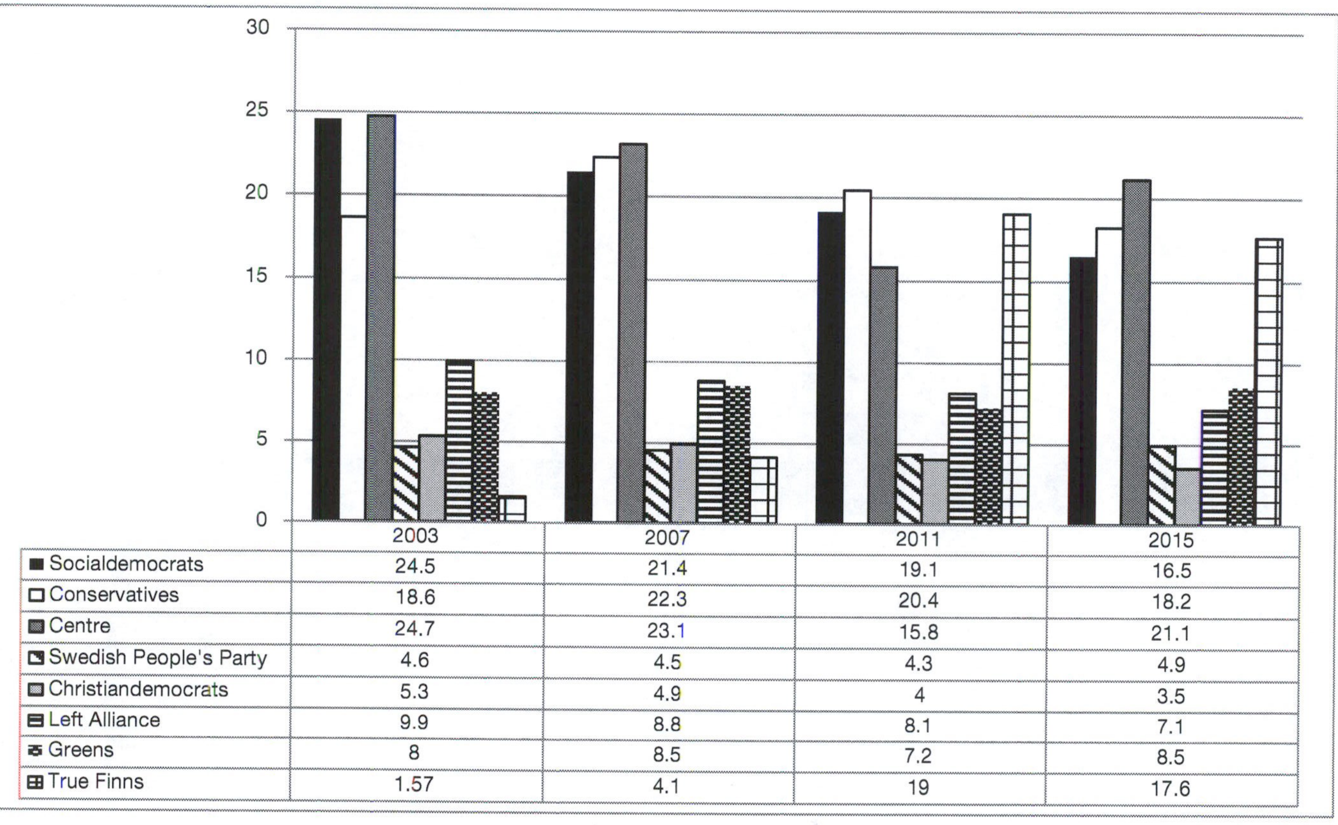

	2003	2007	2011	2015
Socialdemocrats	24.5	21.4	19.1	16.5
Conservatives	18.6	22.3	20.4	18.2
Centre	24.7	23.1	15.8	21.1
Swedish People's Party	4.6	4.5	4.3	4.9
Christiandemocrats	5.3	4.9	4	3.5
Left Alliance	9.9	8.8	8.1	7.1
Greens	8	8.5	7.2	8.5
True Finns	1.57	4.1	19	17.6

Figure 7.13 General elections in Finland, 2000–15

Source: Author's graph based on database of Parties and Elections in Europe (2018).

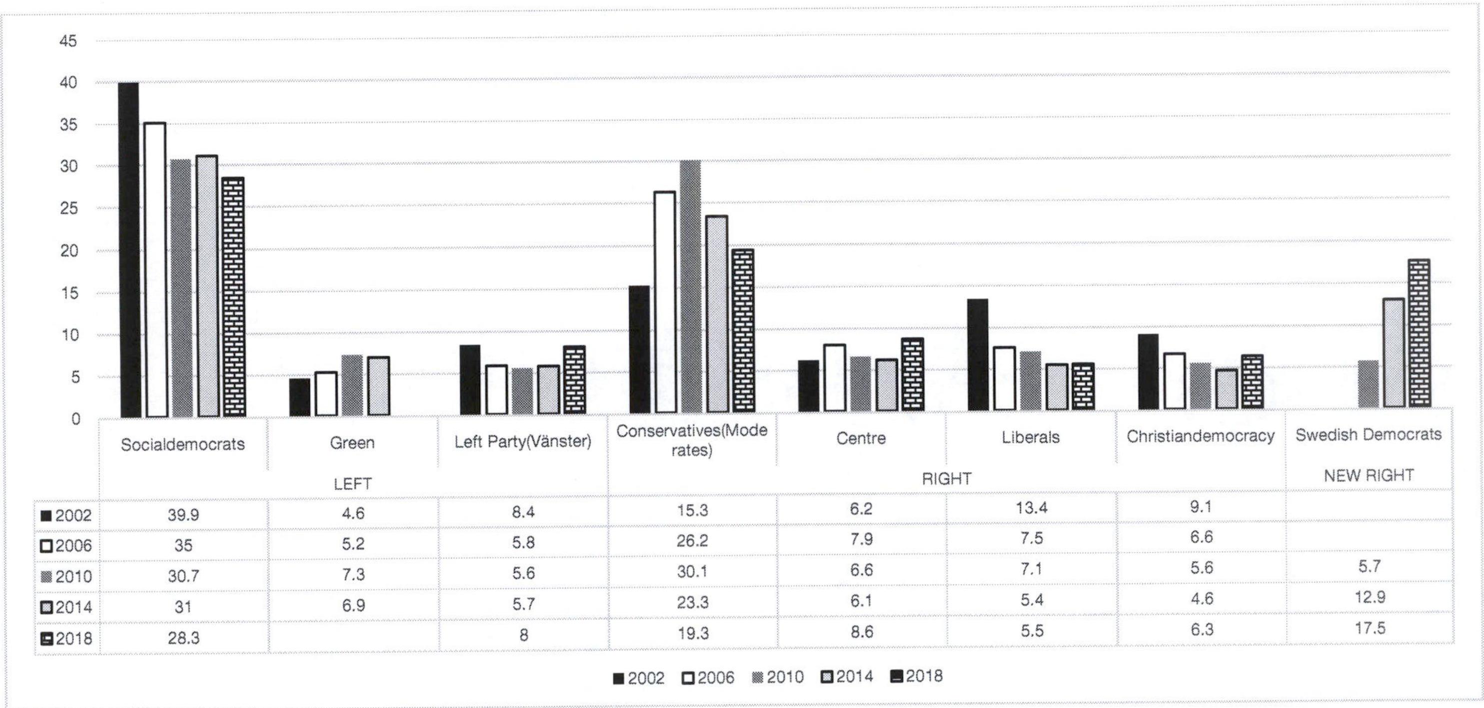

	Socialdemocrats	Green	Left Party(Vänster)	Conservatives(Moderates)	Centre	Liberals	Christiandemocracy	Swedish Democrats
	LEFT			RIGHT				NEW RIGHT
2002	39.9	4.6	8.4	15.3	6.2	13.4	9.1	
2006	35	5.2	5.8	26.2	7.9	7.5	6.6	
2010	30.7	7.3	5.6	30.1	6.6	7.1	5.6	5.7
2014	31	6.9	5.7	23.3	6.1	5.4	4.6	12.9
2018	28.3		8	19.3	8.6	5.5	6.3	17.5

Figure 7.14 General elections in Sweden, 2000–18

Source: Author's graph based on database of Parties and Elections in Europe (2018).

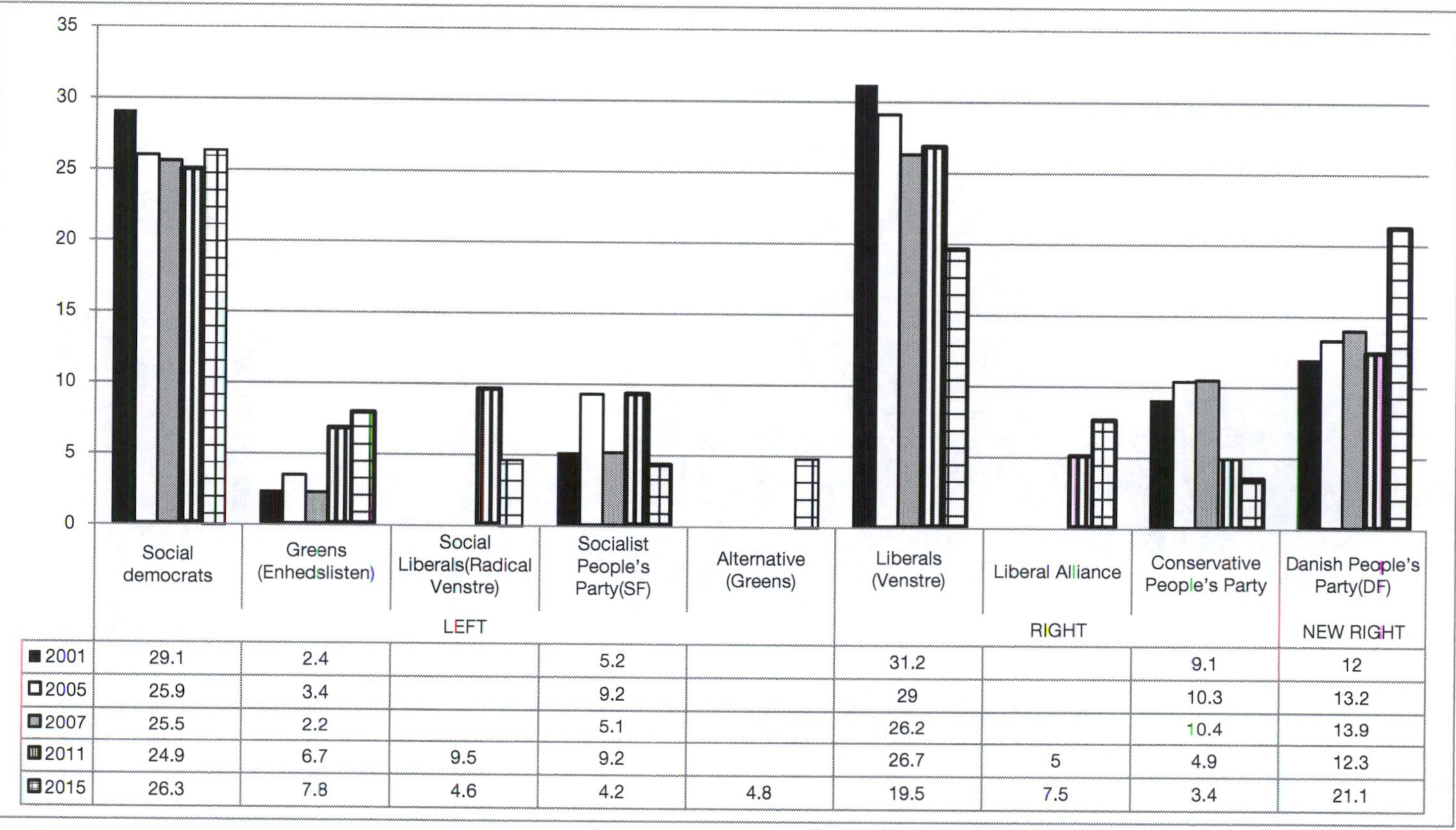

	Social democrats	Greens (Enhedslisten)	Social Liberals(Radical Venstre)	Socialist People's Party(SF)	Alternative (Greens)	Liberals (Venstre)	Liberal Alliance	Conservative People's Party	Danish People's Party(DF)
	LEFT					RIGHT			NEW RIGHT
2001	29.1	2.4		5.2		31.2		9.1	12
2005	25.9	3.4		9.2		29		10.3	13.2
2007	25.5	2.2		5.1		26.2		10.4	13.9
2011	24.9	6.7	9.5	9.2		26.7	5	4.9	12.3
2015	26.3	7.8	4.6	4.2	4.8	19.5	7.5	3.4	21.1

Figure 7.15 General elections in Denmark, 2000–15

Source: Author's graph based on database of Parties and Elections in Europe (2018).

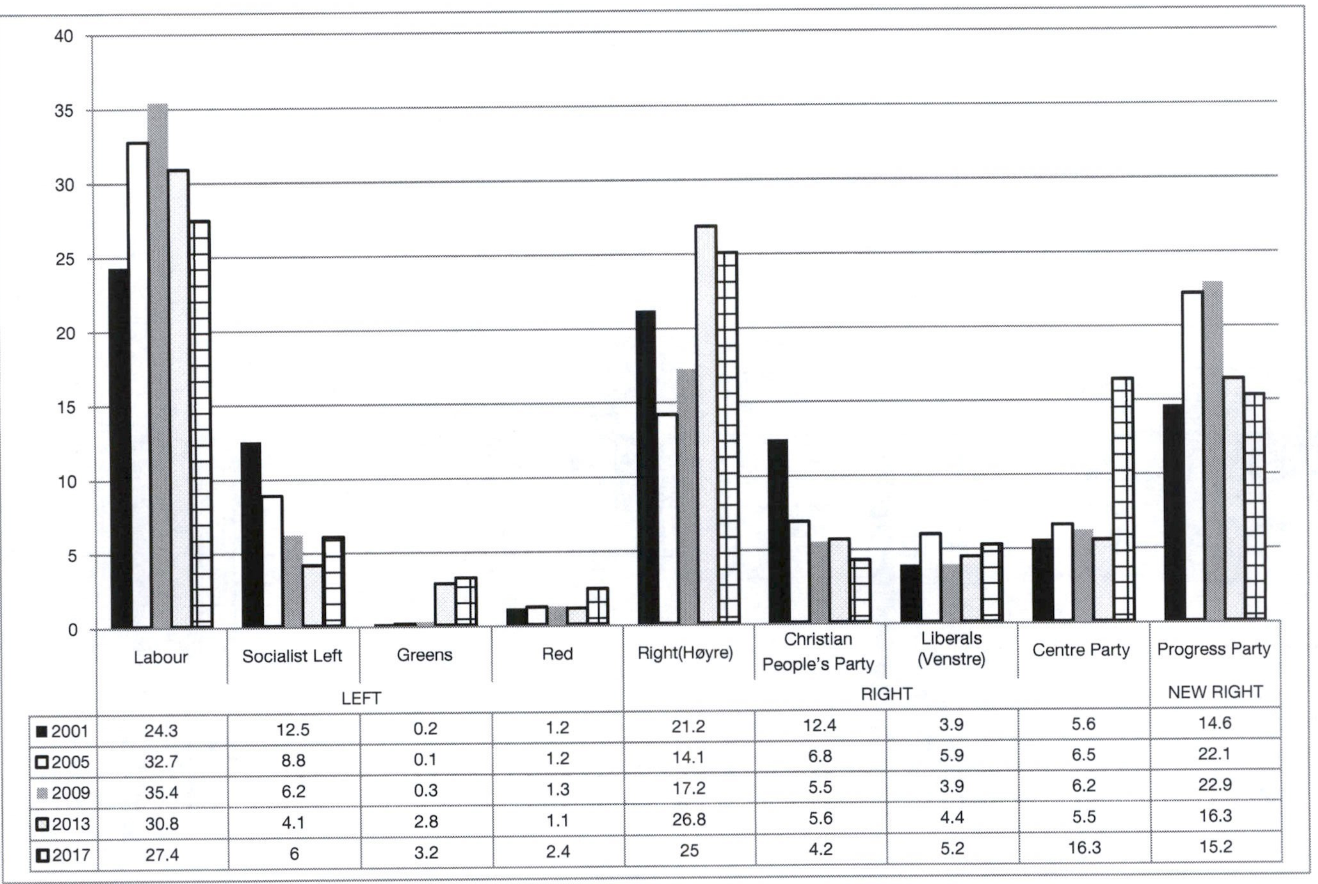

	Labour	Socialist Left	Greens	Red	Right(Høyre)	Christian People's Party	Liberals (Venstre)	Centre Party	Progress Party
2001	24.3	12.5	0.2	1.2	21.2	12.4	3.9	5.6	14.6
2005	32.7	8.8	0.1	1.2	14.1	6.8	5.9	6.5	22.1
2009	35.4	6.2	0.3	1.3	17.2	5.5	3.9	6.2	22.9
2013	30.8	4.1	2.8	1.1	26.8	5.6	4.4	5.5	16.3
2017	27.4	6	3.2	2.4	25	4.2	5.2	16.3	15.2

Figure 7.16 General elections in Norway, 2000–17

Source: Author's graph based on database of Parties and Elections in Europe (2018).

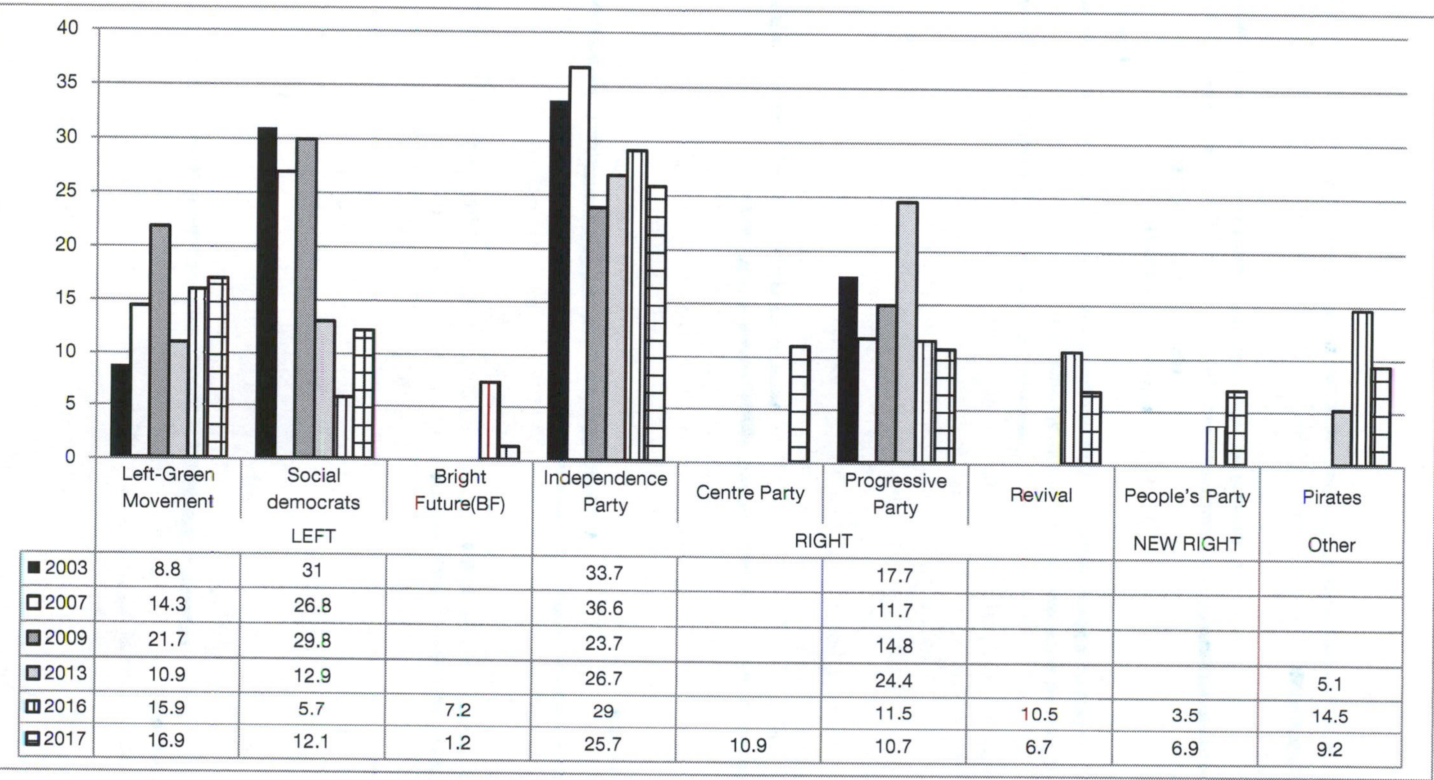

	Left-Green Movement	Social democrats	Bright Future(BF)	Independence Party	Centre Party	Progressive Party	Revival	People's Party	Pirates
	LEFT			RIGHT				NEW RIGHT	Other
2003	8.8	31		33.7		17.7			
2007	14.3	26.8		36.6		11.7			
2009	21.7	29.8		23.7		14.8			
2013	10.9	12.9		26.7		24.4			5.1
2016	15.9	5.7	7.2	29		11.5	10.5	3.5	14.5
2017	16.9	12.1	1.2	25.7	10.9	10.7	6.7	6.9	9.2

Figure 7.17 General elections in Iceland, 2000–17

Source: Author's graph based on database of Parties and Elections in Europe (2018).

The UK and French models: majoritarian democracy at work

The UK

In the UK, the simple majority electoral system tends to lead to a bipolarisation of the party system. The UK model is also the classic majoritarian democracy in Arend Lijphart's typology (see Chapter 4). Two main parties dominate the party and political system, with the main axis of competition being the left-right ideological spectrum: the Labour Party is on the left and the Conservative Party is on the right. However, since the early 1990s, the Liberal Democrats, who are on the left of the Labour Party in many respects, have re-emerged. There has been considerable change in the party system in the UK since the 1960s, with the decline in the class-based vote for the Labour Party contributing to the emergence of an electoral market with spiralling campaign costs (Sanders, 2017: 108–12). Due to the decline of this main cleavage, the party system has become more volatile. The Conservatives clearly are divided about European integration, culminating in the Brexit referendum of June 2016. In spite of the fact that Brexiteers won the referendum, now the party under the leadership of Theresa May is divided between soft (remaining in the Single European Market or Customs Union) and hard Brexiteers (complete break with EU). Labour is divided between the more radical left around Jeremy Corbyn and the more economic liberal New Labour group from Tony Blair's days as leader, the former more Eurosceptic and the latter very pro-European. Today, in 2018, British parties compete in an electoral market that has similar properties to that of the United States. The vast majority of the 650 constituencies are regarded as safe seats for the main parties; however, a small, though increasing, proportion of these seats are leading to real contests between the parties and may change hands from election to election. Moreover, smaller parties, such as the Liberal Democrats, the regionalist Scottish Nationalist Party (SNP) and Plaid Cymru, are also able to create embarrassment for the main parties when they succeed in taking safe seats from them. This was the case during the general elections of 2015, when the SNP was able to win a landslide against Labour in Scotland, becoming the third largest party in the UK.

The majoritarian nature of the UK electoral system creates major distortions in terms of the distribution of seats (Table 7.7). This considerably helps the two main parties, which have greater resources, allowing them to field candidates in all constituencies. The distortion in the distribution became very clear in the general elections of May 2015, in which the Conservative Party with a 36.9 per cent share of the vote got 50.9 per cent of the seats, and the Labour Party with 30.4 per cent share of the vote got 36 per cent of seats. The big loser from election to election has been the Liberal Democratic Party, which got about 7 to 9 per cent of the vote, but only 1.2 per cent of the seats (Green and Prosser, 2015).

More recently, regionalist parties have become important kingmakers at national level. In the 2017 elections, the Conservative Party won the elections, but failed to achieve an absolute majority (Table 7.8). Therefore, Conservative leader Theresa May decided to form a parliamentary legislature agreement with the Democratic Unionist Party (DUP) which had won ten seats (Figure 7.18). Against all the odds, the Labour Party under Jeremy Corbyn succeeded in mobilising the left-wing against Brexit voters and restored the traditional two-party system in the UK.

Table 7.7 The electoral system in general elections in the UK

Electoral system						
	UK	*England*	*Scotland*	*Wales*	*Northern Ireland*	
Number of constituencies	650	533	59	40	18	
Electoral system	Simple plurality system (first-past-the-post)					
Political parties						
National parties			Scottish parties	Welsh parties	Northern Ireland parties	
Social democracy	Liberals	Conservative	Regionalist-Nationalist	Regionalist-Autonomist	Unionist parties	Irish Nationalists
Labour	Liberal Democrat	Conservative and Unionist Party	Scottish National (SNP)	Plaid Cymru	Ulster Unionists (UUP) Democratic Unionists (DUP)	Sinn Fein (SF) Social Democratic and Labour Party (SDLP)

Source: Author.

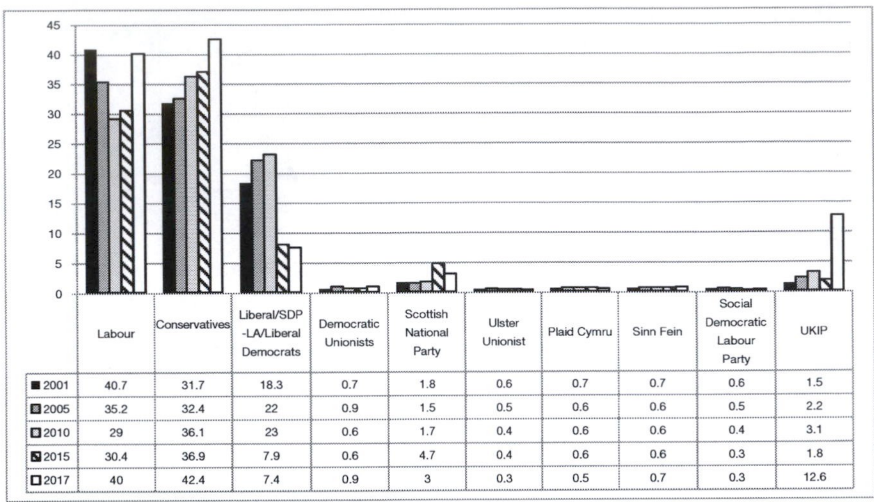

	Labour	Conservatives	Liberal/SDP -LA/Liberal Democrats	Democratic Unionists	Scottish National Party	Ulster Unionist	Plaid Cymru	Sinn Fein	Social Democratic Labour Party	UKIP
2001	40.7	31.7	18.3	0.7	1.8	0.6	0.7	0.7	0.6	1.5
2005	35.2	32.4	22	0.9	1.5	0.5	0.6	0.6	0.5	2.2
2010	29	36.1	23	0.6	1.7	0.4	0.6	0.6	0.4	3.1
2015	30.4	36.9	7.9	0.6	4.7	0.4	0.6	0.6	0.3	1.8
2017	40	42.4	7.4	0.9	3	0.3	0.5	0.7	0.3	12.6

Figure 7.18 General elections in the UK, 2001–17

Source: Author's graph based on database of Parties and Elections in Europe (2018) and *BBC Online* (2018).

Table 7.8 The distribution of seats according to UK region after the 2017 general election (difference with respect to the 2015 general election shown in parentheses)

	England	*Scotland*	*Wales*	*Northern Ireland*	*UK*
Labour Party	227 (+21)	7 (+6)	28 (+3)		262 (+30)
Conservative Party	297 (−22)	13 (+12)	8 (−3)		318 (−13)
Liberal Democratic Party	8 (+2)	4 (+3)	0 (−1)		12 (+4)
Greens	1	0	0	0	1
UKIP	0 (−1)	0	0	0	0
Scottish National Party		35 (−21)			35 (−21)
Plaid Cymru			4 (+1)		4 (+1)
Democratic Unionists				10 (+2)	10 (+2)
Ulster Unionists				0 (−2)	0 (−2)
Sinn Fein				7 (+3)	7 (+3)
Social Democratic and Labour Party				0 (−3)	0 (−3)
Others	0	0	0	1	1
Totals	533	59	40	18	650

Source: *BBC Online* (2018).

In comparison to the Nordic countries, the turnout of the electorate in the UK has been decreasing since the 1970s, reaching an all-time low of 59.6 per cent in the 2005 election. Afterwards, it was between 61–68 per cent. The Brexit referendum has played a major role in mobilising more people to vote, so that the 2017 UK elections became a reflection of the continuing divisions within the country. One major reason seems to be the fact that young people began to realise that they needed to get involved in politics, so they can shape the direction the country is taking.

France

After 1958, the party system of the Fifth Republic was a response to the highly fragmented parliament of the previous regime. The new political system had as its priorities stability and the ability to govern. The new Fifth Republic led to a major change in the electoral system from proportional representation at *département* level to the two-ballot majoritarian system, with a threshold of 12.5 per cent for candidates to reach the second round. Although the electorate continues to be highly fragmented, the majoritarian electoral system forces parties to form coalitions on the right or left in order to increase their overall chances in terms of seats. The main cleavage goes back to the French Revolution, which divided France into a rightwing camp with stronger confessional roots in the Catholic Church, and a leftwing camp, which is secularised and adheres to a staunch republicanism (Tables 7.9 and 7.10).

Due to the electoral system, the party system was for a long time been dominated by a *quadrille bipolaire* (bipolarised four-party system) with a large and small party on the left and the right. On the left, one can find the Socialist Party (PS) and the Communist Party (PCF); on the right the Gaullist Right, which changed its name over time from Rally for the Republic (RPR) (until 2002)/Union for a Popular Movement (UMP) (until 2015)/Les Republicains (LR) (since 2015), and the centrist Union for French Democracy (UDF) (until 2007)/Democratic Movement (MoDem) (since 2007). The Greens tend to work closely with the Socialists. The ideological continuity is much stronger among the left than the right (Bornschier and Lachat, 2009; Cole, 2017: 173–7; Kempf, 2017: 233–44). The relabelling of parties is rather related to personalities who want to become president and then take part in presidential elections. The same happened in the 2017 presidential and legislative elections when Emmanuel Macron created his own supporting party which, for the first time broke, into the polarisation between left and right. Macron's La Republique en Marche (The Republic onwards), more of a pragmatic ideology between left and right, a hybrid party, was able to count on the support of the centrist MoDem. It was the Socialist party in particular that suffered with the positioning of Macron's party between the two poles. Moreover, on the left, the Communist Party had to compete with a former member, the charismatic populist Jean-Luc Meléndron and his France Insoumise (Michel, 2018: 113; Figure 7.19; Tables 7.9 and 7.10). According to Vincenzo Emmanuele, the left-right cleavage seems to be being replaced by an urban-rural cleavage. The largest cities and towns voted for Macron and his party, while the rural areas and small towns voted for Marine Le Pen and her party. What comes to the fore here

Table 7.9 The French electoral system

Electoral system				
System	*Constituencies*	*Election threshold for candidate in first round*	*Threshold for candidates who qualify for second round*	
Two-ballot electoral system	577	At least 25% of the vote	12.5% of vote in first round	
Political parties				
Radical/extreme left	Left	Right	Radical/extreme right	Other
Communist Party (Parti Communist Français – PCF) Indomitable France (La France Insoumise) Radical Party of the Left (Parti Radical de la Gauche – PRG)	Socialist Party (Parti Socialiste – PS)	The Republicans (Les Republicains – LR) Union of Democrats and Independents (Union des Democrates et Independents – UDI)	National Front (Front National – FN)	Greens (Europe Ecologie Les Verts – EELV)
	The Republic onwards (La République en Marche) Democratic Movement (Mouvement Democratique – MoDem)			

Source: Author.

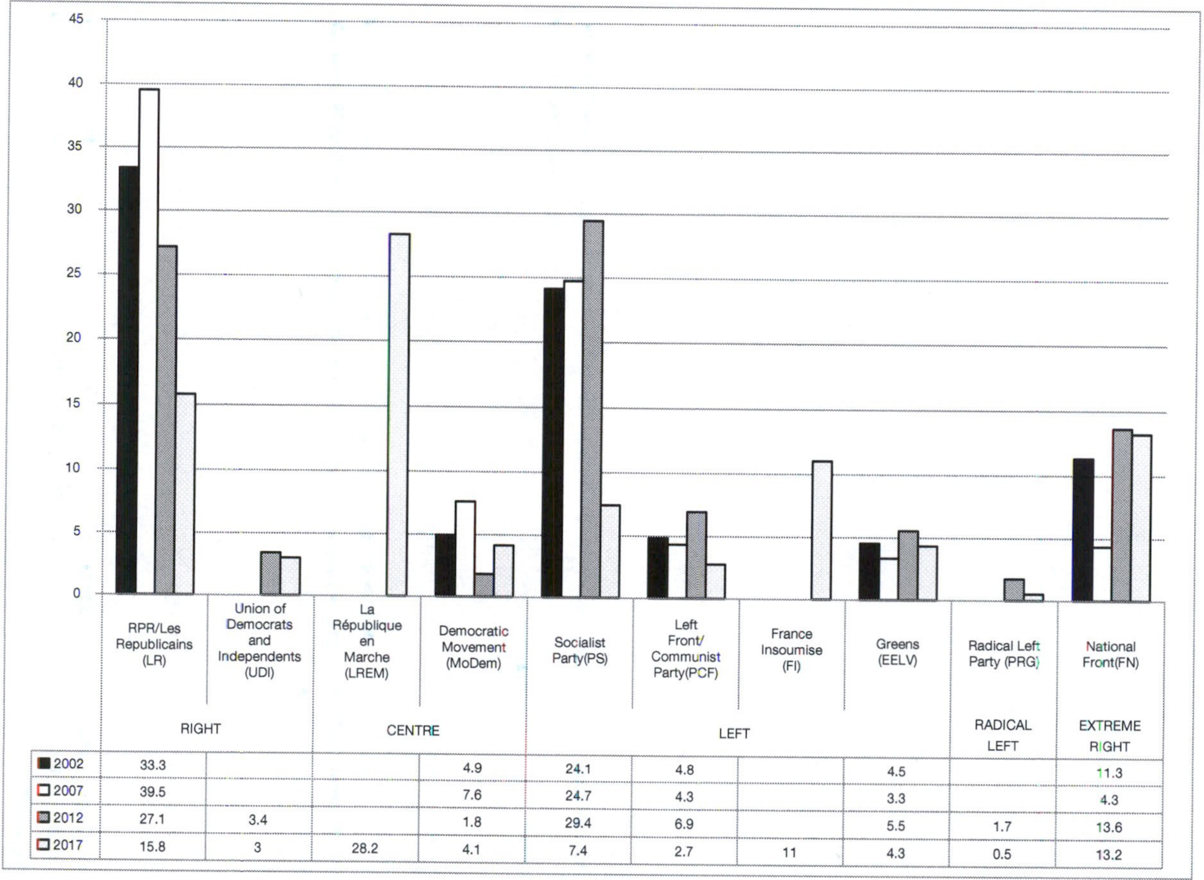

	RPR/Les Republicains (LR)	Union of Democrats and Independents (UDI)	La République en Marche (LREM)	Democratic Movement (MoDem)	Socialist Party(PS)	Left Front/ Communist Party(PCF)	France Insoumise (FI)	Greens (EELV)	Radical Left Party (PRG)	National Front(FN)
	RIGHT		CENTRE		LEFT				RADICAL LEFT	EXTREME RIGHT
2002	33.3			4.9	24.1	4.8		4.5		11.3
2007	39.5			7.6	24.7	4.3		3.3		4.3
2012	27.1	3.4		1.8	29.4	6.9		5.5	1.7	13.6
2017	15.8	3	28.2	4.1	7.4	2.7	11	4.3	0.5	13.2

Figure 7.19 General elections in France, 2002–17

Source: Author's graph based on database of Parties and Elections in Europe (2018).

Table 7.10 The distribution of seats in the first and second rounds in the French general elections, 2017

	First round	*Second round*	*Total*
La Republique en Marche	2	306	308
Les Republicains (LR)		112	112
Democratic Movement (MoDem)		42	42
Socialist Party (PS)		30	30
Union of Democrats and Independents (UDI)	1	17	18
La France Insoumise		17	17
Communist Party (PCF)		10	10
National Front (FN)		8	8
Greens		1	1
Radical Party of the Left (RDG)		3	3
France First (Debout La France)		1	1
Other leftwing parties	1	11	12
Other rightwing parties		6	6
Regionalists		5	5
Other		4	4

Source: Ministère du Interieur (2018).

is the one major cleavage that we can find in most European countries, which is the cleavage between the 'closed' national society and the 'open' globalised one (Emmanuele, 2018b: 91–93). Quite problematic also was the very low turnout at the legislative elections, which was a record low.

Marine Le Pen's FN/RN has been isolated by the other parties due to their anti-immigration and nationalist policies. In 2012 and 2017 the then FN was able to gain three and eight seats respectively in the Assemblée Nationale (Kempf, 2017: 218–25).

For the future, the main question will be whether Macron's new party will be able to change the party system for good, or whether a new polarised party system may emerge. The pace of socioeconomic reforms imposed by president Emmanuel Macron has reduced his popularity.

The Drei-Sat model: Germany, Austria and Switzerland

Although Germany, Austria and Switzerland have distinctive political cultures, they share many commonalities. In spite of different electoral systems, all of them want to achieve the highest level of proportional representation in their respective assemblies.

One of the main characteristics of these three-party systems is that they all have similar parties that belong to the traditional party families, and in all three countries, the traditional cleavages have had their expression in party politics (see Table 7.11). However, Germany and Austria are clearly dominated by a partyocratic structure that leads to cartelisation of politics due to the generous public funding system. The patronage index developed by Peter Mair and his team puts Austria at the top as a result of the generous public party funding system (Sickinger, 2009; Treib, 2012; Von Beyme, 1993, 2017: 166–82). This contrasts heavily with Switzerland, where there is just funding for the parliamentary groups, but not for the political parties or elections (see earlier).

Originally, the German party system could be characterised as a two-and-half party system (Figure 7.20). On the right, is the confessional cleavage represented by the Christian democrats (CDU/CSU). On the left, there are the social democrat (SPD) representatives of the workers-employers cleavage, in spite of their major reform towards a catch-all party in the Bad Godesberg party conference of 1958. A smaller third party are the liberals (FDP), which are always split between those that emphasise economic liberalism and those that are more socially inclined. The FDP was for a long time a kingmaker, because neither of the main two parties was able to achieve an absolute majority. Since 1983, the German party system has become a four-party system, when the Greens were able to achieve representation. At first they were ostracised as a radical party and suspected of being supported by the GDR. However, over time, they became an established party and a governing party in a coalition government of chancellor Gerhard Schröder between 1998 and 2005. After the fall of the Berlin Wall in 1989 and German reunification in 1990, a fifth party emerged which represented mainly the Eastern Länder. It was the transformation of the unity party of the GDR, the SED (Socialist Unity Party of Germany) into the Party of Democratic Socialism (PDS). Later it merged with a splinter of the SPD, the new party Labour and social justice-the electoral choice (WASG) and created the Left Party (die Linke) in 2007. The new party weakened considerably the SPD (Elff and Roßdeutscher, 2017; Von Beyme, 2016: 205–10). Since 2017, Germany has had a six-party system. The conservative new right populist party Alternative for Germany (AfD) achieved representation in the Bundestag. The conservative anti-immigration new right party AfD was founded in 2013 and achieved representation in the European Parliament and some regional parliaments, before becoming a parliamentary group in the Bundestag. After the opening of the borders by chancellor Angela Merkel in the summer 2015, in particular, the AfD gained new élan and was able to mobilise even more voters. While in 2013, the AfD had a 4.7 per cent share of the vote and missed the 5 per cent threshold required for representation, in 2017, the new party got 12.7 per cent and 94 seats. But two MPs decided to leave the party after the elections and are without parliamentary group. The overwhelming majority of voters of the AfD are in the eastern Länder, the former GDR, although there are also voters in the west that voted for the new right-wing party, thereby consolidating it well above the 5 per cent threshold (Siri, 2018).

Although some polarisation between left and right exists, by grouping political parties on the left (SPD, Linke and Greens) and right (CDU/CSU and FDP), no party and, since the legislative elections of 2017, no two parties together on the left or right, have been able to achieve an absolute majority. The only two-party variant is the grand coalition between the CDU/CSU and the SPD, but this

Table 7.11 Political parties in Germany, Austria and Switzerland

	Social Democrats	*Christian Democrats*	*Liberals*	*Greens*	*Die Linke*	*New right populism*
Germany	Sozialdemokratische Partei Deutschlands (SPD)	Christlich-Demokratische Union (CDU) Christlich-Soziale Union (CSU)	Freie Demokratische Partei Deutschlands (FDP)	Grüne/Bündnis '90 (The Greens/ Alliance '90)	Die Linke (The Left)	Alternative für Deutschland (Alternative for Germany – AfD)
Austria	Sozialdemokratische Partei Österreichs (SPÖ)	Österreichische Volkspartei (ÖVP)	Freiheitliche Partei Österreichs (FPÖ) (before 1986) Neues Österreich und Liberales Forum – NEOS (New Austria and Liberal Forum)	Kommunistische Partei Österreichs (KPÖ) Communist Party of Austria (no parliamentary representation)	Grünen-Alternativen Bündnis für die Zukunft Österreichs (BZÖ) (new right party)	Freiheitliche Partei Österreichs (FPÖ) (since 1986) Freedom Party of Austria
Switzerland	Sozialdemokratische Partei der Schweiz (SPS/PS) Social democratic Party of Switzerland	Christlich-Demokratische Volkspartei (CVP) Christian Democratic People's Party (CVP/PPC)	Freisinning Demokratische Partei (FDP/PRD) Liberal Democratic Party of Switzerland	Partei der Arbeit (PdA) Labour Party (very small party)	Grüne Partei der Schweiz (GPS) (Green Party of Switzerland) Grünliberale Partei der Schweiz (GLP) (Greenliberal Party of Switzerland	Schweizerische Volkspartei (SVP/ UDC) Swiss People's Party

Source: Author's compilation.

has only been achieved by a whisker. In 2017, both parties together got 53.5 per cent (Table 7.12), but in 2013 they received 67.2 per cent. This is a problem because the more parties there are in the coalition government, the more there will be political instability. Both Die Linke and the AfD weaken the two main parties. While the CDU/CSU remains the uncontested largest political group of the political system with over 32 per cent, the SPD has been in a permanent crisis since 2005. Although there are different factors that account for this, the lack of leadership or a charismatic strong leader like Gerhard Schröder, Willy Brandt or Helmut Schmidt seems to be one of the major reasons for the crisis (Turner, 2018; Wiliarty, 2018).

The Austrian party system is today a five-party system consisting on the right of the Austrian People's Party, the Freedom Party (FPÖ) and the Liberals (NEOS) and on the left the Social Democratic Party and the Greens. The new right populist Freedom Party is a traditional party of Austria, originally liberal, but after 1986 became a new right populist party led by then leader Jörg Haider. The Liberal Forum, relabelled later as New Austria (NEOS) was a liberal faction that left the Freedom Party in February 1993 as a response to its populist turn. Volatility in the millennium has increased considerably allowing for the emergence of new parties, but not all of them were able to succeed in the long run. In the last elections of 2017, the three traditional parties SPÖ, ÖVP and FPÖ are now of equal electoral strength, reaching between 26 and 30 per cent each. The traditional grand coalition between SPÖ and ÖVP lost considerably in appeal, due to the fact that this had been the main form of government since the late 1940s. The rise of the FPÖ to become one of the dominant parties has remained an important factor for the

Table 7.12 The distribution of seats after the general elections in Germany, 2017

	Share of the vote	*Uninominal*	*PR*	*Included are*		
				Surplus	*Compensatory*	
	Total	*Seats*	*Seats*	*Seats*	*Seats*	*Total seats*
CDU	26.8	185	15	36		200
CSU	6.2	46		7		46
SPD	20.5	59	94	3	19	153
Greens	8.9	1	66		10	67
FDP	10.7		80		15	80
Left Party	9.2	5	64		10	69
AfD	12.6	2	90		11	92
No parliamentary group		1	1			2
		299	410	46	65	709

Source: Bundeswahlleiter (2017).

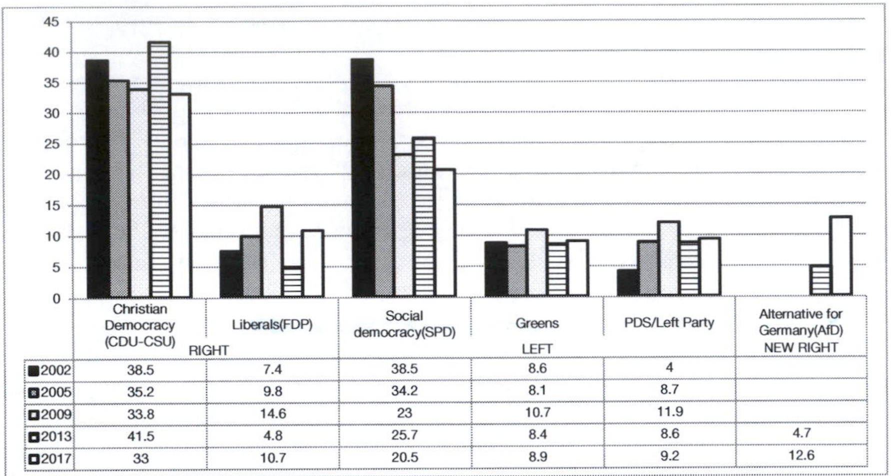

	Christian Democracy (CDU-CSU)	Liberals(FDP)	Social democracy(SPD)	Greens	PDS/Left Party	Alternative for Germany(AfD)
2002	38.5	7.4	38.5	8.6	4	
2005	35.2	9.8	34.2	8.1	8.7	
2009	33.8	14.6	23	10.7	11.9	
2013	41.5	4.8	25.7	8.4	8.6	4.7
2017	33	10.7	20.5	8.9	9.2	12.6

Figure 7.20 General elections in Germany, 2000–17

Source: Author's graph based on database of Parties and Elections in Europe (2018).

political parties in positioning themselves. Only the ÖVP is willing to form coalition governments with the FPÖ, so that since 2000 three such coalitions have been formed in 2000, 2002 and presently after the 2017 general elections. So far the FPÖ has been a responsible party in power (Dolezal and Zeglovits, 2014; Magone, 2017: 132–43; Müller, 2006b; Weisskirchner, 2017) (Figure 7.21).

The Swiss party system has been characterised by the dominance of a group of traditional parties, none of which was able to achieve an absolute majority. The four strongest parties are always represented in government. This 'magic formula' was introduced in 1958 and has since then characterised the allocation of government seats between the political parties. Each member is elected by the joint houses of parliament, and, until 1987, the system worked quite well, leading to stability of the party system. The main political parties were able to achieve approximately the same level of support, so there was no major change in the allocation of seats to the federal council. Until the mid-1990s, the main political parties were the Social Democrats (SPS/PSS), the Radical Democrats (FDP/PRD) and the Christian Democrats (CVP/PDC), each of them being among the parties that received most of the votes as well as the smaller Party of Farmers, Shopowners and Citizens (BGB). Since 1991, the BGB has transformed into a populist anti-immigration and anti-EU party with the name Swiss People's Party (SVP). Their leader was the charismatic businessman Christoph Blocher from the canton Zurich. He introduced a new rightwing populist discourse against increased taxation, immigration and membership of the EU. The rejection of membership of the European Economic Area (EEA) in December 1992 was a key victory for the party. Since then, the popularity of the Swiss People's Party has been increasing from election to election. It is now the largest party with about 30 per cent of the vote. Although Blocher retired from party office, his daughter and wife are strongly involved in the party and he remains an important figure in the background (for more detail, see Ladner, 2004, 2014; see also Vatter, 2014: chapter 4) (Figure 7.22).

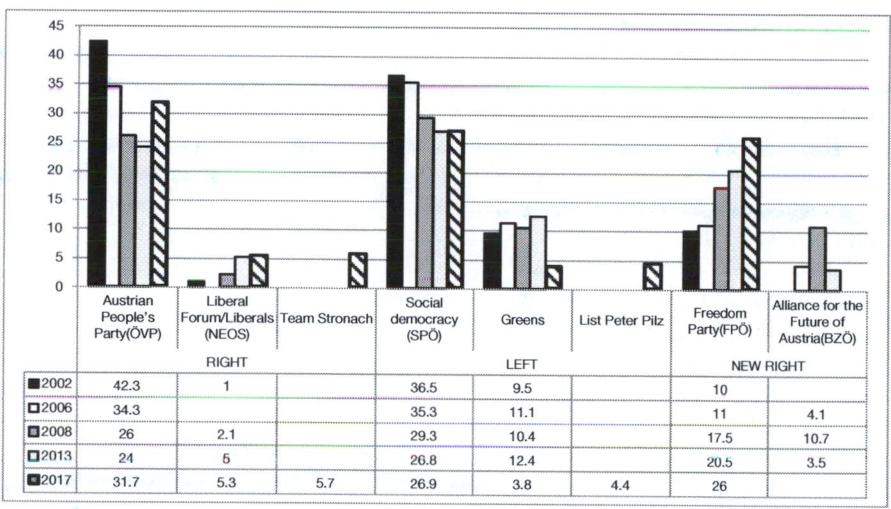

	Austrian People's Party(ÖVP)	Liberal Forum/Liberals (NEOS)	Team Stronach	Social democracy (SPÖ)	Greens	List Peter Pilz	Freedom Party(FPÖ)	Alliance for the Future of Austria(BZÖ)
2002	42.3	1		36.5	9.5		10	
2006	34.3			35.3	11.1		11	4.1
2008	26	2.1		29.3	10.4		17.5	10.7
2013	24	5		26.8	12.4		20.5	3.5
2017	31.7	5.3	5.7	26.9	3.8	4.4	26	

Figure 7.21 General elections in Austria, 2000–18

Source: Author's graph based on database of Parties and Elections in Europe (2018).

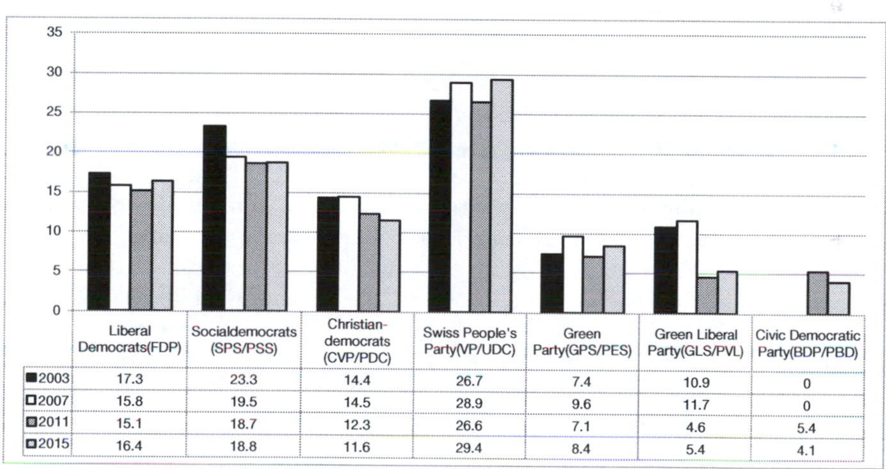

	Liberal Democrats(FDP)	Socialdemocrats (SPS/PSS)	Christian-democrats (CVP/PDC)	Swiss People's Party(VP/UDC)	Green Party(GPS/PES)	Green Liberal Party(GLS/PVL)	Civic Democratic Party(BDP/PBD)
2003	17.3	23.3	14.4	26.7	7.4	10.9	0
2007	15.8	19.5	14.5	28.9	9.6	11.7	0
2011	15.1	18.7	12.3	26.6	7.1	4.6	5.4
2015	16.4	18.8	11.6	29.4	8.4	5.4	4.1

Figure 7.22 General elections in Switzerland, 2000–17

Source: Author's graph based on database of Parties and Elections in Europe (2018).

Party systems and the single transferable vote: Ireland and Malta

Ireland and Malta are the only European countries that use the oldest electoral system in the world (see Table 7.13): the single transferable vote (STV), which is a proportional representation system that allows voters to rank candidates according to their preferences. All preferences are counted, so that it takes a long time to get an accurate result. In a similar way to the UK, MPs are strongly involved with their particular rural or urban constituency. The dangers of clientelism and patronage are always a present reality in this system of party politics (Farrell, 1999: 31–2; Weeks, 2010: 148).

In Ireland, the main cleavage is a historical one, which goes back to the emergence of the Irish Free State out of the British Empire, and the Treaty that was signed with the British government. The main party struggling for independence, Sinn Fein ('Ourselves'), split into two. One party supported the Treaty and became known as Fine Gael ('family group of the Gaels' [Irish]), while the opponents to the Treaty formed Fianna Fail ('the warriors of destiny'). After 1932, Fianna Fail became the predominant party. Fine Gael had a weaker social base and had to form coalitions with other smaller parties, particularly the Labour Party, in order to come to power (Farrell, 1999: 30–1). Similarly to the UK, the Irish party system is traditionally regarded as a two-and-a-half party system, with, in 2010, one predominant party, Fianna Fail (Farrell, 1999: 32; Weeks, 2010: 147).

However, since the late 1980s, there has been a considerable party system change that has led to the emergence of new parties, all of which emerged as breakaway factions of the main parties. One important new party is the Progressive Democrats, which emerged out of a breakaway faction of Fianna Fail in 1987. Previously, in the 1960s and 1970s, Sinn Fein split and one of the new parties became the Workers' Party; then, in 1992, seven MPs of the Workers' Party formed the Left Democrats. Furthermore, the Green Party emerged in the late 1980s. The consequence of all this is that the Irish party system has become fairly volatile in the past few decades (Farrell, 1999: 40–4), with a change of government at almost every election since the 1970s (Figure 7.23).

The finance crisis affected Ireland and its party system considerably. The EU bailout also affected the major parties considerably, but national interest was put above party politics, so that the party system was able to survive these difficult times (Mair, 2008b; Little, 2012, 2017). The mismanagement of the financial crisis by prime minister Brian Cowen's Fianna Fail government in 2010–11 saw the return of Fine Gael to power. It formed a coalition with the Labour party and was able to count on the support of the other parties in parliament due to the dire situation. The party was overwhelmingly defeated in the 2016 elections, but new

Table 7.13 The use of single transferable voting in Ireland (2016) and Malta (2017)

Country	*Number of seats*	*Number and size of constituencies*
Ireland	158 (since 2016, previously 166)	40 constituencies (since 2016, previously 43) • 11 with 5 seats • 16 with 4 seats • 13 with 3 seats
Malta	65 (in 2017, with compensatory seats: 67)	13 constituencies with 5 seats to be elected

Source: Author's own calculations, based on database elections of Ireland (2018) and the election commission of Malta (2018).

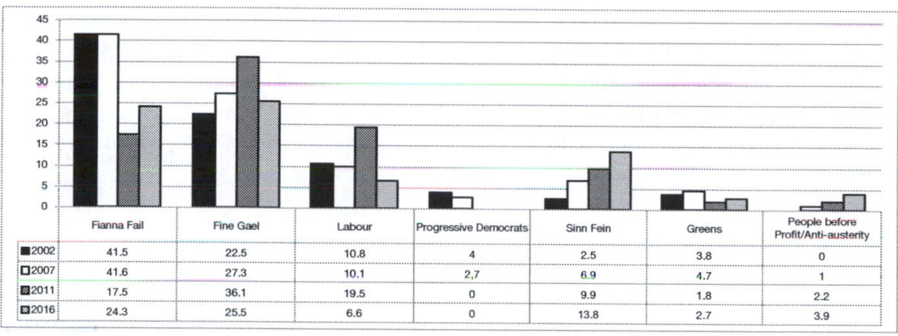

	Fianna Fail	Fine Gael	Labour	Progressive Democrats	Sinn Fein	Greens	People before Profit/Anti-austerity
2002	41.5	22.5	10.8	4	2.5	3.8	0
2007	41.6	27.3	10.1	2,7	6.9	4.7	1
2011	17.5	36.1	19.5	0	9.9	1.8	2.2
2016	24.3	25.5	6.6	0	13.8	2.7	3.9

Figure 7.23 Irish general elections, 2000–16

Source: Author's graph based on database of Parties and Elections in Europe (2018).

leader Leo Varadkar was able to form a single party minority government tolerated by parliament.

Although the Maltese party system is more polarised than in Ireland, the constituency-based networks of clientelism and patronage play an important role in the political system. The Labour Party and the conservative Nationalist Party are the two main parties, regularly alternating in power. Since 2005, there have been thirteen districts with five seats each (a total of sixty-five seats). Because of the complexity of the voting system, some parties were able to get more seats than the actual electoral share. This led to the introduction of a rule in 1982 that the party that gets the most first preference votes will form the government. Another feature of the Maltese party system is that the personal relationship of candidates to their constituencies leads to highly partisan campaigns at local level. This also translates into high turnouts of more than 90 per cent of registered voters. In spite of the complexity of the voting system, the number of spoiled ballot papers is quite low and has been reducing over time (Farrell et al., 1996; Hirczy de Miño and Lane, 1999; Figure 7.24).

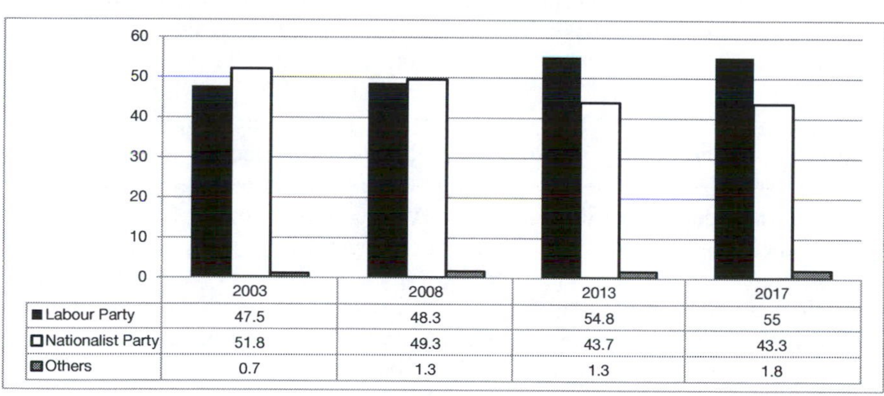

	2003	2008	2013	2017
Labour Party	47.5	48.3	54.8	55
Nationalist Party	51.8	49.3	43.7	43.3
Others	0.7	1.3	1.3	1.8

Figure 7.24 Maltese general elections, 2000–17

Source: Author's graph based on database of Parties and Elections in Europe (2018).

Due to the size of the countries, patronage, clientelism and gerrymandering are features inherent in the party and political system.

In sum, the use of the single transferable vote in Ireland and Malta has produced two quite different party systems. The Irish party system is fragmented, while the Maltese system is characterised by a polarisation of the two main parties.

The Benelux countries

In Belgium, the Netherlands and Luxembourg proportional representation is the electoral system used. Owing to the fragmentation of the party system, political parties have to work together. All three are considered consensus democracies, and Arend Lijphart highlighted that the Netherlands was the country used for his typology of consensus and majoritarian democracies (see Chapter 4).

The most complex case of the three is probably Belgium. The federalisation of Belgium after 1993 led to the establishment of two independent party systems in Wallonia and Flanders, but in spite of these two separate electoral areas with their own dynamics, the political parties are almost the same in the two parts of Belgium. The electoral results in the two electoral arenas are also counted together in terms of the national vote, which means that political parties of the same ideological family are formally separate and independent entities. Nonetheless, their ideological affinity and common history leads to cooperation at national level. The complexity of the Belgian party system started in the 1980s, when the parties divided into two and created their dynamics in the two parts of the country. Moreover, after the 1999 elections, many Belgian parties decided to change their labels in order to appeal to particular electorates. The two regional electoral markets produced an extremely fragmented party system. All parties are quite small in terms of electoral share. The largest party in the 2014 elections was the independentist moderate New Flemish Alliance (N-VA) with 20.3 per cent of the vote, based in Flanders (for more detail, see Deschouwer, 2004, 2009: 106–20).

In Wallonia, the Socialist Party (PS) and the Liberals (MR) dominate the party system. The PS can rely on a strong subculture based on the traditional cleavages. However, de-industrialisation since the 1970s has created a major crisis among this electorate, so that its social basis is eroding steadily. The liberals can rely on a long standing tradition going back to the nineteenth century. It was actually the main party along with the Catholics/Christian Democrats until the end of the nineteenth century. However, PS and MR received just 9 to 12 per cent each in the new millennium and are weaker than the parties in Flanders. The Flemish party system has been quite volatile. Traditionally dominated by the Christian Democrats (CD&V), it has been challenged by the spin-off NV-A that follows similar ideas but wants independence from Belgium. This moderate independentist party sometimes uses populist language and this has been heavily criticised. For a long time, the extreme/new right Vlaams Belang (National Interest) was setting the agenda in Flanders. In 2007, it had reached 12 per cent nationwide, but since then it has been challenged successfully by N-VA, so that in 2014 it declined to just 3.7 per cent. Certainly, Lieven de Winter, Marc Swyngedouw and Patrick Dumont are quite right in questioning whether the Belgian party systems are moving towards Balkanisation due to their high levels of fragmentation. Problems with the coordination of national governance have emerged which affect directly the efficiency of the system, in particular related to coalition formation and governance (André and Depauw, 2015; Delwit, 2011; Deschouwer, 2009: 120–32; De Winter et al., 2006; Van Aelst and Louwerse, 2014; on political parties, see the excellent volume by Delwit et al., 2011) (Figure 7.25).

The Dutch party system changed considerably in the 1970s, with the decline of the Christian democratic parties. As a result of the very friendly electoral system, parties are able to achieve representation quite easily. A political party only needs 0.67 per cent of the vote to gain a seat. This means that the Dutch parliament is highly fragmented, with over ten parties in it. Traditionally, the Christian democrats (CDA), the social democrats (PvDA) and the liberals (VVD) represent the three main subcultures of the country. However, its social base has been eroding since the 1970s, with the 'heartlands' of the Christian democrats, social democrats and liberals (based on class and religion cleavages) being eroded and replaced by a battlefield in which parties have to compete for all the votes. Today, none of the three parties reaches more than 30 per cent of the vote. In 1982, these three parties together gained 82 per cent of the vote, but in the 2012 and 2017 elections this figure had decreased to 59.7 and then 39.3 per cent respectively. Huib Pelikaan, Tom Van der Meer and Sarah De Lange discovered that apart from economic (state intervention-more market) and ethical issues (moral laws-neutral government), a third dimension has been emerging since the 1990s, which comprises the so-called communitarian dimension of parties between those that want a unicultural Dutch culture and those that are supportive of multiculturalism. In the early millennium most parties would place themselves in a pro-market and unicultural position, with only the Groenleft on the other side, followed by the SP and PvDA. As a consequence, the party system changed from a depolicised one to a centrifugal polarised one (Pelikaan et al., 2003: 26, 42).

Traditional Dutch politics was shaken up by the appearance of a charismatic new politician called Pim Fortuyn in 2002. Fortuyn was a professor of sociology at Rotterdam Erasmus University and used very direct language to address issues that were relevant for at least part of the Dutch population, including immigration, policies of integration, and other law and order issues. Although he had a populist rightwing discourse on certain issues, it was fairly liberal on others. Shortly before the elections of 2002, Pim Fortuyn was killed by Volkert van der Graaf, an animal protection activist (who, allegedly, opposed Pim Fortuyn's policies against the Muslim population). The death of Fortuyn led to a considerable share of the vote for his PFL – his party received 17 per cent of the vote and it was interpreted by most commentators as a sympathy vote for him. The PFL became part of the first coalition government of Jan Peter Balkenende (CDA), but their participation did not last long because of the continual infighting of the leaders of the PFL over policy and personal issues (Van Praag, 2003: 16–18; Van Holsteyn and Irwin, 2003). After early elections in 2003, the PFL's share declined to 5.7 per cent and, later, in the 2006 elections it declined further to 0.2 per cent. The party had to dissolve at end of that year. In the 2006 elections, a new populist anti-immigration party called Party of Freedom (PVV), under the leadership of charismatic Geert Wilders, emerged. It won 5.4 per cent of the vote and nine seats. Potentially, PVV could have become the largest party in the Netherlands in the 2017 elections according to the opinion polls, but in the final weeks the VVD was able to surpass it.

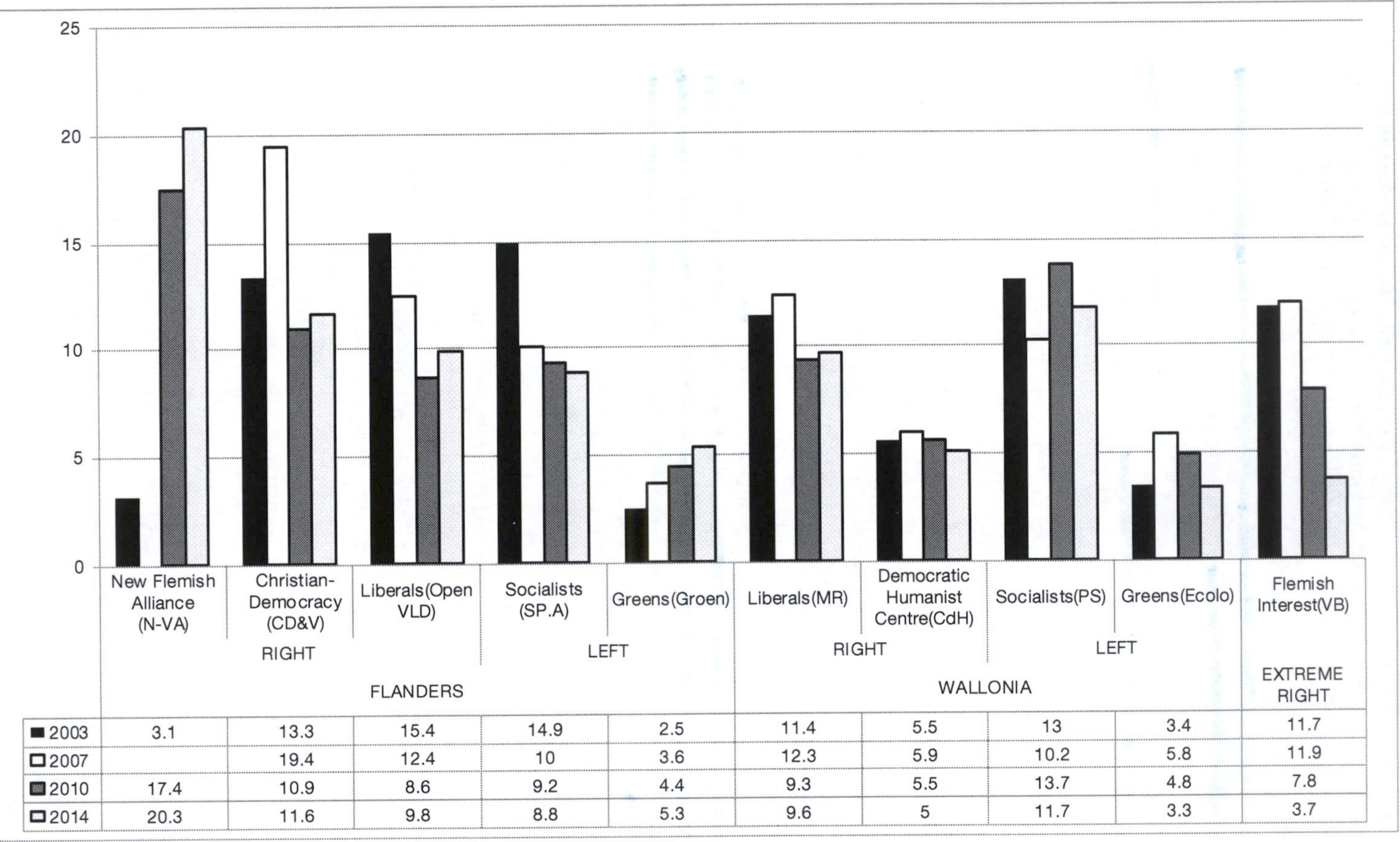

	New Flemish Alliance (N-VA)	Christian-Democracy (CD&V)	Liberals(Open VLD)	Socialists (SP.A)	Greens(Groen)	Liberals(MR)	Democratic Humanist Centre(CdH)	Socialists(PS)	Greens(Ecolo)	Flemish Interest(VB)
2003	3.1	13.3	15.4	14.9	2.5	11.4	5.5	13	3.4	11.7
2007		19.4	12.4	10	3.6	12.3	5.9	10.2	5.8	11.9
2010	17.4	10.9	8.6	9.2	4.4	9.3	5.5	13.7	4.8	7.8
2014	20.3	11.6	9.8	8.8	5.3	9.6	5	11.7	3.3	3.7

Figure 7.25 Belgian general elections, 2000–14

Source: Author's graph based on Parties and Elections in Europe (2018).

The PVV received 13 per cent and VVD 21.2 percent. All this demonstrates that the immigration and integration discussion is far from over in the Netherlands. It also means that the other parties are under pressure to follow tougher policies on immigration. Furthermore, the radical leftwing Socialist Party (SP) achieved a remarkable improvement from 6.3 per cent in 2003 to 16.6 per cent in 2006. One of the main reasons for the rise of the Socialist Party was that the population was extremely dissatisfied with the implementation of quite an austere reform plan on the part of the government that particularly affected the weaker parts of Dutch society. Overall, Dutch parties have become fairly pragmatic and have adjusted to the electoral market. The consensual nature of politics allows for coalition-building based on the results (Thomassen, 2014; Van Holsteyn, 2018; Figure 7.26).

In Luxembourg, the main political parties have been able to keep their central position in the political system. The Christian Socials (CSV) are still the dominant party in the party system and are regularly challenged by the social democrats (LSAP). The third party is the liberal democratic party (DP) which regularly comes to power as part of a coalition government with the CSV or LSAP. In the 2013 elections, DP was able to secure the prime minister's position, in spite of being just the third largest party with 18.3 per cent. Xavier Bettel, former mayor of Luxembourg, leads a coalition government with the LSAP and the Greens. In the 2018 general elections, all three main parties declined in their electoral share, but the Greens increased to 15.1 per cent. Also the Pirate party was able to increase its vote, making the party system more fragmented and volatile. Other smaller parties are the Left Party (De Lénk) and the Alternative Democratic Reform Party (ADR) (Dumont et al., 2009; Figure 7.27).

Turnout in all three countries has been particularly high. Compulsory voting in Belgium and in the Netherlands between 1917 and 1970 were important in keeping the numbers above the 80 per cent threshold. Compulsory voting is still responsible in Belgium and Luxembourg for high turnouts of between 87 and 91 per cent in the past decades. In the Netherlands, it still achieves between 74 and 81 per cent. Although failing to vote will lead to sanctions, in reality in the case of Luxembourg no one has been punished since 1964. It seems that for all three countries it has become a taken for granted obligation that was passed on from generation to generation (*Luxembourg Times*, 4 November 2018).

The Southern European countries

Party systems in Southern Europe have become more bipolarised since the 1980s, and this has led to the establishment of two main parties/electoral coalitions with equal electoral strength as well as two or more smaller parties. Although party systems in Southern Europe have many common features, there are still major differences, for example, between Italy and the democracies of Portugal, Spain and Greece that emerged after 1974–5. During and after the euro and financial crises (2008–15), new party systems emerged in Greece and Spain, while Italy has remained in a state of volatility due to the weak cohesion of parties and party alliances. In spite of high levels of volatility only Portugal's party system has remained more or less intact (for a summary until 2003, see Magone, 2003: chapter 4).

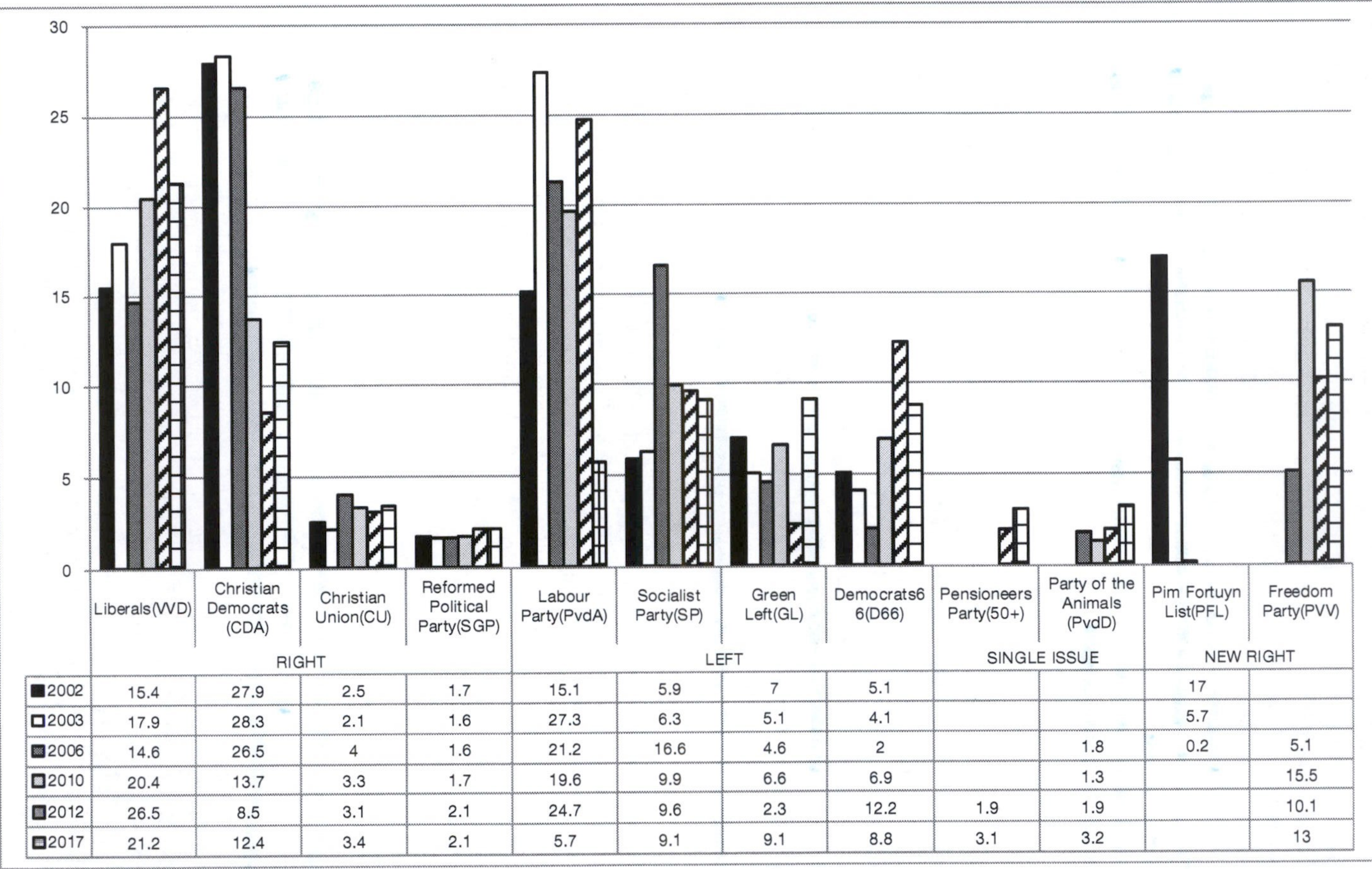

	Liberals(VVD)	Christian Democrats (CDA)	Christian Union(CU)	Reformed Political Party(SGP)	Labour Party(PvdA)	Socialist Party(SP)	Green Left(GL)	Democrats6 6(D66)	Pensioneers Party(50+)	Party of the Animals (PvdD)	Pim Fortuyn List(PFL)	Freedom Party(PVV)
	RIGHT				LEFT				SINGLE ISSUE		NEW RIGHT	
2002	15.4	27.9	2.5	1.7	15.1	5.9	7	5.1			17	
2003	17.9	28.3	2.1	1.6	27.3	6.3	5.1	4.1			5.7	
2006	14.6	26.5	4	1.6	21.2	16.6	4.6	2		1.8	0.2	5.1
2010	20.4	13.7	3.3	1.7	19.6	9.9	6.6	6.9		1.3		15.5
2012	26.5	8.5	3.1	2.1	24.7	9.6	2.3	12.2	1.9	1.9		10.1
2017	21.2	12.4	3.4	2.1	5.7	9.1	9.1	8.8	3.1	3.2		13

Figure 7.26 General elections in the Netherlands, 2000–17

Source: Author's graph based on database of Parties and Elections in Europe (2018).

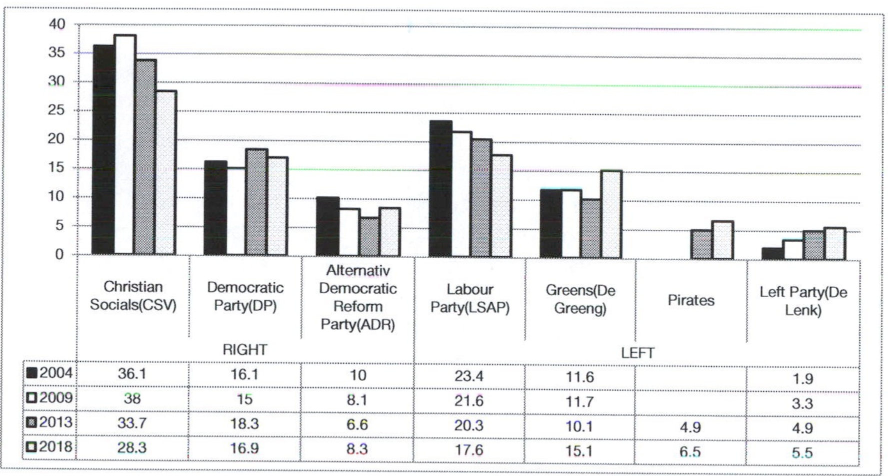

	Christian Socials(CSV)	Democratic Party(DP)	Alternativ Democratic Reform Party(ADR)	Labour Party(LSAP)	Greens(De Greeng)	Pirates	Left Party(De Lenk)
■2004	36.1	16.1	10	23.4	11.6		1.9
□2009	38	15	8.1	21.6	11.7		3.3
▩2013	33.7	18.3	6.6	20.3	10.1	4.9	4.9
□2018	28.3	16.9	8.3	17.6	15.1	6.5	5.5

Figure 7.27 General elections in Luxembourg, 2000–18

Source: Author's graph based on database of Parties and Elections in Europe (2008).

As already mentioned, Italian politics after 1945 has to be divided into two main periods with their respective party systems. Between 1945 and 1992, a party system based on proportional representation led to the creation of an imperfect bipolarism (*bipolarismo imperfetto*) based on a centre-right block around Christian Democracy (DC) and five smaller parties on the one hand, and the Communist Party (PCI) on the other. In the context of the Cold War, Christian Democracy always remained in power in coalition governments with the five smaller parties, to make sure that the Communist Party would not come to power (Hine, 1993). This lack of alternation in power is what is meant by being an imperfect bipolarism (for more detail, see Hine, 1993). However, a decline in the share of the vote of DC and the difficulty of forming stable majorities led to the erosion of the system in the 1980s (Leonardi and Wertman, 1989). Also the Communist Party was looking for a new identity both before and after the fall of the Berlin Wall (Daniels and Bull, 1994). Finally, in 1992, a web of systemic corruption around DC and the other five parties led to the collapse of the party system (Rhodes, 1997).

Since 1993, there have been three electoral systems in place to engineer a majoritarian polarised two-party system. However, such a two-party system only partly materialised due to the fact that most parties had weak party structures. The realignment and polarisation also led to a de-ideologisation of the party programmes and a growing personalisation. The main problem is that the bipolarisation was only partly achieved, because the behaviour of MPs in parliament followed the logics of the pre-1993 political culture, in which personalisation and defections were common. As a consequence, throughout the legislature, the original bipolarisation has been characterised by a process of fragmentation, with new parties emerging in parliament (Tarchi, 2018).

Among the most innovative parties is the former Forza Italia, characterised as a 'firm party' (*partito azienda*) or a 'media-mediated personality party', because it was founded and established by the firms of tycoon Silvio Berlusconi using marketing techniques usually used in business (Seisselberg, 1996: 717). Forza Italia was founded in 1994 and, since then, has been shaping the way the party system has evolved (Donovan, 2015). Berlusconi's party has always been part of the centre-right coalition of parties, which included Northern League and post-fascist new right parties such as National Alliance (AN) or Brothers of Italy (Fratelli di Italia) (Tarchi, 2018).

On the centre-left, the Democratic Party (Partito Democratico – PD) has been the dominant party, able to form a coalition with others to compete with the centre-right block. PD emerged out of the PCI by becoming the Democrats of the Left in 1996, and then with other parties, the PD in 2007 (Bardi, 2007: 720; Ventura, 2018) (Figures 7.28 and 7.29; Table 7.14).

In the 2018 elections, Silvio Berlusconi's Forza Italia was part of the centre-right block with the Lega Nord (LN), which was a regionalist-independentist party in the 1990s, but today it has become a national party with strong anti-immigration positions and the new right/post-fascist Brothers of Italy (FdI). The centre-left is dominated by the Democratic Party (PD). Since 2013, the Italian party system has also had a third populist party, the Five Star Movement (M5S) of Beppo Grillo, presently led by Luigi di Maio, which since 2013 has become the largest party in terms of vote share. In 2018, M5S received 32.7 per cent of the vote. The innovative coalition government between M5S and Lega Nord is still too recent to make an assessment.

In terms of political space, the party system seems to be changing from a left-right system to positive and negative positions towards the EU. Clearly, the legislative elections of 2018 have transformed the Eurosceptic regionalist Lega Nord and Beppe Grillo's M5S into important national parties, challenging Berlusconi's Forza Italia and the Democratic Party (Gianetti et al., 2017).

One of the big successes of democratisation in Portugal, Spain and Greece is that all three party systems were fairly well consolidated until the financial and euro crises. Between 1974 and 2008, there was, generally, continuity of the political parties and also of the electoral share of the vote (Table 7.15). The big exception was Spain in 1982, when the governmental party, the centre-right Union of Democratic Centre (Unión del Centro Democratico – UCD), collapsed

Table 7.14 The main Italian political parties, 2018

Centre-right	*Centre-left*	*Citizens' movements/ populists*
• Forza Italia (FI) • Lega Nord (LN) • Brothers of Italy (Fratelli di Italia –FdI) • We with Italy-Christian Democratic Union (Noi con Italia/Union Democratica Cristiana – NcI-UDC)	• Democratic Party (Partito Democratico) • More Europe (Piú Europe +E) • Other smaller parties including the South Tyrolean People's Party (Südtiroler Volkspartei – SVP)	• Five Star Movement (Movimento 5 Stelle – M5S)

Source: Author.

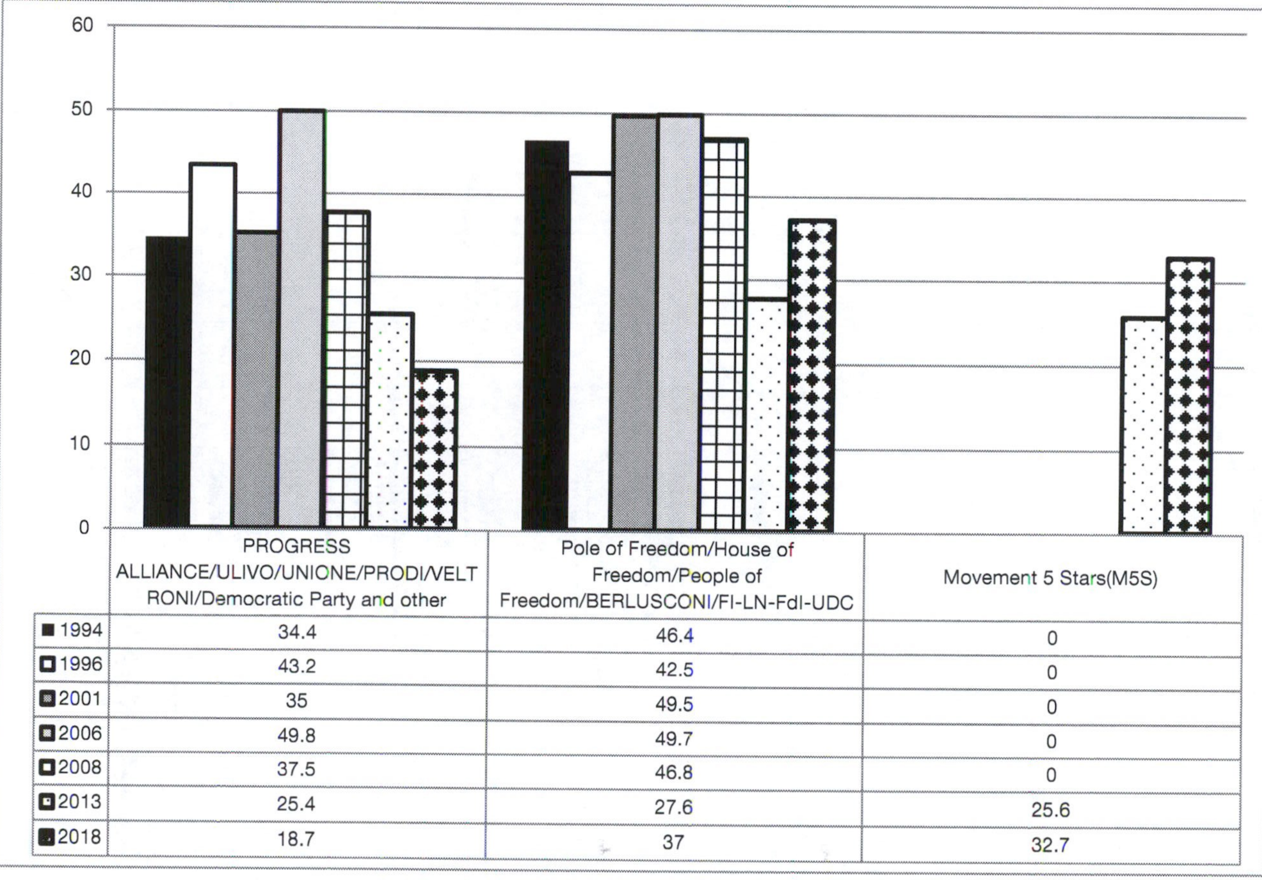

	PROGRESS ALLIANCE/ULIVO/UNIONE/PRODI/VELTRONI/Democratic Party and other	Pole of Freedom/House of Freedom/People of Freedom/BERLUSCONI/FI-LN-FdI-UDC	Movement 5 Stars(M5S)
1994	34.4	46.4	0
1996	43.2	42.5	0
2001	35	49.5	0
2006	49.8	49.7	0
2008	37.5	46.8	0
2013	25.4	27.6	25.6
2018	18.7	37	32.7

Figure 7.28 Elections in Italy according to the two main electoral coalitions/parties, 1994–2018

Source: Author's graph based on database of Parties and Elections in Europe (2018).

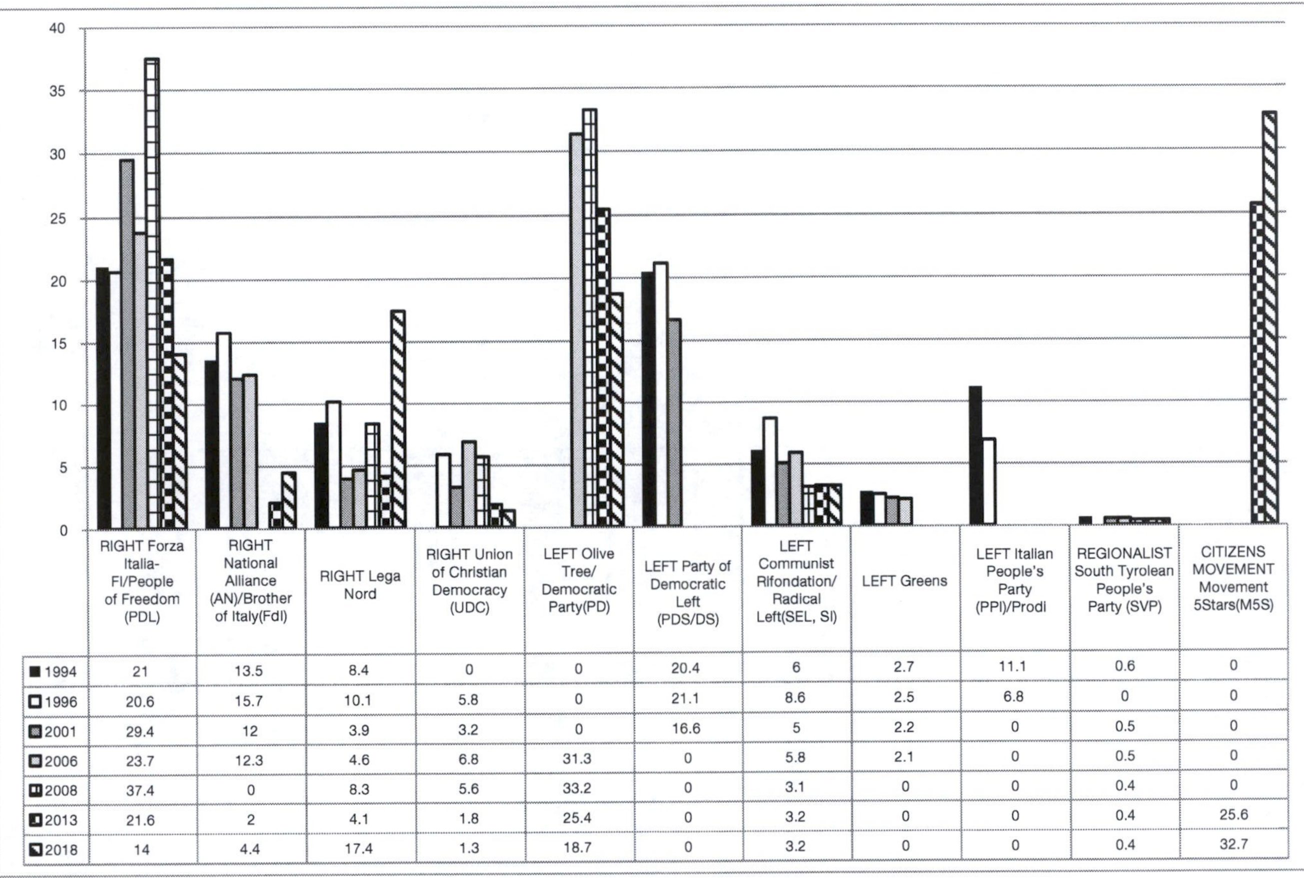

	RIGHT Forza Italia-FI/People of Freedom (PDL)	RIGHT National Alliance (AN)/Brother of Italy(FdI)	RIGHT Lega Nord	RIGHT Union of Christian Democracy (UDC)	LEFT Olive Tree/ Democratic Party(PD)	LEFT Party of Democratic Left (PDS/DS)	LEFT Communist Rifondation/ Radical Left(SEL, SI)	LEFT Greens	LEFT Italian People's Party (PPI)/Prodi	REGIONALIST South Tyrolean People's Party (SVP)	CITIZENS MOVEMENT Movement 5Stars(M5S)
1994	21	13.5	8.4	0	0	20.4	6	2.7	11.1	0.6	0
1996	20.6	15.7	10.1	5.8	0	21.1	8.6	2.5	6.8	0	0
2001	29.4	12	3.9	3.2	0	16.6	5	2.2	0	0.5	0
2006	23.7	12.3	4.6	6.8	31.3	0	5.8	2.1	0	0.5	0
2008	37.4	0	8.3	5.6	33.2	0	3.1	0	0	0.4	0
2013	21.6	2	4.1	1.8	25.4	0	3.2	0	0	0.4	25.6
2018	14	4.4	17.4	1.3	18.7	0	3.2	0	0	0.4	32.7

Figure 7.29 General elections in Italy according to the main parties, 1994–2018

Source: Author's graph based on database of Parties and Elections in Europe (2018)

Table 7.15 The main political parties in Southern Europe

	Social Democrats	*Christian Democrats/ Conservatives*	*Liberals*	*Communists*	*Radical Left*	*Other parties*	*Regionalist-nationalist parties*
Portugal	Socialist Party (Partido Socialista – PS)	Social democratic Party (Partido Socialdemocrata – PSD) Democratic Social Centre-People's Party (Centro Democratico Social-Partido Popular – CDS-PP)		Portuguese communist parties-Green Party Partido Comunista Portugues-Partido Os Verdes – PCP-PEV	Block of the Left (Bloco da Esquerda – BE)	Party of Animals and Nature (Partido dos Animais e Natureza)	
Spain	Partido Socialista Obrero Español (PSOE)	Partido Popular (PP)	Citizens (Ciudadanos – Cs)	United We Can (Unidos Podemos) Rather a coalition of two parties (United Left and Podemos)		Convergencia i Unió (CiU) Partido Nacionalista Vasco (PNV)	Catalonia European and Catalan Democratic Party (PdeCAT) Catalan Republican Left (Esquerra Republicana Catalana – ERC) Basque Country Basque Nationalist Party (Partido Nacionalista Vasco – PNV) Basque Country Rally (Euskal Herria Bildu –EH Bildu) Canary Islands Canary Coalition (Coalición Canaria – CC9
Greece	Panhellenio Sosialistisko Kinima (PASOK)	Nea Dimokratia (ND)		Kommunistiko Komma Ellada (KKE)	Synaspismos tis Rizospastikis Aristeras (Syriza)	Golden Dawn (Chrysi Avyi – XA) The River (To Potami) Independent Greeks (Anexartitoi Ellines – ANEL) Union of Centrists (Einosi Kentron – EK)	

Source: Author.

and contributed to the emergence of the Socialist Party (PSOE) as the dominant party. As already mentioned, Southern European and Central and Eastern European political parties have only partially had a similar development to the more established democracies in the north and west of Europe. From the very beginning, new political groups were cartel parties that were and are still highly dependent on public funding.

In Portugal, the party system has remained almost the same since the founding elections of 1975. Originally a four-party system, it is now a five-party system with two dominant parties, the socialists (PS) and the social democrats (PSD), with an almost equal share of the vote, and three smaller parties – communists (PCP), the radical Block of the Left (BE) and the conservative Democratic Social Centre-People's Party (CDS-PP) all below the 10 per cent threshold. Since 2015, there has also been a sixth single issue party, the Party of Animals and Nature (PAN) with one seat. The three small parties, CDS-PP, PCP-PEV and the new left party BE can be important for coalition government or parliamentary support for the two main parties. In 2015 socialist leader Antonio Costa decided to form a minority government with parliamentary support of the communists and blockists. This has been an innovation in Portuguese politics (see the study by Freire, 2017; Magone, 2014: chapter 5; and Fernandes, 2016b; Lisi, 2015; Figure 7.30).

Since the 2015 general elections in Spain, there are now four main parties in the party system, replacing the former bipartyism consisting of socialists (PSOE) and the People's Party (PP). Two new political parties emerged at the end of the crisis that are shaping the party system and contributing to more instability in the political system (Orriols and Cordero, 2016). On the left, there is Podemos, which in the 2016 general election joined forces in an electoral coalition with the communist party-led United Left (IU) to become Unidos Podemos. Due to the fact that it is difficult for a new party to establish national structures in a short space of time, this alliance strengthens Podemos. Podemos also looked for alliances with small leftwing regionalist parties such as En Marea in Galicia. On the centre-right, PP must now compete with the youthful Ciudadanos (Citizens), which was founded in 2006 in Catalonia. Although Ciudadanos is a liberal party, it clearly occupies the tradition of the centre in the country of previous parties (Rodon and Hierro, 2016; Rodríguez-Teruel et al., 2016; Figure 7.31).

In Greece, the reinforced proportional representation electoral system is conducive to a polarised two-party system. The electoral system favours larger parties against the smaller ones. This is the reason why the two main parties – New Democracy (ND) on the right and Socialists (PASOK) on the left – were able to alternate in power and divide the spoils. No other party was able to achieve a large share of the vote. Such continuity in power was achieved through a web of systemic corruption, patronage and clientelism.

Similarly to Spain, the Greek party system was considerably affected by the financial and euro crises. Basically, the two-party system consisting of socialists (PASOK) and New Democracy (ND) came to an end in the elections of 2012, when in two early elections the socialist party vote collapsed, New Democracy lost votes, and the leftwing populist Left Coalition (Syriza) under the charismatic Alexis Tsipras emerged as a major player after New Democracy. Finally, in the two early elections of 2015, Tsipras's party became the largest one and was able to form a coalition government with the small party Independent Greeks (ANEL).

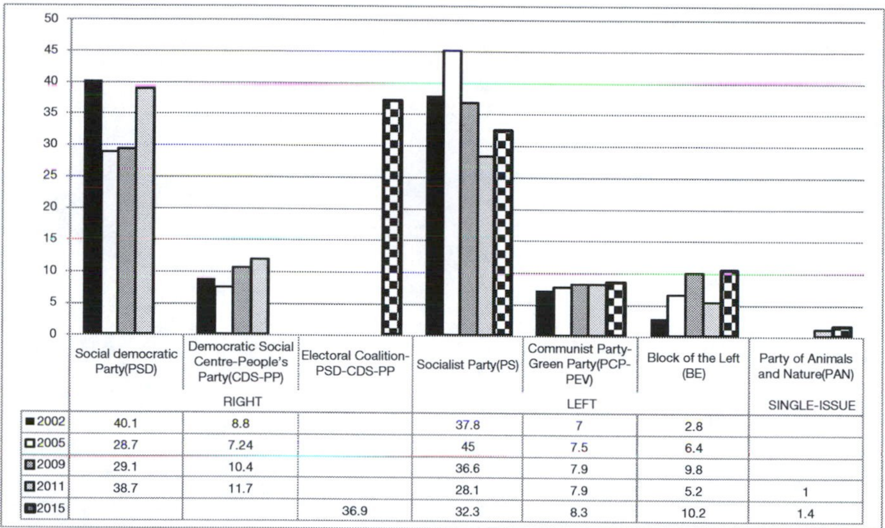

	Social democratic Party(PSD)	Democratic Social Centre-People's Party(CDS-PP)	Electoral Coalition-PSD-CDS-PP	Socialist Party(PS)	Communist Party-Green Party(PCP-PEV)	Block of the Left (BE)	Party of Animals and Nature(PAN)
	RIGHT			LEFT			SINGLE-ISSUE
2002	40.1	8.8		37.8	7	2.8	
2005	28.7	7.24		45	7.5	6.4	
2009	29.1	10.4		36.6	7.9	9.8	
2011	38.7	11.7		28.1	7.9	5.2	1
2015			36.9	32.3	8.3	10.2	1.4

Figure 7.30 General elections in Portugal, 2000–15

Source: Author's graph based on database of Parties and Elections in Europe (2018).

This transformation of the party system was clearly influenced by the fact that the main parties mishandled the sovereign debt crisis and have been engulfed in political corruption scandals for decades. Tsipras promised a populist easy solution to the sovereign debt problem, but in the end his government is doing exactly what he said he would not do during the political campaign (Toloudis, 2017; Tsakatika, 2016; Tsakatika and Eleftheriou, 2013; Tsatsanis and Teperoglou, 2016; Tsirbas, 2016; Vasilopoulou and Halikiopoulou, 2013). A new extreme rightwing party is the fascist Golden Dawn which also gained quite considerable support during the sovereign debt crisis, particularly as a xenophobic, anti-immigration party (Ellinas, 2013; Figure 7.32).

The East Central European countries: Hungary, the Czech Republic, Slovakia, Poland and Slovenia

While the Southern European party systems achieved a considerable level of party system consolidation, in spite of a high level of volatility at the centre, those of Central and Eastern Europe are still in the middle of such a process.

There are several features that can be found in most Central and Eastern European countries. First, democratic political parties are relatively new and have therefore a weak linkage to civil society. They tend to have very weak party organisational structures. Therefore they rely quite a lot on the media to spread their message (Lewis, 2003, 2015; Olson, 1998). Second, party systems are quite volatile due to the emergence of new political parties that try to challenge the still incipiently established parties (Enyedi and Deegan-Krause, 2017: 174–7). Third, such a volatile environment allows for the regular emergence of populist parties

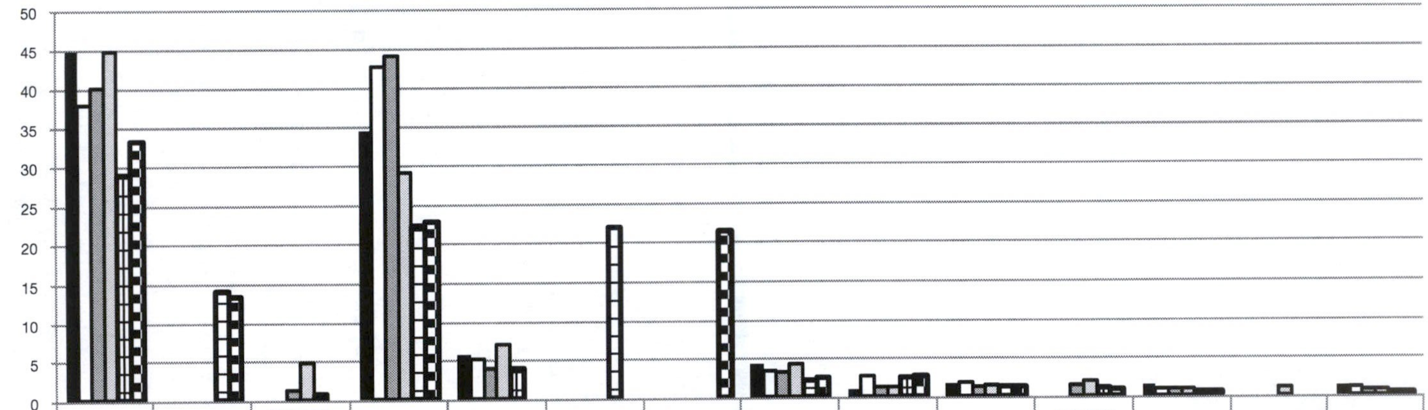

	RIGHT		CENTRE					REGIONALISTS						
	People's Party(PP)	Ciudadanos (Cs)	Union for Democracy and Progress (UPyD)	Socialist Party(PSOE)	United Left(IU)	Podemos	Electoral Coalition Unidos Podemos	Convergence and Union(CiU,CDC,PdeCAT)	Catalan Republican Left(ERC)	Basque Nationalist Party(PNV)	AMAIUR/ Basque Country Rally(EH Bildu)	Galician Nationalist Party(BNG)	Equo (Valencian Regionalists)	Canary Coalition
2000	44.5			34.2	5.5			4.2	0.8	1.5		1.3		1.1
2004	37.7			42.5	5			3.2	2.5	1.6		0.8		0.9
2008	39.9		1.2	43.9	3.8			3	1.2	1.2	1.4	0.8		0.7
2011	44.6		4.7	28.8	6.9			4.2	1.1	1.3	1.9	0.8	0.9	0.6
2015	28.7	13.9	0.6	22	3.7	21.7		2	2.4	1.2	0.9	0.3		0.3
2016	33	13.1		22.6			21.2	2.3	2.6	1.2	0.8	0.2		0.3

Figure 7.31 General elections in Spain, 2000–16

Source: Author's graph based on the database of Parties and Elections in Europe (2018).

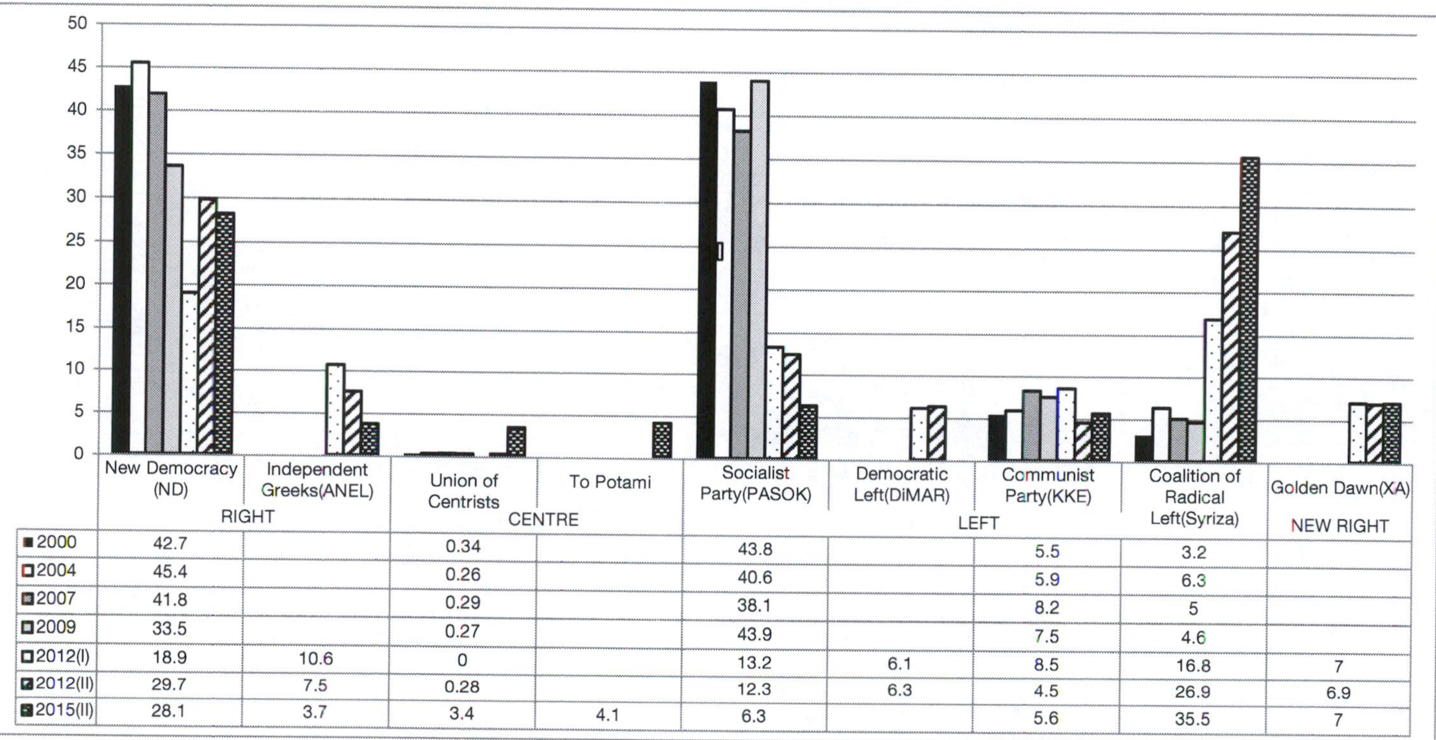

	New Democracy (ND)	Independent Greeks(ANEL)	Union of Centrists	To Potami	Socialist Party(PASOK)	Democratic Left(DIMAR)	Communist Party(KKE)	Coalition of Radical Left(Syriza)	Golden Dawn(XA)
	RIGHT		CENTRE		LEFT				NEW RIGHT
2000	42.7		0.34		43.8		5.5	3.2	
2004	45.4		0.26		40.6		5.9	6.3	
2007	41.8		0.29		38.1		8.2	5	
2009	33.5		0.27		43.9		7.5	4.6	
2012(I)	18.9	10.6	0		13.2	6.1	8.5	16.8	7
2012(II)	29.7	7.5	0.28		12.3	6.3	4.5	26.9	6.9
2015(II)	28.1	3.7	3.4	4.1	6.3		5.6	35.5	7

Figure 7.32 General elections in Greece, 2000–15

Source: Author's graph based on the database of Parties and Elections in Europe (2018).

or anti-establishment parties (Engler, 2016; Hanley and Sikk, 2016; Pirro, 2013). Fourth, parties in Central and Eastern Europe can rely on a generous public funding system, so that they have been cartel parties from the very beginning, more interested in office-seeking. Party regulatory frameworks are rather poorly implemented and enforced (Casal-Bértoa and Van Biezen, 2014a, 2014b). Fifth, party systems are more to the right than in Western Europe, due to the communist legacy. The best cases in this context are Hungary, Poland and the Baltic states. However, sixth, in some countries the former communist parties have become part of social democracy and have been able to keep some power in the political system. This is particularly strong in Bulgaria and Romania. The most prominent scholar of the region, Attila Ágh, has already begun to observe a deconsolidation or decline of democracy in Central and Eastern Europe, due mainly to the decline of trust in politicians and political parties (Ágh, 2017; see also Coman and Tomini, 2014). Nevertheless, the East Central countries are still in a relatively better shape than those of Eastern Europe (Cabada et al., 2014).

Hungary and the Czech Republic were the two countries where party systems consolidated at a very early stage. In the case of Hungary, the early transition led to an advantageous position for the incumbent Communist Party, which transformed itself into a social democratic party. This strategy of the 'reform communists' was practised in most other countries of Central and Eastern Europe (see Table 7.16).

Between 1989 and 2010, the Hungarian party system has evolved towards a majoritarian democracy, resulting from the polarisation between the Social Democrats (former Reform Communists – MSZP) and the Hungarian Civic Union (Fidesz). These are the two main parties that have their respective junior partners for eventual coalition building. The Social Democrats tended to join with the Liberals (SDSZ) while Fidesz joined with the Hungarian Democratic Forum and the Christian Democrats (KDNP). There was a general tendency towards a bipolarised two-party system (Körösényi et al., 2010: 387–98; Figure 7.33).

However, the landslide victory of Victor Orbán in the 2010 elections led to a change of the electoral system in 2012 which was clearly advantageous for his party. We mentioned this earlier in the section on the impact of electoral systems on party systems. The result was a perpetuation of an absolute majority with super majorities for the governing Fidesz-KDNP coalition (Batory, 2016; Kim and Swain, 2015). The leftwing socialists (MSZP) share of the vote declined from 43.2 per cent in 2006 to 11.9 per cent in 2018. Quite problematic is the rise of the xenophobic anti-Roma, anti-immigration and extreme rightwing Jobbik party, which became the second largest party with 19.1 per cent of the vote in 2018. It seems that its success is also due to its anti-capitalist economic programme, which is able to attract many people affected by poverty (Varga, 2014). Both Fidesz-KDNP and Jobbik have used a rather anti-immigration populist language during the political campaign. Due to the over-dominance of Fidesz in governing structures and its tendency to try to control the media, the political opposition is considerably weakened in regular elections (Batory, 2016; Fumarola, 2016). There is a real danger of an 'Orbanisation' of the political system, leading to the kind of 'Hungarian' elections, meaning façade elections, of the nineteenth century (Ágh, 2016; Ilonski and Varnágy, 2014).

The Czech Republic's party system also became consolidated soon after the transition to democracy, but this achievement has been eroding in the new millennium. Originally, the party system was polarised between the umbrella party of the Civic Forum and the orthodox communist party (KSČM). However, KSČM soon became ostracised and isolated due to its anti-systemic attitude towards the new liberal democracy. Soon, this polarisation was replaced by one between the ODS and the newly refounded social democrats (ČSSD). In between there were several smaller parties like the Christian Democrats (KDU-ČSL) and the Greens (SZ) so that about five or six parties were represented in parliament between 1996 and 2013. The consolidated party system began to erode during the Mirek Topolanek (ODS) government between 2006 and 2009. Several factions decided to leave the party and create new political groups. As a consequence, the electoral share of the vote decreased from 35.4 per cent in 2006 to 7.7 per cent in 2013. Also ČSSD's share reduced from 32.3 per cent to 20.5 per cent during this period. The electoral tectonic shift began to emerge in the 2010 elections, in which two new political parties, TOP09 and Public Affairs (VV), fought against political corruption, advocating transparency and accountability, and secured representation in national parliament. TOP09 was carried by mayors and representatives in local politics, while VV was more conservative in financial matters (Balik and Hloušek, 2016; Klvaňova, 2016; Vodička, 2005). In 2010, the new parties achieved 27.7 per cent of the vote and the main losers were the established parties. This dealignment of voters led in 2013 to the emergence of the firm party ANO 2011 (Yes) of food industry and media tycoon Andris Babiš, which became the second largest party after the ČSSD. Meanwhile, in the 2017 parliamentary elections, ANO 2011 became the largest party with 29.6 per cent, and the two former major parties ODS and ČSSD were reduced to 11.3 per cent and 7.7 per cent respectively.

ANO 2011 profited immensely from this dealignment of voters. The party may be referred to as a business-firm party, similar to the rise of Berlusconi's Forza Italia. This is the reason that Babiš is referred to as Babisconi. He created the party from scratch and funded the beginnings of the party organisation using his large agricultural, food and chemicals enterprise. Moreover, he bought one of the most important Czech media groups, the MAFRA media group, which owned two major newspapers MF DNES and Lidové noviny (Hajek, 2017: 279). One of the first studies carried out by Lukáš Hájek on ANO 2011's voting behaviour in the legislature (2013–17) seems to suggest that it is quite a cohesive centrist party. The highly centralised structure seems to be working well (Hájek, 2017). ANO 2011 was a member of the coalition government with ČSSD and the Christian democrats (KDU-ČSL) showing the ability for cooperation and consensual policy-making. After the general elections of 2017, Babiš was able to become the prime minister in a coalition government with the ČSSD. The party system also now includes an anti-immigration new right party called Freedom and Direct Democracy (SPD), which increased its vote from 6.9 per cent in 2013 to 10.6 per cent in 2017. In the last election, the Pirates were also able to get 10.8 per cent (Figure 7.34). All these are signs of a very volatile unconsolidated party system.

After the velvet divorce, Slovakia was dominated by the Movement for Democratic Slovakia (HZDS) under the leadership of Vladimir Mečiar, which received about 35 per cent of the vote and coalesced with smaller parties, among them the extreme rightwing Slovak Nationalist Party (SNS). Mečiar's authoritarian style led to the establishment of a strong coalition of opposition to counteract his exclusionist policies particularly towards the Hungarian minority. He was replaced by prime minister Mikulas Džurinda who built a strong coalition around

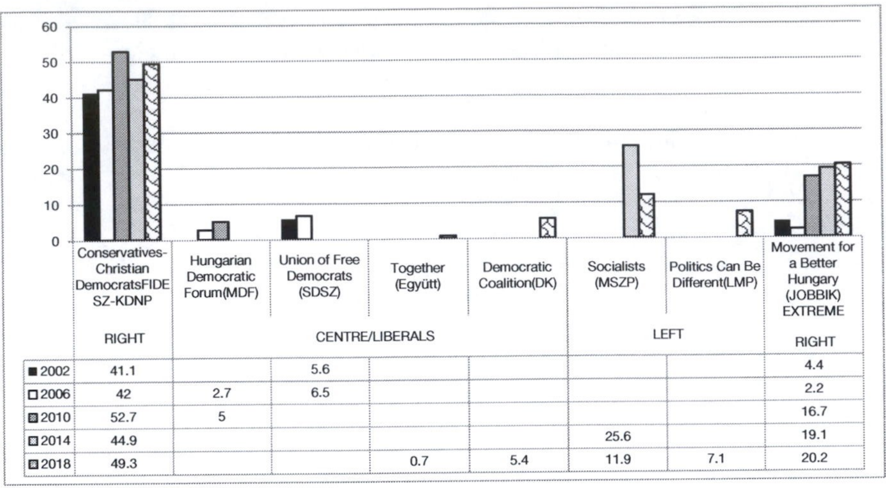

	Conservatives-Christian DemocratsFIDE SZ-KDNP	Hungarian Democratic Forum(MDF)	Union of Free Democrats (SDSZ)	Together (Együtt)	Democratic Coalition(DK)	Socialists (MSZP)	Politics Can Be Different(LMP)	Movement for a Better Hungary (JOBBIK) EXTREME
	RIGHT	CENTRE/LIBERALS				LEFT		RIGHT
2002	41.1		5.6					4.4
2006	42	2.7	6.5					2.2
2010	52.7	5						16.7
2014	44.9					25.6		19.1
2018	49.3			0.7	5.4	11.9	7.1	20.2

Figure 7.33 General elections in Hungary, 2000–18

Source: Author's graph based on database of Parties and Elections in Europe (2018).

the main Christian Democratic Party (SDKU), the Social Democrats (SDL) and the Hungarian Minority (SMK-MKP). The stabilisation of the party system was achieved by Robert Fico and his populist party Social Democracy Direction (SMER). He was able to change the image of the party towards social democracy and has so far been the main governing power. While the two Christian democratic parties SDKU-DS and KDH did not get representation after the 2016 elections, a new liberal, but Eurosceptic party called Freedom and Solidarity (SAS) emerged as the second largest party (Koźbiał, 2017: 135–7). Due to the murder of a Czech investigative journalist, Jan Kuciak, who was investigating political corruption of EU funds in Slovakia connected to the Italian Mafia, Robert Fico had to resign, but his party remains in power under prime minister Peter Pellegrini (*The Guardian*, 15 March 2018; Figure 7.35).

Three major features seem to characterise the Czech Republic and Slovakia. First of all, the high level of volatility. Second, the regular emergence and disappearance of new parties, and third, the important role of political leaders like Vaclav Klaus, Miloš Zeman and Andris Babiš in the Czech Republic and Vladimir Mečiar and Robert Fico in Slovakia. The main cleavage is a socioeconomic one, partly related to supporters or opponents of the free market (Koźbiał, 2017: 140–2).

In Poland, a consolidation of the party system took place only after 2005. Between 1989 and 2005, trade union Solidarity-related political parties emerged on the right, while on the left the former communists became a social democratic party (SLD). Quite an important juncture is the formation of Electoral Action (AWPS), a coalition of rightwing parties, many of them related to Solidarity, which won the 1997 elections but collapsed in 2001. Out of this emerged two parties that have become today's main rivals in the party system. On the one hand, the liberal Civic Platform (PO) and on the other the conservative Law and Justice Party (PiS) (Scszerbiak, 2008: 141, 147; Ziemer, 2013: 201–10). In the 2005 elections, PiS and PO become the two largest parties with 27.0 and 24.1 per cent respectively. Since

Table 7.16 Political parties in East Central Europe, 2018

Country	*Social democrats*	*Conservatives*	*Liberal*	*Centre*	*Christian democrats*	*Other*
Hungary	Magyar Szocialista Párt (MSZP) Hungarian Socialist Party	Fidesz – Magyar Polgári Szövetség (FIDESZ)			Kereszténydemokrata Néppárt (KDNP) Christian Democratic People's Party (in electoral coalition with Fidesz)	Jobbik, Movement for a Better Hungary (extreme right)
Czech Republic	Česká Strana Sociálne Demokratická (ČSSD) Czech Social Democratic Party	Občanská Demokratická Strana (ODS) Civic Democratic Party		ANO 2011 Yes 2011	Kresťanská a Demokratická Unie (KDU–CSL) Christian and Democratic Union (2002: KDU–CSL + US–DEU)	Komunistická Strana Čech a Moravy (KSČM) Communist Party of Bohemia and Moravia Strana Zelenych (SZ) Green Party TOP 09 Swoboda a Primá Democracie (SPD) Freedom and Direct Democracy Ceská Pirátská Strana (Pirati) Pirate Party
Slovakia	Smer – Sociálna Demokracia (SMER–SD) Direction – Social Democracy	Obyčajní Ľudia a Nezávislé Osobnosti (OĽaNO-NOVA) Ordinary People and Independent Personalities Slovenská Národná Strana (SNS) Slovak National Party Sme Rodina (SME-RODINA) We Are Family	Sloboda a Solidarita (SAS) Freedom and Solidarity (Liberal, eurosceptic)		Slovenská Demokratická a Kresťanská Únia (SDKU–DS) Slovak Democratic and Christian Union Krestanskodemokratické Hnutie (KDH) Christian Democratic Movement Sieť (SIEŤ) Network (conservative, Christian-democracy	Most-Hid Bridge (Hungarian minority) Ľudová Strana Naše Slovensko (Ľ'SNS) People's Party Our Slovakia (Far right)
Poland	Sojusz Lewicy Demokratycznej (SLD) Democratic Left Alliance / 2015 as Zjednoczona Lewica (ZL) United Left	Prawo i Sprawiedliwość (PiS) Law and Justice National conservatism)	Nowoczesna (N) Modern		Platforma Obywatelska (PO) Civic Platform (liberal, Christian democracy) Polskie Stronnictwo Ludowe (PSL) Polish People's Party (Christian democracy)	Kukiz'15 (K) (Rightwing populism) Mniejszość Niemiecka (MN) German Minority
Slovenia	Socialni Demokrati (SD) Social Democrats	Slovenska Demokratska Stranka (SDS) Slovenian Democratic Party	Zavezništvo Alenke Bratušek (ZaAB) Alliance of Alenka Bratušek Pozitivna Slovenija (PS) Positive Slovenia Državljanska Lista (DL) Civic List	Stranka Modernega Centra (SMC) Modern Centre Party (Liberal	Slovenska Ljudska Stranka (SLS) Slovenian People's Party Nova Slovenija – Krščanska Ljudska Stranka (NSI) New Slovenia – Christian People's Party	Demokratična Stranka Upokojencev Slovenije (DeSUS) Democratic Pensioners' Party of Slovenia

Source: Author's own compilation.

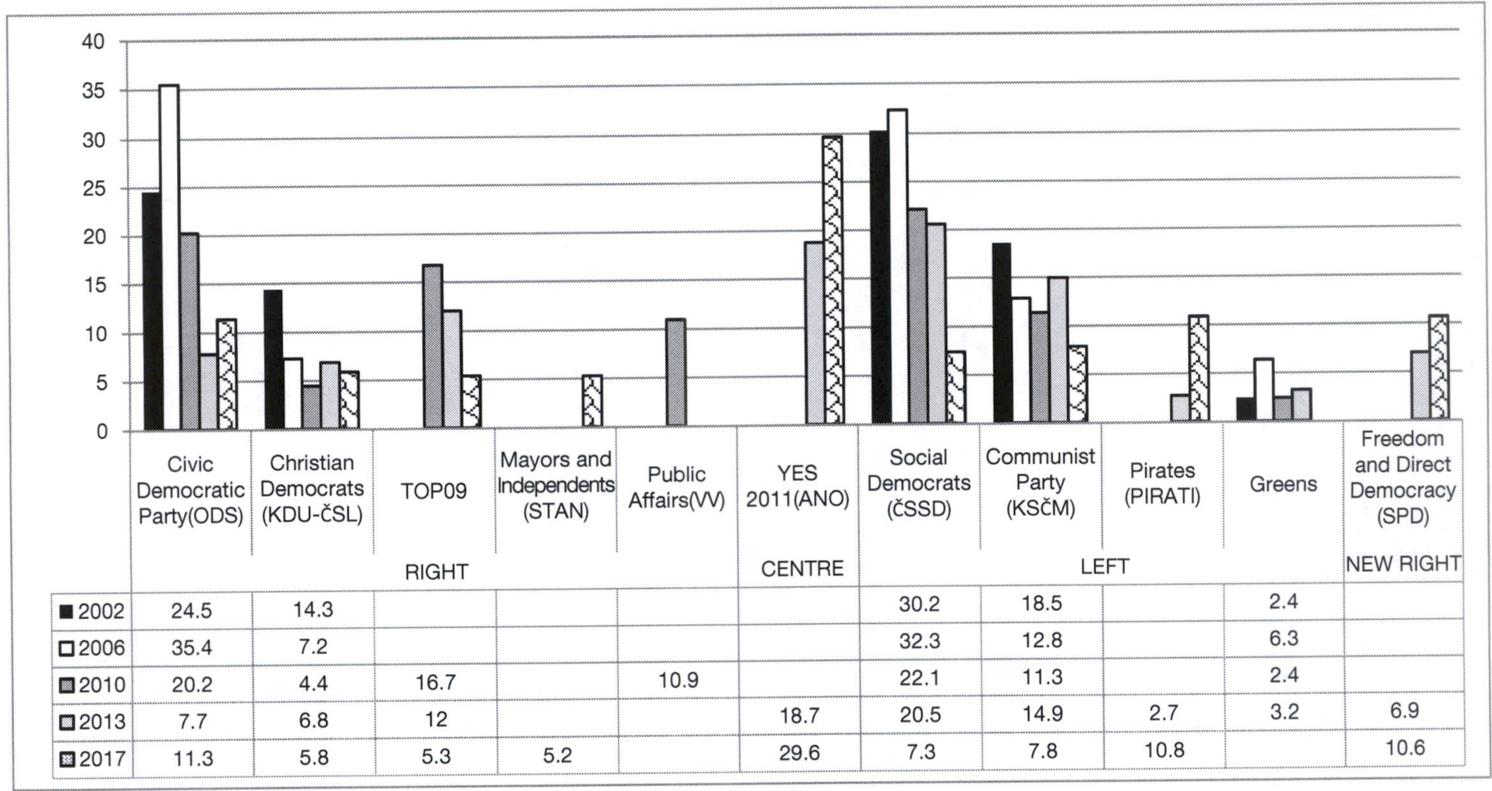

	Civic Democratic Party(ODS)	Christian Democrats (KDU-ČSL)	TOP09	Mayors and Independents (STAN)	Public Affairs(VV)	YES 2011(ANO)	Social Democrats (ČSSD)	Communist Party (KSČM)	Pirates (PIRATI)	Greens	Freedom and Direct Democracy (SPD)
	RIGHT					CENTRE	LEFT				NEW RIGHT
■ 2002	24.5	14.3					30.2	18.5		2.4	
□ 2006	35.4	7.2					32.3	12.8		6.3	
▩ 2010	20.2	4.4	16.7		10.9		22.1	11.3		2.4	
▨ 2013	7.7	6.8	12			18.7	20.5	14.9	2.7	3.2	6.9
▧ 2017	11.3	5.8	5.3	5.2		29.6	7.3	7.8	10.8		10.6

Figure 7.34 General elections in the Czech Republic, 2000–17

Source: Author's graph based on database of Parties and Elections in Europe (2018).

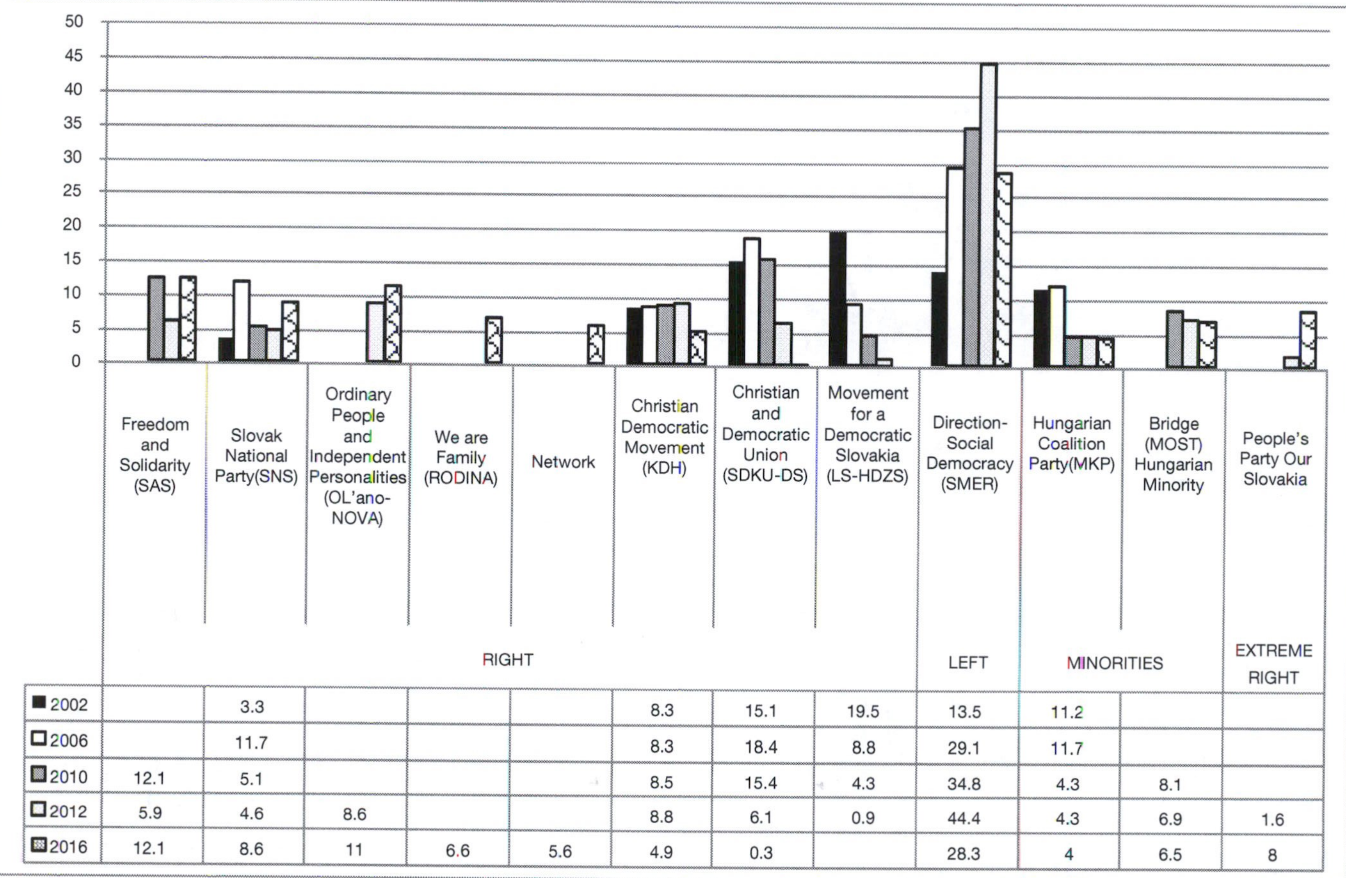

	Freedom and Solidarity (SAS)	Slovak National Party(SNS)	Ordinary People and Independent Personalities (OL'ano-NOVA)	We are Family (RODINA)	Network	Christian Democratic Movement (KDH)	Christian and Democratic Union (SDKU-DS)	Movement for a Democratic Slovakia (LS-HDZS)	Direction-Social Democracy (SMER)	Hungarian Coalition Party(MKP)	Bridge (MOST) Hungarian Minority	People's Party Our Slovakia
	RIGHT								LEFT	MINORITIES		EXTREME RIGHT
2002		3.3				8.3	15.1	19.5	13.5	11.2		
2006		11.7				8.3	18.4	8.8	29.1	11.7		
2010	12.1	5.1				8.5	15.4	4.3	34.8	4.3	8.1	
2012	5.9	4.6	8.6			8.8	6.1	0.9	44.4	4.3	6.9	1.6
2016	12.1	8.6	11	6.6	5.6	4.9	0.3		28.3	4	6.5	8

Figure 7.35 General elections in Slovakia, 2000–16

Source: Author's graph based on database on Parties and Elections in Europe (2018).

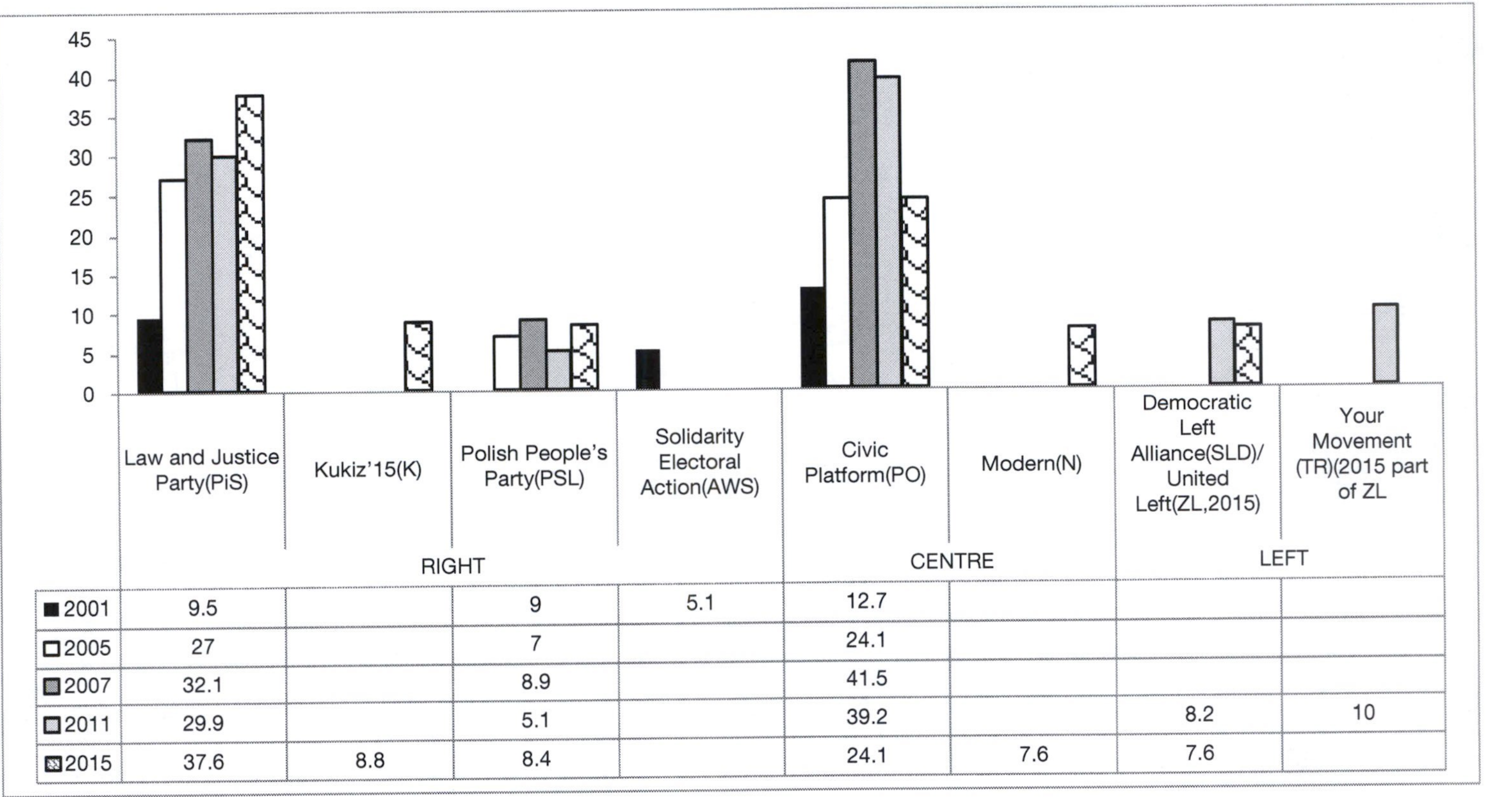

	Law and Justice Party(PiS)	Kukiz'15(K)	Polish People's Party(PSL)	Solidarity Electoral Action(AWS)	Civic Platform(PO)	Modern(N)	Democratic Left Alliance(SLD)/ United Left(ZL,2015)	Your Movement (TR)(2015 part of ZL
2001	9.5		9	5.1	12.7			
2005	27		7		24.1			
2007	32.1		8.9		41.5			
2011	29.9		5.1		39.2		8.2	10
2015	37.6	8.8	8.4		24.1	7.6	7.6	

Figure 7.36 General elections in Poland, 2000–15

Source: Author's graph based on database on Parties and Elections in Europe (2018).

then they have become the two poles of the party system. Between 2007 and 2015, PO was the main governing party in a coalition with the small Polish People's Party (PSL). In 2015, it changed to the PiS, which won an absolute majority of seats, but just 37.6 per cent of share of the vote. Also here, the role of political leaders like Lech Kaczynski (PiS) and Donald Tusk (PO) should be emphasised in the way voters were mobilised for the political parties. The 2015 general elections also led to emergence of new parties in parliament such as the rightwing populist Kukiz'15 and liberal Modern (Nowoczesna). In terms of electoral geography, there are differences between PO and PiS. PO is quite strong in north and west Poland, which is more liberal and younger in terms of population. PO is quite strong in the cities. PiS is rather a party of the rural areas, older people and located in the east and south of the country (Ziemer, 2013: 237–8; Figure 7.36).

Geographically, Slovenia can be placed as part of the western Balkans, but politically it has been part of the Central European pattern of politics. We may divide the trajectory of the Slovenian party system into the periods before and after 2008. Although the former Slovenian communists were instrumental in paving the way towards democracy in the country, the first period is dominated by three parties, namely the Social Democrats (SD), the Democrats (SDS) and the Liberal Democrats (LDS). The dominant party was the LDS, which was able to form governments with other parties between 1992 and 2004 almost without interruption. However, in 2004, the conservative Democratic Party (SDS) won the elections and formed a government with other centre-right parties including the Christian People's Party (NSi), the Slovenian People's Party (SLS) and the Pensioners' Party (DeSUS). Since then, volatility has increased considerably, particularly after the 2008 elections. New parties (Positive Slovenia – PS, Modern Centre Party – SMC) linked to leaders emerged in subsequent elections and then disappeared (Figure 7.37).

Since then volatility has increased considerably such that LDS and Zares did not achieve parliamentary representation in 2011. A new party called Positive Slovenia (PS) appeared from this dealignment but the country is still awaiting a new consolidated realignment. The Social Democrats declined to 30.5 per cent in 2008 and to just 6 per cent in 2014. It means that only the Democratic Party has remained as one of the three major parties and is again the largest party of the country after the 2018 general elections. The second largest became the new party of Marian Šarec, which is linked to a politician of the same name. He was mayor of the small town of Kamnik and is now the prime minister leading a coalition government of five parties. An important smaller party which was part of the original party system of the early 1990s is DeSUS, which still holds the function of kingmaker in coalition-building (Jurek, 2010; Klvaňova, 2016).

In all countries except Poland, turnout is about 60 per cent, but in Poland it is only about 50 per cent, which clearly shows that a large part of the population is alienated from the political system.

The Baltic countries

While the East Central European countries were able to preserve some kind of sovereignty during the Soviet period, this was not the case in the three Baltic states, Lithuania, Latvia and Estonia. They were occupied by Germany during the Second

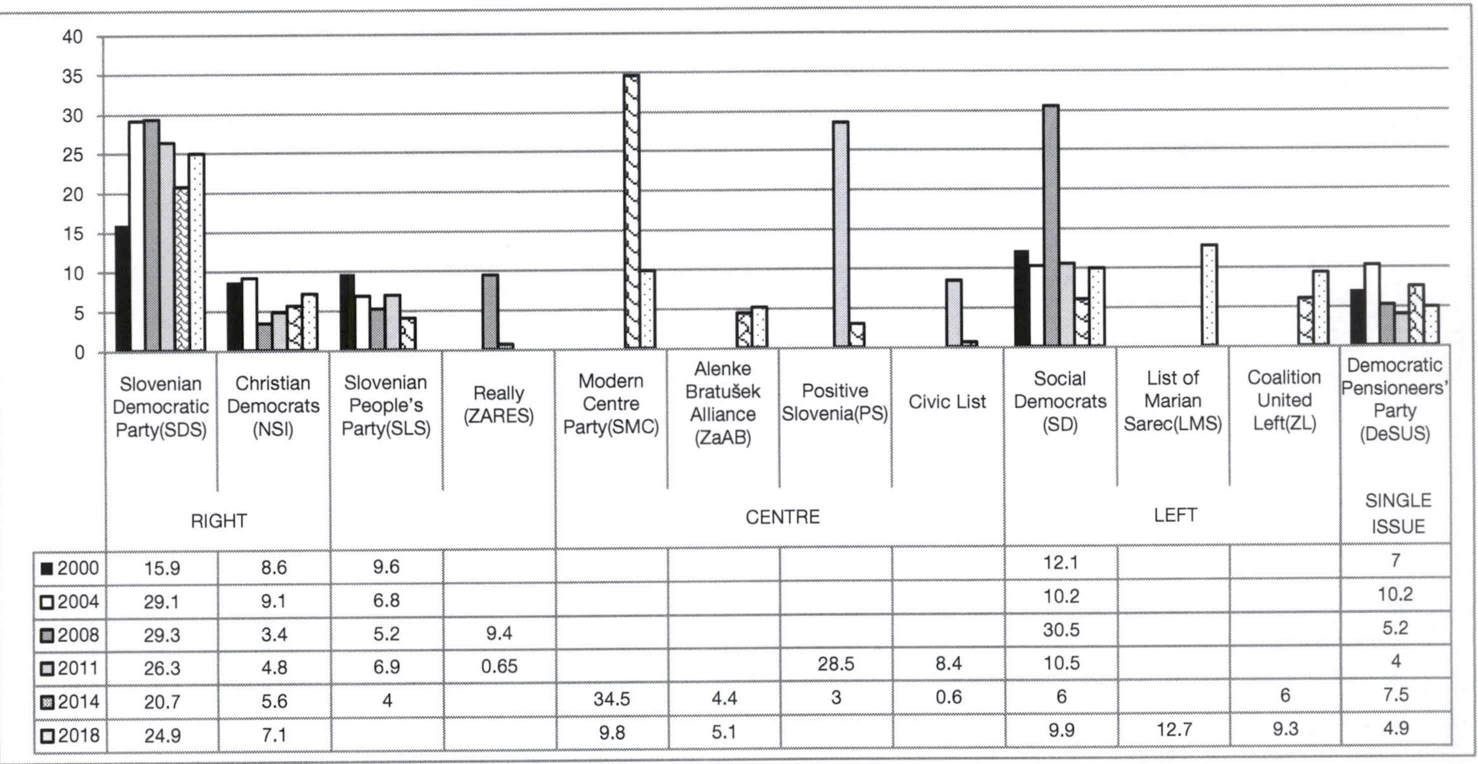

	Slovenian Democratic Party(SDS)	Christian Democrats (NSI)	Slovenian People's Party(SLS)	Really (ZARES)	Modern Centre Party(SMC)	Alenke Bratušek Alliance (ZaAB)	Positive Slovenia(PS)	Civic List	Social Democrats (SD)	List of Marian Sarec(LMS)	Coalition United Left(ZL)	Democratic Pensioneers' Party (DeSUS)
	RIGHT			CENTRE					LEFT			SINGLE ISSUE
2000	15.9	8.6	9.6						12.1			7
2004	29.1	9.1	6.8						10.2			10.2
2008	29.3	3.4	5.2	9.4					30.5			5.2
2011	26.3	4.8	6.9	0.65			28.5	8.4	10.5			4
2014	20.7	5.6	4		34.5	4.4	3	0.6	6		6	7.5
2018	24.9	7.1			9.8	5.1			9.9	12.7	9.3	4.9

Figure 7.37 General elections in Slovenia, 2000–18

Source: Author's graph based on database of Parties and Elections in Europe (2008).

World War in 1942 and were annexed by the Soviet Union in 1944. They became integral republics of the Soviet Union. Their newly found independence after 1991 led to the establishment of political parties, although the strong russification of the population during the Soviet period led to considerable tensions with the Soviet Union and today with Russia. The exclusion of the Russian minority who did not learn either Estonian or Latvian has led to considerable social tensions in these countries. The Ukrainian crisis since March 2014 has increased tensions in the difficult relations with Russia, which has also had an impact on the party systems, particularly in the latest elections of 2014–18 in the respective countries.

Although all three Baltic republics were independent during the interwar period (1918–42), party systems cannot establish any continuity with this period. Instead they can be traced back to the reform (*perestroika*) and transparency (*glasnost*) efforts of Soviet leader Mikhael Gorbachev starting in the mid-1980s. The internal democratisation of the soviet (council system) affected the whole Soviet Union, as well as the three Baltic states. In these elections, three kinds of groups emerged which shaped politics in the Baltic states. First, there was the Popular Front that clearly intended to achieve independence. Second, there was the more nationalist Congress oriented against the Soviet regime, and third, the pro-regime Inter movements. They clearly shaped the early party system, but they collapsed and new parties emerged out of them that were strongly dependent on personalities. Factionalism, fission and fusion in and between parties have remained major characteristics in the three countries, particularly in Latvia (Ágh, 2017; Auers, 2015: 100–1; Saarts, 2011; Table 7.17).

Probably Estonia can be singled out as the most consolidated party system (for the early period see the excellent study by Arter, 1997). It is a five-party system consisting of four main parties, and in spite of a change of labels since 1992, one can trace continuity to the early elections. These are the political and economic liberal Estonian Reform Party (RE), social liberal and agrarian Estonian Centre Party (K), the social democrats (SDE), and the conservative-Christian democratic Fatherland and Respublica (IRL). Both the K and SDE are more inclusive towards the Russian minority; in particular, the former is shaped by the legacy of the Popular Front (Auers, 2015: 109–10). In the 2015 elections these four parties represented 81.4 per cent of the votes. A very positive aspect is that the four political parties work closely together and have been present in coalition governments since the early 1990s. Moreover, two further conservative parties were able to achieve representation – the Estonian Free Party (EVA) and the Conservative People's Party of Estonia (EKRE). Estonia is also a major innovator in terms of elections, because it was the first country to introduce e-voting for all elections in 2007 (Auers, 2015: 84). The highly personalised electoral system was devised by the prominent American-Estonian political scientist Rein Taagepera and contributes to a strong relationship between political personalities and politicians at constituency level. This is reinforced by the small size of the country (Figure 7.38). In the 2018 general elections the Reform Party became the largest party again; however, it needs to form a coalition with the other main parties of the party system.

The Latvian party system is probably the least consolidated of all three countries. In spite of three decades of party system evolution, in 2011 a major overhaul and relabelling of parties took place. The discontinuation of political parties is a frequent strategy used when there are judicial investigations going on

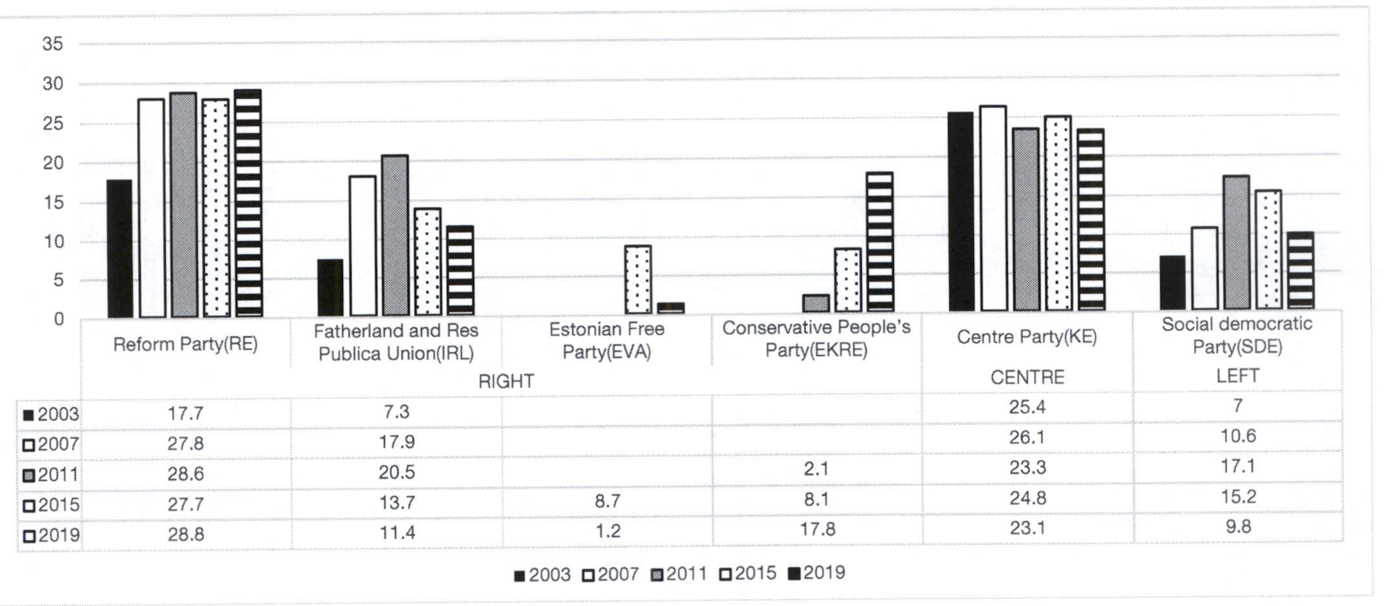

	Reform Party(RE)	Fatherland and Res Publica Union(IRL)	Estonian Free Party(EVA)	Conservative People's Party(EKRE)	Centre Party(KE)	Social democratic Party(SDE)
	RIGHT				CENTRE	LEFT
■2003	17.7	7.3			25.4	7
□2007	27.8	17.9			26.1	10.6
▩2011	28.6	20.5		2.1	23.3	17.1
□2015	27.7	13.7	8.7	8.1	24.8	15.2
□2019	28.8	11.4	1.2	17.8	23.1	9.8

Figure 7.38 General elections in Estonia, 2000–16

Source: Author's graph based on database of Parties and Elections in Europe (2018).

about corruption in illegal electoral campaign and party financing. Moreover, the financial crisis affected Latvia quite badly, so that dissatisfaction with political parties led to high levels of volatility.

The Latvian party system was always quite fragmented, so that coalition government led to quite considerable instability (see Chapter 4). About five parties were important between 1993 and 2010. Latvian Way (LC), which then merged with First Party of Latvia (LPP) in 2007, emerged out of the Popular Front and was a liberal party. The conservative nationalist Fatherland and Freedom party/Latvian National Independence Movement party (TB/LNNK) had about 5 to 14 per cent of the vote, but after 2011 one part joined the quite conservative rightwing National Alliance (NA). The third major party is the agrarian Centre Party-Latvian Peasants Party (LZS), which after 2002 became the Greens and Peasants' Union (ZZS), a merger of several agrarian and regionalist parties. In 1998, the People's Party (TT) emerged as a new party around the charismatic Andris Šķēle and was able to shape politics in the first decade of the new millennium, but in 2011 it was disbanded in order to avoid paying back campaign funding. Last but not least, the centre-right New Era party (JL) was founded around the personality of Einars Repše in 2002. It was a relatively important party during the first decade of the new millennium and still remains central to the political system. JL merged with other parties to form the Unity Party (V) in 2010. JL/V is also the party of European Commissioner Valdis Dombrovskis. In 2011, the Reform party around former president Valdis Zatlers was founded and achieved 20.8 per cent in 2011 elections, but did not achieve representation in 2014. Only the Latvian Russian Union (LKS), the main representative of the Russian minority which achieved 19 per cent of the vote in 2002, and the Russophile Social democratic party-Harmony (SDPS) were excluded from the political system. After 2002, the electorate of LKS eroded, so that the party achieved just 1.48 per cent in the 2014 elections. Harmony (Saskana) is now the uncontested leftwing party and largest party of the party system since 2011. It will certainly be difficult to continue to exclude Harmony from the political system, due to the fact that they are part of the coalition government in the capital Riga. From the five parties that dominated politics before 2011, just three (TB-LNNK, JL, ZZS) survived but only after merging with other parties. Since the 2014 elections, there have been four main parties, which are the centre-right Unity (V) with 21.9 per cent, the conservative National Alliance (NA) with 16.6 per cent, the agrarian-centrist Union of Greens and Farmers (ZZS) with 19.5 per cent, and the social democrats (Saskana-SDPS) with 23 per cent (Figure 7.39). The first three parties were part of the coalition government from 2011. In the legislative elections on 6 October 2018, the three government parties lost badly, and a populist party Who Owns the State (KPV-LV) became the second largest party, after Saskana (Harmony). Also the third largest party is new in the Saeima, the new Conservative Party (JKP). Coalition negotiations will be quite difficult, because no party has an overall majority and nine parties are represented in parliament.

The Lithuanian party system can be placed between the more consolidated Estonian and the less consolidated Latvian ones. The electoral system forces parties to create coalitions on the left and right, in order to be able to move to the second round in the uninominal constituency part. According to Algis Krupavicius, the Lithuanian party system was on the path to stability between 1992 and 2000. Four main parties emerged on the left and right that contributed to the structuring

Table 7.17 Political parties in the Baltic states, 2018

	Social democrats	*Conservatives*	*Liberals*	*Agrarian/Green*	*Centre*	*Other*
Latvia	Sociāldemokrātiskā Partija 'Saskaņa' (SDPS) Social Democratic Party 'Harmony'	Nacionālā Apvienība (NA) National Alliance No Sirds Latvijai (NSL) For Latvia From The Heart Jauna Konservativa Partija (JKP) (New Conservative Party)	Jauna Vienotība (V) (New Unity)	Zaļo un Zemnieku Savienība (ZZS) Greens and Peasants' Union	Latvijas Reģionu Apvienība (LRA) Latvian Alliance of Regions	Kam Pieder Valsts-KPV (Who Owns the State)
Estonia	Sotsiaaldemokraatlik Erakond (SDE) Social Democratic Party	Isamaa erakond(I) Eesti Vabaerakond (EVA) Estonian Free Party Eesti Konservatiivne Rahvaerakond (EKRE) Conservative People's Party of Estonia	Eesti Reformierakond (RE) Estonian Reform Party Eesti	Eestimaa Rohelised (ER) Estonian Greens Eestimaa Rahvaliit (ERL) Estonian People's Union	Keskerakond (K) Estonian Centre Party	
Lithuania	Lietuvos Socialdemokratu Partija (LSDP) Lithuanian Social Democratic Party	Tėvynės Sąjunga – Lietuvos Krikščionys Demokratai (TS–LKD) Homeland Union – Lithuanian Christian Democrats Tvarka ir Teisingumas (TT) Order and Justice	Lietuvos Respublikos Liberalu Sajūdis (LRLS) Liberal Movement of the Lithuanian Republic	Lietuvos Valstiečių ir Žaliųjų Sąjunga (LVŽS) Lithuanian Peasant and Greens Union	Lietuvos Centro Partija (LCP) Lithuanian Centre Party (Centrism; Euroscepticism) Darbo Partija (DP) Labour Party (Centrism, Social liberalism)	Lietuvos Lenku Rinkimu Akcija (LLRA) Lithuanian Poles' Electoral Action (Polish minority)

Source: Author.

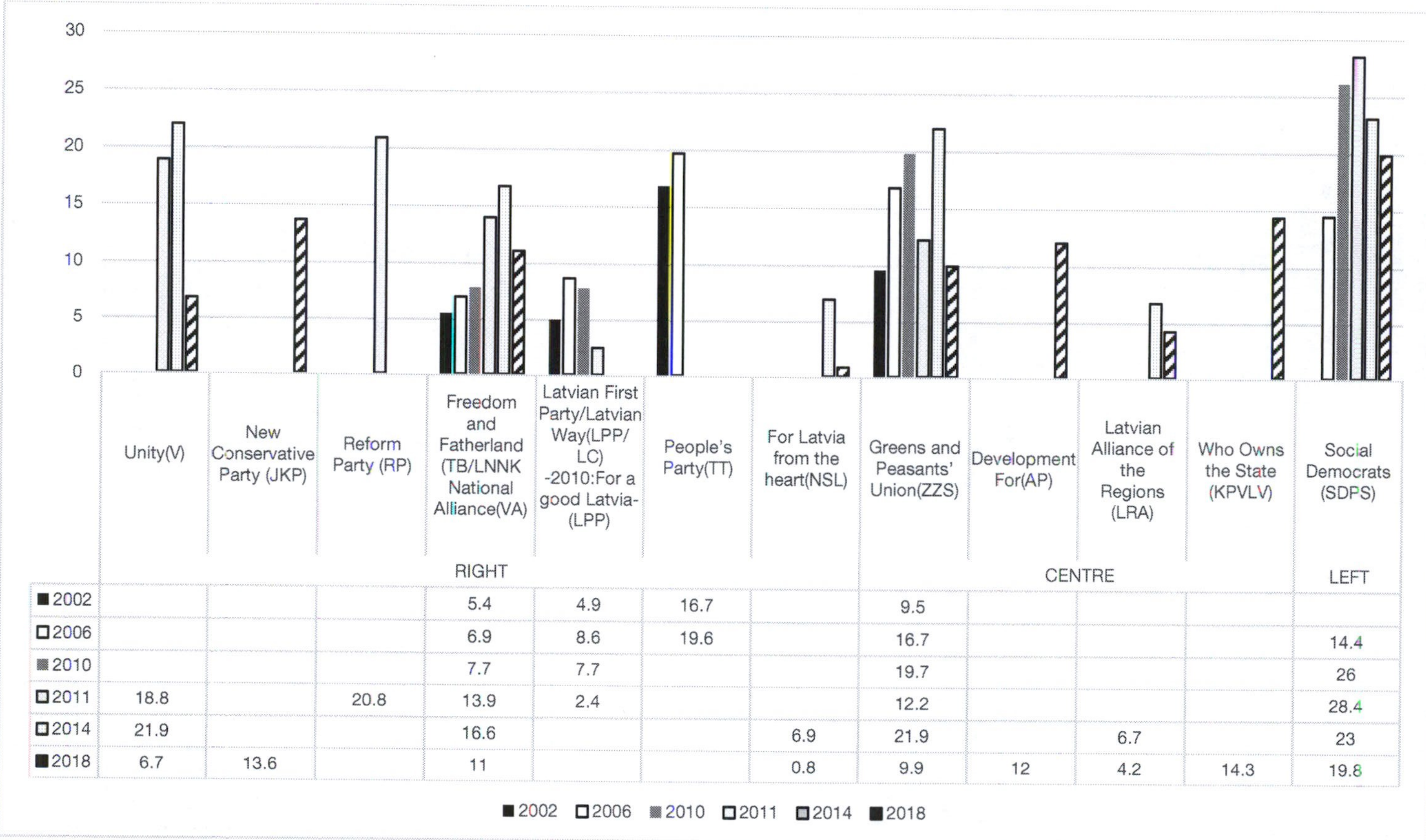

	Unity(V)	New Conservative Party (JKP)	Reform Party (RP)	Freedom and Fatherland (TB/LNNK National Alliance(VA)	Latvian First Party/Latvian Way(LPP/ LC) -2010:For a good Latvia-(LPP)	People's Party(TT)	For Latvia from the heart(NSL)	Greens and Peasants' Union(ZZS)	Development For(AP)	Latvian Alliance of the Regions (LRA)	Who Owns the State (KPVLV)	Social Democrats (SDPS)
	RIGHT							CENTRE				LEFT
■2002				5.4	4.9	16.7		9.5				
□2006				6.9	8.6	19.6		16.7				14.4
▩2010				7.7	7.7			19.7				26
□2011	18.8		20.8	13.9	2.4			12.2				28.4
□2014	21.9			16.6			6.9	21.9		6.7		23
■2018	6.7	13.6		11			0.8	9.9	12	4.2	14.3	19.8

Figure 7.39 General elections in Latvia, 2000–18

Source: Author's graph based on database of Parties and Elections in Europe (2018).

of the party system: Homeland Union (TS), the Christian Democrats (LDKP) and the two social democratic parties (LDDP and LSDP). Homeland Union and the Christian Democrats merged to create TS-LDK in 2008. On the left, the LDDP became part of LSDP in 2001. In this sense, the two blocks have been able to survive until today. However, after 2000 several new parties emerged. Apart from the sudden appearance of the populist Labour Party (DB) in the European Parliament elections of 2004 funded by Russian billionaire Viktor Uspaskish, many other parties have had to deal with factionalism resulting in the formation of new parties. The Lithuanian Green and Peasant Union (LVŽS) emerged in 2001 and remained a small party until the general elections of 2016, when it achieved 21.5 per cent and became the second largest party after the Christian Democrats (TS-LKD) with 21.7 per cent and the largest in terms of seats (54). It has also been the ruling party since 2016. Since 2008, there has also been a liberal party (LRLSS) in the party system. It means that after the 2016 elections, the Lithuanian party system consists of three main parties: the Christian Democrats (TS-LKD), Greens and Peasants (LVŽS) and the social democrats (LSDP), together with other smaller parties including the Liberals. A moderate polarisation between the left around the LSDP and the right around the TS-LKD dominates party politics in Lithuania (Figure 7.40).

The south-eastern model: Bulgaria, Romania and Croatia

The south-eastern pattern of party systems is characterised by strong social democratic parties that emerged out of the former communist parties. As a reaction, liberal anti-communist umbrella parties emerged, which were able to attract the more conservative vote (Table 7.18).

A major problem that affects the three countries today is that electoral integrity is still rather low with regular cases of vote-buying, which does not strengthen trust in the political system (Mares et al., 2017; Volintiru, 2012). Incipient party regulation further undermines a level playing field in terms of electoral competition in Bulgaria and Romania (Kostandinova, 2007; Roper, 2002).

In Bulgaria, we can recognise a polarised multiparty system. On the left is the Bulgarian Socialist Party (BSP) achieving over 40 per cent in the early 1990s, but then decreasing to between 15 and 27 per cent depending on the election. A study of Maria Spirova of 2005 showed that it is the Bulgarian Socialist Party (BSP) that sets the party organisational model for the other parties, therefore such party structures have been more developed in Bulgaria (Spirova, 2005: 606–8, 612–15; 2008, 2014). On the right, several parties have succeeded each other. Presently, the Citizens for European Development in Bulgaria (GERB) led by charismatic former bodyguard Boyko Borisov is the strongest party since its emergence in the 2009 elections. It clearly is able to work closely together with other rightwing political groups such as the conservative Bulgarian National Movement (VMRO-BND), the National Front for the Salvation of Bulgaria (NFSB) and the xenophobic far right Ataka. The latter targets the Turkish minority. Quite an important party is the Movement for Rights and Freedoms (DPS) representing the Turkish minority in Bulgaria. The DPS tends to work mainly with the BSP. Most volatility seems therefore to be happening on the right. It is difficult to predict if

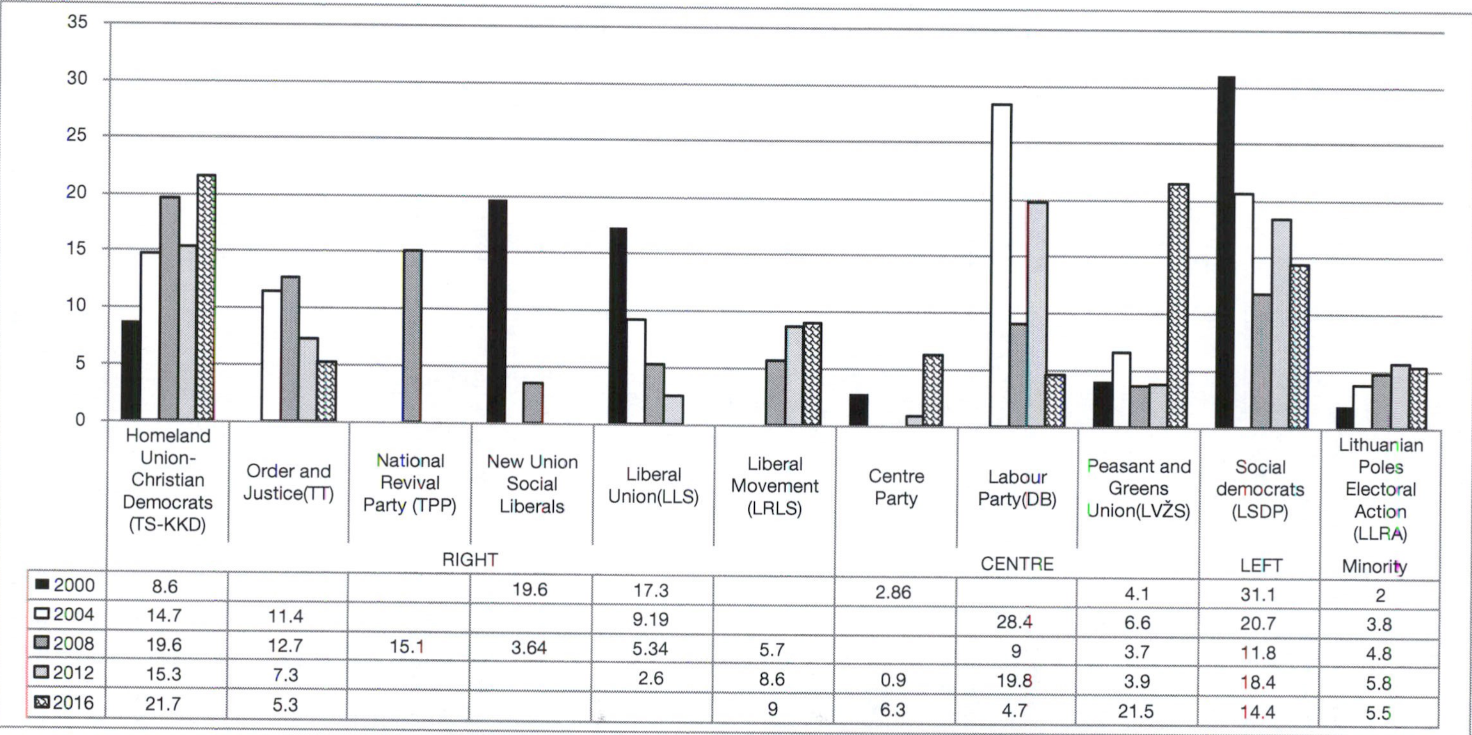

	Homeland Union-Christian Democrats (TS-KKD)	Order and Justice(TT)	National Revival Party (TPP)	New Union Social Liberals	Liberal Union(LLS)	Liberal Movement (LRLS)	Centre Party	Labour Party(DB)	Peasant and Greens Union(LVŽS)	Social democrats (LSDP)	Lithuanian Poles Electoral Action (LLRA)
2000	8.6			19.6	17.3		2.86		4.1	31.1	2
2004	14.7	11.4			9.19			28.4	6.6	20.7	3.8
2008	19.6	12.7	15.1	3.64	5.34	5.7		9	3.7	11.8	4.8
2012	15.3	7.3			2.6	8.6	0.9	19.8	3.9	18.4	5.8
2016	21.7	5.3				9	6.3	4.7	21.5	14.4	5.5

Figure 7.40 General elections in Lithuania, 2000–16

Source: Author's graph based on database of Parties and Elections in Europe (2018).

after Boris Borisov, GERB will be able to survive due to its strong dependency on the leader (Jurek, 2010; Kostadinova, 2007; Rashkova, 2014a, 2014b; Spirova, 2014; Figure 7.41).

In Romania, two parties seem now to dominate the party system. More, concretely the former reform communists, now social democrats (PSD), still control the structures of power. PSD was able to expand its electoral share in 2012 and 2016 to 58.6 and 45.5 per cent respectively. This is certainly related to the charismatic leadership of Victor Ponta. However, he had to resign in 2015 after mass protests over a mishandling of a fire in a nightclub (*The Guardian*, 4 November 2015). The main rival party is the liberal conservative National Liberal Party (PNL) with 20 per cent in the 2016 elections. The PNL has been absorbing many other parties in the centre-right since the 1990s. In spite of this, a new liberal party Alliance of Liberals and Democrats in Europe (ALDE) emerged in the 2016 elections achieving 5.6 per cent of the vote. Another centre-right party is the People's Movement Party (PMP), which achieved 5.4 per cent of the vote in 2016. Certainly a very important party is the Democratic Alliance of Hungarians in Romania (UDMR), representing the Hungarian minority. Save Romania Union (USR) is a new anti-corruption party that also achieved representation in parliament with 8.9 per cent of the vote in 2016. In spite of the volatility, one may regard the Romanian party system as being relatively stable (Figure 7.42). Apart from the low level of electoral integrity, political elites have been using and abusing the electoral system to manipulate majorities. Meanwhile four different electoral systems have been used for elections, as well as constitutional reform (Brett, 2015; Chiva, 2014; Coman, 2015; Jurek, 2010).

A genuine Croatian party system began to emerge only after the death of charismatic leader Franjo Tuđman in 2000. Although the party system was still fragmented, two parties emerged as the dominant ones: the moderate conservative Croatian Democratic Union (HDZ) and the Social Democrats (SDP); each one has been able to achieve between 20 and 35 per cent of the vote. Two smaller parties are the Croatian People's Party–Liberal Democrats (HNS) and the agrarian Croatian Peasants' Party (HSS) and are allied to the SDP. Furthermore, the moderation of politics has contributed to an improvement in the economy and reform efforts of successive Croatian governments. One major problem remains, which is the high level of fragmentation. There are currently fourteen parties represented in parliament (Fink-Hafner, 2008; Jurek, 2010; Preiec and Brown, 2015; Šedo, 2010a; Figure 7.43).

Party system consolidation in the Balkans

In comparison to the Central and Eastern European countries, the Balkans are still in the early process of consolidation, with most party systems still in the making. The legacy of nationalism is still quite strong in Serbia, Bosnia-Herzegovina, Macedonia and Kosovo. The EU has been an important actor in structuring the political process towards more democracy. Nationalism has been a major factor affecting democracy in the region. Only European integration is regarded by the more moderate elites and parts of the population as being able to overcome this vicious cycle of former socialist rule and nationalist populist politics (Stojarová,

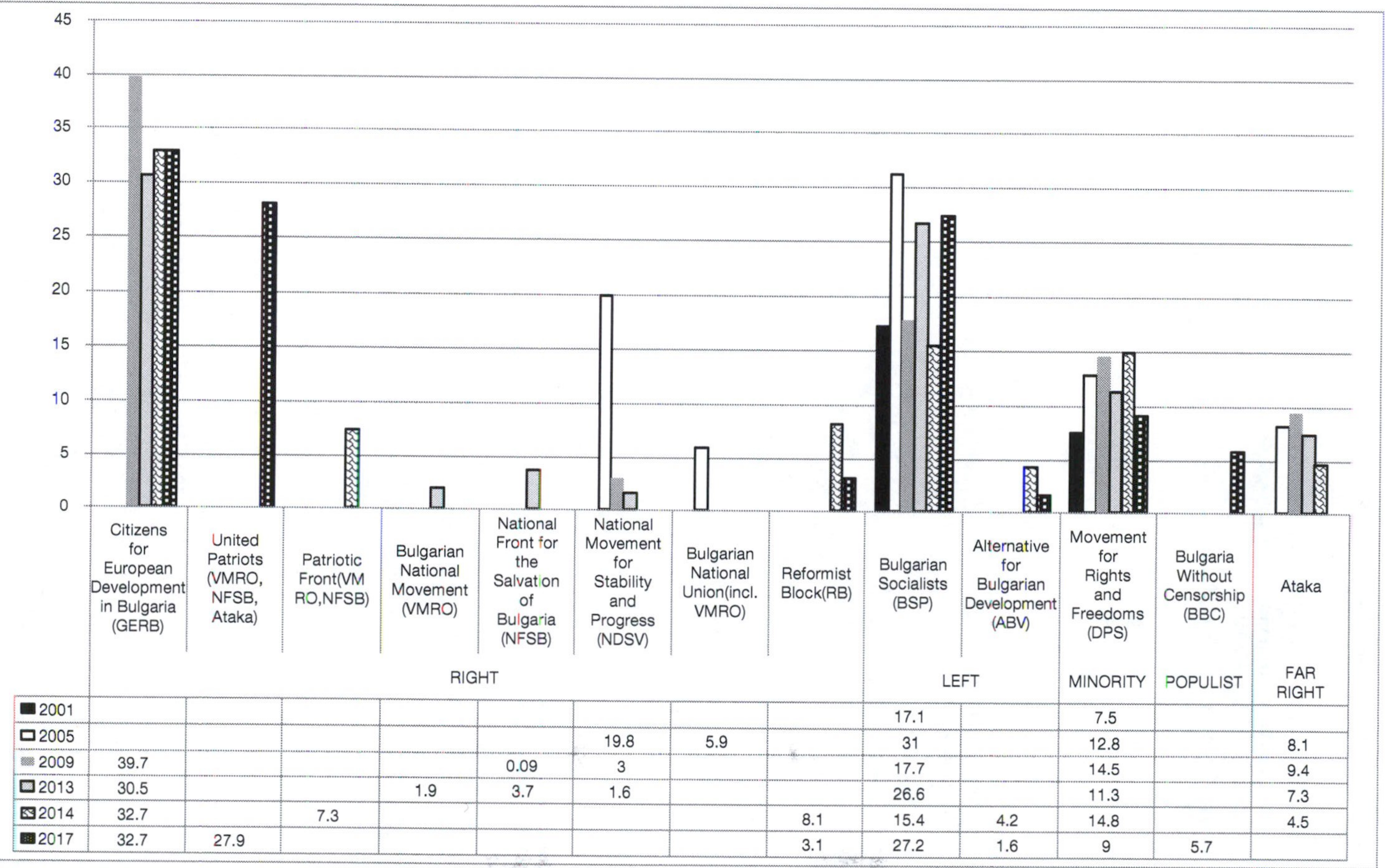

	Citizens for European Development in Bulgaria (GERB)	United Patriots (VMRO, NFSB, Ataka)	Patriotic Front(VM RO,NFSB)	Bulgarian National Movement (VMRO)	National Front for the Salvation of Bulgaria (NFSB)	National Movement for Stability and Progress (NDSV)	Bulgarian National Union(incl. VMRO)	Reformist Block(RB)	Bulgarian Socialists (BSP)	Alternative for Bulgarian Development (ABV)	Movement for Rights and Freedoms (DPS)	Bulgaria Without Censorship (BBC)	Ataka
	RIGHT								LEFT		MINORITY	POPULIST	FAR RIGHT
2001									17.1		7.5		
2005						19.8	5.9		31		12.8		8.1
2009	39.7				0.09	3			17.7		14.5		9.4
2013	30.5			1.9	3.7	1.6			26.6		11.3		7.3
2014	32.7		7.3					8.1	15.4	4.2	14.8		4.5
2017	32.7	27.9						3.1	27.2	1.6	9	5.7	

Figure 7.41 General elections in Bulgaria, 2000–16

Table 7.18 Political parties in Bulgaria, Romania and Croatia, 2018

	Social Democrats	*Christian Democrats/ Conservatives*	*Liberals*	*Nationalists/ extreme right*	*Other*
Bulgaria	Bălgarska Socialističeska Partija (BSP) Bulgarian Socialist Party Alternativa za Bălgarsko Vălgarsko (ABV) Alternative for Bulgarian Development	Grajdani za Evropejsko Razvitie na Bulgaria (GERB) Citizens for European Development of Bulgaria (Conservatism) VMRO – Bălgarsko Nacionalno Dviženie (VMRO-BND) VMRO – Bulgarian National Movement (National conservatism) Nacionalen Front za Spasenie na Bălgaria (NFSB) National Front for the Salvation of Bulgaria (Nationalism) Reformatorski Blok (RB) Reformist Bloc (Conservatism, Christian Democracy)		Nacionalen Săjuz Ataka (Ataka) National Union Attack	Dvizenie za Prava i Svobodi (DPS) Movement for Rights and Freedoms (Turkish minority)
Romania	Partidul Social-Democrat (PSD) Social Democratic Party	Partidul Mişcarea Populara (PMP) People's Movement Party	Partidul National Liberal (PNL) National Liberal Party Allianta Liberalilor si Democratilor (ALDE) Alliance of Liberals and Democrats	Partidul România Mare (PRM) Great Romania Party (small party, 1%)	Uniunea Democrată Maghiară din România (UDMR) Democratic Alliance of Hungarians in Romania Uniunea Salvati România (USR) Save Romania Union
Croatia	Socijaldemokratska Partija Hrvatske (SDP) Social Democratic Party of Croatia	Hrvatska Demokratska Zajednica (HDZ) Croatian Democratic Union Most Nezavisnih Lista (MOST) Independent List Bridge Hrvatska Demokršćanska Stranka (HDS) Croatian Christian Democratic Party	Hrvatska Socijalno Liberalna Stranka (HSLS) Croatian Social Liberal Party Hrvatska Narodna Stranka – Liberalni Demokrati (HNS) Croatian People's Party – Liberal Democrats		Hrvatska Stranka Umirovljenika (HSU) Croatian Party of Pensioners Hrvatska Seljačka Stranka (HSS) Croatian Peasant Party

Source: Author.

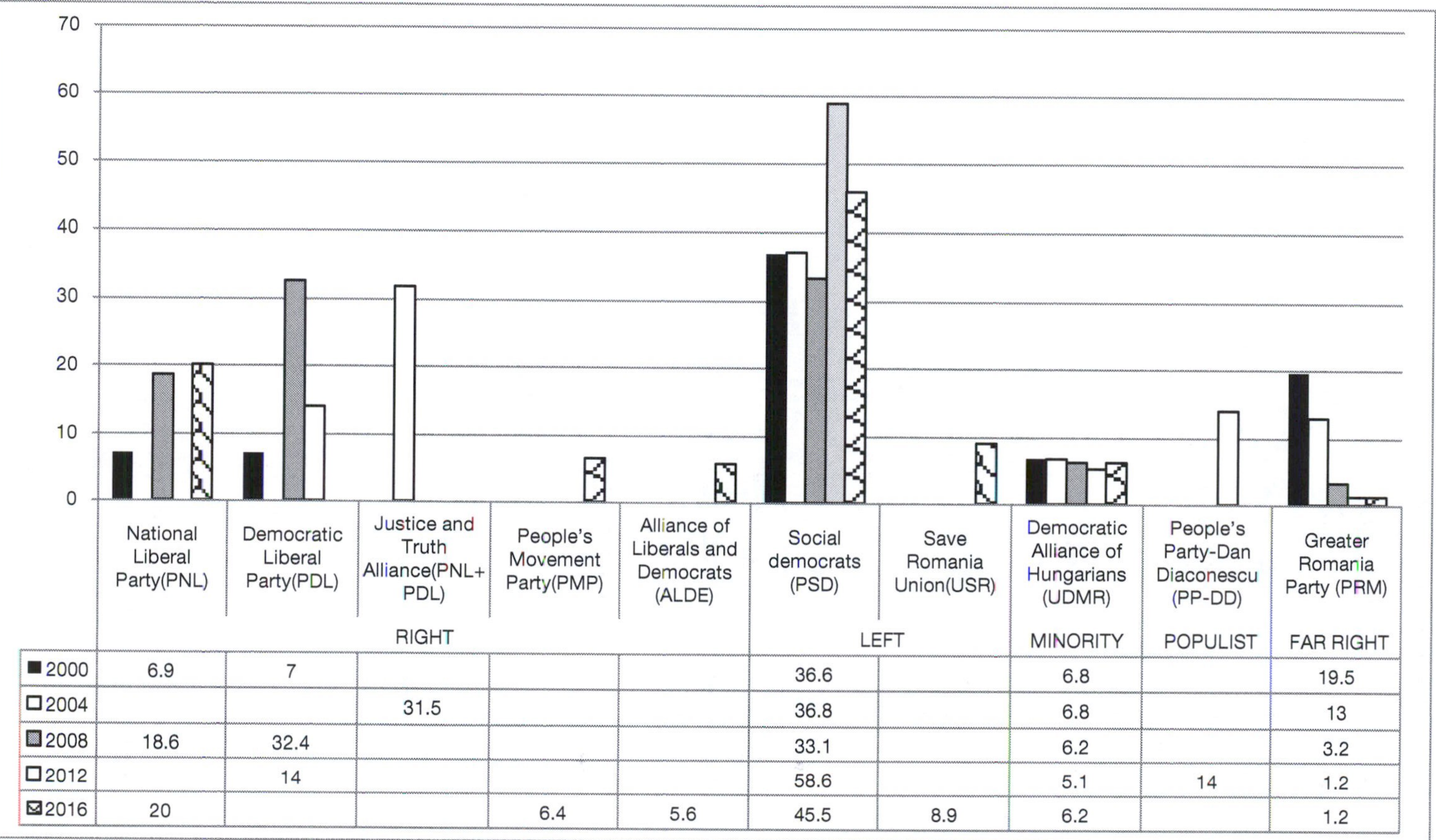

	National Liberal Party(PNL)	Democratic Liberal Party(PDL)	Justice and Truth Alliance(PNL+ PDL)	People's Movement Party(PMP)	Alliance of Liberals and Democrats (ALDE)	Social democrats (PSD)	Save Romania Union(USR)	Democratic Alliance of Hungarians (UDMR)	People's Party-Dan Diaconescu (PP-DD)	Greater Romania Party (PRM)
	RIGHT					LEFT		MINORITY	POPULIST	FAR RIGHT
2000	6.9	7				36.6		6.8		19.5
2004			31.5			36.8		6.8		13
2008	18.6	32.4				33.1		6.2		3.2
2012		14				58.6		5.1	14	1.2
2016	20			6.4	5.6	45.5	8.9	6.2		1.2

Figure 7.42 General elections in Romania, 2000–16

Source: Author's graph based on the database of Parties and Elections in Europe (2018).

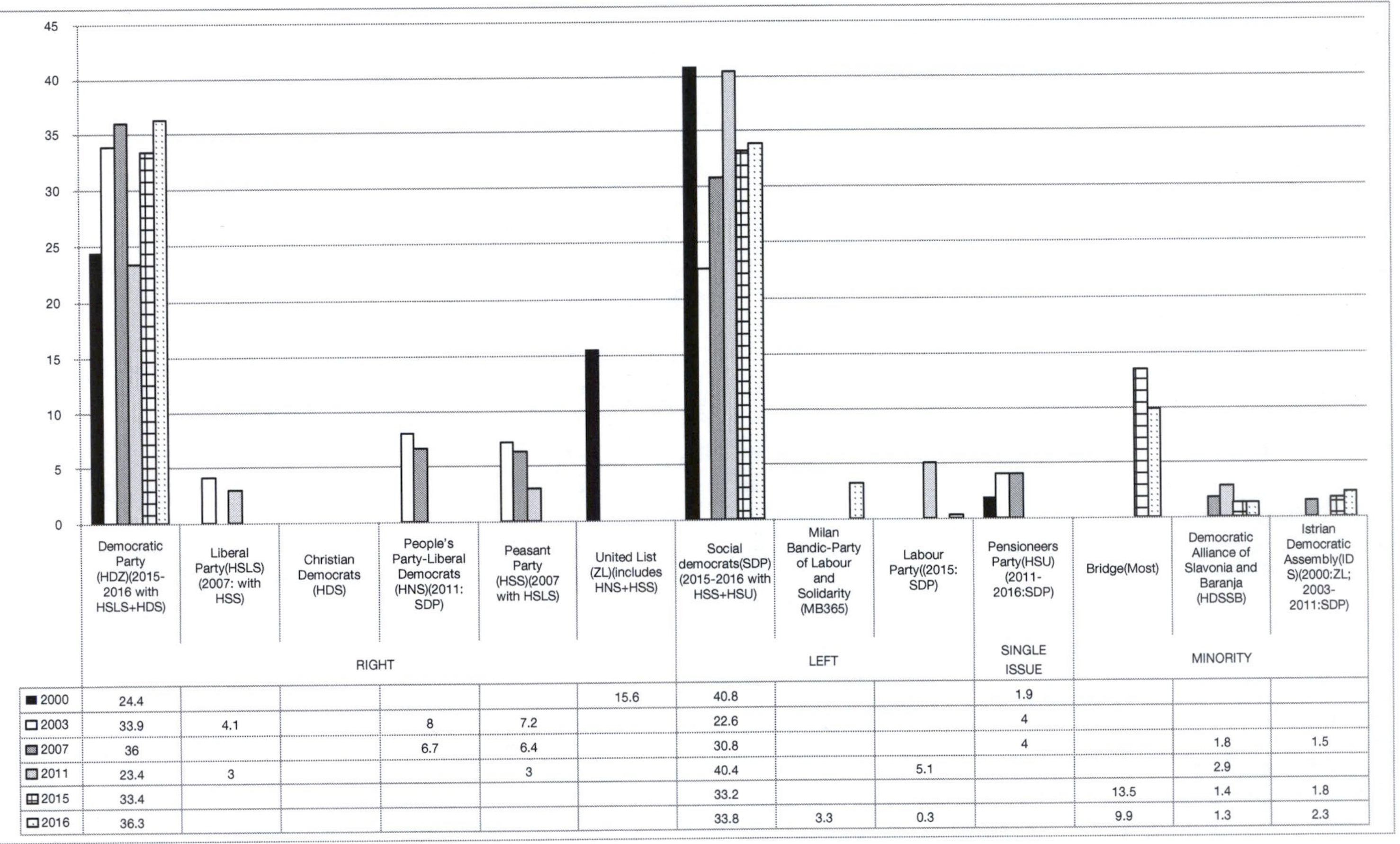

	Democratic Party (HDZ)(2015-2016 with HSLS+HDS)	Liberal Party(HSLS) (2007: with HSS)	Christian Democrats (HDS)	People's Party-Liberal Democrats (HNS)(2011: SDP)	Peasant Party (HSS)(2007 with HSLS)	United List (ZL)(includes HNS+HSS)	Social democrats(SDP) (2015-2016 with HSS+HSU)	Milan Bandic-Party of Labour and Solidarity (MB365)	Labour Party((2015: SDP)	Pensioneers Party(HSU) (2011-2016:SDP)	Bridge(Most)	Democratic Alliance of Slavonia and Baranja (HDSSB)	Istrian Democratic Assembly(IDS)(2000:ZL; 2003-2011:SDP)
	RIGHT						LEFT			SINGLE ISSUE	MINORITY		
2000	24.4					15.6	40.8			1.9			
2003	33.9	4.1		8	7.2		22.6			4			
2007	36			6.7	6.4		30.8			4		1.8	1.5
2011	23.4	3			3		40.4		5.1			2.9	
2015	33.4						33.2				13.5	1.4	1.8
2016	36.3						33.8	3.3	0.3		9.9	1.3	2.3

Figure 7.43 General elections in Croatia, 2000–16

Source: Author's graph based on the database of Parties and Elections in Europe (2018).

2010a, 2010b) A major announcement was made that the Balkan countries may be able to join the EU after 2025 depending on the progress made. The main structuring cleavage still seems to be between left and right. Party success is strongly linked to charismatic personalities. This is the case for Serbia, where the Serbian Progressive Party (SNS) of president Aleksandar Vukcič is the dominant party with 48.3 per cent of vote, and in coalition with the socialists, its main rival since the 2016 elections (Bochsler, 2010; Fink-Hafner, 2008).

Macedonia has also a more or less stable party system. On the one hand, the Democratic Party for Macedonian National Unity (VMRO-DPMNE) remains the strongest party of the party system with 38 to 50 per cent of the vote, while the second largest is the Social Democratic Union of Macedonia (SDSM) with 25 to 37 per cent. There are several small Albanian parties that may become kingmakers (Šedo, 2010c).

Similarly, in Montenegro, the Social Democratic Party dominates the political system with a 40 to 50 per cent share of the vote (for more detail, see Fink-Hafner, 2008; Bieber, 2010). In Albania, two main parties have been dominant since the foundation elections in 1991: the Socialist Party (PS) with about 40 to 48 per cent of the vote, and the liberal Democratic Party with 30 to 40 per cent since 2009 (Stojarová, 2010c, 2010d).

More problematic has been the situation in Bosnia-Herzegovina. After more than a decade of international supervision and political engineering, there is no political party that is able to transcend the national divide (Šedo, 2010b).

In sum, the Balkan party systems are probably still the least consolidated. Apart from their late development, other reasons for this relate to the ethnic composition of the respective countries. The most problematic party system is probably that of Kosovo and Bosnia-Herzegovina, largely because of the polarisation between the different ethnic groups and the respective political parties.

The European Parliament: towards Americanisation of politics?

One characteristic of contemporary European politics is that political parties do not act in just one electoral area, but rather in multiple ones. As already mentioned, there are national general elections and local elections, but for some countries (for example, Spain, Germany, Belgium, France, the UK, Italy, Austria and, increasingly, the Czech Republic, Slovakia and Poland) there are also regional elections. There is now an intertwined dynamic between the different levels of elections within the national territories. Furthermore, political parties also have to campaign for elections to the European Parliament, which have taken place every five years since 1979. One problem of European elections is that they are still characterised by national campaigns. The European issues are not as salient as national issues. This has been changing over time, but factors such as the organisation of national and European elections at the same time leads to a nationalisation of politics. Another factor is that elections take place on different days, not just on one single day. For example, the UK and the Netherlands organise their elections on Thursdays, most other countries on Sundays. In spite of the fact that all EU member countries have to use proportional representation systems, the method differs from country to country (Hix, 2005: 192–6). The most important obstacle to a Europeanisation of elections is probably the fact that nobody knows what the European Parliament does (see Chapter 10). Media reporting on the European Parliament at national level has been at a low level, with the result that European elections are regarded by most voters as second-order (or even third-order) elections after regional and local elections. Low turnout at European elections is particularly widespread in Central and Eastern European countries, with East Central and Eastern Europe having the lowest record (Figure 7.44).

The European Parliament elections bring together all the party families that exist in Europe. Many new political parties in Central and Eastern Europe have had to decide which of the parliamentary groups they wanted to belong to. There are seven parliamentary groups, of which the European People's Party (EPP) is the largest. This party includes Christian democrats, conservatives and some liberals. The second largest but more cohesive is the Party of European Socialists (PES), which clearly has strong relations to the Socialist International. Many communist parties of Central and Eastern Europe transformed themselves into social democratic parties and joined the PES. The third largest group is the European Liberal Democratic and Reform (ELDR) group comprising mainly the liberal parties. Furthermore, on the left, there are the European Green Party and the regionalists (EGP-EFA) and the European United Left– Nordic Green Left (EUL-NGL), which comprises the communists, some new left parties and some of the more left-wing greens from Nordic Europe. On the right, there is the European Conservative Party, which comprises Eurosceptic and national-conservative parties, as well as the soft Eurosceptic Europe of Freedom and Direct Democracy (EFDD) and the more nationalist hard Eurosceptics Europe of Nations and Freedom (ENF) (Hix, 2005: 186–92; Hix and Lord, 1997; Judge and Earnshaw, 2008: chapter 5) (see Table 7.19). Since 2007, parliamentary groups and extra-parliamentary parties can create European political parties and party political foundations. Moreover, these new structures are funded by the European Parliament. Their main task is to promote the idea of European integration in the context of ideological diversity. However, they are not very salient and still dependent on getting their message across through their national representatives (a quite early study is by Hanley, 2008; Peglis, 2015).

In sum, the European electoral arena further reinforces the framing of national politics towards a limited number of party families that have achieved representation in the European Parliament. In this sense, dissemination and cooperation within the parliamentary groups have made political parties more Europeanised. The highest level of Europeanisation can probably be found among the European People's Party, European Socialist Party, European Liberals and the European Greens. More Eurocritical and Eurosceptic voices come from the Radical Left (EUL-NGL), the European Conservatives, and particularly the nationalists (EFDD and ENF).

Conclusions: party politics in Americanised electoral markets

Today, party politics in European countries takes place in Americanised electoral markets. The erosion of encapsulated subcultures in the traditional democracies and the non-existence of them in new democracies has led to the emergence of volatile electoral markets in which parties compete for individual voters. Individual

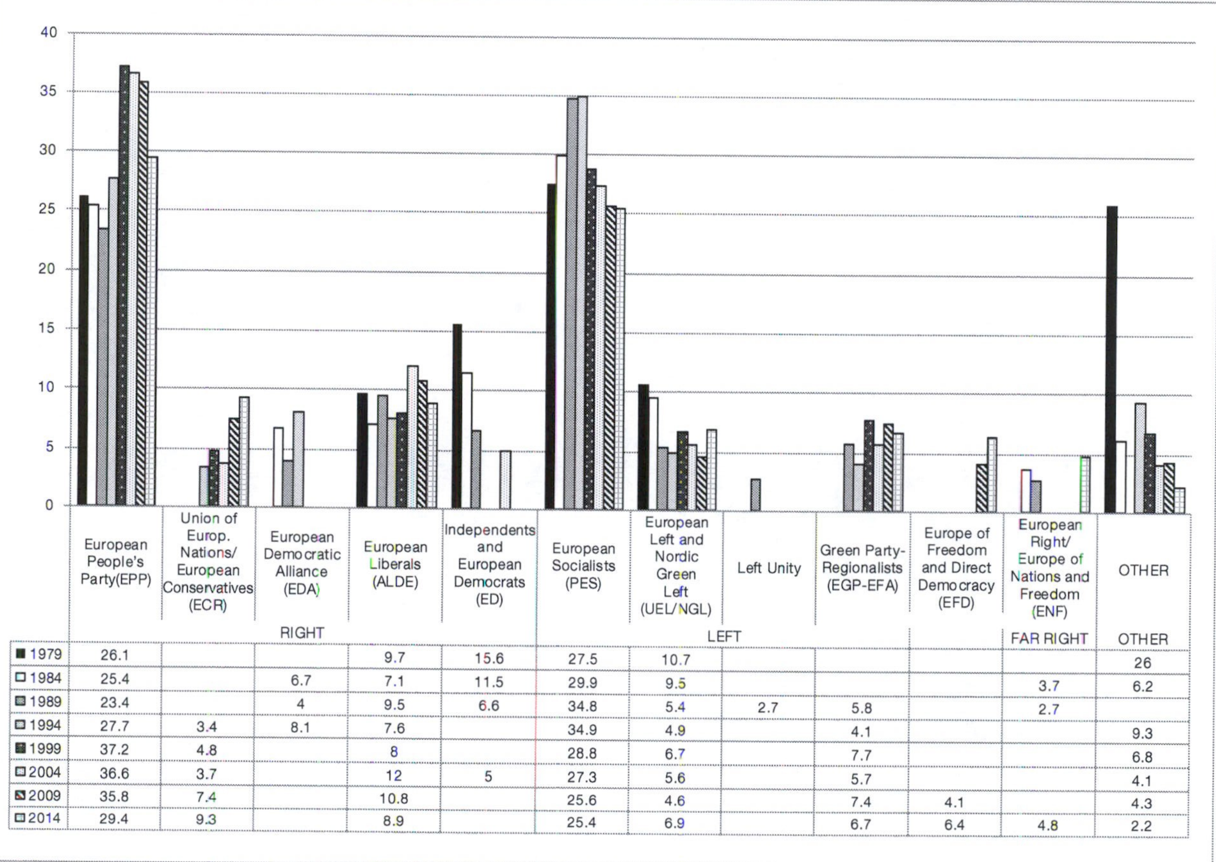

	European People's Party(EPP)	Union of Europ. Nations/ European Conservatives (ECR)	European Democratic Alliance (EDA)	European Liberals (ALDE)	Independents and European Democrats (ED)	European Socialists (PES)	European Left and Nordic Green Left (UEL/NGL)	Left Unity	Green Party-Regionalists (EGP-EFA)	Europe of Freedom and Direct Democracy (EFD)	European Right/ Europe of Nations and Freedom (ENF)	OTHER
1979	26.1			9.7	15.6	27.5	10.7					26
1984	25.4		6.7	7.1	11.5	29.9	9.5				3.7	6.2
1989	23.4		4	9.5	6.6	34.8	5.4	2.7	5.8		2.7	
1994	27.7	3.4	8.1	7.6		34.9	4.9		4.1			9.3
1999	37.2	4.8		8		28.8	6.7		7.7			6.8
2004	36.6	3.7		12	5	27.3	5.6		5.7			4.1
2009	35.8	7.4		10.8		25.6	4.6		7.4	4.1		4.3
2014	29.4	9.3		8.9		25.4	6.9		6.7	6.4	4.8	2.2

Figure 7.44 European Parliament elections 1979–2014 according to share of seats

Source: Author's graph based on database of European Parliament (2018).

Table 7.19 Distribution of seats of the 2014 European Parliament elections, according to countries and parliamentary groups

	EPP	*S&D*	*ALDE*	*Greens*	*ECR*	*GUE/NGL*	*EFD*	*ENF*	*NA*	*Total*
Belgium	4	4	6	2	4			1		**21**
Bulgaria	7	4	4		2					**17**
Czech Republic	7	4	4		2	3	1			**21**
Denmark	1	3	3	1	3	1			1	**13**
Germany	34	27	4	13	6	8	1	1	2	**96**
Estonia	1	1	3	1						**6**
Ireland	4	1	1		1	4				**11**
Greece	5	4			1	6			5	**21**
Spain	17	14	8	5		10				**54**
France	20	13	7	6		4	5	17	2	**74**
Croatia	5	2	2	1	1					**11**
Italy	15	31	1		2	6			5	**73**
Cyprus	1	2			1	2				**6**
Latvia	4	1	1	1	1					**8**
Lithuania	3	2	3	1	1		1			**11**
Luxembourg	3	1	1	1						**6**
Hungary	12	4		2					3	**21**
Malta	3	3								**6**
Netherlands	5	3	7	2	2	3		4		**26**
Austria	5	5	1	3				4		**18**
Poland	22	5			18		1	2	3	**51**
Portugal	8	8	1			4				**21**
Romania	13	14	3		2					**32**
Slovenia	5	1	1	1						**8**
Slovakia	6	4			3					**13**
Finland	3	2	4	1	2	1				**13**
Sweden	4	6	3	4		1	2			**20**
UK	2	20	1	6	19	1	20	1	3	**73**
	219	**189**	**68**	**52**	**71**	**51**	**45**	**36**	**20**	**751**

Source: Own graph based on database of European Parliament (2018).

voters think more in opportunistic rational terms about their choices. The big business of political marketing, including political strategy, further advance the consolidation of electoral market behaviour by parties and individual voters. Furthermore, social media is revolutionising the way parties are communicating with their members and potential voters. Political parties are losing membership and becoming more interested in getting access to public office and public funding in order to sustain the organisation and its functionaries. This is leading to the emergence of the cartel party. European party politics is increasingly multilevel with elections at local, regional, national and European levels

Suggested reading

Broughton, David and Mark Donovan (eds) (1999), *Changing Party Systems in Western Europe*. London: Pinter.

Caramani, Daniele (2004), *The Nationalization of Politics: The Formation of National Electorates and Party Systems in Western Europe*. Cambridge: Cambridge University Press.

Caramani, Daniele (2015), *The Europeanization of Politics. The Formation of a European Electorate and Party System in Historical Perspective*. Cambridge: Cambridge University Press

Casal-Bértoa, Fernando and Ingrid van Biezen (eds) (2014), Party regulation and party politics in post-communist Europe. A Special Issue of *East European Politics*, 30(3).

Farrell, David M. (2000), *Electoral Systems: A Comparative Introduction*. Basingstoke: Palgrave.

Katz, Richard S. and Peter Mair (1995), Changing models of party organization and party democracy. *Party Politics*, 1(1): 5–28.

Mair, Peter (1997), *Party System Change. Approaches and Interpretations*. Oxford: Oxford University Press.

Organisation for Economic Cooperation and Development (OECD) (2016b), *Financing Democracy. Funding of Political Parties and Election Campaigns and the Risk of Policy Capture*. Paris: OECD.

Van Biezen, Ingrid (2003), *Political Parties in New Democracies*. Basingstoke: Palgrave.

Electronic journals

Electoral Studies: Excellent for national election reports.

West European Politics: Excellent on party systems and national election reports.

Party Politics: Excellent on parties and party systems.

European Journal of Political Research: Excellent political data yearbook (PDY): the beginning of each volume, issue 1 (December), holds the national yearly reports of all countries of the EU and other OECD countries. These are accompanied by a dedicated website of the PDY at www.politicaldatayearbook.com/ accessed on 5 November 2018.

Federal and Regional Studies: Excellent source for regional elections, particularly Spain, Belgium, Germany, Austria and the UK.

Websites

International Institute for Democracy and Electoral Assistance (IDEA) (2018), Electoral Systems Design Database at www.idea.int/data-tools/data/electoral-system-design accessed on 5 November 2018.

Parties and Elections in Europe (2018), database on elections of all European countries at: www.parties-and-elections.de/ accessed 6 May 2018.

QUESTIONS FOR REVISION

- What is understood by 'cartel party'? Discuss, using examples from at least two countries.
- Compare the ideologies of the main political party families.
- Why is membership of political parties declining? Discuss, using examples from at least two different countries.
- Compare political parties in 'old' and 'new' democracies. Discuss, using examples from at least two countries.
- What main factors should one take into account when designing an electoral system? Discuss, using examples from at least two countries in Europe.
- Compare the main features of the German and UK electoral systems.
- How stable are the party systems in the Netherlands and France?
- How consolidated are the party systems in Hungary and Poland?

Chapter 8

Interest groups and systems of interest intermediation

- Patterns of interest intermediation and industrial relations at national level
- Towards a multilevel system of interest intermediation
- Conclusions: from national systems of interest intermediation to a multilevel EU governance system
- Suggested reading

In contrast to the United States, interest groups have a closer relationship to national governments in Europe. The European integration process has highlighted that a European social model of capitalism is inherent in all member-states. This European social model includes a continuing consultation with the relevant economic and social partners regarding economic, labour and social policy issues. The tripartite social dialogue is one of the elements of this European model of industrial relations. The three partners are the main business organisations, the trade unions and the government (representing the state). This has now become part of the industrial relations pattern of the EU.

Europe is also characterised by dense civil societies that allow participation of the population in different issues. However, this density varies cross-nationally, with the Nordic countries having the strongest civil societies, and Southern, Central and Eastern European states the lowest.

Patterns of interest intermediation and industrial relations at national level

Europeanisation and globalisation are transforming national patterns of interest intermediation and industrial relations. Figure 8.1 shows four groups of countries and their respective patterns of adjustment.

From rigid interventionist to regulatory flexible neo-corporatism

The European social model of capitalism clearly is more coordinated by a partnership between state and social partners. It fits well into the typology of Varieties of Capitalism proposed by David Soskice and Peter Hall, in which they differentiate

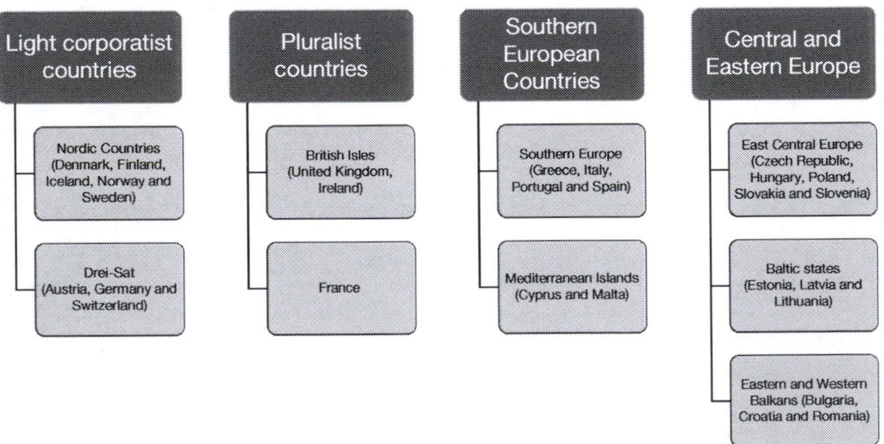

Figure 8.1 Patterns of interest intermediation in Europe

between coordinated market economies (e.g. Germany) and liberal market economies (e.g. the United States). While the former has more elements of inter-firm cooperation, a solid system of industrial relations, an extensive programme of vocational training embedded in the enterprises, and a long-term relationship with financial institutions, also known as the house bank (Hausbank), the latter clearly is more characterised by a competitive behaviour of enterprises, a non-existent system of industrial relations, the lack of an extensive vocational training system and reliance on general education, and more short-term risk funding schemes provided by the financial institutions. Coordinated market economies are incremental innovators, and liberal market economies tend towards risk innovation (Soskice and Hall, 2001: 21–33). This clearly is just a typology, and each country in Europe may have a more or less sophisticated system of coordination. However, the typology is certainly helpful to understand the big difference between US and European capitalism. In reality, we can find myriad socioeconomic coordination models across Europe.

The negative experiences of capitalism in the interwar period and the subsequent Second World War gave rise to a major incentive to move away from uncontrolled non-regulated capitalism. Between 1945 and 1975, the so-called glorious thirties (trentes glorieuses), most Western European countries adopted some kind of a social model of organised capitalism, fostering cooperation between highly unionised trade union confederations and strongly organised business confederations. A kind of tripartite cooperative institutional framework was developed leading to collective bargaining, improvement of workers' rights and strong welfare states. In Central and Eastern Europe, the Soviet Union pushed all the countries to move to a communist regime. The so-called 'people's democracy' established social systems for the working class. In this regard, the social dimension was quite central to European capitalism after the war. In Western Europe, the strong involvement of the traditional social partners in economic and labour market policy was labelled as 'neo-corporatism' or 'tripartite', but there were differences between the countries in this respect as well. 'Corporatism' was part of the economic philosophy of social Catholicism developed in the nineteenth and early twentieth centuries that advocated a harmonious cooperation between interest groups and was against the socialist/communist 'class struggle' between employers and workers, and was also against the 'pluralist', 'non-regulated' approach of pure capitalism. Corporatism was later adopted by Italian fascism and copied by other authoritarian regimes, such as those in Austria (1934–8), Portugal (1926–74) and Spain (1939–78) (a major theorist of corporatism was Mihail Manoilescu; for more, see Schmitter, 1974). 'Neo-corporatism' was a revival of such arrangements, although in a democratic and capitalist context. The 'tripartite' or 'neo-corporatist' approach became important in countries with strong unified trade union confederations and business organisations, such as Sweden, Denmark, Norway, the Netherlands, Belgium and Austria. Alan Siaroff defines neo-corporatism as follows:

> [Within] an advanced industrial society and democratic polity, the coordinated, co-operative, and systematic management of the national economy by the state, the centralised unions, employers, (these latter two co-operating directly in industry), presumably to the relative benefit of all three actors.
>
> (Siaroff, 1999: 177)

Such model was particularly used by small countries with a quite open economy, namely Austria, the Netherlands, Belgium, Luxembourg, Sweden, Denmark, Finland, Norway and Iceland. Many countries, such as the UK, France, Germany and Italy, had neo-corporatist elements in their systems of interest intermediation, but were generally more pluralist. During the glorious thirty years (1945–75) the highly unionised trade union confederations had a strong ideological relationship with the main parties, leading to an intertwined relationship between political and socioeconomic structures (see Table 8.1).

In his seminal studies on neo-corporatism of the 1980s, Peter Katzenstein differentiated between social and liberal corporatism (Katzenstein, 1984: 30; 1985). Social corporatism could rely on strong trade union confederations and socially oriented government policies, while in liberal corporatism there was more equidistance of governments to both trade union confederations and employers. While Austria, Norway and Denmark were characterised as social neo-corporatist, and Switzerland, the Netherlands and Belgium best represented the liberal branch, Germany and Sweden would certainly be placed somewhere between the two (Katzenstein, 1985: 81).

However, since the 1970s, the generous welfare systems and working conditions in these neo-corporatist small states contributed to a loss of competitiveness, and they were required to reform their economic and social systems. Welfare states could no longer grow because the respective economies had difficulties financing them. Instead, reforms were undertaken to link welfare policies to labour market

Table 8.1 The placement of countries according to a neo-corporatism–pluralism continuum

Dominance of neo-corporatism			*Dominance of pluralism*		
Strongly corporatist	*Moderately to strongly corporatist*	*Moderately corporatist*	*Pluralism with some strong corporatism*	*Pluralism with some weak corporatism*	*Pluralist*
Austria	Netherlands	Finland Belgium	Ireland UK (1962–1979)	Central and Eastern European countries	USA Canada UK (since 1980s)
Norway	West Germany (up until 1989)	Luxembourg	Italy Unified Germany (after 1989)		
Denmark		Sweden	France Portugal Spain Greece		

Source: Simplified and amended from Siaroff (1999: 184); this is based on the perceptions of different authors and is, therefore, an inter-subjective assessment. Germany and the UK are the author's own assessment.

activation policies. This 'workfare' approach required most open economies to reduce labour costs that were previously imposed by legislation agreed through tripartite arrangements (see Scharpf, 2000; Schmidt, 2008). Across the EU, after 2005, this approach has been called 'flexicurity' and assumes that the majority of people of working age will have five or six jobs during their lifetime. This means that, instead of job security, the focus should be on employability and lifelong training, in order for people to be able to find employment. In short, 'flexicurity' means flexibility of labour markets, supported by a linked and generous supporting welfare state and the intensive implementation of labour market activation policies (Andersen, 2011; Antoneades, 2005; Bekker, 2018).

According to Franz Traxler (2004), social partners, particularly trade unions, needed to become more flexible in their approach towards the labour market and social policies. Traxler identified a cross-national transformation of neo-corporatism from a rigid interventionist to a light neo-corporatist approach. According to Traxler, this process started in the 1970s and is now leading to the restructuring of the system of intermediation, particularly in terms of wage regulation (Traxler, 2004: 576; see also Schmitter and Grote, 1997: 5–12). As already mentioned, economic and monetary union is a major factor in the revival of some kind of light neo-corporatism across the EU. Governments have to have social partners on board in order to keep disciplined budgetary policies. Therefore, national social pacts have gained in considerable importance since the late 1980s (Hamann and Kelly, 2011, 2015; Hassel, 2009; Pochet et al., 2010).

The following brief look at the individual countries known to have a strong neo-corporatist legacy clearly confirms the theses of Traxler, and Schmitter and Grote (Figures 8.2 and 8.3).

The Nordic countries: from neo-corporatism to network governance

The greatest transformations happened in the Nordic countries. The centralised structures of neo-corporatist coordination and decision-making, particularly in terms of income policy, began to falter in the 1990s. Particularly, business organisations began to withdraw from national wage bargaining coordination and push for more de-centralised enterprise level flexible bargaining. This was particularly visible in Sweden, Finland and Denmark. According to Peter Munk Christiansen the main features of the transformation were that the nature of interest intermediation moved from being encompassing to being just partial. Although there is still use of consultation committees, this has been less generalised and more asymmetrical according to policy area (Christiansen, 2018: 44).

Sweden may be regarded probably as one of the most traditional neo-corporatist country – the strong Trade Union Confederation (Landsorganisationen, LO), founded in 1898, consists of 14 trade union federations comprising in 2018 1.44 million members and the Swedish Enterprises Association (Svensk Näringsliv) was re-founded in 2001 with this new name, although it had existed since 1902 under the name of Swedish Employers' Organisation (Svenska arbetergivarföreningen, SAF). The Svensk Näringsliv comprises 49 organisations with 60, 000 member companies and 1.6 million employees (LO, 2018; SN, 2018). Both remain central to the consensual style of politics with a culture of consultation

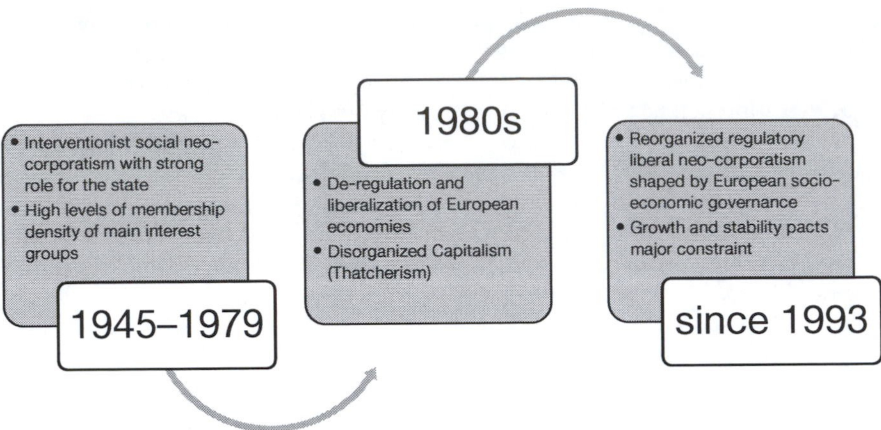

Figure 8.2 The transformation of democratic neo-corporatism in Europe

and integration of relevant interest groups. The most important event leading to the establishment of the neo-corporatist system was probably the Saltjöbaden Agreement of 1938 between the main LO and SAF. The agreement was a trade-off that allowed the Swedish enterprises to rationalise and adjust to the crisis in exchange for a stronger welfare state provided mainly by the state to the workers.

The Swedish model reached its peak between 1960 and the late 1980s, following which Sweden had to deal with a major recession. Throughout the 1950s and 1960s the whole neo-corporatist network was formalised, becoming known as the 'Harpsund Democracy', because prime minister Tage Erlander would meet representatives of relevant socioeconomic interest groups in his seat at Harpsund, a manor house 125 km (100 miles) to the south of Stockholm (Arter, 1997: 162; Götz, 2012: 644). Although globalisation and Europeanisation are transforming the Swedish model, particularly as a result of the growing importance of lobbying by many enterprises, the system of interest intermediation has been rather resilient. The coordinating networks around business confederations and trade union confederation built over decades remain in place, although the state has retreated considerably as well as business organisations. Some crucial institutions that remain are the symbolic Labour Court and the Conciliators' Office (Svensson and Öberg, 2005: 1088–91). However, other more critical studies have identified a considerable decline in Swedish corporatism since the 1990s. The withdrawal of the Swedish business confederation from all the boards of all government agencies in 1991 was the major turning point in this respect. It led to the exclusion of the trade union confederations from the same boards, so that the state could preserve its neutrality towards the two social partners (Lindvall and Sebring, 2005: 1058; Svensson, 2016: 621). This also meant a decline in consultation with the social partners, although consultation remains an important part of the Swedish culture of interest intermediation. It means that today that social partners are engaged in a light patterned wage coordination system allowing for quite considerable flexibility at other levels of the system. Since then, more agreements have been achieved, contributing to an adjustment and restructuring of Swedish industrial relations (Svensson, 2016: 622).

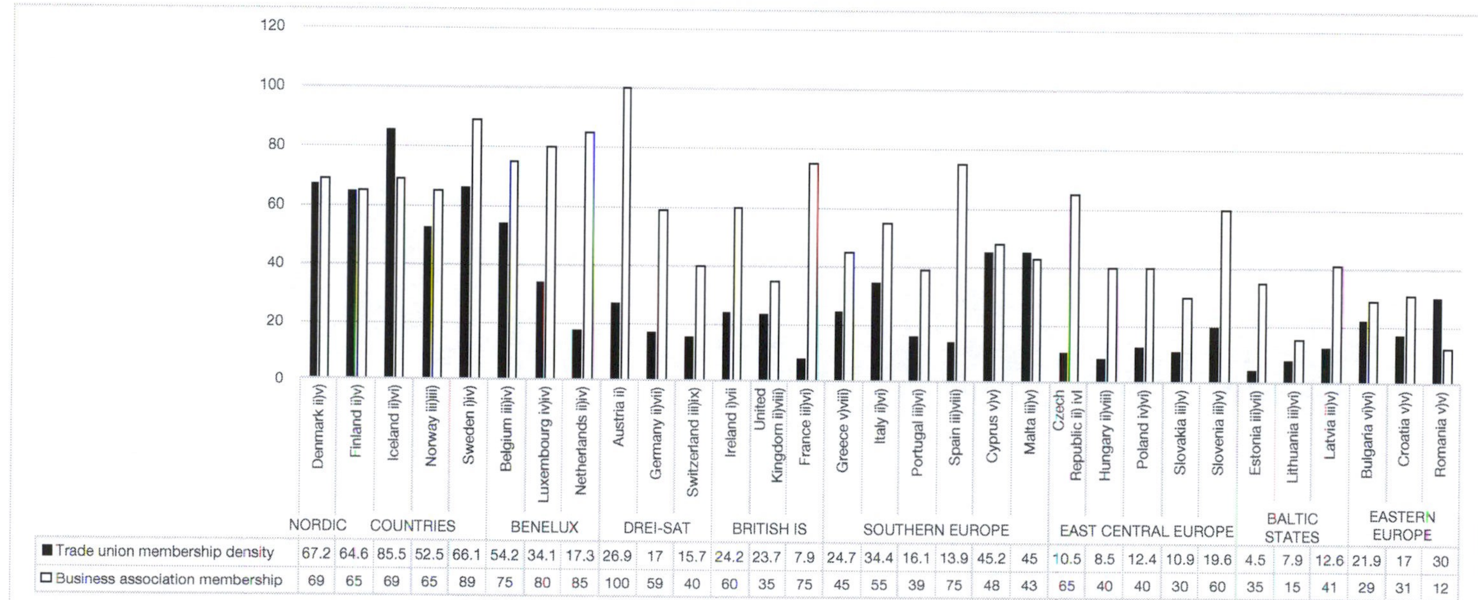

	NORDIC COUNTRIES					BENELUX		
	Denmark ii)v)	Finland ii)v)	Iceland ii)v)	Norway iii)iii)	Sweden i)v)	Belgium iii)v)	Luxembourg iv)v)	Netherlands ii)v)
■ Trade union membership density	67.2	64.6	85.5	52.5	66.1	54.2	34.1	17.3
□ Business association membership	69	65	69	65	89	75	80	85

	DREI-SAT			BRITISH IS		
	Austria ii)	Germany ii)vii)	Switzerland iii)ix)	Ireland i)vii	United Kingdom ii)viii)	France iii)vi)
■ Trade union membership density	26.9	17	15.7	24.2	23.7	7.9
□ Business association membership	100	59	40	60	35	75

	SOUTHERN EUROPE					
	Greece v)viii)	Italy ii)vi)	Portugal iii)vi)	Spain iii)viii)	Cyprus v)v)	Malta iii)v)
■ Trade union membership density	24.7	34.4	16.1	13.9	45.2	45
□ Business association membership	45	55	39	75	48	43

	EAST CENTRAL EUROPE				
	Czech Republic ii) ivl	Hungary ii)viii)	Poland iv)vi)	Slovakia iii)v)	Slovenia iii)v)
■ Trade union membership density	10.5	8.5	12.4	10.9	19.6
□ Business association membership	65	40	40	30	60

	BALTIC STATES			EASTERN EUROPE		
	Estonia iii)vii)	Lithuania iii)vi)	Latvia iii)v)	Bulgaria vi)vi)	Croatia v)v)	Romania v)v)
■ Trade union membership density	4.5	7.9	12.6	21.9	17	30
□ Business association membership	35	15	41	29	31	12

Figure 8.3 Trade union and employers' organisation membership density (estimates)

Source: OECD (2017: 136, 2018b); Country files at Eurofound (2018).

i) 2017 ii) 2016 iii) 2015 iv) 2014 v) 2013 vi) 2012 vii) 2011 ix) own calculations based on figures of the Swiss Employers' Association posted in website 2018.

Similar systems of interest intermediation were established in Denmark, Norway, Finland and Iceland. Denmark was probably the country that adjusted best to the new challenges of globalisation and Europeanisation. In this sense, the role of neo-corporatism has become more flexible and decentralised, while, at the same time, successive governments have directed their whole policy-making process towards labour market activation policies (Campbell and Pedersen, 2007; Due et al., 1995: 145). Similar to Sweden, two major organisations represent the workers and business enterprises. Also in Denmark, there has been a process of merging over the past decades, so that they remain quite strong interest groups. On the one hand, the Danish Confederation of Trade Unions (Landesorganisationer – LO), founded in 1898, represents the workers' and a large part of employees, and on the other, the Danish Employers Confederation (Dansk Arbejdsgiverforening – DA) founded in 1896, is the main organisation representing business enterprises. The LO consists of seventeen trade unions and four federations comprising one million workers and employees, about 50 per cent of unionised workers (LO Denmark, 2018a, 2018b). The DA consists of 14 federations comprising 28,000 member companies (DA, 2018). An additional important player on the side of business enterprises is the Confederation of Danish Industry (Dansk Industri – DI), which was able to restructure itself and include other members from DA in 1992 (Christiansen et al., 2012: 110). It comprises 10,000 company members (DI, 2018). Historically, the Danish system of consensual industrial relations goes back to 1899 through the so-called September agreement, in which both confederations recognised each other and became the major players in the political economy of the country (Christiansen et al., 2012: 107). Denmark is much smaller than Sweden, so that the networking between state, socioeconomic interest groups and civil society organisation is even denser. One particular element gluing it all together is the generous subsidies provided by the state to these organisations that share some administrative tasks, so-called administrative corporatism. The lack of resources in the ministries seems to be a major factor for the inclusion of the expertise and infrastructure of interest groups (Christiansen et al., 2012: 113–14). Similar to Sweden, the neo-corporatist structures have been eroding towards a more flexible system, including informal networks, and a governance approach, including state institutions, civil society and economic interest groups.

In Finland, the most important socioeconomic confederations are the Central Organisation of Finnish Trade Unions (Suomen Ammattiliittojen Keskusjärjestö – SAK) and the Confederation of the Finnish Industries (Elinkeinoelämän keskusliitto – EK). The SAK consists of 18 affiliated federations comprising one million workers and employees (SAK, 2018), while the EK consists of 24 members, 15,300 member companies (96 per cent of small and medium-sized enterprises (SMEs)) employing over 900,000 employees (EK, 2018; SAK, 2018). Neo-corporatism in Finland has been dominated by the trade union confederations, which strategically want to preserve some kind of centralised wage bargaining. Such system was established in 1968, after postwar decades of continuing socioeconomic conflict. This change was due to the participation of leftwing parties in government after the elections in 1966 (Lappalainen and Siisiäinen, 2012: 198). However, the collapse of the Soviet Union led to a substantial increase in unemployment in the 1990s, which gave a stronger bargaining position to the employers' organisations. The neo-corporatist system of intermediation, which was established after the Second

World War, is slowly giving way to more flexible forms of system intermediation (Lappalainen and Siisiäinen, 2012: 201). In 2007, the EK decided to change the rules of engagement in the Finnish neo-corporatist system and withdrew from central coordination, leading to a more flexible decentralised system of collective bargaining (Lappalainen and Siisiäinen, 2012: 202–3).

In Norway, the neo-corporatist mode of interest intermediation was also quite dominant. However, since the late 1970s, major changes have been taking place. In spite of the changing nature of neo-corporatist interest intermediation, according to Tom Christensen in 2005, there were over 3,000 interest groups still formally involved in a vast network of government agencies (Christensen, 2005: 727). The corporatist insiders were certainly the two main socioeconomic partners The two main interest groups are the Norwegian Trade Union Confederation (Landesorganisatjonen – LO) and the Confederation of Norwegian Enterprise (Næringslivets Hovedorganisasjon – NHO). The LO was founded in 1899 and comprised 900,000 workers and employees in 2018 (LO Norge, 2018), while the NHO is a merger of three different employers' organisations and has existed since 1989. One of the main reasons for the latter was to better use the organisational resources available to employers. It represents over 24,000 Norwegian enterprises and consists of 15 federations (NHO, 2018). After decades of expansion of the formalised network of neo-corporatist agencies and boards, a crisis in the system began to emerge. Globalisation and Europeanisation played a particularly strong role in the rethinking of the Norwegian model. A seminal study comparing Norway and Denmark showed that in both countries the number of government corporatist policy preparatory committees in which 'corporatist insider' interest groups were represented declined considerably from 188 (Norway) and 68 (Denmark) in the early 1980s, to 39 (Norway) and 12 (Denmark) respectively in 2005. This continual pushing out of the traditional interest groups from committees dealing with preparatory policy committees led to a growing number of corporatist insiders supplementing their channels of access by lobbying elected politicians in parliament. For corporatist outsiders this has always been the alternative route to gain influence. It means that apart from the fact that both the Storting and Folketing gained in importance and power, the overall interest intermediation system has become more pluralist since the late 1970s (Rommetvedt et al., 2012: 462, 471–6).

Since the devastating financial crisis in Iceland after the collapse of Lehman Brothers, and its impact on the then unsustainable national financial system, there have been more critical studies questioning whether Iceland really is a consensual and neo-corporatist system. In reality, the conflict potential in Icelandic society is much higher than in other Nordic countries. Among the reasons is that the left-wing parties, the socialists and communists, were too weak to have any influence over such a system. Therefore, the Icelandic Confederation of Labour (ASI) could not rely on much support from leftwing parties in government. Rather, Iceland has been dominated by a more conservative nationalist independence party which clearly emphasises the independence of the country. Strong lobbying of agricultural and fisheries lobbies prevented the establishment of rigid neo-corporatist structures like in other Nordic countries. However, since 1964, there has been a slow evolution towards neo-corporatism in wage bargaining, but this is certainly at a much lower level than in the other Nordic countries. A peak in this neo-corporatism was when a tripartite national agreement was signed to bring about better management of wage bargaining and improved working conditions. Between 1990 and 2009, the number of strikes was reduced fundamentally and simultaneously under the leadership of the Independence Party, the main party in coalition governments, there was a considerable shift to neoliberal policies (Jónsson, 2014: 519–20). The US financial crisis of 2008 had a direct effect on the big banks of Iceland and a considerable return to conflictive politics (for more detail, see the excellent study by Bergmann, 2014). Due to strike activity, collective agreements led to partly unsustainable pay awards, which would clearly have implications for economic growth. Since 2013, there has been an agreement to move towards a new negotiation model in Iceland, known as Salek. In 2015, a major collective agreement was reached, but social partners remain rather divided. Trade unionism is quite strong in Iceland. It seems that some institutional transfer is taking place from Norway to Iceland after a major report by an academic, Steinar Holden from the University of Oslo, was commissioned in 2016, so that the country can move to a new model of wage formation. Basically, it is highly influenced by the Norwegian model. The new model should then be monitored by the Icelandic State Conciliation and Mediation Office (SCMO), which so far has not been very respected by the social partners. It is intended to give more powers to the SCMO to achieve a more moderate peaceful approach to wage formation (Holden, 2016; OECD, 2018a: 104–20). ASI has about 123,000 members, which represents over 80 per cent of the working population (ASI, 2018). Other smaller unions for state employees and workers, academics and teachers, are also taking part in bargaining. Similar to other Nordic countries, with the exception of Norway, the high level of union density is related to the Ghent system of unemployment insurance, which allows trade unions to manage these funds, which are also supported by state transfers. The main business organisation is SA-Confederation of Icelandic Enterprise (SA) consisting of six associations which comprise 22,000 business enterprises (SA, 2018).

The Benelux countries

The Dutch neo-corporatist system of interest intermediation contributed to political and economic stability throughout the 1950s and 1960s. At the centre of the Dutch model is the Social and Economic Council (Sociaal en Economische Raad – SER), in which all relevant interest groups are represented, particularly employers' and employees' organisations. However, most socioeconomic agreements are done in the bipartite Foundation for Labour (Stichting van der Arbeid – STAR) behind closed doors. One particular feature of the Dutch system is that the trade union confederations were split along subcultural lines. There were the Catholic (Nederlands Katholieke Vakverbond – NKV), the Protestant Christian democratic (Christelijk Nationaal Vakverbond – CNV) and the socialist (Nederlands Verbond van Vakbewegingen – NVV) trade union confederations, in which over 40 per cent of workers were organised. The Catholic and socialist confederations merged into the Dutch Trade Union Federation (Federatie Nederlandse Vakbeweging – FNV) in 1976. The business organisations were more unified. Between 1945 and 1970, there was a strong integration and consultation of these main social partners.

However, the economic and social crisis of the 1970s led to major reforms by the Dutch coalition government of Christian democrats and liberals from 1982 to 1992. The 'Wassenaar agreement', which was reached by the social partners in 1982, transformed a centralised neo-corporatist system into a decentralised flexible one. Tripartite negotiations with heavy intervention of the state were replaced by bipartite ones between the social partners and a retreat of the state from the economy. The Dutch 'Polder-model' was referred to as an example of the capacity of neo-corporatist systems of interest intermediation to adjust to new realities, but keeping the basic principles of negotiated bargained principles carried by the main interest groups. Parallel to an increase in efficiency of the economic sector, the government strengthened the labour market activation policies (Hemerijck, 1995; Kleinfeld, 2012: 485). Further reforms were undertaken since then in order to keep the Dutch Polder model flexible enough in a globalised world. In terms of labour market policies, the Netherlands adopted its own flexicurity system (for a historical review, see Touwen, 2008, 2014). During the financial and euro crises, high levels of unemployment were avoided by a short-term employment scheme in which Dutch enterprises could shorten the working times of workers, and the rest of the time would be subsidised by the state, which would also provide training programmes for this period. In November 2013, the Modriaan agreement between trade union and business organisations was signed, which further flexibilised the Polder model. Trade union confederations reluctantly supported this new package of erosion of workers' rights (see Keune, 2016, particularly the chapter on the agreements by Hemerijck and Van der Meer, 2016). One of the problems of the Polder model is that trade unionism has been declining over the past decades. The density of unionisation declined from 22.6 in 2000 to 17.3 per cent in 2016 (OECD, 2018b). The main workers' and employees' organisations are the FNV comprising one million members, and the CNV with 287,000 members (CNV, 2018; FNV, 2018). On the employers' side there has been a merging process taking place since the 1980s which has led to the Association of Dutch Enterpreneurs-Dutch Federation of Christian Employers (Vereiniging Nederlandse Ondernemer-Nederlandse Christelijk Werkgeversverbond – VNO-NCW). VNO-NCW represents 120,000 enterprises (VNO-NCW, 2018). Moreover, there is the Royal Association of Small- and Medium-Sized Enterprises (Koningkijke Vereiniging Midden en Kleinbedrijfen Nederland – MKB Nederland) which represents over 150,000 SMEs. The main collective bargaining organisation of employers is the General Association of Employers (Algemeen Werkgevers Vereiniging Netherlands – AWVN), which comprises all relevant business confederations. There is also a Council of Central Business Organisations (Raad van de Centrale Ondernemensorganisationen – RCO) that facilitates exchanges of opinion between the employers' organisations. The organisational density of employers is over 80 per cent.

Belgium was also characterised by a rigid neo-corporatist system of interest intermediation, which made it possible for the state to strongly intervene in the economy between 1945 and 1973. As in the Netherlands, pillarisation of the Christian democratic, socialist and liberal subcultures led to the establishment of three main trade union confederations with different ideological make-ups (Hooghe, 2012: 59). In the 2016 trade union elections, 'social elections', which decide about the composition of the works' council in Belgium, reconfirmed the dominance of Christian democratic trade union confederation ACV-CSV, with 51 per cent of the works' council and 51 per cent in work safety committees, followed by the socialist ABVV-FGTB with 34.9 and 35.9 per cent, and the liberal CGSLB with 12.3 and 12.4 per cent respectively (*La Libre*, 25 May 2016).

In spite of federalisation, trade union confederations in Wallonia and Flanders still work closely together, and in comparison to the political parties' landscape, they are nationally organised. The decline of the political parties has eroded the intertwined relationship of the trade union movement with politics, which was one of the main characteristics of Belgium. Belgian trade unionism has one of the highest organisational levels in Europe. Trade union confederations administer unemployment benefits for their members, also known as the Ghent system and common also in the Nordic countries, leading therefore to one of the highest unionisation levels in Europe. Belgium has become more of a hybrid system, while the Nordic countries still follow the pure system (Ebbinghaus et al., 2011; Vandaele, 2009; Van Rie et al., 2011). The Belgian Employers' Organisation (VBO-FEB) is the main social partner of the trade union confederations. Both are represented in a wide network of state-sponsored government boards, committees and agencies at national, sectoral and company level. Nationally, there is the Central Economic Development Board (Conseil Centrale de l'Economie – CCE/CRB) which comprises the social partners and is an advisory strategic body for mid-term to long-term macroeconomic policies. Moreover, social and labour issues are dealt with in the Central Labour Board (Conseil National du Travail-Nationaal Arbeids Raad – CNT-NAR). These are now quite long-standing institutions that were founded in 1948 and 1952 respectively. However, there is also an informal 'Group of Ten' bipartite caucus of five representatives of trade unions and five representatives of the business organisations that consensually try to sort out concrete socioeconomic measures and agreements, particularly interprofessional agreements and general coordinating and guiding agreements for collective bargaining (*La Libre*, 18 November 2016; *rtbf*, 17 December 2014, 3 July 2017).

Also important is the Federal Planning Bureau (FPB) which is an independent public body providing forecasts and studies to government and social partners. It emulates the well-respected Dutch Central Planning Bureau (CPB) which was established in 1945 and fulfils the same tasks. Last but not least, Belgium has now introduced, similar to Spain, regional economic and social councils that coordinate with the national CCE-CRB and NAR-CNT (Magone, 2017: 261–2).

The 'Luxembourg model' follows closely that of the Netherlands and Belgium. It is extremely vulnerable to developments in other countries, because it is a quite open economy. Most of the workforce is foreign and commuted from neighbouring countries. The social dimension is very important to Luxembourg capitalism in order to achieve a balance between a competitive economy and a cohesive society. The model gained its importance in the crisis of the 1970s, when the steel industry had to lay off a considerable number of workers. Tripartite committees were set up to manage the change and create new, more competitive sectors in the economy (Hirsch, 2010a, 2010b, 2012; Schroen, 2012). Since then, there has been a strong input from the government to strategically think how the Luxembourg social model can be preserved with the support of the social partners. Apart from the social partners, Luxembourg also has one of the most extensive chamber systems of Europe, along with Austria and Slovenia.

Drei-Sat Europe: between neo-corporatism and liberalisation

In Austria, the negative experiences of the interwar period, which led to the establishment of an authoritarian regime (1934–8) by the Christian Social Party and, later, occupation by Nazi Germany, contributed to a more consensual approach to politics and the economy. Furthermore, until 1955, Austria was occupied by Allied troops and therefore was not a free country. The State Treaty (*Staatsvertrag*) of 1955 finally led to its independence. One pillar of the Austrian Second Republic became the informal but well-entrenched social partnership (*Sozialpartnerschaft*) founded in 1957, which led to the establishment of a network of committees to bargain wages centrally and shape national economic policy. The large Austrian Trade Union Confederation (Österreichischer Gewerkschaftsbund – ÖGB), and the Austrian Association of Enterpreneurs (Vereinigung der Österreichischen Industriellen – VÖI; now known as Industriellenvereinigung – IV), and the Labour, Industry and Agriculture Chamber, which historically goes back to the nineteenth century, were all involved in this decision-making process, which was not covered by the constitution (Tálos, 2005, 2006: 426–8). Social partnership remains a foundation of macroeconomic and social management, but it is now more contested by the Freedom party and the Greens in particular as being too linked to the traditional grand coalition parties, the social democrats (SPÖ) and the conservative Christian democrats (ÖVP). Since the 1950s, these two parties have built a system of proportional distribution of spoils and patronage which clearly prevented other parties coming to power (Karlhofer, 2012; Lehmbruch, 1967; Treib, 2012). Therefore, the coalition governments between the ÖVP and the FPÖ between 2000 and 2006, and since 2018 have focused on the liberalisation and decartelisation of Austrian politics (Karlhofer and Tálos, 2006; Tálos, 2005).

Neo-corporatism in Germany remains a major way of solving macroeconomic problems like the financial crisis of 2008–13. The introduction of short working schemes for German enterprises funded by the state during the financial crisis from 2009 to 2011 resembles similar programmes in the Nordic, Benelux countries and Austria. Being the largest economy in the EU does not allow Germany to follow a similar path to the smaller countries, in which the main actors are very few and know each other well. Germany is a federal country which also has to deal with sixteen similar regional economies. In spite of this decentralisation of policy-making, the main social partners are quite centralised allowing for some light coordination and cooperation with successive governments in terms of the economy. The main economic partners in Germany are the German Trade Union Confederation (Deutsche Gewerkschaftsbund – DGB), which comprises one of the largest and most powerful trade unions, IG-Metall, and Vereinte Dienstleistungsgewerkschaft (ver.di), for employees in different service sectors. Unionisation levels have been declining steadily since the 1990s, so that today only slightly more than six million workers and employees (17 per cent) are members of trade unions (OECD, 2018b). On the employers' side, there is the Federation of German Employers (Bund der deutschen Arbeitgeberverbände – BDA) and the Federation of German Industry (Bund der deutschen Industrie – BDI) as the main representatives of business. Because no party is able to win an outright majority in parliament, the German style of politics has moved towards consensual bargaining (Lehmbruch, 1996: 4; 2002: 183). Like in Luxembourg and

Austria, Germany has a well-established chamber system of main economic actors that play an important role in co-managing socioeconomic aspects, particularly the certification of professional and vocational training. Neo-corporatism is quite well established in policy-making processes through committees with interest representation, collective bargaining and, last but not least, the co-determination in the largest enterprises (Rudzio, 2015: 89–95). However, the heydays of neo-corporatism were in the 1960s, but since then the neo-corporatist network has been eroding. One positive feature was the adoption and implementation of the co-determination legislation of 1972 and 1976 which allowed for a strong industrial democracy in the larger enterprises in Germany (for more detail on the history of industrial democracy, see Müller-Jentsch, 2016). According to Wolfgang Streeck and Anke Hassel (2003), the German state had the ability to co-opt important interest groups in civil society into important positions in the political and economic systems of Germany, forcing them to act responsibly (Streeck and Hassel, 2003: 103).

The Helmut Kohl governments (1982–98) introduced some reforms to the labour market and the welfare state, but not in a consistent matter, so that by the end of the twentieth century, Germany was the economic 'sick man' of Europe.

After coming to power in 1998, Chancellor Gerhard Schröder created a neo-corporatist institution called Alliance for Jobs and Training (*Bündnis für die Arbeit*), which was intended to reduce the high level of unemployment, create new jobs and enhance the competitiveness of the German economy. However, after the adoption and implementation of the Hartz reform between 2002 and 2005, the trade union confederation left the committee as a protest against the Hartz reform introducing flexibilisation of the labour market through new atypical forms of work. Moreover, unemployment benefit rules were changed, creating a two-tier system which allowed the amount receivable to be reduced substantially, after one, exceptionally two years, of unemployment (Kemmerling and Bruttel, 2006; Streeck and Hassel, 2003: 114–20). According to Wolfgang Streeck, the financial crisis further contributed to an erosion of the original nationally oriented German system of coordinated market economy (Streeck, 2010). Klaus von Beyme speaks of an erosion of the nationally oriented Deutschland AG (Germany Inc.) system towards pluralism and lobbyism targeting MPs and political parties in Parliament more, of which the conservative CDU/CSU and the liberal FDP have been those that have profited the most financially from this shift (Von Beyme, 2017: 234–9; see Transparency International, 2016). Excellent studies by Wolfgang Streeck, Martin Höpner and their team seem to confirm that the Deutschland AG networks that existed between the banking sector, insurances and major German industrial companies are now being replaced by a more or less successful integration of these large enterprises into an emerging World Inc. along with transnational corporations from other countries. This clearly reduces the capacity for neo-corporatist coordination (Freye, 2009; Höpner and Krempel, 2006; Streeck and Höpner, 2003).

As already mentioned, Switzerland belongs to a liberal variant of democratic corporatism. The large business organisations are quite powerful, while the trade union confederations are integrated into an asymmetrical system of industrial relations. The highly decentralised federalism further undermines a centralised approach to policy-making (Oesch, 2011: 82). In spite of this, the consensual type of Swiss politics also has its translation in neo-corporatist structures. Probably the most important one is the number of expert committees attached to the Swiss bureaucracy formulating policy-making, which includes relevant interest groups. Moreover, legislative drafts are subject to an official consultation period (*Vernehmungslassung*) of registered interest groups which may offer their comments and proposals to a particular document. Negotiating support consensually from the relevant interest groups, above all the quite powerful ones, is an important strategic approach to avoiding a referendum, which is regarded by the administrative and political elites as a symbol of failure in the politics of compromise (Kriesi and Trechsler, 2008: 118–20; Linder, 2005: 122–5; Sciarini, 2014; Vatter, 2014: 179–84). It means that in the pre-parliamentary phase interest groups are already well integrated into the process. The consultation process of interest groups is enshrined in the constitution. However, it seems that lobbying has increased considerably at parliamentary level in the past decades. Due to the opacity of party funding in Switzerland, there is a real danger of party capture by interest groups. Directly elected or recruited representatives of interest groups have established quite complex and effective influencing networks affecting both houses of parliament (*Neue Zürcher Zeitung*, 14 March 2016; Sciarini, 2014: 119).

Interest groups, particularly the social partners, are strongly integrated into the implementation process in a multilevel governance system, comprising the cantonal and national level. The main reason is that the Swiss bureaucratic structure is rather small and needs therefore to rely on the co-responsibility of relevant interest groups to successfully implement policies (Rohrer and Trampusch, 2011; Vatter, 2014: 184–6).

The main trade union confederation, the Swiss Federation of Trade Unions (Schweizerischer Gewerkschaftsbund/Federation Syndicale Suisse – SGB/FSS) and the Christian democratic-dominated Travailsuisse comprise a low number of unionised workers of about 15.3 per cent of the workforce (OECD, 2018b). The neo-corporatist network is therefore biased towards the employers' organisations, which have a substantially higher grade of organisation: the Federation of Swiss Employers (SAV/UPS), Economiesuisse as the consolidated federation of enterprises, the crafts federation (SGB/USAM), the Swiss farmers' confederation (SBV-USB) and the Swiss Association of Bankers (ABV-ASB). Switzerland has always been a country with a strong civil society, particularly in the social and economic sectors (Eichenberger and Mach, 2011; Oesch, 2011).

Tamed pluralism in Europe

Pluralism in a democratic setting refers to 'free competition between a plurality of organised interests and supportive relations between groups and government'. In its ideal form it is a decentralised, unrestricted system (Newton and Van Deth, 2006: 173–4) (see Table 8.2). It means that there is no such thing as a structured integration of social partners in the policy-making process. Rather all interest groups compete for influence by lobbying politicians and civil servants. This may lead to more or less success in ensuring their interests are taken into account.

Table 8.2 The main social partners in social dialogue at supranational level

Organisation	*Constituency*	*Foundation year*	*Organisation*
European Trade Union Confederation (ETUC)	Workers, employees	1973	89 national organisations from 40 countries, 10 European industry federations
BUSINESSEUROPE (former UNICE)	Employers	1958	39 employers' associations from 36 countries,
European Centre of Enterprises with Public Participation and of Enterprises of General Economic Interest (CEEP)	Employers' association for public sector entities (local transport, energy, water ports), networked businesses and, in some countries, local authorities	1961	National sections in 17 countries
European Association of Craft, Small and Medium Sized Enterprises (UEAPME)	European crafts, trades and small businesses	1979	67 member organisations (national cross-sectoral small- and medium-sized enterprises, federation branches) in 34 countries, representing 12 million business enterprises across Europe and comprising 55 million staff
EUROCADRES	Professional and managerial staff representing all branches of industry, public and private services and administrative departments	1993	56 organisations in 24 countries and 8 Federations
European Confederation of Executives and Managerial Staff (CEC)	Professional, managerial and executive staff	1989	European branch federations and 17 national organisations and 9 federations from 14 countries

Source: websites of the respective confederations in 2018.

The UK and Ireland: pluralism par excellence

Traditionally, the UK has followed a largely pluralist tradition (Finer, 1958), although there were influences from the rest of Europe that led to the adoption of neo-corporatist structures in the 1960s and 1970s. Among these was the National Economic Development Council (NEDC) with its regional counterparts ('the Neddies') founded in 1962 but discontinued in the 1980s after Margaret Thatcher came to power; the Manpower Services Commission founded in 1974, also to be replaced by more decentralised structures in 1987; the Health and Safety Commission founded in 1975; and the still important Advisory, Conciliation and Arbitration Service (ACAS) set up in 1976. The latter has been used to solve major industrial disputes in the public sector. It included trade union representatives from the Trade Union Congress (TUC) and the Confederation of Business and Industry (CBI) (Kavanagh, 2001: 193–4). After Margaret Thatcher came to power in 1979, she completely changed the system of interest intermediation to one of deregulated pluralism. While the period between 1945 and 1979 was referred to as a period of 'organised capitalism' because of the inclusion of social partners, the 1980s are often referred to as a period of 'disorganised capitalism' (Johnston, 1993: 129).

Thatcherite liberalisation policies bypassed any consultation with social partners. Some interest groups that had considerable authority in the economy and society lost their power in the battle against prime minister Margaret Thatcher, particularly trade unions (Moran, 1989: 280–92, 293). Thatcher's drive towards US-style neoliberal pluralism had considerable influence on policies concerning the Single European Market as well as in the member-states after 1985. Many of the reforms in France, Germany, Spain, Italy and other countries were influenced by the Thatcherite approach; however, none of these reform efforts had quite the same level of radicalism. In spite of the pluralistic tendencies in the UK, the opportunities to influence legislative processes are more 'framed' than one would expect. When interest groups lobby for specific legislation, there will be a long process of consultation, frequently leading to a Green Paper. Following this, a bill will be drafted and interest groups will have an opportunity to influence the process by lobbying backbenchers and civil servants. After the bill has been approved, interest groups still have the opportunity to influence the implementation process. Moreover, there are 'insider' and 'outsider' interest groups. Insider interest groups, such as the Howard League for Penal Reform or the National Farmers' Union, have special access to the Department of Justice and the Department of Agriculture respectively. The trade-off is that such interest groups have to follow a moderate code of conduct and be able to compromise on legislation in order to preserve their long-term influence. Outsider interest groups have no interest in belonging to an inner circle in this way. They often use radical, uncompromising strategies to achieve their aims. Some interest groups may use direct action or even terrorist tactics in order to publicise their issues. Two specific groups are 'We are Fathers-4-Justice' and 'Greenpeace', which both organise spectacular direct action in order to publicise their issues.

Thatcherism contributed to a move of the UK towards a more Americanised pluralist system, and lobbying has grown since the late 1980s. Cases of sleaze and corruption such as the 'cash for questions' affair in 1996 and the 'cash for honours' in 2006 led to the introduction of stricter guidelines for MPs. In 1994–5 a commission under Lord Nolan was established that created a code of conduct with specific, strict guidelines for MPs. Apart from full declaration of all their business interests, MPs are forbidden to influence legislation on behalf of any group (Jones, 2014: 193).

After the New Labour Party came to power in 1997, prime minister Tony Blair made it clear that the government would remain equidistant from both the CBI and TUC. Therefore, in spite of a strong historical legacy binding the Labour Party to the trade union movement, there has been a move towards a more pragmatic, less ideological approach to industrial relations. This all fits with the process of the professionalisation of socioeconomic interest groups and the separation of certain interests from politics (Jones, 2014: 191–2).

There is an Advisory Committee on Business Appointments (ACOBA) founded in 1975 that normally approves appointments in the private sector of former ministers and politicians and sets the conditions for these appointments. Any politician appointed to private sector positions within a two-year period after leaving office has to seek the advice of the ACOBA. Moreover, there is a two-year ban on lobbying. Quite problematic has been the tendency of former prime ministers like Tony Blair or David Cameron to take advisory jobs in private companies. There is a period of two years in which former politicians are not allowed to lobby on behalf of their clients. Allegedly, Chinese companies have been recruiting these former ministers for lobbying work (*BBC News*, 6 March 2018; *The Guardian*, 28 April 2016).

The government established a Registrar of Consultant Lobbyists in which 141 lobbying firms and 1,398 listed clients are registered. However, in the Registrar of the Chartered Institute of Public Relations, the number of lobbying firms increases to 781 firms, and estimates from the Alliance for Lobbying Transparency puts at 4,000 the number of lobbyists. It is estimated that over £2 billion (€2.3 billion; US$2.7 billion) are spent by firms on lobbying. According to a well-researched article by *Politico*, it seems that Brexit has opened a structure of opportunities for increasing lobbying. The main target of this massive lobbying is the huge Repeal Bill which will copy all the EU legislation into UK law, and then amend or dismiss it accordingly. This is a project for at least a decade, and provides lots of work for lobbyists to influence outcomes (*Politico*, 12 July 2017).

Although the Republic of Ireland was strongly influenced by the British legacy, the smallness of the country has led to the establishment of neo-corporatist structures within an overwhelmingly pluralist system of industrial relations. The culmination of such neo-corporatism was between 1959 and 1982, particularly in terms of wage bargaining at a central level in the tripartite National Wage Agreement. Furthermore, social partners are regularly consulted in the National Economic and Social Council (Elvert, 2012: 322). The main trade union is the Irish Congress of Trade Unions (ICTU), which covers 24–25 per cent of the labour force (about 527,000 people) (Eurofound, 2018; OECD, 2018b). On the employers' side, there is the Irish Business and Employers Organisation (IBEC), which was refounded in 1993, when the confederation of Irish industries and the Federal Union of Employers merged together. Other important business organisations are the Construction Industry Federation (CIF), which profited enormously from the booming 1990s, the Irish Bankers' Federation (IBF) as well as the American

Chamber of Commerce representing about 570 US enterprises based in Ireland (Elvert, 2012: 326–8; Eurofound, 2018). Neo-corporatism becomes important in periods of crisis in the Irish economy, such as, for example, during the 1980s or more recently during the financial crisis. This clearly shows a strong cooperation between the social partners and the government to retain the competitiveness of the Irish economy. The attraction of high technology foreign direct investment is a major aspect of this policy. Social partners and the government realised that adversarial politics is too costly for a vulnerable small open economy. In this context, neo-corporatism is adjusted to keep the liberal market economy going. It is more case of concertation of policy-making than intervening in the economy. Since the 1990s, Irish social partners with the support of the government had been signing a lot of long-term agreements and social pacts like Towards 2016 (2007) for a period of ten years shortly before the crisis. This consensual approach to politics was facilitated by the smallness of the country (Elvert, 2012: 322; Government of Ireland, 2007; Hamann and Kelly, 2011: 61–8). However, the sovereign debt crisis in 2009–11 was a major challenge for the Irish social partnership. EMU social pacts of social coordination were more difficult, particularly for the trade unions. Clearly, this allowed the Irish government to pursue a more neoliberal agenda during this period. In spite of this, social partners remained committed to continuing social partnership (Barnes and Wren, 2012; Regan, 2012) (Figure 8.4).

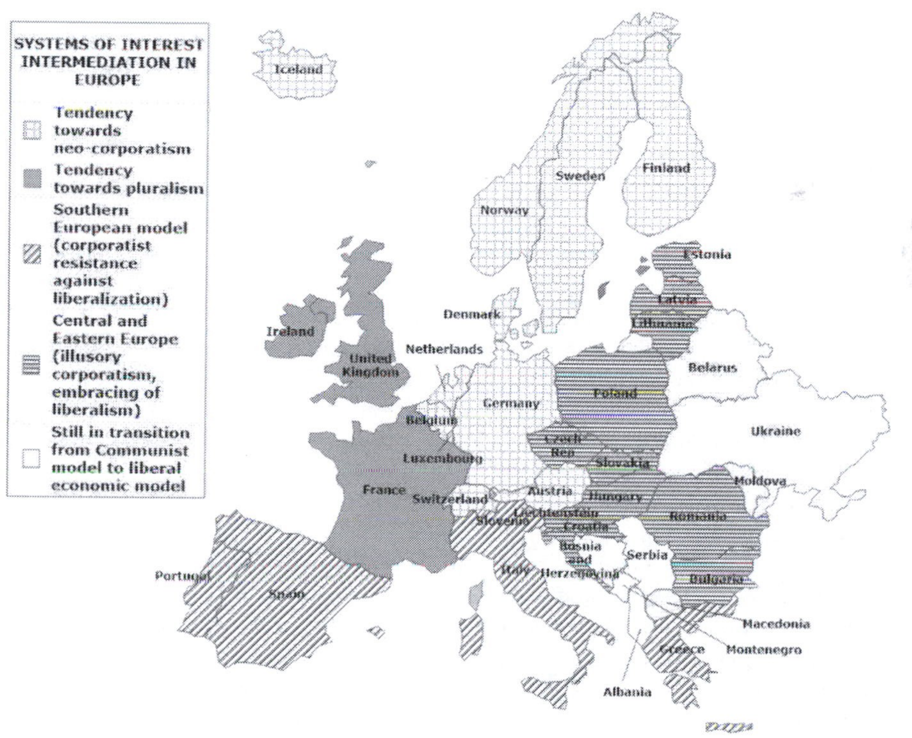

Figure 8.4 Systems of interest intermediation in Europe, 2018

France: from state-led dirigisme to liberalisation

The French model of industrial relations is difficult to classify, largely because of its strong *étatist* tradition. The role of the state in the economy has been a major factor since the beginning of the Fifth Republic. This means that a strong national economy is regarded as part of the overall identity of the country and that the unity of the country should prevail above particular interest groups. According to Alistair Cole, the French system of interest intermediation cannot be referred to as either pluralistic or neo-corporatist. However, it has elements of the two embedded in the political system. The *étatist* political culture of the country does not allow either pluralism or neo-corporatism to dominate. Traditionally, the agricultural sector and their associations have been strongly involved in national policy-making. Neo-corporatist structures were detected there. Furthermore, the *grands corps* of public administration have been instrumental in building neo-corporatist structures in their specific fields (Cole, 2017: 220–3).

Another characteristic of the French model is that trade union confederations are among the weakest in Europe. In 2015, only 7.9 per cent of workers were unionised in one of the five peak organisations (OECD, 2018b). Trade union confederations are ideologically split. There are five important trade union confederations: the communist General Confederation of Labour (CGT), the centrist French Democratic Confederation of Labour (CFDT), the radical left Workers' Force (FO), the Christian democratic French Confederation of Christian Workers (CFTC) and finally the more specialised General Confederation of Cadres (CGE-CGC). The regularly held works' council elections confirmed this fragmented pattern of representation. According to the calculations of representativeness by the ministry of labour based on trade union elections between 2013 and 2017, the CFDT got 26.4 per cent, the communist CGT 24.9 per cent, CGT-FO 15.6 per cent, the CGE-CGC 10.7 per cent and the Christian democratic CFTC 9.5 per cent. They are also the only trade union confederations recognised by the state, because they were able to pass the threshold of at least 8 per cent of cast votes (Ministère du Travail, 31 March 2017: 2).

The employers' organisations are divided according to sizes of enterprise and sectoral membership. The former National Council of the French Employers (CNPF) has been known since 1998 as the Movement of French Enterprises (MEDEF) and it represents mainly the larger business organisations in France. However, this fact is really just a simplification. In reality, the MEDEF represents 70 per cent of firms with fewer than fifty employees (Woll, 2006: 496). The General Confederation of Small and Medium Sized Enterprises and Real Employers (CPME) represents the SMEs, while the National Union of Liberal Professions (Union National des Professions Libérales – UNAPL), founded in 1977, is the association for the liberal professions Finally, there is the Crafts Union (Union Professionelle Artisanale – UPA), which was founded in 1977 as a merger of three major associations. In 2009, a major hospitality association joined UPA, and in 2014 it became U2P. These organisations are the officially recognised business confederations and are able to take part in policy-making.

In terms of representation for tripartite organisations, those listed above are the main official organisations, although there are other smaller employees' and employers' organisations. The weak membership numbers of French associations can be related to the strong individualism of French people as well as a state that distrusts organised interest groups, fearing they may present a challenge to the unity of the country. An important consultative forum is the Economic and Social Committee (Conseil Economique et Social – CES), in which all major interest groups are represented. However, collective bargaining (despite its coverage of over 90 per cent mainly through extension of agreements to wider workforce) and tripartite negotiations have both been rather weak. Between 1983 and the late 1990s, there was a radical shift from a centralised system of industrial relations to a decentralised one at the level of the individual firm (Woll, 2006: 502–3).

French exceptionalism has been eroding since the early 1980s. Apart from globalisation, Europeanisation has been central to this process. The socialist policies of liberalisation after 1983 marked the beginning of a transformation of French capitalism. The internationalisation of the economy was pursued across all sectors of the economy, particularly at regional level. In a comparative study about the impact of Europeanisation on capitalism in the UK, Germany and France, Vivien Schmidt found that in the 1980s and 1990s quite radical transformational changes were taking place in France. France has moved from a 'state-led' to a 'state-enhanced' capitalism since the early 1980s, allowing the market to regulate the economy. This has had a major impact on the system of industrial relations, which is now less dirigiste (Schmidt, 2002: 202–4).

Like most other EU member-states, French interest groups now work in a multilevel setting and have abandoned purely nationally oriented strategies of influence. The French state is also interested in adjusting to Europeanisation processes, so there has been a substantial shift in France towards pluralism, accompanied by a simultaneous withdrawal of the state. French interest groups are now embedded in European-wide transnational interest groups (Eurogroups). Their own financial resources remain weak, as do those of the employers' organisations (Grossmann and Saurugger, 2004; Quittkat, 2006: 222–30). Moreover, these Europeanising effects have a differential impact and are certainly stronger among the business organisations (Saurugger, 2007: 1090).

Since 2002, successive presidents have tried to further the reform and liberalisation of the economy. In particular, labour market reform has been highly contested by the trade union confederations. There is a special responsibility of France, as one of the largest economies of the Eurozone, to set the standards of socioeconomic reform; however, so far this has been difficult. In this context, the old alliances of *étatisme* are being replaced by new ones that were socialised in a more globalised world (for a review and thorough analysis, see Amable, 2016, 2017; Amable et al., 2012). President Emmanuel Macron's presidency since 2017 has focused on domestic reform, particularly by creating better conditions for enterprises, but also on EU reform, in order to strengthen the supranational policy as a shield to deal with the challenges of globalisation. He symbolically stands for changing social alliances and elites at the helm of French political economy.

In sum, European pluralism has tendencies towards neo-corporatism and, apart from the UK, most other pluralist systems of interest intermediation are tamed by neo-corporatist elements.

Southern Europe: the weak state and weak interest groups

The Southern European systems of interest intermediation share some similarities. The weak state and the weak economy, with the exception of northern Italy, are factors that have shaped the way interest intermediation is undertaken in Southern European countries. Clientelism and patronage have played a role in all four countries (Brunazzo and Della Sala, 2016; Magone, 2003, 2016a, 2016b, 2016c; Sapelli, 1995; Schmitter, 1995). However, Europeanisation has led to a 'hollowing out and simultaneous hardening of the state' not just in Italy but also in the other Southern European countries that have reduced the power of such clientelistic and patronage tendencies (Della Sala, 1997). The financial and sovereign debt crisis between 2008 and 2013 affected all four countries of Southern Europe badly, and it is still not clear if the economic model is competitive enough. I would assess that reforms have been stagnating in all four countries, although Spain seems to be the most advanced. This can be dangerous in future crises. The bailout programmes (2010–18) in Portugal, Greece and Cyprus further undermined economic growth, particularly in Greece.

Italy was too big to fail so that clearly avoided any bailout by adopting quite strong austerity measures that led to the establishment of a technocratic government under former European Commissioner Mario Monti in 2011–12, who unilaterally introduced many reforms to the labour market that were then followed up by the Leta (2012–3), Renzi (2013–6) and Gentilone (2016–8) governments (Brunazzo and Della Sala, 2016; Culpepper, 2014; Regalia and Regini, 2018). Due to the fact that the Southern European countries were in the EMU, which constrained national macroeconomic policies, the only way to achieve an adjustment was to lower the wage costs and increase productivity, so that the economies could be competitive again. This led to a quite rapid dismantling of the generous welfare states when contextualised in the rather weak economies, with the exception of northern Italy (Armingeon and Baccaro, 2012).

One characteristic of Italy and other Southern European countries is that they have dualistic economies. The weak state just controls part of the economy, and a substantial part of economic transactions are undertaken in the informal sector (about 29 per cent in Italy in 2017, Spain 25 per cent, Portugal 24 per cent, Greece 31 per cent, Cyprus 31 per cent and Malta 31 per cent, all according to the calculations of Medina and Schneider, 2017: 19–21 and taken the median value). Moreover, both trade union confederations and business organisations are extremely fragmented, the former in ideological terms and the latter sectorially or according to the size of the enterprises, in much the same way as in France. In Italy, there are three main trade union confederations: the former communist General Confederation of Italian Workers (CGIL), the Christian democratic Italian Confederation of Workers' Trade Unions (CISL) and the socialist Union of Italian Workers (UIL). In spite of this fragmentation, trade union confederations are everywhere in society. Some neo-corporatism has existed in Italy since 1948, which has allowed trade union confederations to co-manage many social policies set out by the government. Moreover, they have been quite successful in offsetting the decline in trade unionism in the manufacturing sector, by increasing membership in other branches, among pensioners and immigrants

(Regalia and Regini, 2018: 70–1). For a long time, trade union confederations were close to political parties in the First Republic (1948–92), namely CGIL to the Communist party (PCI), CSIL to Christian Democracy (DC) and UIL to the Socialist Party (PSI). Tangentopoli ended this close relationship (Ceron and Negri, 2017). In 2016, unionisation density was 34.4 per cent (OECD, 2018b). On the employers' side, the Confederation of Industry (CONFINDUSTRIA) is probably the most important, but there are also confederations for trade organisations (CONFCOMMERCIO), for agriculture (CONFAGRICOLTURA) and for crafts (CONFARTIGIANATO). The strong presence of the state in the economy until 1992 was a major factor leading to tangentopoli (kickback city corruption scandal). Many business organisations paid kickbacks to Christian Democracy, the dominant party of the political and party system, to secure contracts for tenders issued by public sector firms. Many of these kickbacks were used for illicit party financing or even personal enrichment (see the classic study on clientela and parentela by La Palombara, 1965; Guzzini, 1994). Since 1992, there has been a process of the hollowing out of the state as a result of the pressures stemming from Europeanisation, particularly the EMU (Della Sala, 1997). In spite of the change of context, both trade union confederations and business organisations are still highly fragmented and therefore financially constrained in terms of shaping political processes.

European integration has been a major uniting element for cooperation between trade unions and business organisations. Several agreements were signed throughout the 1990s which were all related to the EMU. In particular, the Romano Prodi coalition government was able to count on the support of the social partners to join the third phase of the EMU in 1998. Also, during the second Berlusconi government (2001–6), the social partners signed a pact for Italy (Patto per Italia) that concentrated on labour market reform based on a White Book presented by Marco Biagi in 2003; the social partners remained committed to the Biagi law in 2003. The new social pact led to some flexibilisation of industrial relations at the level of the firm. However, the weak state was confronted by weak trade union confederations and weak business organisations. This meant that difficulties of implementation emerged throughout this period (Molina and Rhodes, 2007: 810–16). The financial and sovereign debt crises interrupted this long period of social pacts. As already mentioned, the Berlusconi (2008–11) and particularly the technocratic Mario Monti governments imposed unilaterally several reforms to unemployment benefit and labour market policies, including labour law. In spite of this, the social partners remained committed to social dialogue, particularly SMEs and the trade unions. However, incrementally, the conditions of the labour market have been changing towards flexicurity, but the decentralisation of collective bargaining has still not been taken up by the social partners, in spite of pressure from the government (Colombo and Regalia, 2016; Regalia and Regini, 2018: 71–5).

In Spain, the Workers' Committees (CCOO) and the General Union of Workers (UGT) are the main trade union confederations. In 2015, Spain had one of the lowest unionisation rates of the EU after France, with 13.9 per cent of the working population being members (OECD, 2018b). The crisis affected considerably the trade union movement, which had to deal with an exponential growth in unemployment and was forced into supporting austerity measures and the flexibilisation of the labour market (Magone, 2018: 217–19; for an excellent study on trade unions in Spain, see Hamann, 2012). In contrast, the Spanish Confederation for Business Enterprises (CEOE), which also comprises the Confederation for Small and Medium Sized Enterprises, CEPYME), has been a reliable social partner since 1977 (Brinkmann, 2012; Magone, 2018: 214–17; Nonnell and Medina, 2015).

Europeanisation has played a major role in pushing all three countries towards the European social model by better integrating their social partners into the decision-making process. In Spain, in 1991, the Economic and Social Council (Consejo Económico y Social – CES) was created, and such bodies were also extended to all seventeen autonomous regions. Social pacts, such as the 'Moncloa pacts' during the democratic transition in 1978, have been used extensively in Spain since then. However, most of them were about the flexibilisation of the labour market or pension reform. During the sovereign debt crisis, successive governments tried to instrumentalise social partnerships to gain support for their policies. Eventually, the social dialogue collapsed during Mariano Rajoy's absolute majority government. The so-called 'precariate', young people and women in short-term jobs or the unemployed, increased considerably during the crisis (Magone, 2018: 249–52; Medina et al., 2013; Molina, 2014; Royo, 2013).

In comparison to the larger Southern European countries, the smaller economies of Portugal, Greece and Cyprus were subject to quite tough austerity programmes supervised by the Troika. While Portugal was able to complete its programme between July 2011 and June 2014, and Cyprus between 2013 and March 2016, Greece started its bailout programmes (three bailouts) in 2010 and did not complete them until June 2018. The austerity policies attached to the bailout programme put considerable strains on civil society and the social partners (for more detail, see Magone, 2016a; Kruse, 2016; Visvizi, 2016).

In Portugal, a Permanent Council for Social Concertation (Conselho Permanente de Concertação Social – CPCS) was established in 1984 and became the central body for negotiation of public sector workers' wages. Later, in 1994, it became part of the consultative Economic and Social Council (CES). In a similar way to Spain, Portuguese governments were engaged in establishing social pacts with their social partners. However, the communist-led General Confederation of Portuguese Workers (CGTP) has so far been uncompromising on many issues, while the socialist/social democrat General Union of Workers (UGT) has been more conciliatory and supportive of government efforts to integrate the social partners. The most important employers' organisation is the Confederation of Portuguese Industry (CIP), founded in 1974. The finance and sovereign debt crisis has affected business enterprises considerably, so that they have merged with other associations in order to represent this sector more efficiently. Very important also is the Confederation of Portuguese Farmers (CAP). Alan Stoleroff clearly shows in a seminal study that industrial relations in Portugal are of a rather precarious type. It means that there is a general concern about wages and working conditions, but a general negotiation between the social partners towards industrial democracy, and the relationships between labour and capital, have been rather neglected. This has been reinforced by the fact that union density declined from 60.5 per cent in 1978 to 16.1 in 2014 (Stoleroff, 2016: 107, 110). One consequence of the crisis was the near collapse of collective bargaining, something that also happened in Spain (Stoleroff, 2016: 115–16; Távora and González, 2016). The only big exception seems to be the German factory AutoEuropa in Setúbal, where Volkswagen produces some car models and follows exemplary company-level industrial relations (Stoleroff, 2016: 115–16).

Finally, the Greek system of interest intermediation has been dominated by the main trade union confederation, the Confederation of Labour (GSEE), which comprises all trade union federations. The Confederation of Public Servants (ADEDY), which was fairly close to New Democracy, is in the process of merging with GSEE. GSEE had a close relationship with the socialist party (PASOK), particularly during the Papandreou governments of the 1980s. However, trade union membership has been declining steeply in Greece. In 2013, only 24.7 per cent of the working population was a member of a trade union (OECD, 2018b). In this sense, the business organisations such as the Federation of Greek industries (SEB), the National Confederation of Greek Commerce (ESEE) and the General Confederation of Professional Craftsmen and Small Manufacturers of Greece (GSEBEE) have gained in influence and importance over time. However, according to Dimitris Tsarouhas (2008), both trade union confederations and employees' organisations have been fragmented at the top of the hierarchy. Trade unionism in Greece is still characterised by ideological fragmentation, as in other Southern European countries, in spite of the unitary nature of GSEE (Lavdas, 2005: 302; Lavdas and Chatzigianni 2012: 264; Tsarouhas, 2008: 357–8).

As in Portugal and Spain, Europeanisation has been a major factor in creating social dialogue institutions in Greece. A network of social dialogue institutions, such as the tripartite Economic and Social Committee (OKE), founded in 1994 and emulating the European-level institution, the Fund for Employment and Vocational Training (LAEK) and the Hellenic Institute for Occupational Health and Safety (ELINYAE), are examples of such institutional proliferation. Social pacts have also been used since 1997 as a support for membership of the EMU. However, these policies were not properly coordinated. There have been lots of initiatives, but they were not overarched by a more long-term strategy of growth and stability. There were changes to the highly conflictive pattern of industrial relations up to the late 1980s, in which clientelism and patronage networks of the main political parties with interest groups played an important role (Tsarouhas, 2008: 357–9). One major problem has been what Kostas Lavdas labels 'disjointed corporatism', which comprises the lack of a tradition of social dialogue and tripartism, and the fragmentation of interest groups, allowing an asymmetrical development of neo-corporatist arrangements. The European integration process based on 'competitive' corporatism further complicates the stalled process of social dialogue and reform. In particular, trade unionism has tended to have a defensive attitude towards change, both in the public and private sectors. Clearly, Kevin Featherstone characterised Greece as a financially skewed failed state. Featherstone had already predicted back in 2003 what the problems for the Greek economy would be when joining the EMU (Featherstone, 2003, 2005, 2011; Featherstone and Papadimitriou, 2008; Lavdas, 2005: 306–11; Lavdas and Chatzigianni, 2012: 265–8). The sovereign debt crisis was just a consequence of inertia in terms of structural reforms to adjust to a more competitive globalised economy. Between 2010 and 2018, several austerity measures imposed by the Troika, and then by the Quadriga after the inclusion of the European Stability Mechanism (ESM), were rushed through parliament, but there was a lack of ownership of the policies.

In spite of this, the austerity policies have certainly weakened the rigid system of industrial relations that existed before the crisis (Clauwaert et al., 2017; see Koukiadaki and Kokkinou, 2016; Papadimitriou, 2012).

In spite of the contestation of the austerity packages in Portugal, Spain and Greece that were quite visible in the media, civil societies are rather weak and lack strong organisations like in the Nordic countries, the Benelux, Germany, Austria and Switzerland. According to several surveys, these three countries have an average of about 28 to 35 per cent of people involved in civil society associations, in comparison to the Nordic countries with 70 to 85 per cent. Italy has a slightly more developed civil society, particularly in the north, with about 43 per cent of people involved in associations (Van Deth and Maloney, 2015: 833).

The Mediterranean islands of Cyprus and Malta have similar traits to the continental Southern European countries, but are shaped by the long rule of the Ottoman Empire and then moderated by its British colonial legacy. In both cases, there is a strong level of cooperation between the main socioeconomic interest groups which have strong linkages to their respective ideological parties. The two countries follow a business model which focuses on attracting foreign direct investment. Therefore, they are low-tax countries. Consensual politics between the social partners is a major feature in both countries. In both cases, the system of industrial relations goes back to the 1960s. The codification of labour law and industrial relations took place in the 1970s (Bestler, 2012: 454; Stergiou, 2012: 815–6, 819). In both countries there are tripartite bodies to solve socioeconomic issues. In Malta, there is the Malta Council for Economic and Social Development and the Employment Relations Board, while in Cyprus there are the National Advisory Board and the National Employment Committee (Kalosinatos, 2018). In Cyprus, the role of the ideological orthodox, but pragmatic communist AKEL party clearly contributes a lot to the peaceful resolution of conflict.

In conclusion, the Southern European countries are characterised by a weak state, a weak economy and weak interest groups. In spite of the Europeanisation of the system of interest intermediation, a culture of clientelism and patronage, and of weak states, continues to prevail.

New democracies in Central and Eastern Europe

After forty years of a communist state or socialist regime, most Central and Eastern European countries are still creating systems of interest intermediation that are compatible with a liberal market economy, Europeanisation and globalisation. Such a task is difficult, because depending on the country business organisations are still weak and membership density in trade unions remains low. Moreover, after decades of regimented communist regimes, biased towards the working class and against business, many people avoid associational membership. Therefore many countries have a very low associational involvement (Ost, 2015; Van Deth and Maloney, 2015: 833).

The accession process to the EU has also imposed economic criteria on the Central and Eastern European countries. Moreover, a framework for the implementation of such economic criteria was exported to the Central and Eastern European countries. The tripartite social dialogue has been institutionalised and expanded in all Central and Eastern European countries. This proliferation of new tripartite social dialogue institutions has led to a better integration of employers' and employees' representative organisations. In spite of this, there is still a work in progress in most countries. For example, the high level of associational fragmentation in some countries has created problems of representativeness. Therefore, systems of interest intermediation are still work in progress, although the new rationale is being slowly integrated into economic and social policies. In most countries, according to David Ost, a kind of 'illusory neo-corporatism' dominated by government priorities and always about labour market liberalisation, is the kind of interest intermediation pattern that exists. The fragmentation of representativeness among employees/workers and business representatives further reinforces the role of the state in these tripartite institutions (Comité Économique Sociale Européen, 2002: 137–49; Cox and Mason, 2000; Glaessner, 2013; Mailand and Due, 2004; Ost, 2000).

East Central Europe: the quest for tripartism for the benefit of the economy

The most consolidated system of interest intermediation is probably that of Slovenia, which was able to establish a tradition of social partnership that has become a model for other Central and Eastern European countries. The country was able to follow a path-dependent development that had its origins in the former Yugoslav system of interest intermediation (Grdesic, 2008: 135–8). The tradition of industrial democracy and workers' auto-determination in enterprises in former Yugoslavia played a major role in facilitating the transition to a free market economy. However, one should not generalise this – Croatia and Serbia are still struggling to build a credible system of interest intermediation after the Franjo Tuđman and the Slobodan Milošević authoritarian periods of the 1990s (Grdesic, 2008: 139–47). From early on, Slovenian social partners were integrated in the decision-making process. Therefore, collective bargaining covers between 80 and 100 per cent of workers. The Slovenian constitution defines the upper chamber, the National Council, as a corporatist chamber of vested interests, which is reasonably rare in Europe and can only be found in the Irish Senate. This means that both employers' and employees' organisations and other interest groups are able to shape the legislative process. Moreover, an Economic and Social Council was established in 1994 with consultative powers. Representativeness of socioeconomic groups has been a major problem in Slovenia. Trade unionism is split into four main confederations, of which the Association of Free Trade Unions of Slovenia (ZSSS) is the largest with 150,000 members (2015), and the Confederation of Trade Unions of Slovenia Pergam (PERGAM) is the second largest with 72,000 (2015) members. Moreover, in the public sector there is the large Confederation of Public Sector Trade Unions (KSJS) with 73,400 workers (members). The fourth largest is the splinter Confederation of Trade Unions 90 of Slovenia with 36,000. Unionisation has been declining over the decades to 19.6 per cent in 2015 (OECD, 2018b). The employers' organisations are better organised. The two main employers' organisations are Association of Employers of Slovenia (ZDS) for the larger enterprises and Association of Employers in Craft and Small Business of Slovenia

(ZDOPS) for the SMEs. However, Slovenia, influenced by Austria and the legacy of the Austro-Hungarian monarchy, has a highly sophisticated and developed chamber system which strengthens the organisation of the main socioeconomic groups. It is estimated that in 2013 business organisation membership density was 44 per cent. Moreover, the role of the state in tripartite neo-corporatist concertation of interests is supported by the social partners. Although the Slovenian model of industrial relations has been resilient, the euro and financial crises led to a deterioration towards the 'illusory' corporatism model (Lukšič, 2012: 706–16; Lužar et al., 2018; Mrčela, 2017; Stanojević et al., 2016).

In the Czech Republic, a Council for Economic and Social Agreement (RHSD) was established in 1997; however, interest groups remain weak. The main trade union confederations are the Trade Union Association of Bohemia, Moravia and Silesia (ČMKOS) founded in 1991 and the Association of Autonomous Trade Unions of the Czech Republic (ASO ČR), the former had 60 per cent of union members in 2016. There are other smaller unions, but overall unionisation density was just 10.5 per cent in 2016 and decreasing (OECD, 2018b). There are two main business organisations: the Confederation of Industry of the Czech Republic (SPČR) and the Confederation of Employers' and Entrepreneurs' Associations of the Czech Republic (KZPS ČR). Overall they represent only one-third of all enterprises. The Czech Republic has been a booming economy in which unemployment is quite low, so that the low wages have been highlighted by CMKOŠ. The Czech economy relies on the recruitment of workforce from abroad, particularly from the Ukraine, to maintain their high growth rates (Kyzlinková and Veverková, 2018; Mansfeldová, 2012: 759–67).

Among the Central European countries, Slovakia emerges as having a quite successful system of industrial relations, ensuring steady economic growth, low unemployment and a competitive economy attracting foreign direct investment. The automobile sector is the core of this flexible economy. In spite of a considerable decline in union membership to around 10.9 per cent in 2015 (OECD, 2018b), the country has been characterised by social peace. Trade unionism is quite centralised around the Confederation of Trade Unions of the Slovak Republic (KOZ SR) comprising 96 per cent of all unionised workers. On the employers' side there are two major associations, namely the Federation of Employers Associations of the Slovak Republic (AZZZ SR) and National Union of Employers (RUZ). Tripartism neo-corporatism have existed since the 1990s. In 2007, the consultative Economic and Social Council was established, which comprised the relevant employees/workers, business and civil society groups (Čambáliková, 2012: 683–5, 687–9; Cziria et al. 2018; Kahancová, 2013).

In Hungary, there are nine employers' organisations and several trade union confederations active in tripartite bargaining committees. Among them is the tripartite Permanent Consultative Forum of the Competitive Sector and the Government (VKF) and the National Economic and Social Council (NGTT). While the former deals with interest concertation between business and enterprise, the latter comprises all relevant civil society actors and is a consultative body. However, the fragmentation of both trade unions and business organisations has been a major factor undermining a more stable regime. Trade union membership density was just 8.5 per cent in 2016 and decreasing and business organisation membership density was estimated at 21 per cent in 2013 (OECD,

2018b). Corporatism and social dialogue in Hungary may be labelled as 'illusory' and rather imposed by the government. In reality, successive governments have had a top-down perspective on how to deal with socioeconomic interest and civil society groups. The Viktor Orbán governments after 2010 have exacerbated this governmental approach to interest groups even further (Kiss et al., 2018; Reutter and Träger, 2012: 799–803).

Although the trade union confederation Solidarność was the most important actor in contributing to transition from communism to a liberal democracy in Poland, the interest intermediation system then evolved towards an illusory corporatism pattern, which is also characterised by a high level of fragmentation of the trade unions and business sectors. There are four main organisations representing employers and employees/workers. The largest trade union confederation is All-Poland Alliance of Trade Unions (OPZZ), followed by Independent Self-governing Trade Union Solidarity (NSZZ Solidarność) and Trade Unions Forum (FZZ). On the employers' side, there are the Business Center Club, Confederation Lewiatan, Employers of Poland (RP) and Polish Crafts Association (ZRP) There was a steep decline in trade union membership of over 70 per cent between 1993 and 2003. Recruitment has been difficult, partly due to the communist legacy of compulsory membership (Czarzasty et al., 2014). In 2015, membership density among unions was 11 per cent and the trend was declining, but the membership density of business organisations was only 9 per cent in 2013 (OECD, 2018b). Between 1994 and 2015, the main institution for social partnership was the tripartite Commission for Social and Economic Affairs, but after 2015 the incoming Justice and Law party government changed it to the Council of Social Dialogue (RDS). This has expanded to a network of regionalised councils in the sixteen voivodships, similar to Spain and the Czech Republic. Since the Justice and Law party came to power in 2015, the social dialogue has been strongly dominated by the government; however, the social partners seem to follow a successful cooperation in many areas of industrial relations (Czarzasty, 2018; Matthes, 2012: 569–75; Ziemer, 2013: 254–5).

The Baltic states: the impact of EMU

All Baltic countries are still constructing their system of interest intermediation. There are tripartite social dialogue institutions: the Tripartite National Council (LLRTT) in Lithuania and the National Tripartite Cooperation Council (NTSP) in Latvia that were founded in the 1990s and further expanded and improved before and after accession to the EU in 2004. Estonia did not create a similar all-encompassing social dialogue body, but several specialised ones exist that are related to the Health Insurance Fund (EHIF), Unemployment Fund (EUIF) and professional qualifications (EQA). Both labour and business organisations are quite centralised in Latvia and Estonia, but less so in Lithuania. In Latvia, the Free Trade Union Confederation of Latvia (LBAS) and the Latvian employers' confederation (LDDK) are the main social partners. Similarly, in Estonia, the respective main social partners are the Estonian Trade Union Confederation (EAKL) and the Estonian Employers' confederation (ETTK). In contrast, in Lithuania, trade unionism is split in one large and two smaller confederations. The Lithuanian Federation of Trade Unions (LPSK) is the largest trade union confederation in comparison to the Lithuanian Trade Union 'Solidarumas' (L) and the small Christian democratic Lithuanian Labour Federation (LDF). On the employers' side, there are two main business associations, namely the Lithuanian Confederation of Industrialists (LPK) and the Lithuanian Business Employers' Confederation (LDK). The low level of trade union density in all Baltic states is quite problematic. While in Latvia it decreased from 46 percent in 1992 to 10.8 percent in 2014, in Lithuania and Estonia the figures were even lower at 7–8 per cent trade union density in 2014–5. The same applies to business organisation association membership density, which European Company Survey (2013) estimates put at about 18–20 per cent of enterprises in Lithuania and Latvia, while for Latvia there are no figures. In this constellation, socioeconomic interest groups are rather weak and dominated by the policy choices of respective governments, which are more and more embedded in the constraining policies of the EMU and the European semester. The best example is the recent review of the labour code and the restoration of the social dialogue in Lithuania. However, weak trade unions in the Baltic states allow for potential violations of labour law and working conditions by business enterprises (Blaziene and Zabarauskaite, 2018; Kadarik and Osila, 2018; Karnite, 2018; Reetz and Reutter, 2012a: 171–2; 2012b: 375, 381–2; Reutter, 2012).

The western and eastern Balkans: weak civil society and dominance of the state

In the western and eastern Balkans, civil societies are still quite weak, dominated by state interest and political parties. Political corruption, clientelism and patronage are widespread. Romania is still characterised by a high level of fragmentation on the employees' representation side. In 2018, there were five trade union confederations and five employers' organisations represented in the relevant tripartite bodies. This was achieved by stricter representativeness laws. In comparison to other Western, Southern, East Central and Eastern European countries union density is quite high in Romania with about 30 per cent, while business organisation membership density is low at around 12 per cent in 2013, but such figures are not very reliable. The main tripartite body in Romania is the Economic and Social Council (CES). Moreover, the National Tripartite Council for Social Dialogue (CNTDS) has to be mentioned as an important forum for discussion of major social agreements like the minimum wage. According to the excellent work of Aurora Trif, Romanian industrial relations deteriorated considerably during and after the financial crisis between 2008 and 2013. This clearly led to a growing imbalance of government policy and support towards employers to the detriment of the trade unions (Trif, 2008, 2013: 230–2; 2016).

Bulgaria follows a similar business model of a low-wage economy. Civil society is weak, and the socioeconomic social partners are quite fragmented, but to a lesser extent than in Romania. There are two main trade union confederations of which the larger one is the Confederation of Independent Trade Unions in Bulgaria (CITUB) and the smaller Confederation of Labour Podkreva (Podkreva). On the employers' side there are five representative confederations, although the Confederation of Employers and Industrialists in Bulgaria (KPIB) and the Chamber of Commerce and Industry (BTPP) are the largest both comprising over 500,000 workers and employees under contract. There are two main tripartite bodies enabling the social dialogue. The National Council for Tripartite Cooperation deals mainly with socioeconomic agreements and policies, while the Economic and Social Council (ISS) is a broader consultative body that also includes civil society groups similar to counterparts across Europe. The quality of social dialogue has been rather poor with high levels of contestation and the tendency of the government to impose its policies on the social partners. Some restoration of the social dialogue took place during the crisis, but agreed issues were not implemented by the government. However, the social partners themselves seem to be working together to put forward proposals for the reform of tripartism in Bulgaria (Bernaciak, 2013: 243–5; Hristova-Valtcheva, 2012: 83–9; Markova, 2017; Yordanova, 2018).

Croatia is still developing a functioning tripartite social dialogue system. There are four main trade union confederations of which dependent Trade Unions of Croatia (NHS) and the Union of Autonomous Trade Unions of Croatia (SSSH) are the largest with 100,000 members each. On the employers' side it is more united around the Croatian Employers Association (HUP). The main tripartite body is the Economic and Social Council (GSV). Similar to the previous countries discussed, the government dominates the social dialogue process due to the growing demands of the European institutions to include the social partners in any policy-making decision. However, so far the social dialogue has been highly formal, centralised and dominated by the government. Tensions between employers' and employees' organisations over flexibilisation of Croatian labour have negatively affected the social dialogue (Bejakovic and Klemenčić, 2018; Seperić, 2017: 5–9).

It is expected that the majority of countries in the western Balkans will join the EU during the second half of the 2020s. However, they are still far behind in terms of functioning systems of industrial relations and high levels of associational involvement. They will certainly be obliged to move towards some kind of social partnership model of the EU, but this may take quite a long time to bear fruit.

Towards a multilevel system of interest intermediation

Since the mid-1980s, European integration has become an important factor shaping industrial relations at the national level. The European semester connected to socioeconomic governance requires consultation of social partners at all levels of the EU governance system. Apart from the fact that there is an advisory Economic and Social Committee (EESC) at supranational level that comprises all relevant national business, employees' and civil society organisations, they take part in myriad (267) advisory and regulatory committees (so-called comitology) of the European Commission. Representatives of national interest groups appointed by the government travel regularly between Brussels and the national capitals (European Commission, 2018e: 3). Moreover, national interest groups are members of larger pan-European interest groups (Eurogroups). These Eurogroups are also involved in supranational social dialogue institutions that have been set up since 1985, and in some cases go back to the 1970s. They take part in regular tripartite social summits (TSS) four times a year. A social dialogue committee (SDC) and a quite considerable number of sector social dialogue committees also exist making the cooperation of social partners even denser. Further, they can agree on socioeconomic legislation related to labour markets autonomously, and later this is codified as part of the legal *acquis communautaire*. This European social dialogue is generously funded by the European Commission. The main social partners at European level are the European Trade Union Confederation (ETUC): the Union of Industrial and Employers' Confederations of Europe (UNICE), which changed its name to BUSINESSEUROPE in May 2007, the European Centre of Enterprises with Public Participation (CEEP), the European Association of Craft, Small and Medium-Sized Enterprises (UAPME), the Council of European Professional and Managerial Staff (EUROCADRES), and the European Confederation of Executives and Managerial Staff (CEC) (see Table 8.2).

Conclusions: from national systems of interest intermediation to a multilevel EU governance system

The flexibilisation of industrial relations across the EU is leading to a paradigm shift from rigid structures of interest intermediation, of which the interventionist Keynesian neo-corporatism of the 1960s and 1970s is a good example, to a governance model that allows closer cooperation between the public and private sectors. Instead of the dominance of the tripartite mode of interest intermediation, there is a growing reliance on bipartite governance regimes in different policy fields (self-regulation of social partners with hardly any participation by state actors).

One major factor leading to this transformation is the transition from national to a European single market. There is a growing integration of industrial relations at the national and supranational EU levels.

In sum, Europe is certainly the most developed region in terms of industrial relations, and apart from its legacy, it is also an essential part of the European social model of capitalism propagated by the EU.

Suggested reading

General comparative books

Crouch, Colin (1994), *Industrial Relations and European State Traditions*. Oxford: Oxford University Press.

European Foundation for the Improvement of Living Conditions (Eurofound) (2015), *Industrial Relations in Europe 2014*. Luxembourg: Office of the Official Publications of the European Communities. (Available at: http://ec.europa.eu/social/keyDocuments.jsp?type=0&policyArea=0&subCategory=0&country=0&year=0&advSearchKey=IRIE&mode=advancedSubmit&langId=en (accessed on 24 June 2018).

European Foundation for the Improvement of Living Conditions (Eurofound) (2017), *Developments in Working Life in Europe. EurWork Annual Review 2016*. Luxembourg: Office of the Official Publications of the European Communities. (Available at: //www.eurofound.europa.eu/sites/default/files/ef_publication/field_ef_document/ef1727en.pdf (accessed on 24 June 2018).

Greenwood, Justin (2017), *Organized Interests in the European Union*. Basingstoke: Palgrave.

Schmitter, Philippe (2008), The changing politics of organised interests. *West European Politics*, 31(1): 195–210.

Siaroff, Alan (1999), Corporatism in 24 industrial democracies: meaning and measurement. *European Journal of Political Research*, 36: 175–205.

Traxler, Franz (2004), The metamorphoses of corporatism: from classical to lean patterns. *European Journal of Political Research*, 43(4): 571–98.

Electronic journals

European Journal of Industrial Relations. Excellent articles on industrial relations in East and West.

Transfer. Scientific journal of the European Trade Union Institute dedicated to the study of trade unions and industrial relations.

Websites

Alliance for Lobbying Transparency and Ethics Regulation (ALTER-EU) (2018): excellent critical website monitoring lobbying at EU level at: www.alter-eu.org/ (accessed on 23 June 2018).

European Foundation for the Improvement of Living Conditions (EUROFOUND) (2018): excellent database on different aspects including industrial relations at: www.eurofound.europa.eu (accessed on 23 June 2018).

European Observatory of Working Life (EURWORK) (2018), database with excellent reports on the situation of industrial relations in each European country and country profiles on industrial relations including the candidate countries to accession of the European Union at //www.eurofound.europa.eu/de/observatories/eurwork (accessed on 23 June 2018).

QUESTIONS FOR REVISION

- What are the main features of neo-corporatism? Discuss, using examples from at least two European countries.
- What are the main features of pluralism? Discuss, using examples from at least two European countries.
- Assess the consolidation of interest intermediation systems in Central and Eastern Europe. Discuss, using examples from at least two countries.
- Are we moving towards a European system of industrial relations?
- What positive and negative aspects can you identify in Euro-lobbying?

Chapter 9

Regional and local government in multilevel Europe

- Decentralisation in Europe
- Patterns of territorial administration in Europe
- The European dimension of subnational government
- Conclusions: towards a Europe of the regions
- Suggested reading

Decentralisation in Europe

Stein Rokkan identified the silent revolution taking place in the 1970s and early 1980s which was related to the growing self-confidence and self-consciousness of many European regions (Rokkan and Urwin, 1983: chapter 3). Indeed, since the late 1980s, the centralised nation-state has had to move towards a more decentralised structure as a result of the growing pressure coming from the subnational level, seeking greater autonomy, as well as in response to the challenge of globalisation, which requires a more flexible structure (Christiansen and Jørgensen, 2000). In this regard, the region was identified as probably being a more flexible geographic unit than the nation-state to respond directly to global challenges. Michael Keating characterised this revival of the region as 'new regionalism' (Keating, 1998). The European integration process further contributed to a transformation of centre-periphery relations in each country (Bartolini, 2005; Magone, 2006: chapter 7). The present political geography of Europe has become quite diverse, with some countries being fully fledged federal states (e.g. Austria, Belgium, Germany and Switzerland), others being centralised, despite consequent high costs in terms of inefficiency (e.g. Portugal, Greece, Bulgaria and Romania), and many others developing their own new centre-periphery relations between these two extremes. Many countries remained unitary but decentralised and have de-concentrated their administrative structures (e.g. Sweden, Denmark, Norway, Finland and the Netherlands). All these countries have developed new governance structures that allow a more flexible and dynamic relationship between centre and periphery.

Quite crucial for democracy are strong decentralised, but efficient local governments. The European Charter of Local Self-Government of 1985 is the main benchmarking and good practice document for local authorities and centre-periphery relations in Europe. New member-states in the EU have to implement such principles in order to belong to the community of democratic states. At least three main principles have to be mentioned, that we will, if appropriate, return to throughout the text (Table 9.1). First, the principle of decentralisation of power and democracy to the lower level, based on elected bodies and the right of populations to take part in decision-making concerning their lives (article 3). Second, local government should be legally protected by the constitution and/or other main documents (article 11). Last, appropriate human and financial resources should be allocated to local government, so that these authorities can provide adequate services to citizens (articles 6, 7, 9) (COE, 1985).

Since the late 2000s, there have been attempts to measure regional and local authority/autonomy. This is based on a complex set of several variables. Clearly, autonomy is not the same as quality. This is another aspect that probably needs more detailed study beyond quantitative statistical analysis. In terms of local autonomy, Andreas Ladner, Nikolas Keuffer and Harald Baldersheim present a tentative local autonomy index based on eleven variables: financial transfer system, financial self-reliance, institutional depth, central and regional access, fiscal autonomy, borrowing autonomy, organisational autonomy, administrative supervision, legal protection, policy scope and effective political discretion (Ladner et al., 2016: 331). The typology is not static and may change over time. Indeed, the authors analysed it from 1990 with a cut-off point in 2014 (Table 9.2).

As one can see in Table 9.2, apart from the Nordic countries, and partly the Benelux and German-speaking Europe, there are no regional patterns. Nevertheless,

Table 9.1 National territorial organisations in Europe

	Country	*Regional units*	*Municipalities/communes*
Federal states	Germany	16 Länder	11,059
	Austria	9 Bundesländer	2,100
	Switzerland	20 cantons 6 half cantons	2,231
	Belgium	3 regions 3 cultural communities 10 provinces (5 in Flanders and 5 in Wallonia)	589 308 (Flanders) 262 (Wallonia)
Confederal states	Bosnia-Herzegovina	Confederation of two parts – Bosnian–Croatian Federation 10 cantons – Republika Srpska Just communes, no in-between tier	143 communes Bosnian–Croatian Federation 80 Republika Srpska 61+2 cities
Regionalised unitary states	Spain	17 comunidades autonomas (autonomous communities)	8,124 comunalidades (communes)
	UK	4 regions Scotland Wales Northern Ireland England (9 non-elected subregions)	England 353 Wales 22 Scotland 32 Northern Ireland 11
	Italy	15 regions 5 special regions	107 provinces or metropolitan cities 7,978 communes (2017)
	France	22 regions 4 regions overseas 102 departements (4 outside France)	35,399 communes (2017)
	Poland	16 województwo (regions) 380 powiats (counties) 66 cities with county status	2,478 gminas (communes)
	Czech Republic	13 kraje (regions), and Prague as (hlavni mešto) capital-city region 73 okres (counties)	6,249 communes (out of which 392 urban municipalities and 205 urban municipalites with extended powers)
	Hungary	7 non-elected (regiók) regions 19 elected (mégyek) counties 197 (jarasók) districts	3,178 (közsezek) communes (out of which 106 large communes, 322 town local authorities, 23 town with county rank local authority, 24 capital and district local authority)

Unitary, but decentralised states	Netherlands	12 provinces	430 gemeenten (communes) 27 waterschaapen (water boards)
	Sweden	2 directly elected and 18 non-elected counties	290 kommuner (municipalities)
	Norway	19 fylker (counties)	426 kommuner (municipalities)
	Denmark	5 regioner (regions)	98 kommuner (municipalities)
	Finland	19 maakunta (counties/regional councils) 70 seutukunta (subregions)	311 kunta (communes)
Unitary centralised states	Albania	12 prefekture (counties)	62 bashki (municipalities)
	Bulgaria	6 non-elected planning macro-regions 28 non-elected oblasti (districts)	262 obshtini (municipalities)
	Croatia	20 zupanija (counties)	128 gradovi (towns) and 428 opċine (municipalities)
	Estonia	Central government de-concentrated 15 counties (maakond) for coordinating public policies	One tier local government 15 cities (linnad) and 64 rural municipalities (vallad)
	Greece (since 2011) So-called Kallikratis Plan for local government reform	7 apokentroménes dioikíseis (decentralised administrations) Head appointed by government 13 non-elected coordinating perifereies (regions) 74 directly elected perifereiakés enótites (regional units)	325 dimoi (municipalities)
	Iceland	17 sýslur (provinces) (unofficial)	Just one tier of local government 76 urban and rural municipalities
	Ireland	Just administrative and non-elected three regional assemblies One tier system	31 local authorities (3 city councils, 2 city and country councils and 26 country councils)
	Latvia (reform in 2009)	5 planošana regionu (planning regions) (for EU funding purposes)	110 novads municipalities 9 Republikas Pilseta (Republican cities)
	Lithuania		One tier of local government 60 savivaldybés (municipalities)
	Luxembourg		One tier of local government 115 communes

(continued)

Table 9.1 *(continued)*

Country	*Regional units*	*Municipalities/communes*
Macedonia		One tier of local government 80 opštini municipalities
Portugal	5 non-elected coordinating regiões (regions) (de-concentrated central administration) 2 autonomous elected regions (Madeira and Azores)	308 municipios municipalities (subdivided in 3,091 municipalities) Aggregated coordinating level comprising several municipalities (also related to EU funding, but not only) 2 Metropolitan Areas (Oporto, Lisbon) 20 comunidades intermunicipais (intermunicipal communities)
Romania	41 counties and Bucharest 8 non-elected development regions (related to EU funding management)	103 municipiu (municipalities) 217 towns 2,861 communes
Serbia	29 districts Two autonomous regions Vojvodina Kosovo and Metohija (controversial due to unilateral declaration of independence)	174 units of local government 150 municipalities 23 cities and Belgrade
Slovakia	8 samosprávne kraje elected (regions) 79 districts	About 2,927 obci (municipalities)
Slovenia	58 de-concentrated state administrative units	212 občine (municipalities)

Source: Several sources among which the most important is OECD (2016c) regional policy country profiles.

the Nordic countries seem to set the standards for all other countries (Ladner et al., 2016: 338). The big surprise is Serbia in the first group, which may just be a statistical outlier and difficult to back up with qualitative studies. The high level of debt of Serbian local government seems to be a major constraint for autonomy and is not comparable with the Nordic countries (*Euractiv*, 29 June 2017).

Table 9.3 presents a typology of regional authority based on the studies of a research team led by Liesbet Hooghe and Gary Marks. Like in the previous index, several indices were used to determine this regional authority capacity. They differentiate between variables of self-rule (ability to govern its territory) and shared rule (ability to shape national government policies). Four variables are in the first

Table 9.2 A typology of local autonomy, 2014

	Power of initiation (high)	
	Group 1 *Highest level of autonomy* *(25–37)*	*Group 2* *High level of autonomy* *(20–25)*
Constitutional immunity *High*	**Switzerland** **Finland** **Sweden** **Iceland** **Germany** **Denmark** **Poland** **Lichtenstein** Norway France Italy Austria Serbia	**Belgium** **Netherlands** **Spain** **Portugal** **Luxembourg** **Lithuania** **Bulgaria** Czech Republic Estonia Croatia Macedonia Latvia Romania
	Group three *Low level of autonomy* *(19–16)*	*Group four* *Lowest level of autonomy* *(below 16)*
Constitutional immunity *Low*	**Greece** **Malta** **UK** **Slovenia** **Ukraine** **Turkey** Albania Hungary	**Georgia** **Ireland** **Moldova** Cyprus
	Power of initiation (low)	

Source: Simplified and adapted from Ladner et al. (2016: 342–7). In bold, the core countries of this group since at least 2000.

category, namely institutional depth (level of decentralisation), policy scope (range of competences), fiscal autonomy (level of taxation powers) and representation (endowment with independent legislature and government). In the second category, they also measure four variables: law-making (co-legislation powers with central government), executive control (ability to co-determine policy in intergovernmental meetings), fiscal control (ability to co-determine distribution of national tax revenues) and constitutional reform (ability to co-determine constitutional change) (Marks et al., 2008: 115). Based on their data, I prepared a tentative typology for the period 1999–2010, the latest set of data provided by the authors. Very interesting is seeing Bosnia-Herzegovina in the group with the highest regional authority due to the confederal structure of the country. Moreover, Serbia and Montenegro,

Table 9.3 A typology based on Regional Authority Index in 2008

Group 1 Highest level of authority (above 25)	*Group 2 High level of authority (20–24)*	*Group 3 Middle level of authority*	*Group 4 Low level of authority*
Germany (37)	Austria (23)	Netherlands (17.5)	Croatia (9)
Spain (33.6)	Russian Federation (20.1)	Norway (12)	Czech Republic (9)
Belgium (33.1)	France (20)	Sweden (12)	Poland (8)
Italy (27.3)		United Kingdom (11.2)	Slovakia (8)
Bosnia-Herzegovina (27.1)		Greece (11)	Turkey (8)
Switzerland (26.5)		Hungary (10.9)	Denmark (7.3)
		Romania (10)	Finland (7.3)
			Serbia (6.4)
			Portugal (3.8)
			Ireland (3)
			Latvia (3)
			Lithuania (3)
			Albania (2)
			Bulgaria (2)
			Macedonia (2)
			Slovenia (1)
			Cyprus (0)
			Estonia (0)
			Iceland (0)
			Luxembourg (0)
			Malta (0)
			Montenegro (0)
			Kosovo (0)

Source: Hooghe et al. (2008: 262–74; 2016).

shortly before the independence of the latter, also has high regional authority. Of course, this does not tell us anything about the quality of such regional authority (see Table 9.3).

Typologies are more like orientation maps than in-depth studies, so the following pages will try to delineate more qualitatively the way local and regional government works in the individual countries in comparative perspective.

We now turn to patterns of territorial administration in Europe.

Patterns of territorial administration in Europe

One of the simplest and easiest ways to differentiate patterns of territorial administration was devised by John Loughlin. In a seminal article, Loughlin differentiated between four categories of territorial organisation: federal states, regionalised but unitary states, unitary but decentralised states, and unitary centralised states (Loughlin, 2000; Table 9.4). We have added here a tentative fifth category of a confederal state, because Bosnia-Herzegovina is still far from achieving a reconciliation between the Serbs and the Bosniak-Muslims and Croats (Tables 9.1 and 9.2, Figure 9.1).

Federal states: Germany, Austria, Switzerland and Belgium

The most decentralised countries are in the western central part of Europe: Germany, Austria, Switzerland and Belgium. Germany is by far the largest federalised country in Europe. Since reunification of 1989–90, it consists of sixteen *Länder*. There are ten *Länder* in the west, and six new *Länder* including Berlin in the east. The overall pattern of distribution of budget and personnel is one of cooperative federalism based on consensual agreement and negotiation. The *Länder* are an important stepping stone for national politics, and this is also true vice versa. There is joint policy-making (*Politikverflechtung*) that allows diversity to be set alongside agreed frameworks that set the guidelines and limits for the respective policies. The conference of first ministers (*Konferenz der Regierungschefs*) is important for achieving coordination and harmonisation of policy-making between the *Länder* and the federal

Figure 9.1 The territorial organisation of European countries

Table 9.4 General, central, regional and local government expenditure in the EU and EEA, % of GDP, 2017

		General government	*Central government*	*Regional government*	*Local government*
EU average	EU28	45.8	24.9	4.7	10.7
	Euro-area 19	47.1	21.7	6.4	9.6
Federal states	Belgium	52.2	26.7	19.4	7.1
	Germany	43.9	12.5	13.0	7.9
	Austria	49.1	32.2	9.0	8.3
	Switzerland	34.3	10.7	13.7	7.4
Unitary regionalised states	Spain	41.0	18.8	14.8	5.8
	Italy	48.9	28.8		13.9
	France	56.5	23.1		11.2
	UK	41.1	37.5		9.8
	Poland	41.2	25.0		13.3
	Czech Republic	38.8	28.3		10.6
	Hungary	46.5	33.2		6.3
	Slovakia	40.4	24.7		6.9
Unitary decentralised states	Netherlands	42.6	25.4		13.4
	Sweden	49.1	28.7		25.1
	Finland	53.7	26.4		21.7
	Denmark	51.9	38.2		34.4
	Iceland	50.3	41.0		16.9
	Norway	41.9	30.7		13.0
Unitary centralised states	Luxembourg	26.1	24.9		2.1
	Ireland	43.1	26.3		8.2
	Slovenia	48.0	36.4		3.4
	Greece	42.9	30.9		4.9
	Cyprus	38.1	29.4		1.4
	Malta	36.5	36.5		0.4
	Portugal	45.9	34.6		5.8
	Bulgaria	35.2	23.5		7.1
	Romania	33.4	23.7		8.7
	Croatia	45.3	29.0		11.5
	Estonia	40.2	34.3		9.8
	Latvia	38.0	22.7		10.2
	Lithuania	33.3	21.8		7.8

Source: Eurostat (2018a).

government. There are also several intergovernmental meetings between the ministers of the *Länder* governments, which allow more specialised discussions between the representatives of the *Länder* and the federal government

(*Ressortministerkonferenzen*) to take place. Moreover, a complex network of committees between the federal government and the *Länder* has been established over the last sixty years, making the decision-making process less transparent and accountable (Figure 9.2).

The *Länder* have exclusive competences in education, culture, policing, media and local government, but have to share a bulk of other competences with

Figure 9.2 The *Länder* in Germany

the federal government. According to Wolfgang Rudzio, most of the interesting domestic policy areas are shared between the *Länder* and the federal government (Rudzio, 2016: 338). One of the main reasons is that there are general principles underlying the governance of the Federal Republic of Germany. First, there is the general principle of creating a level playing field across the country in terms of life chances and quality of life. Second, in spite of diversity, the economic and legal conditions are intended to be largely the same in all parts of the country. This sets boundaries for policy-makers at the regional level. Despite this small number of exclusive competences, the *Länder* are central to implementation of federal policies, so that Germany is characterised by an executive federalism (*Verwaltungsföderalismus*). According to Rudzio, there is no dualist structure between federal level and *Länder* as is common in the United States and Canada, but rather an integrated one in which there is cooperation (Rudzio, 2016: 339–40).

The *Länder* have their own governments and parliaments, which are elected every four years. This has become an important factor for the dynamics of domestic politics. Positive or negative results at regional elections may create problems for a party that is represented in the federal government in Berlin, because representatives of the regional governments are represented in the Bundesrat, the upper chamber of German parliament. Changing majorities in the Bundesrat due to regional elections of individual *Länder* throughout the four-year period may undermine or enhance the coalition government in power. *Länder* also have a suspensive veto power in the upper chamber of the national parliament, the Bundesrat (Federal Council), and a final veto in a limited number of areas.

Austria has a similar territorial structure to Germany with nine *Bundesländer*. The only major difference is that it is more centralised in terms of competences and there is more emphasis on executive federalism. This has to do with the Austrian historical legacy in which Vienna was the centre of

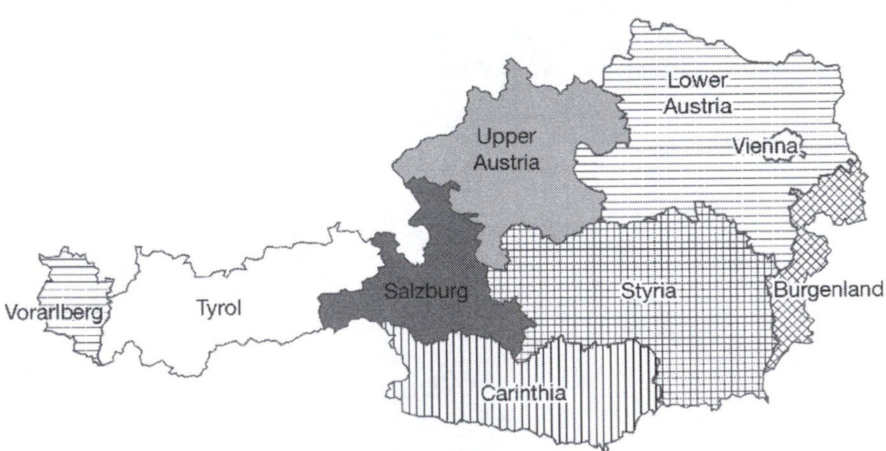

Figure 9.3 The federal territorial organisation of Austria

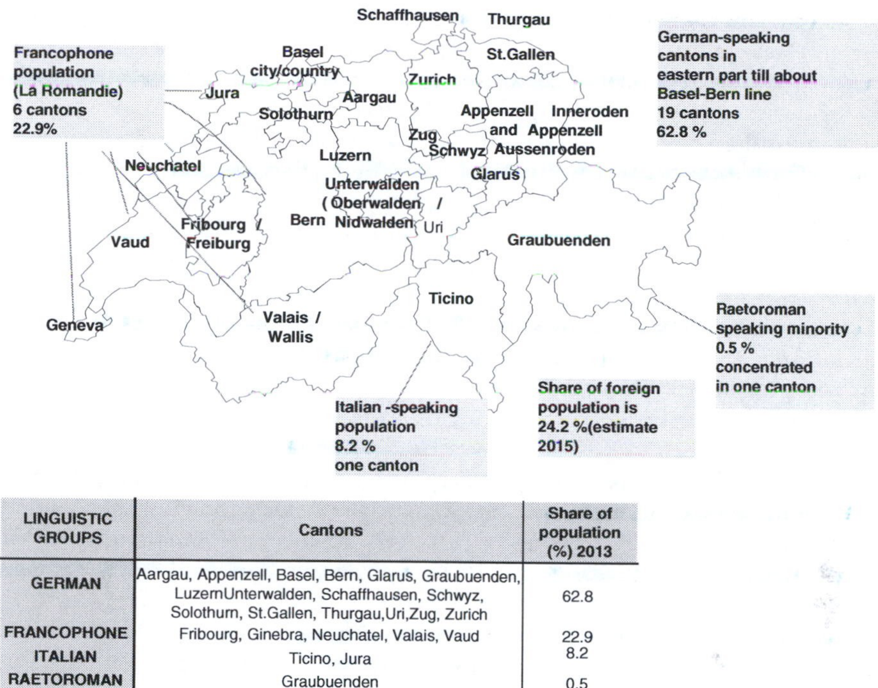

LINGUISTIC GROUPS	Cantons	Share of population (%) 2013
GERMAN	Aargau, Appenzell, Basel, Bern, Glarus, Graubuenden, LuzernUnterwalden, Schaffhausen, Schwyz, Solothurn, St.Gallen, Thurgau,Uri,Zug, Zurich	62.8
FRANCOPHONE	Fribourg, Ginebra, Neuchatel, Valais, Vaud	22.9
ITALIAN	Ticino, Jura	8.2
RAETOROMAN	Graubuenden	0.5
		24.2% (2015)

Figure 9.4 The federal structure of Switzerland and attached table of linguistic groups

Source: *Der Neue Fischer Weltalmanach* (2018: 404, 410).

administration and the political system was highly centralised. From 1945, the historical legacy shaped the way the country has been organised up to the present day. However, Austria is one of the most decentralised countries of the EU in financial terms (Pelinka and Rosenberger, 2003: 223–32). In a similar way to Germany, there are regular elections to a regional parliament (*Landtag(e)*) every four years. Also, since the 1960s, an informal conference of first ministers (*Konferenz der Landeshauptleute*) regularly takes place. Last, but not least, the regional parliaments send representatives to the Bundesrat (Federal Council), the upper chamber of the national parliament. However, in comparison to the German system, the Austrian Bundesrat is fairly weak, and their representatives are appointed by the regional parliaments according to their strength. They lack human and financial resources to do their jobs (see Magone, 2017: 184; see Chapter 5) (Figure 9.3).

Switzerland is the most decentralised of the three countries, although the central government has gained in importance since 1945. There are twenty cantons and six half cantons, each with their own parliament and government (see Figure 9.4). Because of the high level of decentralisation, intergovernmental structures are of great importance in order to achieve the harmonisation and coordination of policies. This fragmentation and high level of autonomy create major administrative problems, and some policy areas, such as taxation, are still far from harmonised. The consequence is the establishment of a very expensive administrative structure because most cantons are small. Coordination takes place through the conference of cantonal governments (Konferenz der Kantonalregierungen – KdK) established in 1993. It comprises a myriad of 500 horizontal inter-cantonal conferences per year. Quite important are the sixteen conferences of directors responsible for different policy areas (*Direktorenkonferenz*) (Bolleyer, 2006: 400–1; see also Magone, 2017: 227–8; see also Table 9.2). Although more centralisation from the federal government has been happening, cantons have, through the KdK, quite a lot of possibility to shape the central government-cantonal relationship, which has become known as a participatory federalism (*Mitwirkungsföderalismus*) (Steytler, 2017: 60–8). The historical legacy of the twenty cantons and six half cantons have produced varieties of Swiss democracy; however, all of them are characterised by a high level of consensus, and some isomorphism processes may take place (Vatter, 2002). The cantons are also represented in the symmetrical bicameralism of the Swiss parliament, namely in the Council of Estates (*Ständerat*) consisting of forty-six members. Members are elected by a first-past-the-post system and it is a more reflective consensual chamber (Magone 2017: 182–3; also see Chapter 5).

Belgium is the youngest federal state in Europe. It was established after the ratification of the new constitution in 1993. This was the culmination of a process of decentralisation that had been taking place since the 1960s. Meanwhile there were six state reforms, the latest in 2014, which included a redesigning of the Senate as the chamber of the subnational units. At the centre was an ongoing latent conflict between the Francophone region of Wallonia and the Flemish-speaking region of Flanders. Although there is a third German linguistic group, in the east of Belgium, it has remained outside the major conflict between the two regions. Before the Second World War, when Wallonia dominated the unitary state, the Flemish-speaking population felt disadvantaged in Belgium. After the Second World War, Flanders gradually became the richest part of Belgium and began to demand greater autonomy. Moreover, the population ratio between the two parts of Belgium became inverted. Although before the Second World War, the majority of the population was living in Wallonia, in the 1960s there was a larger share of the population in Flanders. Since the 1960s, there has been a process of decentralisation and also some separation of the two populations (I would rather characterise this as 'civilised ethnic cleansing', pushed more by Flanders). Piecemeal reforms were undertaken so that greater autonomy could be granted to the three regions. However, this period was also characterised by many conflicts (Leton and Miroir, 1999). The new federal structure comprises six subnational units: three regions and three cultural communities. The three regions are Flanders, Wallonia and Brussels. and the cultural communities are the Flemish, Francophone and German communities. The Flemish region and community have merged and built one government. There are also attempts of coordination and even fusion, between the regional government of Wallonia and the Francophone community, but in terms of boundaries this is more difficult. One characteristic of Belgian politics is that there is no national party system. There are now two party systems, one in Wallonia and the other in Flanders, and, depending on the national strength of each party in each of the two regions, they then negotiate a coalition government at national level. Less known, is that there is a third party system in the German community.

Pro-independence political parties emerged just in Flanders. From the 1990s to 2007, the extreme rightwing anti-immigration Flemish Interest (Vlaamse Belang, until 2004 named Vlaams Blok – VB) dominated the independence discourse, but since then the more moderate New Flemish Alliance (Nieuw-Vlaamse Alliantie – N-VA) has taken its place. Although a moderate party, N-VA uses a new right populist discourse sometimes close to VB, which creates tensions at federal level. In contrast to VB, which was avoided by the other parties by a *cordon sanitaire*, N-VA has been the main party in the five-party coalition under Walloon liberal prime minister Charles Michel since 2014. According to a 2014 election survey, Marc Swyngedouw and his team discovered that a larger minority of 32.6 per cent are happy with the status quo, and a declining minority of 36.4 per cent want more competences to be devolved to the regions. Just a small minority of 6.4 per cent want a separation of the two communities (Swyngedouw et al., 2015: 15; see Figure 9.5).

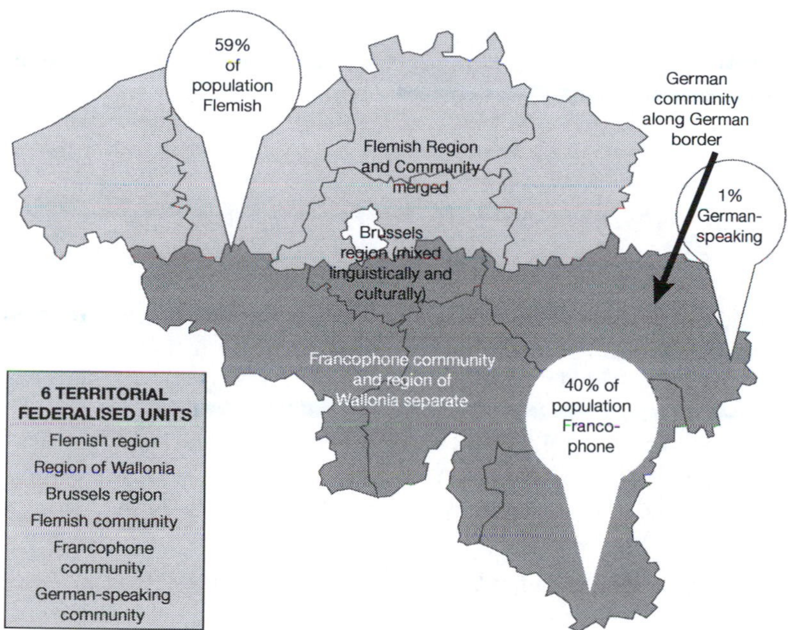

Figure 9.5 The federal structure of Belgium

A confederal state: Bosnia-Herzegovina

Local government in Bosnia-Herzegovina is organised in a confederal manner, with two separated local systems, one in the Croatian-Bosnian federation and another in the Republika Srspka. This clearly allows for a continuing consolidation of the partition of the country along ethnic lines (Jenne, 2009: 277–80). Moreover, issues related to government inefficiency, slow development of a market economy and political corruption have prevented greater progress in bringing the ethnic communities closer together (Bideleux and Jeffries, 2007b: 399–404). Several studies confirm that local government is poor in terms of efficiency in both parts of the Federation, and the population is dissatisfied with the provision of public services, particularly access to water (Bojičić-Dželilović, 2011: 25; McNeil et al., 2009; Zlopaka, 2008: 180). The two parts have different local government structures: in the Bosnian-Croatian Federation there are ten cantons, which are treated as federal units and are different in size and level of competences, and eighty municipalities; the Republika Srpska is far more centralised with only one local government tier, sixty-one municipalities and two cities (Zlopaka, 2008: 182–8). In both parts of the country, centralisation is dominant. The only major difference is that in the Bosnian-Croatian Federation centralisation takes place at cantonal level, while in the Republika Srpska it comes from the central government (Zlopaka, 2008: 199). Indeed, the ten cantons are rather powerful mini-states challenging the centre (Bojičić-Dželilović, 2011: 5). In spite of all this, more recent studies seem to show varieties in performance of local government depending on the quality of leadership, but funding and models in the international community are not enough to change the situation. More important is to understand the local informal politics on a case-by-case approach and to try to create virtuous circles complementing new and old rules of the game (see the excellent study by Pickering and Jusić, 2017).

Regionalised unitary states: Spain, Italy, France, the UK, Poland, the Czech Republic, Hungary and Slovakia

The regionalised unitary states can be divided into two broad categories: those that allow autonomy because of the strong regional consciousness of some parts of the country (such as Spain, the UK and, to some extent, Italy) and those that are engaged in administrative decentralisation and de-concentration (such as France, Italy, Poland, the Czech Republic, Hungary and Slovakia). The former want to accommodate centre-periphery tensions, while the latter want to modernise the state through the introduction of more flexible decentralised structures.

Spain: a successful model of democratisation and decentralisation

Among the first group, Spain is probably the most interesting case. In the constitution of 1978, Spain was defined as a 'state of autonomies'. This was a compromise between the Francoist right, which wanted to preserve the unitary nature of Spain, and the leftwing democratic opposition, which was keen to move towards a federal structure and, if not, at least to restore the autonomy of the historical regions of Catalonia, the Basque Country and Galicia, all of which had their own languages. However, between 1979 and 1982, the granting of autonomy to the historical regions led to a movement towards the creation of autonomous communities in other parts of the country. At the end of 1982, there were seventeen autonomous communities, some with a comprehensive level of autonomy, which included policing and education, and others with lower levels of autonomy. Four regions were able to achieve a considerable level of autonomy according to article 151: Andalucia, the Basque Country, Galicia and Catalonia. The others had autonomy conceded through article 143, which allowed for a limited autonomy. However, all autonomous communities were granted directly elected regional parliaments and their own executives (Figure 9.6).

Such an asymmetrical construction of the state of autonomies has been continuously reviewed by governments of the then two main parties, the People's Party (Partido Popular – PP) and the Socialist Party (Partido Socialista Obrero Español – PSOE), leading to a considerable decentralisation of the former highly centralised political system.

Between 2004 and 2011, the Zapatero government pushed for further decentralisation and allowed for a review of the statutes of the autonomous regions. The most controversial was the Catalan Statute, which led to major opposition by the

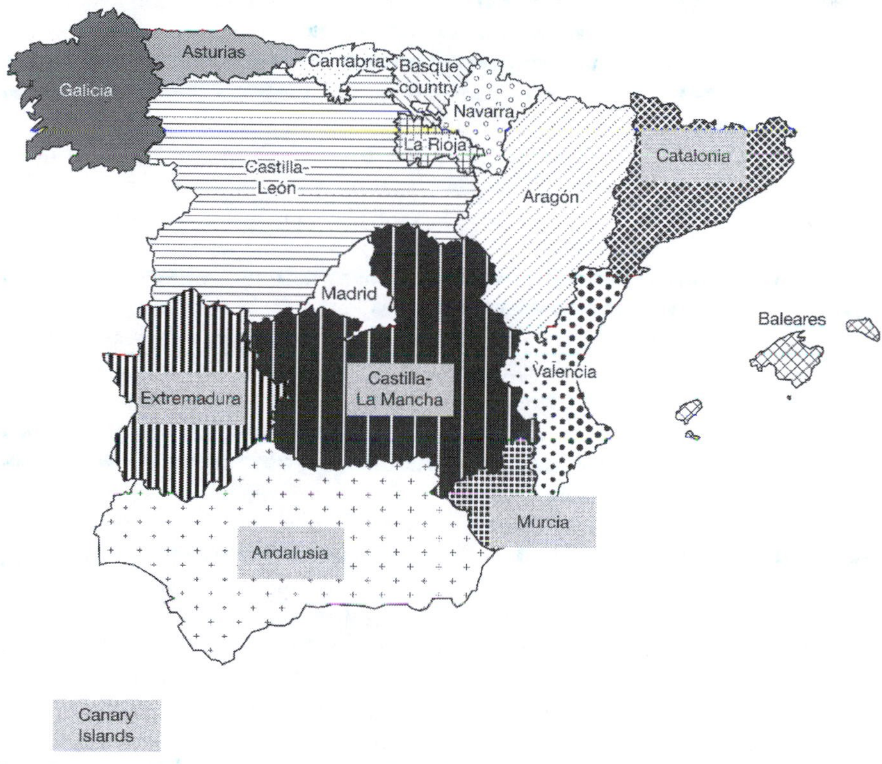

Figure 9.6 The autonomous communities in Spain

PP under Mariano Rajoy. In 2006, PP requested the constitutional court review the revised Catalan Statute on its constitutionality. One particular issue of contention was the use of the word 'nation' for Catalonia in the statute. The more radical conservative factions inside the PP regarded this as an assault on the unity of Spain. Article 2 of the Spanish constitution regards Spain as an indissoluble nation, but it recognises the right to autonomy of nationalities and regions. However, the different historical communities in Spain do regard themselves as nations and would like to change the Spanish constitution to enshrine the pluri-national identity of the country. The country could follow the UK model, which allows for a full acknowledgment of the different nationalities – Scottish, Welsh, Irish and English – within the state. Apart from the Catalan Statute, several other autonomous communities undertook review processes. Although the Catalan Statute was approved and confirmed in a referendum in Catalonia on 18 June 2006, a lot of articles in it were rejected by the constitutional court on 27 June 2010. Since then, the pro-independence movement has gained in strength through its main organisation the National Catalan Assembly (Assemblea Nacional Catalana – ANC) founded in 2012. It started organising local pro-independence referendums leading to two illegal independence referendums on 9 November 2014 and 1 October 2017 in order to force independence. In both cases, the constitutional court declared the referendums against the constitution, which regards the Spanish nation as indissoluble. The peak of this process (also known in Catalan as the *procés*) was the unilateral declaration of independence (*Declaración unilateral de independencia-DUI*) on 27 October 2017, declared as null and void by the constitutional court on 8 November 2018. The leaders of the *procés* are now being prosecuted by the Spanish authorities. Some of them fled the country, including former president Carles Puigdemont. One major problem for the pro-independence supporters is the fact that so far Catalan society is divided into two equal blocks. Overall, it seems that the pro-Spanish party may be in the majority according to the opinion polls. However, the Catalan pro-independence movement has been gaining ground over the decades (Magone, 2018: 183–99).

The relationship between the Spanish government and the Basque government has also been characterised by difficulties. Between 2001 and 2008, former Basque president Juan José Ibarretxe presented his plan for an independence referendum (Ibarretxe plan), but this was rejected by the Cortes in Madrid. After a period of single minority government under Basque president Patxi Lopez (PSOE), PNV returned to power after the elections of 2012. New moderate Basque leader Iñigo Urkullu was able to form a government with support from the socialists, and in 2016 a coalition government. Urkullu is a supporter of Basque independence, but he is a realist and moderate in working towards that aim. For a long time, the major issue in the Basque Country has been the fight against nationalist terrorism perpetrated by the Basque separatist organisation Basque Country and Freedom (Euskadi ta Askatasuna – ETA). ETA was active between 1959 and 2 May 2018 and demanded independence from Spain. Between 1959 and 2018, 853 people died as a consequence of their terrorist attacks, two-thirds in the Basque Country and the rest in other autonomous communities (*20 Dias*, 6 May 2018). Since 2003 both the PP and PSOE governments have reinforced their fight against the terrorist organisation. The new law of political parties, ratified in 2002, forbids any association of political parties with terrorist organisations. This allowed the Spanish government, after a judicial process, to forbid the existence of parties connected to ETA. This strategy paid off, because ETA declared its disbandment on 3 May 2018 and decommissioned all their weapons in 2017 and 2018 under the supervision of an international team of intermediaries.

Spanish intergovernmental relationships have increased over time through forty-one so-called top-down sectorial conferences (*conferencias sectoriales*) related to policy areas. Furthermore, the Zapatero government introduced the conference of presidents, which has decision-making powers on issues related to the autonomous communities. It is comprised of the Spanish prime minister, known as *El Presidente* in Spain, and the presidents of the seventeen autonomous communities. Since 2004, there have been six such conferences (Magone, 2018: 161–5).

The UK: an incomplete model

When the New Labour government under the leadership of Tony Blair came to power in 1997, devolution of powers to Scotland, Wales and Northern Ireland were top priorities. In November 1997, two referendums in Scotland and Wales led to the approval of the establishment of a Parliament in Scotland and an Assembly in Wales. Such a bold move by the first Blair government was perceived by many (especially in the Conservative Party) as the dismantling of the UK; however, for the Labour government, it was part of a major modernisation of the constitution of the UK, which also entailed transformations in the House of Lords (see Chapter 5), in the judiciary (see Chapter 6) and other parts of the political system. After more than two decades of devolution, it can be assessed as being very successful in Wales and Scotland, but Northern Ireland's Assembly is currently suspended. The Scottish Parliament and Executive have been able to develop their own policies in education and health, which are now quite distinctive from those of England. This variable geometry has led to new questions about the equity of opportunities across the territory. While the Welsh Assembly, the Scottish Parliament after 1997 and the Northern Ireland Assembly after 2007 profited considerably from the new territorial arrangements, the advantages became less clear for England, the largest part of the UK. Attempts by former deputy prime minister John Prescott to implement English regions across the territory through referendums failed after a rejection in the referendum for the North East by an overwhelming majority of 78 per cent against 22 per cent on 4 November 2004 (*BBC News*, 5 November 2004).

The most difficult process was probably that for Northern Ireland, which required strong negotiating skills by the UK government. Prime minister Tony Blair followed in the footsteps of John Major in trying to achieve a reconciliation between the nationalist Sinn Fein on the one hand and the loyalist Ulster Democratic Party (DUP) and Ulster Unionist Party (UUP) on the other. US Senator George J. Mitchell was appointed to mediate in the negotiation process, but this took a decade to become reality. Finally, a power-sharing agreement between Sinn Fein and the DUP was reached that allowed the restoration of devolution to take place. In spite of regular conflicts, power-sharing in Northern Ireland can be regarded as a success story until recently. It also allowed for the geographical integration of the Northern Ireland territory with the Republic of Ireland within the EU after the border was removed as part of the peace process. However, after

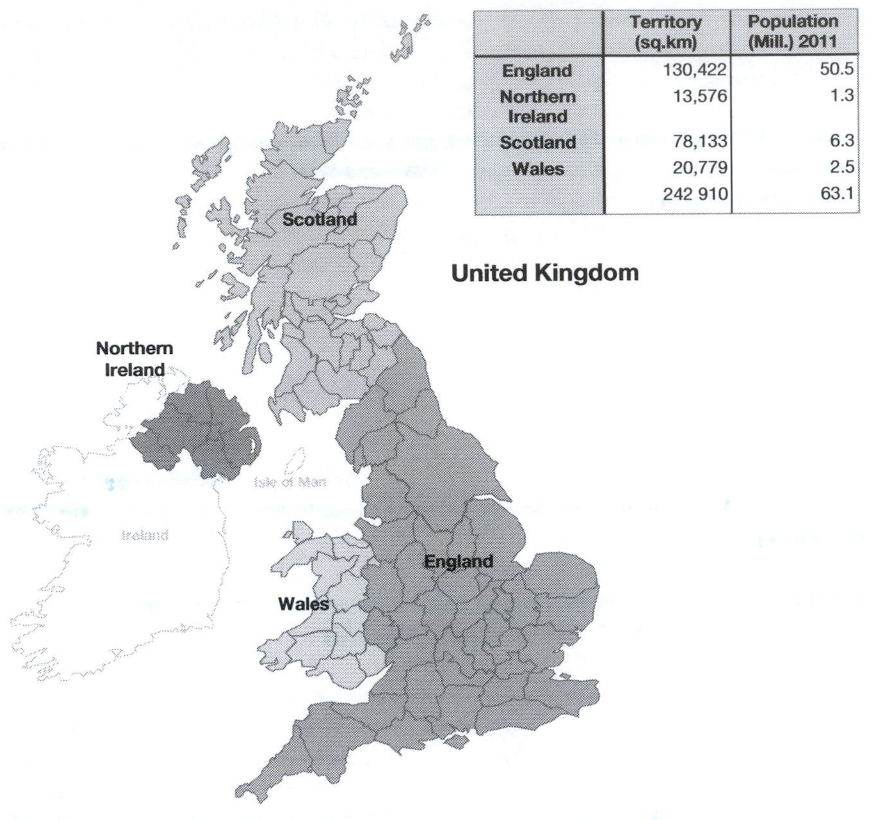

	Territory (sq.km)	Population (Mill.) 2011
England	130,422	50.5
Northern Ireland	13,576	1.3
Scotland	78,133	6.3
Wales	20,779	2.5
	242 910	63.1

Figure 9.7 The regionalised structure of the UK after 1997

two decades of a successful power-sharing arrangement, Brexit negotiations may put the open borders policy between the two countries at risk. This could signify a return to the partition of the island with eventual implications for the peace process.

Since 2007, the dominant party in Scotland has been the pro-independence Scottish National Party (SNP), a moderate leftwing party. Policy-making in Scotland is deviating considerably from that of England and Wales towards egalitarian politics, taking small countries, such as Denmark, as a model. In 2011, the SNP achieved an absolute majority with 44 per cent and 69 out of 129 seats. Therefore, first minister Alex Salmond decided to organise a referendum on independence. In contrast to the Spanish case, successful negotiations with the UK government took place. However, the referendum on 18 September 2014 led to a victory of the 'no' vote with 55.3 per cent against the 'yes' camp with 44.7 per cent. The turnout was quite high at 84.3 per cent (*BBC News*, 19 September 2014). Similarly to Northern Ireland, the Brexit vote has mobilised the SNP, now under first minister Nicola Sturgeon, to ask for a second referendum, because the vast majority of the Scottish population wants to stay in the EU. On 28 March 2017, the Scottish parliament voted by a majority of ten votes for negotiations with the UK government for a second referendum. However, after the general elections of 8 June 2017 during which she suffered heavy losses in her party to the Conservatives, Sturgeon decided to put the referendum on hold. One of the reasons was that there was no popular majority for independence at that particular time (*The Guardian*, 28 March 2017, 27 June 2017).

In Wales, the Party of Wales (Plaid Cymru – PC) supports more autonomy, but it is not the dominant party. This place is occupied by the Labour Party.

Italy: increased powers for the regions in the Second Republic

Among the second group of countries of regionalised unitary states, Italy has to be regarded as a hybrid case because of the regional mobilisation of the northern regions by the Northern League in the 1990s. Umberto Bossi's movement was instrumental in transforming the then highly centralised regional and local government system, leading the new political parties of the Second Republic to advocate federal or quasi-federal reform of centre-periphery relations (Mazzoleni, 2009: 141–4).

The regionalisation of Italy was enshrined in the constitution of 1948, although elected regions were only established in 1970. This delayed the process of decentralisation and de-concentration inherited from fascism. In total, twenty regions were established, of which fifteen were ordinary regions and five special regions. The special regions were established where linguistic or ethnic minorities were considered, such as Vale d'Aosta (French-speaking minority), Trentino-Adige (German-speaking minority) and Friuli-Venezia Giulia (Croat and Slovene minorities) or for those with island status such as Sicily and Sardinia. Most devolution in competences and budgetary terms took place in the 1970s. Until the collapse of the First Republic in 1992, the regional governments had very limited powers and constrained budgetary means. The regions were regarded as extended arms of the Italian government. This meant that Italian regions had almost no autonomy (Hine, 1993: 269). The political structure comprises a regional assembly elected every five years and a regional executive (*giunta regionale*) that implements the policies.

In spite of this, some regions have done better than others. According to a seminal study by Robert Putnam with Bob Leonardi and Laura Nanetti undertaken in the late 1980s, the northern regions were doing considerably better than the southern regions. Historical legacy factors like the city-states of the Middle Ages and early modern times combined with government efficiency were presented as reasons for the gap between north and south (Putnam, 1994: 152–62). The findings of Putnam and his team help to explain the major gap between north and south in terms of gross domestic product per capita. In spite of the anti-Mafia movement that emerged out of civil society in the 1990s and the successes of law enforcement, the role of the Mafia in capturing public services in local government cannot be underestimated. They clearly explain some of the underdevelopment of the Mezzogiorno (southern Italy) in relation to northern Italy (Jamieson, 1998: 152–3; see also an overall assessment by Paoli, 2007; Bull and Baudner, 2004) (Figure 9.8).

After several failed attempts to revise the constitution in the Second Republic after 1992, the political elites agreed on a piecemeal approach. Since 1993, a major restructuring of the regional and local government has been taking place.

Figure 9.8 The administrative regions in Italy

In 2001, there was a major revision of Chapter V of the constitution related to regional and local government. The piecemeal reform is still going on and affects the whole design of regional and local government, including direct elections of regional presidents and city mayors. Moreover, new electoral systems with a tendency towards majoritarianism were adopted for regional and local elections. Furthermore, more competences in policy-making as well as decentralisation of human and financial resources have reduced centralisation by Rome (Baldini and Vassalo, 2001: 127–32; Cotta and Verzichelli, 2016: 192).

According to Maurizio Cotta and Luca Verzichelli, this 'Americanisation of regional politics' resulted in many regional presidents being called 'governor', an allusion to the same term used for the leaders of the individual states in the United States (Cotta and Verzichelli, 2007: 188–9). There were attempts to move towards fully fledged federalism, including a model of fiscal federalism, but this was rejected in a referendum in June 2006 (Cotta and Verzichelli, 2016: 194).

One major problem is that the piecemeal approach of permanent reform since 1993 has put the whole system under pressure, because political parties are not working consensually towards a commonly agreed model of territorial politics. Gianfranco Baldini and Brunetta Baldi even speak of an incomplete failed federalisation. A lot has to do with the different designs of the centre-left and centre-right parties (Baldi and Baldini, 2014: 102; Bull and Pasquino, 2007: 671–2; Mazzoleni, 2009: 144–6).

In spite of Italian unification, a strong regional consciousness characterises the country, which is still relevant today. However, regional political parties are almost non-existent in Italy, apart from the Northern League (Lega Nord – LN) that emerged as a collection of smaller leagues in the 1980s and is now a national party. In the 1990s, the LN evolved to a major junior partner of the Berlusconi governments and focused on reform of the state. It had a discourse against the bureaucracy in Rome and its dominance by the southerners. It was also quite xenophobic in relation to the Muslim population. There were even calls for independence of the northern part of Italy, so-called 'Padania', comprising the territory north of the Po river. However, at the end of the 1990s, leader Umberto Bossi and his party became more moderate. Since 2013, new leader Matteo Salvini has transformed the regional party into a national one, and after the general elections of 2018, it formed a coalition government with the citizens' populist 5 Star party. In this regard, the LN has been an important force of transformation of Italian politics, particularly in territorial politics, since the late 1990s (on the early development of the LN, see Diamanti, 1996; Biorcio and Securo, 2013; Passarelli, 2014; Vercesi, 2015). Both LN and 5 Star Movement are able to mobilise high levels of dissatisfaction in Italian society. This clearly confirms that since the 1970s Italy has been a dissatisfied society and easy prey for populist parties with easy solutions (see Taylor, 2018; Morlino and Tarchi, 1996, 2006; Silver et al., 2018).

France: from centralisation to regionalisation

French administrative regionalisation started in the 1960s as a consequence of the new regional planning philosophy, which comprised the Constituencies of Regional Action and Commissions of Regional Economic Development (Circonscriptions d'Action Régionale et des Commissions de Developpement Économique Régional – CODER) in 1964 and the Public Regional Bodies (Établissements Public Regionaux) in 1972 (Balme, 1998a: 182).

Directly elected regions were legally only established in 1982, and the first elections took place in 1986. Before that regions did exist but consisted of appointed members coming from the *départements*. The highly centralistic tradition of the Napoleonic state began to be quite inefficient in a period of growing Europeanisation and globalisation. In spite of the centralistic tendencies of the French state, the territorial structure was and remains highly fragmented and, in terms of competences, quite confusing. There are over 35,300 local authorities, and they remain important in the political system, out of which 94 per cent have up to 5,000 inhabitants and comprise 37.7 per cent of the population. Above the local authorities there are the traditional ninety-six *departements*. In between are the non-elected pragmatically established 1,264 inter-communal public corporations (Etablissement publique de cooperation intercommunale – EPCI) and the 10,585 Voluntary Intercommunal Syndicates (Syndicats intercommunaux á vocations uniques ou multiples – SIVU and SIVOM) designed to achieve more efficiency of communal public policy by creating economies of scale (DGCL, 2018). On top of all this are the twenty-one administrative regions of continental France, Corsica and the autonomous government of four overseas islands (French Guyana, Guadeloupe, Martinique and Reunion) outside France. As part of a major territorial reform during the François Hollande presidency of 2014

Figure 9.9 The administrative regions in France

Note: There are further five islands outside France with autonomy status: Saint Barthelemy and Saint Martin, both in the Caribbean; Saint Pierre and Miquelon on the Atlantic coast of Canada; Wallis and Fortune; and French Polynesia in the Pacific Ocean.

Source: Interior Ministry of France.

and 2015, the competences between communes, cities and regions were changed and a new regional map adopted. The consequence was that in 2016, several regions were merged and now there are just twelve administrative regions in continental France, Corsica and five overseas islands (French Guyana, Guadeloupe, Martinique, Reunion and additionally Mayotte) The representatives of the eighteen regions altogether are elected for six years and have increased competences of strategic policy-making (Cole, 2017: 138–40) (Figure 9.9).

According to Andrew Knapp and Vincent Wright, the decentralisation process of the 1980s and 1990s contributed to three important improvements: subsidiarity, rationalisation and democratisation. After decades of centralistic decision-making, regionalisation allowed these to be taken at a more appropriate level, thus reinforcing better services for citizens. This also allowed the rationalisation of services caught between centralisation and fragmentation. The new tier allowed these services and territorial organisation to be more efficient. Last, but not least, all this contributed to a democratisation of the policy and decision-making process, allowing for more access points for citizens (Knapp and Wright, 2001: 365–9). In spite of all this, Alistair Cole is clearly more critical emphasising that the myriad layers of public administration (labelled as *mille-feuille institutionel*) have increased the complexity and fragmentation. Moreover, competences are poorly assigned to each level, so that competition between the tiers, even when there is some definition of competences, is the daily practice of local government in France (Cole, 2018: 150–4).

In spite of the historical legacy of centralism, weak regional consciousness still exists in Brittany and, more so, in Corsica, where several separatist groups tried to gain independence through political violence. However, the separatist movement is ideologically divided, allowing the French state to continue to control the territory (De Calle and Fazi, 2008). Nevertheless, on 3 and 10 December 2017 in the regional elections in Corsica, the coalition of parties Pé a Corsica (PAC) (consisting of Femu Corsica-Let's Make Corsica and Corsica Libera-Free Corsica) was able to get forty-one seats (out of sixty-three) and achieve an absolute majority. PAC is rather moderate and wants more autonomy, but the island is extremely dependent on funding from central government. Apart from autonomy, there is a demand for acknowledging the same status for the Corsican language as French. A continuing problem is the terrorist Corsican National Liberation Front (FLNC), which is still in existence (*The Guardian*, 11 December 2017; La Calle, 2015: chapter 3).

Remaking local and regional government in East Central Europe: Poland, Czech Republic, Slovak Republic and Hungary

European integration and the enlargement process was a major factor shaping the development of the new territorial organisation in the Central and Eastern European countries. After decades of a centralised communist regime, decentralisation was an important issue in all these countries. In particular, the need to adjust to the EU multilevel governance system was a major incentive to undertake reform. Besides, the forthcoming large amounts of EU structural funds played a major role in reshaping the territorial structure (Brusis, 2002, 2014; Bruszt, 2008; Jacoby, 2005; Scherpereel, 2010). However, until the end of the 1990s, the political parties had difficulty in coming to an agreement about how decentralisation and regionalisation should be implemented. Regionalisation took place mainly in Poland, the Czech Republic, the Slovak Republic and Hungary, although the extent has been much more limited in these countries than in Western European ones.

Polish regionalisation goes back to the communist period in which the subnational government was subordinated to the centre. Throughout the 1990s there was a restructuring of the Polish territorial organisation. In 1998, the forty-five small regions (*województwo*) were replaced by sixteen directly elected large ones. A large number of them had some regional tradition (German minority in Upper Silesia), while others were created taking account of minorities or other factors (Czernielewska, 2004; Dembinska, 2013). The intermediate structure of counties (*powiat*) that existed until 1974 was restored in 1998, resulting now in 380 counties out of which 314 are rural and 66 are cities of county status. Moreover, there are 2,479 municipalities (*gmina*), out of which 1,566 are rural and 608 mixed urban-rural (AER, 2017; Swianiewicz, 2006: 11; 2011). It is probably too early to make an assessment, but the Polish model of regionalisation bears similarities to the French model. It has limited budgetary means and limited competences, but it is essential for the coordination of regional policy-making (AER, 2017; Swianiewicz, 2006: 14; 2011). The regions have become a very important tier in strategically planning the socioeconomic development of the region, in particular due to the incoming EU structural funds (Ziemer, 2013: 155).

A similar process of redesigning the territorial structure of the country took place in the Czech Republic. Throughout the 1990s, the new structures of local government were implemented, although it was only in 1999 that an agreement was reached on regionalisation. In the end, the political parties agreed on the creation of thirteen regions (*kraj*) and the independent region of the city of Prague. The first regional elections for the new regions took place in 2000, and for the city of Prague in 2002 (Illner and Vajdova, 2006: 11–18). One of the reasons for the delay was the resistance of the Civic Forum (ODS) of Vaclav Klaus to the implementation of regionalisation, which was enshrined in the constitution of 1992. However, the European Commission clearly pressed the Czech government to implement some kind of regional structure in order to better absorb the structural funds for which the country would be eligible when it joined the EU (Baun and Marek, 2006: 412–13). The overall rationale of the regions is to develop a regional policy that is compatible with the national strategies. It has competences that are shared with the national government. Among these competences are spatial planning and regional development, education, culture, transport and communication, health care, social welfare, environment and the protection of public order (Illner and Vajdova, 2006: 30–1). However, the Czech regions are highly dependent on government grants to fulfil their function, and autonomy in terms of funding is quite limited. In spite of this, after five electoral cycles, regionalisation has gained an important place in Czech politics. Normally, there are important mid-term second-order elections supporting or punishing incumbent national governments. Quite important is the fact, that apart from the Civic Party (ODS) and the social democrats (ČSSD), the communists are very well represented at local and regional level, forcing ČSSD in some cases to enter into alliances with a normally ostracised political group. This has contributed to a change from orthodoxy to a more pragmatic coalitional support by the communists (Baun and Marek, 2006: 418–19; Ryšavý, 2013: 639–40).

Similar to Poland and Hungary, Slovakia was characterised by Paweł Swianiewicz as belonging to a group of champions of decentralisation of Central and Eastern Europe due to the fragmentation of local government and fiscal decentralisation (Swianiewicz, 2014: 303). Over 70 per cent of the 2,890 communes have less than 1,000 inhabitants and represent just 16 per cent of the population. Similar to Poland and Hungary, the high level of fragmentation makes the system highly expensive, and reforms towards an amalgamation programme have been rather avoided by the national political elites (Klimóvsky, 2015: 15). However, Slovakia is predominantly rural (OECD, 2016c). After the velvet divorce, pressure coming from the EU led to a rushed programme of territorial restructuring between 2000 and 2002. In 2002, the directly elected self-governing regions (*kraje*) were introduced, which are responsible for subnational management of the structural funds. The territorial division in eight regions was taken over from the Meciar government that had introduced it in 1996. However, the main purpose then was to create an intermediate tier that would avoid giving any majority to the Hungarian majority leaving in the south of the country. Therefore this gerrymandering took no account of geographical and historical bases. Moreover, they were matched by a de-concentrated representation of the central government, emphasising the unitary nature of the state. In between communes and the eight kraje are seventy-nine districts (*okresy*) used mainly for economies of scale in the delivery of public services (Bochsler and Szöcsik, 2013: 436–7; Halás and Klapka, 2017: 1474–7).

Similarly, throughout the 1990s, there was discussion about the merits of decentralisation and regionalisation between the leftwing and rightwing parties in Hungary. The local government act of 1990 created a situation of complete freedom for the establishment of local government units. This led to the establishment of a very fragmented local government which clearly not only became unmanageable but also was very expensive (Kovacs, 2011: 9–11), but bankruptcy and high levels of debt were the result of this policy (Kovacs, 2011: 12). Directly elected county regions were established in 1994. In total nineteen county regions (*megye*) were established, with on average about 537,000 inhabitants in each region. The regions were established primarily to facilitate the coordination and implementation of EU structural funds, but the financial devolution process in respect of these regions has been slow and cumbersome (Rószás, 2004: 80–7). Below and above the counties, there were micro-regions facilitating economies of scale between communes, and seven non-elected administrative macro-regions, with a regional development council consisting of central government representatives and local representatives, steering regional development policies. As a result, the local and regional government system became even less clear in terms of competences. Since the early 1990s, the county level has almost disappeared in terms of competences (Palné Kovacs, 2012: 14–22; 2015: 6–9). In 2010, the incoming Viktor Orbán government streamlined the existing system towards centralisation through the new Law on Local Self-Government (2011). It introduced a programme to pay off all the debts of the communes, but simultaneously to gain more control over local authorities. The macro- and micro-regions were abolished, and instead the directly elected counties became a central tier in the local authority system. However, the roles of county commissioners as representatives of de-concentrated central administration were reinforced, so that counties became strongly dominated by the government. Moreover, according to Ilona Palné Kovacs, the EU structural funds are now managed directly by central government with a low input by the counties. According to her, the already weak tier of the counties became even weaker, and therefore are the big losers of the reforms. The directly elected county assemblies are rather single issue organisations dealing with development policy (Palné Kovacs, 2015: 12–13, 15; Palné Kovacs et al., 2017). Between communes and counties, a new tier called the districts was introduced to achieve economies of scale in public services delivery. There are 175 districts across Hungary, and 23 in the capital Budapest (Palné Kovacs, 2015: 17; Palné Kovacs et al., 2017). The 2010 and 2014 county and local elections showed clearly that the conservative Fidesz is in control of most of the local level, and the major challengers of the new right populist and xenophobic Jobbik and the social democrats (MSZP) are ideologically so far apart that they are unable to bring about a coalition against the national and local government party (Palné Kovacs, 2015: 14; Palné Kovacs et al., 2017).

Unitary decentralised states: the Netherlands, Denmark, Sweden, Finland and Norway

Among the unitary decentralised states are the Netherlands and the Nordic countries. All of them are unitary states, but the administration is extremely decentralised. All these advanced democracies have also moved towards new forms of governance that allow for a stronger cooperation between the public and private sectors as well as allowing civil society to shape the policy-making process. Due to their unitary nature, we will just give a brief overview.

The Dutch state model goes back to the reforms introduced by Johan Rudolf Thorbecke after 1848. This is relevant, because this was the beginning of the democratisation of the Netherlands. In the Local Government and Provincial Acts of 1851 a three-tier system consisting of central government, twelve provinces and the municipalities at the bottom was enshrined. Human and financial resources are quite decentralised. Provincial governments are coordinating structures with limited funding. They are elected and also appoint the members of the Senate according to the proportional results in each province. Clearly the local government is the most important, representing the wish to strengthen bottom-up democracy. Therefore, local autonomy was given quite a strong role in the new state model. However, this 'positive power' of municipal autonomy should be constrained by the supervising 'negative power' of the provinces (Toonen, 1990: 287).There is strong cooperation between the three levels in terms of policy-making, also known as co-governance. This comprises about 70 to 80 per cent of the local government agenda. Simply put they are extended arms of central government with some discretion in implementation (Breeman et al., 2015: 34). There is a strong commitment by Dutch policy-makers to strengthen local civil society (citizens' assembly, referendums, consultation) in order to achieve a citizen friendly local public administration (Hendriks and Tops, 2003: 311; Kickert, 2000: 55; VNG, 2008: 31–2). Apart from these territorial structures, the Netherlands has the unique directly elected twenty-three water board (waterschappen) governments who look after the network of water channels and the management of the dyke system (OECD, 2014b: 203–4, 225–6).

The Nordic countries have decided to move towards more competitive regions or similar structures. Clearly, adjustment to globalisation and Europeanisation are important considerations. There is some cross-national institutional transfer going on, but in spite of their similarities, there are still major national differences in this development. Very important is the quest to develop more flexible competitive subnational structures to meet the demands of a globalised world economy (Hörnström, 2013: 430–3).

Denmark has been at the forefront in creating more efficient structures. It has been engaged in the reform of local government since the 1970s. The main rationale was to make local government more efficient and de-concentrated. Meanwhile, in 2007, a second major overhaul of the local government system took place, reducing the number of municipalities to ninety-eight. Moreover, the fourteen counties were abolished and replaced by five regions, which are just in charge of primary and secondary healthcare. Furthermore, the new regions have no taxation powers and are dependent on transfer grants from the central government and municipalities. One reason for the reform was the growing problem of attracting professional staff to public services in small communities, so that economies of scale became an important issue. Another important reason was the lack of clarity about the competences between municipal and county level. The creation of economies of scale in the municipalities, which went from an average population size of 19,451 to 55,217, also allowed the counties to be abolished and the creation of the single-purpose regions for primary and secondary healthcare (Kjaer et al., 2010: 571–2; Vrangbæk, 2010). This reform was not supported by all political parties and secured only a narrow victory in parliament. However, liberal prime minister Lars Løkke Rasmussen was skilful in getting the right alliances particularly with the municipalities and their associations in order to achieve the result (Broom-Hansen et al., 2012: 80–7). In terms of public expenditure, subnational government represents two-thirds of the national total (this is similar to Finland and Sweden). The welfare state is a central aspect of the decentralised Danish system. It is too early to make assessment, but a first study seems to show that elected backbench councillors have lost both influence and power, and that central government priorities have become more strongly emphasised at the local level (Kjaer et al., 2010: 576, 582–3; Kjaer and Elklitt, 2010).

In Sweden, Finland and Norway, a similar decentralisation of public services and public expenditure has been taking place since the late 1970s. In Sweden, the process of rationalisation of local government took place between 1950 and 1970. Until 1955, the Swedish local government was fragmented into 2,500 municipalities – a very large number in comparison to the 290 today. Since the 1990s, Sweden has been engaged in a restructuring of its territorial governance system. The basic system consists of 21 elected counties (*landssting*) and 290 municipalities (*kommuner*), which are in no hierarchical relationship to each other and can overlap. Counties tend to focus on the management of healthcare, particularly the hospitals, and 90 per cent of the budget is assigned to this (Bäck, 2007: 18). There are now bodies of regional cooperation (*regional samwerksorgan*) between the counties and the municipalities, which have coordinating functions for the overall county (Bäck, 2007: 25).

In 2007, the parliamentary Committee on Public Sector Responsibility proposed the replacement of the twenty-one county councils with six to nine larger regions, which was approved by all political parties. In 2010, the island of Gotland and the county of Halland became regions (Lidström, 2011: 278, 409–10; Niklasson, 2016: 407–8). As is happening in many other countries, according to Christine Hudson, there has been a major shift from government to a governance system, in which stakeholders in regional policy are included in the whole process of decision-making. This was not very difficult for Sweden, because of the political culture of consultation with relevant stakeholders that was already in existence. However, other aspects relating to new public management (for example public–private partnerships, the establishment of less rigid structures and the activation of the regional stakeholders for regional policy) were introduced in the present reforms (Hudson, 2005: 314, 320). In sum, Sweden is slowly moving to a regionalised unitary system, due to the need to better coordinate policies in an existing European multilevel governance system (see Feltenius, 2015).

In Finland, in contrast to Denmark and Sweden, there were strong protests against the amalgamation of municipalities between 1965 and 1980, so that the number of municipalities in Finland remained fairly high (it was only reduced by 100) (Sandberg, 2005: 18). In 2017, Finland's subnational government consisted of 18 counties including the capital Helsinki and 311 municipalities. There are also over 200 joint municipal authorities for regional policy coordination in particular areas. Additionally, Finland has granted self-government to the Åland Islands (with their own local government act) (Kuntaliitto, 2017a, 2017b; Sandberg, 2005: 9–15; Sjoblöm, 2011: 245–8). However, also in Finland, non-elected administrative regions were set up to deal with incoming EU structural and investment funds and regional planning. There are now eighteen regional councils dealing with regional development and planning, and there are also other regional structures dealing with other specific policies (Hörnström, 2013: 435; Kuntaliitto, 2017a, 2017b; Sandberg, 2005: 9–15; Sjoblöm, 2011: 245–8). This allows for better coordination of the one-tier local system.

In Norway, local government consists of 19 counties (*fylkestinge*) and 428 municipalities (*Kommuner*). The Local Government Act of 1992, updated and amended in 2005, is the main document defining competences and tasks. At the local level, an amalgamation process of municipalities has taken place. Since the 1950s and 1960s, the number of municipalities has declined from 774 to 428 today. (Baldersheim and Fimreite, 2005: 765, 770; Baldersheim and Rose, 2011: 286–7). And there is pressure at national level to reduce the present number even further. A first attempt by the government failed in 2009 due to the resistance of county governors and the ministries of central government, which were able to convince the cabinet. However, a second attempt in 2016 seems to have been more successful. The present discussion is to reduce the nineteen counties to ten larger units with more comprehensive competences, particularly regional development and planning. An expert committee was put in charge of coming up with proposals (Baldersheim and Fimreite, 2005: 768; Bloom-Hansen et al., 2012: 79–87; Higdem and Hagen, 2017: 13–14; Rose, 2006: 21–2).

Unitary centralised states: the micro-states, Southern, Central and Eastern Europe and the Baltics

The micro-states: Iceland, Luxembourg, Cyprus, Malta and the Baltic states

Countries such as Luxembourg, Latvia, Estonia, Lithuania and Slovenia do not need high levels of decentralisation, because both populations and territories are quite small. All of them have a one-tier local government. The small countries below one million and their small territories ensure that this centralisation does not affect equity across the territory. Even here, one can observe the processes of reform, particularly in Luxembourg, which is engaged in a process of amalgamation of small communes, hoping to reduce them from 130 to 105 (*Luxemburger Wort*, 31 December 2017; *Tageblatt*, 29 September 2017). Most of the population of Iceland lives in the capital Reykjavik, so that just 12 per cent of public expenditure is spent in the seventy-two local authorities.

In the Baltic states and Slovenia there was, of course, debate about creating some kind of decentralised regional structures to better absorb the structural funds. All three Baltic republics have implemented some kind of non-elected administrative regional structures that are, in essence, extended de-concentrated bodies representing the central government at the regional level. All three countries are engaged in a rationalisation process of the local government, which has been quite fragmented in the past (OECD, 2016c: Lithuania, Latvia, Estonia factsheets; Pukis, 2015; Sootla and Kattai, 2011: 581–6; Vaiciuniene and Nefas, 2011: 625–7; Vilka, 2011: 614–17). Moreover, Estonia remains a champion of e-government, particularly at the local level. In both Latvia and Estonia, the Harmony-Social Democratic Party and the Center Party representing the Russian-speaking population are quite strong at the local level. In Latvia, the Harmony-Social democratic party is the leading party in the government coalition in the capital Riga, and the same applies to the Center Party in Tallinn.

In the islands of Malta and Cyprus, local politics is quite important, due to the networks of clientelism and patronage. Structures are adjusted to the small territories with 68 local councils in Malta, and 30 urban councils and 350 rural communities in Cyprus. In addition, the Northern Republic of Turkish Cyprus has a further 130 local councils. We should also add Slovenia to this group. Slovenia has a population of roughly 2 million. In spite of major reforms, it is still constructing its new local government system. Presently it has 212 municipalities. Most of them are still too small and are a major obstacle to economies of scale. A major attempt at reform was undertaken in 2008, but the economic crisis led to an abrupt interruption. Slovenian local government lacks enough human and financial resources (OECD, 2016c: Slovenia, 2018c; Pevcin, 2015; Pinterić, 2015: 17; Ploštajner, 2008: 39–43).

The unitary centralised states in Ireland, Southern Europe, Eastern Europe and the Balkans

The Irish local system is strongly influenced by the British legacy, although after independence it developed its own structures. Attempts at decentralisation were made in the new millennium, but the 2010–14 crisis led to developments going in the opposite direction. The main objective was to create economies of scale for the provision of public services at local level. Since the adoption of the Local Government Reform Act in 2014, the then 114 local councils were merged into 31 local government units (3 city councils, 2 city and country councils and 26 county councils). The six former non-elected regional authorities were replaced by three regional assemblies. Most competences of the former non-elected regions were passed on to the new local government units. A first study by Aeodh Quinlivan seems to suggest that the 'big is beautiful' centralised approach of imposing a new local government structure may have created a major democratic deficit. However, it is too early to make an assessment. Professional managers were appointed to deal with the operational policy-making process and the management of the specific local council. They are appointed by an independent local appointments committee and are a distinctive feature in comparison to other European government systems (Quinlivan, 2006: 25–7; 2017: 113–4; 117–19).

In Southern Europe, the decentralising efforts of Spain and Italy (see earlier) are in clear contrast to the highly centralised countries of Greece and Portugal.

Democratisation after 1974 did not change the highly centralised Greek administrative structure, which has concentrated most of its administration in the two cities of Athens and Thessaloniki. In Greece, centralisation is a legacy of the history of unification of the country (*einosis*). The fear of disintegration of the Greek territory remains part of the administrative culture. There have been several reforms since the late 1990s to rationalise the highly fragmented Greek local government. One should mention the important Capodistria reform of 1999 which led to the merger of 5,775 city and rural municipalities (*dimoi*) into 1,033 municipalities. Ten years later, the Kallikratis reform reduced these even further to 325. The threshold for urban municipalities is 2,000 inhabitants. Moreover, the once-elected fifty-four prefectures were reduced to thirteen directly elected regions (*perifereies*). Furthermore, there are seven non-elected de-concentrated state administrations and seventy-four de-concentrated regional units for administrative purposes (Hlepas, 2005; Hlepas and Getimis, 2011: 416–21; OECD, 2016c: Greece). The Kallikratis reform coincided with the sovereign debt crisis, so that although both developments were separate, they became intrinsically linked, because it also involved financial reforms of local government. Quite a considerable number of cutbacks affecting particularly civil servants' wages and pensions were introduced. State transfers were reduced from 63 per cent in 2011 to 53 per cent in 2015, which had to be matched by own tax revenues or by making cuts. In spite of this, in a seminal study, Sandra Cohen and Nikolaus Hlepas found local governments were quite resilient and innovative in dealing with the crisis. Due to overspending in the past, there was a lot of leeway in becoming more efficient in spending (Cohen and Hlepas, 2017: 138–9).

Portuguese local government today consists of 308 directly elected municipalities, and the 2 autonomous regions of the island archipelagos of the Azores and Madeira located in the Atlantic. The constitution allows for the introduction of directly elected administrative regions in Portugal, but similarly to Hungary and Slovenia, the political elites of the main parties were not able to agree on a model. Moreover, a referendum in 1998 led to a rejection by two-thirds of voters, though it was non-binding, because less than 50 per cent of the eligible electorate turned out to vote. As an alternative, similar to most countries of Europe, legislation in 2013 allowed for the creation of so-called inter-municipal communities (Comunidades Inter-municipais – CIM) and greater metropolitan areas (Grandes Areas Metropolitanas – GAM). In 2017, there were twenty-one CIMs and two GAMs in Lisbon and Oporto. Their main purpose is to create economies of scale for public policy, public services and the management of the EU structural and investment funds. Moreover, continental Portugal has five de-concentrated regional commissions for coordination and development which deal with implementation of central government public policies as well as the management of the structural and investment funds (Magone, 2014a: chapter 9). In 2016, both Portugal and Greece were among the countries with the lowest local expenditure of the national total with 12 per cent and 7 per cent respectively, corresponding to 5.61 and 3.53 of GDP respectively (OECD, 2018c).

Similar centralised unitary countries are Bulgaria, Romania and Croatia. In Bulgaria, the main subnational directly elected tier consists of 265 municipalities (*obshtini*). Above this are twenty-eight districts (*oblasti*), which are merely extended de-concentrated structures of central government. They are in charge of implementing and coordinating regional policy. Moreover, six planning macro-regions (*rayone za planirane*) at NUTS 2 were established in order to implement the structural funds better. In spite of this restructuring of the Bulgarian local government system, not enough funding from central government was allocated for local communities to fulfil their tasks, and their own revenues remain quite limited. Political corruption and the lack of transparency and accountability are still major problems (Nikolova, 2007: 239–42; 2011: 668–72, 676–9; OECD, 2016; Troeva, 2015). The Romanian subnational government consists of 42 counties (*judete*) and Bucharest, 320 towns (*orase*) of which 113 are larger towns (*municipii*), and 2,861 communes (*commune*). These are directly elected non-hierarchical tiers. Moreover, in the counties there are also forty-one prefectures (similar to the French model) of which prefects are appointed by the central government to oversee the county and local government. In a similar way to Bulgaria, eight NUTS 2 level administrative regions were created to coordinate regional development. In spite of major changes since the early 1990s, subnational government is still highly fragmented, preventing the establishment of economies of scale, particularly at village level. Increased competences and tasks over the years have not been accompanied by the respective funding. However, since 2014, there have been major efforts to further decentralise competences to local government and also to reduce the existing fragmentation (Bondar, 2014; Dobre, 2009; 2011: 694–702, 706–7; Nikolov, 2006: 14–16; OECD, 2016c: Romania).

Although legislation on territorial organisation goes back to 1992 and 1993, Croatia started reforming its local government after 2002. The role of international organisations and NGOs cannot be underestimated here. This has been a work in progress which was reinforced during the process of accession to the EU. In 2016, the Croatian two-tier system consisted of 20 counties (*županijas*) and the city of Zagreb in the upper tier, and 556 lower-tier local government units, comprising 128 towns (*grad*) and 428 municipalities (OECD, 2016c: Croatia). Since 2004, there have been programmes of decentralisation strongly influenced by the international community, focusing on devolution of competences, human and financial resources. However, they have not been very successful in overcoming the still high level of fragmentation of local government. County councils are responsible for regional development (Budak et al., 2004: 666–9; Government of Croatia, 2018; Klarić, 2017).

Although these Central and Eastern European countries have already made some considerable progress towards more efficient subnational government structures, such democratisation of local government has been more difficult in the western Balkans. European integration and conditionality reform programmes for accession have been important factors in regime transformation. According to the road map of enlargement of the EU, priority will be given to the candidate countries of the Balkans: Montenegro, Macedonia and Serbia. All of these countries have very inefficient structures, characterised by fragmentation, misallocation and lack of human and finance resources, and pre-modern patterns of interpersonal exchange such as clientelism, patronage and political corruption. Unfortunately, the western Balkans remain negative examples of state capture and systemic corruption by business and criminal networks, particularly in Serbia, Bosnia-Herzegovina, Macedonia, Montenegro, Albania and Kosovo. The local level is an important equation in this situation. The highly centralised programming of the EU and the central governments of the western Balkans rather perpetuates the situation. More consultation with relevant stakeholders at local level, fostering a bottom-up approach, would certainly be an important additional strategy (an excellent regular publication on the problems of fiscal decentralisation is NALAS, 2017a, 2017b; European Parliament, 2017; on clientelism and patronage, see Cvejić, 2016; Heinrich Böll Foundation, 2017).

The European dimension of subnational government

The European integration process has led to growing cooperation between the regional and local authorities. There are several aspects related to a Europeanisation of subnational government. The emergence of the multilevel governance system of the EU has opened up new access points to regions and local authorities beyond the main gatekeeper, the EU. According to Gary Marks and his team, in the 1980s and 1990s regions were able to gain influence at the supranational level through a 'multiple crack' policy (Marks et al., 1996: 45). The Treaty of Maastricht rationalised this process of access by creating the Committee of Regions and Local Authorities, an advisory body of the European Commission. It consists of 350 regional and local authority representatives that sit according to political parties. Many regional offices were set up in Brussels to facilitate lobbying and networking. According to the official list posted on the website of the Committee of the Regions (CoR), there were 136 local and regional offices based in Brussels (CoR, 2018; Greenwood, 2017: 181–5). Access is asymmetrical due to the amount of resources available to different regions and local authorities (Marks et al., 2002). A major factor leading to this activity has been the structural and investment funds of the EU, which have represented more than one-third of the supranational budget since 1988. This also includes cross-border and inter-regional programmes fostering cooperation between European regions and local authorities.

Conclusions: towards a Europe of the regions

This chapter assesses the growing importance of subnational government in European politics. Decentralisation of most territorial organisations began to be widespread in the 1980s and 1990s. Such transformations were encouraged by several factors, including the European integration process. This chapter, following a slightly changed typology of John Loughlin, differentiates national territorial organisations in five main categories: federal states, confederal states, regionalised unitary states, unitary decentralised states and unitary centralised states.

Suggested reading

Loughlin, John, Frank Hendriks and Anders Lidström (eds) (2011), *The Oxford Handbook of Local and Regional Democracy in Europe*. Oxford: Oxford University Press.

Yoder, Jennifer A. (2013), *Crafting Democracy: Regional Politics in Central and Eastern Europe*. Lanham, MD: Rowman and Littlefield Publishers.

QUESTIONS FOR REVISION

- What are the main forms of territorial organisation in Europe? Discuss, using examples for each form.
- Compare the advantages and disadvantages of devolution in the UK and Spain.
- Discuss the challenges to the federalisation of Belgium since 1993.
- How efficient are federal countries? Discuss, using examples from at least two countries.
- Are we moving towards a Europe of the regions? Discuss, using examples from at least two countries.

Chapter 10

National politics and the European Union

- European integration from the Schuman Plan to the Lisbon Treaty of 2009
- The institutional framework of the supranational level of the EU
- Europeanisation of national politics and Euromestication
- National governments, parliaments and judiciaries in the EU multilevel governance system
- The growing importance of European public policy
- Conclusions: the intertwinedness of the EU multilevel governance system
- Suggested reading

European integration from the Schuman Plan to the Lisbon Treaty of 2009

The Franco–German reconciliation that has been taking place since 1950 is the major factor contributing to a sustained process towards European integration. Partly as an initiative of French Foreign Minister Robert Schuman, the so-called 'Schuman plan', partly as a desire of the US Truman administration, the supranational European Community for Steel and Coal (ECSC) was founded in 1952 (Clemens et al., 2008: 96–7). Further processes of integration took place in 1957 with the Treaty of Rome leading to the European Economic Community (EEC) and Euratom. After several attempts at creating a supranational organisation through a big bang approach, politicians became more modest and followed a 'small steps' (petit pas) approach towards European integration (see Box 10.1). The revival of the European Community in the 1980s during the Jacques Delors presidency 1985–95, led then to a considerable upgrading of the project. Several Treaty revisions such as the Single European Act in 1987, the Treaty of the European Union in 1993, the Treaty of Amsterdam in 1999 and the Nice Treaty of 2003 contributed to the emergence of the EU as we know it today. There was an attempt to develop this main document into a constitutional treaty in 2004–5, but two referendums in France (May 2005) and the Netherlands (June 2005) led to its failure to achieve ratification. Finally, in 2009, the Treaty of Lisbon, which was almost identical to the Constitutional Treaty, was adopted. This is the main 'constitutional' treaty of the EU as it stands today (see Figures 10.1, 10.2, 10.3 and 10.4; Box 10.1).

Box 10.1 The founding fathers of the European Union

Robert Schuman (1886–1963)

French foreign minister between 1948 and 1952, on 9 May 1950 Schuman presented the 'Schuman plan', which led to the establishment of the European Community of Steel and Coal (ECSC) in 1952. He began the Franco–German reconciliation process. He was president of the European Parliament between 1958 and 1960.

Jean Monnet (1888–1979)

Monnet was a French civil servant who developed the 'Schuman plan', which led to the foundation of the ECSC. He also became its first High Commissioner between 1952 and 1955. However, he became disillusioned about the slow pace of integration and founded his own movement called the 'United States of Europe'.

Konrad Adenauer (1876–1967)

German chancellor between 1949 and 1963, Adenauer was the main partner, with Robert Schuman, in the processes of French–German reconciliation and European integration. In 1963, Adenauer signed a Treaty of Friendship with his

(continued)

(continued)

French counterpart, Charles de Gaulle. This treaty was to institutionalise Franco–German cooperation, which lay at the heart of European integration.

Walter Hallstein (1901–82)

A German law professor at Frankfurt University before and after the Second World War, Hallstein became the first president of the Commission of the European Communities between 1958 and 1966. Influenced strongly by the devastating consequences of Nazi rule, he was a tireless worker for the predominance of the rule of law over national power interests. Today's European Commission and the European Court of Justice (ECJ) have become such important institutions due to the founding work of Hallstein.

Altiero Di Spinelli (1907–86)

An Italian communist politician, Spinelli was Commissioner for Industry and Technology between 1970 and 1976. After three years as an MP in the Italian parliament, he was elected to the European Parliament in 1979. As a member of the European Parliament he became one of its most active leaders. He also became associated with the draft version of the Treaty of the European Union.

Paul-Henri Spaak (1899–1972)

Spaak was a Belgian foreign minister, and later prime minister, who was an enthusiastic supporter of European integration. He was instrumental in drafting the treaty leading to the formation of the European Economic Community and Euratom in 1958.

Joseph Bech (1887–1975)

Before, during and after the Second World War, Bech was the foreign minister (1937–53) and then prime minister (1953–57) of Luxembourg and was an enthusiastic supporter of European integration. As representative of his country, he played a crucial role in the foundation of the ECSC, the European Economic Community (EEC) and Euratom.

Johan Willem Beijen (1897–1976)

A pragmatic businessman who became Dutch foreign minister between 1952 and 1956, he presented his 'Beijen plan' for the creation of a European single market at the Messina conference of 1955. He was supported by Paul Henri Spaak. This Dutch–Belgian plan then became the EEC in 1957.

Sicco Mansholt (1908–95)

Like Spinelli, Mansholt was a federalist and convinced European. He was a farmer and during the Second World War an active resistance fighter against

Nazi occupation in the Netherlands. He was minister for agriculture in the Netherlands between 1945 and 1956. In 1958, he became the vice-president of the new Commission of the EEC under the leadership of Walter Hallstein. In this period, he developed the Common Agricultural Policy (CAP). In 1972–3, he became the president of the Commission.

Source: based on European Commission (2018b).

Starting in 1985, the new president of the European Commission, Jacques Delors, transformed the role of the European Community within a decade. Until that date, the member-states had the pace of the European integration process under control, whereas from 1985 onwards the pace was set by the European Commission. During the incumbency period of Jacques Delors, the number of policy legislative initiatives increased exponentially. This incrementalism of policy-making reached its peak in 1995 but then declined when Delors was succeeded by other less charismatic commissioners, such as Jacques Santer, Romano Prodi and Manuel Durão Barroso (Pollack, 1994, 2000).

In Chapter 3, we referred to the work of Stefano Bartolini, who identified the European integration process as a new stage of development in European politics. There is a political restructuring process between national political systems and the EU taking place that is qualitatively transforming European politics (Bartolini, 2005: 366).

The 1980s and 1990s can be identified as an important juncture in this process. The qualitative difference before and after 1985 was that these European policies put member-states under permanent pressure to transpose a huge amount of legislation into national law, with the goal of achieving the completion of the SEM.

The institutional framework of the supranational level of the EU

This permanent European policy-making pressure since 1985 enhanced the importance of the supranational institutions of the European Commission and the European Parliament over time (Box 10.2). Although the centre of decision-making still lies in the Council of Ministers, the incrementalism of policy-making strengthened the position of the European Commission as the motor of European integration. This triadic relationship has become even closer since the late 1980s. They are known as trilogues normally brokered by the country holding the rotating presidency of the EU. Negotiations on policy decisions are taken behind closed doors and are characterised by a lack of transparency; however, a very large part is agreed consensually (for more detail, see Häge and Naurin, 2013; Reh, 2014). The intergovernmental Council of Ministers of the European Union now has only few areas in which the representatives vote by unanimity. Today, a majority of policies are shared

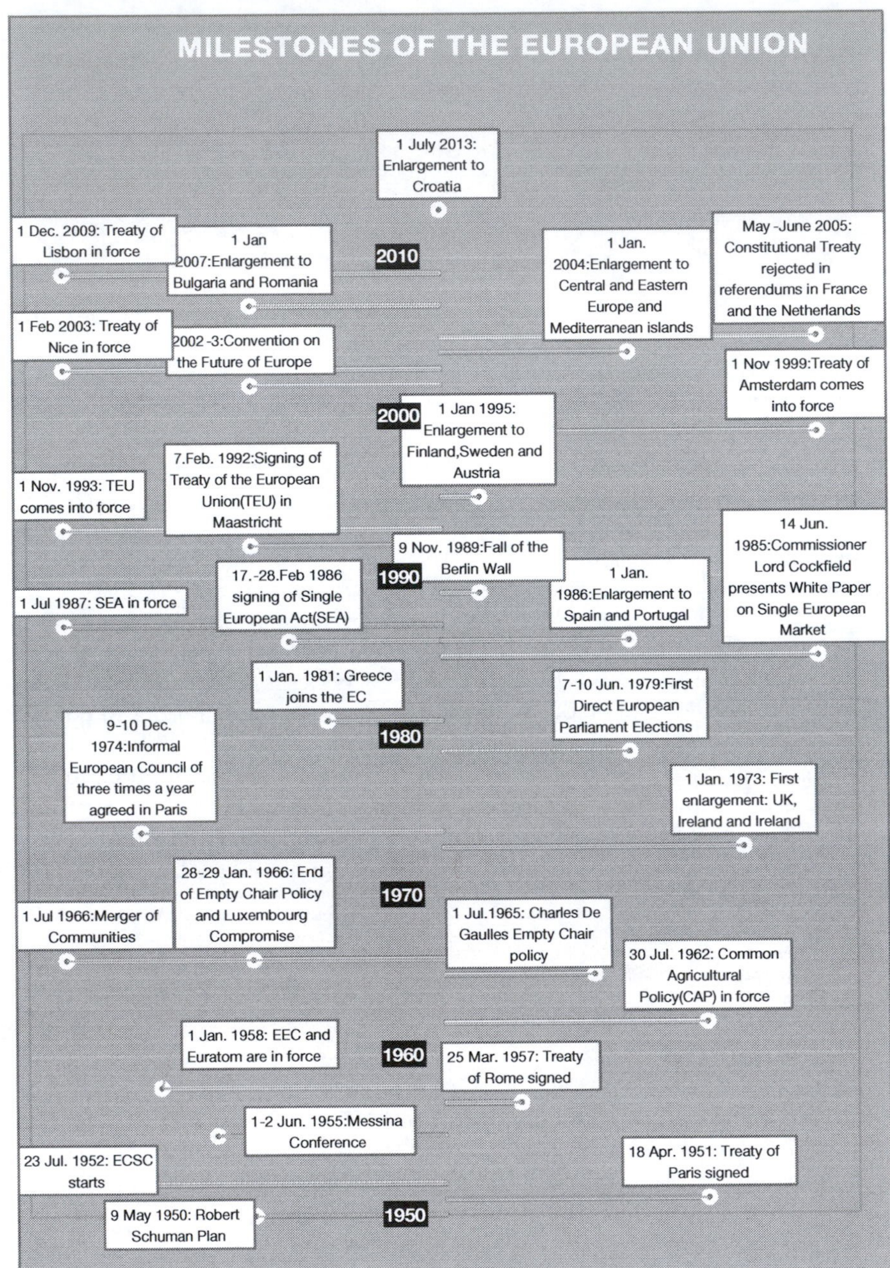

Figure 10.1 Milestones of European integration

Source: Author's graph based on data from European Commission (2018b).

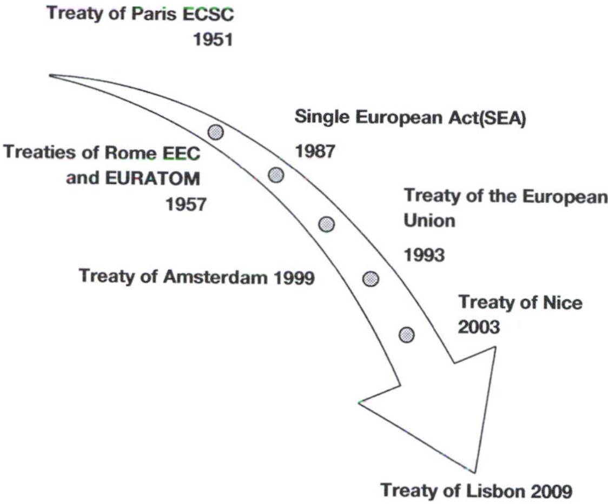

Figure 10.2 The incremental legal basis for the EU since 1951

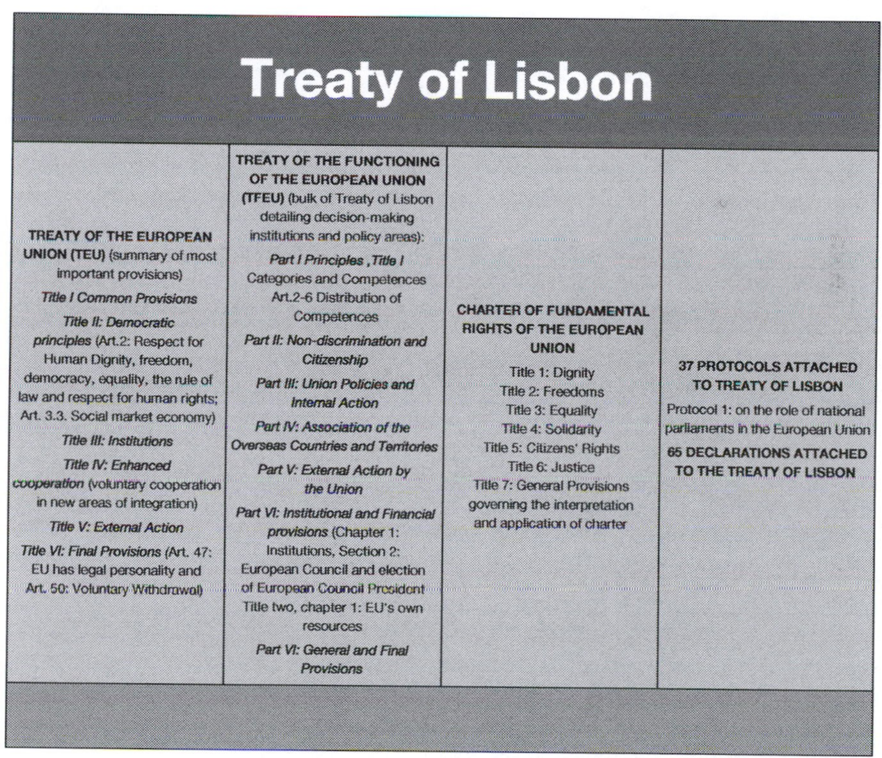

Figure 10.3 The structure of the Treaty of Lisbon

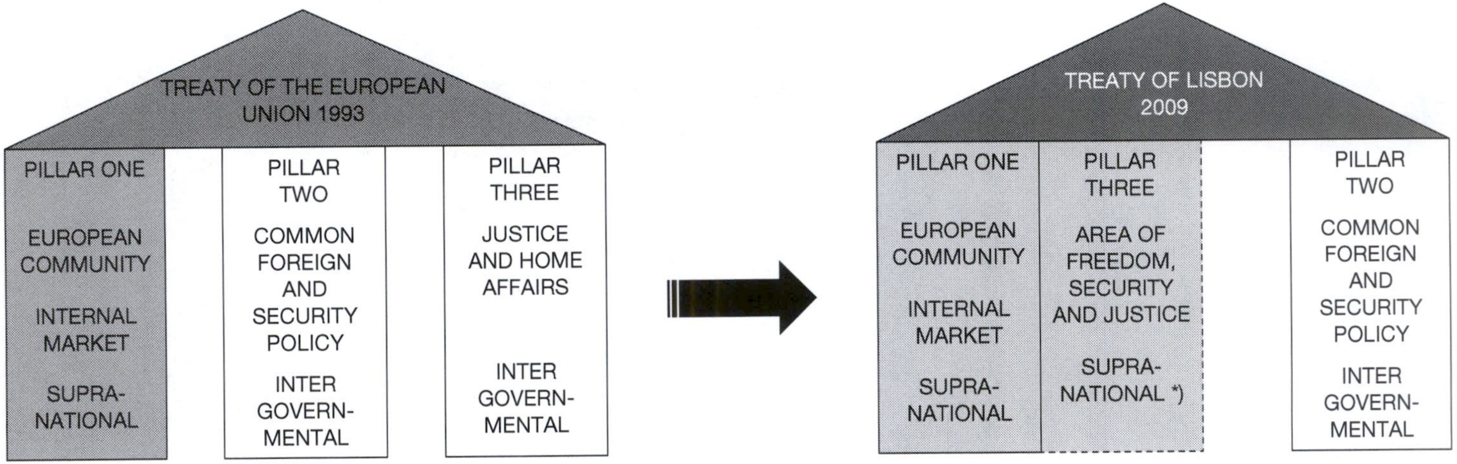

TREATY OF THE EUROPEAN UNION 1993

PILLAR ONE
EUROPEAN COMMUNITY
INTERNAL MARKET
SUPRA-NATIONAL

PILLAR TWO
COMMON FOREIGN AND SECURITY POLICY
INTER GOVERN-MENTAL

PILLAR THREE
JUSTICE AND HOME AFFAIRS
INTER GOVERN-MENTAL

TREATY OF LISBON 2009

PILLAR ONE
EUROPEAN COMMUNITY
INTERNAL MARKET
SUPRA-NATIONAL

PILLAR THREE
AREA OF FREEDOM, SECURITY AND JUSTICE
SUPRA-NATIONAL *)

PILLAR TWO
COMMON FOREIGN AND SECURITY POLICY
INTER GOVERN-MENTAL

Figure 10.4 The structure of the Treaties of the European Union (1993) and Lisbon (2009)

*) Note: Most areas are still in progress towards communitarisation due to resistance of member-states, conflicting national and European logics, or lack of human and financial resources; refugee crisis symbolises a certain stalemate in this process.

between the supranational institutions and the member-states, and most policy areas are decided by a qualified majority in the Council of Ministers. Since the Treaty of Maastricht of 1993, the role of the directly elected European Parliament has been enhanced through the co-decision procedure, now known as the ordinary legislative procedure. In spite of differences, a majority of legislation is approved consensually. Roughly, 80 per cent of legislative proposals are decided by consensus without a vote, and in just 20 per cent, particularly in the policy areas of agriculture, fisheries and the single market, a vote may be required. The organisational culture of the EU is based on consensus, and most policy areas are negotiated in the around 150 highly specialised working committees (2018) consisting of highly specialised national negotiators of the member-states. However, these national skilled negotiators are part of a transeuropean network that is geared towards compromise. They are socialised into this existing organisational culture over time. There are no winners and losers in negotiation processes, and if there are, this is a good way for everybody to feel they are a winner. In the Council of Ministers most of the negotiations have already taken place in the working committees, which show the limits of absolute positions so that ministers comply with the result (see Lewis and Jeffrey, 2015: 224–9; on the Council committees see Häge, 2016; on the EU as a consensus democracy, see Kalina, 2012; Schmidt 2002). Difficult legislative bills are discussed in a conciliation committee, consisting of representatives of the Council of Ministers and the European Parliament (Wallace, 2005: 49–66). In spite of its low-key presence at national level, the European Parliament has become a central player in the decision-making process and shaping of a European deliberative space (for more, see Hix et al., 2007; Judge and Earnshaw, 2008). Furthermore, the institutional triadic is complemented by an independent European Court of Justice that oversees and makes judgements on the correct implementation of European law. So far, this has been the most innovative part of the European integration process. Since the 1950s, the has EU accumulated a huge quantity of European legal documents as well as decisions based on case work, making European law quite complex. This process has led to the merging of different European traditions into one overarching legal system, which is above national law. Today, most national law is, in effect, translated European law, because of the adjustments governments make to comply with supranational legislation (Wallace, 2005: 69–74). If we take Germany as an example for most countries, an excellent empirical study by Sven Hölscheidt and Tilman Hoppe seems to suggest that by May 2010, 67 per cent, probably even 80 per cent (if legislation related to agriculture is taking into account due to the Common Agricultural Policy) of parliamentary adopted national German legislation goes back to the transposition of EU law (Hölscheidt and Hoppe, 2010: 546–7; less overwhelming numbers are reported by Brouard et al., 2013 for other countries at about 25 per cent on average, excluding agriculture). This clearly seems to confirm partly what former president Jacques Delors said in a speech in 1988, that in twenty years 80 per cent of national legislation will be of European origin. The so-called 'myth' propagated by Delors in 1988 may have become reality, at least in the German case (see Figure 10.5).

Box 10.2 The institutions of the European Union

The European Commission

The main administrative machinery of the EU is the European Commission. It is a supranational institution with the aim of progressing the European integration process. Therefore, it is often referred to as the 'motor' of European integration. It has the right to initiate legislation, which is then forwarded to the Council of Ministers and the European Parliament. It comprises over 32,196 European civil servants (2018) who are divided between thirty-seven directorates-general and services (such as the Statistical Office or the Office for Official Publications) and several other agencies (such as the European Foundation for the Improvement of Living Conditions (EUROFOUND), the European Environment Agency (EEA), FRONTEX (for border control coordination), and the European Union Agency for Fundamental Rights (FRA)).

Since the European Parliament elections of 2014 (the so-called *Spitzenkandidatenwahl*) the main candidate of the largest party is normally appointed as president of the European Commission after confirmation by the European Council. Presently there are twenty-eight commissioners, one from each member-state. Such a European Commission is perceived as being too large, due to the fact that there is not enough work for all commissioners. It also makes it more difficult to achieve consensus, one of the features of decision-making in the European Commission (for more detail, see Cini, 2015; Peterson, 2017).

The Council of Ministers of the European Union and the European Council

While the European Commission is a supranational institution, the Council of Ministers and the European Council is an intergovernmental one. It is the institution in which the governments of the member-states are represented. Its main task is to adopt legislative proposals of the European Commission increasingly together with the European Parliament. This so-called ordinary legislative procedure requires the approval of legislative proposals by both institutions before it can become law.

The Council of Ministers of the European Union has grown over time. It has a general-secretariat, with 2,770 civil servants in 2018, which supports the work of the Council of Ministers. The Council secretariat is chaired by the general secretary, who at the moment is the Dane Jeppe Tranholm-Mikkelsen.

Most of the work is done by the ten formations of the Council of Ministers of the member-states. They take decisions that were already decided at subaltern 150 working groups and the Committee of Permanent Representatives (COREPER I and II). The legislative programme is normally coordinated by the country that is the incumbent of the rotating presidency of the Council of Ministers. This is an important task, because legislation needs about six to eighteen months to be adopted. Therefore, since 2010, a group of three countries, the so-called trio presidency (the incumbent, the previous president and the subsequent one) are strongly involved in the coordination of the legislative programme over an eighteen-month period. Since the Treaty of Lisbon, the presidency of the Council of Ministers has lost its competences in Common Foreign and Security Policy (CFSP) and has been downgraded from a political to a now technical role.

Although the European Council has existed informally since 1972, after a proposal by French president Georges Pompidou it only became a new institution after the adoption of the Treaty of Lisbon. The European Council consists of the heads of government and state chiefs and is presided over by a permanent president appointed for thirty months by the European Council, which is renewable. So far there have been two presidents: Herman van Rompuy (2009–14) and since 2014 the former Polish prime minister Donald Tusk. The main task of the president is to coordinate the work of the Council and represent the EU internationally. The European Council meets four times a year, and sometimes more often when there are major problems like the financial or refugee crises. It sets the strategic guidelines for the future development of the EU and makes 'history-making' decisions (Peterson and Bomberg, 1999: 10–16; on the Council of Ministers and European Council, see Wessels, 2016; Lewis and Jeffrey, 2015).

The European Parliament

The European Parliament has evolved from a mere consultative and appointed assembly to a decision-making legislature that is directly elected. The direct election of the European Parliament was introduced in 1979. Since then, there have been seven elections. After the 2014 elections there were 751 members elected by a proportional representation system, which differs in detail between the countries, for a five-year period. They are organised according to seven parliamentary party groups (for more detail see Chapter 7).

The powers of the European Parliament have evolved over time. According to Wolfgang Wessels, the Lisbon Treaty increased the number of articles covered by the co-decision procedure to 38.8 per cent, and reduced the non-participation share to 26.7 per cent (Wessels, 2008: 124).

The European Parliament still has three different seats: Strasbourg, Brussels and Luxembourg. Strasbourg remains the main seat for plenary sessions, while committee meetings and parliamentary group meetings take place in Brussels. Luxembourg holds a large part of the administration of the European Parliament (for more detail, see Raunio, 2015; Hix et al., 2007; Judge and Earnshaw, 2008).

The ECJ

One of the great achievements of the EU was the creation of its own supranational European law, which overrides national law. Today, most national legal systems are simply transpositions of European law. The ECJ, based in Luxembourg, has the highest instance of dealing with judicial decisions relating

(continued)

(continued)

to the internal market, but also, increasingly, it deals with other issues as well. It consists of twenty-eight judges, one for every member-state.

Since the 1950s, the ECJ has emerged as an important player in shaping the European integration process. Many decisions of the ECJ have led to changes in European and national law. Although most of the ECJ's decisions have been to do with the internal market and competitive policy, they have also had, indirectly, political, social and cultural implications.

The European Commission, member-states, corporate organisations and individuals can all file complaints to the ECJ. Decisions by the ECJ are binding, but the enforcement mechanisms are still in the making. It is quite astonishing how decisions of the ECJ are complied with, despite the absence of enforcement mechanisms. In recent years, the ECJ has created a network of judicial authorities at national level in order to increase its efficiency in making decisions (for further information, see Chapter 6).

The workload has been increasing considerably in the past decades, so that a major reform of the judicial structure has been taking place since 2015. Its main goal has been to reduce the accumulated workload over the years, so that the number of judges in the General Court has doubled. Critics regarded this as waste of tax payers' money, and contradicting the trend in member-states' judiciaries to cut resources and become more efficient. The new structure comprises the Court of Justice and a General Court. The reformed ECJ main court consists of twenty-eight judges and eleven advocates, while the General Court comprises forty-five judges. The main difference between the courts is that the Court of Justice deals with the more important cases, while the General Court is responsible for the bulk of routine cases as well as European civil service cases (on the ECJ and for a critical discussion of the reform, see Blauberger and Schmidt, 2017; Dehousse, 2016; *Politico*, 14 June 2016).

The supranational level and the member-states are integral to a dynamic systemic whole, so that several authors characterise the EU as a political system. Nevertheless, Hix makes clear that the EU is not a state in the historical sense: it is a supranational organisation (Hix, 2005: 2–9). Sovereignty still lies with the member-states, although, as William Wallace asserts, because of the transfer of competences in key policy areas, the EU is a 'post-sovereign polity' based on 'shared pooled sovereignty' (Wallace, 1999, 2005). Although the Treaty of Lisbon recognises the EU as an international legal entity, a majority of member-states and citizens are reluctant to have a super-state above them, one of the main reasons behind Brexit. So far, the EU has been based on treaties, not on an overarching constitution, which would be essential to build a federal state. According to Wolfgang Wessels, Andreas Maurer and Jürgen Mittag, the process of systemic integration between the different levels of governance, particularly the national and supranational, can be called 'fusion'. This fusion between the levels is taking time. It is a process of ups and downs, but eventually it will lead to more supranational integration (Wessels et al., 2003: 14).

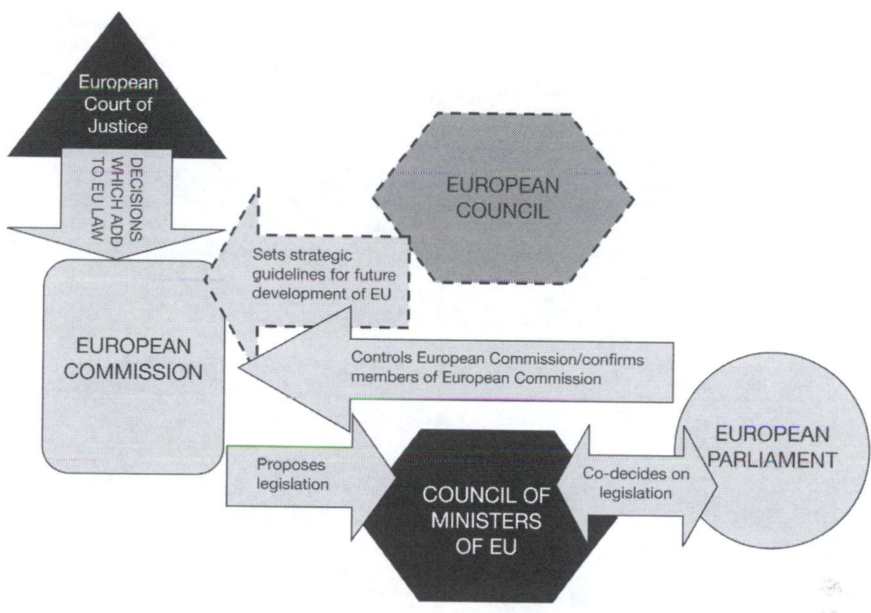

Figure 10.5 The core EU supranational decision-making system

This supranational and national integration of levels is best exemplified by what we can call the 'transnational level'. This where officials from both national and supranational institutions work together, preparing policy-making initiatives and engaging in decision-making processes. This occurs particularly in the 150 working groups and the Committee of Permanent Representatives (COREPER), and the 277 advisory, examination and regulatory scrutiny groups attached to the European Commission (the so-called comitology) consisting of national representatives of the main stakeholders and representatives of Europe-wide interest groups related to the policy area. The input of comitology shapes European legislation or its implementation and regulation (for more detail, see Blom-Hansen, 2011; Dehousse, 2003: 800; Dehousse et al., 2014; see also Bach, 1995; European Commission, 2017e: 4; Maurer et al., 2000: 37, 41) (see Figure 10.6).

This means that, in order to study contemporary national political systems in Europe, we need to take into account the systemic nature of the EU. Although diversity between European national political systems still persists and will not disappear in the near future, there have also been processes of convergence and institutional adjustments.

Europeanisation of national politics and Euromestication

The previous section showed that, since 1985, there has been a growing integration between national and supranational politics. This Europeanisation is increasingly complemented by a 'domestication' of European politics (Euromestication), in which

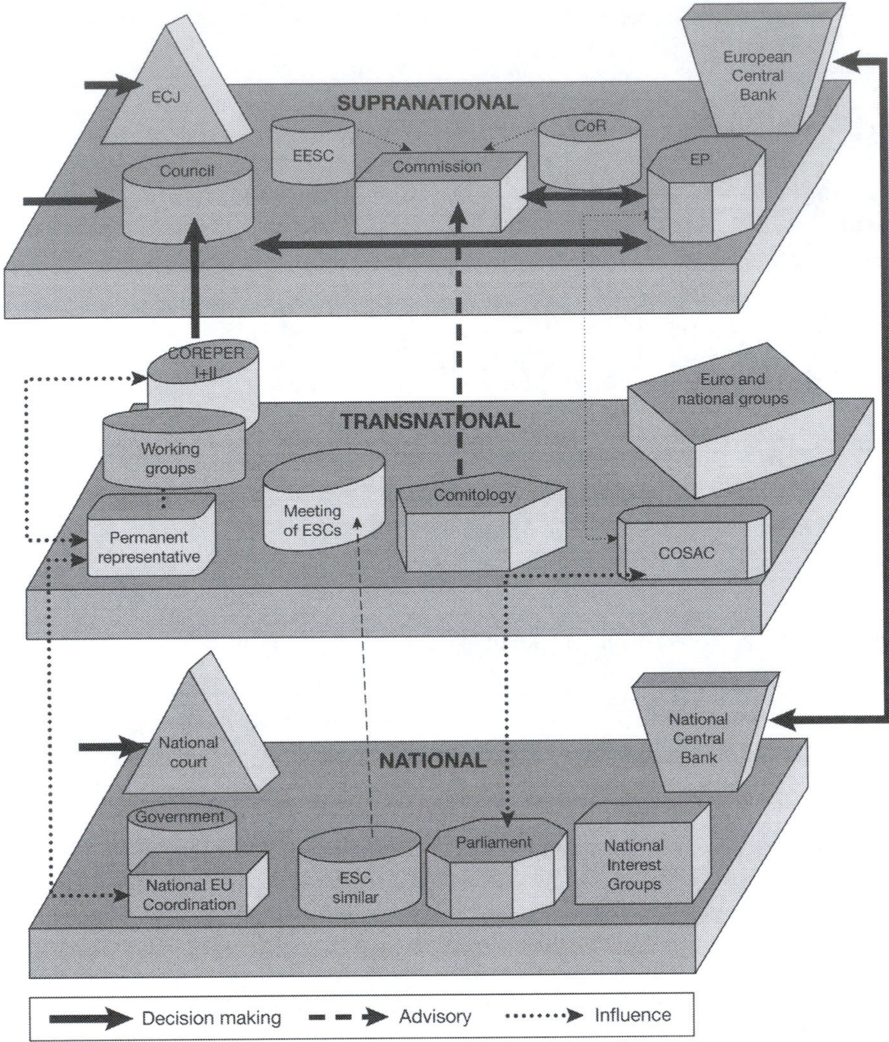

Figure 10.6 The multilevel governance system of the EU

national actors (national governments, national legislatures, civil society, transeuropean networks) try to shape the future and ongoing policies of the EU. Tanja Börzel and Thomas Risse characterise this as the *uploading* of preferences by national actors to the supranational level (in our language here, the Euromestication) and the *downloading* of supranational policies to the national level (in our language, the Europeanisation of national politics) (Börzel and Risse, 2003: 62). Both processes are intertwined and systemic. In another study, Börzel refers to downloading as Europeanisation and uploading as European integration (Börzel, 2005: 46). Although Börzel is right about Europeanisation, I would argue that the uploading process may be better defined as the domestication of European politics, whereas European integration would be the overarching intertwined dynamic of the two processes.

In this volume, we have concentrated mainly on Europeanisation processes and less on Euromestication processes. The main reason for this is that we are interested in comparing different countries. This means that our main territorial level of analysis is, and remains, the national level. Although it is important to contextualise such national politics in the new EU political system, our main focus remains the discussion of the similarities and differences between European countries. It is also very important to differentiate between vertical top-down and horizontal Europeanisation. The vertical top-down Europeanisation is simply the process of the integration of policies defined at supranational level into national politics, policy-making or polity. Horizontal Europeanisation refers to the coordination of policies through specific soft governance methods, for example the open method of coordination, which allows best practice and benchmarking to be adopted by the member-states (Radaelli, 2003: 41) (see Figure 10.7).

Top-down vertical Europeanisation of national politics

As already mentioned, this process of Europeanisation refers to the period since 1985, when member-states had to implement, in a very short period of time, several policies designed at supranational level in order to implement the SEM (see Table 10.1). The SEM programme comprised over 280 directives that had to be implemented between 1985 and the end of 1992. After 1992 further directives were introduced in order to finetune legislation in many areas. Apart from the right legal transposition into national law, national governments also had to find mechanisms to monitor the working of such directives in reality. Europeanisation as such is, therefore, a never-ending process and part of the systemic nature of European integration. Although Europeanisation processes simultaneously shape policy, politics and polity, it is important to differentiate analytically between the three, so that partial Europeanisation processes can also be better understood. Moreover, it is important to add a cultural dimension and consider, in particular, how elites and populations in each of the respective countries may adjust their attitudes towards the new EU political system. This means that Europeanisation processes are complex and can be characterised by parallel, but different, timeframes. Changes in attitudes may take a long time (for more detail, see Ladrech, 2010; Figure 10.7, Box 10.3).

Box 10.3 The Europeanisation of national politics and the domestication of European politics

The Europeanisation of national politics

A very thorough definition by Claudio Radaelli, influenced by Robert Ladrech (1994):

> Processes of (a) construction, (b) diffusion and (c) institutionalisation of formal and informal procedures, policy paradigms, styles, 'ways of

(continued)

(continued)

> doing things', and shared beliefs and norms that are first defined and consolidated in the making of EU public policy and politics and then incorporated in the logic of domestic discourse, identities, political structures, and public policies.
>
> (Radaelli, 2003: 31)

- *Top-down Europeanisation*: The decisions taken at the supranational level are implemented at the national level, leading to a change of institutions or policy-making processes (e.g. structural funds).
- *Horizontal Europeanisation*: The voluntary process of convergence of institutions or policy styles across the EU. This is achieved through a light coordination structure at the centre, combined with a continuous review and monitoring of the process (e.g. employment, economic governance, convergence in public administration styles).

Euromestication (European/transnational domestication)

Individual member-states or alliances of member-states may formulate new ideas and policy proposals that are successful at the national level and upload at supranational level (e.g. economic governance through 'Merkozy' based on German stability culture principles).

Probably, the most sophisticated one has been presented by Christopher Knill and Dirk Lehmkuhl. They differentiate between three forms of top-down Europeanisation. The first one is labelled as positive Europeanisation, meaning that member-states adopt policies based on a design developed at supranational level. The second form is 'negative' Europeanisation, which lacks a design or model and is a mere enforcement of directives. The third form is the cultural transformation of attitudes and ways of thinking in relation to the European integration process. It is a process of overcoming the poor fit between the supranational and national levels (Knill and Lehmkuhl, 2002).

According to Börzel, Europeanisation can be measured according to a continuum that stretches from no change to high change. In between, she includes inertia/resistance, retrenchment/'negative change' (both are low change), absorption, accommodation/'peripheral change' (medium change) and transformation/systemic change (high change) (Börzel, 2005: 59). She also highlights that the level of transformation is dependent on mediating factors, such as the number of institutional veto points (president, judiciary, parliament, subnational actors), supporting formal institutions, or a cooperative informal culture (Börzel, 2005: 49–58). This makes the process of Europeanisation in each individual country fairly complex. We may therefore assert that there is a high degree of variation in the top-down Europeanisation of member-states. Paradoxically, as already mentioned, best compliance can be found in the Eurosceptic Nordic countries, the UK and the Netherlands, while France, Germany, Belgium, Italy and Greece are rather less compliant.

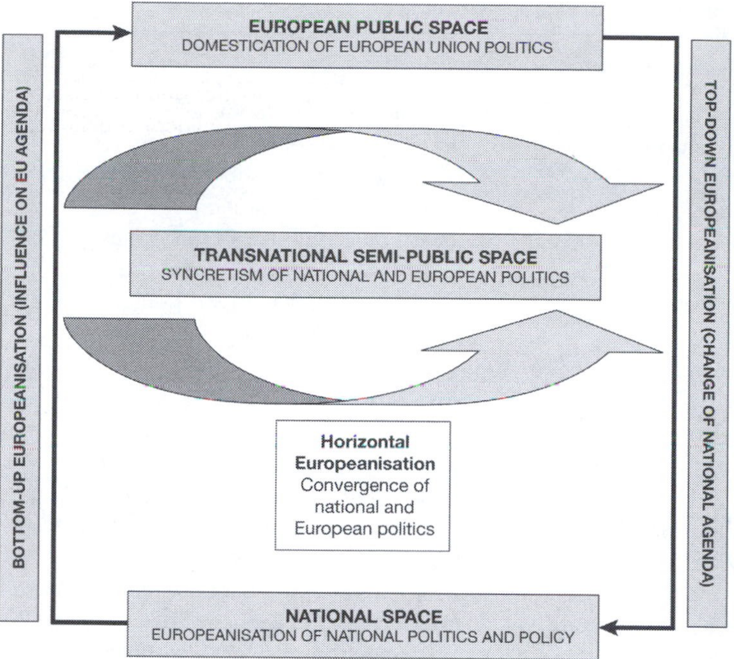

Figure 10.7 The dimensions of the Europeanisation of national politics and the domestication of European politics

Horizontal Europeanisation or transnationalisation of politics

This form of Europeanisation is less formalised and less well framed than vertical Europeanisation. Horizontal Europeanisation can be observed in policy areas in which member-states resist calls for supranationalisation, for example in areas such as economic policy, social policy, employment policy, immigration policy, education policy and public administrative reform. The methods of horizontal Europeanisation include, for example, the open method of coordination (OMC), formalised as one of the European integration methods in the extraordinary European Council of Lisbon, 23–4 March 2000. The OMC had been applied primarily to the coordination of employment policies since 1998, but also economic governance. The OMC is a soft form of governance, which has a minimal coordinating structure at supranational level. It sets guidelines for each member-state in a particular policy area and is a medium- to long-term instrument of policy-making (Borrás and Jacobsson, 2004: 188–9). Other soft methods are benchmarking and good practice, based on voluntary adherence to it.

Bottom-up Euromestication

The 'uploading' of preferences, as referred to by Tanja Börzel and Thomas Risse, requires that national, subnational and, sometimes, transnational actors contribute

Table 10.1 The dimensions of top-down Europeanisation

Layers	*Institutions/actors*	*Description*
The political system	• Central government • Parliament • Judiciary • Regional and local government • Public administration	• The impact of European integration on the political elite, the core executive, parliament, courts, subnational government and public administration • Pressures to adjust to European integration; it also includes constitutional change
Decision-making system	• Political parties • Interest groups • Organised civil society	• The role of intermediary organisations in shaping the decision-making process • This impact may have interactions with aggregated interest groups at the supranational level, which have been characterised as European organised civil society (Eurogroups)
Public policy space	• Public administration • Policy networks • Private actors • Business enterprises	• The implementation of policies designed at the supranational level • It requires cooperation between government, civil society and economic actors
Political cultural space	• Political elites • Population • Interest groups • Social movements	• Political expression for and against European integration • Establishment of social movements related to the European integration process • Linkage between political parties and voters • National political culture and European integration (knowledge of EU matters and institutions; support for the EU; benefits of the EU)

Source: Adapted from Magone (2004: 13).

to the Euromestication of debates about European integration. However, the best examples of Euromestication were probably the two conventions that led to the drafting of the Charter of Fundamental Citizens' Rights in 2002 and the constitutional treaty in 2003, respectively. The multilevel European deliberative space led to the intervention of intellectuals, think-tanks, interest groups, politicians, national parliaments and subnational parliaments in order to put forward their particular contributions. This transformed the nature of the debate. For the European Convention on the Charter of Fundamental Citizens' Rights, 70 civil society organisations submitted 900 contributions, while for the European Convention on the Constitutional Treaty 547 organisations (including think-tanks and national interest groups) sent 1,251 contributions; these figures do not include the contributions at national and subnational levels (Magone, 2006: 179). In this sense, the whole European integration process has become more deliberative and the trend seems to be to include more and more actors in order to legitimise and democratise the outcome. In most initiatives of the European Commission, there is a lengthy consultation process that allows the public to send their views on the proposal. Also the debate on the bailout for Greece led to a Euromestication of the discussion in a multilevel setting. The peak of the discussion was the exchange of opinions between German finance minister Wolfgang Schäuble and Greek finance minister Yannis Varoufakis in the first half of 2015. Also the refugee crisis in 2015 led to a major multilevel debate across Europe with Germany and chancellor Angela Merkel at the centre.

Differentiated integration

One major challenge for the EU is that some countries are not integrated in all policy areas. This has been characterised as differentiated integration. The UK has been the best example of differentiated integration in the EU. The UK, Sweden, Denmark, Poland, the Czech Republic, Hungary, Bulgaria, Romania and Croatia are not part of the Economic and Monetary Union (EMU). Just the Danish krone is pegged to the euro. In Justice and Home Affairs (Area of Freedom, Security and Justice – AFSJ), the UK and Ireland opted out of the Schengen Area, and Bulgaria, Romania, Croatia and Cyprus are still waiting to be members, a delay related to their poor progress in judicial reform (Leuffen et al., 2013).

National governments, parliaments and judiciaries in the EU multilevel governance system

The governments of the member-states are also involved in policy-making at the supranational level. As already mentioned, the Council of Ministers of the European Union consists of the Council of Ministers of the individual states. National government ministers of a particular policy area meet with their counterparts regularly in Brussels and Luxembourg. There are ten Council Formations, of which those of the economic and finance ministers and foreign ministers are among the most important. They meet once a month. In contrast, ministers for education and other less central areas meet twice a year. They are supported by a highly skilled staff in the twenty-eight national permanent representations, and all legislation has to go through a negotiation process in the 150 working committees and COREPER (Hussein, 2015). In this regard, member-states are in charge of the European legislative process, against the general misperception that the EU imposes legislation on the member-states. In reality, the governments of the member-states are central to decision-making and most decisions are taken by consensus (Figures 10.8 and 10.9).

National parliaments and the EU: an asymmetrical top-down Europeanisation

Since the late 1980s, the EU has considerably expanded its legislative activity and policy-making powers. As already mentioned, the Delors myth that 80 per cent of national legislation derives from supranational acts could have become reality, although a unified methodology to measure it has been lacking (Brouard et al., 2013

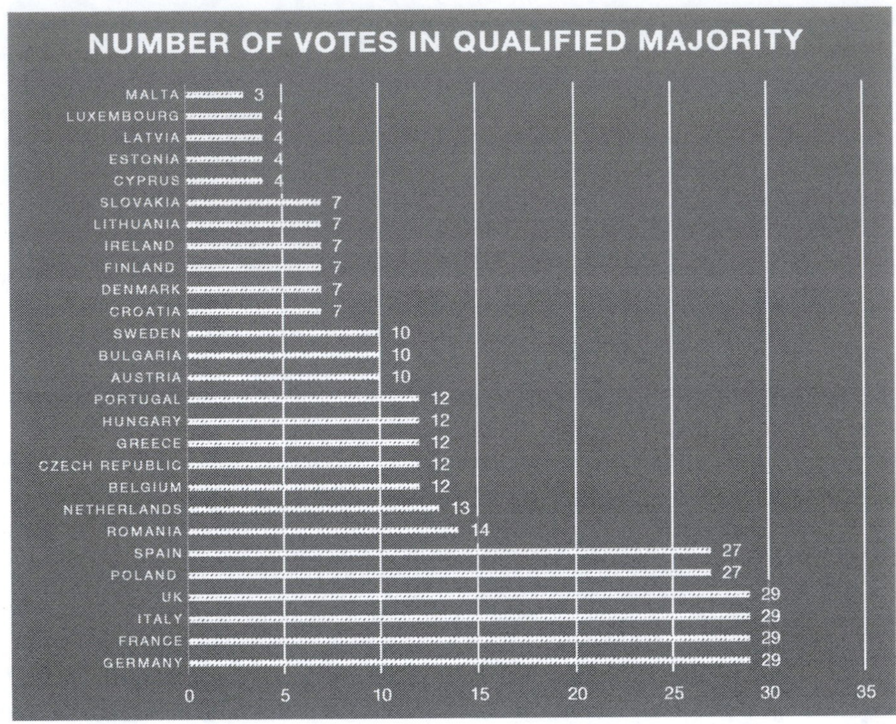

Figure 10.8 The distribution of votes in the Council of Ministers after the Treaty of Lisbon

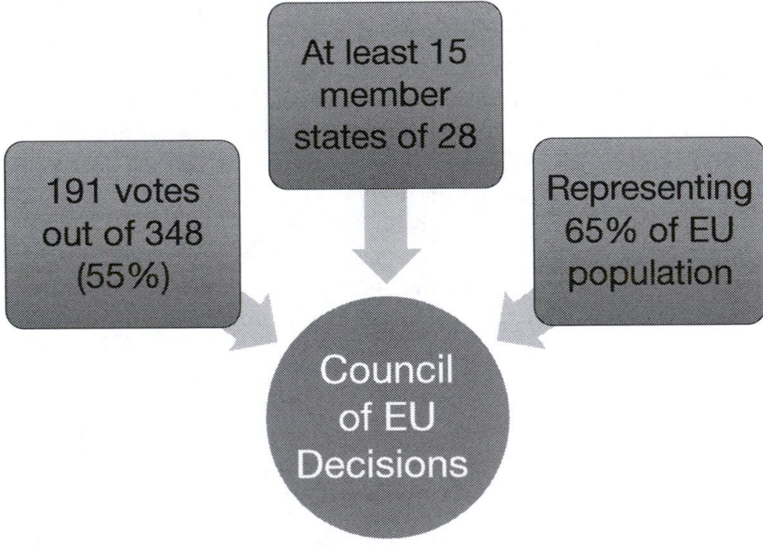

Figure 10.9 Decision-making by the qualified majority, according to the Treaty of Lisbon

has quite low figures for several analysed countries, around 25 per cent, but agriculture is not included; my cautious assessment is just for Germany and is based on Hölscheidt and Hoppe, 2010: 546–7). Clearly, in the emergence of this multilevel governance system, the democratic deficit has increased considerably. In particular, the national parliaments and the European Parliament have not been able to compensate for this transfer of powers to the supranational level with more accountability and control powers. While the European Parliament has gained in powers, they are still not enough to hold the European Commission accountable for their actions. In 1999, the EU was able to dismiss the Jacques Santer European Commission because of the many cases of clientelism and corruption that had accumulated over the decades. The main consequence was a major reform of the European Commission by the UK Commissioner Neil Kinnock in 2001 (Cini, 2015: 240–2).

Even more problematic is the sidelining of national parliaments in the emerging new political system. In this sense, John O'Brennan and Tapio Raunio speak of a 'de-parlamentarisation' of national political systems. De-parlamentarisation means that 'the development of European integration led to an erosion of parliamentary control over executive office holders. The argument about de-parlamentarisation is based both on constitutional rules and on the political dynamics of the EU policy process' (O'Brennan and Raunio, 2007: 2). This de-parlamentarisation has been taking place with greater intensity since the early 1990s.

Therefore, after the introduction of the principle of subsidiarity into the Treaty of Maastricht in 1993, a protocol was added giving rights of information to national parliaments. In the Treaty of Lisbon, the protocol on the national parliaments and the EU introduced a political dialogue with the European Commission which consists of informing legislatures about forthcoming legislation eight weeks before it is discussed in the respective institutions. If one-third of parliaments raise objections based on infringements of national competences (subsidiarity), the European Commission has to reconsider the legislative act, which is also known as giving a 'yellow card'. In the area of freedom, security and justice (home affairs), only a quarter of legislatures are needed to utter such reservations. This can be upgraded to an 'orange card' if half of national parliaments raise reservations. In this case, the European Commission has to offer a better justification as to why the legislative act should be decided at supranational level. National parliaments have to be informed about internal security issues and have the right to ask for a review six months after the new legislation has come into force (Auel and Neuhold, 2017; Gattermann and Hefftler, 2015). The European Commission is obliged to write an annual report on the relationship between the EU and national parliaments (European Commission, 2017c: 2–3). However, quantity in opinions does not mean that such opinions are of a high quality. For example, the Swedish Riksdag has submitted twenty-three opinions, out of which more than half (twelve) are well reasoned, while Italy has sent eighty-one and only three were well reasoned (European Commission, 2017d: 2). Furthermore, 18.4 per cent of opinions were directed towards directorate-general Migration and Home Affairs, a clear reflection of the ongoing refugee crisis (European Commission, 2017d: 8).

Probably the most salient events exposing the loss of power of national parliaments and the increase of the democratic deficit were the financial and euro crises. Most parliaments of the Eurozone had to rush fast-track legislation of a quite complex nature in order to approve their share of the bailout for Greece (three times),

Ireland, Portugal, Cyprus and Spain. Although the bailouts were loans to the countries with sovereign debt problems, it clearly led to considerable opposition in many parliaments such as in Finland, Slovakia, Austria and Germany (for a comparative study, see the excellent research by Auel and Höing, 2015; Wonka, 2016).

As already mentioned in previous chapters the quality of parliamentarianism is still quite uneven cross-nationally. This has a direct reflection on the way different parliaments scrutinise European legislation ex ante and control their governments. Paradoxically, there is now a quite extensive literature on this topic, more than on the actual processes of national domestic parliamentarianism. According to the literature, there are at least four patterns of parliamentarianism in dealing with EU matters: European player (European Parliament), multilevel players/policy-shapers (Denmark, Finland, Germany), national players/debating parliaments (France, the UK) and slow adapters/scrutiny laggards (Spain, Greece, Belgium, Luxembourg). If we exclude the European Parliament as a European player, Denmark, Finland and Sweden are the main examples of multilevel players/policy-shapers. It means that this group of countries is strong and efficient in controlling the European policies of governments and play a role ex ante in legislation. In the Danish case, government members have to attend a meeting before they go to Brussels and are set clear limitations in their mandate to negotiate (so-called parliamentary reservation). One of the main reasons is the strength of Eurosceptic parties such as the Danish People's Party (Dansk Folkeparti – DF) in the Danish Folketing, the True Finns in the Finnish Eduskunta and the Swedish Democrats (Sverigedemokraterna – SD) in the Swedish Riksdag (Christensen, 2015; Hegeland, 2016; Raunio, 2016). Germany and the Netherlands also belong to this group, but with lower mechanisms of scrutiny and government control. Moreover, Germany's Bundestag and Bundesrat have been dominated by Euroenthusiastic parties, so that their scrutiny of EU matters and ex ante control of governments is more moderate than in the Nordic countries. The Lisbon Treaty and the sovereign debt crisis have contributed to an upgrading of the powers of the Bundestag in shaping EU policy matters A major factor were complaints to the constitutional court which led to landmark decisions on behalf of the Bundestag (Höing, 2016). Moreover, the soft Eurosceptic, more nationally oriented Alternative for Germany (Alternative für Deutschland – AfD) may change this pro-European parliamentary consensus towards more critical tunes. Similarly, the Netherlands has moved slowly to this pattern after decades of support for European integration. Since 2006, the Dutch parliament has upgraded their procedures in the lower house, due to the fact that most resources are there, and it tries to improve the efficiency of scrutiny with the upper house, the Eerste Kamer. Since 2002, the Pim Fortuyn List (PFL) and then the Party of Freedom (Partij van der Vrijheid of Geert Wilders) have contributed to a more Eurosceptic profile of Dutch society in general and Dutch parliament in particular (Högenauer, 2016; Magone, 2017).

A second pattern is the so-called national players or debating parliaments, which comprises most legislatures such as France, the UK, Italy, Austria and Portugal. Poland and Hungary also belong to this group, but one has always to treat this typological classification with caution due to the ongoing threats to the rule of the law in the two countries since 2015 and 2010 respectively. All these legislatures are clearly overwhelmed by the EU legislation, and also the governments are quite strong, so it is difficult to control them. However, they try to compensate by being more active in informing the population about the latest developments.

A third pattern is the slow adapters, or EU scrutiny and control laggards, which include pro-European Belgium, Luxembourg, but also Bulgaria, Cyprus and Greece. These parliaments have proforma mechanisms of scrutiny and control, but they are rather superficial.

Since 1993 the European Parliament and the national parliaments meet regularly in the Conference of European Affairs Committees (CEAC/French acronym COSAC). They meet twice a year in the countries of the rotating presidency of the Council of Ministers. This is an important opportunity to forge coalitions and compare notes on ongoing legislation. They have also established an interparliamentary information network (IPEX) between the EU and the national parliaments in order to be kept informed of all pending EU legislation. All this is coordinated by the European Parliament. National parliaments also have delegations attached to the European Parliament in order to improve coordination and efficiency in their work in the context of the EU multilevel governance system (European Parliament, 2018; Hefftler and Gattermann, 2016; Neyer, 2014: 134–5).

The emergence of a multi-level European judicial and legal space

The multilevel linkages of the executive and legislative branches have to be complemented by the judicial one. This is still an under-researched area in European politics, because it is traditionally the domain of legal experts. Since 1952 the ECJ has produced a large number of landmark rulings, particularly on the supremacy of EU over national law (see case Costa/ENEL, 1964), and the vertical and horizontal direct effect of EU law which allows individuals and private firms in some provisions to invoke European law before national and European courts (see case Van Gend en Loos, 1963). Over time, the ECJ has expanded its scope to other areas, including Justice and Home Affairs and the European Charter of Fundamental Rights. The space for Freedom, Security and Justice has allowed for a large number of national home affairs policies to become transnational or even supranational. Probably the most innovative element is the establishment of the European Public Prosecutor's Office with a network of national offices, which is due to be operational by 2020 shortly before the new EU budget comes into force (for more see Chapter 6 and later in this chapter).

The resources of the EU and the member-states

There is a general lack of knowledge about the distribution of financial and human resources between the EU and member-states. In reality, the EU spends about 1 per cent of the gross national income (GNI) of the total EU economy that totalled €14.8 trillion in 2016. However, this has been declining since the late 1980s, in spite of enlargement from twelve to twenty-five countries and the expansion of new policy areas. While in multiannual financial framework (MFF) 1993–1999 1.18 per cent of GNI was allocated to the supranational level, in MFF 2014–2020 it had declined to 0.96 per cent. In 2016, the EU spent €155 billion (2 per cent), while the member-states together spent €6.9 trillion (98 per cent) of public expenditure. The member-states spend forty-six times more than the EU supranational level (European Commission, 2018c: 58). Only the federal budget (without the Länder budgets) of Germany in 2016 was more than double that of the EU, at €311 billion (Bundesministerium der Finanzen, 2017). This clearly shows that there is a misallocation of resources, which hinders any attempts by the EU to be a serious global player.

This also applies to the human resources which are quite highly skilled, but still not enough for the growing tasks assigned to the EU at supranational level. In 2015, according to the calculations of Christopher Huggins, the EU comprised 46,356 staff (including all the institutions and agencies). Also according to Huggins, Birmingham City Council had 33,457 staff working for just 1.1 million people. In comparison, Slovenia has about this number of civil servants for a population of slightly over 2.1 million, while Germany with the largest population of 83 million has over 2.8 million civil servants. Overall, all member-states have roughly over 14 million civil servants, which is about 2.4 per cent of the overall population (Spanish Presidency, 2010: 9). In contrast, the EU civil service is roughly 0.01 per cent in relation to the total population of 508 million. All this shows that there is a lack of ambition to make the emerging EU political system stronger at the core. Any increase in the budget would be welcome so that the EU can play a more important role in economic governance, in asylum and migration matters, and certainly in internal security of the European space of freedom, security and justice, and external defence.

Another major problem is the uneven distribution of the funding available to the EU. Taking into account inflation, the EU budget for 2018 increased to €160.1 billion, out of which a staggering 37 per cent was allocated to the Common Agricultural Policy (CAP) for just 3 per cent of the working population. In the late 1980s and in 1993, a doubling of the budget took place under the Delors presidency in 1988 and then again in 1993, which led to the emergence of the territorial, economic and social cohesion fund, which is the main redistributive mechanism of the EU to the poorer regions of the EU, mainly located in Southern, Central and Eastern Europe. In contrast, global Europe gets just 6 per cent (see Figure 10.10). These so-called European Structural and Investment Funds (ESIF) are used for modernisation projects of public infrastructures and enterprises and investment in human resources. For the MFF 2021–2027, the European Commission has overhauled the present structure by reducing the share of the CAP in the budget and moving it to the external and internal security policies of the EU (European Commission, 2018g). However, the ceiling will remain at about 1 per cent of EU GNI (Figure 10.11).

The growing importance of European public policy

As already mentioned, all member-states of the EU are under considerable pressure at the supranational level to implement policies designed to make them more compatible with the emerging European internal market. After the enlargement of the EU it has a market of 508 million citizens (2017). Even after a Brexit, it will comprise 443 million people. The completion of the internal market remains probably the most important task for the EU to achieve. The internal market is based

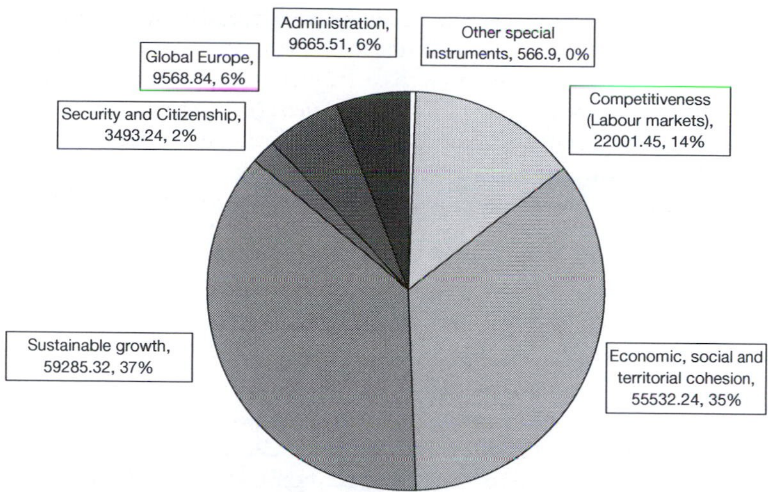

Figure 10.10 Annual budget 2018 in billion € and percentage share of items

Source: European Commission (2018d).

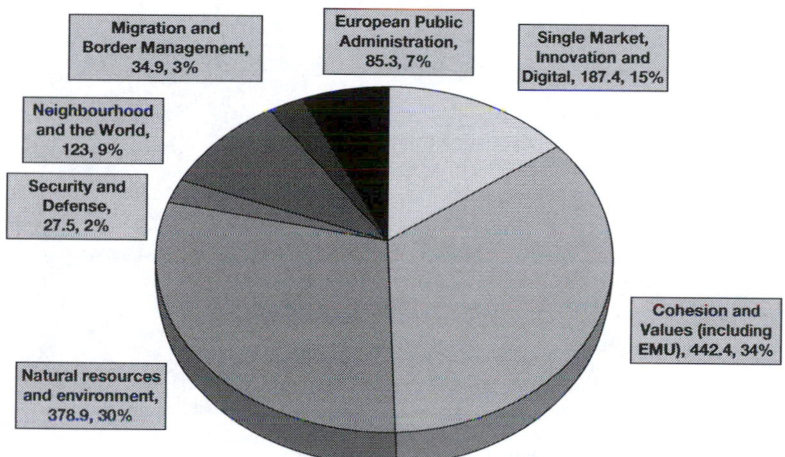

Figure 10.11 Multi-annual financial framework 2021–2027 proposed by the European Commission

Source: European Commission (2018h).

on four main freedoms: freedom of movement, freedom of goods, freedom of capital and freedom of services. Since 1985, all member-states have been engaged in an accelerated process of European integration that has led to the establishment of several policy regimes in order to transform national economies into a large unified market. However, trade barriers, national resistance and the lack of a European internal market culture like in the United States have prevented integration from being more advanced. Reports on the first two decades suggest that the growth of the overall economy has been modest, and the countries closer to the core of the single market, in particular Germany, have profited the most. In Western Europe, Germany, Denmark, Finland and Austria have profited most in terms of increased income for their populations, while Italy, Spain, Portugal, Greece and the UK have had a much lower increase in income (Bertelsmann Stiftung, 2014: 27–29; Egan and Guimarães, 2017; Eich and Vetter, 2013).

We will now briefly delineate some of the key policies that are being Europeanised and restricting the manoeuvrability of member-states and contributing to convergence of policy styles and outcomes: economic and monetary union (EMU), the constraints on welfare states, European cohesion agricultural and environmental policies, and policies related to the refugee crisis. There are three groups of competences of the EU and the member-states. As Figure 10.12 shows, there are some competences that were transferred to the EU, those that are shared with the member-states and those that are exclusive competences of the EU with some input at the European level.

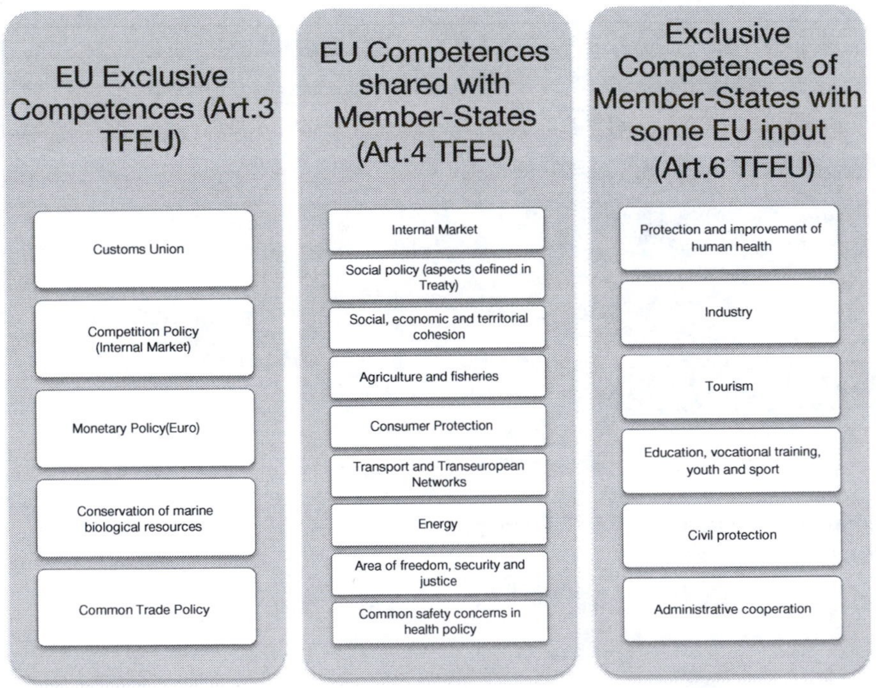

Figure 10.12 Catalogue of competences of the EU and the member-states in the Treaty of Lisbon

Source: Based on article 3–6 of the Treaty of the Functioning of the European Union.

Economic and monetary policy: a core area of European integration

The Treaty of the European Union adopted in 1993 represented the end of a nationally dominated EU and the beginning of a supranational dynamics due to the policies of convergence necessary to implement EMU. Three stages were introduced in order to achieve enough convergence between the economies by 1999, when eleven countries qualified to be part of the project. In 2001, Greece also qualified to become a member of EMU, although there were already questions about the manipulation of the accounting statistics used, following advice from Goldman Sachs who were paid €300 million for their services (Lewis, 2012: 62–3).

One major problem of EMU is that it is based on two quite distinct pillars. On the one hand, a supranational monetary policy pillar with the European Central Bank (ECB) as the main actor providing currency and prices and wages stability by keeping inflation low, and on the other, an intergovernmental pillar of nineteen economic policies of the Eurozone member-states which are monitored by the European Commission and the Eurogroup (a subcommittee of the Council for Economy and Finances – ECOFIN, a formation of the Council of the European Union). Such exercise of surveillance and convergence of policies was to be achieved through two major criteria: Eurozone member-states should keep their yearly public deficit at 3 per cent and public debt at 60 per cent of GDP respectively (the so-called Maastricht criteria). Moreover, each country agreed on a Stability and Growth Pact (SGP) towards economic convergence between member-states with the European Commission (McNamara, 2005: 143–7). Between 1999 and 2012 the mechanism of surveillance was quite lax leading to continuing infringements of the Maastricht criteria and the SGP, including a cartel-like exemption given to Germany and France in 2004, in spite of complaints from smaller states about this fact (see the thorough study by Blavoukos and Pagoulatos, 2008). A study by the well-known quite conservative Leibnitz Institute for Economic Research attached to the University of Munich, states that between 1999 and 2015 member-states infringed 165 times, out of which 114 times (69 per cent) were not allowed. France emerges as the top country with eleven disallowed infringements, followed by Portugal and Greece with ten, Italy eight and Germany five. Outside the Eurozone, the UK emerges as the leader with eight disallowed infringements. However, countries were able to infringe without being fined, when normally a payment of 0.2 to 0.5 per cent of GDP would be due. This clearly shows that politics remains strong and selective in the application of infringement procedures, thereby compromising the seriousness of the exercise (see *Die Presse*, 12 July 2016; for the table of infringements, see CESinfo Munich, 2016).

In spite of this deficiency, EMU was quite successful in its first decade until the US financial crisis spilled over onto the European continent in 2009 and 2010 (for a positive assessment of EMU in its first decade, see Enderlein and Verdun, 2009a and their special issue, 2009b). The global financial crisis was a major threat to the euro. One of the main reasons for the collapse of the fiscal discipline of the member-states was the ad hoc national bailouts for the respective banking sectors that were affected by the toxic assets of US subprime mortgages sold to

European banks. This led to severe consequences for national budgets and an inability to keep to the agreed Maastricht criteria. Therefore, quite a lot of countries had to redraft their SGPs with the European Commission.

During the establishment of EMU, there were already concerns that the Southern European countries would have difficulties in periods of crisis. They would certainly be vulnerable to asymmetrical shocks. The financial crisis in the United States had a spillover effect on Greece and then on other Southern European countries as well as on Ireland.

The Southern, Central and Eastern Europe countries were considerably affected by the crisis, as was Ireland. Southern Europe countries and Ireland had profited immensely from cheap money at low interest rates that were available with the introduction of EMU. However, most of this cheap money was spent on consumption, instead of investment in the production sector. This led to highly indebted households, and in some countries, governments. The global financial crisis just exacerbated this. Greece, Ireland, Italy, Portugal, Cyprus and Spain were affected by a severe sovereign debt crisis as a consequence. This was due to the distrust of the markets of the economies in these countries, which, as a consequence, led to the drying up of funding due to the increase in the yields of national sovereign bonds. Quite an important role in influencing the markets were the three US rating agencies Moody's, Fitch, and Standard and Poor's, which entered into a competition for downgrading the sovereign bonds of these countries. In the markets, these countries became known as the PIIGS (Portugal, Ireland, Italy, Greece and Spain), albeit Cyprus was not included (Armingeon and Baccaro, 2012a, 2012b; Duman, 2017; Jessop, 2014).

While the problems of Ireland, Portugal, Cyprus, Italy and Spain were related to the banking sector and the bailouts, Greece was also a case of statistical accounting fraud which had degenerated over the years to create a large hole in public finances. It was the first country to ask for support from the EU, although in the Treaty of Lisbon it is enshrined that no bailout shall be given to Eurozone member-states in order to avoid a precedent leading to a transfer union of funds from the richer to the poorer countries (the so-called bailout clause, article 125). However, the situation in Greece was so dire during 2010 that the Franco-German partnership, personified by German chancellor Angela Merkel and French president Nicolás Sarkozy, so-called 'Merkozy', developed an intergovernmental compromise solution outside the treaties that appealed to the solidarity between Eurozone countries. Greece would receive a bailout of €110 billion in 2010, but in return it had to implement a very strict austerity programme to reform the country. However, political and administrative inertia and the very high public debt led to two further bailouts of €130 billion and €86 billion in 2012 and 2015 respectively. Greece only completed the bailout programme in 2018, after almost a decade of austerity measures monitored by regular visits by a team consisting of the European Commission, the ECB and the IMF, the so-called Troika. After 2015, the new European Stability Mechanism (ESM) was added to the monitoring team, it became known as the 'Quadriga' (on the discussion in the German Bundestag, see Hennessy, 2017; Schwarzer, 2014; Wonka, 2016; on the Greek bailouts, see Lim et al., 2018; Visvizi, 2014, 2016). The contagion of the Greek sovereign debt crisis also led to similar bailouts in Ireland (€67.5 billion, 2010–13), Portugal (€78 billion, 2011–14), Cyprus (€10 billion, 2013–15) as well as a softer one for Spain

(2012) which was used just for the ailing banking sector (*CNBC*, 10 March 2016; Connaughton, 2016; Kruse, 2016; Magone 2014c, 2016b; Wheelan, 2013). All this led to the creation of a permanent bailout fund in October 2012, the ESM, comprising €700 billion and mainly consisting of guarantees (*BBC News*, 7 July 2015; Pisani-Ferry et al., 2013). While in 2017 Portugal, Cyprus and Spain had a public debt of 125.7, 98.0 and 99.0 per cent of GDP respectively, Ireland had decreased its levels from 119.4 per cent at the end of the programme in 2014 to 68 per cent by the end of 2017. An amazing achievement and only possible by keeping continuing fiscal discipline and a firm debt payment policy until the programme ends. It means that Ireland is almost achieving the Maastricht criteria and is creating more space for policy-making (Eurostat, 2018b). Ireland had paid back the share of the IMF loan in the bailout by the end of 2017, but still owed €45.4 billion to its European partners, including the UK (*Irish Times*, 21 December 2017).

After the PIIGS, it was only Italy that escaped any bailout interference, however, leading to the introduction of a Monti technocratic government with very strict austerity measures in 2012–13. Even today, the ailing banking sector remains a major problem for Italy, but also for the Eurozone due to the size of Italy's economy (Brunazzo and Della Sala, 2016; Bull, 2018; Culpepper, 2014).

The original 'Merkozy' intergovernmental ad hoc solution developed a dynamics of its own afterwards. The contagion effects of the Greek case led to a positive spillover effect on economic and monetary governance in which transformative leadership played a role. The economic governance pillar was tightened even further with a stronger surveillance of national budgets through a new open coordination mechanism, the so-called European semester. Prevention and correction mechanisms were devised to prevent any systemic crisis across the EU. This means that the EU has the right to see the drafts of national budgets to check on their sustainability before they are approved by national parliaments. This clearly demonstrates a major problem of democratic accountability. The big winner of this move towards a streamlining of economic governance was the European Commission (Bressanelli and Chelotti, 2016; Verdun, 2013; Verdun and Zeitlin, 2017). In addition, an intergovernmental Treaty on Stability, Coordination and Governance in the Economic and Monetary Union (TSCG), also known as the Fiscal Compact, was signed on 2 March 2012 which obliges all countries of the Eurozone to include a limit on the debt level in their constitutions or crucial budgetary documents (the so-called 'debt brake'). Only the UK and the Czech Republic refused to sign the agreement as they were not intending to join the Eurozone (Schweiger, 2014: 76–8).

The monetary policy pillar was better equipped to deal with the crisis, because the ECB was an independent institution and had two excellent successive presidents during the crisis which complemented the efforts of the European Commission and the Eurogroup in the economic pillar.

The two presidents of the ECB during the crisis, the French Jean-Claude Trichet (2003–11) and Mario Draghi (since 2011; also known as 'Super-Mario') were key players in navigating EMU through the difficult global financial crisis. In particular, the leadership of Mario Draghi led to the introduction of a repertoire of new instruments such as political communication, the outright monetary transactions of 2012 (buying sovereign bonds of crisis countries), and quantitative easing (buying sovereign bonds across the EU to push up inflation to 2 per cent) in 2015 (see Verdun, 2017). His speech on 26 July 2012 became famous, in which he asserted:

> Within our mandate, the ECB is ready to do whatever it takes to preserve the euro. And believe me, it will be enough.
>
> (Draghi, 2012)

This proactive approach against the speculation of international markets contributed considerably to the improvement of the economic situation in the Eurozone.

The next MFF 2021–2027 has prioritised the strengthening of economic governance among other areas. A Franco-German agreement will allow for a modest separate budget for economic governance and the transformation of the ESM into a proper European Monetary Fund (EMF). These new institutions and rules will probably all be integrated into a future review of the Lisbon Treaty. Overall support for the euro in Eurozone countries and other countries in the EU is quite high (see Figure 10.13).

Overall, the crisis has rather strengthened the euro. This solidarity test was based on trial and error, and certainly lessons were learned from the ill design of the troika. Globally, the euro has become a strong alternative to the dollar, even if it lost ground during the global financial crisis. In early July 2018, 61.24 per cent of allocated reserves in foreign currencies were in US dollars, 20.15 per cent in euros (2009: 28 per cent), the pound sterling 4.68 per cent, Japanese yen 4.81 per cent, and the Chinese yuan 1.39 per cent (*Reuters*, 1 July 2018).

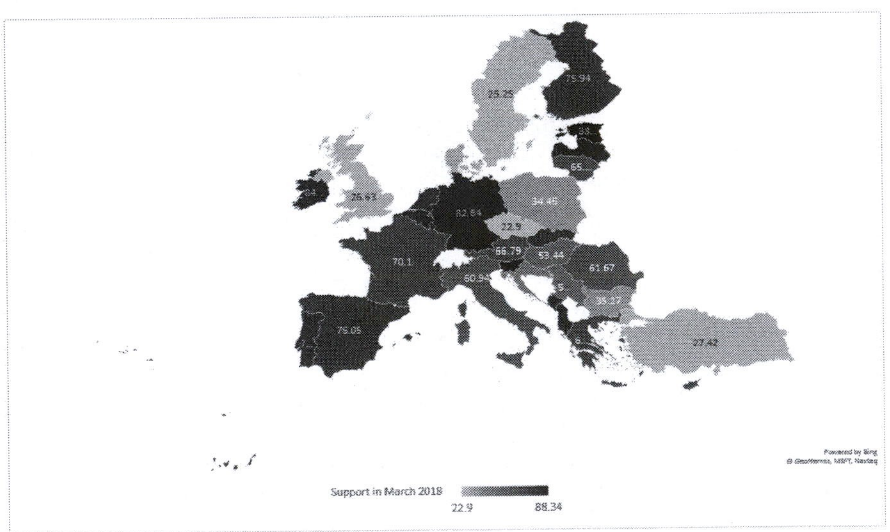

Figure 10.13 Support for the single European currency in percentage, March 2018

Source: Eurobarometer (2018).

From welfare to workfare states: the growing importance of flexicurity

According to Gösta Esping Andersen, three worlds of welfare capitalism existed at the end of the 1970s: the Nordic/social democratic, the continental/conservative and the Anglo-Saxon welfare states. The Nordic/social democratic model is financed through universal taxation and is quite generous in terms of benefits. The working population offers its labour as commodity in the market. According to him, the weaker the welfare state, the higher will be the commodification of labour level in a particular country. The stronger the welfare state, the lower will be the commodification of labour. It means that the Nordic model has the highest level of decommodification. The conservative Bismarckian welfare model, common in Germany, the Benelux, Austria and France is funded by shared contributions of employers and employees and also offers a high level of decommodification to people. However, the role of the state in filling the shortfall in funding has become a permanent feature of the system. The Anglo-Saxon model provides more of a basic welfare state like in the United States, but is more generous in other countries such as the UK. It is funded mainly through universal taxation. In the past decades, further hybrid models were added, namely the Southern European and the Central and Eastern European models in the 1970s and 1990s respectively. The former is a rather hybrid system between conservative and Anglo-Saxon, and the latter strongly influenced by the liberal Anglo-Saxon model. The Southern European model is characterised by a quite late development, with the exception maybe of Italy, while the Central and Eastern European model had to deal with the transition from a communist unsustainable welfare state to a market-oriented one creating a high level of inequalities, particularly in the Baltic states, Romania and Bulgaria (Esping-Andersen, 1990; Ferrera, 2008; Hemerijk, 2013, 2018).

Until the late 1970s, welfare states were designed to redistribute the accumulated wealth of the country, so that low-income social groups were able to improve their quality of life and also their life chances, particularly for the subsequent generation. Generous benefits for family, housing, education and social policy contributed to a more egalitarian society. Such redistributive policies were reasonably generous in the Nordic countries, continental Europe and the UK, but less so in Southern Europe. This became known as the glorious thirty years (trentes glorieuses, 1945–75). Such strong welfare states were concentrated in all democratic Western European countries and were funded by a booming post-war economy (for a history of welfare states, see Kaelble, 2007).

However, in the mid-1970s and 1980s, the European economy began to stagnate and welfare state costs became a heavy burden on national budgets. Since then, European national governments have been engaged in restructuring their generous welfare states, particularly in Western Europe (Scharpf, 2000; Schmidt, 2008).

Since 2000, this goal has been more strongly embedded in a wider Lisbon (2000–2010) and presently Europe 2020 strategy (2010–2020). This so-called strategisation of the future of the EU intends to make Europe more competitive in relation to the United States, Japan and China. The Europe 2020 strategy has three pillars, namely smart growth (innovation in research and development), sustainable growth (reconciliation of economic growth with the environment by investing in renewable energy sources) and inclusive growth (by expanding employment to 75 per cent of the population and reducing poverty) (Eurostat, 2017: 27, 57, 109, 132).

In this context, member-states have been engaged in restructuring their welfare states by linking them to an increase in people integrated into the labour market. The main paradigm shift is from welfare to workfare state policies. In the EU, the common concept is called flexicurity, meaning flexible labour markets combined with generous welfare states and labour market activation policies. The latter requires employment agencies to ensure the employability of people who may become unemployed. It follows the Danish model which is also common in most Nordic countries (Antoniades, 2008; Bekker, 2018; Tsarouhas and Ladi, 2013; Zeitlin, 2017). One of the reasons for such a paradigm shift is that the European population is decreasing. While in 2015, the EU represented 6 per cent of the world's population, it will shrink to 4 per cent and become much older in 2060, while in other continents, particularly in Africa and Asia, the population will continue to grow at a considerably higher rate (European Commission, 2017f: 8). It means that fewer and fewer people will contribute to welfare and pension systems, making the European social model unsustainable. A generous but legal immigration policy is one solution to the problem; another is that people have to work longer (Hay and Wincott, 2012; Hemerijck, 2013, 2018).

Probably the greatest problem is that the quality of welfare states is quite asymmetrical across the EU, both in terms of social benefits and inequality levels. One can find major differences between the Nordic and conservative welfare states with rather generous social benefits systems and low inequality levels, the Anglo-Saxon system with still high social benefits but high levels of inequality, and then the Southern, Central and Eastern European countries with low social benefits systems and high inequality, the big exceptions being the Czech Republic and Slovenia (Figures 10.14, 10.15 and 10.16).

European regional policy: the impact of the Structural and Investments Fund

As already mentioned, the EU lacks, like in any federal system, mechanisms of interterritorial compensation. However, since the 1970s, attempts have been made to provide some funds for development projects. For a long time, the only redistribution mechanism was the CAP in the agricultural sector. After enlargement to include Greece, Portugal and Spain in the 1980s, some mechanism of interterritorial compensation was developed which now is an important part of the small budget of the EU. As Figure 10.10 shows, about €55 billion (35 per cent of the budget) is allocated annually to structural and investment programmes developed in the member-states. This funding has been allocated mainly to the less-developed regions of Southern, Central and Eastern Europe. There have been five multi-annual programmes (1989–1993; 1994–1999; 2000–2006; 2007–2013; 2014–2020). Most funding is invested in modernising infrastructures, upgrading human resources and supporting innovation of enterprises.

Meanwhile, there have been three decades of cohesion policy and a considerable amount of policy learning by the European Commission and the

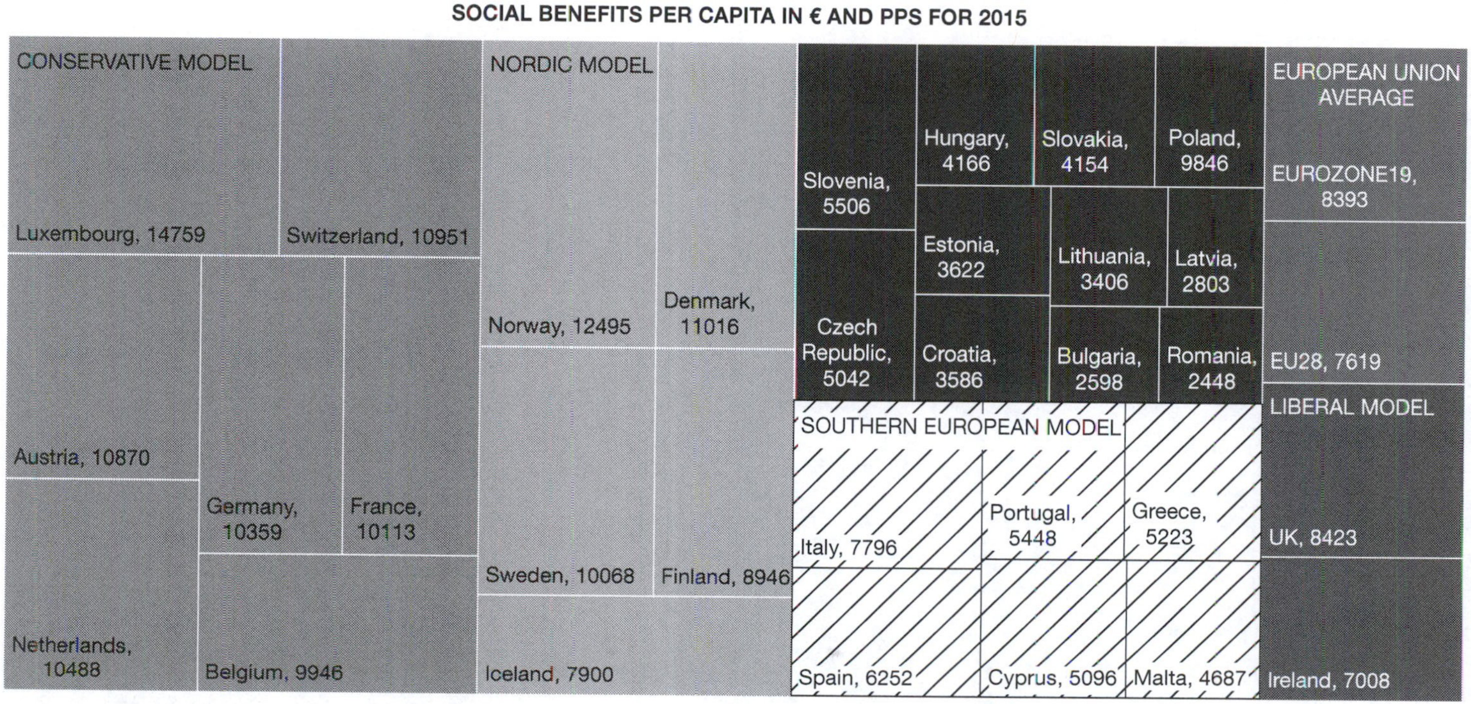

SOCIAL BENEFITS PER CAPITA IN € AND PPS FOR 2015

CONSERVATIVE MODEL
Luxembourg, 14759
Switzerland, 10951
Austria, 10870
Germany, 10359
France, 10113
Netherlands, 10488
Belgium, 9946

NORDIC MODEL
Norway, 12495
Denmark, 11016
Sweden, 10068
Finland, 8946
Iceland, 7900

Slovenia, 5506
Hungary, 4166
Slovakia, 4154
Poland, 9846
Estonia, 3622
Lithuania, 3406
Latvia, 2803
Czech Republic, 5042
Croatia, 3586
Bulgaria, 2598
Romania, 2448

SOUTHERN EUROPEAN MODEL
Italy, 7796
Portugal, 5448
Greece, 5223
Spain, 6252
Cyprus, 5096
Malta, 4687

EUROPEAN UNION AVERAGE
EUROZONE19, 8393
EU28, 7619

LIBERAL MODEL
UK, 8423
Ireland, 7008

Figure 10.14 Social expenditure in the member-states of the EU according to regions (in euros, in power purchasing standard (PPS))

Source: Author's own graph based on Eurostat (2018c).

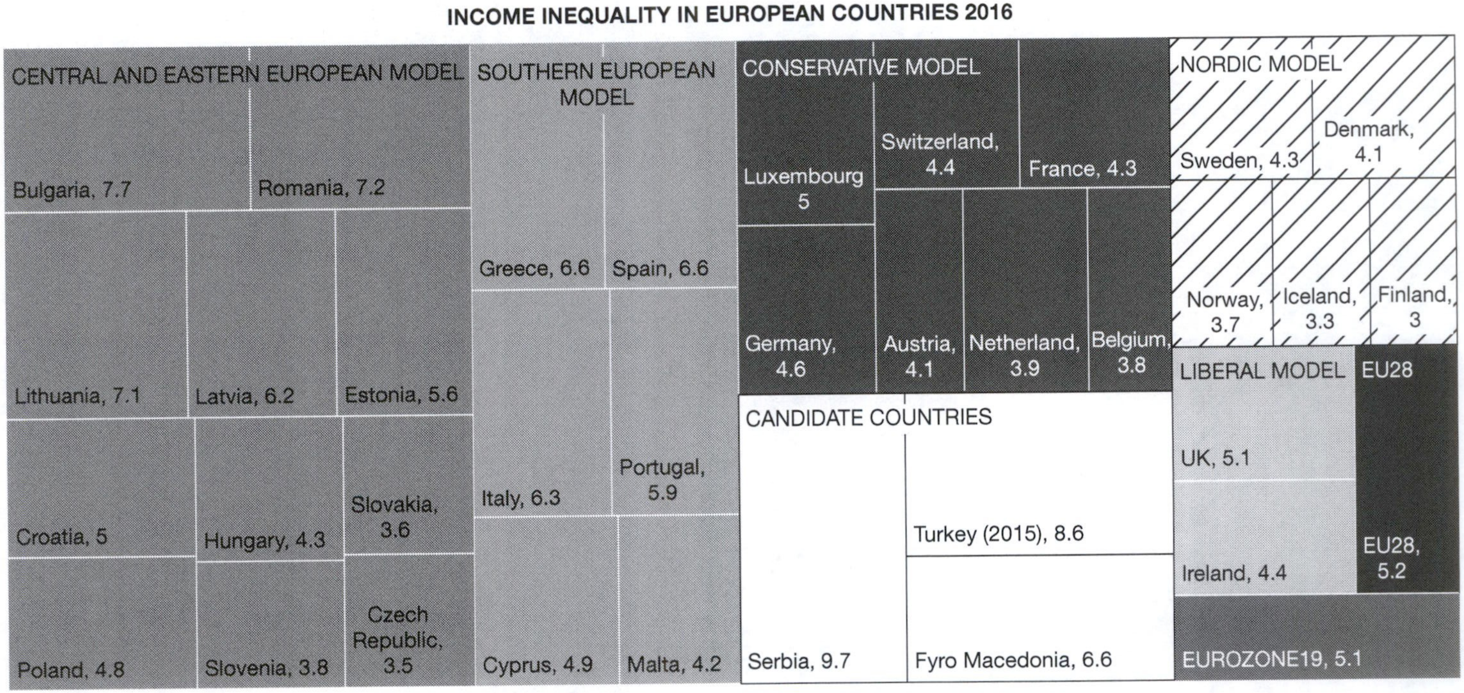

Figure 10.15 Income inequality in member-states of the EU

Source: Author's own graph based on Eurostat (2018d).

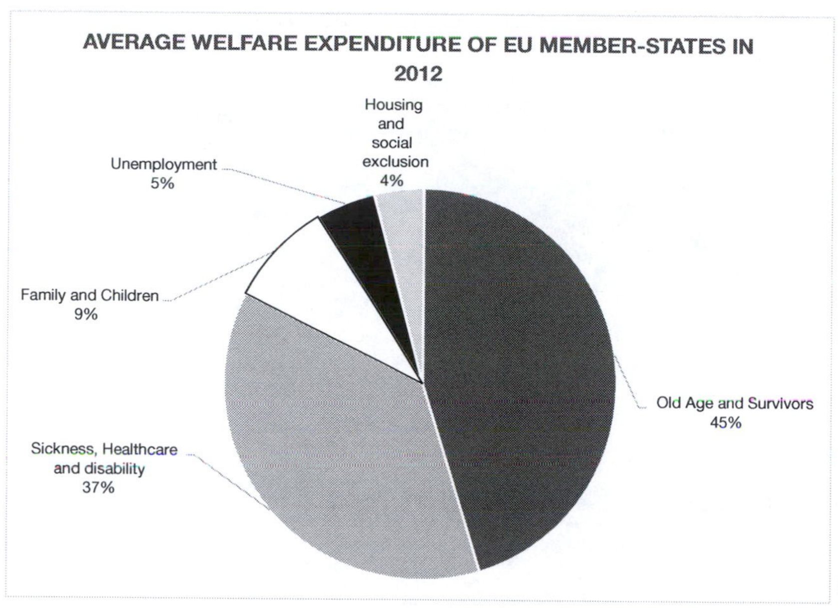

Figure 10.16 The structure of social protection expenditure in the EU-25, 2012

Source: Author's own graph based on European Union (2016).

member-states. While in the beginning large infrastructure projects were quite common, particularly in Southern Europe, there has been a paradigm shift of investment to the productive sector, particularly private enterprises and human resources. In the fifth common support framework 2014–2020, there are just three main categories of regions: less-developed regions (with GDP per capita below 75 per cent of EU average) with an allocation of 51 per cent of the €352 billion for the period; transition regions (with GDP per cent between 75 and 90 per cent) with an allocation of 10.5 per cent; and more developed regions (with GDP above 90 per cent) with 16 per cent of the budget. The rest of the funding is split among other programmes such as the Cohesion Fund (18 per cent) for large infrastructure projects, transnational and cross-border European Territorial Cooperation programmes (2.6 per cent), the Youth Employment Initiative (YEI) set up during the crisis to combat youth unemployment (2.5 per cent), and Outermost or Sparsely Populated Northern populations (0.5 per cent). The vast bulk of funding goes to Poland (25 per cent), Italy (9 per cent), Spain (8 per cent), Czech Republic (7 per cent), Romania (7 per cent), Hungary (7 per cent), Portugal (5 per cent) and Greece (5 per cent), meaning that eight out of twenty-eight countries receive 73 per cent of the funding, and all of them at the southern, central and eastern peripheries of the EU (European Commission, 2018g).

The structural policies are negotiated between the national government and the European Commission, and a common support framework is agreed between the specific national governments. However, European cohesion policy is now linked to the Europe 2020 strategy, so that most indicators are geared to finding

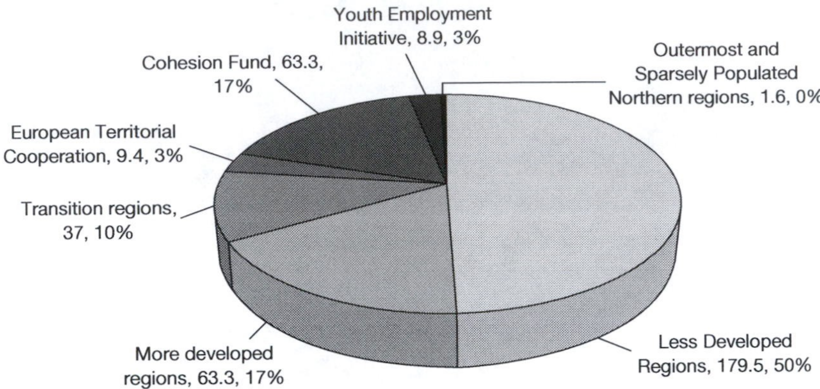

Figure 10.17 Indicative allocation of structural funds, 2014–20 by item

Source: European Commission (2018g).

out if the investment is leading to more competitive economies. Furthermore, the rule of law criteria, particularly in view of challenges by conservative Hungarian and Polish governments, will become an important criteria for discussion in the future, particularly in the context of MFF 2021–2027 negotiations. So far the Central and Eastern countries have protested vehemently about the rule of law conditionality (*EU Observer*, 30 April 2018; *Financial Times*, 19 February 2018; Figure 10.17).

The greening of the Common Agricultural Policy (CAP)

Clearly, the most important item in the EU remains the CAP for agriculture, spending in 2018 37.03 per cent of the total €160 billion budget for just 3 per cent of the working population (European Commission, 2018d). This clearly is a legacy of the past, when food security was an important issue after the war. However, European agriculture has become highly efficient and is regularly over-producing for the market. Therefore, the EU has been reforming the CAP over time. Environmental aspects have become more important in allocating funding to farmers, so that farmers may receive direct payments for not cultivating and taking care of the rural landscape. Also investment in rural tourism facilities has become a way of changing the economy of the rural areas. In view of global competition, European farmers are still highly subsidised and protected by the CAP, which clearly raises questions about global justice in free trade in the agricultural sector. Most of the funding is still spent in direct payments to farmers (Roederer-Rynning, 2014: 211–18).

Environmental policy: a crucial piece of the European model of capitalism

Although incidental environmental policy-making existed before the adoption of the Single European Act in 1987, of which the car emissions directive of the early 1980s was regarded as a milestone, only since then has environmental policy been an integrated part of all other policies.

The number of directives, decisions and regulations on the environment have increased considerably since the late 1980s. While in the 1960s and 1970s there were mainly one or two pieces of EC/EU legislation per year on the environment, this increased to over twenty in the 1980s, over forty in the 1990s and over eighty between 2000 and 2004 (Lenschow, 2005: 308; 2014).

Since the 1990s, the EU has been able to play an important role in pushing for cooperation in environmental policy by being proactive in the Rio de Janeiro UN environment conference in 1992, and signing up to the UN Convention on Climate Change (Kyoto Protocol) in 1998. Lately, after more than a decade of negotiations, a new major worldwide Climate Change Agreement was adopted by the United Nations conference in Paris in November 2015.

As already mentioned, the Europe 2020 strategy has set three main targets, namely that greenhouse emissions shall be lowered by 20 per cent in comparison to 1990s levels, 20 per cent of energy shall come from renewables and there shall be a 20 per cent increase in energy efficiency. In 2015, according to figures from the EU, in comparison to 1990 greenhouse emissions fell by 22.1 per cent, 16.7 per cent of energy came from renewables, and energy efficiency is on target, but still with problems in primary energy consumption (European Commission, 2017: 99). Although the EU is a global leader in environmental policy initiatives, there are still major differences between the regions and countries of this regional supranational organisation. The highest standards of environmental policy are kept in the Nordic countries, the UK, the Benelux countries, France, Germany, Switzerland and Austria. Lower standards can be found in Southern, Central and Eastern Europe. Ronald Inglehart, influenced by Abraham Maslow's pyramid of hierarchy of needs, identified a new younger generation that has post-materialist values which entail a more sustainable environmental, social friendly way of life and emphasising post-industrial 'self-expressive' values. This contrasts to the older generations of materialists that still are ideologically framed by an exponential growth model of consumption and 'survival' values (Inglehart, 1977; Inglehart and Welzel, 2005). Based on Eurobarometer data of 2008 (I could not find any more recent survey), we may find more post-materialists in the Nordic countries, the Benelux, Austria, Switzerland, Germany, France and the UK and less so in Southern, Central and Eastern Europe (Eurobarometer, 2008: 69; Figure 10.18).

Justice and home affairs: the impact of the refugee crisis in the summer of 2015

Until 2015, the EU had an internal market without borders between the member-states, but neglected to establish procedures to control its external borders. This

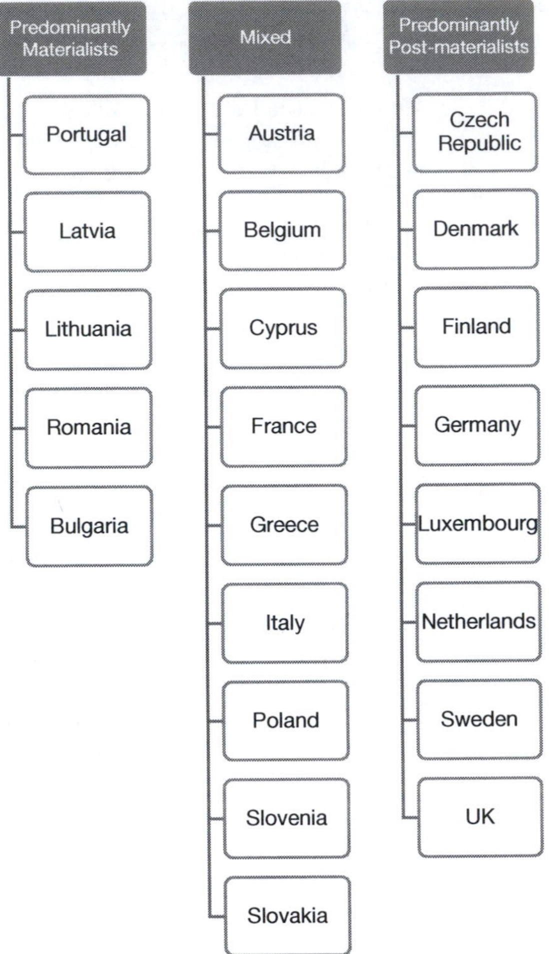

Figure 10.18 Mapping materialists and post-materialists in the EU member-states, 2008

Source: Own typology based on data from Eurobarometer (2008: 69).

was a fatal mistake which led to the refugee crisis. The European integration process is work in progress and it takes quite a while for member-states to recognise problems within it. This was the case in economic governance, and it is also now in the way the EU manages its borders and the refugee crisis.

The refugee crisis of the summer of 2015 put the still incipient protection of the external borders of the EU in the spotlight. The Syrian civil war led to an exponential growth in the number of refugees coming to Europe by crossing the Mediterranean. Large numbers of them were helped by criminal people smuggler gangs. This has now become a mass phenomenon, so that the southern borders of the EU are faced with a management crisis.

In 2015, the peak year, 972,500 refugees crossed the Mediterranean Sea, 80 per cent mainly through Turkey and then to the Greek islands. About 50 per cent were Syrians, 20 per cent Afghans and 7 per cent Iraqis (UNCHR, 2015). About 3,670 people tragically died at sea (IOM, 2018). Numbers have been coming down since then. While in 2016, 362,753 still crossed the Mediterranean, in 2017 it decreased to 172,371. By the end of October 2018, the figures were at 97,857, much lower than in the previous years (IOM, 2018).

This was possible after an agreement between the EU and Turkey to prevent refugees coming to Greece, and simultaneously, most Balkan countries and Hungary closed their borders to prevent refugees coming to Northern Europe. Turkey is paid about €3 billion a year to honour this deal (*Euractiv*, 5 January 2017, 4 April 2016). The new main route has become the Libya-Italy one, which is even more dangerous than coming through Greece and the Balkans. Desperate appeals of successive Italian governments to get a European solution to the refugee problem were either ignored or just followed up with good intentions, without concrete actions. The situation is even more complex, because quite a number of NGOs have rescue ships (such as the Aquarius belonging to NGO SOS Mediterranée or Lifeline) located in international waters between Libya and Italy, and actively save many refugees from drowning (*CNN*, 26 June 2018, 4 July 2018). In June 2018, the new coalition government between the Northern League and the Five Stars Movement under prime minister Giuseppe Conte decided not to allow rescue ships to anchor in Italian ports, and the same happened in Malta. Rescue ships like the German Lifeline were confiscated and charges brought against the captain and the crew, as aiding the people smugglers. Prime minister Conti proposed an agency to coordinate migrant arrivals. Interior minister Matteo Salvini has been quite active in blocking migrant arrivals in Italy (*Euractiv*, 4 June 2018, 20 July 2018, 24 July 2018). Therefore, refugees are trying to come to Europe through other routes, namely to Spain (*Euractiv*, 31 July 2018).

The original idea of distributing asylum seekers across the EU was abandoned due to the quite considerable resistance of the Visegrad group (Czech Republic, Slovakia, Hungary and Poland); however, an alternative is still to be found. A new compensation mechanism was proposed which entails that countries that do not accept refugees have to pay a solidarity fee for each refugee they have rejected. Apparently, the proposal was for a figure of €250,000. I think this is a recipe for further conflict. Probably a compromise on a lower sum may be found (European Commission, 2018i).

All these issues belong to the Area of Freedom, Security and Justice (AFSJ), which deals with all internal freedoms, security and legal aspects of the internal market. This is work in progress and therefore any thrusts for further integration depend on external pressures such as the refugee crisis.

The origins of the AFSJ go back to the 1970s as networks of national officials began to cooperate in different aspects related to internal security and judiciary matters. The best example is the Trevi group in 1975 that was created to coordinate better the fight against terrorism. The next milestone was the Schengen agreement of 1985 which included France, Germany and the Benelux. However, this was only implemented in 1990 and came into being only in 1995. The internal market programme was a major catalyst for the establishment of the Schengen Area. Compensatory measures had to be established to ensure internal security. Therefore, the Dublin Convention I (1997), II (2003) and III (2013) were established to control asylum applications across the EU. The Treaty of Maastricht ratified in 1993 introduced a third pillar of home and justice affairs. The Schengen agreement still remained outside. Through a system of differentiated integration as happened for EMU, the Schengen Agreement became part of the Treaty of Amsterdam. The UK, Ireland and Denmark were able to negotiate opt-outs. While the UK and Ireland are not part of a Schengen Area, they cooperate in some judicial and police cooperation areas. Denmark participates in Schengen, but mainly through an international law agreement. In spite of these differences, the inclusion of the Schengen agreement has to be regarded as a milestone towards more European integration. A continuing incrementalism of policies has also improved the acquis in this area. Ambitious plans like in the Tampere Council in 1999, The Hague and Stockholm programmes of 2005 and 2010 further reinforced this AFSJ area. The Nice and Lisbon Treaty consolidated this part of the treaties (Leuffen et al. 2013: 222–9). Many policy areas were transferred from the third to the first pillar (EC Pillar) becoming then supranational policies. In spite of this permanent incrementalism of policies, the area was always under-resourced until 2015. Since then it has been increasing fairly quickly. In 2018, the budget for AFSJ increased to €3.5 billion, which looks like a considerable amount, but in the context of the EU budget is just 2.2 per cent of €160 billion (European Commission, 2018i).

The AFSJ is a quite complex area because it includes both supranational as well as intergovernmental/transgovernmental policies. The development of these policies is quite uneven and clearly dominated by the necessity to achieve more efficiency in transnational cooperation. The most developed areas are those that interface with the external world, while internal policies are still in the making. Such external policies are related to border management such as visa, asylum and migration policies. The internal policies are more related to police cooperation and judicial cooperation in civilian and criminal matters. Police cooperation and judicial cooperation in criminal matters are the less integrated areas (Lavenex, 2015: 370–3). The refugee crisis triggered thrusts towards more efficiency of the existing instruments. Databases like the Visa Information System (VIS), the Schengen Information System (SIS) and Eurodac became more integrated and are now operated by one single agency, the European Union Agency for the Operational of Large-Scale IT Systems in the Area of Freedom, Security and Justice (EU-LISA), which has existed since 2012 (EU-LISA, 2016). A common European asylum system (CEAS) was adopted in the Tampere Council of the European Union of 1999, but member-states, particularly in Central Europe had difficulties dealing with the ongoing supranationalisation of asylum policies leading to major conflicts with its Western partners, particularly Germany and Luxembourg (*Euractiv*, 13 July 2016). Meanwhile, any decision on a reform of the CEAS has been postponed. On 28–9 June 2018, the reform proposal of the European Commission was discussed at the European Council and included control centres outside Europe and voluntary regional disembarkation centres for refugees rescued at sea. Moreover, a review of Dublin III (so-called Dublin IV) was also discussed (*Euractiv*, 2018).

Parallel to this the European Commission is developing a European migration policy by trying to create partnerships with third countries. This so-called partnership framework is a major acknowledgment that the EU will continue to be a target for migration waves and it needs to create order and structure in these processes. It is a double strategy of reducing the causes for migration in third countries, and providing an orderly legal migration to Europe from these countries. The European Commission wants to raise up to €62 billion in order to invest in third countries. Africa is a particularly targeted continent in this respect. All this will be more and more combined with the external policies of the EU. There will be a process of synergy focusing on the European interests.

The most important agencies in the AFSJ are Frontex-European Border and Coast Guard which has dealt with border management since 2004. It must always rely on member-states to conduct some parts of the policies, like return flights. The staff of Frontex have been upgraded and comprise a pool of 1,500 people. More funding will be available to acquire material resources (probably vessels). Europol, founded in 1998, is just a coordinating structure, far from being a kind of 'European police'. Cepol is the European police school training national staff and has existed since 2000. As already mentioned, EU-LISA has managed the coordination and harmonisation of databases since 2012. The European Asylum Support Office (EASO) is being upgraded to perform more efficiently in the revised CEAS. This has been so far a dormant agency, but now it has acquired an important role maintaining standards of protection for asylum seekers across the EU (European Commission, 2018i).

Conclusions: the intertwinedness of the EU multilevel governance system

The EU has become a political system. This means that supranational and national levels are intrinsically linked. The EU multilevel governance system is a myriad of intertwined downloading and uploading processes that have become systemic over time.

National political systems are embedded in the EU multilevel governance system. This creates greater complexity and also a quest for better coordination of governmental and parliamentary work at different levels. European political systems are undergoing such a transition today.

Suggested reading

Börzel, Tanja (2005), Europeanization: How the European Union interacts with the member-states. In: Simon Bulmer and Christian Lequesne (eds), *The Member-States of the European Union*. Oxford: Oxford University Press, pp. 45–69.

Hix, Simon and Bjørn Høyland (2011), *The Political System of the European Union*, third edition. Basingstoke: Palgrave.

Ladrech, Robert (2010), *The Europeanization of National Politics*. Basingstoke: Palgrave.

QUESTIONS FOR REVISION

- Define the concept of 'Europeanisation' and give examples from different European countries.
- What is the role of the Council of the European Union in the EU political system?
- Discuss the role of national parliaments in the EU multilevel governance system.
- How much autonomy have member-states in relation to the supranational institutions of the EU?
- How democratic is the EU?

Chapter 11

The political systems of the wider Europe

Russia, Turkey, Ukraine, Moldova, Belarus and Georgia

- The wider European common house and geopolitics
- Neo-patrimonialism, political corruption and façade democracies
- Russia: the re-emergence of a superpower
- The limits of export of the Russian model: 'managed democracy' in Ukraine, Georgia and Moldova
- Belarus: the last dictatorship of Europe
- Turkey: between democracy and dictatorship
- The eastern partnership of the EU: the need for a recalibration
- Conclusions: the struggle for democracy, rule of law and economic prosperity in wider Europe
- Suggested reading

The wider European common house and geopolitics

After giving a quite thorough overview of the political systems of core Europe in comparative perspective it is important to look at the wider Europe countries. These are countries on the periphery of core Europe, that culturally and geo-strategically have played just a marginal, but still important role in European history. In this context, we include Russia, Ukraine, Belarus, Moldova and Turkey. Even farther way, one could add Georgia and even Armenia as part of wider Europe, although this is certainly overstretching what is commonly understood as Europe.

We focus here primarily on the domestic problems of the neo-patrimonial defective democracies of these countries of wider Europe. In spite of this, it is important to mention the present context of an overarching conflict between the United States and Russia, a kind of new Cold War with its new arms race. Many attempts by the EU to further its influence in terms of a peace project is sometimes in contradiction with US interests in the Eurasian world island, a major strategic concept going back to British geostrategist Harold Mackinder. Post-soviet states are therefore divided in terms of their allegiance either to the EU/United States or Russia, complicating even further their route towards sustainable democracies. Unfortunately, geopolitics still plays an important role in calculations in foreign policy establishments in the United States and Russia (Brzezinski, 1997: 46–7; Hahn, 2018: 46–65; Mackinder, 1919). However, in the twenty-first century this has become the obsolete thinking of the past. More difficult, but interesting is to build something new, such as the proposal on the Common European House of former Soviet leader Michail Gorbachev (Gorbachev, 1989). This would imply a collective security architecture based on the resources of the Organisation for Cooperation and Security in Europe (OSCE) in a multipolar global governance context. Such an approach would make NATO obsolete over time, particularly if the EU were able to create its own army for defence and peace-keeping and building. This could be established alongside a major trading relationship between the EU and the Eurasian Economic Union. The side effects of this partnership would probably have a positive spillover effect on democracy and the rule of law in post-Soviet states. For this to happen, we need bold leaders in the EU, Russia and certainly also in the United States.

In the following pages we will concentrate therefore mainly on the domestic political systems of this Western Eurasian core area. We will also discuss Turkey and the problems of the Eastern partnership of the EU.

Neo-patrimonialism, political corruption and façade democracies

All countries of the post-Soviet space are characterised by neo-patrimonialism, political corruption and façade democracies. For our purposes, the countries we are interested in here are Russia, Ukraine, Georgia, Moldova and Belarus.

Neo-patrimonialism means that many elites from the post-Soviet states were able to capture strategic positions inside the state in these countries after the collapse of the Soviet Union at the end of 1991. In particular, the state economic enterprises were captured by oligarchs close to the parties of power. Politicians are strongly connected to these oligarchs, so that a takeover of the state has been sustained until now (for Russia, see Harding, 2011). The origins of the concept go back to Max Weber who referred to patrimonialism as the form of government in the early modern period up until the French and industrial revolutions, being then slowly replaced by a legal-bureaucratic neutral government and administration (Weber, 1968: chapter XIII). Neo-patrimonialism can be considered a form of rule during transitions from a pre-modern capitalist or even modern planning economy to a modern liberal market economy and democracy. It clearly is a mixed system with pre-modern and modern features. This neo-patrimonial rule is rather non-transparent and non-accountable, leading therefore to considerable political corruption in these countries. It is the use and abuse of public resources by ruling elites for their own strategies to remain in power, including corrupt networks of patronage and clientelism. The longer neo-patrimonial elites stay in power, the higher the level of systemic corruption leading to kleptocratic forms of behaviour. The neo-patrimonial state has established legal-bureaucratic structures, a judiciary and a more or less functioning market economy. However, ruling elites use these structures to advance their personal interests or in order to retain power. In the worst case scenario, one can speak of state capture by powerful business oligarchs and criminal bosses who are intertwined with the political elite, obscuring lines of separation between, on the one hand, legal and on the other, informal and criminal procedures. State capacity is hindered by these networks of systemic corruption. Neo-patrimonialism can be found in many countries in Africa, Asia, Latin America and in the post-Soviet states (Bach, 2011: 286–9; Kelsall, 2012; Robinson, 2017: 349–53).

One of the reasons for the emergence of a neo-patrimonial rule in the post-Soviet states and also in the Central and Eastern European countries, was the very difficult triple transition from a one-party communist system to liberal democracy. The triple transition was a political transition from a communist dictatorship to liberal democracy, an economic transition from a planning economy to a liberal market economy, and a social transition from a communist welfare state to a social democratic/liberal workfare state. It means also a cultural transition from a system emphasising egalitarianism under a *nomenklatura* (ruling elite) to a liberal democracy emphasising competition under a system based on alternation of power under consensually agreed rules of the game. Time is a major factor allowing for this transition to happen, which is reinforced by socialisation agencies – school, work, political parties, trade unions – and allows the long-term perspective to change the political culture towards a genuine democratic pluralist behaviour. So far, this long-term perspective of education towards democracy has been neglected by international democracy promotion agents.

If not corrected, political corruption then becomes systemic and endemic pervading all aspects of life, similar to what happened in Italy between 1948 and 1992, and is probably happening in Romania today through the dominance of the social democratic party (PSD) (Gallagher, 2005, 2009).

Apart from neo-patrimonialism and systemic corruption, most of these countries are façade democracies with a low level of electoral integrity. It means even the formal regular elections that make up the basic condition of a formal democracy are regularly rigged by the political leaders in power. There is a vast industry of 'political technologists' in Russia that regularly get jobs from parties in power in post-Soviet republics and are in charge of manufacturing the 'right results' in elections.

This tradition of 'political technologists' may be compared to the political strategists in US elections, with one very important difference – that they clearly use all means to get the right result, including carousel voting, vote buying or manipulation of early voting. However, sometimes such attempts may go wrong, if civil society groups are on alert like during the Orange revolution in the Ukraine in November-December 2004, or the Rose Revolution in 2003 in Georgia. A common approach of this 'directed democracy' is that important leaders of the opposition are disqualified, put in prison or intimidated before election day. The model of such 'directed democracy' is Russia, which has been developing this kind of political system now for decades (Wilson, 2005a, 2005b: 108–9, 2011: 217).

All these façade democracies have democratic constitutions which clearly emphasise the rule of law and the separation of powers. Most of these constitutions are revised documents used in the Soviet period, so that they clearly emphasise continuity rather than a break with the past. Moreover, most of them have adopted a semi-presidential or almost presidential system with a directly elected president. The rule of law is undermined by the actions of the government or a judiciary that is far from being independent. We can find similar tendencies in Bulgaria and Romania, but the extent of the lack of independence and corruption of the post-Soviet judiciaries is much greater.

Moreover, parliamentarianism is extremely weak and dominated by the parties of power managed by the executive. In some cases, like in Ukraine, oligarchs have bought their seats and use parliament to foster their interests with other oligarchs (Leschtschenko, 2017; Wilson, 2005a: 149).

Most international democracy indices are from the West, so that there are some biased towards the post-Soviet countries, particularly Russia. Excluding US indices, particularly Freedom House, due to their Cold War history of bias towards Russia, we are left with two European ones that give at least a general idea because they are multidimensional. The first one is the yearly democracy index of *The Economist* (Table 11.1) and the second one is the Bertelsmann Transformation Index with one dimension being about democracy (Table 11.2). However, one has always to add that the model of these indices is about liberal democracy connected to a capitalist market economy; it is the hegemonic model of the predominantly capitalist world system (Wallerstein, 2011). In spite of this, from our perspective of European politics, the model of a liberal economy linked to a capitalist market economy is the one that is dominant in the European continent and at the centre of the EU and the Council of Europe, so that any comparison has to take the model of the European regional community of democratic states (Whitehead, 2001: 395–8) as the benchmark.

In 2017, *The Economist* puts Georgia, Moldova and Ukraine regularly in the hybrid democracy category, between flawed and authoritarian democracy, while Russia is clearly an authoritarian democracy. In 2018, the Bertelsmann Transformation Index characterised Georgia, Moldova and Ukraine as defective democracies, and Russia as a moderate autocracy. If we take the definition of Wolfgang Merkel of defective democracy, it means that one or more than one of the five partial regimes of a functioning embedded democracies is not working. The partial regimes are (1) the electoral regime through a high level of electoral integrity, (2) political liberties, (3) civil rights, (4) horizontal accountability as a genuine separation of powers and (5) effective power to govern, meaning that only democratically elected people should hold power, not extra-constitutional groups (Merkel, 2004: 37–43). He differentiates then between four kinds of defective democracy: exclusive (no democratic rights for parts of the population), domain democracy (exclusion of the population from certain power areas due to the dominance of veto powers such as the military), illiberal democracy (weak judiciary unable to limit executive and legislative, weak rule of law) and delegative democracy (legislative and judicative power are too weak to rein in executive power; the checks and balance do not function) (Merkel, 2004: 49–52) (Table 11.2).

Probably, the best performing country is Georgia, which has been improving in all democracy indices and also in terms of the corruption perception index (CPI). At position 46 in the CPI Georgia seems to be moving towards a virtuous cycle, while Armenia (107), Moldova (122), Azerbaijan (122), Ukraine (130) and Russia (135) are still very corrupt countries. As a dictatorship Belarus is in

Table 11.1 A typology of European countries and the United States according to the democracy index, 2017 (in parentheses European countries)

Types of democracy	*Countries*
Full democracies	Norway, Iceland, Sweden, Denmark, Ireland, Finland, Switzerland, Netherlands, Luxembourg, Germany, UK, Austria, Malta, Spain (14)
Flawed democracies	United States, Italy, Portugal, France, Belgium, Czech Republic, Cyprus, Lithuania, Greece, Latvia, Slovakia, Bulgaria, Poland, Hungary, Croatia, Romania, Serbia (17)
Hybrid regimes	Albania, *Moldova, Georgia, Ukraine*, Montenegro, Macedonia, *Turkey*, Bosnia-Herzegovina, *Armenia* (9)
Authoritarian regimes	*Russia, Belarus* (2)

Source: Own table based on *The Economist* (2018).

Wider Europe countries in italics.

Table 11.2 Bertelsmann transformation index of new democracies, just Central, East and wider European countries, 2018

Types of democracy	*Countries*
Consolidating democracy	Czech Republic, Poland, Estonia, Latvia, Lithuania, Slovakia, Slovenia, Croatia, Romania, Bulgaria
Defective democracy	Hungary, Bosnia-Herzegovina, Serbia, Montenegro, Albania and Macedonia, Romania, *Georgia, Moldova*
Very defective democracy	*Turkey, Armenia*
Moderate autocracy	*Belarus, Russia*
Hard autocracy	*Azerbaijan*

Source: Own table based on Bertelsmann (2018).

Wider Europe countries in italics.

88th place, which is better than the previously mentioned supposed democracies. Turkey has been deteriorating in terms of the CPI and is now on placed 88th as well (TI, 2018).

In terms of democratic quality, press freedom is probably one of the most important categories. The reporters without borders freedom of press index allows us to have a general view of the situation in each of the countries studied in this chapter. In 2017, the best scores for press freedom were found in Norway (place 1), Sweden (2) and Netherlands (3). The worst cases in the EU were Hungary (53) and Poland (58), which have a problematic situation with press freedoms. The best places of the countries studied was Georgia (61), Armenia (80) and Moldova (81), followed by Ukraine (101) where press freedom is still problematic. Russia (149), Belarus (155) and Turkey (157) have a bad problem with press freedoms. Azerbaijan (163) has a very bad issue with press freedoms (RSF, 2018).

In terms of political systems, Ukraine, Moldova, Georgia and Russia are defective semi-presidential democracies, while Belarus is a dictatorship with regular elections. In the next pages, we will briefly discuss the main features of each political system and its latest developments.

Russia: the re-emergence of a superpower

After the end of the Soviet Union on 25 December 1991, a new constitution was elaborated which was strongly influenced by the French model. On 12 December 1993 over 60 per cent of the population voted for the new constitution. Apart from federalism, the constitution of the new Russian federation was semi-presidential, though putting more emphasis on the powers of the president and reducing the power of the prime minister to a mere technocratic implementation of policies. In principle, a straightforward separation of powers between executive, the two-chamber parliament and the judiciary is enshrined in the constitution, but in reality the old Soviet culture soon pervaded the way politics was done in the country. In this regard, the separation of powers is rather a proforma than reality in Russia. The president was originally elected for two terms of four years, but this was changed in 2008 to two terms of six years (article 81 of Russian constitution). The president appoints the prime minister and key figures in the government. Moreover, s/he can rule by decree if there is strong opposition in parliament. However, the prime minister has to be confirmed by the lower house, otherwise after two attempts, the president may call for new elections. Parliament consists of two houses, the upper house Council of the Federation and the lower house the Duma. Originally, members to the Federation Council were directly elected, but since 1995 the appointment has become more controlled by the centre. Formally appointed representatives of each of the eighty-five regional parliaments and executives are members of the Federation Council. However, the selection is strongly influenced by the party in power, United Russia (White, 2011: 64). The lower chamber, the Duma consisting of 450 MPs, is directly elected, but the electoral system was changed several times. Between 1993 and 2008 it was elected by a mixed parallel system of half of MPs being elected by a first-past-the-post system and half of MPs being elected by proportional representation in one large constituency by closed list and the largest remainder system. Parties have to achieve a 5 per cent threshold. It was a system inspired by the German electoral law but without having its equalising effects, because it was parallel. Originally a 7 per cent threshold was in place but this was lowered to 5 per cent at a later stage. Between 2007 and 2011, a proportional representation system was in place with the same 5 per cent threshold. However, the return of Putin to the presidency in May 2012 led to a new change towards the old system. This MMP parallel system is certainly easier by controlling most seats in the single member constituencies elected by majority. If the party in power does well in this part of the election, it can easily control the other part and create disproportional majorities.

In the 1990s, Russia under Boris Yeltsin (1991–2000) was quite weak, so that it did not pose a major threat to the United States or the EU. Actually, it had gained a secure place in the one world of US-led economic liberalism and liberal democracy. A lot of US money as democracy assistance was poured into Russia to allow the country to make a transition to a liberal democracy and a capitalist economy. However, it seems that most of the implementation of this funding was poorly monitored by the US government and just ended up reinforcing the emergence of a Mafia-state. The Mafia-state was controlled by oligarchs who were able to enrich themselves during the economic shock therapy which led to a rapid transition from a Soviet planning economy to a liberal market one. This was due by a fast and quite chaotic privatisation of state enterprises that opened a structure of opportunity to make considerable fortunes for these oligarchs. In many ways, the oligarchs were able to capture the state and dominate policy-making. President Boris Yeltsin was too weak to change this situation. Moreover, he was part of this vast network of corruption and patronage (Sakwa, 2000: 294, 2016b: 4–20).

The ailing Russian economy had to deal with the legacy of the Soviet Union, which included the reduction of a large armed forces which was built up during the Cold War. In 1998, the rouble collapsed leading to major problems for the Russian economy. The Boris Jelzin period was also characterised by a high level of government instability (MacKenzie and Curran, 2002: 399–402).

Parliament was able to challenge the governments of Jelzin, leading to six different prime ministers between 1992 and 2000. On 16 August 1999, he appointed Vladimir Putin, a former agent of the Soviet secret services KGB (Committee for State Security) as the new prime minister, who in 2000 became the new president of Russia and was re-elected in 2004. Clearly, the much younger Putin was able to improve considerably the Russian economy, using mainly the oil and gas resources to upgrade the country's infrastructure and welfare system. After the constitutionally allowed two terms, Putin was replaced by his prime minister Dmitry Medvedev who clearly was a loyal partner in the quest to restore the reputation of the country again. In 2008, the constitution was changed and a term was expanded to six years. In 2012 Putin returned to the presidency and was re-elected in 2018. Medvedev became the new prime minister. In this regard, both politicians became a tandem in government that replaced each other. It will be interesting what will happen after 2024, when the second term of Putin expires.

Meanwhile, one can speak of a 'directed, managed façade', certainly a defective democracy as Wolfgang Merkel defined earlier. This is a highly personalistic-clientelistic political system tailored towards the needs of the Russian leader. One characteristic of this system is a parliament that is dominated by political parties that support Putin. Putin's present party is 'United Russia', which has been characterised as a party of power, meaning that the 'administrative resources' of the state are used to manufacture elections. So-called 'political technologists' are used to achieve the right result in presidential and parliamentary elections. It should always be above 50 per cent, while in 2011 it had achieved just 49.32 per cent. In 2016, after returning to the old electoral system, it reached 54.2 per cent (see Wilson, 2005a).

The legislature is rather a rubber-stamp parliament; other parties in parliament support Putin's party. The second largest are the communist party led by Gennadyi Zyuganov, who clearly supports Putin in restoring the strength of the country abroad. Moreover, connections between Putin and the post-Soviet leaders still remain intact. Before 1999, they were the strongest party in the Duma, but after Putin came to power and used the party of power electoral strategy, they have achieved between 12 and 20 per cent of the votes. In 2011, they achieved 19.19 per cent, but in 2016 just 13.34 per cent. The third largest party are the Liberal Democrats, but the name is deceiving, because in reality it is a rightwing nationalist party led by Vladimir Zhirinovsky. Due to its ideology there is a strong affinity to the nationalist policies of Vladimir Putin. In 1993, it was the largest party with over 22 per cent, but then it declined to between 8 and 13 per cent. In 2016, the party received 13.14 per cent of the votes. A fourth party of this 'cartel' supporting Putin is Just Russia led by Sergey Mironov. The party emerged in 2007 as a merger of several smaller parties and is a social democratic party pushing for welfare policies in the country. It regularly achieves over 13 per cent of the vote, also in the elections of 2016. Genuine opposition is rather excluded from parliament by different political technological methods. One of the most important methods is the use of fake candidates or parties in order to confuse the electorate and reduce the votes of genuine parties (for more detail, see Hutcheson, 2012; Laverty, 2015; Oversloot and Verheul, 2006: 391–8; Roberts, 2012; White, 2012; Wilson, 2005a).

This has negative consequences for Russian parliamentarianism. The Duma and Federation Council have become rubber-stamping legislative chambers which clearly approve most of the legislation proposed by government. This is also ensured by vast networks based on favours, clientelism and patronage (Remington, 2008). A quite important study on the composition of the Russian Duma shows that managers and businessmen are a major category making up about 30 to 40 per cent of the chamber. Many managers of state-owned businesses are also part of this large group. They also belong to the largest party in the Duma, United Russia. Also the military is highly represented in the Duma, the so-called militocracy, but they are not direct representatives of the military, but rather linked to business enterprises related to the arms industry. They are mainly commercial lobbyists (Gaman-Golutvina, 2014: 251–2).

Elections in Russia are far from having a high level of electoral integrity (OCSE, 2016, 2018). On the contrary, the work of the real opposition is rather impeded, and critical voices like Gary Kasparov, the former chess world champion, were imprisoned before the elections of 2012 (*The Telegraph*, 24 August 2012) and Alexej Navalny in 2018 (*Die Zeit*, 14 June 2017; *Deutsche Welle*, 23 June 2017).

One major problem among others for Russia is the still incipient rule of law. President Putin was able to wrest control of the country from the rule of criminal organisations and the wild Mafia-state of the early 1990s, but such groups still exist and operate in a more sophisticated way. They clearly have penetrated the legitimate Russian and global economy, strengthening their positions. They were able to expand globally, particularly to the United States. It is alleged that the Kremlin may keep contacts with these criminal organisations and use them in certain opportunistic ways (Harding, 2011). The high level of corruption, the personalistic-clientelistic and patronage network of Russian politics, and the continuation of illegal raids on business corporations have undermined the confidence of investors in the country. A lack of transparency and accountability have characterised Russian politics so far. There have been corporate raids (*rederstvo*), the most prominent case being Michail Khodorkovsky and his oil company Yukos. It seems that Khodorkovsky had political ambitions of his own in the early period of Putin's rise. This led to the confiscation of his business enterprise Yukos by the state based on the charge that it had not paid taxes. Khodorkovsky was put in prison for a decade between 2004 and 2014. He was released as part of an amnesty programme of the Kremlin just shortly before the Winter Olympics of 2014. He is now in Switzerland and tends not to get too involved in Russian politics (for more detail, see Sakwa, 2016a). However, the Khodorkovsky case is just one among many. According to figures from an excellent report written by Louise Shelley and Judy Dean and based on figures presented by President Putin, there were 200,000 such cases of economic crimes in 2014, out of which just 15 per cent led to a conviction, while 83 per cent of legitimate owners lost control over their businesses (Cohen, 2016; Harding, 2011; Holmes, 2008; Shelley and Dean, 2016: 10).

Since the collapse of the Soviet Union, Soviet leaders have tried to create some kind of loose federation with the former Soviet Republics, but distrust of Russia's intentions in the 'near abroad' has undermined this project. Moreover, the frozen conflicts strategy of Russia has not been conducive to creating good relations with its neighbours. More recently, Putin has been strongly engaged in building a Eurasian Economic Union. However, this project has very few members. At the moment just Russia, Armenia, Belarus, Kazakhstan and Kyrgyzstan are members. According to the website, the GDP is $2.2 trillion, representing 3.7 per cent of world exports and 2.3 per cent of world imports. One has to qualify this with the fact that most of the GDP comes from Russia ($1.83 trillion) (EAEU, 2018). In spite of the fact that most countries are either façade democracies or dictatorships, the EAEU could strategically turn out to be quite important in the future, bolstering the ambitions of Russia as a superpower. However, the Georgia and Ukraine crises of 2008 and 2014 respectively have undermined considerably the attractiveness of the project. Of course, US (control of Eurasia and Russian containment) and European interests (Eastern partnership) in the post-Soviet economies are major factors for this clash of projects (Krickovic and Bratersky, 2016; Libman and Vinokurov, 2018; Smith, 2016).

In sum, the Russian establishment seems to regard 'managed' democracy as a necessary transition stage towards more pluralism after the collapse of the Soviet Union. Grigorii Yavlinsky, a liberal that headed the small party Yabloko and who was critical of the Kremlin until 2003, before succumbing to the strategies of political technology and administering resources, argued in 2002 in an interview in the *St Petersburg Times* that Russian democracy is a 'Potemkin village whose façade merely looks European' (quoted from White, 2007: 212).

The limits of export of the Russian model: 'managed democracy' in Ukraine, Georgia and Moldova

Most countries of the post-Soviet space have developed authoritarian or hybrid forms of democracy. In many ways, the Russian model of 'managed democracy' was exported to all countries. However, after three decades of such hybrid systems the coercive approach of the Russian federation towards influencing politics in some countries has been rather counterproductive (Delcour, 2015; Delcour and Wolczuk, 2015). Ukraine, Georgia and Ukraine are good examples of an emerging rift between the oligarchisation of politics and a growing opposition from civil society. US and EU involvement do not explain alone the Coloured Revolutions, but their work over several decades with civil society associations was an important additional help (Nodia et al., 2017). In the next sections we discuss the cases of the defective democracies of the Ukraine, Georgia and Moldova, and then the dictatorship of Belarus under president Aljaksandr Lukashenka.

Ukraine: oligarchic 'managed democracy' between East and West

The Russian model is emulated in all post-Soviet states, but to different degrees. In terms of affection, historical legacy and geostrategic interests, the Ukraine is regarded as the most important country for Russia. Ukraine, Belarus and Russia share a common history that goes back to the Kiever Rus founded by Scandinavian Vikings in 980 and lasted as an empire until 1240, before being destroyed by the Mongols. This glorious empire was strongly influenced by Constantinople/Byzantium. Today's Ukraine emerged only in 1991, although there have been periods of the past in which territorial parts of the Ukraine were independent and part of a national history like the Hetmanate which existed between 1648 and 1764. Any kind of Ukrainian entity was always under considerable pressure from its neighbours Poland and Russia. Therefore, in 1654, the treaty of Pereyaslav led to the submission of the Hetmanate to the Russian Empire. Ekaterina II (1762–92) abolished the Hetmanate and fully incorporated it into Russia. There were attempts during the First World War and Second World War to achieve an independence federation (Boekh and Völkl, 2007: 54–64; Plokhy, 2015: chapters 18 and 19; Wilson, 2015: chapters 3–5). During the Second World War, the independence movement was spearheaded by nationalist groups such as the Organisation of Ukrainian Nationalists (OUN) and the Ukrainian Liberation Army (UPA), a legacy that still haunts Ukraine today, because they are well-networked and a have power basis in the United States (see Hahn, 2018). Paradoxically, the contiguous Ukrainian territory which is larger than any other country of Europe, namely 603,000 square kms, but less than one-tenth of that of Russia are a result of border changes imposed by Soviet Russia between 1917 and 1945 on its neighbours (Boeckh and Völkl, 2007: 125). The Crimea was a present from the Supreme Soviet to the Ukraine as a sign of brotherly love of Russia for its neighbour and as part of the 300-year celebration of the Pereyaslav Treaty in 1954, in the firm belief that the Soviet Union would endure for ever (Boeckh and Völkl, 2007: 155).

Although 78 per cent are Ukrainians and 17 per cent are Russians, there are also over 130 nationalities over the territory. Also in terms of language, 68 per cent have Ukrainian as their mother tongue, but 30 per cent have Russian, but there are also other minorities with a vast array of mother tongues. Many Ukrainians speak both Ukrainian and Russian, so that the influence of Russia in Ukraine will remain an important factor. It means that Ukraine is a real bridge between Europe and Russia. It remains geostrategically a crucial country for Russia, and it seems also for the United States in their quest for control of the Eurasian space.

On 24 August 1991 an overwhelming majority of the Ukrainian Soviet parliament proclaimed de facto independence of the Ukraine. On 1 December 1991, a referendum on independence was held leading to 92 per cent voting for it. On the same day, presidential elections were held which led to the victory of Leonid Kravchuk of 61.29 per cent over his rival Vyaschelav Chornovil with 23.27 per cent (Wilson, 2005a: 156–71).

One basic problem of the new Ukrainian state is that the old Soviet elite remained more or less in place. Moreover, no constituent assembly elections took place for the drafting of a new democratic constitution. The composition of parliament remained the same, because no new parliamentary elections were called. Therefore, Kravchuk could rely on the old administrative structure to build his power. Similar to Russia, several regional clans were able to seize important state enterprise assets. Among these clans, the most well known were based in the east in Donetzk and Dniepropetrovsk around the coal and energy sectors respectively, and in Kiev around the banking business (Wilson, 2005a: 41–2). Clearly, the transition from Soviet autocracy to liberal democracy, and from planned to market economy, was a major structure of opportunity for these clans to enrich themselves. Kravchuk built a similar system of 'managed' democracy as in Russia achieving manufactured majorities for its policies. The dominant party remained the communist party. The first post-Soviet parliamentary elections took place on 27 March 1994. Although the communist party had lost a considerable number of votes, it continued to be the largest group. Parliament was quite fragmented with a lot of small parties. In June-July 1994, president Kravchuk lost to Leonid Kuchma in the second round of the presidential elections. However, Kuchma continued on the path of building a 'managed' democracy, particularly due to the fact he was re-elected in 1999. One major turning point for the end of the Kuchma period was the kidnapping and murder of Ukrainian journalist Georgiy Gongadze in 2000, who had set up the online newspaper *Pravda* (*The Truth*). His murder was allegedly linked to Kuchma, so that a major movement started against him. A movement called 'Ukraine without Kuchma' was established in order to bring him down (Wilson, 2005a: 51–2). The opposition led by Viktor Yuschenko, the former president of the Nationalbank and prime minister, and Yuliya Timoshenko were able to do well in the 2002 parliamentary elections. In the 2004 presidential elections, Kuchma was not able to run for a third time, although the constitutional court had strangely supported it (Wilson, 2005a: 79–80). He tried to get his prime minister Viktor Yanukovich elected as his successor. However, attempts to steal the election in 2004 led to the Orange Revolution in November-December that year. A third run-off between Yunakovich and Yuschenko led to the victory of the latter. He became the new president and appointed Yuliya Timoshenko as his prime minister. In spite of a dynamic beginning, Yuschenko had difficulties push through crucial reforms in public administration and the economy. In the 2010 elections, he was replaced by Viktor Yanukovich. New president Yanukovich restored the old Kuchma order with even more vehemence, leading to growing protests from the population. The Euromaidan of 2013–14 was a very heterogenous movement against Yanukovich policies. One factor that triggered the Ukraine crisis was the refusal of President Yanukovich to sign a free trade agreement with the EU. He clearly used the EU negotiations to get a better deal from Russia, particularly also in terms of the gas business. The radicalisation of the Euromaidan put Yanukovich under considerable pressure. In the end, he fled the country and the government was taken over by the three main parties of the Ukrainian opposition, at the forefront being Arseniy Jatzenyuk from the nationalist Fatherland party (Batkivshchyna), Vitaliy Klitschko from moderate centrist Alliance of liberal Reformers (UDAR) and Oleh Tyahnybok from the rightwing nationalist Freedom Party (Swoboda). President Yanukovich is fully to blame for the Euromaidan, mainly due to his decisions and policies over the four years that he was in power. Russia was certainly backing Yanukovich and interested in keeping him in power. However, the role of the EU and the United States in bringing down the legitimate government of Ukraine is certainly a matter for discussion. Both have encouraged regime change through its actions. US politicians such as Senator John McCain and Assistant State Secretary Victoria Nuland took part in events of Euromaidan and therefore unduly contributed to the destabilisation of the country (Sakwa, 2016b; Wilson, 2014; see quite critical comments by Hahn, 2018: 187; for a more pro-nationalist and anti-Russian account, see Kuzio, 2017). The anti-Russian Lithuanian EU presidency was far from being an honest neutral broker as is required as incumbent of the position. More distance to the events and research will be necessary to reconstruct what happened during Euromaidan. It has been quite problematic finding out the truth about the events of 20 February in which so many innocent people died after snipers opened fire from the roofs of buildings in Maidan square. Officially, Berkut policemen have been blamed for carrying out the shootings, but alternative versions seem to allege that rightwing nationalists were involved (see Hahn, 2018, 196–205; see the forensic work of Katchanovski, 2015); however, the truth is still out there due to the lack of a proper thorough investigation by the Ukrainian authorities.

The geopolitical territorial price that the Ukraine had to pay was high, leading to the illegal occupation of Crimea by Russia and the indirect support for separatists in the eastern regions of Donetzk and Luhansk. Crimea is geopolitically important for Russia, because the Russian fleet is based there. In 1997, a leasing agreement was signed with the Ukraine, so that the Russian fleet could stay there for twenty years. The treaty had been renewed by president Viktor Yanukovich allowing Russians to stay until 2046, with a five-year additional renewal option. However, with the coup d'état of nationalists and pro-Europeans on 22 February 2014, Putin perceived this as a geopolitical change in the balance of forces, which motivated a fast intervention to seize Crimea (for more detail, see Hahn, 2018: 225–35). The civil war in the eastern regions is part of a strategy of 'frozen conflicts' to prevent Ukraine becoming fully integrated in the West (for more detail, see Hahn, 2018: chapter 9). In this regard, both the United States and the EU have made mistakes in their strategic calculations in relation to Russia's possible behaviour (see Friedman, 2014; Hahn, 2018; Mearsheimer, 2014).

Many hopes were linked to the oligarch Petro Poroshenko when he became president on 25 May 2014. However, one major negative aspect was that he did not divest his business interests which included his Roshen corporation with factories in Ukraine, Hungary and Lithuania and his private TV5 station (Hahn, 2018: 289–90). Moreover, in 2016, it was discovered that he had offshore accounts according to the Panama papers, showing that he had evaded billions of US dollars in tax (Hahn, 2018: 289–90). Before and after the Euromaidan, the IMF and the EU poured considerable funding into the Ukraine in exchange for public administration, market regulatory and transparency reforms. According to a European audit report, a considerable amount of funding provided by the EU is not accounted for. It disappeared in the non-transparent complex administrative structure of the Ukraine (see the damaging report of the European Audit Court, 2016). In reality, Poroshenko is a man of the old system and he uses the same methods of 'managed' democracy. His first prime minister Arseniy Yatsenyuk was unable to get the reforms needed underway and had to resign after a long battle trying to remain in power (Willershausen, 2016). Quite worrying has been a Ukrainisation policy in education, which tends to reduce the importance of minority languages in school. However, a lack of funding did not lead to the policy being widely adopted (Osipian, 2018). More problematic have been attempts by successive presidents to rewrite the history of Ukraine and whitewash the Ukrainian nationalists of OUN and UPA, and allegedly minimising the role these nationalist groups and Ukraine played as perpetrators in the Jewish holocaust. This Ukrainisation was started during the Yushenko presidency, which also entailed a rewriting and falsifying of history pushed very much by the nationalist lobbies in the Ukraine and the United States (see Hahn, 2018: 142–8).

One major problem that remains is the parliament, which clearly is accustomed to horse trading deals. While after the Orange Revolution 300 out 450 MPs were millionaires, this did not change very much according to MP and journalist Serhii Leshenko after Euromaidan. In a more detailed study, Elena Semenova found out that between 1994 and 2002 over one-fifth of MPs were managers and civil servants respectively; in this sense continuity seems to be very much the case (Leschtschenko, 2017; Semenova, 2014: 276–7; Wilson, 2005b: 149). The presidential and government majority is manufactured along centrist political parties. However, the composition of parliament is changing from election and election. One of the reasons is certainly the manipulation of the electoral system, which was changed at least three times. Another is that the party system is not consolidated; parties do not last many parliamentary terms and are built around personalities (Crowther, 2011; Thames, 2016; Whitemore, 2003, 2005, 2014). Another major problem for parliamentarianism in the Ukraine is the high turnover of MPs in parliament. After the 2014 elections, 56 per cent of MPs were elected for the first time. This clearly presents a daunting task in terms of professionalisation (Fedorenko et al. 2016: 618).

Very damaging for the transition to democracy has been the late adoption of a new post-Soviet constitution in 1996. It took five years to negotiate a new constitution. Since then, it has been a major source of contention between the Russophile parties and the opposition. It has been changed several times according to the party in power (Gallina, 2014: 506–10).

In sum, Ukraine still remains trapped in the old system due to the continuing state capture by the oligarchs. The 2019 Ukrainian presidential elections will show if Poroshenko will remain in power or if a new leader emerges. At the time of writing, Poroshenko is struggling to reach the second round in the opinion polls. In front of him is the popular television comedian Volodymyr Zelensky and behind him Yulia Timoshenko.

Georgia and Moldova: the Russian model in two poor countries

The Russian model is also reproduced in other countries of the post-Soviet space. However, Georgia has been able to reduce some of this impact since the 2003 Rose Revolution. Georgia became independent from the Soviet Union in 1991. In 2017, the estimated population was about 3.59 million in a territory of 69,700 square km. Although the large majority of the population is ethnic Georgian, there are territorial pockets dominated by Russian-speaking populations, more concretely in South Ossetia in the north neighbouring the Russian republic of North Ossetia-Alania and Abkhazia on the northern part of the Black Sea coast. South Ossetia is about 3,900 square km and about 53,000 Russian speaking people live there, while Abkhazia comprises 8,660 square km and a predominantly Russian-speaking population of 253,000. Overall, this is roughly 9 per cent of the overall Georgian population and 20 per cent of the territory.

Soon after independence, the two regions became hot spots for ethnic conflict leading to war. One of the reasons for the war was the radical ethnonationalist policies of the first president of the country, Zviad Gamsakhurdia, who was then removed from power and killed in 1992. One of the main reasons for the war was the wish of the two breakaway republics to stay within the former Soviet Union. Moreover, Gamsakhurdia's ethnonationalism was anti-Russian and exclusionist of other ethnic groups. This clearly created bad conditions for a roadmap towards a new Georgia as Gamsakhurdia had wanted to achieve (Berglund and Blauvelt, 2016: 14–21; on this period, see Jones, 2015: chapter 3).

He was replaced by the well-known foreign minister of the late Soviet Union Edvard Shverdnadze in 1992. He had to make concessions to Russia, which took control of the two breakaway regions of South Ossetia and Abkhazia. Russia was allowed to have troops stationed in the two territories. Shverdnadze was able to gain control over the rest of territory between 1992 and 1994. He was able also to develop policies towards the civic integration of minorities. Finally, in 1995, he was overwhelmingly elected the president of Georgia. Similar to Russia and Ukraine, he used the state resources to remain in power, which was used to 'manage' elections throughout his period. In 1995, a new constitution was adopted by the Georgian parliament which clearly confirmed the already existing political system of semi-presidentialism (Aprasidze, 2016: 90).

However, in 2003, a major revolt led by Mikheil Saakashvili forced president Shevardnadze to resign. This so-called Rose Revolution followed similar tactics to those leading to the resignation of former Serbian president Slobodan Milosevic, which was based on non-violence and civil disobedience protests organised by a US-sponsored civil society youth organisation called Otpor (Resistance), allegedly funded by USAID and US party foundation the National Democratic Institute (NDI). They used the surrogate Georgian civil society organisation

Kmara! (Enough!) to reproduce the same kind of momentum to oust president Shevardnadze (Hahn, 2018: 100–2; Kakachia and Lebadnidze, 2016: 136–8) . Clearly civil society organisations close to Saakashvili were trained by US democracy promotion programmes which allowed for regime change. Indeed, this becomes even more evident when we take into consideration that civil society is weak and highly dependent on external funding, mainly from international donors. Moreover, civil society organisations tended to support just Saakashvili, even though he was becoming authoritarian, at least after 2008. This uncritical approach to civil society has been a characteristic of both US and European organisations (Kakachia and Lebadnidze, 2016: 134–46; Pokleba, 2016).

However, Saakashvili was not an entirely unknown politician in Georgia when he came to power. In fact, he was part of the establishment – he was justice minister (2000–1) during the Shevardnadze presidencies. In this sense, he knew the process of the managed system and could apply it while in power.

Saakashvili became president and introduced major reforms to deregulate the economy, fight criminal groups and recover taxes and money owed to the state. His policies bore fruit leading to an increase in income into state coffers, which was used to improve the ailing public services. Moreover, crime was reduced considerably. All this was overshadowed by rather unorthodox methods of the police and the judiciary to restore law and order in the country, bypassing the elementary rule of law principles such as the presumption of innocence and non-use of violence to extract confessions. Moreover, like Shevardnadze before him, he abused the state resources to manipulate elections, harass the opposition and control the media (Kakachia and Lebanidze, 2016: 149–51).

By 2012, a growing discontent emerged with protests against Saakashvili leading to a peaceful transition to the more pro-Russian Georgian Dream party funded by Bidnidze Ivashvili, the richest person in Georgia. One of the reasons was the failed attempt to reintegrate South Ossetia into Georgia in 2008, which then led to unilateral declarations of independence by the two enclaves controlled by the Russian army. An independent report of the EU confirmed that it was Saakashvili's government that first attacked South Ossetia, but it blamed both sides for the unnecessary escalation of the conflict (*Der Spiegel*, 21 September 2009; Independent Fact-Finding Mission, 2009; Lanskoy and Areshidze, 2008).

Saakashvili was re-elected in the 2008 presidential elections, but there was a growing opposition to his policies of managed democracy, including the control of television. In the 2012 elections, the more pro-Russian Georgian Dream party was able to win the elections, and president Saakashvili had to appoint the leader of the party, Bidniza Ivanishvili to be the next prime minister. One year later, Giorgi Margvelashvili, the candidate from Georgian Dream, became the new president. One of the positive aspects of this alternation of power was that it was peaceful, in spite of the resistance of president Saakashvili (for an account of the parliamentary elections of 2012, see Fairbanks and Gugushvili, 2013).

Since then, the Georgian Dream party of Ivanishvili has dominated the political system. One major fear of the opposition is that his powerful economic status may be a major impediment preventing Saakashvili's United National Movement coming to power again (Kakachia and Lebadnidze, 2016: 150–153). Indeed, in 2016, Georgian Dream won the parliamentary elections again with an absolute majority. Ivanishvili and his party reset the relationship with Russia and the EU towards a more equidistant approach. One of the major foreign policy choices was to improve relations with Russia, but keeping the strong ties with the EU and NATO at the same time. In 2018, Georgian Dream was able to secure their candidate, the independent Salome Zurabishvili, as president. According to the constitutional reform, this will also be the last time that direct elections to the presidency will take place. Afterwards, the president will be elected by parliament.

Moldova emerged as an independent country when the Soviet Union began to disintegrate. It comprises a population of 3.4 million people in a territory of 33,842 square km. Similarly to Georgia, Transnistria declared its independence from Moldova in 1990 leading then to a civil war that only ended with a ceasefire in 1992. One of the major reasons for the ethnic conflict was that Transnistria is inhabited by a predominantly Russian and Ukrainian population and wanted to stay in the Soviet Union or any federation that may emerge from it. Due to the civil war, Russian troops occupied the separatist enclave and remain there today. Tensions between Moldova and Transnistria remain. It comprises a population of over 475,000 in a territory of 3,567 square km, 19 per cent and 10 per cent of Moldova respectively. The majority population of Moldova speaks Moldovan, which is a local dialect of Romanian. In the Soviet Union, Moldavian used the Cyrillic alphabet, but after independence they switched to the Latin alphabet, probably to demonstrate a closer relationship to Romania. By far the largest party is the Communist Party of the Republic of Moldavia (PCRM), which is led by Vladimir Voronin and tends to have a quite positive image of the former Soviet Union (on the communist party, see Tudoroiu, 2011a).

Between 1991 and 1997, a popular front government under the presidency of Mircea Snergu was in charge, to be followed by Petru Lucinschi, a candidate of the Democratic Agrarian party who was incumbent until 2001. He tried to change the constitution of 1994 to gain more powers, but this was prevented by the opposition parties in parliament. Instead, a full parliamentary system with an indirectly elected president was introduced (Fruhstorfer, 2014: 368–71; Tudoroiu, 2011a: 299).

Between 2001 and 2009, the communist Vladimir Voronin was able to win the presidency, which was now indirectly elected by parliament. Similar to the other post-Soviet states, he used 'managed democracy' methods to remain in power that clearly were accompanied by state capture strategies leading allegedly to the enrichment of the leadership. Voronin's son Oleg emerged as a very rich man estimated to own a $2 billion fortune (Tudoroiu, 2011a: 299–301, 312). However, in the 5 April 2009 elections a similar wave of protests as the colour revolutions in Georgia 2003 and Ukraine 2004 led to a repressive crackdown of the opposition. It seems that a similar strategy using social media, particularly Twitter, was used to protest against alleged electoral fraud. It seems also that civil society organisations sponsored by the United States have been involved in these protests. Allegedly Serbian activists related to the US-sponsored civil society organisations took part in these protests and were expelled from the country. The Soros Foundation sponsored independent exit polls which contradicted the official results (Tudoroiu, 2011a: 301–2).

However, the crackdown certainly damaged the image of the communist party, which tried to push through its candidate in the Moldovan parliament consisting of 101 MPs. The proportional representation system had allocated sixty seats to the communist party and forty-one to the opposition. It meant, that the communist party was short by one seat to elect the president. The opposition refused to give this one seat to elect the communist candidate, so that new elections were called for 29 July 2009. In these early elections, the communist party lost votes and seats. It now had forty-eight seats in parliament, still being the largest party, but they were beaten by the electoral coalition Alliance of European Integration (AEI) consisting of four parties: the liberal democratic party (PLDM, eighteen seats), the liberal party (PL, fifteen seats), the democratic party (PDM, thirteen seats) and Our Moldova (AMN, seven seats). Together they had the absolute majority with fifty-three seats. However, the AEI was quite an unstable coalition, with one of the parties, the democratic party, being a splinter of the communist party led by Voronin's rival Marian Lupu. In the 2010 early elections the majority of the three main parties of AEI increased to fifty-nine seats, and Our Moldova was not able to achieve representation (Tudoroiu, 2014: 659–61).

Between 2010 and 2012, no president could be elected by parliament due to the lack of a quorum of sixty-one seats (three fifths majority), so that the president of parliament became the interim president of the republic. In total, there were three acting presidents. Due to the stalemate, the constitution was changed to allow for the reintroduction of a direct election of the president. A referendum on the direct election of the president should have taken place on 5 September 2010, but the referendum failed, because it did not pass the already very low threshold of 33 per cent of the voting population. The low turnout meant it reached only 30 per cent, in spite of the fact that over 87 per cent of those who did vote, voted yes (Fruhstorfer, 2016: 371–3).

The stalemate was overcome when three MPs of the communist party left the party and voted for a new independent president, Nicolas Timofti, in January 2012. He remained in place until 23 December 2016, being replaced by the directly elected Igor Dodon from the party of socialists. The main reason for the direct election of Igor Dodon was a constitutional ruling issued in March 2016 that declared unconstitutional the constitutional reform of 2000, which had changed the Moldovan political system from a semi-presidential to a parliamentary one.

In the 2014 elections, we see a new phenomenon emerging which is part of Soviet-style 'managed' elections. The socialist party of Moldova, led by Igor Dodon and strongly associated with the communist party, became the largest party, but the two parties were not able to achieve an absolute majority with their forty-six seats. Instead the three-party coalition AEI lost votes but was able to keep the absolute majority in parliament with fifty-five seats. However, since the direct election of Igor Dodon on 23 December 2016, there has been a tense cooperation between president Dodon and prime ministers from AEI ruling the country. One particular difference is the orientation of president Dodon towards Russia, and AEI towards the EU. Dodon was able to secure observer status in the EAEU, against the will of the AEI coalition. In this sense, we have here two different foreign policies in the Moldovan government. In spite of the alternation in power, the AEI coalition showed similar behaviour to the former communists. Many former communists just opportunistically switched sides, in order to preserve their influence or power. Similar to other neo-patrimonial Russian-style hybrid democracies, the coalition used its power to control the judiciary through networks of influence. This is the case of businessman Vladimir Plahotniuc who just changed camps in order to preserve his interests. Although Moldova is the poorest country in Europe, oligarchs are present here also and are able to capture the state. This is reinforced by the fact that Marian Lupu of the democratic party was a major player in the communist party before 2009. In this sense, instead of a renewal, the neo-patrimonial Russian style model will continue to dominate politics in Moldova (*Euractiv*, 29 May 2017, 25 September 2017; Timoroiu, 2014: 661–4; 670–3).

Major problems in Moldova are the lack of a national Moldovan identity. Moldovanism tends to be linked to the old Soviet system and represented by the electorate of the communist and socialist parties, while a more Romanian identity is emphasised by the pro-European parties (Danero Iglesias, 2015: 861–5). Moldova has been characterised as a state without a nation, in contrast to Catalonia or Scotland (Friedman, 2011: 44, 49). A third major problem is the high level of unemployment and the emigration of young people to EU countries, estimated at 900,000 (about 35 per cent of the population). Last but not least, civil society is quite weak, and a more passive rural population (57 per cent) dominates the social structure of the country (Timoroiu, 2011b).

The EU has been engaged in Moldova through the Eastern partnership programme, but results from moves towards democratic change and rule of law have been rather poor (Bosse, 2010).

Belarus: the last dictatorship of Europe

As already mentioned, Belarusian history is intertwined with that of Russia and the Ukraine. All have as their founding myth the Kiever Rus (987–1240), the three East Slavic brother nations. Similar to Ukraine, there was never a sustainable independent state before 1991. A history of Belarus has been intrinsically intertwined with that of the Russian Empire and then the Soviet Union. Like in the Ukrainian case, Belarusian territory and population have always been under pressure from its neighbours Poland and Russia. The present borders and territory of Belarus, like most other post-Soviet states, goes back to the First World War and Second World War in which the Soviet army was able to annex further regions to the west (based on Wilson, 2011). Geostrategically, Belarus is very important to Russia due to the fact that it functions as a buffer in the northern European plain starting in Poland and allowing for a fast movement of troops towards Russia. Both Hitler and Napoleon used this northern European plain to advance towards the Soviet Union and the Russian Empire, respectively, and the latter also towards Berlin (Friedman, 2011: 9). Although there is a Belarusian language in different versions, Russian remains a major language of the country. In 1995, a positive referendum gave Russian the status of second official language (Wilson, 2011: 124). At least until the millennium, president Lukashenka used Russian as the language of governmental stability, while Belarusian was portrayed as the language of the opposition, which wants instability through its mass protests (Goujon, 1999: 665–73).

The Belarusian Socialist Soviet Republic was strongly integrated into the Soviet Union. It used the mythology of the partisans of the Second World War that fought against Nazi Germany as an important historical-symbolic asset in order to gain political and economic support from the political leadership in the Soviet Union (Leshchenko, 2008: 1420). The pro-Russian communist elites reluctantly declared the independence of Belarus in parliament in 1991 (Wilson, 2011: 150).

The post-Soviet Belarus comprises a population of 9.5 million and extends itself over a very large territory of 207,595 square km.

Between 1992 and 1994, the political leadership under Viacheslaw Kebich kept a close relationship with Russia's Yeltsin. In March 1994, a new constitution replaced the amended constitution of 1972. In general terms, one could say that it was a copycat of the Russian constitution, in which semi-presidentialism became the new government model.

The first presidential elections took place in June 1994, in which Aliaksandr Lukashenka was able to win comfortably in the first and second rounds, with 44.8 per cent and 80.1 per cent respectively. His main rival Kebich only reached 19.9 per cent (McMahon, 1997). Little by little, Lukashenka began to move the new political system towards authoritarianism. This was done through different mechanisms.

First, he clearly began to sideline the political parties in parliament by creating new clone parties that would be more friendly towards his regime. It meant that political technology and administering resources were used and abused to manufacture a pro-Lukashenka super majority in each subsequent election (Wilson, 2011: 192, 208, 227).

Second, this super majority was achieved due to the changes to the constitution that Lukashenka undertook through mega referendums in 1995, 1996 and 2004. In the first referendum there were four questions, of which the extension of powers of the president towards parliament was the most important and was approved with over 77 per cent of the vote (Wilson, 2011: 174). In the second mega referendum there were seven questions, four for the president and three for parliament. The most important one was the question on a new constitution designed by Lukashenka, which was approved with over 70 per cent. Moreover, the population decided against the abolition of the death penalty (Wilson, 2011: 178–83). Finally, in 2004, Lukashenka gained approval in the third referendum to abolish the limits to his presidency, so that he could now rule forever. Although Lukashenka had a good chance of getting his way in all the referendums, allegedly there was a massive manipulation of the results (Marples and Pervushina, 2005: 23–6).

Third, Lukashenka has used Russian-style political technology to manipulate elections since at least 1999. We mentioned earlier some of these techniques used in other post-Soviet states, but the favourite so far has been the so-called early voting. It means that many people in factories or students in universities are already voting before the election, otherwise they may lose their job or have problems with their studies (Marples and Pervushina, 2005: 20; Wilson, 2011: 217). Due to the lack of transparency of the Central Electoral Commission, manipulation of the vote can happen extensively. In particular, the December 2010 presidential elections ended in chaos due to the subsequent protests alleging rigging of the results (Crabtree, 2015: 1; Padhol and Marples, 2010: 5, 11–14). According to Andrew Wilson, early voting has been increasing steadily from 3.2 per cent in the 1994 parliamentary elections to 14.6 per cent in the 2001 presidential elections and to a staggering 31.3 per cent in the 2006 presidential elections (Wilson, 2011: 217). Since 2006, the use of fake exit polls became also part of the inventory of political technology (Wilson, 2011: 218).

Such a sophisticated control of the electoral and political process has been established over time, preventing the emergence of a colour revolution sponsored by the West. Indeed, the Belarusian case shows the ability of authoritarian regimes to learn in relation to coloured revolutions backed by the West, and then of disseminating these lessons among similar post-Soviet states including Russia (Hall, 2017).

Fourth, Lukashenka kept the 'one socialism in one country' more or less intact until 2008. It meant that the old Soviet system still remained in place and gave quite strong socioeconomic stability. Instead of the privatisation of state enterprises, they remained public entities. This clearly allowed for a quite egalitarian society with a very low Gini coefficient, which measures income inequality as well as low income disparity. Lukashenka created a national ideology which emphasises close ties to Russia, but emphasising as well Belarusian sovereignty (Leshchenko, 2008: 1422–2).

Political, economic and social stability is very appealing to any population. The generous welfare state allows Lukashenka to sustain a quite strong social basis consisting mainly of the older parts of the population which lived in the Soviet Union, and workers and the population living in the rural areas. Moreover, more women tend to vote for Lukashenka than men, and people with lower levels of education (MacAllister and White, 2016: 364–7, 369).

The business model of president Lukashenka is highly dependent on oil and gas revenues and the refinery industry, and has been used to cross-subsidise ailing state enterprises and the welfare system. Lukashenka and his son Victar are at the top of a kleptocratic state similar to other post-Soviet states; however, they have been rather moderate at doing it (Wilson, 2011: 243–4). However, this became skewed during the 2008 economic crisis and the US sanctions against Russia.

Meanwhile, Lukashenka has been power since 1994. The survival of the regime is very dependent on the state of the Russian economy. There is a strong bond between the two countries, but the Ukraine crisis has certainly shown the limits of the sovereignty of Belarus. Moreover, Lukashenka did not recognise de jure the annexation of Crimea, just de facto recognising it as part of Russia. This was a major theme in the 2015 presidential elections (*Belarus in Focus*, 22 April 2016; Radio Free Europe, 23 March 2014). There is a fear that Belarus could be next.

Lukashenka has been very keen to diversify his foreign policy and to increase contacts with the EU (Crabtree et al., 2016: 2). However, this has been used to geostrategically rebalance Russian power and show Russian president Vladimir Putin that it is better to sustain the Belarusian rentier state, otherwise his government may seek alternatives.

Turkey: between democracy and dictatorship

The wider Europe also includes Turkey on the southeastern part of Eurasia. Turkish and European history have been intertwined over the centuries. However, one has to differentiate between the period before and after 1923. Until 1920, the Ottoman Empire was one the major players in European history. It clearly was able to project considerable power against a quite fragmented Europe. This still remains an important source of identity for Turkey today, in spite of having moved from a sultanate to a republic.

In 1923, the new Republic of Turkey was proclaimed and Mustafa Kemal Pascha became the head of state. The new constitution abolished the sultanate and the califate, and a major legislative programme was introduced in order to modernise the country towards European standards. One particular element of this modernisation programme was the separation of politics and religion, something that still today is quite unique in the Islamic world. The basic problem was that such an approach was difficult to sustain without repressive methods against religious groups. Apart from the fact that over 70 per cent of the population was illiterate, they were traditionally devoted Muslims (Davison, 1968: 128–43).

Between 1923 and 1939, Mustafa Kemal Pascha, also known as Atatürk (father of the Turks) established a one-party education dictatorship towards a Western model of democracy. Atatürk often used emergency law to get through his agenda. The principles of such new republic were republicanism, populism, etatism, secularism and reformism (Dodd, 1979: 98).

The postwar period starts with a democratisation process allowing for a pluralist party system; however, the tutelary role of the military remained a major constraint, particularly directed towards radical religious-based parties. This conflict between the tutelary role of the military to preserve Atatürk's secularised state legacy and the growing importance of religious-based parties has been at the crux of the development of democracy in Turkey. Several military coups took place in 1960, 1971 and 1980 in order for religious-based parties to either come to power or end their term in power. Changes in 1961, 1971 and 1980 to the constitution further restricted the role of religious-based parties in the political system. A so-called national security council controlled by the military was enshrined in the constitution. Among the leaders that were deposed by the military were Adnan Menderes (1960), Turgut Özal (1971) and Necmattin Erbakan (1998). However, all these more religious-inspired leaders were able little by little to increase the space for religious-based parties and improve considerably the access of the population to religious institutions. Probably, one of the most important achievements was to gain official approval for parallel religious-based so-called Imam Hatip high schools which worked in parallel with lay state schools. The number of students in the Imam Hatip high schools was low, but since the new millennium the Justice and Development Party (AKP) has created the conditions for a considerable expansion (see Dreßler, 2017: 27).

Since 2002, the AKP party of Tayip Recep Erdogan, who also went to an Imam Hatip high school, has been in power (Schweizer, 2016: 297). The AKP learned a lot from previous experiences of religious-based parties and followed a pragmatic approach to politics focusing mainly on the economy. The AKP is a centrist moderate party using Turkish nationalist populism when they need the support of other parties. Moreover, the charismatic personalities of the leadership, particularly Erdogan and Abdullah Gül, played a major role in attracting voters from all spectrums (Alpan, 2016; Gidengil and Karakoc, 2016; Ocakli, 2017). One major achievement of the AKP was to reduce the power of the military by putting the national security council under civilian control through a constitutional reform in 2003. The AKP was able to secure support from other parties in the Grand National Assembly. Erdogan had been a victim of this military tutelage in 1998 when he had to go to prison for reciting a poem of a famous lay poet. He was only released one year after the electoral victory of his party.

A further step was to get his ally, Abdullah Gül, who had replaced him as prime minister while he was in prison until 2003, to be elected president of the republic in parliament. This clearly was against the convention of the Kemalist constitution that a military person should be president and oversee the political process. Although duly elected, the constitutional court annulled the election. New general elections in 2007 only increased the majority of AKP and, in a second attempt, Gül was elected president (Çarkoğlu, 2007).

A third step was the constitutional reform of 2010 which allowed for the direct election of the president. However, the AKP was not able to change the constitution towards a US-style presidential or French-style semi-presidential system. The powers of the president remained formal. The first directly elected president was Erdogan in 2014, replacing the one-term president Gül. The weakening of the military in the new constitution allowed the Erdogan government to indict the leadership of the military. Between 2011 and 2013, several military including nineteen top generals were tried and convicted with long sentences. This was done mainly by state attorneys, judges and police officers linked to the Gülen movement, which was a major ally of Erdogan's AKP. A major break with the Gülen movement took place in 2013. In that year, a major corruption scandal became known, after judges began to indict high-ranking ministers and members of the AKP, including Erdogan's son Bilal. This clearly was very damaging for Erdogan's party. The main reason for this rift between the Gülen movement and the AKP was the repressive way the AKP government dealt with the Gezi Park protesters in July 2013. Most protesters were young people who wanted to prevent half the park being used to build a mall. Environmental activists and other young protesters decided to occupy the park. They used new social media to mobilise the population against the intentions of Erdogan. Soon the movement was about more than the Gezi Park and was a channel for many grievances related to the expansion of the AKP's power (Dohrn, 2017: 34–5; Özen, 2015).

From 2013 onwards, the AKP government began to target all possible adversaries or critics of the party, particularly the press. Within five years, all printing media and television came under the control of the government. Moreover, journalists were put in prison, so undermining the pluralist order that existed at least until 2007 (Karasu, 2017; Yilmaz, 2016). The daily newspaper *Zaman*, controlled by the Gülen movement, was taken over by the AKP on 14 December 2014 (Schweizer, 2016: 412). According to *Newsweek*, in September 2018 150 journalists were in prison, 180 media outlets closed down and 2,500 journalists lost their jobs (*Newsweek*, 18 September 2018).

Since 2014, Erdogan has tried to achieve a further constitutional reform to increase his powers. However, the AKP failed in the June and November 2015 elections to get a two-thirds majority, which clearly prevented him from achieving constitutional reform without support from other parties. The two contests were undertaken under a climate of terror, not only from Islamic state but also allegedly from state security forces against the Kurds, as well as the Kurdish separatist group PKK. Moreover, the contest was not fair due to the control of the media by the government and the partisan support of Erdogan for the AKP, in spite of the fact that he was president of the republic and should have acted in a neutral manner towards all political parties. Furthermore, resources of the state were used to fund some of the meetings of the AKP, which clearly shows similarities to the use of administrative resources in the post-Soviet states (for more detail, see Kemahlıoğlu, 2016). In May 2016, the AKP tried to achieve the two-thirds quorum by introducing a new terrorism law which allowed the prosecution of MPs, particularly the Kurdish HDP. On 15–16 July he used a failed military coup attempt to stage a civilian countercoup eliminating any adversaries from the political system and civil society. He introduced emergency laws to purge adversaries from political and judiciary institutions, particularly those linked to the Gülen movement (Martens, 2017).

He maintained emergency rule throughout two very important events, the referendum on the new presidential constitution on 16 April 2017 and the new presidential elections of 3 May 2018. Only after these elections were over did Erdogan decide to end emergency rule. However, the repressive measures against his adversaries remained in place. On both occasions, in spite of the unfair conditions under which adversaries were able to campaign, he was able to win the contests with very narrow margins. Just 51.41 and 52.59 per cent voted for the new constitution and for him in the first round of the presidential elections respectively (Esen and Gümüşçü, 2017). One major problem is that he still remains president of the AKP party, violating any ethical principles of neutrality and being the president of all Turks. Electorally, Erdogan relied more and more on votes from the nationalist MHP party in order to compensate for the lost votes from the centre due to his actions (on the support for presidentialism, see Aytaç et al., 2017).

Similar to most of the wider Europe countries, the rule of law was certainly a major victim of this political restructuring of Turkey. Through the purges, the judiciary has become an instrument of power of the AKP (Saatçioğlu, 2016).

Certainly the most urgent problem for president Erdogan and the AKP government is the never-ending conflict with the Kurdish population. The terrorist organisation PKK has played a major role in challenging the dominance of the state in the Kurdish-dominated regions. Moreover, the growing self-confidence of the Kurdish minorities in Iraq and Syria after the respective wars is putting Turkey in a considerable national security dilemma. However, any solution to the Kurdish problem has to be political, not military, and so far this has been a quite difficult option for a rigid Turkish nationalism (Gürbey, 2017: 16–17).

In sum, it seems that Turkey is heading to a façade democracy similar to those of the post-Soviet states.

The Eastern partnership of the EU: the need for a recalibration

Following the end of the Cold War, the EU has been developing a foreign policy towards its neighbourhood countries. It started with the Euro-Mediterranean partnership with the southern rim of the Mediterranean being agreed after Spain's initiative in Barcelona in 1995 (Gillespie, 1997). This so-called Barcelona process envisaged the creation of a large Euro-Mediterranean market including the EU countries, the Maghreb, the Mashreq and the Middle Eastern countries. The outcome would be a Euromorph single market, meaning that all these countries had to adopt the *acquis communautaire* in order to be part of the market. Although a democracy clause was included in the association agreements, most of the provisions were related to the *acquis communautaire*. The majority of these countries are rather neo-patrimonial defective or fragile democracies (Morocco, Lebanon, Jordan) or dictatorships (Egypt, Libya, Syria). Just Israel could be regarded as a functioning democracy, but rather repressive in relation to the annexed territories of Palestine. The Palestine Authority was also included in the programme, and the EU spent considerable funding building their structures (Gillespie, 1997; Magone, 2018: 298–9).

After a decade, the Euro-Mediterranean partnership was stagnating somewhat, and it was used by the EU in the fight against terrorism (Gillespie, 2006). By 2008, the Euro-Mediterranean partnership was replaced by a softer version, the Union for the Mediterranean (UfM), initiated by president Nicolás Sarkozy during the French presidency of 2008. UfM has been developing projects for the Mediterranean, but private funding is still lacking, so that very few projects have been approved (Gillespie, 2011; Katsaris, 2015). The Arab Spring of 2011 further undermined the reputation of the EU, which had been working closely with dictators like Ben Ali in Tunisia and Hosni Mubarak in Egypt. Today, the EU's main preoccupation is to control migration waves coming from the southern rim of the Mediterranean, so that again realistic interests prevail over idealistic ones (see the assessment of Börzel and Lebanidze, 2017; Boogaerts et al., 2016).

In 2004, after the big enlargement to Central and Eastern Europe, the EU decided to incorporate the Euro-Mediterranean partnership in the all-encompassing European Neighbourhood Policy (ENP), which focused on more long-term projects in the post-Soviet states. Similar to the Euro-Mediterranean partnership, it intended to help all countries, with the exception of Russia which had a special programme, to become more similar to the EU. The overall aim was to transform these countries into functioning democracies and markets that were compatible with the EU.

After a Polish-Swedish initiative, the Eastern partnership was born in 2008. This new initiative was more ambivalent than the still existing overarching ENP. The countries targeted were Ukraine, Georgia, Moldova, Azerbaijan and Armenia.

Such a partnership was upgraded during the Lithuanian presidency of the EU in the second half of 2013, which envisaged association agreements towards a Deep and Comprehensive Free Trade Area (DCFTA). Particularly, three countries would qualify for it: Ukraine, Georgia and Moldova. Historically, it is not a coincidence that Poland, Sweden and Lithuania have been the main initiators of the Eastern partnerships. All three countries have been intertwinedly involved in the history of Moldova, Ukraine and Belarus. One positive decision of EU member-states is that the Eastern partnership has no membership perspective. A membership of Ukraine in the EU without first achieving very good relations of trust and cooperation with Russia would become a disruptive, even conflictive, permanent crisis for the EU. This is also valid for NATO. It could even lead to a breakup of the country. The best way to involve Russia is to take the EAEU seriously, because it has lots of potential, and the EU single market regulatory framework, in spite of the autocratic or defective democracy nature of its members, could slowly shape this regional project over a long period of time as well. For Ukraine, Georgia, Moldova, Azerbaijan and Armenia it would be a win-win situation. However, this will only be possible if the EU is able to convince Russia of a new genuine partnership comprising also the security dimension. So far, the Russian perspective has been negative about the ENP and the Eastern partnership. In the present form, the EU tends to reinforce old stereotypes about Russia and rigid boundaries between East and West, instead of 'transforming' it in the sense of a peace project (Delcour, 2015).

As I have shown in these pages, democratisation and market reform will only be possible when state capture and kleptocracy are reduced to substantially and the rule of law begins to prevail in the Eastern partnership countries. So far the signs are rather bleak. Moreover, the few resources that the EU is spending should be used more efficiently, doing less but better. Funding should only exist first to strengthen democracy, the rule of law and the respective enforcement forces such as police and the judiciary, before dealing with market reform (see a kind of assessment of international assistance by Sasse, 2013).

Conclusions: the struggle for democracy, rule of law and economic prosperity in wider Europe

Wider Europe can be regarded as a natural geographical border of core Europe. It clearly belongs to other political traditions than core Europe. It is probably also the natural geographical borders of the EU. Beyond this frontier, the EU and its values will have difficulties being asserting, particularly if we consider the limited resources of the supranational organisation.

Suggested reading

Börzel, Tanja A. and Bidzina Lebanidze (2017), The transformative power of Europe beyond enlargement: the EU's performance in promoting democracy in its neighbourhood. *East European Politics*, 33(1): 17–35.

Brzezinski, Zbigniew (1997), *The Grand Chessboard. America's Primacy and Its Geostrategic Imperatives*. New York: Basic Books

Hahn, Gordon M. (2018), *Ukraine Over the Edge: Russia, the West and the New Cold War*. Jefferson: McFarland and Company

Nodia, Ghia (ed.) (2016), *25 Years of Independent Georgia: Achievements and Unfinished Projects*. Tbilisi: Konrad Adenauer Foundation and Ilia State University Press, pp. 91–129.

QUESTIONS FOR REVISION

- Assess the relationship between the EU and Russia.
- What are the main reasons for the Ukraine crisis of 2014?
- Is Moldova a viable nation-state? Discuss using examples.
- What are the main achievements and challenges of the Eastern partnership of the EU?
- How important is geopolitics to understanding the post-Soviet space?

Chapter 12

Conclusions

Reinventing Europe

- Learning from each other: diversity and convergence of European politics
- Mediatisation and electoral markets in Europe
- A multilevel governance system: European, national, regional and local
- Flexible means of communication: positive and critical issues of e-government and e-democracy
- Towards multicultural societies? The challenge of immigration
- The unification of the continent as an historical milestone: towards a region of democratic peace and stability
- The borders of the EU: Turkey and the post-Soviet space
- Conclusions: the rise of post-sovereign European politics

Learning from each other: diversity and convergence of European politics

One particular characteristic of European politics is the number of states that exist across the continent. Most of these states are small, but there are also larger states such as Germany, the UK, France and Italy. There are also medium-sized countries such as Spain, Poland and Romania. The diversity of political systems also shows that national path-dependency has been important for all these countries. The French semi-presidential system was established because the Fourth Republic was not stable and efficient enough; since it was proclaimed in 1958, French politics has become more predictable and stable. The Napoleonic political culture played a major role in shaping the figure of the president in France. Furthermore, the French model was taken over by many other countries, such as Portugal, Finland, Poland, Romania, Bulgaria, Lithuania and Slovakia. However, each country has created a different balance between institutions. This means that institutional transfer is constantly taking place between the different countries, but each country adjusts the transferred institutions to their own national political cultures. Hungary for example, emulated many of the German institutions, particularly the model of a Chancellor democracy, but the electoral system has led to a majoritarian type of democracy instead of the consensual style prevalent in Germany.

One particular element of European politics is institutional transfer within a region. The Nordic countries are a good example in this respect. There has been permanent institutional transfer between all five Nordic countries, so that they now look very similar. Although Finland is a semi-presidential democracy, the Nordic institutional transfer has contributed to the establishment of similar institutions in the judiciary and in the legislature, so that the political systems have become very alike. In Chapter 6 it was possible to see how the judiciary of all these countries converged to a Nordic model; this has also been visible among the countries with romance languages, which overwhelmingly adopted the Napoleonic code.

Another important aspect of institutional transfer has been among party systems. The established party families, which found their highest expressions in the European political party federations in the European parliament, have contributed to the stabilisation of many party systems in Southern, Central and Eastern Europe. The panoply of political parties is increasingly framed by traditional party families. New political parties have difficulty in staying outside the existing groups in the European Parliament. If they are not part of a parliamentary group, they are sidelined from important decision-making processes. Europeanisation of party politics has become an important aspect of contemporary European politics.

Mediatisation and electoral markets in Europe

Contemporary European politics is increasingly dominated by the media. The permanent media campaign has become an important feature of how politics is communicated to the public. The importance of 'spin doctors', electoral strategists, media managers and focus groups is changing the nature of representation in European politics. The marketisation of politics has transformed the way political parties conduct elections. The end of the mass party and its replacement by the cartel party has created a more economistic approach to politics. Indeed, we can speak of a political economy of electoral politics. Political parties are engaged in product marketing, so that now representation is constructed through the market and the media. This is an inversion of the representation process, which used to be more of a bottom-up, social movement. Such manipulation of representation can be observed particularly in Southern Europe and Central and Eastern Europe. The best example is the creation of the firm–party Forza Italia by Silvio Berlusconi in 1994. Berlusconi was able to use the knowledge of his business empire to create a new party and used product marketing strategies to achieve victory in the March 1994 elections. Since then, Italian politics has become much more Americanised and bipolarised between the left and the right. The model was followed by other countries – in the UK (Tony Blair and New Labour), France (Nicolas Sarkozy and the Union for the People's Movement, UMP and Emmanuel Macron with his La Republique en Marche) and Germany (Gerhard Schröder and the German Social Democratic Party – SPD).

This also means that political and electoral campaigns have led to a spiralling of costs. In spite of generous public funding in many European countries, there is still a need to raise even more money from private donors, creating problems of accountability and transparency. The dangers of political corruption, clientelism and patronage then become very real. Political corruption is still a major problem in Central and Eastern European countries, and, at least partly, is related to party politics. The tangentopoli affair in Italy in 1993 highlighted the dangers of systemic corruption over several decades. The Helmut Kohl affair, when he refused to disclose all the transactions of a DM2 million secret fund to a committee in the Bundestag between 1999 and 2002 is a good example. In France, the Elf scandal involved foreign minister Roland Dumas, who was convicted but then acquitted by a higher court because he was not aware that his mistress had given him presents sponsored by Elf (*The Guardian*, 13 November 2003).

This political economy of electoral campaigns also led to the 'cash for honours' affair in 2006–7 in the UK. Many private donors allegedly made donations or loaned money to the Labour Party with very low interest rates (close to zero) in return for future honours (lordships). Also allegedly, this had been common practice of all the UK political parties. Prime minister Tony Blair was interviewed three times by the London Metropolitan Police. In the end, the investigation was closed, with nobody being prosecuted.

This means that a 'crisis of representation' related to partyocracy in many European countries is leading to the emergence of leftwing and rightwing populist parties across Europe. Even the Netherlands, one of the countries where political parties have the highest scores in terms of trust, has seen the emergence of populist parties, for example Pim Fortuyn List (2002–7) and, since 2005, the Party of Freedom (Partij van Vrijheid – PvV) of Geert Wilders, who is against an 'Islamisation of Europe' and the 'European super-state'. Such a populist backlash can be found, for example, in Austria, where, since the mid-1980s, the Freedom Party (FPÖ) has gained steadily electorally and has been able to change the political culture of the country. In the new millennium, the FPÖ was in power in a coalition with the conservative People's Party (ÖVP) between 2002 and 2006, and again since March 2018. In the presidential elections of 2017, the FPÖ candidate Norbert Hofer made it to the second round, and lost just 7 percentage points to Green candidate Alexander van der Bellen. In Germany, the anti-immigration and soft Eurosceptic Alternative for Germany (AfD) is now dominating the debate by highlighting mistakes in the refugee policy of the grand coalition between the Christian democrats (CDU/CSU) and the social democrats (SPD). It is now the leader of the opposition in the Bundestag, it being the third largest party. A similar situation is happening in Sweden with the rise of anti-immigration Swedish Democrats(SD).

A multilevel governance system: European, national, regional and local

Another aspect of European politics is that the traditional sovereign nation-state has been replaced by an integrated cooperative post-sovereign state within a multilevel governance system. The 'post-sovereign' state, as defined by William Wallace, works together with other states to resolve concrete problems (see Chapter 10). The European integration process led to the establishment of an EU political system that includes not only national and supranational levels but also subnational and global levels. This means that, since the 1980s, there has been a growth in the complexity of the way politics is run. The post-sovereign state operates in a globalised world, in which many policy areas are shared with other countries. This creates a high level of global and European interdependency that limits the possibilities for individual countries to move alone in most policy areas. Among these policy areas are the environment, global trade arrangements and security issues. Moreover, at subnational level regions and local authorities have become more self-confident and develop international networks or engage in cross-border cooperation. Some regions, such as Flanders, Wallonia, Catalonia and Scotland, regard themselves as stateless nations. They have developed their own paradiplomacy parallel to the national governments.

The multilevel governance system is also a new structure of opportunities for non-governmental organisations (NGOs) and civil society associations. Many NGOs have become global players and tend to use the different levels to influence policy. In the EU, the supranational level has seen an increase in Eurogroups. This means that there has been a growing politicisation of the European integration process (Marks and Steenbergen, 2004).

Flexible means of communication: positive and critical issues of e-government and e-democracy

This growth of complexity has made the analysis of European politics more interesting, but also more challenging. The nation-state as such is only one of many actors that have emerged since the early 1980s. A thorough analysis needs to take into account all other levels and the interactions between three kinds of actors: political institutions, private economic and civil society actors. Governance is characterised by a high level of dynamics and flexibility that contrasts heavily with the rigid nation-state of the 1950s and 1960s. One of the reasons for this flexibility is that there is a continuing process of adjustment to new globalised and Europeanised realities. This also means that the institutions of national political systems have become more flexible. The new mobile technologies and, of course, the internet have changed our understanding of the state. E-government and e-democracy have become new tools in the way democratic governments create a direct link to citizens.

There are also other more critical issues that may emerge from this increasing use of new technologies. The 'big brother' state, as described in George Orwell's *1984*, may yet become a reality. Digital televisions create an interactive platform that can lead to a better service for the customer but also to greater control by the state and large private corporations. The high number of surveillance cameras in European countries is important to preserve security, but could also lead to the surveillance state and all its negative implications.

A turning point of the debate was Edward Snowden's revelations about the programme of the US National Security Agency (NSA) to spy on everything using sophisticated electronic surveillance mechanisms. As a whistleblower he decided to move abroad, getting asylum in Russia, and although he really has done a heroic great service to democracy and the citizens of the world, he was indicted by the US government as a traitor (see Lyon, 2015; Murakami and Wright, 2015).

The potential and threat of social media have become more evident in the 2010s. It is used both for information as well as disinformation. A good example is the targeting of voters through social media profiles undertaken by the UK company Cambridge Analytica with allegedly the known or unknown cooperation of Facebook and used by the campaign of presidential candidate Donald J. Trump during the US elections of 2016 (*The Guardian*, 17 March 2018). Such phenomena related to the manipulation of social media have been detected in Europe. According to data traffic records, allegedly Russian networks used manipulated social media to try to influence the campaign during the Brexit referendum in 2016 and the Catalan illegal referendum on 1 October 2017 (*El Pais*, 1 October 2017). It seems that new hybrid warfare is becoming part of the inventory of fighting the adversary or enemy. Citizens and voters need to be educated to look critically at ideologically manufactured news, both in terms of consent or dissent (Herman and Chomsky, 1988; Hoffstetter, 2016).

Towards multicultural societies? The challenge of immigration

In spite of the social differences, lifestyles have converged across Europe. We cannot speak of a European society, but the cultural traits of most European countries are fairly similar. Social stratification has become comparable across all countries. The dominance of the services sector, a declining industrial sector and a very small, but efficient agricultural sector are the characteristics of the main employment sectors in Europe. However, there are still substantial differences between Western and Eastern Europe. Poland and Romania, for example, still have very large agricultural sectors. In spite of this, European integration will certainly lead to a decrease in the number of people working in the agricultural sector.

Since the early 1950s, Western Europe has experienced several immigration waves. Today we have multicultural societies in most Western European countries.

Many children of immigrants have become integrated in the new societies and become citizens of the country. This multiculturalism if socially integrated is a source of wealth and diversity for the country and society. All northern countries have a very multicultural outlook, which is probably strongest in the UK, Germany, France and the Netherlands.

Meanwhile, the Southern European countries, which were emigration countries, have become new targets for immigrants. The population of Spain has been growing considerably, at least in part due to the number of immigrants that have come to the country since the early 1990s. Spain is also the most multicultural society in Southern Europe.

Overall, immigration has increased considerably in the same period. The main reason is that we now have global immigration movements from the southern hemisphere to the northern one, and from east to west. All this leads to new challenges for European societies. The decline of populations in most countries is leading to a necessary rethinking about immigration. Apart from more coordination between EU member-states in relation to immigration policy, integration today also requires a European dimension, because most immigrants, like most European citizens, have to be more mobile in the context of an emerging single European market.

The refugee crisis in the summer of 2015 was a wake-up call. It showed that not all parts of the European populations welcome refugees. On the contrary, the new processes of globalisation have led to divisions within national societies. The majority of populations seem to deal well with new challenges, but a large minority feels threatened in their way of life. Their response to the refugee crisis is more of a national one leading to the rise of new right or extreme rightwing parties. European integration further reinforces this social divide within and across the EU. Thomas Risse identified different subcultures oriented towards further European integration. On the one hand there are the Europeans supporting the values that the EU embodies, such as democracy, rule of law, human rights, freedom and equality. They are open-minded and willing to thinking in supranational and international terms. They are high-skilled and more mobile. On the other, there are the exclusive nationalists that reject European integration due to their strong attachment to their nation-state. They have less transnational interactions. They have low levels of education and are blue collar workers. In between, there is a third group of inclusive nationalists that have Europe as their secondary identity. They tend to side with the first group, but it remains an ambiguous group that may also swing to more nationalist positions. The perception of the EU of this middle group will determine how the EU evolves in the future (Risse, 2010: 49).

The unification of the continent as an historical milestone: towards a region of democratic peace and stability

In the past millennium, the European nations went to war with each other and concentrated their energies in trying to achieve supremacy over their neighbours. Such national behaviour started to change after 1945, after two 'European' civil wars in 1914–18 and 1939–45. The division of Europe soon afterwards contributed to a change of mentalities among European political elites. Such diffusion of behaviour was reinforced by the democratic nature of regimes in most European countries. The Franco-German reconciliation in the early 1950s must be regarded as the beginning of such a change in mentality. The creation of the European Communities in the 1950s allowed a new Europe based on democratic peace to be established. In spite of the Cold War, which was dominated by the United States and Russia, Europeans on both sides of the Iron Curtain contributed to this unification process. The legendary Ostpolitik of Hans-Dietrich Genscher towards East Germany and Poland cannot be underestimated. It created conditions for dialogue, in spite of the differences of regimes. Václav Havel's heroic fight for democracy and human rights as a member of the Charta 77, along with other dissidents in Czechoslovakia, was a further contribution to the European integration process. The Solidarity protest movement in Poland in the 1980s contributed immensely to the change from an authoritarian dictatorship under General Jaruzelski to a semi-presidential democracy. The Iron Curtain began to be porous on the border between Austria and Hungary in 1989. Many East Germans fled the country through Hungary and Austria and moved to West Germany. Finally, on 9 November 1989, the fall of the Berlin Wall ended the division of Europe. West and East became part of a new era in Europe and European integration became a central process.

However, war still continued to shape the continent. In 1991, the Balkan wars erupted and confirmed that divisive nationalisms were still creating wars in Europe. The wars lasted until 1999. Since then nationalist and ethnic divisions have continued to prevail in the Balkans. The United Nations, with a strong contribution from NATO and the EU, sent peacekeeping forces and civilian reconstruction teams to improve the situation in these countries. From the former Yugoslav states, only Slovenia was able to escape the atrocities of war and move peacefully towards European integration. In spite of this positive example, in the massacre of Srebrenica in 1995 by Bosnian-Serbs against Bosniaks allegedly carried out by Radko Mladiç, over 8,000 Bosnian men and boys were killed on 11–13 July 1995. This was characterised by the United Nations as genocide and awakened memories of the Holocaust against the Jewish population by the National Socialist regime during the Second World War and the Rwanda genocide against the Tutsis perpetrated by the Hutus in April–July 1994. This atrocious event was even more shocking because peacekeepers did not intervene and allowed the massacre to take place. Most of these soldiers were Dutch, so the Dutch government, after a damaging report, decided to resign before the end of the legislature on 15 April 2002 (*BBC News*, 16 April 2002). Today, Bosnia-Herzegovina still exists as a country because of the presence of the international community. The mistrust between Bosnian-Serbs, Bosniaks and Bosnian-Croats has prevented reconciliation. All institutions are controlled, or at least monitored, by the High Representative for Bosnia-Herzegovina who is also the Special Representative of the EU. The Serbian Republic (Republika Srpska) remains outside the federation as an autonomous entity.

The growing tension between Serbia and the Albanian Kosovo Liberation Army (KLA) in 1999 led again to the intervention of the international community through NATO. The bombardment of Serbia created the conditions for a settlement, in which the international peacekeeping forces could be deployed. In February 2008, almost a decade after the conflict, Kosovo was recognised as an independent country by the United States, most European countries (apart from Spain, Greece, Romania, Slovakia, Cyprus and Bosnia-Herzegovina), and some countries in Latin America, Africa and Asia. However, Russia and China, partly because of their own centre-periphery relations, did not recognise its independence. A major issue was that it was unilaterally declared. Russia was quite solidarous with Serbia against illegal NATO bombardment, and the bond between the two Slavic countries is quite strong. Kosovo continues to be a major divisive issue in Serbia, where the Europeanists want to move on and focus their energies on becoming part of the EU, while the nationalists regard Kosovo as part of Serbia and remain intransigent. This will be a most difficult problem in a process of integration of the Balkan countries starting after 2026. Serbia, Macedonia, Montenegro and Albania are now candidate countries, while the more problematic cases of Bosnia-Herzegovina and Kosovo are not. It is important that the EU first dismantles the networks of state capture and kleptocracy in these countries before allowing them to join.

In spite of these negative events of contemporary European politics, the overall thrust has so far been towards peace. In 2004, after a decade of democratisation, liberalisation and restructuring of economy, politics and society a major enlargement eastwards, comprising ten countries and the Mediterranean islands of Malta and Cyprus, took place. It is changing the nature of European politics. In 2007, Bulgaria and Romania also joined the EU, followed by Croatia in 2013.

The borders of the EU: Turkey and the post-Soviet space

Although Turkey is a candidate country, the growing authoritarian features of the country under president Tayip Recep Erdogan has destroyed any hopes of achieving membership. In order to achieve this, president Erdogan must reverse all these repressive measures, including reinstating everybody that was purged from state institutions just because they held a different opinion from him.

The proposed membership of Turkey has, so far, been a divisive issue in Europe. The supporters claim that the EU would set an example of cosmopolitanism by integrating a largely Muslim country, which is oriented towards the West and has participated actively in European fora since the 1960s. Moreover, Turkey has a large market of over 88 million people. And, as a political actor, it would certainly be an asset to the EU when dealing with conflicts in the Middle East.

The sceptics regarding the eventual membership of Turkey refer to the fact that it would be too costly to integrate the country, because of the lower level of development of regions in the eastern part of the country. Moreover, there are still many outstanding problems in Turkish democracy, such as human rights issues. Furthermore, some refer to the religion issue and tend to follow a loose or more concrete vision of Europe as a Christian community (Giscard D'Estaing). Turkey's membership is opposed particularly in France and Austria, and both countries intend to conduct a referendum on it after all negotiations have been undertaken. This is a further hurdle that is affecting the process of Turkish integration into the EU.

This leads us to the question of where the borders of the EU are or should be. In my view, after an eventual Balkan enlargement, and possibly the Moldavian-speaking part of Moldova, the EU has reached its borders. Any expansion to the post-Soviet space would need excellent relations with Russia. The EU has been built so far on the cheap, with the United States paying for the security of the continent. This tandem of EU and NATO is regarded as a threat by Russia, which regards the post-Soviet space as its sphere of influence. In this regard, Ukraine and Georgia should not be offered membership as long as EU-Russia relations and also those of these countries with Russia have improved. In both countries there are frozen conflicts that cannot be resolved without a trust-building engagement with Russia. Although Moldova also has a frozen conflict with Transnistria, it would be desirable to organise a referendum to ask the Moldavian population if it wants to become part of Romania. This would clarify the choices of the country.

Conclusions: the rise of post-sovereign European politics

The European integration process since 1985 has transformed European politics towards a multilevel governance system. The erosion of national sovereignty has exerted major pressure on the move towards post-sovereign regimes of cooperation. Therefore, national politics is now intertwined with supranational European and global politics. We can observe this globalised and Europeanised politics in the processes of institutional transfer, mediatisation and marketisation of electoral markets and party politics, the use of flexible ways of communication, and the growing cooperation in immigration and integration policies. The financial crisis of 2008–13, which originated the United States, was a major challenge for the European socioeconomic model. The refugee crisis of 2015 put the EU under considerable pressure. However, without the EU probably all these crisis would have led to even worse outcomes. Overall, the EU as a regional community of democratic states, in spite of Brexit, will remain the greatest success of European cooperation in an increasingly turbulent world.

References

Ágh, Attila (1994), *The Emergence of East Central European Parliaments: The First Steps*. Budapest: Hungarian Centre for Democracy Studies.

—— (1998), *The Politics of Central Europe*. London: SAGE.

—— (2003), *Anticipatory and Adaptive Europeanization in Hungary*. Budapest: Hungarian Centre for Democracy Studies.

—— (2016), The Decline of Democracy in East-Central Europe. *Problems of Post-Communism*, 63(5–6): 277–87.

—— (2017), Declining Systemic Trust in the Political Elite in the EU's New Member States: The Divergence Between East-Central Europe and the Baltic States. *Baltic Journal of Political Science*, 6: 27–49.

—— and Gabriela Ilonski (1996), *Parliaments and Organised Interests: The Second Steps*. Budapest: Hungarian Centre for Democracy Studies.

—— and Sandór Kurtán (1995), *Democratization and Europeanization in Hungary: The First Parliament 1990–1994*. Budapest: Hungarian Centre for Democracy Studies.

Alpan, Başak (2016), From AKP's 'Conservative Democracy' to 'Advanced Democracy': Shifts and Challenges in the Debate on 'Europe'. *South European Society and Politics*, 21(1): 15–28.

Alþýðusamb and Íslands (Icelandic Confederation of Labour-ASI) (2018), Icelandic Confederation of Labour (ASI). www.asi.is/engpol/ (accessed on 25 June 2018).

Althingi (2011), Ársskýrsla Alþingis 2010–2011. Reykjavik: Althingi. www.althingi.is/pdf/arsskyrsla2010.pdf (accessed on 29 October 2018).

—— (2016), Ársreikningur 2015. Reykjavik: Althingi. www.althingi.is/pdf/Arsreikningar/Arsreikningur_Althingis_2015.pdf (accessed on 29 October 2018).

—— (2018), Ársskýrslur 1999–2010. www.althingi.is/um-althingi/utgefid-efni/arsskyrslur-althingis/ (accessed on 19 February 2018).

Amable, Bruno (2016), The Political Economy of the Neoliberal Transformation of French Industrial Relations. *Industrial and Labor Relations Review*, 69(3): 523–50.

—— (2017), *Structural Crisis and Institutional Change in Modern Capitalism. French Capitalism in Transition*. Oxford: Oxford University Press.

——, Elvire Guillaud and Stefano Palombarini (2012), Changing French Capitalism: Political and Systemic Crises in France. *Journal of European Public Policy*, 9(8): 1168–87.

Anderson, M.S. (1963), *Europe in the Eighteenth Century 1713–1783*. London: Longman.

Andersen, Torben M. (2011), *A Flexicurity Labour Market in the Great Recession: The Case of Denmark*. Discussion Paper No. 5710, May 2011.

Andeweg, Rudy and Galen Irwin (2014), *The Politics and Governance in the Netherlands*, fourth edition. Basingstoke: Palgrave.

André, Audrey and Sam Depauw (2015), A Divided Nation? The 2014 Belgian Federal Elections. *West European Politics*, 38(1): 228–37.

Andreev, Svetlozar A. (2008), Semi-Presidentialism in Bulgaria: The Cyclical Rise of Informal Powers and Individual Political Ambitions in a 'Dual Executive'. In: Robert Elgie and Sophia Moestrup (eds), *Semi-Presidentialism in Central and Eastern Europe*. Manchester: Manchester University Press, pp. 32–50.

Antoniades, Andreas (2008): Social Europe and/or global Europe? Globalization and Flexicurity as Debates on the Future of Europe. *Cambridge Review of International Affairs*, 21(3): 327–46.

Aprasidze, David (2016), 25 Years of Georgia's Democratization: Still Work in Progress. In: Ghia Nodia (ed.), *25 Years of Independent Georgia: Achievements and Unfinished Projects*. Tbilisi: Konrad Adenauer Foundation and Ilia State University Press, pp. 91–129.

Aristotle (323 BC, 1992), *The Politics*. London: Penguin Books.

Armingeon, Klaus and Lucio Baccaro (2012), The Sorrows of Young Euro: The Sovereign Debt Crisis of Ireland and Southern Europe. In: Nancy Bermeo and Jonas Pontusson (eds), *Coping with Crisis. Government Reactions to the Great Recession*. New York: Russell Foundation, pp. 162–97.

Arter, David (1999), *Scandinavian Politics Today*. Manchester: Manchester University Press.

—— (ed.) (2007), *Comparing and Classifying Legislatures*. London: Frank Cass.

—— (2011), Taking the Gilt off the Conservatives' Gingerbread: The April 2011 Finnish General Election. *West European Politics*, 34(6): 1284–95.

—— (2015), A 'Pivotal Centre Party' Calls the Shots: The 2015 Finnish General Election. *West European Politics*, 38(6): 1345–53.

Assemblée Nationale (2018), Statistiques de l'activité parlamentaire. From 11th to 15th legislature. www2.assemblee-nationale.fr/15/statistiques-de-l-activite-parlementaire (accessed on 15 February 2018).

Assembleia da República (2018a), Deputados e Grupos Parlamentares/Estatuto Remuneratório e outros Direitos dos Deputados. www.parlamento.pt/DeputadoGP/Paginas/EstatutoRemuneratorioDeputados.aspx (accessed on 16 February 2018).

—— (2018b), Yearly Statistical Reports in Section Atividade Parlamentar e Processo Legislativo. www.parlamento.pt/ActividadeParlamentar/Paginas/Relatorios-e-estatisticas.aspx (accessed on 22 February 2018).

Auel, Katrin and Oliver Höing (2015), National Parliaments and the Eurozone Crisis: Taking Ownership in Difficult Times? *West European Politics*, 38(2): 375–95.

—— and Christine Neuhold (2017), Multi-Arena Players in the Making? Conceptualizing the Role of National Parliaments Since the Lisbon Treaty. *Journal of European Public Policy*, 24(10): 1547–61.

Auers, Daunis (2015), *Comparative Politics and Government in the Baltic States: Estonia, Latvia and Lithuania in the 21st Century*. Basingstoke: Palgrave.

Auffermann, Burkhard (2009), Das politische System Finnlands. In: Wolfgang Ismayr (ed.), *Die politischen Systeme Westeuropas*. Wiesbaden: Springer VS, pp. 183–216.

Aylott, Nicholas (2005), 'President Persson': How Did Sweden Get Him? In: Thomas Poguntke and Paul Webb (eds), *The Presidentialization of Politics: A Comparative Study of Modern Democracies*. Oxford: Oxford University Press, pp. 176–98.

Baboš, Pavol and Darina Malová (2016), Czech Republic. In: Andreas Bågenholm and Liam Weeks (eds), *Political Data Yearbook 2015*. Special issue of *European Journal of Political Research*, 56(1): 231–6.

Bach, Daniel C. (2011), Patrimonialism and Neopatrimonialism: Comparative Trajectories and Readings. *Commonwealth & Comparative Politics*, 49(3): 275–94.

Bach, Maurizio (1995), *Die Bürokratisierung Europas: Verwaltungseliten, Experten und Politische Legitimation in Europa*. Frankfurt a. M.: Campus.

Badó, Attila (2014), Die Versuche zur Reform des ungarischen Justizwesens nach der Systemwende: Gerichtsebenen und zentrale Verwaltung. In: Badó Attila and Detlev W. Belling (eds), *Rechtsentwicklungen aus europäischer Perspektive im 21. Jahrhundert [European Perspectives on Legal Developments in the 21st Century]*. Potsdam: Universitätsverlag Potsdam, pp. 11–53.

Bale, Tim (2011), *The Conservative Party. From Thatcher to Cameron*. Cambridge: Polity.

Balik, Stanislav and Vit Hloušek (2016), The Development and Transformation of the Czech Party System after 1989. *Acta Politologica*, 8(2): 103–17.

Barnes, Lucy and Anne Wren (2012), The Liberal Model in the Crisis: Continuity and Change in Great Britain and Ireland. In: Nancy Bermeo and Jonas Pontusson (eds), *Coping with Crisis: Government Reactions to the Great Recession*. New York: Russell Foundation, pp. 287–324.

Bartolini, Stefano (2000), *The Political Mobilization of the European Left, 1860–1980: The Class Cleavage*. Cambridge: Cambridge University Press.

—— (2005), *Restructuring Europe: Centre Formation, System Building, and Political Structuring between the Nation State and the European Union*. Oxford: Oxford University Press.

—— and Peter Mair (1990), *Identity, Competition and Electoral Volatility: The Stabilisation of European Electorates 1885–1985*. Cambridge: Cambridge University Press.

Batory, Agnes (2016), Populists in Government? Hungary's 'System of National Cooperation. *Democratization*, 23(2): 283–303.

Bauman, Zygmunt (2001), *The Individualized Society*. Cambridge: Polity.

Beck, Ulrich (2008), *Weltrisikogesellschaft*. Frankfurt a. M.: Suhrkamp.

Behnen, Michael (2002), Bürgerliche Revolution und Reichsgründung (1848–71). In: Martin Vogt (ed.), *Deutsche Geschichte: Von den Anfängen zur Gegenwart*. Frankfurt a. M.: Fischer, pp. 451–516.

Behrendt, Christian (2013), The Process of Constitutional Amendment in Belgium. In: Xenophon Contiades (ed.), *Engineering Constitutional Change: A Comparative Perspective on Europe, Canada and USA*. London: Routledge, pp. 35–50.

Bekker, Sonja (2018), Flexicurity in the European Semester: Still a Relevant Policy Concept? *Journal of European Public Policy*, 25(2): 175–92.

Bell, John (2006), *Judiciaries within Europe: A Comparative Review*. Cambridge: Cambridge University Press.

Benz, Arthur (2009), *Politik im Mehrebenen Systemen. Ein Lehrbuch*. Wiesbaden: Verlag für Sozialwissenschaften.

Bergman, Torbjörn (1993), Formation Rules and Minority Governments. *European Journal of Political Research*, 23(1): 55–66.

—— and Thomas Larue (2004), The regime parlamentaire en Suède. In: Olivier Costa, Eric Kerrouche and Paul Magnette (eds), *Vers un renouveau du parlamentarisme en Europe?* Brussels: Éditions Université Libre de Bruxelles, pp. 231–54.

Bergmann, Eirikur (2014), *Iceland and the International Financial Crisis: Boom, Bust and Recovery*. Basingstoke: Palgrave.

Bernaciak, Magdalena (2013), Social Dialogue Revival or 'PR Corporatism'? Negotiating Anti-Crisis Measures in Poland and Bulgaria. *Transfer* 19(2): 239–51.

Bertelsmann Stiftung (2014), *20 Jahre Binnenmarkt: Wachstumseffekte der zunehmenden europäischen Integration*. Gütersloh: Bertelsmann Stiftung.

—— (2018a), Policy Performance and Governance Capacities in the OECD and EU Sustainable Governance Indicators 2018. www.sgi-network.org/docs/2018/basics/SGI2018_Overview.pdf (accessed on 23 November 2018).

—— (2018b), Bertelsmann Transformation Index 2018. www.bti-project.org/de/laenderberichte/ (accessed on 13 September 2018).

Bestler, Anita (2012), Malta. In: Werner Reutter (ed.), *Verbände und Verbandssysteme in den Ländern der Europäischen Union*. Wiesbaden: Springer Verlag, pp. 445–76.

—— and Arno Waschkuhn (2009), Das politische System Maltas. In: Wolfgang Ismayr (ed.), *Die politischen Systeme Westeuropas*. Wiesbaden: Verlag für Sozialwissenschaften, pp. 868–90.

Bideleux, Robert and Ian Jeffries (2007a), *A History of Eastern Europe: Crisis and Change*. London: Routledge.

—— (2007b), *The Balkans: A Post-Communist History*. London: Routledge.

Bíroság (2018), The Courts in Hungary. https://birosag.hu/en (accessed on 2 November 2018).

Black, Harold D., George Gebel and Robert R. Newton (1984), The Centenary of the Prime Meridian and of International Standard Time. *Johns Hopkins APL Technical Digest*, 5(4): 381–9.

Blauberger, Michael and Susanne K. Schmidt (2017), The European Court of Justice and its Political Impact. *West European Politics*, 40(4): 907–18.

Blavoukos, Spyros and George Pagoulatos (2008), Negotiating in Stages: National Positions and the Reform of the Stability and Growth Pact. *European Journal of Political Research*, 47(2): 247–67.

Blaziene, Inga and Rasa Zabarauskaite (2018), Working Life in Lithuania. www.eurofound.europa.eu/country/lithuania (accessed on 27 June 2018).

Blondel, Jean (1973), *Comparative Legislatures*. London: Prentice-Hall.

—— (1995), *Comparative Government: An Introduction*. London: Prentice Hall.

—— and Darina Malová (2007), *Governing New European Democracies*. Basingstoke: Palgrave.

—— and Ferdinand Müller-Rommel (eds) (1997 [1988]), *Cabinets in Western Europe*, second edition. Basingstoke: Palgrave.

—— (eds) (2001a), *Cabinets in Eastern Europe*. Basingstoke: Palgrave.

—— (2001b), Poland. In: Jean Blondel and Ferdinand Müller-Rommel (eds), *Cabinets in Eastern Europe*. Basingstoke: Palgrave, pp. 50–61.

Bochsler, Daniel (2010), The Party System of Serbia. In: Vera Stojarová and Peter Emerson (eds), *Party Politics in the Western Balkans*. London: Routledge, pp. 99–118.

—— and Edina Szöcsik (2013), The Forbidden Fruit of Federalism. Evidence from Romania and Slovakia. *West European Politics*, 36(2): 426–46.

Bodnar, Adam and Łukasz Bojarski (2012), Judicial Independence in Poland. In: Anja Seibert-Fohr (ed.), *Judicial Independence in Transition*. Wiesbaden: Springer Verlag, pp. 667–78.

Boeckh, Katrin and Ekkehard Völkl (2007), *Ukraine. Von der Roten zur Orangenen Revolution*. Regensburg: Pustet.

Bojičić-Dželilović, Vesna (2011), Decentralisation and Regionalisation in Bosnia-Herzegovina: Issues and Challenges, LSEE Papers on Decentralisation and Regional Policy. Research paper nr. 2. http://eprints.lse.ac.uk/63572/ (accessed on 15 July 2016).

Bolleyer, Nicole (2006), Intergovernmental Arrangements in Spanish and Swiss Federalism: The Impact of Power-Concentrating and Power-Sharing Executives on Intergovernmental Institutionalization. *Regional and Federal Studies*, 16(4): 385–408.

Bondar, Florin (2014), Quality of Government and Decentralization in Romania. *International Social Research Review*, 4(1): 5–25.

Bonoli, Giuliano, Silja Häusermann (2011), Swiss Welfare Reforms in a Comparative European Perspective: Between Retrenchment and Activation. In: Christine Trampusch and André Mach (eds), *Switzerland in Europe: Continuity and Change in the Swiss Political Economy*. London: Routledge, pp. 186–204.

Boogaerts, Andreas, Clara Portela and Edith Drieskens (2016), One Swallow Does Not Make Spring: A Critical Juncture Perspective on the EU Sanctions in Response to the Arab Spring. *Mediterranean Politics*, 21(2): 205–25.

Bornschier, Simon and Romain Lachat (2009), The Evolution of the French Political Space and Party System. *West European Politics*, 32(2): 360–83.

Borrás, Susana and Kerstin Jacobsson (2004), The Open Method of Coordination and New Governance Patterns in the EU, *Journal of European Public Policy*, 11(2): 185–208.

Börzel, Tanja (2005), Europeanization: How the European Union Interacts with Its Member States. In: Simon Bulmer and Christian Lequesne (eds), *The Member States of the European Union*. Oxford: Oxford University Press, pp. 25–44.

——, Tobias Hofmann and Diana Panke (2012), Caving In or Sitting It Out? Longitudinal Patterns of Non-Compliance in the European Union. *Journal of European Public Policy*, 19(4): 454–71.

—— and Bidzina Lebanidze (2017), The Transformative Power of Europe Beyond Enlargement: The EU's Performance in Promoting Democracy in its Neighbourhood. *East European Politics*, 33(1): 17–35.

—— and Thomas Risse (2003), Conceptualizing the Domestic Impact of Europe. In: Kevin Featherstone and Claudio M. Radaelli (eds), *The Politics of Europeanization*. Oxford: Oxford University Press, pp. 57–80.

—— (2018), From the Euro to the Schengen Crises: European Integration Theories, Politicization, and Identity Politics. *Journal of European Public Policy*, 25(1): 83–108.

Bosse, Giselle (2010), The EU's Relations with Moldova: Governance, Partnership or Ignorance? *Europe-Asia Studies*, 62(8): 1291–1309.

Bréchon, Pierre (2000), Religious Voting in a Secular France. In: David Broughton and Hans-Martien ten Napel (eds), *Religion and Mass Electoral Behaviour in Europe*. London: Routledge, pp. 97–117.

Breeman, Gerard, Peter Scholten and Arco Timmermans (2015), Analysing Local Policy Agendas: How Dutch Municipal Executive Coalitions Allocate Attention. *Local Government Studies*, 41(1): 20–43.

Bressanelli, Edoardo and Nicola Chelotti (2016), The Shadow of the European Council: Understanding Legislation on Economic Governance. *Journal of European Integration*, 38(5): 511–25.

Brett, Daniel (2015), Fiddling While Rome Burns: Institutional Conflict and Party Politics in Romania since 2007. *Südosteuropa*, 63(1): 47–74.

Brinkmann, Sören (2012), Spanien. In: Werner Reutter (ed.), *Verbände und Verbandssysteme in den Ländern der Europäischen Union*. Wiesbaden: Springer Verlag, pp. 723–52.

Brinton, Crane (1934), *A Decade of Revolution 1789–1799*. New York: Harper & Brothers.

—— (1952), *The Anatomy of Revolution*. New York: Prentice-Hall.

Brouard, Sylvain, Olivier Costa and Thomas König (eds) (2013), *The Europeanization of Domestic Legislatures: The Empirical Implications of the Delors' Myth in Nine Countries*. Wiesbaden: Springer VS.

——, Olivier Costa, Eric Kerrouche and Tinette Schnatterer (2013), Why Do French MPs Focus More on Constituency Work than on Parliamentary Work? *Journal of Legislative Studies*, 19(2): S141–S159.

Browne, Wayles (2017), Serbo-Croatian Language. Britannica Online. www.britannica.com/topic/Serbo-Croatian-language (accessed on 18 October 2017).

Brunazzo, Marco and Vincent della Sala (2016), Italy between Transformismo and Transformation. In: José M. Magone, Brigid Laffan and Christian Schweiger (eds), *Core–Periphery Relations in the European Union: Power and Conflict in a Dualist Political Economy*. London: Routledge, pp. 216–27.

Brunclík, Milos and Michal Kubát (2016), The Czech Parliamentary Regime After 1989: Origins, Developments and Challenges. *Acta Politologica*, 8(2): 5–29.

Brusis, Martin (2002), Between EU Requirements, Competitive Politics and National Traditions: Re-Creating Regions in the Accession Countries of Central and Eastern Europe. *Governance*, 15(4): 531–59.

—— (2014), Paths and Constraints of Subnational Government Mobilization in East-Central Europe. *Regional & Federal Studies*, 24(3): 301–19.

—— (2017), Core Executives in Central Europe. In: Adam Fagan and Petr Kopecký (eds), *Routledge Handbook of East European Politics*. London: Routledge, pp. 55–66.

Bruszt, László (2008), Multi-level Governance: The Eastern Versions – Emerging Patterns of Regional Developmental Governance in the New Member States. *Regional & Federal Studies*, 18(5): 607–27.

Brzezinski, Zbigniew (1965), *The Soviet Block: Unity and Conflict*. Cambridge, MA: Harvard University Press.

—— (1997), *The Grand Chessboard. America's Primacy and Its Geostrategic Imperatives*. New York: Basic Books.

Bucur, Cristina (2012a), Romanian Politics in 2012 Has Been Marked by a Rocky Cohabitation between Victor Ponta's Government and President Traian Basescu. Blog. http://blogs.lse.ac.uk/europpblog/2012/12/26/2012-in-romanian-politics/ (accessed on 21 December 2017).

—— (2012b), Romania's President Băsescu Remains Suspended, Despite Surviving the Impeachment Referendum Brought Against Him. Blog. http://blogs.lse.ac.uk/europpblog/2012/08/07/romania-president-impeachment/ (accessed on 21 December 2017).

—— (2012c), In Romania, Electoral Reform is Taking a Backwards Step, to the Benefit of the Ruling Parties. Blog. http://blogs.lse.ac.uk/europpblog/2012/05/30/romania-elections/ (accessed on 21 December 2017).

—— (2017), Bulgaria: Who Got What in Borisov III Cabinet? Semipresidentialism One. http://presidential-power.com/?cat=87 (accessed on 21 December 2017).

Budak, Jelena, Dubravka Jurlina Alibegović and Jelena Šišinački (2004), Local Government and Development in Croatia: Are We Lost In Transition? *Ekonomski Pregled*, 55(7–8): 660–73.

Bull, Martin J. (2018), In the Eye of the Storm: The Italian Economy and the Eurozone Crisis. *South European Society and Politics*, 23(1): 13–28.

—— and Joerg Baudner (2004), Europeanization and Italian Policy for the Mezzogiorno. *Journal of European Public Policy*, 11(6): 1058–76.

—— and Gianfranco Pasquino (2007), A Long Quest in Vain: Institutional Reforms in Italy. *West European Politics*, 30(4): 670–91.

Bulmer, William Elliott (2014), Constrained Majoritarianism: Westminster Constitutionalism in Malta. *Commonwealth & Comparative Politics*, 52(2): 232–53.

Bundesamt für Justiz (2017a), Gerichte des Bundes und der Länder am 15. Mai 2017 (ohne Dienst- und Ehrengerichtsbarkeit). www.bundesamt.de (accessed on 1 November 2018).

—— (2017b), Zahl der Richter, Richterinnen, Staatsanwälte, Staatsanwältinnen und Vertreter, Vertreterinnen des öffentlichen Interesses in der Rechtspflege der Bundesrepublik Deutschland am 31. Dezember 2016. www.bundesjustizamt.de/DE/SharedDocs/Publikationen/Justizstatistik/Richterstatistik_2016.pdf?__blob=publicationFile&v=2 (accessed on 1 November 2018).

Bundesministerium der Finanzen Deutschland (12 January 2017), Vorläufiger Haushaltsabschluss 2016. Pressemitteilung. www.bundesfinanzministerium.de/Content/DE/Pressemitteilungen/Finanzpolitik/2017/01/2017-01-12-pm02.html (accessed on 2 August 2018).

Bundesministerium für Justiz (2014), *The Austrian Judicial System*. Wien: Bundesministerium für Justiz. www.justiz.gv.at/web2013/file/8ab4ac8322985dd501229ce2e2d80091.de.0/broschuere_oesterr_justiz_en_download.pdf (accessed on 1 November 2018).

Bundestag (2014), *Basic Law for the Federal Republic of Germany*. Berlin: Deutscher Bundestag. www.btg-bestellservice.de/pdf/80201000.pdf (accessed on 23 September 2017).

—— (2018a), Abgeordnete. www.bundestag.de/abgeordnete/ (accessed on 10 February 2018). Information on resources is below the biographies, not easy to find.

—— (2018b), Parlamentsdokumentation. You can find statistics on the cited legislatures Statistik der Gesetzgebung-Überblick 13.-19.Wahlperiode individual pdf reports for each legislature. www.bundestag.de/dokumente/parlamentsdokumentation/parlaments dokumentation/197500 (accessed on 10 February 2018).

Bundesrat (2018a), *Die Arbeit des Bundesrates im Spiegel der Zahlen*. www.bundesrat.de/SharedDocs/downloads/DE/statistik/gesamtstatistik.pdf;jsessionid=7CFB418FF3B4743F414C5C8B456C5045.2_cid391?__blob=publicationFile&v=9 (accessed on 15 February 2018).

—— (2018b), *Der Bundesrat/Sekretariat*. www.bundesrat.de/DE/bundesrat/sekretariat/sekretariat-node.html;jsessionid=690A2C3E32ADE97F0DF85D5548BB1EED.1_cid365 (accessed on 29 October 2018).

Bundeswahlleiter (2017), *Endgültige Sitzberechnung und Verteilung der Mandate bei der Bundestagswahl 2017*. www.bundeswahlleiter.de/dam/jcr/dd81856b-7711–4d9f-98dd-91631ddbc37f/btw17_sitzberechnung.pdf (accessed on 5 November 2018).

Bundeszentrale für Politische Bildung (2014), Einnahmen und Ausgaben der Parteien. www.bpb.de/politik/grundfragen/parteien-in-deutschland/zahlen-und-fakten/42237/einnahmen-und-ausgaben (accessed on 8 March 2019).

Burch, Martin (1988), The United Kingdom. In: Jean Blondel and Ferdinand Mueller-Rommel (eds), *Cabinets in Western Europe*. Basingstoke: Macmillan, pp. 17–32.

Buzogány, Aron (2017), Illiberal Democracy in Hungary: Authoritarian Diffusion or Domestic Causation? *Democratization*, 24(7): 1307–25.

Cabada, Ladislav, Vit Hloušek and Petr Jurek (2014), *Party Systems in East Central Europe*. Lanham: Lexington Books.

Čambáliková, Monika (2012), Slowakei. In: Werner Reutter (ed.), *Verbände und Verbandssysteme in den Ländern der Europäischen Union*. Wiesbaden: Springer Verlag, pp. 671–98.

Campbell, John L. and Ove K. Pedersen (2007), The Varieties of Capitalism and Hybrid Success Denmark in the Global Economy. *Comparative Political Studies*, 40(3): 307–32.

Capano, Gilberto and Marco Giuliani (2003), The Italian Parliament: In Search of a New Role? In: Cristina Leston Bandeira (ed.), *Southern European Parliaments in Democracy*, special issue of *Journal of Legislative Studies*, 9(2): 8–34.

Capo Giol, Jordi (2003), The Spanish Parliament: The New Rules of the Game. In: Cristina Leston Bandeira (ed.), *Southern European Parliaments in Democracy*, special issue of *Journal of Legislative Studies*, 9(2): 85–106.

Caramani, Daniele (2000), *The Societies of Europe. Elections in Western Europe since 1815. Elections by Constituencies*. Basingstoke: Palgrave.

—— (2004), *The Nationalization of Politics: The Formation of National Electorates and Party Systems in Western Europe*. Cambridge: Cambridge University Press.

—— (2015), *The Europeanization of Politics. The Formation of a European Electorate and Party System in Historical Perspective*. Cambridge: Cambridge University Press.

Çarkoğlu, Ali (2007), A New Electoral Victory for the 'Pro-Islamists' or the 'New Centre-Right'? The Justice and Development Party Phenomenon in the July 2007 Parliamentary Elections in Turkey. *South European Society & Politics*, 12(4): 501–19.

Carr, Raymond (1999), *España, 1808–1975*. Barcelona: Ariel.

Casal-Bértoa, Fernando and Ingrid van Biezen (2014), Party Regulation and Party Politics in Post-Communist Europe. *East European Politics*, 30(3): 295–314.

Cassese, Sabino (2003), The Age of Administrative Reform. In: Jack Hayward and Anand Menon (eds), *Governing Europe*. Oxford: Oxford University Press, pp. 128–38.

Castells, Manuel (2000), *The Power of Identity. Volume II of The Information Age: Economy, Society and Culture*. London: Blackwell.

Ceccarini, Luigi and Fabio Bordignon (2017), Referendum on Renzi: The 2016 Vote on the Italian Constitutional Revision. *South European Society and Politics*, 22(3): 281–302.

Cecchini, P., M. Catinat and A. Jacquemin (1988), *The European Challenge 1992: The Benefits of a Single Market*. Aldershot: Wildwood House.

Centre for European Studies-Institute for Economic Research Munich (CESInfo) (26 May 2016), EU-Staaten rissen Defizit-Kriterium in 165 Fällen. www.cesifo-group.de/de/ifoHome/presse/Pressemitteilungen/Pressemitteilungen-Archiv/2016/Q2/pm-20160523_EU-Staaten-Defizit.html (accessed on 2 August 2018).

Cerny, Philip G.(1990), *The Changing Architecture of Politics. Structure, Agency, and the Future of the State*. London: SAGE.

Ceron, Andrea and Fedra Negri (2017), Trade Unions and Political Parties in Italy (1946–2014): Ideological Positions and Critical Junctures. *South European Society and Politics*, 22(4): 491–508.

Chiva, Cristina (2014), EU Accession and Party Competition in Postcommunist Romania. *Southeast European and Black Sea Studies*, 14(1): 65–82.

Christensen, Mette Bukjaer (2016), The Danish Folketing and EU Affairs? Is the Danish Model of Parliamentary Scrutiny Still the Best Practice. In: Claudia Hefftler, Christine Neuhold, Olivier Rozenberg and Julie Smith (eds), *The Palgrave Handbook of National Parliaments and the European Union*. Basingstoke: Palgrave, pp. 275–90.

Christensen, Tom (2005), The Norwegian State Transformed? *West European Politics*, 28(4): 721–39.

Christiansen, FJ and HB Seeberg (2016), Cooperation between Counterparts in Parliament from an Agenda-Setting Perspective: Legislative Coalitions as a Trade of Criticism and Policy. *West European Politics*, 39(6): 1160–80.

Christiansen, Peter Munk (2018), Still the Corporatist Darlings? In: Peter Nedergaard and Anders Wivel (eds), *The Routledge Handbook of Scandinavian Politics*. London: Routledge, pp. 36–48.

——, Birgitta Niklasson and Patrik Öhberg (2016), Does Politics Crowd Out Professional Competence? The Organisation of Ministerial Advice in Denmark and Sweden. *West European Politics*, 39(6): 1230–50.

——, Asbjørn Sonne Nørgaard and Niels C. Sidenius (2012), Dänemark. In: Werner Reutter (ed.), *Verbände und Verbandssysteme in den Ländern der Europäischen Union*. Wiesbaden: Springer Verlag, pp. 101–28.

Christiansen, Thomas and Knud Jørgensen (2000), Transnational Governance 'Above' and 'Below' the State: The Changing Nature of Borders in the New Europe. *Regional and Federal Studies*, 10(2): 62–77.

Christelijk Nationaal Vakverbond (CNV) (2018), Geschiedenis. www.cnv.nl/over-cnv/organisatie/geschiedenis/?L=0%2525252525252F (accessed on 25 June 2018).

Cianetti, Licia (12 October 2013), The Fall of the Latvian Government After the Riga Supermarket Tragedy Has Exposed Deep Divisions in the Country's Political System. Blog. http://blogs.lse.ac.uk/europpblog/2013/12/10/the-fall-of-the-latvian-government-after-the-riga-supermarket-tragedy-has-exposed-deep-divisions-in-the-countrys-political-system/ (accessed on 23 December 2017).

—— (8 October 2014), The Governing Parties Survived Latvia's Election, But the Issue of the Country's Russian-Speaking Minority Remains Centre-Stage. Blog. http://blogs.lse.ac.uk/europpblog/2014/10/08/the-governing-parties-survived-latvias-election-but-the-issue-of-the-countrys-russian-speaking-minority-remains-centre-stage/ (accessed on 23 December 2017).

Cidoncha Martín, Antonio (2011), El Senado y su reform (un clásico de nunca acabar). *Revista Juridica de la Universidad Autonoma de Madrid*, 23: 167–206.

Cini, Michele (2015), The European Commission after the Reform. In: José M. Magone (ed.), *Routledge Handbook of European Politics*. London: Routledge, pp. 235–47.

Clauwaert S., Z. Rasnača and M-E. Liakopoulou (2017), The Crisis and National Labour Law Reforms: A Mapping Exercise. Country Report: Greece. Etui.org (accessed on 25 June 2018).

Clemens, Gabriele, Alexander Reinfeldt and Georg Wille (2008), *Geschichte der europäischen Integration. Ein Lehrbuch*. Paderborn: Schöningh/UTB.

Clogg, Richard (1998), *A Concise History of Greece*. Cambridge: Cambridge University Press.

Coakley, John (2000), The Foundations of Statehood. In: John Coakley and Michael Gallagher (eds), *Politics in the Republic of Ireland*, third edition. London: Routledge, pp. 1–31.

Cobban, Alfred (1963), *A History of Modern France. Volume 2: 1799–1945*. Harmondsworth: Penguin Books.

Cohen, Ariel (2016), Corporate Raiding, Russian Style. *Huffington Post*, 16 June 2016, updated on 17 May 2017.

Cohen, Sandra and Nikolaus Hlepas (2017), Financial Resilience of Greek Local Government. In: Ileanna Steccolini, Martin Jones and Iris Saliterer (eds), *Governmental Financial*

Resilience. International Perspectives on How Local Government Face Austerity. Bingley: Emerald Publishing Limited, pp. 153–72.

Cole, Alistair (2017), *French Politics and Society*, third edition. London: Routledge.

Colino, César and José A. Olmeda (2012), El Estilo de Gobierno y Liderazgo. In: César Colino and Ramón Cotarelo (eds), *España en Crisis. Balance de la Segunda Legislatura de Rodriguez Zapatero*. Valencia: Tirant Humanidades, pp. 75–108.

—— and Eloisa del Pino (2015), National and European Patterns of Public Administration and Governance. In: Magone, José (ed.), *Routledge Handbook of European Politics*. London: Routledge, pp. 611–39.

Colombo, Sabrina and Regalia Ida (2016), Changing Joint Regulation and Labour Market Policy in Italy During the Crisis: On the Edge of a Paradigm Shift? *European Journal of Industrial Relations*, 22(3): 295–309.

Coman, Emmanuel Emil (2015), Electoral Reform in Romania: From the Need for Party System Consolidation to Concern for Improved Quality of Representation. *Südosteuropa. Zeitschrift für Politik und Gesellschaft*, 63(1): 75–94.

Coman, Ramona and Luca Tomini (2014), A Comparative Perspective on the State of Democracy in Central and Eastern Europe. *Europe-Asia Studies*, 66(6): 853–58.

Comité Economique et Sociale Européen (2002), *La societé civile organisée en Pologne, Republique tchéque, Slovakie et Hongrie*. Brussels: CES.

Committee of the Regions and Local Authorities (CoR) (2018), List of Regional Offices in Brussels. https://cor.europa.eu/en/members/Documents/regional-offices-organisations.pdf (accessed on 16 July 2018).

Congreso de Diputados (2017), Régimen Económico y Ayudas De Los Señores Diputados. 27 July 2017. www.congreso.es/portal/page/portal/Congreso/Congreso/Diputados/RegEcoyProtSoc/regimen_economico_diputados.pdf (accessed on 15 February 2018).

—— (2018), Database of 'Initiativas'. www.congreso.es/portal/page/portal/Congreso/Congreso/Iniciativas (accessed on 16 February 2018).

Connaughton, Bernadette (2016), Confronting Interrelated Crises in the EU's Western Periphery Steering Ireland–EU Relations Back to the Centre. In: José M. Magone, Brigid Laffan and Christian Schweiger (eds), *Core–Periphery Relations in the European Union: Power and Conflict in a Dualist Political Economy*. London: Routledge, pp. 166–78.

Connolly, Eileen and Eunan O'Halpin (2000), The Government and the Governmental System. In: John Coakley and Michael Gallagher (eds), *Politics in the Republic of Ireland*. London: Routledge, pp. 249–70.

Conradt, David P. (2001), *The German Polity*, seventh edition. New York: Longman.

Conseil Supérieur de la Magistrature (CSM) (2017), *Rapport d' Activité 2016*. Paris: CSM. www.ladocumentationfrancaise.fr/rapports-publics/174000541/index.shtml (accessed on 1 November 2018).

Consejo General del Poder Judicial (CGPJ) (2016), *The Spanish Judiciary in Figures 2015*. Madrid: CGPJ. file:///C:/Users/Jos%C3%A9/Downloads/2015%20-%20The%20Spanish%20Judiciary%20in%20figures_1.pdf (accessed on 1 February 2017).

—— and Transparency International (TI) (2015), *Encuesta de ámbito nacional a todos los jueces o magistrados en servicio activo*. www.poderjudicial.es/cgpj/es/Poder-Judicial/Consejo-General-del-Poder-Judicial/Actividad-del-CGPJ/Encuestas/Encuestas-a-la-Carrera-Judicial/VI-Encuesta-a-la-Carrera-Judicial--Encuesta-de-ambito-nacional-a-todos-los-jueces-o-magistrados-en-servicio-activo-2015 (accessed on 6 July 2017).

Contiades, Xenophon (ed.), *Engineering Constitutional Change. A Comparative Perspective on Europe, Canada and USA*. London: Routledge.

Cotta, Maurizio (1994), The Rise and Fall of the 'Centrality' of the Italian Parliament: Transformation of the Executive-Legislative Subsystem after the Second World War. In: Gary W. Copeland and Samuel C. Patterson (eds), *Parliaments in the Modern World: Changing Institutions*. Ann Arbor: University of Michigan Press, pp. 59–84.

—— and Francesco Marangoni (2015), *Il Governo*. Bologna: Il Mulino.

—— and Luca Verzichelli (2008), *Political Institutions in Italy*. Oxford: Oxford University Press.

—— (2016), *Il Sistema politico in Italia. Terza edizione*. Bologna: Il Mulino.

Council of Europe/Commission on Democracy through Law (Venice Commission) (2012), Opinion on the Cardinal Acts on the Judiciary That Were Amended Following the Adoption of Opinion Cdl-Ad (2012)001 on Hungary Adopted by the Venice Commission at its 92nd Plenary Session (Venice, 12–13 October 2012). Strasbourg: Council of Europe. www.venice.coe.int/webforms/documents/default.aspx?pdffile=CDL-AD (2012)020-e (accessed on 2 November 2018).

—— (2017), Poland Opinion on the Draft Act Amending the Act on the National Council of The Judiciary, On the Draft Act Amending the Act on the Supreme Court, Proposed by the President of Poland, and on the Act on the Organisation of Ordinary Courts Adopted by the Venice Commission at Its 113th Plenary Session (8–9 December 2017). Strasbourg: Council of Europe. www.venice.coe.int/webforms/documents/default.aspx?pdffile=CDLAD (2017)031-e (accessed on 2 November 2018).

Courts Service (2017), *Explaining the Courts. An Information Booklet*. Dublin: Courts Service. www.courts.ie/Courts.ie/library3.nsf/(WebFiles)/A15BCA388D64C09C80257DFC003EA21C/$FILE/Explaining%20the%20Courts%20Complete%20booklet%20for%20web.pdf (accessed on 1 November 2018).

Cox, Terry M. and Bob Mason (2000), Interest Groups and the Development of Tripartism in East Central Europe. *European Journal of Industrial Relations*, 6(3): 325–47.

Crabtree, Charles, Christopher J. Fariss and Paul Schuler (2016), The Presidential Elections in Belarus, October 2015. *Electoral Studies*, 42(6): 304–7.

Crampton, R.J. (2002), *The Balkans Since the Second World War*. London: Longman.

Crespy, Amandine and Vivien Schmidt (2014), The Clash of Titans: France, Germany and the Discursive Double Game of EMU Reform. *Journal of European Public Policy*, 21(8): 1085–1101.

Crowther, William E. (2011), Second Decade, Second Chance? Parliament, Politics and Democratic Aspirations in Russia, Ukraine and Moldova. *The Journal of Legislative Studies*, 17(2): 147–71.

—— and Steven D. Roper (1996), A Comparative Analysis of Institutional Development in the Romanian and Moldovan Legislatures. In: David M. Olson and Philip Norton (eds), *The New Parliaments of Central and Eastern Europe*. London: Frank Cass, pp. 133–60.

Culpepper, Pepper D. (2014), The Political Economy of Unmediated Democracy: Italian Austerity under Mario Monti. *West European Politics*, 37(6): 1264–81.

Cvejić, Slobodan (ed.) (2016), Informal Power Networks, Political Patronage and Clientelism in Serbia and Kosovo. Belgrade: SECONS. http://crdp-ks.org/wp-content/uploads/2016/05/Informal-Power-Networks-Political-Patronage-and-Clientelism-in-Serbia-and-Kosovo1.pdf (accessed on 25 November 2018).

Czarzasty, Jan (2018), Poland: Working Life. www.eurofound.europa.eu/sites/default/files/wpef18040.pdf (accessed on 27 June 2018).

——, Katarzyna Gajewska and Adam Mrozowicki (2014), Institutions and Strategies: Trends and Obstacles to Recruiting Workers into Trade Unions in Poland. *British Journal of Industrial Relations*, 52(1): 112–35.

Czernielewska, Malgorzata, Christos J. Paraskevopoulos and Jacek Szlachta (2004), The Regionalization Process in Poland. An Example of 'Shallow' Europeanization? *Regional & Federal Studies*, 14(3): 461–95.

Cziria, Ludovit, Rastislav Bednárik and Miroslava Kordošová (2018), Slovakia: Developments in Working Life. www.eurofound.europa.eu/sites/default/files/wpef18043.pdf (accessed on 27 June 2018).

Dallara, Cristina (2014), *Democracy and Judicial Reforms in South-East Europe. Between the EU and the Legacies of the Past*. Wiesbaden: Springer Verlag.

Danero Iglesias, Julien (2015), An Ad Hoc Nation. *East European Politics & Societies*, 29(4): 850–70.

Dansk Arbejdsgiverforening (DA) (2018), About DA. www.da.dk/ (accessed on 25 June 2018).

Dansk Industri (DI) (2018), About DI. https://di.dk/English/AboutDI/Pages/confederation.aspx (accessed on 25 June 2018).

Davison, Roderic H. (1981), *Turkey: A Short History*. Walkington: Eothen Press.

Dehousse, Franklin with collaboration of Benedetta Marsicola (2016), *The Reform of the EU Courts (II). Abandoning the Management Approach by Doubling the General Court*. Egmont Papers 63. Brussels: Egmont-Royal Institute of International Affairs. www.egmontinstitute.be/content/uploads/2016/03/ep83.pdf.pdf?type=pdf (accessed on 2 August 2016).

Dehousse, R., A. Fernández Pasarín and J. Plaza (2014), How consensual is comitology? *Journal of European Public Policy*, 21(6): 842–59.

Dehousse, Renaud (2003), Comitology: Who Watches the Watchmen? *Journal of European Public Policy*, 10(5): 798–813.

Delcour, Laura (2015), Between the Eastern Partnership and Eurasian Integration: Explaining Post-Soviet Countries' Engagement in (Competing) Region-Building Projects. *Problems of Post-Communism*, 62(6): 316–27.

Delcour, Laure and Kataryna Wolczuk (2015), Spoiler or Facilitator of Democratization? Russia's Role in Georgia and Ukraine. *Democratization*, 22(3): 459–78.

Della Sala, Vincent (1997), Hollowing Out and Hardening the State: European Integration and the Italian Economy. *West European Politics*, 20(1): 14–33.

—— (1998), The Relationship between the Italian Parliament and Government. In: Philip Norton (ed.), *Parliaments and Governments in Western Europe*. London: Frank Cass, pp. 73–93.

Delwit, Pascal (2011), Partis et systèmes de partis en Belgique en perspective. In: Pascal Delwit, Benoit Pilet and Emilie van Haute (eds), *Les Partis Politiques en Belgique*. Brussels: Edition de l'Université de Bruxelles, pp. 6–33.

Dembinska, Magdalena (2013), Ethnopolitical Mobilization without Groups. Nation-Building in Upper Silesia. *Regional & Federal Studies*, 23(1): 47–66.

De Montesquieu, Baron Charles de Secondat (1973), *De l'Esprit des Lois*. Two volumes. Paris: Éditions Garnier.

Deschouwer, Kris (2004), Political Parties and Their Reactions to the Erosion of Voter Loyalty in Belgium: Caught in a Trap. In: Peter Mair, Wolfgang C. Müller and Fritz Plasser (eds), *Political Parties and Electoral Change: Party Responses to Electoral Markets*. London: SAGE, pp. 179–206.

—— (2009), *The Politics of Belgium. Governing a Divided Society*. Basingstoke: Palgrave.

De Waal, Thomas and Balász Jarábik (2018), Bessarabia's Hopes and Fears on Ukraine's Edge. Carnegie Europe. https://carnegieeurope.eu/2018/05/24/bessarabia-s-hopes-and-fears-on-ukraine-s-edge-pub-76445 (accessed on 13 September 2018).

De Winter, Lieven (1998), Parliaments and Governments in Belgium: Pioneers of Partyocracy. In: Philip Norton (ed.), *Parliaments and Governments in Western Europe*. London: Frank Cass, pp. 97–122.

——, Donatella della Porta and Kris Deschouwer (1996), Comparing Similar Countries: Italy and Belgium. In: Kris Deschouwer, Lieven de Winter and Donatella della Porta (eds), *Partitocracies between Crises and Reforms: The Cases of Italy and Belgium*, a Special issue of *Res Publica*, 2: 215–36.

——, Arco Timmermans and Patrick Dumont (2000), Belgium: On Government Agreements, Evangelists, Followers, and Heretics. In: Wolfgang C. Muller and Kaare Strøm (eds), *Coalition Governments in Western Europe*. Oxford: Oxford University Press, pp. 300–55.

Dimitrov, Vesselin (2006), Bulgaria: A Core at All Odds. In: Vesselin Dimitrov, Klaus H. Goetz and Helmut Wollmann (eds), with contributions by Radoslaw Zubek and Martin Brusis, *Governing after Communism: Institutions and Policy Making*. Lanham: Rowman and Littlefield, pp. 159–201.

Dinan, Desmond (2004), *Europe Recast: A History of the European Union*. Basingstoke: Palgrave.

Di Scala, Spencer (1995), *Italy: From Revolution to Republic, 1700 to the Present*. Boulder: Westview Press.

Di Virgilio, Aldo (2005), Francia: le molte risorse del primo ministro. In: Gianfranco Pasquino (ed.), *Capi di governo*. Bologna: Il Mulino, pp. 41–72.

Dobre, Ana (2009), The Dynamics of Europeanisation and Regionalisation: Regional Reform in Romania. *Perspectives on European Politics and Society*, 10(2): 181–94.

—— (2011), Romania: From Historical Regions to Local Decentralization via the Unitary State. In: John Loughlin, Frank Hendriks and Anders Lidström (eds), *The Oxford Handbook of Local and Regional Democracy in Europe*. Oxford: Oxford University Press, pp. 685–712.

Dodd, Clement Henry (1979), *Democracy and Development in Turkey*. Beverley: Eothen Press.

Dohrn, Kristina (2017), Die Gülen Bewegung: Entstehung und Entwicklung eines muslimischen Netzwerks. *Aus Politik und Zeitgeschichte*, 9–10: 18–22.

Dolezal, Martin and Eva Zeglovits (2014), Almost an Earthquake: The Austrian Parliamentary Election of 2013. *West European Politics*, 37(3): 644–52.

Domstol Administrasjonen (n.d.), The Courts of Norway. Oslo: Domstole Administrasjonen. www.domstol.no/globalassets/upload/da/internett/domstol.no/domstoladministrasjonen/publikasjoner/doad_domstolene-i-norge_engelsk.pdf (accessed on 2 November 2018).

Domstolsstyrelsen (2015), A Closer Look at the Courts of Denmark. www.domstol.dk/om/publikationer/HtmlPublikationer/Profil/Profilbrochure%20-%20UK/profil brochure_uk.pdf (accessed on 1 November 2018).

Donovan, Mark (2015), Berlusconi's Impact and Legacy: Political Parties and the Party System. *Modern Italy*, 20(1): 11–24.

Dorey, Peter (2004), Le Parlement en Grande-Bretagne. In: Olivier Costa, Eric Kerrouche and Paul Magnette (eds), *Vers un renouveau du parlamentarisme en Europe?* Brussels: Éditions Université Libre de Bruxelles, pp. 107–30.

Dorn, Walter L. (1963), *Competition for Empire, 1740–1763*. New York: Harper & Row.

Draghi, Mario (2012), Speech at the Global Investment Conference in London, 26 July 2012. www.ecb.europa.eu/press/key/date/2012/html/sp120726.en.html (accessed on 2 August 2018).

Dreßler, Markus (2017), Erdoğan und die fromme Generation: Religion und Politik in der Türkei. *Aus Politik und Zeitgeschichte*, 9–10: 23–29.

Državni, Zbor (2000–2014), Report on National Assembly's Work in the Parliamentary Term for the Periods 1996 – 2000, 2004–2008, 2008–2012, 2012–2016. www.dz-rs.si/wps/portal/Home/deloDZ/Publikacije/PorocilaDZ/!ut/p/z1/04_Sj9CPykssy0xPLMnMz0vMAfIjo8zinfyCTD293Q0N3C0CzAwczYzc_SxDDY28fU30wwkpiAJKG-AAjgZQ_d6e_sGWToaOBv6Whm4GnqHG7ibGviEGBr5GYP0E7cdjAQH9BbmhoaGOiooAqAZJsg!!/dz/d5/L2dBISEvZ0FBIS9nQSEh/p0/IZ7_BNR5IKG10G8P60A62GN9U12KM3=CZ6_BNR5IKG10G8P60A62GN9U12KM4=LA0=Ejavax.servlet.include.path_info!QCPGalleryBrowserPubView.jsp==/#Z7_BNR5IKG10G8P60A62GN9U12KM3 (accessed on 17 February 2018).

Due, Jesper, Jorgen Steen Petersen, Lars Kjerulf and Carsten Stroby (1995), Adjusting the Danish Model: Towards Centralised Decentralisation. In: Colin Crouch and Franz Traxler (eds), *Organised Industrial Relations in Europe: What Future?* Aldershot: Avebury, pp. 121–50.

Düllfer, Jost (2002), Deutschland als Kaiserreich (1871–1918). In: Martin Vogt (ed.), *Deutsche Geschichte: Von den Anfängen bis zur Gegenwart*. Frankfurt a. M.: Fische, pp. 517–615.

Duman, Özgün Sarımehmet (2017), The Political Economy of the Eurozone Crisis. Competitiveness and Financialization in PIIGS. *Journal of Balkan and Near Eastern Studies*, 20(3): 211–29.

Dumont, Patrick, Fernand Fehlen and Philippe Poirier (2009), Politisches System, politische Parteien und Wahlen. In: Wolfgang H. Lorig and Mario Hirsch (eds), *Das politische System Luxemburgs*. Wiesbaden: Verlag für Sozialwissenschaften, pp. 155–89.

Dumont, Patrick and Lieven de Winter (2000), Luxembourg: Stable Coalitions in a Pivotal Party System. In: Wolfgang C. Müller and Kaare Strøm (eds), *Coalition Governments in Western Europe*. Oxford: Oxford University Press, pp. 399–432.

Duverger, Maurice (1970), *Institutions et Droit Constitutionel*, eleventh edition. Paris: Presses Universitaires de France.

Dyson, Kenneth (2000), EMU as 'Europeanization': Convergence, Diversity and Contingency. *Journal of Common Market Studies*, 38(4): 645–66.

—— and Kevin Featherstone (1996), Italy and EMU as '*Vincolo Esterno*: Empowering the Technocrats and Transforming the State. *South European Society and Politics*, 1(2): 272–99.

Ebbinghaus, Bernhard, Claudia Göbel and Sebastian Koos (2011), Social Capital, 'Ghent' and Workplace Contexts Matter: Comparing Union Membership in Europe. *European Journal of Industrial Relations*, 17(2): 107–24.

Ebbinghaus, Bernhard and Jelle Visser (1997), Der Wandel der Arbeitsbeziehungen im westeuropäischen Vergleich. In: Stefan Hradil and Stefan Immerfall (eds), *Die westeuropäischen Gesellschaften im Vergleich*. Opladen: Leske & Budrich, pp. 333–76.

Eduskunta (2017), The Parliament of Finland 2016. Helsinki: Eduskunta. www.eduskunta.fi/EN/tietoaeduskunnasta/Documents/2016_VUOSIKERTOMUS_ENGLANTI_NETTI.pdf (accessed on 6 February 2018).

Eesti Kohtud (2018), Estonian Court System. www.kohus.ee/en/estonian-courts/estonian-court-system (accessed on 2 November 2018).

Egan, Michelle and Maria Helena Guimarães (2017), The Single Market: Trade Barriers and Trade Remedies. *Journal of Common Market Studies*, 55(2): 294–311.

Eich, Theresa and Stefan Vetter (2013), Der EU-Binnenmarkt nach 20 Jahren Erfolge, unerfüllte Erwartungen und weitere Potenziale. EU Monitor. Deutsche Bank Research. www.dbresearch.de/PROD/RPS_DE-PROD/Der_EU-Binnenmarkt_nach_20_Jahren%3A_Erfolge%2C_unerf%C3%BC/RPS_DE_DOC_VIEW.calias?rwnode=PROD0000000000435630&ProdCollection=PROD0000000000444482 (accessed on 2 August 2018).

Eichenberger, Pierre and André Mach (2011), Organized Capital and Coordinated Market Economy: Swiss Business Interest Associations between Socio-Economic Regulation and Political Influence. In: Christine Trampusch and André Mach (eds), *Switzerland in Europe. Continuity and Change in the Swiss Political Economy*. London: Routledge, pp. 63–81.

ElectionsIreland.Org (2018), General Election to 32nd Dail on Friday 26 February 2016. https://electionsireland.org/results/general/32dail.cfm (accessed on 5 November 2018).

Elgie, Robert (2000), Political Leadership: The President and the Taoiseach. In: John Coakley and Michael Gallagher (eds), *Politics in the Republic of Ireland*. London: Routledge, pp. 232–48.

—— (ed.) (2001), *Divided Government in Comparative Perspective*. Oxford: Oxford University Press.

—— (2003), *Political Institutions in Contemporary France*. Oxford: Oxford University Press.

—— and Sophie Moelstrup (eds) (2008), *Semi-Presidentialism in Central and Eastern Europe*. Oxford: Oxford University Press.

Elinkeinoelämän keskusliitto (EK) (2018), About Us: The Voice of Finnish Business. https://ek.fi/en/about-us/ (accessed on 25 June 2018).

Ellinas, Antonis A. (2013), The Rise of Golden Dawn: The New Face of the Far Right in Greece. *South European Society and Politics*, 18(4): 543–65.

Elster, Jon, Claus Offe and Ulrich K. Preuss (1998), *Institutional Design in Post-Communist Societies: Rebuilding the Ship at Sea*. Cambridge: Cambridge University Press.

Elvert, Jürgen (2012), Irland. In: Werner Reutter (ed.), *Verbände und Verbandssysteme in den Ländern der Europäischen Union*. Wiesbaden: Springer Verlag, pp. 317–44.

Emanuele, Vincenzo (2018a), Dataset of Electoral Volatility and its Internal Components in Western Europe (1945–2015). Rome: Italian Center for Electoral Studies. http://dx.doi.org/10.7802/1112. www.vincenzoemanuele.com/dataset-of-electoral-volatility.html (accessed on 11 May 2018).

—— (2018b), The Hidden Cleavage of the French Election: Macron, Le Pen and the Urban-Rural Conflict. In: Lorenzo De Sio and Aldo Paparo (eds), *The Year of Challengers? Issues, Public Opinion, and Elections in Western Europe in 2017*. Rome: Centro Italiano per Studi Elettorale (CISE), pp. 151–158. https://cise.luiss.it/cise/wp-content/uploads/2017/12/CISE010_2018_10EN_A4.pdf (accessed on 10 May 2018).

Enderlein, Henrik and Amy Verdun (2009a), EMU's teenage Challenge: What Have We Learned and Can We Predict from Political Science? *Journal of European Public Policy*, 16(4): 490–507.

—— (eds) (2009b), *Ten Years of EMU: What Have We Learned in Political Science?* Special issue of *Journal of European Public Policy*, 16(4).

Engels, Friedrich (1974 [1844]), *The Condition of the Working Class in England*. Frogmore: Panther.

Engler, Sarah (2016), Corruption and Electoral Support for New Political Parties in Central and Eastern Europe. *West European Politics*, 39(2): 278–304.

Enyedi, Zsolt and Kevin Deegan-Krause (2018), Voters and Parties in Eastern Europe. In: Adam Fagan and Petr Kopecký (eds), *Routledge Handbook of East European Politics*. London: Routledge, pp. 169–83.

Eriksen, Svein (1988), Norway. In: Jean Blondel and Ferdinand Müller-Rommel (eds), *Cabinets in Western Europe*. Basingstoke: Macmillan, pp. 183–96.

Esen, Berk and Şebnem Gümüşçü (2017). A Small Yes for Presidentialism: The Turkish Constitutional Referendum of April 2017. *South European Society and Politics*, 22(3): 303–26.

Esping-Andersen, Gösta (1990), *The Three Worlds of Welfare Capitalism*. Princeton: Princeton University Press.

—— (ed.) (1995), *Changing Classes: Stratification and Mobility in Post-Industrial Societies*. London: SAGE.

Eurobarometer (2008), Eurobarometer 69.1. Values of Europeans. Conducted March-May 2008, Publication November 2008. http://ec.europa.eu/commfrontoffice/publicopinion/archives/eb/eb69/eb69_values_en.pdf (accessed on 1 August 2018).

Eurobarometer Interactive (2018), Longitudinal Archive of Attitudes of European Integration. http://ec.europa.eu/commfrontoffice/publicopinion/index.cfm/Chart/index (accessed on 16 February 2018).

European Agency of European Union Agency for the Operational of Large-Scale IT Systems in the Area of Freedom, Security and Justice (EU-LISA), Testing the Borders of the Future: Smart Borders Pilot. www.eulisa.europa.eu/Publications/Reports/Smart%20Borders%20-%20The%20results%20in%20brief.pdf (accessed on 1 August 2018).

European Commission (2010), Handbook on Integration for Policy Makers and Practitioners. Luxembourg: Office of the Official Publications of the European Union. https://ec.europa.eu/home-affairs/sites/homeaffairs/files/e-library/docs/handbook_integration/docl_12892_168517401_en.pdf (accessed on 9 November 2017).

—— (2017a), European Innovation Scoreboard 2017. Main Report. Brussels: European Commission. http://ec.europa.eu/DocsRoom/documents/24829 (accessed on 8 November 2017).

—— (2017b), Report from the Commission to the European Parliament and the Council on Progress in Romania under the Co-Operation and Verification Mechanism. https://ec.europa.eu/info/sites/info/files/comm-2017-751_en.pdf (accessed on 17 February 2018).

—— (2017c), Report on Progress in Bulgaria under the Co-operation and Verification Mechanism. Brussels, 15.11.2017 COM (2017), 750 final. Brussels: European Commission. https://ec.europa.eu/info/sites/info/files/comm-2017-750_en_0.pdf (accessed on 23 November 2018).

—— (2017d), Annual Report 2016 on Relations between the European Commission and National Parliaments. Brussels, 30.6.2017 COM (2017), 601 final. https://eur-lex.europa.eu/resource.html?uri=cellar:186cfcb2-5d72-11e7-954d-01aa75ed71a1.0001.02/DOC_1&format=PDF (accessed on 2 August 2018).

—— (2017e), Report From The Commission on the Working of Committees during 2016. Brussels, 16.10.2017. COM (2017), 594 final. http://ec.europa.eu/transparency/regcomitology/docs/annual_report_2016_en.pdf (accessed on 17 November 2018).

—— (2017f), Reflection Paper on the Future of Europe. Brussels: European Commission. https://ec.europa.eu/commission/sites/beta-political/files/white_paper_on_the_future_of_europe_en.pdf (accessed on 17 November 2018).

—— (2018a), Transparency Register. http://ec.europa.eu/transparencyregister/public/homePage.do?locale=en#en (accessed on 27 June 2018).

—— (2018b), The Founding Fathers of the European Union. https://europa.eu/european-union/about-eu/history/founding-fathers_en (accessed on 2 August 2018).

—— (2018c), The European Union. What it Does and What it Is. Luxembourg: Office of Publications of the European Union. https://publications.europa.eu/en/publication-detail/-/publication/715cfcc8-fa70–11e7-b8f5–01aa75ed71a1/language-en (accessed on 2 August 2018).

—— (2018d), Budget. Annual Budget. http://ec.europa.eu/budget/annual/index_en.cfm (accessed on 1 August 2018).

—— (2018e), Report From The Commission On The Working Of Committees During 2017. Brussels, 11.10.2018 COM (2018), 675 final. http://ec.europa.eu/transparency/regcomitology/docs/annual_report_2017_en.pdf (accessed on 11 November 2018).

—— (2018f), A Modern EU Budget for a Union that Protects, Empowers and Defends. Factsheet. https://ec.europa.eu/commission/sites/beta-political/files/budget-proposals-modern-eu-budget-may2018_en.pdf (accessed on 17 November 2018).

—— (2018g), Cohesion Policy. Available Budget. Financial Allocations 2014–2020. http://ec.europa.eu/regional_policy/en/funding/available-budget/ (accessed on 4 August 2018).

—— (2018h), Available Budget. 2014–2020. http://ec.europa.eu/regional_policy/en/funding/available-budget/ (accessed on 1 August 2018).

—— (2018i), Common European Asylum System (CEAS). https://ec.europa.eu/home-affairs/what-we-do/policies/asylum_en (accessed on 24 November 2018).

European Commission for the Efficiency of Justice (CEPEJ) (2018), European Judicial Systems. Efficiency and Quality of Justice. Strasbourg: CEPEJ. www.coe.int/en/web/cepej/special-file-publication-2018-edition-of-the-cepej-report-european-judicial-systems-efficiency-and-quality-of-justice (accessed on 1 November 2018).

European Council (1993), European Council in Copenhagen 21–22 June 1993: Conclusions of the Presidency. Doc 93/3 22 June 1993. Brussels, 11.10.2018 COM (2018), 675. www.consilium.europa.eu/media/21225/72921.pdf (accessed on 23 November 2018).

European Court of Auditors (2016), EU Assistance to Ukraine. A Special Report. Luxembourg: Office of the Official Publications of the European Union. www.eca.europa.eu/Lists/ECADocuments/SR16_32/SR_UKRAINE_EN.pdf (accessed on 13 September 2018).

European Foundation for the Improvement of Living Conditions (Eurofound) (2015), Industrial Relations in Europe 2014. Luxembourg: Office of the Official Publications of the European Communities. http://ec.europa.eu/social/keyDocuments.jsp?type=0&policyArea=0&subCategory=0&country=0&year=0&advSearchKey=IRIE&mode=advancedSubmit&langId=en (accessed on 24 June 2018).

—— (2016), *Role of the Social Partners in the European Semester*. Luxembourg: Publications Office of the European Union.

—— (2017), Developments in Working Life in Europe. EurWork Annual Review 2016. Luxembourg: Office of the Official Publications of the European Communities. www.eurofound.europa.eu/sites/default/files/ef_publication/field_ef_document/ef1727en.pdf (accessed on 24 June 2018).

—— (2018), EURWORK Observatory Database. www.eurofound.europa.eu/de/observatories/eurwork (accessed on 28 June 2018).

European Institute for Gender Equality (2015), Gender Equality Index 2015. http://eige.europa.eu/gender-statistics/gender-equality-index (accessed on 25 September 2017).

European Parliament (2017), Anti-Corruption Efforts in the Western Balkans. www.europarl.europa.eu/thinktank/en/document.html?reference=EPRS_BRI(2017)599417 (accessed on 16 July 2018).

—— (2018), European Parliament Relations with National Parliaments. www.europarl.europa.eu/relnatparl/en/home/latest-news.html (accessed on 2 July 2018).

European Social Survey (ESS) (2002–2016), Round 1 (2002) to 8 (2016), Data File Edition 1.0. NSD: Norwegian Centre for Research Data, Norway – Data Archive and Distributor of ESS Data for ESS ERIC. www.europeansocialsurvey.org/ (accessed on 25 November 2018).

European Union (2012), The Treaty of the European Union. Consolidated Version. Official Journal of the European Union (OJEU) C326/13 26.10.2012. http://eur-lex.europa.eu/resource.html?uri=cellar:2bf140bf-a3f8-4ab2-b506-fd71826e6da6.0023.02/DOC_1&format=PDF (accessed on 26 September 2017).

—— (2016), Social Protection Committee Annual Report 2016. In: Review of the Social Protection Performance Monitor and Developments in Social Protection Policies. European Union: Office of Official Publications of the European Union. http://ec.europa.eu/social/main.jsp?catId=738&langId=en&pubId=7936&visible=0&preview=cHJldkVtcGxQb3J0YWwhMjAxMjAyMTVwcmV2aWV3 (accessed on 2 June 2017).

Eurostat (2017), Smarter, Greener and Inclusive? Indicators to Support the Europe 2020 Strategy. Luxembourg: Publications Office of the European Union. http://ec.europa.eu/eurostat/documents/3217494/8113874/KS-EZ-17-001-EN-N.pdf/c810af1c-0980-4a3b-bfdd-f6aa4d8a004e (accessed on 1 August 2018).

—— (2018a), Total General Expenditure as % of GDP. http://ec.europa.eu/eurostat/tgm/refreshTableAction.do?tab=table&plugin=1&pcode=tec00023&language=en (accessed on 17 July 2018).

—— (2018b), General Gross Government Debt. http://ec.europa.eu/eurostat/tgm/table.do?tab=table&init=1&language=en&pcode=sdg_17_40&plugin=1 (accessed on 2 January 2018).

—— (2018c), Social Benefits Per Head of Population in € and in Power Purchasing Standard (Social Protection). http://ec.europa.eu/eurostat/tgm/table.do?tab=table&plugin=1&language=en&pcode=tps00107 (accessed on 4 August 2018).

—— (2018d), Income Quintile Share Ratio (S80/S20) By Sex. http://ec.europa.eu/eurostat/tgm/table.do?tab=table&plugin=1&language=en&pcode=tessi180 (accessed on 4 August 2018).

—— (2018e), Population on 1 January by Age Group, Sex and Citizenship. http://appsso.eurostat.ec.europa.eu/nui/submitViewTableAction.do (accessed on 3 March 2019).

—— (2019a), Employment by Sex, Age and Economic Activity (from 2008 onwards, NACE Rev. 2). http://appsso.eurostat.ec.europa.eu/nui/show.do?dataset=lfsq_egan2&lang=en (accessed on 4 March 2019).

—— (2019b), Employment Rate by Sex, Age Group 20–64. https://ec.europa.eu/eurostat/tgm/table.do?tab=table&init=1&language=en&pcode=t2020_10&plugin=1 (accessed on 4 March 2019).

—— (2019c), Total Public Expenditure 2017. https://ec.europa.eu/eurostat/tgm/table.do?tab=table&init=1&language=de&pcode=tec00023&plugin=1 (accessed on 8 March 2019).

Eythórsson, Grétar Thór and Detlef Jahn (2009), Das politische System Islands. In: Wolfgang Ismayr (ed.), *Die politischen Systeme Westeuropas*. Wiesbaden: Verlag für Sozialwissenschaften, pp. 195–218.

Fairbanks, Charles H., Jr. and Alexi Gugushvili (2013), A New Chance for Georgian Democracy. *Journal of Democracy*, 24(1): 116–27.

Farrell, David M. (1999), Ireland: A Party System Transformed? In: David Broughton and Mark Donovan (eds), *Changing Party Systems in Western Europe*. London: Pinter, pp. 30–47.

—— (2000), *Electoral Systems. A Comparative Introduction*. Basingstoke: Palgrave.

——, M. Mackerras and I. McAllister (1996), Designing Electoral Institutions: Varieties of STV Systems. *Political Studies*, 44: 24–43.

Featherstone, Kevin (2003), Greece and EMU: Between External Empowerment and Domestic Vulnerability. *Journal of Common Market Studies*, 41(5): 923–40.

—— (2005), 'Soft' Co-Ordination Meets 'Hard' Politics: The European Union and Pension Reform in Greece. *Journal of European Public Policy*, 12(4): 733–50.

—— (2011), The Greek Sovereign Debt Crisis and EMU: A Failing State in a Skewed Regime. *Journal of Common Market Studies*, 49(2): 193–217.

—— and Dimitris Papadimitriou (2008), *The Limits of Europeanization. Reform Capacity and Policy Conflict in Greece*. Basingstoke: Palgrave.

—— (2013), The Emperor Has No Clothes! Power and Resources within the Greek Core Executive. *Governance: An International Journal of Policy, Administration, and Institutions*, 26(3): 523–45.

—— (2015), *Prime Ministers in Greece. The Paradox of Power*. Oxford: Oxford University Press.

Federatie Nederlandse Vakbeweging (FNV) (2018), Over de FNV. www.fnv.nl/over-fnv/ (accessed on 25 June 2018).

Fedorenko, Kostyantyn, Olena Rybiyand and Andreas Umland (2016), The Ukrainian Party System Before and After the 2013–2014 Euromaidan. *Europe-Asia Studies*, 68(4): 609–30.

Feltenius, David (2016), Subnational Government in a Multilevel Perspective. In: Jon Pierre (ed.), *The Oxford Handbook of Swedish Politics*, first edition. Oxford: Oxford University Press, pp. 383–98.

Fernandes, Jorge M. (2016a), Intra-Party Delegation in the Portuguese Legislature: Assigning Committee Chairs and Party Coordination Positions. *The Journal of Legislative Studies*, 22(1): 108–28.

—— (2016b), The Seeds for Party System Change? The 2015 Portuguese General Election. *West European Politics*, 39(4): 890–900.

Ferguson, Niall (2007), *Empire: How Britain Made the Modern World*. London: Penguin.

Ferrera, Maurizio (1996), The Southern Model of Welfare State in Social Europe. *Journal of European Social Policy*, 6(1): 17–37.

—— (2005), *The Boundaries of Welfare: European Integration and the New Spatial Politics of Social Protection*. Oxford: Oxford University Press.

—— (2008), The European Welfare State: Golden Achievements, Silver Achievements. *West European Politics*, 31(1): 82–107.

——, Anton Hemerijk and Martin Rhodes (2000), *O Futuro da Europa Social: Repensar o Trabalho e a Protecção Social na Nova Economia*. Lisbon: Celta.

Field, Bonnie (2009), Minority Government and Legislative Politics in a Multilevel State: Spain under Zapatero. *South European Society and Politics*, 14(4): 417–34.

—— (2016), *Why Minority Governments Work: Multilevel Territorial Politics in Spain*. Basingstoke: Palgrave.

Fiers, Stefaan and André Krouwel (2005), The Low Countries: From 'Prime Minister' to President–Minister. In: Thomas Poguntke and Paul Webb (eds), *The Presidentialization of Politics: A Comparative Study of Modern Democracies*. Oxford: Oxford University Press, pp. 269–88.

Filos, Altana (2008), The Judicial and Legal System. In: James Ker-Lindsay and Hubert Faustann (eds), *The Government and Politics of Cyprus*. Oxford: Peter Lang, pp. 169–84.

Finer, Hermann (1949), *Theory and Practice of Government*. London: Methuen.

Finer, Samuel E. (1958), *Anonymous Empire. A Study of the Lobby in Great Britain*. London: Pall Mall.

—— (1970), *Comparative Government*. London: Penguin Press.

—— (1999), *The History of Government*, 3 volumes. Oxford: Oxford University Press.

Fink-Hafner, Danica (2008), Europeanization and Party System Mechanics: Comparing Croatia, Serbia and Montenegro. *Journal of Southern Europe and the Balkans*, 10(2): 167–81.

Finotelli, Claudia and Giuseppe Sciortino (2013), Through the Gates of the Fortress: European Visa Policies and the Limits of Immigration Control. *Perspectives on European Politics and Society*, 14(1): 80–101.

Der Neue Fischer Weltalmanach (2018), Frankfurt a. M.: Fischer Verlag.

Fleckenstein, Timo (2012), The Politics of Labour Market Reforms and Social Citizenship in Germany. *West European Politics*, 35(4): 847–68.

Fleiner, Thomas (2013), Constitutional Revision: The Case of Switzerland. In: Xenophon Contiades (ed.), *Engineering Constitutional Change. A Comparative Perspective on Europe, Canada and USA*. London: Routledge, pp. 337–58.

Flora, Peter (1999), Introduction and Interpretation. In: Peter Flora with Stein Kuhnle and Derek Urwin (eds), *State Formation, Nation-Building and Mass Politics in Europe: The Theory of Stein Rokkan*. Oxford: Clarendon Press, pp. 1–91.

—— with Stein Kuhnle and Derek Urwin (eds) (1999), *State Formation, Nation-Building and Mass Politics in Europe. The Theory of Stein Rokkan*. Oxford: Clarendon Press.

Folketing (2017), *Året, Der Gik, I Folketinget: Beretning om Folketingsåret 2016–17*. Copenhagen: Folketing.

—— (2018a), Rigsretten. www.ft.dk/folkestyret/domstolene/rigsretten (accessed on 6 February 2018).

—— (2018b), Året der gik i Folketinget, 2008–17. www.ft.dk/da/dokumenter/bestil-publikationer/publikationer?f___publicationcategory=%u00e5rsberetninger (accessed on 19 February 2018).

Føllesdal, Andreas (2006), Political Consumerism as a Change and Challenge. In: Michele Micheletti, Andreas Føllesdal and Dietlind Stolle (eds), *Politics, Products, and Markets: Exploring Political Consumerism. Past and Present*. New Brunswick: Transaction Publishers, pp. 3–20.

Fomarola, Andrea (2014), Fidesz and Electoral Reform: How to Safeguard Hungarian Democracy. EUROPP, 21 March 2016. http://blogs.lse.ac.uk/europpblog/2016/03/21/fidesz-and-electoral-reform-how-to-safeguard-hungarian-democracy/ (accessed on 13 May 2018).

Foundethakis, Penelope (2003), The Hellenic Parliament: The New Rules of the Game. In: Cristina Leston Bandeira (ed.), *Southern European Parliaments in Democracy*, Special issue of *Journal of Legislative Studies*, 9(2): 85–106.

Franciscis, Maria Elisabetta de and Rosella Zannini (1992), Judicial Policy-Making in Italy: Constitutional Court. In: Mary L. Volcansek (ed.), *Judicial Politics and Policy-Making in Western Europe*, Special issue of *West European Politics*, 15(3): 68–79.

Freire, André (2017), *Para lá da geringonça: O governo de esquerdas em Portugal e na Europa*. Lisbon: Edições Contraponto.

Freye, Saskia (2009), *Führungswechsel: Die Wirtschaftselite und das Ende der Führungselite*. Frankfurt a. M.: Campus.

Friedman, George (2011), *Borderlands: A Geopolitical Journey in Eurasia*. Austin: Stratfor.

—— (19 December 2014), Interview with Kommersant. www.kommersant.ru/doc/2636177 (accessed on 13 September 2018).

—— (2015), *Flashpoints: The Emerging Crisis in Europe*. New York: Doubleday.

Friedrich, Carl J. (1952), *The Age of Baroque, 1610–60*. New York: Harper & Row.

—— (1966), *Totalitarian Dictatorship and Democracy*. New York: Praeger.

Fruhstorfer, Anna (2016), Moldova. In: Anna Fruhstorfer and Michael Hein (eds), *Constitutional Politics in Central and Eastern Europe: From Post-Socialist Transition to the Reform of Political Systems*. Wiesbaden: Springer VS, pp. 359–87.

—— and Michael Hein (eds) (2016), *Constitutional Politics in Central and Eastern Europe: From Post-Socialist Transition to the Reform of Political Systems*. Wiesbaden: Springer VS.

—— and Barbora Moormann-Kimáková (2016), Czech Republic. In: Anna Fruhstorfer and Michael Hein (eds), *Constitutional Politics in Central and Eastern Europe: From Post-Socialist Transition to the Reform of Political Systems*. Wiesbaden: Springer VS, pp. 39–63.

Gabanyi, Anneli Ute (2010), Das politische System Rumäniens. In: Wolfgang Ismayr (ed.), *Die politische Systeme Osteuropas*. Wiesbaden: Springer Verlag, pp. 525–62.

Gallagher, Michael (1991), Proportionality, Disproportionality and Electoral Systems. *Electoral Studies*, 10(1): 33–51.

—— (2010a), The Oireachtas: Parliament and President. In: John Oakley and Michael Gallagher (eds), *Politics in the Republic of Ireland*. London: Routledge, pp. 198–229.

—— (2010b), The Changing Constitution. In: John Oakley and Michael Gallagher (eds), *Politics in the Republic of Ireland*. London: Routledge, pp. 73–108.

—— (2018), Election Indices Dataset. www.tcd.ie/Political_Science/people/michael_gallagher/ElSystems/Docts/ElectionIndices.pdf (accessed on 11 May 2018).

Gallagher, Tom (2005), *Modern Romania: The End of Communism, the Failure of Democratic Reform, and the Theft of a Nation*. New York: New York University Press.

—— (2009), *Romania and the European Union. How the Weak Vanquished the Strong*. Manchester: Manchester University Press.

—— and Viorel Andrievici (2008), Political Irresponsibility Without Constitutional Safeguards. In: Robert Elgie and Sophia Moestrup (eds), *Semi-Presidentialism in Central and Eastern Europe*. Manchester: Manchester University Press, pp. 138–58.

Gallina, Nicole (2016), Ukraine. In: Anna Fruhstorfer and Michael Hein (eds), *Constitutional Politics in Central and Eastern Europe: From Post-Socialist Transition to the Reform of Political Systems*. Wiesbaden: Springer VS, pp. 495–518.

Gaman-Golutvina, Oxana (2014), Parliamentary Representation and MPs in Russia: Historical Retrospective and Comparative Perspective. In: Elena Semenova, Michael Edinger and Heinrich Best (eds), *Parliamentary Elites in Central and Eastern Europe: Recruitment and Representation*. London: Routledge, pp. 261–83.

Ganshof, F.L. (1964), *Feudalism*. New York: Harper & Row.

Gattermann, Katjana and Claudia Hefftler (2015), Beyond Institutional Capacity: Political Motivation and Parliamentary Behaviour in the Early Warning System. *West European Politics*, 38(2): 305–34.

Geisler, Alexander and Ulrich Sarcinelli (2002), Modernisierung von Wahlkämpfen und Modernisierung von Demokratie? In: Andreas Dörner and Ludgera Vogt (eds), *Wahlkämpfe: Betrachtungen über ein demokratisches Ritual*. Frankfurt a. M.: Suhrkamp, pp. 43–67.

Gemenis, Kostas and Roula Nezi (2014), Government-Opposition Dynamics during the Economic Crisis in Greece. *The Journal of Legislative Studies*, 21(1): 14–34.

Gerkrath, Jörg (2013), Constitutional Amendment in Luxembourg. In: Xenophon I. Kontiades (ed.), *Engineering Constitutional Change. A Comparative Perspective on Europe, Canada, and the USA*. London: Routledge, pp. 229–56.

Gerth, H.H. and C. Wright Mills (eds) (1946), *Essays from Max Weber*. New York: Oxford University Press.

Gherghina, Sergiu and Michael Hein (2016), Romania. In: Anna Fruhstorfer and Michael Hein (eds), *Constitutional Politics in Central and Eastern Europe: From Post-Socialist Transition to the Reform of Political Systems*. Wiesbaden: Springer VS, pp. 173–97.

Giddens, Anthony (1992), *Sociology*. Cambridge: Polity Press.

—— (1998), *The Third Way: The Renewal of Social Democracy*. Cambridge: Polity Press.

—— and Philip W. Sutton (2016), *Sociology*, eighth edition. Cambridge: Polity.

Giannetti, Daniela, Andrea Pedrazzani and Luca Pinto (2017), Party System Change in Italy: Politicising the EU and the Rise of Eccentric Parties. *South European Society and Politics*, 22(1): 21–42.

Gidengil, Elisabeth and Ekrem Karakoc (2016), Which Matters More in the Electoral Success of Islamist (Successor) Parties: Religion or Performance? The Turkish case. *Party Politics*, 22(3): 325–38.

Gierke, Otto von (1996), *Political Theories of the Middle Ages*. Bristol: Thoemme Press.

Gillespie, Richard (ed.) (1997), *The Euro-Mediterranean Partnership. Political and Economic Perspectives*. London: Frank Cass.

—— (2006), Onward But Not Upward: The Barcelona Conference of 2005. *Mediterranean Politics*, 11(2): 271–8.

—— (2011), Adapting to French 'Leadership'? Spain's Role in the Union for the Mediterranean. *Mediterranean Politics*, 16(1): 59–78.

Giuffrida, Fabio (2017), *The European Public Prosecutor's Office: King without Kingdom?* Research Report, 2017/03. Brussels: Centre for European Policy Studies.

Glaessner, Vera (2013), Central and Eastern European Industrial Relations in the Crisis: National Divergence and Path-Dependent Change. *Transfer*, 19(2): 155–69.

Goetz, Klaus H. and Helen Z. Margetts (1999), The Solitary Center: The Core Executive in Central and Eastern Europe. *Governance: An International Journal of Policy and Administration*, 12(4): 425–53.

Goodman, Sara Wallace (2015), Immigration Policy-Making in Europe. In: José M. Magone (ed.), *Routledge Handbook of European Politics*. London: Routledge, pp. 809–25.

Goossens, Jurgen and Pieter Cannoot (2015), Belgian Federalism after the Sixth State Reform. *Perspectives on Federalism*, 7(2): 29–55.

Gorbachev, Mikhail (1989), Address Given by Mikhail Gorbachev to the Council of Europe (Strasbourg, 6 July 1989). www.cvce.eu/content/publication/2002/9/20/4c021687–9 8f9–4727–9e8b-836e0bc1f6fb/publishable_en.pdf (accessed on 12 September 2018).

Götz, Norbert (2012), Schweden. In: Werner Reutter (ed.), *Verbände und Verbandssysteme in den Ländern der Europäischen Union*. Wiesbaden: Springer Verlag, pp. 641–70.

Goujon, Alexandra (1999), Language, Nationalism, and Populism in Belarus. *Nationalities Papers*, 27(4): 661–77.

Government of Croatia (2018), About Croatia/Political Organisation/Counties. http://croatia.eu/article.php?lang=2&id=30 (accessed on 16 July 2018).

Grant, Moyra (2009), *The UK Parliament*. Edinburgh: University Press.

Grdesic, Marko (2008), Mapping the Paths of the Yugoslav Model: Labour Strength and Weakness in Slovenia, Croatia and Serbia. *European Journal of Industrial Relations*, 14(2): 133–51.

Green, Jane and Christopher Prosser (2016), Party System Fragmentation and Single-Party Government: The British General Election of 2015. *West European Politics*, 39(6): 1299–1310.

Green, V.H. (1974), *Renaissance and Reformation: A Survey of European History between 1450 and 1660*. London: Edward Arnold.

Greenwood, Justin (2017), *Interest Representation in the European Union*. Basingstoke: Palgrave.

Grossman, Emiliano and Sabine Saurugger (2004), Challenging French Interest Groups: The State, Europe and the International Political System. *French Politics*, 2(2): 203–20.

Group of States Against Corruption (Groupe des Etats Contre la Corruption – GRECO) (2015), *Zweiter Zwischenbericht über die Konformität der Schweiz 'Strafbestimmungen' (SEV 173 und 191, GPC 2). Transparenz der Parteienfinanzierung. Dritte Evaluationsrunde*. Veröffentlicht. Greco RC-III (2015) 6. Zwischenbericht, 17 August. www.bj.admin.ch/dam/data/bj/sicherheit/kriminalitaet/korruption/grecoberichte/ber-iii-2015–6f-d.pdf (accessed on 13 May 2018).

—— (2018), www.coe.int/en/web/greco (accessed on 13 May 2018).

Government of Ireland (2007), Towards 2016. Ten-Year Framework Social Partnership Agreement 2006–2015. Dublin: Stationery Office. www.welfare.ie/en/downloads/Towards201626June06.pdf (accessed on 11 November 2018).

Government of Sweden (2017), The Constitution. www.government.se/how-sweden-is-governed/the-constitution/ (accessed on 26 September 2017).

Grotz, Florian and Ferdinand Müller-Rommel (eds) (2011), *Regierungssysteme in EU Member-Staaten. Die neuen EU-Staaten in Vergleich*. Wiesbaden: Springer Verlag.

Guillorel, Hervé (1981), France: Religion, Periphery, State and Nation-Building. In: Per Torsvik (ed.), *Mobilization, Centre-Periphery Structures and Nation-Building: A Volume in Commemoration of Stein Rokkan*. Bergen: Universitetsforlaget, pp. 390–428.

Gürbey, Gülistan (2017), Erneute Gewalteskalation im Türkischen-Kurdischen Konflikt. *Aus Politik und Zeitgeschichte*, 9–10: 10–17.

Guzzini, Stefano (1994), La longue nuit de la Première République: L'implosion clientéliste en Italie. *Revue Française de Science Politique*, 44(6): 979–1013.

Häge, Frank M. (2016), Committee Decision-Making in the Council of the European Union. *European Union Politics*, 8(3): 299–328.

—— and Daniel Naurin (2013), The Effect of Codecision on Council Decision-Making: Informalization, Politicization and Power. *Journal of European Public Policy*, 20(7): 953–71.

Hahn, Gordon M. (2018), *Ukraine Over the Edge: Russia, the West and the New Cold War*. Jefferson: McFarland and Company.

Hájek, Lukáš (2016), Left, Right, Left, Right . . . Centre: Ideological Position of Andrej Babiš's ANO. *Czech Journal of Political Science*, 3: 235–71.

Halás, Marián and Pavel Klapka (2016), Functionality versus Gerrymandering and Nationalism in Administrative Geography: Lessons from Slovakia. *Regional Studies*, 51(10): 1568–79.

Hall, Stephen G.F. (2017), Preventing a Colour Revolution: The Belarusian Example as an Illustration for the Kremlin? *East European Politics*, 33(2): 162–83.

Haller, Max (1997), Klassenstruktur und Arbeitslosigkeit: Die Entwickling zwischen 1960 und 1990. In: Stefan Hradil and Stefan Immerfall (eds), *Die westeuropäischen Gesellschaften im Vergleich*. Opladen: Leske & Budrich, pp. 377–428.

Halperin, Ernst (1957), *Der siegreiche Ketzer: Titos Kampf gegen Stalin*. Cologne: Politik und Wirtschaft.

Hamann, Kerstin (2012), *The Politics of Industrial Relations: Labor Unions in Spain*. New York: Routledge.

—— and John Kelly (2011), *Parties, Elections and Policy Reforms in Western Europe: Voting For Social Pacts*. London: Routledge.

—— (2015), Social Pacts and Changing Systems of Interest Intermediation. In: José M. Magone (ed.), *Routledge Handbook of European Politics*. London: Routledge, pp. 777–92.

Hanley, David (1996), Introduction: Christian Democracy as a Political Phenomenon. In: David Hanley (ed.), *Christian Democracy in Europe: A Comparative Perspective*. London: Continuum, pp. 1–11.

—— (2008), *Beyond the Nation State: Parties in the Era of European Integration*. Basingstoke: Palgrave.

—— (2015), Outside Their Comfort Zone? National Parties, European Parliament Groups and Transnational Parties. In: José M. Magone (ed.), *Routledge Handbook of European Politics*. London: Routledge, pp. 590–607.

Hanley, Séan and Alan Sikk (2016), Economy, Corruption or Floating Voters? Explaining the Breakthroughs of Anti-Establishment Reform Parties in Eastern Europe. *Party Politics*, 22(4): 522–33.

Hansen, Kasper M. and Karina Kosiara-Pedersen (2017), Nordic Voters and Party Systems. In: Peter Nedergaard and Anders Wivel (eds), *The Routledge Handbook of Scandinavian Politics*. London: Routledge, pp. 114–23.

Harding, Andrew (2017), *The Fundamentals of Constitutional Courts*. Constitution Brief, April 2017. Stockholm: International Institute for Elections and Democracy Assistance (IDEA). www.idea.int/sites/default/files/publications/the-fundamentals-of-constitutional-courts.pdf (accessed on 3 November 2018).

Harding, Luke (2011), *Mafia State. How One Reporter Became an Enemy of the Brutal New Russia*. London: Guardianbooks.

Harmsen, Robert and Karen McAuliffe (2015), The European Courts. In: José M. Magone (eds), *Routledge Handbook of European Politics*. London: Routledge, pp. 263–80.

Harrington, James (1656), *The Commonwealth of Oceana*. London: Livewell Chapman. www.archive.org (accessed on 25 November 2018).

Harvey, J. and L. Bather (1982), *The British Constitution and Politics*, fifth edition. Basingstoke: Macmillan.

Hassel, Anke (2009), Policies and Politics in Social Pacts in Europe. *European Journal of Industrial Relations*, 15(7): 7–26.

Hay, Colin and Daniel Wincott (2012), *The Political Economy of European Welfare Capitalism*. Basingstoke: Palgrave Macmillan.

Hayward, Jack E.S. (1987), *Governing France: The One and Indivisible Republic*. London: Weidenfeld & Nicolson.

—— and A. Menon (eds) (2003), *Governing Europe*. Oxford: Oxford University Press.

Hazell, R. (2008), Conclusion: Where Will the Westminster Model End up? In: R. Hazell (ed.), *Constitutional Futures Revised: Britain's Constitution to 2020*. Basingstoke: Palgrave Macmillan, pp. 285–300.

Hefftler, Claudia and Katjana Gattermann (2016), Interparliamentary Cooperation in the European Union: Patterns, Problems, Potential. In: Claudia Hefftler, Christine Neuhold, Olivier Rozenberg and Julie Smith (eds), *The Palgrave Handbook of National Parliaments and the European Union*. Basingstoke: Palgrave, pp. 94–115.

Hefftler, Claudia, Christine Neuhold, Oliver Rozenberg and Julie Smith (eds) (2016), *The Palgrave Handbook of National Parliaments and the European Union*. Basingstoke: Palgrave.

Hegeland, Hans (2016), Swedish Parliament and EU Affairs: From Reluctant Player to Europeanized Actor. In: Claudia Hefftler, Christine Neuhold, Oliver Rozenberg and Julie Smith (eds), *The Palgrave Handbook of National Parliaments and the European Union*. Basingstoke: Palgrave, pp. 425–43.

Heidar, Knut (1995), Norway. In: Ruud Koole and Peter Mair (eds), *European Journal of Political Research: Political Data Yearbook 1994*, 28(3/4): 446–7.

Heinrich Böll Stiftung (2017), Southeastern Europe: Captured States in the Balkans. Special issue *Perspectives*. www.boell.de/sites/default/files/perspectives_-_09–2017_-_web.pdf?dimension1=division_osoe (accessed on 16 July 2018).

Hemerijck, Anton C. (1995), Corporatist Immobility in the Netherlands. In: Colin Crouch and Franz Traxler (eds), *Organized Industrial Relations in Europe: What Future?* Aldershot: Avebury, pp. 189–216.

—— (2013), *Changing Welfare States*. Oxford: Oxford University Press.

—— (2018), Social Investment as a Policy Paradigm. *Journal of European Public Policy*, 25(6): 810–27.

—— and Marc van der Meer (2016), Nieuw Nederlands polderen Van brede sociale akkoorden naar 'ad hoc' hervormingscoalities. In: Maarten Keune (ed.), *Nog steeds een Mirakel? De Legitimiteit van der Polder Model in de Eenentwintigste Eeuw*. Amsterdam: Amsterdam University Press, pp. 167–95.

Hennessy, Alexandra (2017), Good Samaritans vs. Hardliners: The Role of Credible Signalling in Greek Bailout Negotiations. *Journal of Common Market Studies*, 55(4): 744–61.

Herman, Edward S. and Noam Chomsky (1988), *Manufacturing Consent: The Political Economy of the Mass Media*. New York: Pantheon Books.

Higdem, Ulla and Aksel Hagen (2015), Norway and the Regions. In: Assembly of the European Regions, Report on the State of Regionalisation 2017. Observatory on Regionalisation. https://drive.google.com/file/d/0B94jJjQLXnl-UlZ2TnQ1NmNGNDQ/view (accessed on 16 July 2018).

Hine, David (1993), *Governing Italy: The Politics of Bargained Pluralism*. Oxford: Oxford University Press.

Hinz, Wolfram (2013), Von 'Merkozy' zu 'Merkollande'? *Aus Politik und Zeitgeschichte*, 1(3): 23–29.

Hirczy de Miño, Wolfgang and John C. Lane (1999), Malta: STV in a Two-Party System. In: Shaun Bowler and Bernard Grofman (eds), *Elections in Australia, Ireland and Malta under the Single Transferable Vote: Reflections on an Embedded Institution*. Ann Arbor: University of Michigan Press, pp. 178–204.

Hirsch, Mario (2010a), Luxembourg. La coordination tripartite à l'épreuve, Grande Europe n° 21, juin 2010 – La Documentation française. www.ladocumentationfrancaise.fr/pages-europe/d000515-luxembourg.-la-coordination-tripartite-a-l-epreuve-par-mario-hirsch/article (accessed on 10 July 2015).

—— (2010b), The Luxembourg Model Has Reached Its Limits: Sozialpartnership and Tripartite Arrangements Work Only under Fair Weather Conditions. Paper presented at the Politocologenetmaal 2010 (Workshop 1B: European Integration and Consensus Making in the Low Countries. KU Leuven 28 May 2010).https://soc.kuleuven.be/web/files/11/72/W1B-122.pdf (accessed on 24 February 2016).

—— (2012), Sind Konkordanz-, Konsens und Drei-Partnermodelle 'Schönwetter-Veranstaltungen'? Der Beispiel Luxemburg. In: Stefan Köppl and Uwe Krannenpohl (eds), *Konkordanzdemokratie: Ein Demokratietyp der Vergangenheit*. Baden-Baden: Nomos, pp. 117–32.

Hix, Simon (2005), *The Political System of the European Union*. Basingstoke: Palgrave.

—— and Christopher Lord (1997), *Political Parties in the European Union*. Basingstoke: Palgrave.

Hix, Simon, Abdul G. Noury and Gérard Roland (2007), *Democratic Politics in the European Parliament*. Cambridge: Cambridge University Press.

Hlepas, Nikolaus-Komninos (2005), *Grécia: La Democratització a través de la Descentralització?* Colleció Món Local 14. Barcelona: Universitat Autonoma de Barcelona – Institut de Ciencies Politiques i Socials.

Hobsbawn, E.J. (1964), *The Age of Revolution, 1789–1848*. London: Cardinal.

—— (1984), *The Age of Capital, 1848–1975*. London: Meridian Classic.

—— (1987), *The Age of Empire, 1875–1914*. London: Weidenfeld & Nicolson.

—— (1994), *The Age of Extremes. The Short Twentieth Century, 1914–1991*. London: Abacus.

—— (2000), *Nations and Nationalism since 1780. Programme, Myth, Reality*. Cambridge: Cambridge University Press.

Hoensch, Jörg K.(1989), *A History of Modern Hungary. 1867–1986*. London, New York: Longman.

Hoffstetter, Yvonne (2016), *Das Ende der Demokratie: Wie die künstliche Intelligenz die Politik übernimmt und uns entmündigt*. Munich: C. Bertelsmann.

Högenauer, Anna-Lena (2016), Dutch Parliament and European Affairs: Decentralizing Scrutiny. In: Claudia Hefftler, Christine Neuhold, Olivier Rozenberg and Julie Smith (eds), *The Palgrave Handbook of National Parliaments and the European Union*. Basingstoke: Palgrave, pp. 252–73.

Höing, Oliver (2016), With a Little Help of the Constitutional Court: The Bundestag on its Way to an Active Policy Player. In: Claudia Hefftler, Christine Neuhold, Olivier Rozenberg and Julie Smith (eds), *The Palgrave Handbook of National Parliaments and the European Union*. Basingstoke: Palgrave, pp. 191–208.

Holden, Einar (2016), A New Model for Wage Formation in Iceland. 9 August 2016. http://rikissattasemjari.is/wp-content/uploads/2017/05/New-Model-for-Wage-Formation-in-Iceland.pdf (accessed on 25 June 2018).

Holmes, Leslie (2008), Corruption and Organised Crime in Putin's Russia. *Europe-Asia Studies*, 60(6): 1011–31.

Hölscheidt, Sven and Tilman Hoppe (2010), Der Mythos vom 'europäischen Impuls' in der deutschen Gesetzgebungsstatistik. *Zeitschrift für Parlamentsfragen*, 41(3): 543–51.

Hooghe, Liesbet and Gary Marks (2001), *Multilevel Governance and European Integration*. Lanham: Rowman and Littlefield.

—— (2018), Cleavage Theory Meets Europe's Crises: Lipset, Rokkan, and the Transnational Cleavage. *Journal of European Public Policy*, 25(1): 109–35.

——, Arjan H. Schakel, Sandi Chapman Osterkatz, Sara Niedzwiecki and Sarah Shair-Rosenfield (2016), *Measuring Regional Authority: A Postfunctionalist Theory of Governance, volume I*. Oxford: Oxford University Press.

Hooghe, Liesbet, Arjan H. Schakel and Gary Marks (2008), Appendix B: Country and Regional Scores. *Regional and Federal Studies*, 18(2–3): 259–74.

Hooghe, Marc (2012), Belgien. In: Werner Reutter (ed.), *Verbände und Verbandssysteme in den Ländern der Europäischen Union*. Wiesbaden: Springer Verlag, pp. 55–74.

Hopflinger, Francois (1997), Haushalts- und Familienstrukturen im intereuropäischen Vergleich. In: Stefan Hradil and Stefan Immerfall (eds), *Die westeuropäischen Gesellschaften im Vergleich*. Opladen: Leske & Budrich, pp. 97–138.

Höpner, Martin and Lothar Krempel (2006), Ein Netzwerk in Auflösung: Wie die Deutschland AG zerfällt. 5 July 2006. www.mpifg.de/aktuelles/themen/doks/Netzwerk_in_Aufloesung-w.pdf (accessed on 25 June 2016).

Hörnström, Lisa (2013), Strong Regions within the Unitary State: The Nordic Experience of Regionalization. *Regional & Federal Studies*, 23(4): S427–S443.

House of Lords (2018), Lords by Party, Type of Peerage and Gender. www.parliament.uk/mps-lords-and-offices/lords/composition-of-the-lords/ (accessed on 9 February 2018).

Hristova-Valtcheva, Katia (2012), Bulgarien. In: Werner Reutter (ed.), *Verbände und Verbandssysteme in den Ländern der Europäischen Union*. Wiesbaden: Springer Verlag, pp. 75–100.

Hudson, Christine (2005), Regional Development Partnerships in Sweden: Putting the Government Back in Governance? *Regional and Federal Studies*, 15(3): 311–27.

Huizinga, Johan (1955), *The Waning of the Middle Ages: A Study of the Forms of Life, Thought, and Art in France and the Netherlands in the Fourteenth and Fifteenth Centuries*. Harmondsworth: Penguin.

Huntington, Samuel (1991), *The Third Wave: Democratization in the Late Twentieth Century*. Norman: University of Oklahoma Press.

Hustedt, Thurid and Heidi H. Salomonsen (2017), Political Control of Coordination? The Roles of Ministerial Advisers in Government Coordination in Denmark and Sweden. *Public Administration*, 95(2): 393–406.

Hutcheson, Derek S.(2012), Party Cartels Beyond Western Europe: Evidence from Russia. *Party Politics*, 19(6): 907–24.

Ignazi, Piero (1997), New Challenges: Postmaterialism and the Extreme Right. In: M. Rhodes, P. Heywood and V. Wright (eds), *Developments in West European Politics*. Basingstoke: Macmillan, pp. 300–19.

Ikstens, Jaňis (2014), Latvia. In: Andreas Bågenholm, Kevin Deegan-Krause and Liam Weeks (eds), *Political Data Yearbook 2013*. Special issue of *European Journal of Political Research*, 53(1): 198–204.

—— (2016), Latvia. In: Daniele Caramani, Kevin Deegan-Krause and Liam Weeks (eds), *Political Data Yearbook 2015*. Special issue of *European Journal of Political Research*, 55(1): 164–7.

Illner, Michael and Zdenka Vajdova (2006), *El govern territorial a la República Txeca després de la transformació del sistema*. Barcelona: Universitat Autonoma de Barcelona – Institut de Ciencies Politiques i Socials.

Ilonszki, Gabriella (2007), From Minimal to Subordinate: A Final Verdict? The Hungarian Parliament 1990–2002. *Journal of Legislative Studies*, 13(1): 38–58.

—— and Réka Várnagy (2014), From Party Cartel to One-Party Dominance: The Case of Institutional Failure. *East European Politics*, 30(3): 412–27.

Immerfall, Stefan (1995), *Einführung in den europäischen Gesellschaftsvergleich: Ansätze, Problemstellungen, Befunde*. Passau: Wissenschaftsverlag Richard Rothe.

—— (1997), Soziale Integration in den westeuropäischen Gesellschaften: Werte, Mitgliedschaft und Netzwerke. In: Stefan Hradil and Stefan Immerfall (eds),

Die westeuropäischen Gesellschaften im Vergleich. Opladen: Leske & Budrich, pp. 139–73.

Independent Fact Finding Mission on the Conflict in Georgia (2009), Report. Three Volumes. www.echr.coe.int/Documents/HUDOC_38263_08_Annexes_ENG.pdf (accessed on 14 September 2018).

Inglehart, Ronald (1977), *The Silent Revolution: Changing Values and Political Styles*. Princeton: Princeton University Press.

—— (2008), Changing Values among Western Publics from 1970 to 2006. *West European Politics*, 31(1): 130–46.

—— and Christian Welzel (2005), *Modernization, Cultural Change and Democracy: The Human Development Sequence*. Cambridge: Cambridge University Press.

International Institute of Democracy and Electoral Assistance (IDEA) (2014), *Funding of Political Parties and Election Campaigns: A Handbook on Political Finance*. Stockholm: IDEA www.idea.int/sites/default/files/publications/funding-of-political-parties-and-election-campaigns.pdf (accessed on 13 May 2018).

—— (2018a), Political Financing Database. www.idea.int/data-tools/data/political-finance-database (accessed on 5 November 2018).

—— (2018b), Electoral System Design Database. www.idea.int/data-tools/data/electoral-system-design (accessed on 5 November 2018).

International Organization of Migration (IOM) (2018), Mediterranean Migrant Arrivals Reach 97,857 in 2018; Deaths Reach 1,987. www.iom.int/news/mediterranean-migrant-arrivals-reach-97857-2018-deaths-reach-1987 (accessed on 17 November 2018).

Interparliamentary Union (IPU) (2018), New Parline Database. https://data.ipu.org/ (accessed on 5 November 2018).

Ismayr, Wolfgang (ed.) (2009), *Die politische Systeme Westeuropas*. Wiesbaden: Verlag für Sozialwissenschaften.

—— (2010), Die politischen Systeme Osteuropas im Vergleich. In: Wolfgang Ismayr (ed.), *Die politischen Systeme Osteuropas*. Wiesbaden: Springer Verlag, pp. 9–79.

Israel, Jonathan I. (1998), *The Dutch Republic: Its Rise, Greatness, and Fall 1477–1806*. Oxford: Oxford University Press.

Jäckle, Sebastian and Pascal D. König (2017), The Dark Side of the German 'Welcome Culture': Investigating the Causes Behind Attacks on Refugees in 2015. *West European Politics*, 40(2): 223–51.

Jaremba, Urszula (2014), *National Judges as EU Law Judges: The Polish Civil Law System*. Leiden: Martinus Nijhoff Publishers.

Jasiewicz, Krzystof and Agnieska Jasiewicz-Betkiewicz (2016), Poland. In: Andreas Bågenholm, Kevin Deegan-Krause and Liam Weeks (eds), *Political Data Yearbook 2015*. Special issue of *European Journal of Political Research*, 55(1): 204–15.

—— (2017), Poland. In: Andreas Bågenholm, Kevin Deegan-Krause and Liam Weeks (eds), *Political Data Yearbook 2015*. Special issue of *European Journal of Political Research*, 56(1): 214–22.

Jastramskis, Mažvidas and Ainė Ramonaitė (2016), Lithuania. In: Andreas Bågenholm, Kevin Deegan-Krause and Liam Weeks (eds), *Political Data Yearbook 2015*. Special issue of *European Journal of Political Research*, 55(1): 168–74.

Jessop, Bob (2002), *The Future of the Capitalist State*. London: Polity Press.

—— (2014), Variegated Capitalism, das Modell Deutschland, and the Eurozone Crisis. *Journal of Contemporary European Studies*, 22(3): 248–60.

Johansson, Karl Magnus and Tapio Raunio (2010), Organizing the Core Executive for European Union Affairs: Comparing Finland and Sweden. *Public Administration*, 88(3): 649–64.

Johnston, R.J. (1993), The Rise and Decline of the Corporate Welfare State: A Comparative Analysis in Global Context. In: Peter J. Taylor (ed.), *Political Geography of the Twentieth Century: A Global Analysis*. London: Belhaven Press, pp. 117–70.

Jones, Bill (2014), Pressure Groups. In: Bill Jones and Philip Norton (eds), *Politics UK*, sixth edition. Harlow: Pearson-Longman, pp. 178–201.

—— and Philip Norton (eds) (2014), *Politics UK*, sixth edition. Harlow: Pearson-Longman.

Jones, Stephen (2015), *Georgia: A Political History since Independence*. London and New York: I.B. Tauris.

Jónsson, Guðmundur (2014), Iceland and the Nordic Model of Consensus Democracy. *Scandinavian Journal of History*, 39(4): 510–28.

Joppke, Christian (2007), Beyond National Models: Civic Integration Policies for Immigrants in Western Europe. *West European Politics*, 30(1): 1–22.

—— (2014), Europe and Islam: Alarmists, Victimists, and Integration by Law. *West European Politics*, 37(6): 1314–35.

—— (2017), Civic Integration in Western Europe: Three Debates. *West European Politics*, 40(6): 1153–76.

Judge, David and David Earnshaw (2008), *The European Parliament*. Basingstoke: Palgrave.

Juncker, Jean Claude (2017), The State of the Union 2017. https://ec.europa.eu/commission/state-union-2017_en (accessed on 28 September 2017).

Jungar, Ann-Cathrine (2017). Continuity and Convergence: Populism in Scandinavia. In: Peter Nedergaard and Anders Wivel (eds), *The Routledge Handbook of Scandinavian Politics*. London: Routledge, pp. 147–60.

Jurek, Petr (2010), The Institutionalization of Party Systems: Bulgaria, Romania, Croatia and Slovenia in a Comparative Perspective. *Politics in Central Europe*, 6(1): 110–23.

Kadarik, Ingel and Liina Osila (2018), Estonia: Developments in Working Life. www.eurofound.europa.eu/sites/default/files/wpef18026.pdf (accessed on 27 June 2018).

Kaelble, Hartmut (2007), *Sozialgeschichte Europas: 1945 bis zur Gegenwart*. Munich: Beck.

Kahancová, Marta (2013), The Demise of Social Partnership or a Balanced Recovery? The Crisis and Collective Bargaining in Slovakia. *Transfer*, 19(2): 171–83.

Kakachia, Kornely and Bidzina Lebanidze (2016), Georgia's Protracted Transition: Civil Society, Party Politics and Challenges to Democratic Transformation. In: Gia Nodia (ed.), *25 Years of Independent Georgia: Achievements and Unfinished Projects*. Berlin: Konrad Adenauer Foundation, pp. 130–61.

Kälin, Walter (2002), Justiz. In: Ulrich Klöti, Peter Knoepfel, Hans-Peter Kriesi, Wolf Linder and Yannis Papadopoulos (eds), *Handbuch der Schweizer Politik*. Zurich: Neue Züricher Verlag, pp. 187–208.

Kalina, Ondřej (2012), Die Europäische Union als Konkordanzsystem im Demokratie dilemma. In: Stefan Köppl and Uwe Krannenpohl (eds), *Konkordanzdemokratie: Ein Demokratietyp der Vergangenheit?* Baden-Baden: Nomos, pp. 189–215.

Kalosinatos, Pavlos (2018), Cyprus: Developments in Working Life 2017. www.eurofound.europa.eu/sites/default/files/wpef18023.pdf (accessed on 26 June 2018).

Kalyvas, Stathis N. and Kees van Kersbergen (2010), Christian Democracy. *Annual Review of Political Science*, 13: 183–209.

Kaniouk, Petr and Vít Hloušek (2013), Europe and the Czech Presidential Election of January 2013. Election Briefing No 72. www.sussex.ac.uk/webteam/gateway/file.php?name=epern-election-briefing-number-74.pdf&site=266 (accessed on 21 December 2017).

Karasimeonov, Georgi (1996), The Legislature in Post-Communist Bulgaria. In: David M. Olson and Philip Norton (eds), *The New Parliaments of Central and Eastern Europe*. London: Frank Cass, pp. 40–59.

Karasu, Kristina (2017), Die Wahrheit hinter Gittern: Presse- und Meinungsfreiheit in der Türkei. *Aus Politik und Zeitgeschichte*, (9–10): 18–22.

Karlhofer, Ferdinand (2012), Österreich. In: Werner Reutter (ed.), *Verbände und Verbandssysteme in den Ländern der Europäischen Union*. Wiesbaden: Springer Verlag, pp. 521–50.

—— and Emmerich Tálos (eds) (2006), *Sozialpartnerschaft: Österreichische und Europäische Perspektiven*. Vienna: LIT.

Karlsson, Christer (2014), Comparing Constitutional Change in European Union Member States: In Search of a Theory. *Journal of Common Market Studies*, 52(3): 566–81.

—— (2016a), Explaining Constitutional Change: Making Sense of Cross-National Variation among European Union Member States. *Journal of European Public Policy*, 23(2): 255–75.

—— (2016b), Comparing Constitutional Change in European Union Member States: In Search of a Theory. *Journal of Common Market Studies*, 52(3): 566–81.

—— and Katarina Galic (2016), Constitutional Change in Light of European Union Membership: Trends and Trajectories in the New Member States. *East European Politics*, 32(4): 446–65.

Karnite, Raita (2018), Working Life in Latvia. www.eurofound.europa.eu/country/latvia (accessed on 27 June 2018).

Karvonen, Lauri (2014), *Parties, Governments, and Voters in Finland: Politics under Fundamental Societal Transformation*. Colchester: ECPR Press.

Kasapović, Mirjana (2008), Semi-Presidentialism in Croatia. In: Robert Elgie and Sophie Moestrup (eds), *Semi-Presidentialism in Central and Eastern Europe*. Manchester: Manchester University Press, pp. 51–64.

Kassim, Hussein (2015), The National Coordination of EU Policy. In: José M. Magone (ed.), *Routledge Handbook of European Politics*. London: Routledge, pp. 686–707.

Katchanovski, Ivan (2015), The 'Snipers' Massacre' on the Maidan in Ukraine. Paper Prepared for Presentation at the Annual Meeting of American Political Science Association in San Francisco, 3–6 September 2015. www.researchgate.net/profile/Ivan_Katchanovski/publication/266855828_The_Snipers'_Massacre_on_the_Maidan_in_Ukraine/links/5a83a7f7a6fdcc6f3eb295a5/The-Snipers-Massacre-on-the-Maidan-in-Ukraine.pdf (accessed on 14 September 2018).

Katsaris, Angelos (2015), Managing Climate Change in the Mediterranean: The Union for the Mediterranean and the Challenges of Fragmentation. In: *Mediterranean Politics*, 20(2): 288–94.

Katz, Richard (2015), Party System Change in Western Europe. In: José M. Magone (ed.), *Routledge Handbook in European Politics*. London: Routledge, pp. 494–511.

—— and Peter Mair (1992), The Membership of Political Parties in Western Democracies. In: Ruud Koole and Peter Mair (eds), *European Data Yearbook 1992*. Special issue of *European Journal of Political Research*, 22: 329–45.

—— (1995), Changing Models of Party Organization and Party Democracy. *Party Politics*, 1(1): 5–28.

—— (2002), The Ascendancy of the Party in Public Office: Party Organizational Change in Twentieth-Century Democracies. In: Richard Gunther, José Ramón Montero and Juan J. Linz (eds), *Political Parties: Old Concepts and New Challenges*. Oxford: Oxford University Press, pp. 113–35.

Katzenstein, Peter (1984), *Corporatism and Change: Austria, Switzerland and the Politics of Industry*. Ithaca: Cornell University Press.

—— (1985), *Small States in World Markets: Industrial Policy in Europe*. Ithaca: Cornell University Press.

—— (1987), *Policy and Politics in West Germany: The Growth of a Semisovereign State*. Philadelphia: Temple University Press.

Kavanagh, Dennis (2001), *British Politics: Continuities and Change*. Oxford: Oxford University Press.

Keating, Michael (1998), *The New Regionalism in Western Europe: Territorial Restructuring and Political Change*. Cheltenham: Edward Elgar.

—— (2008), Thirty Years of Territorial Politics. *West European Politics*, 31(1): 60–81.

Kelsall, Tim (2012), Neo-Patrimonialism, Rent-Seeking and Development: Going with the Grain? *New Political Economy*, 17(5): 677–82.

Kemahlıoğlu, Özge (2015), Winds of Change? The June 2015 Parliamentary Election in Turkey. *South European Society and Politics*, 20(4): 445–64.

Keman, Hans and Ferdinand Müller-Rommel (eds) (2012), *Party Government in the New Europe*. London: Routledge.

Kemmerling, Achim and Oliver Bruttel (2006), 'New Politics' in German Labour Market Policy? The Implications of the Recent Hartz IV Reforms for the German Welfare State. *West European Politics*, 29(1): 90–112.

Kempf, Udo (2017), *Das politische System Frankreichs*, fourth edition. Wiesbaden: Springer VS.

Kerrouche, Eric (2006), The French Assemblée nationale: The Case of a Weak Legislature? *The Journal of Legislative Studies*, 12(3–4): 336–65.

Keune, Maarten (ed.) (2016), *Nog steeds een Mirakel? De Legitimiteit van der Polder Model in de Eenentwintigste Eeuw*. Amsterdam: Amsterdam University Press. http://polderboek.nl/wp-content/uploads/2013/03/Nog-steeds-een-mirakel-De-legitimiteit-van-het-poldermodel-in-de-eenentwintigste-eeuw.pdf (accessed on 25 June 2018).

Kickert, Walter J.M. (2000), *Public Management Reforms in the Netherlands: Social Reconstruction of Reform Ideas and Underlying Frames of Reference*. Delft: Uitgeverij Eburon.

—— (2004), *History of Governance in the Netherlands*. The Hague: Elsevier.

Kim, Dae Soon and Nigel Swain (2015), Party Politics, Political Competition and Coming to Terms with the Past in Post-Communist Hungary. *Europe-Asia Studies*, 67(9): 1445–68.

Kipke, Rüdiger (2010), Das politische System der Slowakei. In: Wolfgang Ismayr (ed.), *Die politischen Systeme Osteuropas*. Wiesbaden: Springer VS, pp. 317–56.

Kirby, David (2006), *A Concise History of Finland*. Cambridge: Cambridge University Press.

Kirchheimer, Otto (1965), Der Wandel des westeuropäischen Parteiensystems. *Politische Vierteljahresschrift*, 6: 20–41.

Kiss, Ambrus, Annamaria Kunert, Károly György and Pál Belyó (2018), Hungary: Developments in Working Life 2017. www.eurofound.europa.eu/sites/default/files/wpef18031.pdf (accessed on 27 June 2018).

Kitschelt, Herbert (1995a), A Silent Revolution in Europe? In: Jack Hayward and Edward C. Page (eds), *Governing the New Europe*. Cambridge: Polity Press, pp. 123–65.

—— (1995b), *The Transformation of European Social Democracy*. Cambridge: Cambridge University Press.

—— (1997), European Party System: Continuity and Change. In: Martin Rhodes, Paul Heywood and Vincent Wright (eds), *Developments in West European Politics*. Basingstoke: Macmillan, pp. 131–50.

Kjaer, Ulrik and Jørgen Elklit (2010), Local Party System Nationalisation: Does Municipal Size Matter? *Local Government Studies*, 36(3): 425–44.

Kjaer, Ulrik, Ulf Hjelmar and Asmus Leth Olsen (2010), Municipal Amalgamations and the Democratic Functioning of Local Councils: The Case of the Danish 2007 Structural Reform. *Local Government Studies*, 36(4): 569–85.

Klarić, Mirko (2017), Problems and Developments in the Croatian Local Self-Government. *Zbornik radova Pravnog fakulteta u Splitu*, 54(4): 807–23.

Kleinfeld, Ralf (2012), Niederlande. In: Werner Reutter (ed.), *Verbände und Verbandssysteme in den Ländern der Europäischen Union*. Wiesbaden: Springer Verlag, pp. 477–520.

Klimovský, Daniel (2015), Slovakia as Decentralization Champion: Reality or Myth? *Regions Magazine*, 298(1): 14–16.

Klvaňova, Alena (2016). Institutionalization of the Czech and Slovenian Party System. *Slovak Journal of Political Sciences*, 16(3): 244–65.

Knapp, Andrew and Vincent Wright (2001), *The Government and Politics of France*, fourth edition. London: Routledge.

Knill, Christopher and Dirk Lehmkuhl (2002), The National Impact of European Union Regulatory Policy: Three Europeanization Mechanisms. *European Journal of Political Research*, 41: 255–80.

Koenigsberger, H.G. (1987), *Medieval Europe 400–1500*. London: Longman.

Kommisrud, Arne (2009), *Historical Sociology and Eastern European Development*. Lanham: Lexington Books.

Kopecký, Petr and Peter Mair (2012), Party Patronage as an Organizational Resource. In: Kopecký, Petr, Peter Mair and Maria Spirova (eds), *Party Patronage and Party Government in European Democracies*. Oxford: Oxford University Press, pp. 3–16.

—— and Maria Spirova (eds) (2012), *Party Patronage and Party Government in European Democracies*. Oxford: Oxford University Press.

Körösényi, Gabor, G. Fodor and Jürgen Dieringer (2010), Das politische System Ungarns. In: Wolfgang Ismayr (eds), *Die politischen Systeme Osteuropas*. Wiesbaden: Springer VS, pp. 357–418.

Kosař, David (2016), *Perils of Judicial Self-Government in Transitional Societies*. Cambridge: Cambridge University Press.

Kosiara-Pedersen, Karina (2016), Tremors, No Earthquake: The 2015 Danish Parliamentary Election. *West European Politics*, 39(4): 870–8.

Kostadinova, Tatiana (2007), The Impact of Finance Regulations on Political Parties: The Case of Bulgaria. *Europe-Asia Studies*, 59(5): 807–27.

Koukiadaki, Aristea and Chara Kokkinou (2016), Deconstructing the Greek System of Industrial Relations. *European Journal of Industrial Relations*, 22(3): 205–19.

Koźbiał, Krzysztof (2017), The Evolution of the Party Systems of the Czech Republic and the Slovak Republic After the Disintegration of Czechoslovakia. Comparative analysis. *Przegląd Politologiczny*, 22(4): 133–44.

Krašovec, Alenka and Damjan Lajh (2008), Slovenia: Weak Formal Position, Strong Informal Influence? In: Robert Elgie and Sophia Moestrup (eds), *Semi-Presidentialism in Central and Eastern Europe*. Manchester: Manchester University Press, pp. 201–18.

Krickovic, Andrej and Maxim Bratersky (2016), Benevolent Hegemon, Neighborhood Bully, or Regional Security Provider? Russia's Efforts to Promote Regional Integration after the 2013–2014 Ukraine Crisis. *Eurasian Geography and Economics*, 57(2): 180–202.

Kriesi, Hans-Peter and Alexander H. Trechsel (2008), *The Politics of Switzerland: Continuity and Change in a Consensus Democracy*. Cambridge: Cambridge University Press.

Krüger, F. K. (1914), Judicial System of the German Empire with Reference to Ordinary Jurisdiction. *California Law Review* 124(2–3): 124–36.

Krupavičius, Algis (2008), Semipresidentialism in Lithuania: Origins, Developments and Challenges. In: Robert Elgie and Sophia Moestrup (eds), *Semi-Presidentialism in Central and Eastern Europe*. Manchester: Manchester University Press, pp. 65–84.

Kruse, Thorsten (2016), The Troika's New Approach to Resolving a Financial Crisis in a Eurozone Member State. In: José M. Magone, Brigid Laffan and Christian Schweiger (eds), *Core–Periphery Relations in the European Union: Power and Conflict in a Dualist Political Economy*. London: Routledge, pp. 150–204.

Kühn, Zdeněk (2011), Judicial Independence in Central-Eastern Europe: The Experience of the 1990s and 2000s. *The Lawyer Quarterly*, 1(1): 31–42.

Kuhnle, Stein (1981), Emigration, Democratization and the Rise of the European Welfare States. In: Per Torsvik (ed.), *Mobilization, Centre-Periphery Structures and Nation-Building: A Volume in Commemoration of Stein Rokkan*. Bergen: Universitetsforlaget, pp. 501–23.

Kuntaliitto (Local Finland) (2017), Finnish Municipalities and Regions. www.localfinland.fi/expert-services/finnish-municipalities-and-regions (accessed on 16 July 2018).

Kuzio, Taras (2017), *Putin's War Against Ukraine. Revolution, Nationalism and Crime*. Self-published on CreateSpace.

Kyzlinková, Renata and Sona Veverková (2018), Czech Republic: Developments in Working Life 2017. www.eurofound.europa.eu/sites/default/files/wpef18024.pdf (accessed on 27 June 2018).

La Calle Robles, Luis de (2015), *Nationalist Violence in Postwar Europe*. Cambridge: Cambridge University Press.

—— and Fazi, André (2010), Making Nationalists out of Frenchmen? Substate Nationalism in Corsica. *Nationalism and Ethnic Politics*, 16(3–4): 397–419.

Ladner, Andreas (2004), *Stabilität und Wandel von Parteien und Parteiensystemen*. Wiesbaden: Verlag Sozialwissenschaften.

—— (2014), Politische Parteien. In: Peter Knoepfel, Yannis Papadopoulos, Pascal Sciarini, Adrian Vatter and Silja Häusermann (eds), *Handbuch der Schweizer Politik*. Zürich: Verlag Neue Zürcher Zeitung, pp. 361–89.

——, Nicolas Keuffer and Harald Baldersheim (2016), Measuring Local Autonomy in 39 Countries (1990–2014). *Regional & Federal Studies*, 26(3): 321–57.

Ladrech, Robert (1994), Europeanization of Domestic Politics and Institutions: The Case of France. *Journal of Common Market Studies*, 32(1): 69–88.

—— (2010), *The Europeanization of National Politics*. Basingstoke: Palgrave.

Lagrådet (2018), Council on Legislation. http://lagradet.se/ (accessed on 29 October 2018).

La Justice du Grand Duché du Luxembourg (2017), La justice en chiffres 2016. Luxembourg: La Justice du Grand Duché du Luxembourg. https://justice.public.lu/dam-assets/fr/publications/justice-en-chiffres/La-justice-en-chiffres-2016.pdf (accessed on 1 November 2018).

Landfried, Christine (1992), Judicial Policy-Making in Germany: The Federal Constitutional Court. In: Mary L. Volcansek (ed.), *Judicial Politics and Policy-Making in Western Europe*, Special issue of *West European Politics*, 15(3): 50–67.

Landsorganisationen i Denmark (LO Denmark) (2018a), Affiliated Unions and Cartels. https://lo.dk/en/about-lo/affiliated-unions-and-cartels/ (accessed on 25 June 2018).

---- (2018b), An introduction to LO: The Danish Confederation of Trade Unions. Copenhagen: Landsorganisationen. https://lo.dk/wp-content/uploads/2017/03/160125-0935-an-introduction-to-lo-web.pdf (accessed on 25 June 2018).

Landsorganisasjonen i Norge (LO Norge) (2018), Welcome to LO Norway. www.lo.no/language/English/ (accessed on 25 June 2018).

Landsorganisationen (LO) Sweden (2018), This is LO. www.lo.se/english/this_is_lo (accessed on 24 June 2018).

Lane, Thomas (2002), Lithuania: Stepping Westward. In: David J. Smith, Artis Pabriks, Aldis Purs and Thomas Lane (eds), *The Baltic States: Estonia, Latvia and Lithuania*. London: Routledge.

Lanskoy, Miriam and Giorgi Areshidze (2008), Georgia's Year of Turmoil. *Journal of Democracy*, 19(4): 154–68.

La Palombara, Joseph (1964), *Interest Groups in Italian Politics*. Princeton: Princeton University Press.

Lappalainen, Pertti and Martti Siisiäinen (2012), Finnland. In: Werner Reutter (ed.), *Verbände und Verbandssysteme in den Ländern der Europäischen Union*. Wiesbaden: Springer Verlag, pp. 179–210.

Lavdas, Kostas A. (2005), Interest Groups in Disjointed Corporatism: Social Dialogue in Greece and European 'Competitive Corporatism'. *West European Politics*, 28(2): 297–316.

—— and Efthalia Chatzigianni (2012), Griechenland. In: Werner Reutter (ed.), *Verbände und Verbandssysteme in den Ländern der Europäischen Union*. Wiesbaden: Springer Verlag, pp. 247–74.

Lavenex, Sandra (2015), Justice and Home Affairs: Institutional Change and Policy Continuity. In: Helen Wallace, Mark A. Pollack and Alasdair R. Young (eds), *Policy Making in the European Union*. Oxford: Oxford University Press, pp. 367–87.

—— (2016), Multilevelling EU External Governance: The Role of International Organizations in the Diffusion of EU Migration Policies. *Journal of Ethnic and Migration Studies*, 42(4): 554–70.

Laverty, Nicklaus (2015), The 'Party of Power' as a Type. *East European Politics*, 31(1): 71–87.

Lazdiņš, Jānis (2016), Continuity of the Judicial Power in the Republic of Latvia: Preconditions and Necessity. *Juridiskā zinātne /Law*, 9: 58–77.

Lees-Marshment, Jennifer (2004), *The Political Marketing Revolution: Transforming the Government of the UK*. Manchester: Manchester University Press.

Legislation UK (2009), Political Parties and Elections Act 2009. www.legislation.gov.uk/ukpga/2009/12/contents (accessed on 13 May 2017).

Lehmbruch, Gerhard (1967), *Proporzdemokratie: Politisches System und die politische Kultur in der Schweiz und Österreich*. Recht und Staat in Geschichte und Gegenwart. Eine Sammlung von Vorträgen und Schriften aus dem Gebiet der Gesamten Staatswissenschaften. Tübingen: J.C.B. Mohr (Paul Siebeck).

—— (1996), Die korporative Verhandlungsdemokratie. *Swiss Political Science Review*, 2(4): 1–41.

—— (2002), Quasi-Consociationalism in German Politics: Negotiated Democracy and the Legacy of the Westphalian Peace. In: Jürg Steiner and Thomas Ertman (eds), *Consociationalism and Corporatism in Western Europe: Still the Politics of Accommodation?* Special issue of *Acta Politica*, 37(1/2): 175–93.

Leibfried, Stephan and Michael Zürn (eds) (2006), *Transformations of the State?* Cambridge: Cambridge University Press.

Lenschow, Andrea (2005), Environmental Policy. In: Helen Wallace, William Wallace and Mark Pollack (eds), *Policy-Making in the European Union*. Oxford: Oxford University Press, pp. 305–27.

Léonard, Sarah and Christian Kaunert (2016), Beyond Stockholm: In Search of a Strategy for the European Union's Area of Freedom, Security, and Justice. *European Politics and Society*, 17(2): 143–9.

Leonardi, Robert and Douglas Wertman (1989), *Italian Christian Democracy: The Politics of Dominance*. Basingstoke: Palgrave Macmillan.

Lesaffer, R.C.H. (2004), A Short Legal History of the Netherlands. In: H.S. Taekema (ed.), *Understanding Dutch Law*. The Hague: Boom Juridische Uitgevers, pp. 31–58.

Leschtschenko, Sergej (5 May 2017), Markenzeichen Korruption. www.zeit.de/politik/ausland/2017-04/ukraine-korruption-regierung-bekaempfung-serhij-leschtschenko-abgeordneter (accessed on 13 September 2018).

Leshchenko, Natalia (2008), The National Ideology and the Basis of the Lukashenka Regime in Belarus. *Europe-Asia Studies*, 60(8): 1419–33.

Leston-Bandeira, Cristina (2004), *From Legislation to Legitimation*. London: Routledge.

—— and André Freire (2003), Internalising the Lessons of Stable Democracy: The Portuguese Parliament. In: Cristina Leston-Bandeira (ed.), *Southern European Parliaments in Democracy*, Special issue of *Journal of Legislative Studies*, 9(2): 56–84.

Leton, André and André Miroir (1999), *Les conflits communautaires en Belgique*. Paris: Presses Universitaires de France.

Leuffen, Dirk, Berthold Rittberger and Frank Schimmelfennig (2013), *Differentiated Integration: Explaining Variation in the European Union*. Basingstoke: Palgrave Macmillan.

Lewis, Jeffrey (2015), The Council of the European Union and the European Council. In: José M. Magone (ed.), *Routledge Handbook of European Politics*. London: Routledge, pp. 219–34.

Lewis, Michael (2012), *Boomerang: Travels in the New Third World*. New York: W.W. Norton and Company.

Lewis, Paul G. (2003), *Political Parties in Post-Communist Eastern Europe*. London: Routledge.

—— (2015), Parties and Party Systems in Central and Eastern Europe. In: José M. Magone (ed.), *The Routledge Handbook of European Politics*. London: Routledge, pp. 512–31.

Lhotta, Roland, Jörn Ketelhut and Helmar Schöne (eds) (2013), *Das Lissaboner Urteil: Staat, Demokratie und europäische Integration im 'verfassten politischen Primärraum'*. Wiesbaden: Springer VS.

Libman, Alexander and Evgeny Vinokurov (2018), Autocracies and Regional Integration: The Eurasian Case. *Post-Communist Economies*, 30(3): 334–64.

Lidström, Anders (2011), Sweden: Party-Dominated Subnational Democracy under Challenge? In: John Loughlin, Frank Hendriks und Anders Lidström (eds), *The Oxford Handbook of Local and Regional Democracy in Europe*. Oxford: Oxford University Press, pp. 261–81.

Lijphart, Arend (1975), *The Politics of Accommodation: Pluralism and Democracy in the Netherlands*. Berkeley: University of California Press.

—— (1984), *Democracies: Patterns of Majoritarian and Consensus Government in Twenty-One Countries*. New Haven: Yale University Press.

—— (2009 [1999]), *Patterns of Democracy: Government Forms and Performance in Thirty-Six Countries*. New Haven: Yale University Press .

Lim, Darren J., Michalis Moutselos and Michael McKenna (2018), Puzzled Out? The Unsurprising Outcomes of the Greek Bailout Negotiations. *Journal of European Public Policy*, 26(3): 325–343.

Linder, Wolf (2005), *Schweizerische Demokratie: Institutionen, Prozesse, Perspektiven*. Bern: Haupt.

Lindvall, Johannes and Joakim Sebring (2005), Policy Reform and the Decline of Corporatism in Sweden. *West European Politics*, 28(5): 1057–74.

Linek, Lukás and Zdenka Mansfeldová (2007), The Parliament of the Czech Republic 1993–2004. *Journal of Legislative Studies*, 13(1): 12–37.

Lipset, Seymour Martin and Stein Rokkan (1967), Cleavage Structures, Party Systems and Voter Alignments: An Introduction. In: Seymour Martin Lipset and Stein Rokkan (eds), *Party Systems and Voter Alignments: Cross-National Perspectives*. New York: The Free Press, pp. 1–64.

Lisi, Marco (2015), *Party Change, Recent Democracies, and Portugal: Comparative Perspectives*. Lanham: Lexington Books.

Little, Conor (2011), The General Election of 2011 in the Republic of Ireland: All Changed Utterly? *West European Politics*, 34(6): 1304–13.

—— (2017), The Irish General Election of February 2016: Towards a New Politics or an Early Election? *West European Politics*, 40(2): 479–88.

Lobo, Marina Costa (2005), The Presidentialization of Portuguese Democracy? In: Thomas Poguntke and Paul Webb (eds), *The Presidentialization of Politics: A Comparative Study of Modern Democracies*. Oxford: Oxford University Press, pp. 269–88.

Lopez Calvo, José (1996), *Organización y funcionamiento del gobierno*. Madrid: Tecnos.

Loughlin, John (2000), Regional Autonomy and State Paradigm Shifts in Western Europe. *Regional and Federal Studies*, 10(2): 10–34.

Lukšič, Igor (2010), Das politische System Sloweniens. In: Wolfgang Ismayr (eds), *Die politischen Systeme Osteuropas*. Wiesbaden: Springer VS, pp. 773–836.

—— (2012), Slowenien. In: Werner Reutter (ed.), *Verbände und Interessengruppen in den Ländern der Europäischen Union: Aktualisierte und erweiterte Auflage*. Wiesbaden: Springer VS, pp. 699–722.

Lüthi, Ruth (2014), Parlament. In: Peter Knoepfel, Yannis Papadopoulos, Pascal Sciarini, Adrian Vatter and Silja Hausermann (eds), *Handbuch der Schweizer Politik*. Zürich: Verlag Neue Zürcher Zeitung, pp. 169–218.

Lužar, Barbara, Ana Selan and Tanja Čelebič (2018), Slovenia: Developments in Working Life 2017. www.eurofound.europa.eu/sites/default/files/wpef18044.pdf (accessed on 27 June 2018).

Lyon, D. (2015), The Snowden Stakes: Challenges for Understanding Surveillance Today. *Surveillance and Society*, 13(2): 139–52.

MacAllister, Ian and Stephen White (2016), Lukashenka and His Voters. *East European Politics and Societies and Cultures*, 30(2): 360–30.

MacKenzie, David J. and Michael W. Curran (2002), *Russia and the USSR in the Twentieth Century*, fourth edition. Belmont: Wadsworth Publishing.

Mackinder, Halfold J.(1919), *Democratic Ideals and Reality. A Study in the Politics of Reconstruction*. London: Constable and Company.

Madeley, John (2000), Reading the Runes. The Religious Factor in Scandinavian Electoral Politics. In: David Broughton and Hans-Martien ten Napel (eds), *Religion and Mass Electoral Behaviour in Europe*. London: Routledge, pp. 28–43.

Magalhães, Pedro C., Carlo Guarnieri and Yorgos Kaminis (2006), Democratic Consolidation, Judicial Reform, and the Judicialization of Politics in Southern Europe. In: Richard

Gunther, P. Nikiforos Diamandouros and Dimitri A. Sotiropoulos (eds), *Democracy and the New State in the New Southern Europe*. Oxford: Oxford University Press, pp. 138–96.

Magnette, Paul (2004), Le parlementarisme dans une démocratie de compromis: Reflexions sur le cas belge. In: Olivier Costa, Eric Kerrouche and Paul Magnette (eds), *Vers un renouveau du parlamentarisme en Europe?* Brussels: Éditions Université Libre de Bruxelles, pp. 91–106.

Magone, José M. (1997), *European Portugal: The Difficult Road to Sustainable Democracy*. Basingstoke: Macmillan.

—— (2003), *The Politics of Southern Europe: Integration into the European Union*. Westport: Praeger.

—— (2004), *The Developing Democracy of Portugal in the European Union*. New Brunswick: Transaction Publishers.

—— (2006), *The New World Architecture: The Role of the European Union in the Making of Global Governance*. New Brunswick: Transaction Publishers.

—— (2009), Europe and Global Governance. In: Chris Rumford (ed.), *SAGE Handbook of European Studies*. London: SAGE, pp. 277–94.

—— (2013), Constructing a Regional Democratic Community in Europe: An Assessment of the Impact of European Organisations on Multilevel Governance after 1945. In: Alice Cunha, Aurora Almada and Yvette Santos (eds), *Portugal e as Organizações Internacionais: Comportamentos, Mensagens e Impactos*. Lisbon: A fonte da palavra-Observatório politico, pp. 39–74.

—— (2014a), *The Politics in Contemporary Portugal: Democracy Evolving*. Boulder: Lynne Rienner.

—— (2014b), Divided Europe? Euroscepticism in Central, Eastern and Southern Europe. In: K.N. Demetriou (ed.), *The European Union Crisis: Explorations in Representation and Democratic Legitimacy*. Heidelberg: Springer, pp. 33–57.

—— (2014c), Portugal is Not Greece. Policy Responses to the Sovereign Debt Crisis and the Consequences for the Portuguese Political Economy. *Perspectives on European Politics and Society*, 15(3): 346–60.

—— (2016a), Portugal as the 'Good Pupil of the European Union': Living under the Regime of the Troika. In: José M. Magone, Brigid Laffan and Christian Schweiger (eds), *Core–Periphery Relations in the European Union: Power and Conflict in a Dualist Political Economy*. London: Routledge, pp. 179–89.

—— (2016b), The Politics of Troika Avoidance: The Case of Spain. In: José M. Magone, Brigid Laffan and Christian Schweiger (eds), *Core–Periphery Relations in the European Union: Power and Conflict in a Dualist Political Economy*. London: Routledge, pp. 205–15.

—— (2016c), From 'Superficial' to 'Coercive' Europeanization in Southern Europe: The Lack of Ownership of National Reforms. In: José M. Magone, Brigid Laffan and Christian Schweiger (eds), *Core–Periphery Relations in the European Union: Power and Conflict in a Dualist Political Economy*. London: Routledge, pp. 87–98.

—— (2017), *The Statecraft of Consensus Democracies in a Turbulent World: A Comparative Study of Austria, Belgium, Luxembourg, the Netherlands and Switzerland*. London: Routledge.

—— (2018), *Contemporary Spanish Politics*, third edition. London: Routledge.

——, Brigid Laffan and Christian Schweiger (eds) (2016a), *Core–Periphery Relations in the European Union: Power and Conflict in a Dualist Political Economy*. London: Routledge.

—— (2016b), The European Union as a Dualist Political Economy: Understanding Core-Periphery Relations. In: José M. Magone, Brigid Laffan and Christian Schweiger (eds), *Core–Periphery Relations in the European Union: Power and Conflict in a Dualist Political Economy*. London: Routledge, pp. 1–16.

Mailand, Mikkel and Jesper Due (2004), Social Dialogue in Central and Eastern Europe: Present State and Future Development. *European Journal of Industrial Relations*, 10(2): 179–97.

Mair, Peter (1993), Myths of Electoral Change and the Survival of Traditional Parties: The 1992 Stein Rokkan Lecture. *European Journal of Political Research*, 24(2): 121–33.

—— (1997), *Party System Change: Approaches and Interpretations*. Oxford: Oxford University Press.

—— (2008a), Electoral Volatility and the Dutch Party System: A Comparative Perspective. *Acta Politica*, 43(2–3): 235–43.

—— (2008b), How Ireland Voted 2007: The Full Story of Ireland's General Election. *West European Politics*, 31(3): 627–8.

—— (2013), *Ruling the Void. The Hollowing Out of Western Democracy*. London: Verso.

—— and Ingrid van Biezen (2001), Party Membership in Twenty Democracies (1980–2000). *Party Politics*, 7(1): 5–21.

Mair, Peter, Wolfgang C. Müller and Fritz Plasser (eds) (2004), *Political Parties and Electoral Change: Party Responses to Electoral Markets*. London: SAGE.

Malová, Darina and Dana Sivaková (1996a), The National Council of the Slovak Republic: Between Democratic Transition and National State-Building. In: David M. Olson and Philip Norton (eds), *The New Parliaments of Central and Eastern Europe*. London: Frank Cass, pp. 108–32.

—— (1996b), The National Council of the Slovak Republic: The Development of a National Parliament. In: Attila Ágh and Gabriella Ilonski (eds), *Parliaments and Organized Interests: The Second Steps*. Budapest: Hungarian Centre for Democracy Studies, pp. 342–64.

Manko, R. (2007), Is the Socialist Legal Tradition 'Dead and Buried'? The Continuity of Certain Elements of Socialist Legal Culture in Polish Civil Procedure. *Private Law in European Context Series*, 10: 83–103.

Marangoni, Francesco and Luca Verzichelli (2015), From a Technocratic Solution to a Fragile Grand Coalition: The Impact of the Economic Crisis on Parliamentary Government in Italy. *The Journal of Legislative Studies*, 21(1): 35–53.

Mares, Isabela, Aurelian Muntean and Tsveta Petrova (2017), Pressure, Favours, and Vote-Buying: Experimental Evidence from Romania and Bulgaria. *Europe-Asia Studies*, 69(6): 940–60.

Marks, Gary, Richard Haesly and Heather Mbaye (2002), What do Subnational Offices Think They are Doing in Brussels? *Regional and Federal Studies*, 12(3): 1–24.

Marks, Gary, Liesbet Hooghe and Arjan H. Schakel (2008), Measuring Regional Authority. *Regional and Federal Studies*, 18(2–3): 111–21.

Marks, Gary, Francois Nielsen, Leonard Ray and Jane Salk (1996), Competencies, Cracks and Conflicts: Regional Mobilization in the European Union. In: Gary Marks, Fritz W. Scharpf, Philippe C. Schmitter and Wolfgang Streeck (eds), *Governance in the European Union*. London: SAGE, pp. 40–63.

Marks, Gary, Fritz W. Scharpf, Philippe C. Schmitter and Wolfgang Streeck (eds) (1996), *Governance in the European Union*. Thousand Oaks: SAGE.

Marks, Gary and Marco R. Steenbergen (eds) (2004), *European Integration and Political Conflict*. Cambridge: Cambridge University Press.

Marples, David R. and Lyubov Pervushina (2005), Belarus: Lukashenko's Red October. *Problems of Post-Communism*, 52(2): 19–28.

Martens, Michael (2017), Der gescheiterte Putsch und seine Folgen. *Aus Politik und Zeitgeschichte*, (9–10): 4–7.

Masci, David, Elisabeth Sciupac and Michael Lipka (2015), Gay Marriage Around the World. Pew Research Center. Religion and Public Life 26 June 2016. www.pewforum.org/2015/06/26/gay-marriage-around-the-world-2013/ (accessed on 17 December 2016).

Mason, David S.(2018), *A Concise History of Modern Europe: Liberty, Equality, Solidarity*. Cambridge: Cambridge University Press.

Massari, Oreste (2005), Gran Bretagna: Verso la presidenzializzazione? In: Gianfranco Pasquino (ed.), *Capi di governo*. Bologna: Il Mulino, pp. 109–27.

Mateju, Petr, Blanka Rehakova and Geoffrey Evans (1999), The Emergence of Class Politics and Class Voting in Postcommunist Russia. In: Geoffrey Evans (ed.), *The End of*

Class Politics? Class Voting in Comparative Perspective. Oxford: Oxford University Press, pp. 231–53.

Matthes, Claudia-Yvette (2012), Polen. In: Werner Reutter (ed.), *Verbände und Verbandssysteme in den Ländern der Europäischen Union*. Wiesbaden: Springer Verlag, pp. 551–82.

Mattson, Ingvar (2015), Parliamentary Committees. In: Jon Pierre (ed.), *The Oxford Handbook of Swedish Politics*. Oxford: Oxford University Press, pp. 679–89.

Mau, Steffen, Roland Verwiebe (2009), *Die Sozialstruktur Europas*. Konstanz: UTB-UVK Verlagsgesellschaft.

Maurer, Andreas, Jürgen Mittag and Wolfgang Wessels (2003), Theoretical Perspectives on Administrative Interaction in the European Union. In: Thomas Christiansen and Emil Kirchner (eds), *Committee Governance in the European Union*. Manchester: Manchester University Press, pp. 23–44.

Maurer, Andreas and Wolfgang Wessels (2001), National Parliaments after Amsterdam: From Slow Adapters to National Players. In: Andreas Maurer and Wolfgang Wessels (eds), *National Parliaments on their Ways to Europe: Losers or Latecomers?* Baden-Baden: Nomos, pp. 425–75.

Maurer, Lynn M (2008a), *El Poder del Parlamento: Congreso y políticas públicas en España*. Madrid: Centro de Estudios Politicos y Constitucionales.

—— (2008b), The Power of Committees in the Spanish Congress of Deputies. In: Bonnie N. Field and Kerstin Haman (eds), *Democracy and Institutional Development: Spain in Comparative Theoretical Perspective*. Basingstoke: Palgrave, pp. 90–109.

Mazower, Marc (1998), *Dark Continent: Europe's Twentieth Century*. London: Penguin.

Mazzoleni, Martino (2009), The Italian Regionalisation: A Story of Partisan Logics. *Modern Italy*, 14(2): 135–50.

McMahon, Margery A. (1997), Aleksandr Lukashenka, President, Republic of Belarus. *Communist Studies and Transition Politics*, 13(4): 129–37.

McNamara, R. Kathleen (2005), Economic and Monetary Union. Innovation and Challenges for the Euro. In: Helen Wallace, William Wallace and Mark Pollack (eds), *Policy-Making in the European Union*. Oxford: Oxford University Press, pp. 141–60.

McNeil, Mary, Andre Herzog, Sladjana Cosic, and PRISM Research (2009), *Citizen Review of Service Delivery and Local Governance in Bosnia and Herzegovina*. New York: World Bank.

McNemanin, Iain (2008), Semi-Presidentialism and Democratization in Poland. In: Robert Elgie and Sophia Moestrup (eds), *Semi-Presidentialism in Central and Eastern Europe*. Manchester: Manchester University Press, pp. 120–37.

Meadows, Dennis L. (1972), *The Limits of Growth*. New York: Universe Books.

Mearsheimer, John L.(2014), Why the Ukraine Crisis Is the West's Fault: The Liberal Delusions That Provoked Putin. *Foreign Affairs*, 93(5): 1–12.

Medina, Leandro and Friedrich Schneider (2017), Shadow Economies Around the World: New Results for 158 Countries Over 1991–2015. April 10. CESifo Working Paper Series No. 6430. https://ssrn.com/abstract=2965972 (accessed on 25 June 2018).

Medina Iborra, Ivan, Joaquim Molins and Carmen Navarro Gomez (2013), El Papel de los Actores Sociales en Tiempos de Crisis. *Barataria: Revista Castellano-Manchega de Ciencias Sociales*, 15: 161–78.

Meinecke, Friedrich (1998), *Macchiavellism: The Doctrine of Raison d'État and its Place in Modern History*. New Brunswick: Transaction Publishers.

Mendelski, Martin (2018), The Rule of Law. In: Adam Fagan and Petr Kopecký (eds), *The Routledge Handbook of East European Politics*. London: Routledge, pp. 113–25.

Merkel, Wolfgang C. (1996), Institutionalisierung und Konsolidierung der Demokratien in Osteuropa. In: E. Sandschneider and D. Segert (eds), *Systemwechsel 2: Die Institution alisierung der Demokratie*. Opladen: Leske & Budrich, pp. 73–112.

—— (2004), Embedded and Defective Democracies. *Democratization*, 11(5): 33–58.

Meyer-Sahling, Jan-Hinrik and Kim Sass Mikkelsen (2016), Civil Service Laws, Merit, Politicization, and Corruption: The Perspective of Public Officials from Five East European Countries. *Public Administration*, 94(4): 1105–23.

Mezey, M. (1979), *Comparative Legislatures*. Durham, NC: Duke University Press.

Michalka, Wolfgang (2002), Das Dritte Reich (1933–45). In: Martin Vogt (ed.), *Deutsche Geschichte: Von den Anfängen bis zur Gegenwart*. Frankfurt a. M.: Fischer, pp. 694–775.

Michel, Elie (2018), Macron with a Comfortable Majority Undermined by Record Low Turnout. In: Lorenzo De Sio and Aldo Paparo (eds), *The Year of Challengers? Issues, Public Opinion, and Elections in Western Europe in 2017*. Rome: Centro Italiano per Studi Elettorale (CISE), pp. 113–14. https://cise.luiss.it/cise/wp-content/uploads/2017/12/CISE010_2018_10EN_A4.pdf (accessed on 10 May 2018).

Micheletti, Andreas Føllesdal and Dietlind Stolle (eds) (2006), *Politics, Products, and Markets: Exploring Political Consumerism. Past and Present*. New Brunswick: Transaction Publishers.

Milward, Alan S. (1984), *The Reconstruction of Western Europe 1945–1951*. London: Methuen.

Ministère de la Justice (2018), Chiffres-clés de la justice. www.justice.gouv.fr/statistiques-10054/chiffres-cles-de-la-justice-10303/ (accessed on 1 November 2018).

Ministère de l'Interieur (2018), Résultats des élections législatives 2017. www.interieur.gouv.fr/Elections/Les-resultats/Legislatives/elecresult__legislatives-2017/(path)/legislatives-2017/index.html (accessed on 24 November 2018).

Ministère du Travail (2017), Résultats de la mesure de l'audience pour la représentativité syndicale 2017. Paris, 31 March 2017. http://travail-emploi.gouv.fr/IMG/pdf/communique-de-presse-nouvelle-mesure-de-l_audience-syndicale.pdf (accessed on 25 June 2018).

Ministry of Justice (20 July 2017), Judicial diversity statistics. www.judiciary.uk/publications/judicial-statistics-2017/ (accessed on 1 November 2018).

Molina, Oscar (2014), Self-Regulation and the State in Industrial Relations in Southern Europe. Back to the Future? *European Journal of Industrial Relations*, 20(1): 21–36.

—— and Martin Rhodes (2007), Industrial Relations and the Welfare State in Italy: Assessing the Potential of Negotiated Change. *West European Politics*, 30(4): 803–29.

Möller, Tommy (2015), The Parliamentary System. In: Jon Pierre (ed.), *The Oxford Handbook of Swedish Politics*. Oxford: Oxford University Press, pp. 115–29.

Molnár, Miklós (2001), *A Concise History of Hungary*. Cambridge: Cambridge University Press.

Montero, José Ramón (1998), Sobre las preferencias electorales en España: Fragmentación y polarización (1977–93). In: Pilar del Castillo (ed.), *Comportamiento politico y electoral*. Madrid: CIS, pp. 51–124.

Montgomery, Kathleen (2006), Politics of Hungary. In: Gabriel A. Almond, Russell J. Dalton, G. Bingham Powell Jr. and Kaare Strøm (eds), *European Politics Today*. New York: Pearson Longman, pp. 403–56.

Moran, Michael (1989), Industrial Relations. In: Henry Drucker, Patrick Dunleavy, Andrew Gamble and Gillian Peele (eds), *Developments in British Politics*. Basingstoke: Macmillan, pp. 279–94.

Morlino, Leonardo and Mario Tarchi (1996), The Dissatisfied Society: The Roots of Political Change in Italy. *European Journal of Political Research*, 30(1): 41–63.

—— (2006), La societá insoddisfatta I suoi nemici: I partiti nella crisi italiana. In: Leonardo Morlino and Marco Tarchi (eds), *Partiti e caso italiano*. Bologna: Il Mulino, pp. 207–43.

Moury, Catherine (2013), *Coalition Government and Party Mandate. How Coalition Agreements Constrain Ministerial Action*. London: Routledge.

Mrčela, Aleksandra Kanjuo (2017), Working Life in Slovenia. www.eurofound.europa.eu/country/slovenia (accessed on 27 June 2018).

Mudde, Cas (2004), The Populist Zeitgeist. *Government and Opposition*, 39(4): 542–63.

Müller, Jan-Werner (2010), *Verfassungspatriotismus*. Frankfurt a. M.: Suhrkamp.

Müller, Wolfgang C. (2000), Austria: Tight Coalitions and Stable Government. In: Wolfgang C. Müller and Kaare Strøm (eds), *Coalition Governments in Western Europe*. Oxford: Oxford University Press, pp. 86–125.

—— (2006a), Das Regierungssystem. In: Herbert Gottweis, Helmut Kramer, Volkmar Lauber, Wolfgang C. Müller and Emmerich Tálos (eds), *Politik in Österreich: Das Handbuch*. Vienna: Manzsche Verlags- und Universitätsbuchhandlung, pp. 105–18.

—— (2006b), Parteiensystem. In: Herbert Gottweis, Helmut Kramer, Volkmar Lauber, Wolfgang C. Müller and Emmerich Tálos (eds), *Politik in Österreich: Das Handbuch*. Vienna: Manzsche Verlags- und Universitätsbuchhandlung, pp. 279–304.

—— and Kaare Strøm (eds) (2000a), *Coalition Governments in Western Europe*. Oxford: Oxford University Press.

—— (2000b), Coalition Governance in Western Europe: An Introduction. In: Wolfgang C. Müller and Kaare Strøm (eds), *Coalition Governments in Western Europe*. Oxford: Oxford University Press, pp. 1–31.

Müller-Jentsch, Walther (2016), Formation, Development and Current State of Industrial Democracy in Germany. *Transfer*, 22(1): 45–62.

Murakami Wood, D. and S. Wright. 2015. Editorial: Before and After Snowden. *Surveillance and Society*, 13(2): 132–8.

Næringslivets Hovedorganisasjon (NHO) (2018), About NHO. www.nho.no/en/about-nho/About-NHO/ (accessed on 25 June 2018).

Nalewajko, Ewa and Włodzimierz Wesołowski (2007), Five Terms of the Polish Parliament. *Journal of Legislative Studies*, 12(1): 59–82.

Nalepa, Monika (2016), Party Institutionalization and Legislative Organization: The Evolution of Agenda Power in the Polish Parliament. *Comparative Politics*, 48(3): 353–72.

Nannestad, Peter (2009), Das politische System Dänemarks. In: Wolfgang Ismayr (ed.), *Die politischen Systeme Westeuropas*. Opladen: Leske & Budrich, pp. 65–106.

Narodna rada slovenskey republiku (2018), Štatistiky a prehľady. www.nrsr.sk/web/?sid=nrsr/dokumenty/statistiky_a_prehlady (accessed on 16 February 2018).

Narud, Hanne Marthe (2003), Norway: Professionalization – Party-Oriented and Constituency-Based. In: Jens Borchert and Jırgen Zeiss (eds), *The Political Class in Advanced Democracies: A Comparative Handbook*. Oxford: Oxford University Press, pp. 298–319.

——, Knut Heidar and Tore Grønlie (2014), *Stortingets historie 1964–2014*. Oslo: Fakbokforlaget.

—— and Kaare Strøm (2000), Norway: A Fragile Coalition Order. In: Wolfgang C. Muller and Kaare Strøm (eds), *Coalition Governments in Western Europe*. Oxford: Oxford University Press, pp. 158–91.

Network of Associations of Local Authorities of Local Authorities in South-Eastern Europe (NALAS) (2017a), *Fiscal Decentralization Indicators for South-East Europe: 2006–2015*. Skopje: NALAS.

—— (2017b), NALAS Position Paper: Western Balkans in the Loop – Local Governments and their Associations as Key Stakeholders in the EU Integration Process. www.nalas.eu/News/WB_Position (accessed on 16 July 2018).

Neumann, Franz (1942), *Behemoth: The Structure and Practice of National Socialism*. Oxford: Oxford University Press.

Newell, James L. (2006), Characterising the Italian Parliament: Legislative Change in Longitudinal Perspective. *The Journal of Legislative Studies*, 12(3–4): 386–403.

Newman, Bruce I. (1999), *The Mass Marketing of Politics: Democracy in an Age of Manufactured Images*. London: SAGE.

Newton, Kenneth and Jan W. Van Deth (2006), *Foundations of Comparative Politics*. Cambridge: Cambridge University Press.

Neyer, Jürgen (2014), Justified Multi-Level Parliamentarism: Situating National Parliaments in the European Polity. *The Journal of Legislative Studies*, 20(1): 125–38.

Nieuwbeerta, Paul and Nan Dirk De Graaf (1999), Traditional Class Voting in 20 Postwar Societies. In: Geoffrey Evans (ed.), *The End of Class Politics? Class Voting in Comparative Perspective*. Oxford: Oxford University Press, pp. 23–56.

Niklasson, Lars (2016), Challenges and Reforms of Local and Regional Governments in Sweden. In: Jon Pierre (ed.), *The Oxford Handbook of Swedish Politics*, first edition. Oxford: Oxford University Press, pp. 399–413.

Nikolov, Marjan (2006), Country Report: Local Borrowing in Romania. In: Marjan Nikolov (ed.), *The Future of Local Government Finance: Cases Studies of Romania, Bulgaria and Macedonia*. Skopje: Centre for Economic Analysis, pp. 5–37.

Nikolova, Pavlina (2007), Bulgarian Subnational Authorities on the Road in the EU. In: Mario Kölling, Stelios Stavridis and Natividad Fernández Sola (eds), *The International Relations of the Regions: Subnational Actors, Para-Diplomacy and Multi-Level Governance*. Zaragoza: University of Zaragoza, pp. 237–55.

—— (2011), Bulgaria: The Dawn of a New Era of Inclusive Subnational Democracy? In: John Loughlin, Frank Hendriks and Anders Lidström (eds), *The Oxford Handbook of Local and Regional Democracy in Europe*. Oxford: Oxford University Press, pp. 685–713.

Nodia, Ghia (ed.) (2016), *25 Years of Independent Georgia: Achievements and Unfinished Projects*. Tbilisi: Konrad Adenauer Foundation and Ilia State University Press, pp. 91–129.

—— with the participation of Denis Cenuşă and Mikhail Minakov (2017), *Democracy and Its Deficits: The Path Towards Becoming European-Style Democracies in Georgia, Moldova and Ukraine*. Brussels: Centre for European Policy Studies, Working Document Nr. 2017/12, December 2017. www.ceps.eu/system/files/WD2017_12_GNodia_DemoAndDeficits.pdf (accessed on 14 September 2018).

Nonnell, Rosa and Ivan Medina (2016), Las Organizaciones Empresariales en España. In: Joaquim Molins, Iván Medina Iborra and Luz Muñoz Márquez (eds), *Los grupos de interés en España: La influencia de los lobbies en la política española*. Madrid: Tecnos, pp. 177–210.

Nordsieck, Wolfram (2017), *Parties and Elections in Europe*. Norderstedt: Books on Demand.

Norkus, Zenona (2013), Parliamentarism versus Semi-Presidentialism in the Baltic States: The Causes and Consequences of Differences in the Constitutional Frameworks. *Baltic Journal Of Political Science*, 2: 7–28.

Norris, Pippa (1997), Introduction: The Rise of Postmodern Political Communications? In: Pippa Norris (ed.), *Politics and the Press: The News Media and Their Influences*. Boulder: Lynne Rienner, pp. 1–17.

—— (2001), The Twilight of Westminster? Electoral Reform and its Consequences. *Political Studies*, 49(5): 877–900.

——, Ferran Martínez i Coma and Max Grömping (2015), The Year in Elections, 2014. The World's Flawed and Failed Contests. Report February 2015. https://static1.squarespace.com/static/58533f31bebafbe99c85dc9b/t/590ecfdf2e69cf3d4b41b093/1494142955363/The+Year+in+Elections%2C+2014+Final+11_02_2015.pdf (accessed on 13 May 2018).

——, Thomas Wynter and Sarah Cameron (2018), Corruption and Coercion: The year in 2017. The Electoral Integrity Project. Report, March 2018. https://static1.squarespace.com/static/58533f31bebafbe99c85dc9b/t/5aa60e298165f533f6462e58/1520832089983/The+Year+in+Elections+2017.pdf (accessed on 13 May 2018).

Norton, Philip (1998a), Introduction: The Institution of Parliaments. In: Philip Norton (ed.), *Parliaments and Governments in Western Europe*. London: Frank Cass, pp. 1–15.

—— (1998b), Old Institution, New Institutionalism? Parliament and Government in the UK. In: Philip Norton (ed.), *Parliaments and Governments in Western Europe*. London: Frank Cass, pp. 17–43.

—— (2014), The Crown. In: Bill Jones and Philip Norton (eds), *Politics UK*. London: Routledge, pp. 272–93.

—— and D.M. Olson (eds) (2007), Post-Communist and Post-Soviet Legislatures, Special issue of *Journal of Legislative Studies*, 13(1).

Nousiainen, Jaakko (1988), Finland. In: Jean Blondel and Ferdinand Müller-Rommel (eds), *Cabinets in Western Europe*. Basingstoke: Macmillan, pp. 213–33.

Nugent, Neill (2004), *European Union Enlargement*. Basingstoke: Palgrave.

O'Brennan, John and Tapio Raunio (2007), Introduction: Deparliamentarization and European Integration. In: John O'Brennan and Tapio Raunio (eds), *National Parliaments within the European Union: From 'Victims' of Integration to Competitive Actors?* London: Routledge, pp. 1–26.

Ocaklı, Feryaz (2017), Islamist Mobilisation in Secularist Strongholds: Institutional Change and Electoral Performance in Turkey. *South European Society and Politics*, 22(1): 61–80.

Oesch, David (2011), Swiss Trade Unions and Industrial Relations after 1990. A History of Decline and Renewal. In: Christine Trampusch and André Mach (eds), *Switzerland in Europe: Continuity and Change in the Swiss Political Economy*. London: Routledge, pp. 82–102.

Oireachtas (2018), Houses of Oireachtas. www.oireachtas.ie/parliament/ (accessed on 15 February 2018).

Oliveira Marques, A.H. (1983), *Historia de Portugal. 2: Do Renascimento ás Revoluções Liberais*. Lisbon: Palas Editores.

Olson, David M. (1998), Party Formation and Party System Consolidation in the New Democracies of Central Europe. *Political Studies*, 46(3): 432–64.

—— and Philip Norton (1996), Legislatures in Democratic Transition. In: David M. Olson and Philip Norton (eds), *The New Parliaments of Central and Eastern Europe*. London: Frank Cass, pp. 1–15.

O'Malley, Eoin and Shane Martin (2010), The Government and the Taoiseach. In: John Coakley and Michael Gallagher (eds), *Politics of the Republic of Ireland*. London: Routledge, pp. 295–326.

Organisation for Economic Cooperation and Development (OECD) (2014a), *Spain: From Administrative Reforms to Continuous Improvement*. Paris: OECD. www.keepeek.com/Digital-Asset-Management/oecd/governance/spain-from-administrative-reform-to-continuous-improvement_9789264210592-en#.WJYgP1PhBqw#page1 (accessed on 4 February 2017).

—— (2012), *Slovenia. Towards a Strategic and Efficient State*. Paris: OECD. www-oecd-ilibrary-org.ezproxy.hwr-berlin.de/docserver/9789264173262-en.pdf?-expires=1543079945&id=id&accname=oid021244&checksum=B0D6C9DD7C7AC9AA065BD14078838779 (accessed on 24 November 2018).

—— (2014b), *OECD Territorial Reviews: Netherlands 2014*. Paris: OECD. www.keepeek.com/Digital-Asset-Management/oecd/urban-rural-and-regional-development/oecd-territorial-reviews-netherlands-2014_9789264209527-en#page1 (accessed on 16 July 2018).

—— (2015a), *Lithuania: Fostering Open and Inclusive Policy Making*. OECD Public Governance Reviews. Paris: OECD.

—— (2015b), *Government at a Glance*. Paris: OECD.

—— (2016a), Latvia's Accession to the OECD. www.oecd.org/latvia/latvia-accession-to-the-oecd.htm (accessed on 23 December 2017).

—— (2016b), *Financing Democracy: Funding of Political Parties and Election Campaigns and the Risk of Policy Capture*. Paris: OECD.

—— (2016c), Regional Country Profiles. Single Factsheets for Each OECD Country, But Also Other Countries. www.oecd.org/regional/regional-policy/country-profiles.htm (accessed on 15 July 2018).

—— (2017a), *OECD Employment Outlook 2017*. Paris: OECD.

—— (2017b), Government at a Glance Database. https://stats.oecd.org/index.aspx?queryid=78408 (accessed 8 March 2019).

—— (2018a), *OECD Economic Surveys Iceland*. Paris: OECD.

—— (2018b), Trade Union Density in Membership. https://stats.oecd.org/Index.aspx?DataSetCode=TUD (accessed on 25 June 2018).

—— (2018c), OECD Fiscal Decentralisation Database. www.oecd.org/tax/federalism/fiscal-decentralisation-database.htm (accessed on 16 July 2018).

Organisation for Security and Cooperation in Europe (OSCE) (2014), Parliamentary Elections in Hungary. 6 April 2014. OSCE/ODIHR Limited Election Observation Mission Final Report. www.osce.org/odihr/elections/hungary/121098?download=true (accessed on 13 May 2018).

—— (2016), Russian Federation State Duma Elections 18 September 2016. OSCE/ODIHR Election Observation Mission. Final Report. Warsaw: OSCE, 23 December 2016. www.osce.org/odihr/elections/russia/290861?download=true (accessed on 13 September 2018).

—— (2018), Russian Federation Presidential Election 18 March 2018. Odihr Election Observation Mission. Final Report. Warsaw: OSCE, 6 June 2018. www.osce.org/odihr/elections/383577?download=true (accessed on 13 September 2018).

Orriols, Lluis and Guillermo Cordero (2016), The Breakdown of the Spanish Two-Party System: The Upsurge of Podemos and Ciudadanos in the 2015 General Election. *South European Society and Politics*, 21(4): 469–92.

Országgyülés (Hungarian National Assembly) (2018a), Electing Members of the National Assembly. www.parlament.hu/web/house-of-the-national-assembly/election-of-the-members-of-parliament (accessed on 16 February 2018).

—— (2018b), Legislation-Figures. www.parlament.hu/web/house-of-the-national-assembly/interpellations-submitted-and-addressed-broken-down-by-submitter (accessed on 16 February 2018).

Osipian, Ararat L. (29 January 2018), The Language of Discord: Ukrainian, Hungarian, Romanian, Russian. *New Eastern Europe* http://neweasterneurope.eu/2018/01/29/language-discord-ukrainian-hungarian-romanian-russian/ (accessed on 13 September 2018).

Osipova, Sanima (2014), Die Entstehung der Gerichtsverfassung nach der Gründung der Republik Lettland. *Jurisdiska zinatne/Law*, 7: 32–44. www.lu.lv/fileadmin/user_upload/lu_portal/apgads/PDF/Juristu-zurn_7.pdf (accessed on 3 November 2018).

Ost, David (2000), Illusory Corporatism in Central and Eastern Europe: Neoliberal Tripartism and Postcommunist Political Identities. *Politics and Society*, 28(4): 503–30.

—— (2015), Class after Communism: Introduction to the Special Issue. In: David Ost (ed.), Class after Communism. Special issue of *East European Politics, Societies and Cultures*, 29(3): 543–64.

Oubiña, Daniel Casal (2012), Tejer y Destejer: La Actividad Legislativa. In: César Colino and Ramón Cotare (eds), *España en Crisis: Balance de la Segunda Legislatura de Rodriguez Zapatero*. Valencia: Tirant Humanidades, pp. 109–36.

Overbeek, Henk (1991), *Global Capitalism and National Decline: The Thatcher Decade in Perspective*. London: Unwin Hyman.

Oversloot, Hans and Ruben Verheul (2006), Managing Democracy: Political Parties and the State in Russia. *Journal of Communist Studies and Transition Politics*, 22(3): 383–405.

Özen, Hayriye (2015), An Unfinished Grassroots Populism: The Gezi Park Protests in Turkey and Their Aftermath. *South European Society and Politics*, 20(4): 533–52.

Pabriks, Artis and Aldis Purs (2002), Latvia: The Challenges of Change. In: Artis Pabriks, Aldis Purs and Thomas Lane (eds), *The Baltic States: Estonia, Latvia and Lithuania*. London: Routledge.

Padhol, Ukadzimir M. and David R. Marples (2011), The 2010 Presidential Election in Belarus. *Problems of Post-Communism*, 58(1): 3–16.

Pallaver, Günther (2005), Austria: La centralità del canciliere. In: Gianfranco Pasquino (ed.), *Capi di governo*. Bologna: Il Mulino, pp. 13–40.

Palné Kovacs, Ilona (2012), Local Governance in Hungary: The Balance of the Last 20 Years. Discussion Paper nr. 83. Budapest: Centre for Regional Studies of Hungarian Academy of Sciences. https://discussionpapers.rkk.hu/index.php/DP/article/view/2359/4413 (accessed on 16 July 2018).

—— (2015), Regionalism in Hungary. The Assembly of European Regions (ed.), *Report on the State of Regionalization in Europe 2017*. AER Observatory of Regionalization. https://drive.google.com/file/d/0B94jJjQLXnl-RGU1RURXVGI0Zjg/view (accessed on 16 July 2018).

——, Ákos Bodor, István Finta, Zoltán Grünhut, Péter Kacziba and Gábor Zongor (2017), Farewell to Decentralisation: The Hungarian Story and its General Implications. *Croatian and Comparative Public Administration*, 16(4): 789–816.

Paoli, Letizia (2007), Mafia and Organised Crime in Italy: The Unacknowledged Successes of Law Enforcement. *West European Politics*, 30(4): 854–80.

Papadimitriou, Costas (2013), *The Greek Labour Law Face to the Crisis: A Dangerous Passage Towards a New Juridical Nature*. European Labour Law Network (ELLN) Working Paper 3/2013. www.labourlawnetwork.eu/working_paper/working_papers/prm/201/0/index.html (accessed on 25 June 2018).

Papadimitriou, Dimitris and David Phinnemore (2008), *Romania and the European Union: From Marginalisation to Membership*. London: Routledge.

Papaioannou, Elias (2011), The Injustice of the Justice System. https://greekeconomistsforreform.com/wp-content/uploads/injustice_Papaioannou.pdf (accessed on 3 November 2018).

—— and Stavroula Karatza (2018), The Greek Justice System: Collapse and Reform. In: Costas Meghir, Christopher A. Pissarides, Dimitri Vayanos and Nikolaos Vettas (eds), *Beyond Austerity: Reforming the Greek Economy*. Cambridge: MIT Press, pp. 519–88.

Parties and Elections in Europe (2018), Database on National Elections in European Countries. www.parties-and-elections.eu/countries.html (accessed on 5 November 2018).

Pasquino, Gianfranco (1995), Italy: A Democratic Regime under Reform. In: Josep Colomer (ed.), *Political Institutions in Europe*. London: Routledge, pp. 138–69.

—— (2015a), The Presidents of the Republic. In: Erik Jones and Gianfranco Pasquino (eds), *Oxford Handbook of Italian Politics*. Oxford: Oxford University Press, pp. 82–94.

—— (2015b), Governments in European Politics. In: José M. Magone (ed.), *Routledge Handbook of European Politics*. Oxford: Oxford University Press, pp. 295–310.

—— and Marco Valbruzzi (2017), Italy Says No: The 2016 Constitutional Referendum and its Consequences. *Journal of Modern Italian Studies*, 22(2): 145–62.

Passarelli, Gianluca (2014), Crossing the Rubicon . . . and Back: Twenty Years of the Italian Northern League. *South European Society and Politics*, 19(2): 289–94.

Pedersen, Karina and Tim Knudsen (2005), Denmark: Presidentialization in a Consensual Democracy. In: Thomas Poguntke and Paul Webb (eds), *The Presidentialization of Politics: A Comparative Study of Modern Democracies*. Oxford: Oxford University Press, pp. 159–75.

Pedersen, Mogens N. (1979), The Dynamics of European Party System Systems: Changing Patterns of Electoral Volatility. *European Journal of Political Research*, 7(1): 1–26.

Peglis, Michalis (2015), How Can European Political Parties Maximise Their Success in the 2019 Elections? *European View*, 14(1): 21–30.

Pelikaan, Huib, Tom van der Meer and Sarah De Lange (2003), The Road from a Depoliticized to a Centrifugal Democracy. *Acta Politica*, 38(1): 23–49.

Pelinka, Anton and Sieglinde Rosenberger (2003), *Österreichische Politik: Grundlagen, Strukturen, Trends*. Vienna: WUV.

Pernice, Ingolf (2015), The EU as a 'Citizens' Joint Venture: Multilevel Constitutionalism and Open Democracy in Europe. In: José M. Magone (ed.), *Routledge Handbook of European Politics*. London: Routledge, pp. 184–201.

Peterson, John (2017), Juncker's Political European Commission and an EU in Crisis. *Journal of Common Market Studies*, 55(2): 349–67.

—— and Elizabeth E. Bomberg (1999), *Decision-Making in the European Union*. Basingstoke: Macmillan.

Pettai, Vello and Ülle Madise (2006), The Baltic Parliaments: Legislative Performance from Independence to EU Accession. *Journal of Legislative Studies*, 12(3–4): 291–310.

Pevcin, Primož (2014), Local Government Cost Function: Case Study Analysis for Slovenian Municipalities. *Zagreb International Review of Economics & Business*, 17(1): 79–86.

Pew Research (2017), Europe's Growing Muslim Population: Muslim's Are Projected to Increase in Share of Europe's Population Even With No Migration. Report 29 November 2017. www.pewforum.org/2017/11/29/europes-growing-muslim-population/ (accessed on 3 March 2019).

Peyer, Hans Conrad (1978), *Verfassungsgeschichte der alten Schweiz*. Zurich: Schultheiss Polygraphischer Verlag.

Piccio, D.R. (2012), *Party Regulation in Europe: Country Reports, The Legal Regulation of Political Parties*, Party Law in Modern Europe Working Paper Series, No. 18. www.partylaw.leidenuniv.nl/uploads/wp1812a.pdf (accessed on 24 November 2018).

Pickering, Paula and Mirna Jusić (2017), Making Local Government Work Better: How Local and Internationally Sponsored Institutions Interact to Influence Performance in Bosnia-Herzegovina. *Governance*, 31(4): 665–82.

Pinteric, Uroš (2015), Postponed Regionalization of Slovenia. *Regions Magazine*, 298(1): 16–17.

Pinto, António Costa and André Freire (2005), *O Poder dos Presidentes: A República Portuguesa em Debate*. Lisbon: Campo da Comunicação.

Pinto, Luca (2015), The Time Path of Legislative Party Switching and the Dynamics of Political Competition: The Italian Case (1996–2011). *The Journal of Legislative Studies*, 21(3): 323–41.

Pirro, Andrea L.P. (2014), Populist Radical Right Parties in Central and Eastern Europe: The Different Context and Issues of the Prophets of the Patria. *Government and Opposition*, 49(4): 599–628.

Pisani-Ferry, Jean, André Sapir and Guntram B. Wolff (2013), *EU-IMF Assistance to Euro-Area Countries: An Early Assessment*. Brussels: Bruegel. http://bruegel.org/wp-content/uploads/imported/publications/1869_Blueprint_XIX_-_web__.pdf (accessed on 29 September 2017).

Ploštajner, Zlata (2008), Small and Smaller: What is the Smallest? Local Self-Governance in Slovenia. In: Zdravko Zlopaka (ed.), *Block by Block: It's Good to Build Well – Models of Organisation of Local Self-Governance*. Banja Luka: Enterprise Development Agency, pp. 36–77.

Pochet, Philippe, Maarten Keune and David Natali (2010), After the Euro and Enlargement: Social Pacts in the EU. Brussels: European Trade Union Institute (ETUI). www.etui.org/Publications2/Books/After-the-euro-and-enlargement-social-pacts-in-the-EU (accessed on 24 June 2018).

Poguntke, Thomas (2005), A Presidentializing Party State? The Federal Republic of Germany. In: Thomas Poguntke and Paul Webb (eds), *The Presidentialization of Politics. A Comparative Study of Modern Democracies*. Oxford: Oxford University Press, pp. 63–87.

—— and Paul Webb (2005), The Presidentialization of Politics in Democratic Societies: A Framework for Analysis. In: Thomas Poguntke and Paul Webb (eds), *The Presidentialization of Politics. A Comparative Study of Modern Democracies*. Oxford: Oxford University Press, pp. 1–25.

Pokleba, Nino (2016). Civil Society in Georgia: Expectations versus Reality. *Southeast European and Black Sea Studies*, 16(2): 235–53.

Polanyi, Karl (1944), *The Great Transformation*. New York: Rinehart.

Poli, Davide (2005), Svezia: piu poteri ma piu competitori? In: Gianfranco Pasquino (ed.), *Capi di governo*. Bologna: Il Mulino, pp. 281–309.

Political Data Yearbook Interactive (2018), www.politicaldatayearbook.com/ (accessed on 9 November 2017).

Pollitt, Christopher and Geert Bouckaert (2004), *Public Management Reform: A Comparative Analysis*. Oxford: Oxford University Press.

Polsby, Nelson (1968), The Institutionalisation of the US House of Representatives. *American Political Science Review*, 62(1): 144–68.

Preiec, Tena and Stuart Brown (2015), Croatian Elections: A Final Look at the Parties and the Campaign. EUROPP, 7 November 2015. http://blogs.lse.ac.uk/europpblog/2015/11/07/croatian-elections-a-final-look-at-the-parties-and-the-campaign/ (accessed on 12 May 2018).

Pridham, Geoffrey (ed.) (1985), *The New Mediterranean Democracies: Regime Transitions in Spain, Greece and Portugal*. London: Frank Cass.

—— (1999), *The Dynamics of Democratization: A Comparative Approach*. New York: Continuum.

—— (2005), *Designing Democracy: EU Enlargement and Regime Change in Post-Communist Europe*. Basingstoke: Palgrave.

Pukis, Maris (2015), Regionalism in Latvia. In: Assembly of European Regions (AER) (ed.), *Report on the State of Regionalization in 2017*. https://drive.google.com/file/d/0B94jJjQLXnl-YVZzNDBqUmZGU2s/view (accessed on 18 July 2018).

Quinlivan, Aodh (2006), *El govern local a la Republica d'Irlanda. Col-lecció Món Local 20*. Barcelona: Universitat Autonoma de Barcelona – Institut de Ciencies Politiques i Socials.

—— (2017), Reforming Local Government: Must It Always Be Democracy versus Efficiency? *Administration*, 65(2): 109–26.

Quittkat, Christine (2006), *Europäisierung der Interessenvermittlung: Französische Wirtschaftsverbände zwischen Beständigkeit und Wandel*. Wiesbaden: Verlag für Sozialwissenschaften.

Parau, Cristina E. (2015), Explaining Governance of the Judiciary in Central and Eastern Europe: External Incentives, Transnational Elites and Parliamentary Inaction. *Europe-Asia Studies*, 67(3): 409–42.

Plokhy, Serhij Mykolajovyč (2015), *The Gates of Europe: A History of Ukraine*. New York: Basic Books.

Pollack, Mark (1994), Creeping Competence: The Expanding Agenda of the European Community. *Journal of Public Policy*, 14(2): 95–140.

—— (2000), The End of Creeping Competence? EU Policy Making Since Maastricht. *Journal of Common Market Studies*, 38(3): 519–38.

Radaelli, Claudio (2003), The Europeanization of Public Policy. In: Kevin Featherstone and Claudio M. Radaelli (eds), *The Politics of Europeanization*. Oxford: Oxford University Press, pp. 27–56.

Rae, Douglas (1967), *The Political Consequences of Electoral Laws*. New Haven: Yale University Press.

Rashkova, Ekaterina (2014a), The Decline in Support for Bulgaria's Socialist Party Could Be the First Step in a Rebalancing of the Country's Party System. Blog. http://blogs.lse.ac.uk/europpblog/2014/10/10/the-decline-in-support-for-bulgarias-socialist-party-could-be-the-first-step-in-a-rebalancing-of-the-countrys-party-system/ (accessed on 11 May 2018).

—— (2014b), Party System at Work: The 2014 Legislative Election in Bulgaria. *Österreichische Zeitschrift für Politikwissenschaft*, 44(1): 67–71.

Raunio, Tapio (2015), European Parliament. In: José M. Magone (ed.), *Routledge Handbook in European Politics*. London: Routledge, pp. 248–62.

—— (2016), The Finnish Eduskunta and the European Union: The Strengths and Weaknesses of a Mandating System. In: Claudia Hefftler, Christine Neuhold, Olivier Rozenberg and Julie Smith (eds), *The Palgrave Handbook of National Parliaments and the European Union*. Basingstoke: Palgrave, pp. 406–424.

—— and Teija Tiilikainen (2004), *Finland in the European Union*. London: Routledge.

Reetz, Axel and Werner Reutter (2012a), Estland. In: Werner Reutter (ed.), *Verbände und Verbandssysteme in den Ländern der Europäischen Union*. Wiesbaden: Springer Verlag, pp. 165–78.

—— (2012b), Lettland. In: Werner Reutter (ed.), *Verbände und Verbandssysteme in den Ländern der Europäischen Union*. Wiesbaden: Springer Verlag, pp. 371–93.

Regalia, Ida and Marino Regini (2018), Trade Unions and Employment Relations in Italy during the Economic Crisis. *South European Society and Politics*, 23(1): 63–79.

Regalia, Marta (2018), Electoral Reform as an Engine of Party System Change in Italy. *South European Society and Politics*, 23(1): 81–96.

Regan, Aidan (2012), The Political Economy of Social Pacts in the EMU: Irish Liberal Market Corporatism in Crisis. *New Political Economy*, 17(4): 465–91.

Regeringskansliet (2015), *The Swedish Judicial System*. Sweden: Ministry of Justice. www.government.se/49ec0b/contentassets/9ebb0750780245aeb6d5c13c1ff5cf64/the-swedish-judicial-system.pdf (accessed on 1 November 2018).

Reh, Christine (2014), Is Informal Politics Undemocratic? Trilogues, Early Agreements and the Selection Model of Representation. *Journal of European Public Policy*, 21(6): 822–41.

Rehder, Britta (2015), Judicial Politics in Europe: Constitutional Courts in Comparative Perspective. In: José M. Magone (ed.), *Routledge Handbook of European Politics*. London: Routledge, pp. 386–98.

Remington, Thomas (2008), Patronage and the Party of Power: President–Parliament Relations Under Vladimir Putin. *Europe-Asia Studies*, 60(6): 959–87.

Reporters without Borders (RSF) (2018), RSF Index 2018: Hatred of Journalism Threatens Democracies.https://rsf.org/en/rsf-index-2018-hatred-journalism-threatens-democracies (accessed on 13 September 2018).

Reutter, Werner (2012), Litauen. In: Werner Reutter (ed.), *Verbände und Verbandssysteme in den Ländern der Europäischen Union*. Wiesbaden: Springer Verlag, pp. 393–416.

—— and Hendrik Träger (2012), Ungarn. In: Werner Reutter (ed.), *Verbände und Verbandssysteme in den Ländern der Europäischen Union*. Wiesbaden: Springer Verlag, pp. 783–809.

Rhodes, Martin (1997), Financing Party Politics in Italy: A Case of Systemic Corruption. *West European Politics* 20(1): 54–80.

Rhodes, R.A.W. (1996), The New Governance: Governing without Government. *Political Studies*, 44(4): 652–67.

—— (1997), *Understanding Governance: Policy Networks, Governance, Reflexivity and Accountability*. Buckingham: Open University Press.

Richter, Solveig and Saša Gavrić (2010), Das politische System Bosnien-Herzegovinas. In: Wolfgang Ismayr, Solveig Richter and Markus Söldner (eds), *Die politischen Systeme Osteuropas*. Wiesbaden: Verlag für Sozialwissenschaften, pp. 837–95.

Riedel, Sabine (2010), Das politische System Bulgariens. In: Wolfgang Ismayr (ed.), *Die politische Systeme of Osteuropas*. Wiesbaden: Verlag für Sozialwissenschaften, pp. 677–728.

Rifkin, Jeremy (2004), *The European Dream: How Europe's Vision of the Future is Quietly Eclipsing the American Dream*. Cambridge: Polity Press.

Riigigoku (Parliament of Estonia) (2015), Riigikogu XII Koosseis. Statistikat ja ülevaateid Talinn: Riigigoku. www.riigikogu.ee/wpcms/wp-content/uploads/2014/11/Riigikogu-XII-koosseis-Statistikat-ja-levaated.pdf (accessed on 29 October 2018).

—— (2018), www.riigikogu.ee/riigikogu/riigikogu-komisjonid/ (accessed on 17 February 2018).

Riksrevisionen (National Audit Agency-Sweden) (2018), www.riksrevisionen.se/om-riksrevisionen.html (accessed on 29 October 2018).

Risse, Thomas (2010), *Community of Europeans? Transnational Identities and Public Spaces*. Ithaca: Cornell University Press.

Roberts, Geoffrey K. (2000), The Ever-Shallower Cleavage: Religion and Electoral Politics in Germany. In: David Broughton and Hans-Martien ten Napel (eds), *Religion and Mass Electoral Behaviour in Europe*. London: Routledge, pp. 61–7.

Roberts, Sean P. (2012), United Russia and the Dominant-Party Framework: Understanding the Russian Party of Power in Comparative Perspective. *East European Politics*, 28(3): 225–40.

Robinson, Neil (2017). Russian Neo-Patrimonialism and Putin's 'Cultural Turn'. *Europe-Asia Studies*, 69(2): 348–66.

Rodon, Toni and María José Hierro (2016), Podemos and Ciudadanos Shake up the Spanish Party System: The 2015 Local and Regional Elections. *South European Society and Politics*, 21(3): 339–57.

Rodríguez-Teruel, Juan, Astrid Barrio and Oscar Barberà (2016), Fast and Furious: Podemos' Quest for Power in Multi-level Spain. *South European Society and Politics*, 21(4): 561–85.

Roederer-Rynning, Christilla (2015), The Common Agricultural Policy: The Fortress Challenged. In: Helen Wallace, Mark A. Pollack and Alasdair R. Young (eds), *Policy-Making in the European Union* seventh edition. Oxford: Oxford University Press, pp. 196–219.

Rohrer, Linda and Christine Trampusch (2011), Continuity and Change in the Swiss Vocational Training System. In: Christine Trampusch and André Mach (eds), *Switzerland in Europe: Continuity and Change in the Swiss Political Economy*. London: Routledge pp. 144–61.

Rokkan, Stein (1980), Eine Familie von Modellen für die vergleichende Geschichte Europas. *Zeitschrift für Soziologie*, 9(2): 118–28.

——, with Peter Flora, Stein Kuhnle and Derek Urwin (eds) (1999), *State Formation, Nation-Building and Mass Politics in Europe. The Theory of Stein Rokkan*. Oxford: Oxford University Press.

—— and Derek W. Urwin (1983), *Economy, Territory and Identity: Politics of West European Peripheries*. London: SAGE.

Roller, Elisa (2002), Reforming the Senate? Mission Impossible. *West European Politics*, 25(4): 69–92.

Rommetvedt, Hilmar (2015), The Norwegian Storting: A Less Predictable Parliament. www.psa.ac.uk/sites/default/files/ROMMETVEDT%20-%20The%20Norwegian%20Storting_1.pdf (accessed on 6 February 2018).

—— and Frode Veggeland (2017). Parliamentary Government and Corporatism at the Crossroads: Principals and Agents in Norwegian Agricultural Policymaking. *Government and Opposition*, 1–25. doi:10.1017/gov.2017.32.

——, Gunnar Thesen, Peter Munk Christiansen and Asbjørn Sonne Nørgaard (2012), Coping With Corporatism in Decline and the Revival of Parliament: Interest Group Lobbyism in Denmark and Norway, 1980–2005. *Comparative Political Studies*, 46(4): 457–85.

Roper, Steven D.(2002), The Influence of Romanian Campaign Finance Laws on Party System Development and Corruption. *Party Politics*, 8(2): 175–92.

Rose, Lawrence E. (2006), *Noruega: El govern local en la cruilla*. Col-léció Món Local 17. Barcelona: Universitat Autonoma de Barcelona – Institut de Ciencies Politiques i Socials.

Rose, Richard (1995), Dynamics of Democratic Regimes. In: Jack Hayward and Ed Page (eds), *Governing the New Europe*. Oxford: Polity Press, pp. 67–92.

—— (2006), Politics in England. In: Gabriel A. Almond, Russell J. Dalton, G. Bingham Powell Jr. and Kaare Strøm (eds), *European Politics Today*. New York: Pearson Longman, pp. 84–133.

Rosenau, James N. (2000), Governance, Order and Change in World Politics. In: James N. Rosenau and Ernst Otto Czempiel (eds), *Governance Without Government: Order and Change in World Politics*. Cambridge: Cambridge University Press, pp. 1–29.

Ross, Cameron (ed.) (2004), *Russian Politics under Putin*. Manchester: Manchester University Press.

Ross, Christopher (1995), *Jacques Delors and European Integration*. Cambridge: Polity Press.

Rószás, Arpád (2004), Regional Policy in Hungary: Institutional Preparations for EU Accession. In: Attila Ágh (ed.), *Europeanization and Regionalization: Hungary's Accession*. Budapest: Hungarian Centre for Democracy Studies, pp. 78–112.

Rothmayr Allison, Cristine and Frédéric Varone (2014), Justiz. In: Peter Knoepfel, Yannis Papadopoulos, Pascal Sciarini, Adrian Vatter and Silja Häusermann (eds), *Handbuch der Schweizer Politik*. Zurich: Verlag Neue Zürcher Zeitung, pp. 219–42.

Royo, Sebastián (2013), *Lessons From the Economic Crisis in Spain*. Basingstoke: Palgrave Macmillan.

Rudé, George (1980), *Revolutionary Europe: 1783–1815*. Glasgow: Fontana.

Rudzio, Wolfgang (2015), *Das politische System der Bundesrepublik Deutschland: Aktualisierte und erweiterte Auflage*. Wiesbaden: Verlag der Sozialwissenschaften.

Ryšavý, Dan (2013), Czech Counties after a Dozen Years of Regionalization. Continuity and Novelties after County Elections 2012. *Regional & Federal Studies*, 23(5): 631–42.

Saalfeld, Thomas (1998), The German Bundestag: Influence and Accountability in a Complex Environment. In: Philip Norton (ed.), *Parliaments and Governments in Western Europe*. London: Frank Cass, pp. 44–72.

—— (2000), Germany: Stable Parties, Chancellor Democracy, and the Art of Informal Democracy. In: Wolfgang C. Müller and Kaare Strøm (eds), *Coalition Governments in Western Europe*. Oxford: Oxford University Press, pp. 32–85.

Saarts, Tonis (2011), Comparative Party System Analysis in Central and Eastern Europe: The Case of the Baltic States. *Studies in Transition States and Societies*, 3(3): 83–104.

Saatçioğlu, Beken (2016), De-Europeanisation in Turkey: The Case of the Rule of Law. *South European Society and Politics*, 21(1): 133–46.

Sakwa, Richard (2000), Democracy Assistance: Russia's Experience as Recipient. In: Peter Burnell (ed.), *Democracy Assistance: International Co-operation for Democratization*. London: Frank Cass, pp. 288–314.

—— (2016a), *Putin and the Oligarch: The Khodorkovsky-Yukos Affair*. New York: I.B. Tauris.

—— (2016b), *Frontline Ukraine: Crisis in the Borderlands*. New York: I.B. Tauris.

Samtök atvinnulífsins (Confederation of the Icelandic Enterprise-SA) (2018), SA Confederation of Icelandic Enterprise. https://sa.is/sa-confederation-of-icelandic-enterprise (accessed on 25 November 2018).

Sandberg, Siv (2005), *El govern local a Finlandia*. Col·lecció Món Local 16. Barcelona: Universitat Autonoma de Barcelona – Institut de Ciencies Socials.

Sanders, David (2017), The UK's Changing Party System: The Prospects for Party Realignment at Westminster. *Journal of the British Academy*, 5: 91–124.

Sanford, George (2001), *Democratic Government in Poland: Constitutional Politics Since 1989*. Basingstoke: Palgrave.

Santos, Boaventura de Sousa and Conceição Gomes (2011), *O sistema judicial e o desafio da complexidade social: novos caminhos para o recrutamento e formação dos magistrados*. http://opj.ces.uc.pt/pdf/Relatorio_Formacao_16Jun.pdf (accessed on 15 July 2012).

Santos, Boaventura de Sousa, Maria Manuel Leitão Marques, João Pedroso and Pedro Lopes Ferreira (1996), *Os tribunais nas sociedades contemporâneas: o caso português*. Porto: Editora Afrontamentos.

Sapelli, Giulio (1995), *Southern Europe since 1945: Tradition and Modernity in Portugal, Spain, Italy, Greece and Turkey*. London: Longman.

Sarvilinna, Sami (2007), Court Administration in Finland. *Scandinavian Studies in Law*, 51: 591–605.

Sasse, Gwendolyn (2013), Linkages and the Promotion of Democracy: The EU's Eastern Neighbourhood. *Democratization*, 20(4): 553–91.

Sassoon, Donald (1997), *One Hundred Years of Socialism: The West European Left in the Twentieth Century*. London: Fontana Press.

Saurugger, Sabine (2007), Differential Impact: Europeanizing French Non-State Actors. *Journal of European Public Policy*, 14(7): 1079–97.

Scarrow, Susan (2003), Germany: The Mixed-Member System as a Political Compromise. In: Matthew Soberg Shugart and Martin P. Wattenberg (eds), *Mixed-Member Electoral Systems*. Oxford: Oxford University Press, pp. 55–69.

Scharpf, Fritz W. (2000), The Viability of Advanced Welfare States in the International Economy: Vulnerabilities and Options. *Journal of European Public Policy*, 7(2): 190–228.

Schefbeck, Günther (2006), Das Parlament. In: Herbert Dachs, Peter Gerlich, Herbert Gottweis, Helmut Kramer, Volker Lauber, Wolfgang C. Müller and Emmerich Tálos (eds), *Politik in Österreich: Das Handbuch*. Vienna: Manz, pp. 139–67.

Scherpereel, John A. (2010), EU Cohesion Policy and the Europeanization of Central and East European Regions. *Regional & Federal Studies*, 20(1): 45–62.

Schiemann, John W. (2004), Hungary: The Emergence of Chancellor Democracy. *Journal of Legislative Studies*, 10(2–3): 128–41.

Schlipphak, Bernd and Oliver Treib (2017), Playing the Blame Game on Brussels: The Domestic Political Effects of EU Interventions against Democratic Backsliding. *Journal of European Public Policy*, 24(3): 352–65.

Schmidt, Helmut (5 October 2000), Wer nicht zu Europa gehört Türkei, Rußland, Ukraine, Weißrußland: Sie alle sind große Nationen und wichtige Partner der EU. Aber keine geeigneten Kandidaten für die Erweiterung. *Die Zeit*, 41/2000. www.zeit.de/2000/41/Wer_nicht_zu_Europa_gehoert (accessed on 18 September 2017).

Schmidt, Manfred G. (2002), The Consociational State: Hypotheses Regarding the Political Structure and Potential for Democratization in the European Union. In: Jürg Steiner and Thomas Ertman (eds), *Consociationalism and Corporatism in Western Europe: Still the Politics of Accommodation?* Special issue of *Acta Politica*, 37(2–3): 213–27.

Schmidt, Vivien (2002), *The Future of European Capitalisms*. Oxford: Oxford University Press.

—— (2005), *Democracy in Europe: The EU and National Institutions*. Oxford: Oxford University Press.

—— (2008), European Political Economy: Labour Out, State Back In, Firm to the Fore. *West European Politics*, 31(1–2): 302–20.

Schmitter, Philippe C. (1974), Still the Century of Corporatism? *The Review of Politics*, 36(1): 85–131.

—— (1995), Organized Interests and Democratic Consolidation in Southern Europe. In: Richard Gunther, P. Nikiforos Diamandouros and Hans-Jürgen Puhle (eds), *The Politics of Democratic Consolidation: Southern Europe in Comparative Perspective*. Baltimore: Johns Hopkins University Press, pp. 284–314.

—— (2008), The Changing Politics of Organised Interests. *West European Politics*, 31(1): 195–210.

—— and Jürgen Grote (1997), *The Corporatist Sysiphus: Past, Present and Future*. Florence: EUI working papers, SPS 97/4.

Schröder, Konrad (1993), Many Languages, One World. In: Monica Shelley and Margaret Winck (eds), *What is Europe? Aspects of European Diversity*. London: Routledge, pp. 13–64.

Schroen, Michael (2012), Luxemburg. In: Werner Reutter (ed.), *Verbände und Verbandssysteme in den Ländern der Europäischen Union*. Wiesbaden: Springer Verlag, pp. 417–44.

Schwarzer, Daniela (2013), Deutschland und Frankreich und die Krise im Euro-raum. *Aus Politik und Zeitgeschichte*, 1(3): 30–36.

—— (2014), Building the Euro Area's Debt Crisis Management Capacity with the IMF. *Review of International Political Economy*, 22(3): 599–625.

Schweiger, Christian (2014), *The EU and the Global Crisis: New Varieties of Capitalism*. Cheltenham: Edward Elgar.

Schweizer, Gerhard (2016), *Türkei verstehen: Von Atatürk bis Erdoğan*. Stuttgart: Klett-Cotta.

Sciarini, Pascal (2014), Eppure si muove: The Changing Nature of the Swiss Consensus Democracy. *Journal of European Public Policy*, 21(1): 116–32.

Seawright, David (2000), A Confessional Cleavage Resurrected? The Denominational Vote in Britain. In: David Broughton and Hans-Martien ten Napel (eds), *Religion and Mass Electoral Behaviour in Europe*. London: Routledge, pp. 44–60.

Sebők, Miklós, Csaba Molnár and Bálint György Kubik (2017), Exercising Control and Gathering Information: The Functions of Interpellations in Hungary (1990–2014). *The Journal of Legislative Studies*, 234: 465–83.

Secretariat General des Affaires Européennes (SGAE) (2018), Organisation. www.sgae.gouv.fr/cms/sites/sgae/accueil/le-sgae/organisation.html (accessed on 22 October 2018).

Šedo, Jakub (2010a), The Party System of Croatia. In: Vera Stojarová and Peter Emerson (eds), *Party Politics in the Western Balkans*. London: Routledge, pp. 73–84.

—— (2010b). The Party System of Bosnia-Herzegovina. In: Vera Stojarová and Peter Emerson (eds), *Party Politics in the Western Balkans*. London: Routledge, pp. 85–98.

—— (2010c), The Party System of Macedonia. In: Vera Stojarová and Peter Emerson (eds), *Party Politics in the Western Balkans*. London: Routledge, pp. 167–79.

Seiler, Daniel Louis (2015), The Legacy of Stein Rokkan for European Polities: A Short Tribute. In: José M. Magone (ed.), *Routledge Handbook of European Politics*. London: Routledge, pp. 41–51.

Seima (Parliament of Latvia) (2018), www.saeima.lv/en (accessed on 17 February 2018).

Seimas (Parliament of Lithuania) (2018), www.lrs.lt/sip/portal.show?p_k=2 (accessed on 17 February 2018).

Seisselberg, Jörg (1996), Conditions of Success and Political Problems of a Media-Mediated Personality-Party: The Case of Forza Italia. *West European Politics*, 19(4): 715–43.

Sejm (2018), Prace Sejmu (Work of Sejm): Dane Statystyczne (Statistical Data). www.sejm.gov.pl/sejm7.nsf/page.xsp/prace_sejmu (accessed on 16 February 2018).

Semenova, Elena (2014), Parliamentary Representation in Post-Communist Ukraine: Change and Stability. In: Elena Semenova, Michael Edinger and Heinrich Best (eds), *Parliamentary Elites in Central and Eastern Europe: Recruitment and Representation*. London: Routledge, pp. 261–83.

Senato of Italian Parliament (2018), Statistiche sull'attività legislative XIII-XVII Legislature. www.senato.it/leg/17/BGT/Schede/Statistiche/Iniziativa//DDLPerIniziativa.html (accessed on 15 February 2018).

Seperiċ, Darko (2017), Croatia: Annual Review of Industrial Relations and Social Dialogue. Bratislava: Friedrich Ebert Stiftung. http://library.fes.de/pdf-files/bueros/bratislava/14468.pdf (accessed on 27 June 2018).

Service public federale justice (SPFJ) (2017a), Rapport annuel 2016. Just 2020 droit devant. Brussels: SPFJ. https://justice.belgium.be/sites/default/files/2017–09_rapport_annuel_spfj_fr-nl.pdf (accessed on 1 November 2018).

—— (2017b), Court of the Future: Plus Accessible et Plus Prompt, et Ainsi Plus Equitable. Brussels: SPFJ. www.koengeens.be/policy/court-of-the-future (accessed on 1 November 2018).

Shelley, Louise and Judy Deane (2016), *The Rise of Reiderstvo: Implications for Russia and the West*. Phoenix: Tracc Consulting LLC. www.reiderstvo.org/sites/default/files/The_Rise_of_Reiderstvo.pdf (accessed on 13 September 2018).

Siaroff, Alan (1999), Corporatism in 24 Industrial Democracies: Meaning and Measurement. *European Journal of Political Research*, 36(2): 175–205.

Sickinger, Hubert (2009), *Politikfinanzierung in Österreich*. Vienna: Czernin.

Silberman, Bernard S. (1993), *Cages of Reason: The Rise of the Rational State in France, Japan, the United States and Great Britain*. Chicago: Chicago University Press.

Silver, Laura, Courtney Johnson and Kyle Taylor (30 May 2018), The Populist Parties That Shook up Italy's Election. Fact Tank. Numbers in the News. Pew Research. www.pewresearch.org/fact-tank/2018/05/30/views-of-italian-populist-party-supporters/ (accessed on 15 July 2018).

Siri, Jasmin (2018), The Alternative for Germany after the 2017 Election. *German Politics*, 27(1): 141–5.

Smith, David J. (2002), Estonia: Independence and European Integration. In: David J. Smith, Artis Pabriks, Aldis Purs and Thomas Lane (eds), *The Baltic States: Estonia, Latvia and Lithuania*. London: Routledge.

Smith, Karen E. (2004), *The Making of EU Foreign Policy: The Case of Eastern Europe*, second edition. Basingstoke: Palgrave.

Soeffner, Hans-Georg and Dirk Tänzler (2002), Medienwahlkämpfe-Hochzeiten ritueller Politik inszenierung. In: Andreas Dörner and Ludgera Vogt (eds), *Wahl-kämpfe: Betrachtungen über ein demokratisches Ritual*. Frankfurt a. M.: Suhrkamp, pp. 92–114.

Sootla, Georg and Kersten Kattai (2011), Estonia: Challenges and Lessons of the Development of Local Autonomy. In: John Loughlin, Frank Hendriks and Anders Lidström (eds), *The Oxford Handbook of Local and Regional Democracy in Europe*. Oxford: Oxford University Press, pp. 576–95.

Soskice, David and Peter A. Hall (2001), An Introduction to Varieties of Capitalism. In: David Soskice and Peter A. Hall (eds), *Varieties of Capitalism: The Institutional Foundations of Comparative Advantage*. Oxford: Oxford University Press, pp. 1–68.

Soufan Group (2015), *Foreign Fighters: An Updated Assessment of the Flow of Foreign Fighters into Syria and Iraq*. New York: Soufan Group. http://soufangroup.com/wp-content/uploads/2015/12/TSG_ForeignFightersUpdate3.pdf (accessed on 29 September 2017).

Spirova, Maria (2005), Political Parties in Bulgaria. Organizational Trends in Comparative Perspective. *Party Politics*, 11(5): 611–22.

—— (2008), Europarties and Party Development in EU-Candidate States: The Case of Bulgaria. *Europe-Asia studies*, 60(5): 791–808.

—— (2014), Party Politics in Bulgaria Has Become Completely Nonsensical. http://blogs.lse.ac.uk/lsee/2014/09/25/mariaspirovapartypoliticsinbulgariahasbecomecompletely nonsensical/ (accessed on 12 May 2018).

Språkrådet (2017), Nynorsk in Norway. www.sprakradet.no/Vi-og-vart/Om-oss/English-and-other-languages/English/Nynorsk_in_Norway/ (accessed on 18 October 2017).

Stanojević, Miroslav, Aleksandra Kanjuo Mrčela and Maja Breznik (2016), Slovenia at the Crossroads: Increasing Dependence on Supranational Institutions and the Weakening of Social Dialogue. *European Journal of Industrial Relations*, 22(3): 281–94.

Statistics Norway (2017), Municipalities, By Language Used in Administration. Bokmål and nynorsk (SY 236). www.ssb.no/282171/municipalities-by-language-used-in-administration.bokmal-and-nynorsk-sy-236 (accessed on 18 October 2017).

Stelzer, Manfred (2013), Constitutional Change in Austria. In: Xenophon Contiades (ed.), *Engineering Constitutional Change: A Comparative Perspective on Europe, Canada and USA*. London: Routledge, pp. 7–34.

Stergiou, Andreas (2012), Zypern. In: Werner Reutter (ed.), *Verbände und Verbandssysteme in den Ländern der Europäischen Union*. Wiesbaden: Springer Verlag, pp. 809–37.

Stojarová, Vera (2010a), Legacy of Communist and Socialist Parties in the Western Balkans. In: Vera Stojarová and Peter Emerson (eds), *Party Politics in the Western Balkans*. London: Routledge, pp. 26–41.

—— (2010b), Nationalist Parties and the Party Systems of the Western Balkans In: Vera Stojarová and Peter Emerson (eds), *Party Politics in the Western Balkans*. London: Routledge, pp. 42–58.

—— (2010c), The Party System of Albania. In: Vera Stojarová and Peter Emerson (eds), *Party Politics in the Western Balkans*. London: Routledge, pp. 180–9.

—— (2010d), The Party System of Kosovo. In: Vera Stojarová and Peter Emerson (eds), *Party Politics in the Western Balkans*. London: Routledge, pp. 151–66.

Stoleroff, Alan (2016), The Portuguese Labour Movement and Industrial Democracy: From Workplace Revolution to a Precarious Quest for Economic Justice. *Transfer*, 22(1): 101–19.

Stone, Alec (1992), Where Judicial Politics Are Legislative Politics: The French Constitutional Council. In: Mary L. Volcansek (ed.), *Judicial Politics and Policy-Making in Western Europe*, Special issue of *West European Politics*, 15(3): 29–49.

Stone Sweet, Alec (2000), *Governing With Judges: Constitutional Politics in Europe*. Oxford: Oxford University Press.

—— (2004), *The Judicial Construction of Europe*. Oxford: Oxford University Press.

Storey, Hugh (1995), Human Rights and the New Europe: Experience and Experiment. *Political Studies*, XLIII: 131–51.

Storting (2016), The Norwegian Parliament. Oslo: Storting. www.stortinget.no/globalassets/pdf/hovedbrosjyre-div-spraak/stortingetnorgesnasjonalforsamling_eng_web.pdf (accessed on 6 February 2018).

—— (2017), Stortinget 2015–16. Oslo: Stortinget. www.stortinget.no/globalassets/pdf/brosjyrer_rapporter/stortinget_2015_2016_bm.pdf (accessed on 17 February 2018).

Stoykova, Pavlina (2007), Parliamentary Involvement in the EU Accession Process: The Bulgarian Experience. In: John O'Brennan and Tapio Raunio (eds), *National Parliaments within the European Union: From 'Victims' of Integration to Competitive Actors?* London: Routledge, pp. 255–71.

Streeck, Wolfgang (2010), *Re-Forming Capitalism: Institutional Change in the German Political Economy*. Oxford: Oxford University Press.

—— and Anke Hassel (2003), The Crumbling Pillars of Social Partnership. *West European Politics*, 26(4): 101–24.

—— and Martin Höpner (2003), *Alle Macht dem Markt: Fallsstudien zur Abwicklung der Deutschland AG*. Frankfurt a. M.: Suhrkamp.

Strøm, Kaare, Wolfgang C. Müller and Torbjörn Bergman (eds) (2008), *Cabinets and Coalition Bargaining: The Democratic Life Cycle in Western Europe*. Oxford: Oxford University Press.

Strøm, Kaare, Hanne Marthe Narud and Henry Valen (2005), A More Fragile Chain of Governance in Norway. *West European Politics*, 28(4): 781–806.

Suomen Ammattiliittojen Keskusjärjestö (SAK) (2018), This is SAK. www.sak.fi/en/this-is-sak (accessed on 25 June 2018).

Surubaru, Neculai-Cristian (2015), Governing a Dysfunctional State: The Challenges Facing Romania's New Technocratic Government. Blog. http://blogs.lse.ac.uk/europpblog/2015/11/25/governing-a-dysfunctional-state-the-challenges-facing-romanias-new-technocratic-government/ (accessed on 23 December 2017).

Svensk Närigsliv (2018), About Us. www.svensktnaringsliv.se/english/about-us_563030.html (accessed on 24 June 2018).

Svensson, Torsten (2016), The Swedish Model of Industrial Relations. In: Jon Pierre (ed.), *Oxford Handbook of Swedish Politics*. Oxford: Oxford University Press, pp. 612–27.

—— and Perola Öberg (2005), How are Coordinated Market Economies Coordinated? Evidence from Sweden. *West European Politics*, 28(5): 1075–100.

Swallow, Charles (1973), *The Sick Man of Europe. Ottoman Empire to Turkish Republic, 1789–1923*. Tonbridge: E. Benn.

Swianiewicz, Paweł (2006), Polónia. *El Govern Local a Polónia: La Transició de l'Estat Centralitzat Autoritari al Sistema d'Autogovern*. Colleció Món Local 21. Barcelona: Universitat Autonoma de Barcelona – Institut de Ciencies Politiques i Socials.

—— (2011), Poland: Europeanization of Subnational Government. In: John Loughlin, Frank Hendriks and Anders Lidström (eds), *The Oxford Handbook of Local and Regional Democracy in Europe*. Oxford: Oxford University Press, pp. 480–504.

—— (2014), An Empirical Typology of Local Government Systems in Eastern Europe. *Local Government Studies*, 40(2): 292–311.

Swyngedouw, Marc, Koen Abts, Sharon Haute, Jolien Galle and Bart Meuleman (2015), Het Communautaire In De Verkiezingen Van 25 Mei 2014: Analyse Op Basis Van De Postelectorale Verkiezingsonderzoeken 1991–2014. Onderzoeksverslag Centrum voor Sociologisch Onderzoek (CeSO) Instituut voor Sociaal en Politiek Opinieonderzoek (ISPO) CeSO/ISPO/2015–1. https://soc.kuleuven.be/ceso/ispo/

downloads/Het%20communautaire%20in%20de%20verkiezingen%20van%20 2014.pdf (accessed on 6 May 2016).

Szczerbiak, Aleks (2008), *Poland Within the European Union. New Awkward Partner or New Heart of Europe?* London: Routledge.

Taggart, Paul (1998), A Touchstone of Dissent: Euroscepticism in Contemporary European Party Systems. *European Journal of Political Research*, 33: 363–88 (particularly pp. 365–6).

—— (2000), *Populism*. Buckingham: Open University Press.

—— (2004), Populism and Representative Politics in Contemporary Europe. *Journal of Political Ideologies*, 9(3): 269–88.

Tálos, Emmerich (2005), Vom Vorzeige zum Auslaufmodell? Österreichs Sozialpartnerschaft 1945 bis 2005. In: Ferdinand Karlhofer and Emmerich Tálos (eds), *Sozialpartnerschaft: Österreichische und Europäische Perspektiven*. Vienna: LIT, pp. 185–209.

—— (2006), Sozialpartnerschaft: Austrokorporatismus am Ende? In: Herbert Dachs, Peter Gerlich, Herbert Gottweis, Helmut Kramer, Volkmar Lauber, Wolfgang C. Müller and Emmerich Talos (eds), *Politik in Österreich: Das Handbuch*. Vienna: Manzsche Verlag, pp. 425–42.

Taras, Ray (2006), Politics in Poland. In: Gabriel A. Almond, Russell J. Dalton, G. Bingham Powell Jr. and Kaare Strøm (eds), *European Politics Today*. New York: Pearson Longman, pp. 349–401.

Tarchi, Marco (2018), Voters without a Party: The 'Long Decade' of the Italian Centre-Right and its Uncertain Future. *South European Society and Politics*, 23(1): 147–62.

Tauber, Joachim (2010), Das politische System Litauens. In: Wolfgang Ismayr (eds), *Die politischen Systeme Osteuropas*. Wiesbaden: Springer VS, pp. 171–208.

Távora, Isabel and Pilar González (2016), Labour Market Regulation and Collective Bargaining in Portugal During the Crisis: Continuity and Change. *European Journal of Industrial Relations*, 22(3): 251–65.

Taylor, Kyle (2 March 2018), Many Italians are Deeply Pessimistic Ahead of General Election. Fact tank. News in the Numbers. *Pew Research*. www.pewresearch.org/fact-tank/2018/03/02/many-italians-are-deeply-pessimistic-ahead-of-general-election/ (accessed on 15 July 2018).

Thames, Frank (2016), Electoral Rules and Legislative Parties in the Ukrainian Rada. *Legislative Studies Quarterly*, 41(1): 35–59.

The Economist Intelligence Unit (EUI) (2018), The Economist Intelligence Unit Democracy Index 2017. https://infographics.economist.com/2017/DemocracyIndex/ (accessed on 13 September 2018).

Thomassen, J.J.A., Carolien van Ham and R.B. Andeweg (2014), *De wankele democratie: Heeft de democratie haar beste tijd gehad?* Amsterdam: Prometheus Bert Bakker.

Thomson, David (1972), *Europe Since Napoleon*. Harmondsworth: Penguin.

Tiesu Administracija (2018), The Court Administration Judicial System in Latvia. Riga: Tiesu Administracija. www.ta.gov.lv/UserFiles/TA_buklets_ENG.pdf (accessed on 2 November 2018).

Tilly, Charles (1981), Sinews of War. In: Per Torsvik (ed.), *Mobilization, Centre-Periphery Structures and Nation-Building: A Volume in Commemoration of Stein Rokkan*. Bergen: Universitets forlaget, pp. 108–26.

Toloudis, Nicholas (2017), The New Constitutionalism, Disciplinary Neoliberalism, and the 2015 Greek Election. *New Political Science*, 39(3): 333–49.

Toonen, Theo J. (1990), The Unitary State as a System of Co-governance: The Case of the Netherlands. *Public Administration*, 68(3): 281–6.

Touwen, L. Jeroen (2008), How Does a Coordinated Market Economy Evolve? Effects of Policy Learning in the Netherlands in the 1980s. *Labor History* 49(4): 439–64.

—— (2014), *Coordination in Transition: The Netherlands and the World Economy 1950–2010*. Leiden: Brill.

Transparency International (TI) (2016), Nebeneinkünfte und Interessenkonflikte von Mitgliedern des Bundestages. www.transparency.de/fileadmin/Redaktion/

Publikationen/2016/16–12–09-Bericht_Nebeneinkuenfte_und_Interessenkonflikte-Transparency-Deutschland.pdf (accessed on 25 June 2018).

—— (2017), Global Corruption Barometer 2017. www.transparency.org/news/feature/global_corruption_barometer_citizens_voices_from_around_the_world (accessed on 18 November 2018).

—— (2018), Corruption Perception Index 2017. www.transparency.org/news/feature/corruption_perceptions_index_2017 (accessed on 13 September 2018).

Trauner, Florian (2016), Asylum Policy: The EU's 'Crises' and the Looming Policy Regime Failure. *Journal of European Integration*, 38(3): 311–25.

Traxler, Franz (2004), The Metamorphoses of Corporatism: From Classical to Lean Patterns. *European Journal of Political Research*, 43(4): 571–98.

Treib, Oliver (2012), Party Patronage in Austria: From Reward to Control. In: Petr Kopecký, Peter Mair and Maria Spirova (eds), *Party Patronage and Party Government in European Democracies*. Oxford: Oxford University Press, pp. 31–53.

Trif, Aurora (2008), Opportunities and Challenges of EU Accession: Industrial Relations in Romania. *European Journal of Industrial Relations*, 14(4): 461–78.

—— (2013), Romania: Collective Bargaining Institutions under Attack. In: *Transfer*, 19(2): 227–37.

—— (2016), Surviving Frontal Assault on Collective Bargaining Institutions in Romania: The Case of Manufacturing Industries. *European Journal of Industrial Relations*, 22(3): 221–34.

Troeva, Vesselina (2015), Regionalism in Bulgaria. In: Assembly of European Regions (AER), Report on the State of Regionalization in Europe. *Observatory on Regionalization in Europe*. https://drive.google.com/file/d/0B94jJjQLXnl-VDlwNnpEVUFGN0U/view (accessed on 16 July 2018).

Tsakatika, Myrto (2016), SYRIZA's Electoral Rise in Greece: Protest, Trust and the Art of Political Manipulation. *South European Society and Politics*, 21(4): 519–40.

—— and Costas Eleftheriou (2013), The Radical Left's Turn towards Civil Society in Greece: One Strategy, Two Paths. *South European Society and Politics*, 18(1): 81–99.

Tsarouhas, Dimitri (2008), Social Partnership in Greece: Is There a Europeanization Effect? *Comparative Political Studies*, 14(3): 347–65.

Tsatsanis, Emmannouil and Eftichia Teperoglou (2016), Realignment under Stress: The July 2015 Referendum and the September Parliamentary Election in Greece. *South European Society and Politics*, 21(4): 427–50.

Tsirbas, Yannis (2016), The January 2015 Parliamentary Election in Greece: Government Change, Partial Punishment and Hesitant Stabilisation. *South European Society and Politics*, 21(4): 407–26.

Tuchman, Barbara (1962), *Guns of August*. Basingstoke: Macmillan.

Tudoroiu, Theodor (2011a), Communism for the Twenty-first Century: The Moldovan Experiment. *Journal of Communist Studies and Transition Politics*, 27(2): 291–321.

—— (2011b), Structural Factors vs. Regime Change: Moldova's Difficult Quest for Democracy. *Democratization*, 18(1): 236–64.

—— (2014), Democracy and State Capture in Moldova. *Democratization*, 22(4): 655–78.

Turner, Ed (2018), The SPD at the Bundestagswahl 2017: Die Hoffnung stirbt zuletzt? *German Politics*, 27(1): 119–23.

Tweede Kamer (2014), *De staat van de Tweede Kamer 2013*. Tweede Kamer de Staten-Generaal 2. Vergadejaar 2013–4. Statistical overview provided by the Library of the Tweede Kamer.

Ulam, Adam (1998), *The Bolsheviks: The Intellectual and Political History of the Triumph of Communism in Russia*. Cambridge, MA: Harvard University Press.

United Kingdom Parliament (2001–17), Public Bills Statistics. www.parliament.uk/business/publications/house-of-lords-publications/records-of-activities-and-membership/public-bills-statistics/ (accessed on 10 February 2018).

United Nations (2016), *Human Development Report 2016: Human Development for Everyone*. New York: United Nations Development Programme. http://hdr.undp.

org/sites/default/files/2016_human_development_report.pdf (accessed on 19 September 2017).

—— (2017), Framework Convention on Climate Change. http://unfccc.int/paris_agreement/items/9485.php (accessed on 29 September 2017).

—— (2018), International Criminal Tribunal for the Former Yugoslavia 1993–2017. www.icty.org/ (accessed on 15 July 2018).

United Nations High Commissioner for Refugees (UNHCR) (22 December 2015), A Million Refugees and Migrants Flee to Europe in 2015. www.unhcr.org/news/press/2015/12/567918556/million-refugees-migrants-flee-europe-2015.html# (accessed on 1 August 2015).

Úrad vlády Slovenskej republiky (2017), *Výročná Správa*. Bratislava: Úrad vlády Slovenskej republiky.

Vainikka, Joni Tuomas (2016), Finland's Parliamentary Election 2015: Certainty of the Result with Uncertainty of the Outcome. *Regional & Federal Studies*, 26(2): 269–85.

Van Aelst, Peter and Tom Louwerse (2014), Parliament without Government: The Belgian Parliament and the Government Formation Processes of 2007–2011. *West European Politics*, 37(3): 475–96.

Van Biezen, Ingrid (2003), *Political Parties in New Democracies: Party Organization in Southern and East-Central Europe*. Basingstoke: Palgrave.

—— (2014), *On Parties, Party Systems and Democracy: Selected Writings of Peter Mair*. Colchester: European Consortium for Political Research.

——, Peter Mair and Thomas Poguntke (2012), Going, Going, . . . Gone? The Decline of Party Membership in Contemporary Europe. *European Journal of Political Research*, 51(1): 24–56.

Van Biezen, Ingrid and Petr Kopecký (2014), The Cartel Party and the State: Party–State Linkages in European Democracies. *Party Politics*, 20(2): 170–82.

Van Biezen, Ingrid and Thomas Poguntke (2014), The Decline of Membership-Based Politics. *Party Politics*, 20(2): 205–16.

Vandaele, Kurt (2009), The Ghent-System, Temporary Unemployment and the Belgian Trade Unions since the Economic Downturn. *Transfer*, 15(3–4): 589–96.

Van Der Hecke, Steven (ed.) (2004), *Christian Democratic Parties in Europe Since the End of the Cold War*. Leuven: Leuven University Press.

Van Deth, Jan W. and William A. Maloney (2015), Associations and Associational Involvement in Europe. In: Magone, José M. (ed.), *Routledge Handbook of European Politics*. London: Routledge, pp. 826–42.

Van Holsteyn, Joop J.M. (2018), The Dutch Parliamentary Elections of March 2017. *West European Politics*, 41(6): 1364–77.

—— and Galen A. Irwin (2000), The Bells Toll No More: The Declining Influence of Religion on Voting Behaviour in the Netherlands. In: David Broughton and Hans-Martien ten Napel (eds), *Religion and Mass Electoral Behaviour in Europe*. London: Routledge, pp. 75–96.

—— (2003), Never a Dull Moment: Pim Fortuyn and the Dutch Parliamentary Election of 2002. *West European Politics*, 26(2): 41–66.

Van Praag, Philip (2003), The Winners and Losers in a Turbulent Political Year. *Acta Politica*, 38(1): 5–22.

Van Rie, Tim, Ive Marx and Jeroen Horemans (2011), Ghent Revisited: Unemployment Insurance and Union Membership in Belgium and the Nordic Countries. *European Journal of Industrial Relations*, 17(2): 125–39.

Varga, Mihai (2014), Hungary's 'Anti-Capitalist' Far-Right: Jobbik and the Hungarian Guard. *Nationalities Papers*, 42(5): 791–807.

Várnagy, Réka and Gabriella Ilonszki (2017), The Conflict Between Partisan Interests and Normative Expectations in Electoral System Change: Hungary in 2014. *Corvinus Journal of Sociology and Social Policy*, 8(1): 3–24.

Vasilopoulou, Sofia and Daphne Halikiopoulou (2013), In the Shadow of Grexit: The Greek Election of 17 June 2012. *South European Society and Politics*, 18(4): 523–42.

Vatter, Adrian (2002), *Kantonale Demokratien im Vergleich: Entstehungsgründe, Interaktionen und Wirkungen politischer Institutionen in den Schweizer Kantonen*. Opladen: Leske & Budrich.

—— (2014), *Das politische System der Schweiz*. Baden-Baden: Nomos.

Ventura, Sofia (2018), The Italian Democratic Party from Merger to Personalism. *South European Society and Politics*, 23(1): 181–96.

Vercesi, Michelangelo (2015), Owner Parties and Party Institutionalisationin Italy: Is the Northern League Exceptional? *Modern Italy*, 20(4): 395–410.

Verdun, Amy (2013), The Building of Economic Governance in the European Union. *Transfer: European Review of Labour and Research*, 19(1): 23–35.

—— (2017), Political Leadership of the European Central Bank. *Journal of European Integration*, 39(2): 207–21.

—— and Jonathan Zeitlin (2017), Introduction: The European Semester as a New Architecture of EU Socioeconomic Governance in Theory and Practice. *Journal of European Public Policy*, 25(2): 137–48.

Vereiniging Nederlandse Ondernemer-Nederlandse Christelijk Werkgeversverbond-VNO-NCW (2018), Wie zijn we en wat doet VNO-NCW. www.vno-ncw.nl/over-vno-ncw/wat-doet-vno-ncw (accessed on 25 June 2018).

Verfassungsgerichtshof (2018), Geschichte in section Verfassungsgerichtshof. www.vfgh.gv.at/index.de.html (accessed on 3 November 2018).

Verney, Susannah (2011), Euroscepticism in Southern Europe: A Diachronic Perspective. *South European Society and Politics*, 16(1): 1–29.

Verzichelli, Luca (1995), The New Members of Parliament. In: Richard S. Katz and Piero Ignazi (eds), *Italian Politics: The Year of the Tycoon*. Boulder: Westview Press, pp. 115–34.

—— (2003), Much Ado about Something? Parliamentary Politics in Italy Amid the Rhetoric of Majority Rule and an Uncertain Party System. *Journal of Legislative Studies*, 9(3): 35–55.

—— (2004), Le parlement italien est-il encore une institution central? Le renouveau de la démocratie parlementaire en Italie. In: Olivier Costa, Eric Kerrouche and Paul Magnette (eds), *Vers un renouveau du parlamentarisme en Europe?* Brussels: Éditions Université Libre de Bruxelles, pp. 131–58.

Vigour, Cécile (2013), French MPs and Law-Making: Deputies' Activities and Citizens' Perceptions. *The Journal of Legislative Studies*, 19(2): 219–45.

Vilka, Inga (2011), Latvia: Experiments and Reforms in Decentralization. In: John Loughlin, Frank Hendriks and Anders Lidström (eds), *The Oxford Handbook of Local and Regional Democracy in Europe*. Oxford: Oxford University Press, 598–617.

Visvizi, A. (2014), From Grexit to Grecovery: The paradox of the Troika's engagement with Greece. *Perspectives on European Politics and Society*, 15(3): 335–45.

—— (2016), Greece and the Troika in the Context of the Eurozone crisis. In: José M. Magone, Brigid Laffan and Christian Schweiger (eds), *Core–Periphery Relations in the European Union: Power and Conflict in a Dualist Political Economy*. London: Routledge, pp. 149–65.

Vocelka, Karl (2002), *Geschichte Österreichs: Kultur-Gesellschaft-Politik*. Munich: Wilhelm Heyne.

Vodička, Karel (2005), *Das politische System Tschechiens: Lehrbuch*. Wiesbaden: Verlag für Sozialwissenschaften.

Voermans, Wim J.M. (2013), The Constitutional Revision Process in the Netherlands: Sensible Security Valve or Cause of Constitutional Paralysis? In:Xenophon Contiades (ed.), *Engineering Constitutional Change: A Comparative Perspective on Europe, Canada and USA*. London: Routledge, pp. 257–73.

Vogt, Martin (2002), Deutschland von der Bonner 'Wende' zu den Problemen der Einheit (1982–96). In: Martin Vogt (ed.), *Deutsche Geschichte: Von den Anfängen bis zur Gegenwart*. Frankfurt a. M.: Fischer, pp. 888–970.

Volintiru, Clara (2012), Clientelism: Electoral Forms and Functions in the Romanian Case Study. *Romanian Journal of Political Science*, 12(1): 35–66.

Von Beyme, Klaus (1984), *Parteien in westlichen Demokratien*. Munich: Piper.
—— (1993), *Die politische Klasse im Parteienstaat*. Frankfurt a. M.: Suhrkamp.
—— (1996), Party Leadership and Change in Party Systems: Towards a Postmodern Party State? *Government and Opposition*, 31(2): 135–59.
—— (2017), *Das politische System der Bundesrepublik Deutschland: Eine Einführung*, twelfth edition. Wiesbaden: Springer Verlag.
Wallace, William (1999), The Sharing of Sovereignty: The European Paradox. *Political Studies*, 47(3): 503–21.
—— (2005), Post-Sovereign Governance: The EU as a Partial Polity. In: Helen Wallace, William Wallace and Mark A. Pollack (eds), *Policy-Making in the European Union*. Oxford: Oxford University Press, pp. 483–503.
Wallerstein, Immanuel (2011), *The Modern World System*, four volumes. Berkeley: University of California Press.
Weber, Eugen, (1977), *Peasants into Frenchmen: The Modernization of Rural France 1870–1914*. London: Chatto & Windus.
Weber, Max (1922), *Grundriss der Sozialökonomik: Wirtschaft und Gesellschaft*. Tübingen: C.B. Mohr.
—— (1934), *Die protestantische Ethik und der Geist des Kapitalismus*. Tübingen: C.B. Mohr.
—— (1968), *Economy and Society. An Outline of Interpretive Sociology*. Berkeley: California University Press.
Weeks, Liam (2010), Parties and Party Systems. In: John Coakley and Michael Gallagher (eds), *Politics in the Republic of Ireland*. London: Routledge, pp. 137–67.
Wegs, J. Roberts and Robert Ladrech (2006), *Europe Since 1945: A Concise History*. Basingstoke: Palgrave.
Weisskirchner, Manès (2017), Die österreichische Nationalratswahl 2017, MIDEM-Bericht 01/17, Dresden. www.stiftung-mercator.de/media/downloads/3_Publikationen/2018/Maerz/MIDEM_Bericht_2017-1.pdf (accessed on 10 May 2018).
Welan, Manfred (2000), Regierungsbildung insbesondere 1999/2000. Diskussionspapier 80-R-2000, February. Wien: Universität für Bodenkultur-Institut für Politik, Wirtschaft und Recht. https://wpr.boku.ac.at/wpr_dp/dp-80.pdf (accessed on 22 October 2018).
Wessels, Wolfgang (2008), *Das politische System der Europäischen Union*. Wiesbaden: Verlag für Sozialwissenschaften.
—— (2016), *The European Council*. Basingstoke: Palgrave.
——, Andreas Maurer and Jürgen Mittag (2003), The European Union and Member-States Analysing Two Arenas Over Time. In: Wolfgang Wessels, Andreas Maurer and Jürgen Mittag (eds), *Fifteen Into One? The European Union and Its Member States*. Manchester: Manchester University Press, pp. 3–28.
Wheelan, Karl (2013), Ireland's Economic Crisis: The Good, the Bad and the Ugly. www.karlwhelan.com/Papers/Whelan-IrelandPaper-June2013.pdf (accessed on 2 August 2018).
White, David (2007), Victims of a Managed Democracy? Explaining the Electoral Decline of the Yabloko Party. *Democratizatsiya*, 15(2): 209–29.
White, Stephen (2011), *Understanding Russian Politics*. Cambridge: Cambridge University Press.
Whitehead, Laurence (2001), Democratic Regions, Ostracism, and Pariahs. In: Laurence Whitehead (ed.), *The International Dimension of Democratization: Europe and the Americas*, expanded version. Oxford: Oxford University Press, pp. 395–412.
Whitmore, Sarah (2003), Faction Institutionalization and Parliamentary Development in Ukraine. *Journal of Communist Studies and Transition Politics*, 19(4): 41–64.
—— (2005), State and Institution Building Under Kuchma. *Problems of Post-Communism*, 52(5): 3–11.
—— (2014), Political Party Development in Ukraine. Applied Knowledge Services. *Governance, Social Development, Humanitarian, Conflict*. www.gsdrc.org/docs/open/hdq1146.pdf (accessed on 14 September 2018).

Wiliarty, Sarah Elise (2018), The State of the CDU. *German Politics*, 27(1): 113–18.
Willershausen, Florian (11 April 2016), Der gescheiterte Pharisäer Jazenjuk. *Wirtschaftswoche*. www.wiwo.de/politik/ausland/ukraine-premier-tritt-zurueck-der-gescheiterte-pharisaeer-jazenjuk/13430022.html (accessed on 13 September 2018).
Williams, E.N. (1999), *The Ancien Regime in Europe: Government and Society in the Major States 1648–1789*. London: Pimlico.
Wilson, Andrew (2005a), *Ukraine's Orange Revolution*. New Haven: Yale University Press.
—— (2005b), *Virtual Politics: Faking Democracy in the Post-Soviet World*. New Haven: Yale University Press.
—— (2011), *Belarus: The Last European Dictatorship*. New Haven: Yale University Press.
—— (2014), *Ukraine Crisis: What It Means for the West*. New Haven: Yale University Press.
—— (2015), *The Ukrainians: Unexpected Nation*, fourth edition. New Haven: Yale University Press.
Wintr, Jan, Marek Antoš and Jan Kysela (2016), Direct Election of the President and its Constitutional and Political Consequences. *Acta Politologica*, 8(2): 145–63.
Witte, Els, Jan Craeybeckx and Alan Meynen (2009), *Political History of Belgium: From 1830 Onwards*. Brussels: VUB University Press.
Woll, Cornelia (2006), National Business Associations Under Stress: Lessons from the French Case. *West European Politics*, 29(3): 489–512.
Wollmann, Hellmut (1996), Institutionenbildung in Ostdeutschland: Neubau, Umbau und 'schöpferische Zerstörung'. In: Max Kaase, Andreas Eisen, Oscar W. Gabriel, Oskar Niedermayer and Hellmut Wollmann (eds), *Politisches System: Band 3 of Berichte zum sozialen und politischen Wandel in Ostdeutschland*. Opladen: Leske & Budrich, pp. 47–153.
Wonka, Arndt (2016). The Party Politics of the Euro Crisis in the German Bundestag: Frames, Positions and Salience. *West European Politics*, 39(1): 125–44.
World Bank (2017), GDP Per Capita, PPP (Current International $). https://data.worldbank.org/indicator/NY.GDP.PCAP.PP.CD?locations=AU-TD (accessed on 20 September 2017).
World Bank (2019) World Bank Indicators Database. https://data.worldbank.org/indicator/ (accessed on 4 March 2019).
World Economic Forum (WEF) (2016), Global Gender Gap Report 2016. Geneva: WEF. www3.weforum.org/docs/GGGR16/WEF_Global_Gender_Gap_Report_2016.pdf (accessed on 20 September 2017).
World Justice Project (WJP) (2018), Rule of Law Index 2018–9. Interactive Database. http://data.worldjusticeproject.org/ (accessed on 3 November 2018).
Yılmaz, Gözde (2016), Europeanisation or De-Europeanisation? Media Freedom in Turkey (1999–2015). *South European Society and Politics*, 21(1): 147–61.
Yordanova, Gabriela (2018), Bulgaria: Working Life in 2017. www.eurofound.europa.eu/sites/default/files/wpef18021.pdf (accessed on 27 June 2018).
Zajc, Drago (2007), Slovenia's National Assembly 1990–2004. *Journal of Legislative Studies*, 13(1): 83–98.
Zakošek, Nemad and Tomislav Maršić (2010), Das politische System Kroatiens. In: Wolfgang Ismayr (ed.), *Die politischen Systeme Osteuropas*. Wiesbaden: Verlag für Sozialwissenschaften, pp. 773–836.
Zbytniewska, Karolina (2017), Political Analyst: Romania is Undergoing a Second 'Democratic' Revolution. www.euractiv.com/section/central-europe/interview/milewski-romania-is-undergoing-a-democratic-revolution/ (accessed on 12 November 2017).
Zeitlin, Jonathan (2017), Introduction: The European Semester as a New Architecture of EU Socioeconomic Governance in Theory and Practice. *Journal of European Public Policy*, 25(2): 137–48.
Zervakis, Peter A. and Gustav Auernheimer (2009), Das politische System Griechenlands. In: Wolfgang Ismayr (ed.), *Die politischen Systeme Westeuropas*. Opladen: Leske & Budrich, pp. 819–58.

Zervakis, Peter A. and Tasos Costeas (2010), Das politische Systeme Zyperns. In: Wolfgang Ismayr (ed.), *Die politischen Systeme Osteuropas*. Wiesbaden: Verlag für Sozialwissenschaften, pp. 1097–157.

Z'Graggen, Heidi (2009), *Die Professionalisierung von Parlamenten im historischen und internationalen Vergleich*. Bern: Haupt.

Ziemer, Klaus (2013), *Das politische System Polens*. Wiesbaden: VS Springer.

Zlopaka, Zdravko (2008), It Won't Build By Itself: Local Self-Governance in Bosnia-Herzegovina. In: Zdravko Zlopaka (ed.), *Block by Block: It's Good To Build Well – Models of Organisation of Local Self-Governance*. Banja Luka: Enterprise Development Agency, pp. 179–206.

Zubek, Radoslaw (2001), A Core in Check: The Transformation of the Polish Core Executive. *Journal of European Public Policy*, 8(6): 911–32.

—— (2008), *Core Executive and Europeanization in Central Europe*. Basingstoke: Palgrave.

—— (2011), Core Executives and Coordination of EU Law Transposition: Evidence from New Member States. *Public Administration*, 89(2): 433–50.

Index